Planning and Managing the Experience Economy in Tourism

Rui Augusto Costa
GOVCOPP, University of Aveiro, Portugal

Filipa Brandão
GOVCOPP, University of Aveiro, Portugal

Zelia Breda
GOVCOPP, University of Aveiro, Portugal

Carlos Costa
GOVCOPP, University of Aveiro, Portugal

A volume in the Advances in Hospitality, Tourism, and the Services Industry (AHTSI) Book Series

Published in the United States of America by
IGI Global
Business Science Reference (an imprint of IGI Global)
701 E. Chocolate Avenue
Hershey PA, USA 17033
Tel: 717-533-8845
Fax: 717-533-8661
E-mail: cust@igi-global.com
Web site: http://www.igi-global.com

Copyright © 2022 by IGI Global. All rights reserved. No part of this publication may be reproduced, stored or distributed in any form or by any means, electronic or mechanical, including photocopying, without written permission from the publisher.
Product or company names used in this set are for identification purposes only. Inclusion of the names of the products or companies does not indicate a claim of ownership by IGI Global of the trademark or registered trademark.
    Library of Congress Cataloging-in-Publication Data

Names: Costa, Rui, 1975- editor.
Title: Planning and managing the experience economy in tourism / Rui
   Augusto Costa, Filipa Brandão, Zélia Breda, Carlos Costa.
Description: Hershey, PA : Business Science Reference, 2022. | Includes
   bibliographical references and index. | Summary: "This book provides
   contributed chapters on not only the tourist experience but also the
   growing importance in the economy in tourism and addresses issues such
   as tourism planning, innovation, and development, both at product and
   destination level, include the design of unique, memorable, and
   authentic experiences in order to assure tourism competitiveness"--
   Provided by publisher.
Identifiers: LCCN 2021030069 (print) | LCCN 2021030070 (ebook) | ISBN
   9781799887751 (hardcover) | ISBN 9781799887768 (paperback) | ISBN
   9781799887775 (ebook)
Subjects: LCSH: Tourism--Planning.
Classification: LCC G155.A1 P559 2022 (print) | LCC G155.A1 (ebook) | DDC
   338.4/791--dc23
LC record available at https://lccn.loc.gov/2021030069
LC ebook record available at https://lccn.loc.gov/2021030070

This book is published in the IGI Global book series Advances in Hospitality, Tourism, and the Services Industry (AHTSI) (ISSN: 2475-6547; eISSN: 2475-6555)

British Cataloguing in Publication Data
A Cataloguing in Publication record for this book is available from the British Library.

All work contributed to this book is new, previously-unpublished material. The views expressed in this book are those of the authors, but not necessarily of the publisher.

For electronic access to this publication, please contact: eresources@igi-global.com.

Advances in Hospitality, Tourism, and the Services Industry (AHTSI) Book Series

Maximiliano Korstanje
University of Palermo, Argentina

ISSN:2475-6547
EISSN:2475-6555

Mission

Globally, the hospitality, travel, tourism, and services industries generate a significant percentage of revenue and represent a large portion of the business world. Even in tough economic times, these industries thrive as individuals continue to spend on leisure and recreation activities as well as services.

The Advances in Hospitality, Tourism, and the Services Industry (AHTSI) book series offers diverse publications relating to the management, promotion, and profitability of the leisure, recreation, and services industries. Highlighting current research pertaining to various topics within the realm of hospitality, travel, tourism, and services management, the titles found within the AHTSI book series are pertinent to the research and professional needs of managers, business practitioners, researchers, and upper-level students studying in the field.

Coverage

- Health and Wellness Tourism
- Tourism and the Environment
- Hotel Management
- International Tourism
- Casino Management
- Customer Service Issues
- Service Management
- Cruise Marketing and Sales
- Service Design
- Leisure & Business Travel

IGI Global is currently accepting manuscripts for publication within this series. To submit a proposal for a volume in this series, please contact our Acquisition Editors at Acquisitions@igi-global.com or visit: http://www.igi-global.com/publish/.

The Advances in Hospitality, Tourism, and the Services Industry (AHTSI) Book Series (ISSN 2475-6547) is published by IGI Global, 701 E. Chocolate Avenue, Hershey, PA 17033-1240, USA, www.igi-global.com. This series is composed of titles available for purchase individually; each title is edited to be contextually exclusive from any other title within the series. For pricing and ordering information please visit http://www.igi-global.com/book-series/advances-hospitality-tourism-services-industry/121014. Postmaster: Send all address changes to above address. © © 2022 IGI Global. All rights, including translation in other languages reserved by the publisher. No part of this series may be reproduced or used in any form or by any means – graphics, electronic, or mechanical, including photocopying, recording, taping, or information and retrieval systems – without written permission from the publisher, except for non commercial, educational use, including classroom teaching purposes. The views expressed in this series are those of the authors, but not necessarily of IGI Global.

Titles in this Series

For a list of additional titles in this series, please visit: http://www.igi-global.com/book-series/advances-hospitality-tourism-services-industry/121014

Prospects and Challenges of Community-Based Tourism and Changing Deographics
Ishmael Mensah (University of Cape Coast, Ghana) and Ewoenam Afenyo-Agbe (University of Cape Coast, Ghana)
Business Science Reference • © 2022 • 300pp • H/C (ISBN: 9781799873358) • US $195.00

Challenges and New Opportunities for Tourism in Inland Territories Ecocultural Resources and Sustainable Initiatives
Gonçalo Poeta Fernandes (CITUR, Polytechnic Institute of Guarda, Portugal)
Business Science Reference • © 2022 • 295pp • H/C (ISBN: 9781799873396) • US $195.00

Rebuilding and Restructuring the Tourism Industry Infusion of Happiness and Quality of Life
André Riani Costa Perinotto (Universidade Federal do Delta do Parnaíba, Brazil) Verônica Feder Mayer (Federal Fluminense University, Brazil) and Jakson Renner Rodrigues Soares (Universidade da Coruña, Spain & Universidade Estadual do Ceará, Brazil)
Business Science Reference • © 2021 • 330pp • H/C (ISBN: 9781799872399) • US $195.00

Handbook of Research on the Impacts and Implications of COVID-19 on the Tourism Industry
Mahmut Demir (Isparta University of Applied Sciences, Turkey) Ali Dalgıç (Isparta University of Applied Sciences, Turkey) and Fatma Doğanay Ergen (Isparta University of Applied Sciences, Turkey)
Business Science Reference • © 2021 • 906pp • H/C (ISBN: 9781799882312) • US $415.00

Socio-Economic Effects and Recovery Efforts for the Rental Industry Post-COVID-19 Strategies
Maximiliano Korstanje (University of Palermo, Argentina)
Business Science Reference • © 2021 • 281pp • H/C (ISBN: 9781799872870) • US $195.00

Risk, Crisis, and Disaster Management in Small and Medium-Sized Tourism Enterprises
Diego R. Toubes (University of Vigo, Spain) and Noelia Araújo-Vila (University of Vigo, Spain)
Business Science Reference • © 2021 • 308pp • H/C (ISBN: 9781799869962) • US $195.00

Resiliency Models and Addressing Future Risks for Family Firms in the Tourism Industry
Anita Zehrer (MCI The Entrepreneurial School, Austria) Gundula Glowka (MCI The Entrepreneurial School, Austria) Katrin Magdalena Schwaiger (MCI The Entrepreneurial School, Austria) and Victoria Ranacher-Lackner (MCI The Entrepreneurial School, Austria)
Business Science Reference • © 2021 • 361pp • H/C (ISBN: 9781799873525) • US $195.00

701 East Chocolate Avenue, Hershey, PA 17033, USA
Tel: 717-533-8845 x100 • Fax: 717-533-8661
E-Mail: cust@igi-global.com • www.igi-global.com

EDITORIAL ADVISORY BOARD

Angélica Bock, *Federal Institute of Education, Science, and Technology of São Paulo, Brazil*
Marília Durão, *University Portucalense, Portugal*
Maria Gorete Dinis, *Polytechnic Institute of Portalegre, Portugal*
Ricardo Guerra, *Polytechnic Institute of Guarda, Portugal*
Dália Liberato, *Polytechnic Institute of Porto, Portugal*
Isabel Pinto Oliveira, *Polytechnic Institute of Viseu, Portugal*
Dina Ramos, *University of Aveiro, Portugal*
Márcio Ribeiro Martins, *Polytechnic Institute of Bragança, Portugal*
Manuel Salgado, *Polytechnic Institute of Guarda, Portugal*
Josefina Salvado, *ISCET, Portugal*
Sérgio Teixeira, *ISLA, Portugal*
Armando Luis Vieira, *University of Aveiro, Portugal*
Andreia Vitória, *University of Aveiro, Portugal*

Table of Contents

Preface xvi

Acknowledgment xxvii

Section 1
Tourism Destinations

Chapter 1
Cognitive Science of Tourism Experiences 1
  Noel Scott, University of the Sunshine Coast, Australia & Edith Cowan University, Australia
  Ana Claudia Campos, University of Algarve, Portugal

Chapter 2
Destination's Image and Tourism Experiences 22
  Gökhan Akel, Antalya Akev University, Turkey

Chapter 3
Prioritization of the Destination Attributes: The Case of Fethiye, Turkey 44
  Özgür Davras, Süleyman Demirel University, Turkey

Section 2
Experiences and Tourism Supply

Chapter 4
Conditions of Network Engagement: The Quest for a Common Good 69
  Veronika Trengereid, Western Norway University of Applied Sciences, Norway & Nord University, Norway

Chapter 5
Hospitality in the Experience Economy 85
  Aditya Ranjan, Jamia Millia Islamia, India
  Shweta Chandra, Jamia Millia Islamia, India
  Rohan Bhalla, Jamia Millia Islamia, India
  Sumedha Agarwal, Sharda University, India

Chapter 6
Corporate Museum Experiences in Enogastronomic Tourism 107
    Mario Ossorio, University of Campania "Luigi Vanvitelli", Italy

Chapter 7
If You're Happy, I'm Happy: Emotion Contagion at a Tourist Information Center 122
    Ondrej Mitas, Breda University of Applied Sciences, The Netherlands
    Marcel Bastiaansen, Breda University of Applied Sciences, The Netherlands & Tilburg
      University, The Netherlands
    Wilco Boode, Breda University of Applied Sciences, The Netherlands & Tilburg University,
      The Netherlands

Chapter 8
New Paradigms of the Tourist Guide Profession 141
    Ilídia Carvalho, Lusíada University, Lisbon, Portugal

Section 3
Managing Experiences in Tourism Products

Chapter 9
Innovative Certifications in Adventure Tourism: Attributes and Diffusion 161
    Dorthe Eide, Nord University, Norway
    Anne-Mette Hjalager, University of Southern Denmark, Denmark
    Marcus Hansen, Wrexham Glyndwr University, UK

Chapter 10
Community-Based Tourism Experiences in Nepal: A Path to Sustainable Tourism in the Post-
COVID-19 Era 176
    Sandeep Basnyat, Macao Institute for Tourism Studies (IFTM), China
    Trijya Kafle, Nepal College of Management, Nepal

Chapter 11
Surfing the Creative Wave: Designing Surfing as a Creative Tourism Experience 189
    Rui Carvalho, GOVCOPP, University of Aveiro, Portugal & ISLA Santarém, Portugal
    Patrícia Reis, GOVCOPP, University of Aveiro, Portugal & ISLA Santarém, Portugal &
      Polytechnic Institute of Leiria, Portugal

Chapter 12
Wellness Tourism Experience on the Rise Post COVID: Behavioural Demand Trends and
Expectations 215
    Nasim Hekmat, University Portucalense, Portugal
    Makhabbat Ramazanova, University Portucalense, Portugal
    Jorge Marques, University Portucalense, Portugal
    Joana Alegria Quintela, University Portucalense, Portugal

Section 4
Smart-Based Experiences

Chapter 13
Developing Smart Experiences 239
    Abbie-Gayle Johnson, The Hong Kong Polytechnic University, Hong Kong

Chapter 14
Experience Toward Smart Tour Guide Apps in Travelling: An Analysis of Users' Reviews on
Audio Odigos and Trip My Way 255
    Arvind Mahajan, Lovely Professional University, India
    Sana Maidullah, Lovely Professional University, India
    Mohammad Rokibul Hossain, Premier University, Bangladesh

Chapter 15
Accessible Tourism Experiences in Smart Destinations: The Case of Breda (Netherlands) 274
    Fatih Ercan, Zonguldak Bülent Ecevit University, Turkey

Section 5
Authenticity

Chapter 16
Authenticity in Tourism Experiences: Determinants and Dimensions 302
    Sumedha Agarwal, Sharda University, India
    Priya Singh, Jamia Millia Islamia, India

Chapter 17
Promoting the Tourist Experience Economy in LEDCs Through Authentic Fair-Trade
Handicrafts: A Conceptual Framework 318
    Peter Marwa Ezra, Clemson University, USA
    Lauren Duffy, Clemson University, USA

Compilation of References 337

About the Contributors 397

Index 405

Detailed Table of Contents

Preface xvi

Acknowledgment xxvii

Section 1
Tourism Destinations

Chapter 1
Cognitive Science of Tourism Experiences 1
  Noel Scott, University of the Sunshine Coast, Australia & Edith Cowan University, Australia
  Ana Claudia Campos, University of Algarve, Portugal

While other disciplinary approaches such as sociology and anthropology are important, this chapter introduces a cognitivist psychology approach to experience research. Such theoretical discussion may seem of little practical use, but the chapter argues that it is fundamental to understanding how and why experiences are created. The chapter applies theory and concepts from cognitive science (cognitive psychology and neuroscience) in the study of tourism experiences. This provides a different psychological paradigm to the behavioural approach currently in use in much research. The chapter describes the scope of cognitive psychology and neuroscience, its main concepts of cognitive psychology (perception, attention, emotion, memory, consciousness, learning), and their neuronal basis (neuroscience). These concepts are then applied in three topic areas related to tourism experiences: decision making, emotion, and attention. Several applications to tourism experience research are noted. Finally, the chapter discusses the way cognitive psychology concepts can be used in tourism research.

Chapter 2
Destination's Image and Tourism Experiences 22
  Gökhan Akel, Antalya Akev University, Turkey

The development of world tourism and the increase in the number of tourism destinations has led to the development of competition. Therefore, to gain a competitive advantage, efforts to create a destination image have gained importance. It is necessary to create an image for the destinations and communicate this image clearly to the visitor. An accurate and effective strategy should be pursued in the creation of the destination image, and the impression and perception that will create behavioural intention should be given importance. It is very important to include tourism experiences because of the undeniable necessity of managing and marketing services and experience in tourism. Destination image consists of the sum of the information individuals have about a region, their experiences, and impressions. Therefore, effective and efficient use of tourism experiences is very important for a positive destination image.

Chapter 3
Prioritization of the Destination Attributes: The Case of Fethiye, Turkey 44
    Özgür Davras, Süleyman Demirel University, Turkey

This chapter aims to identify the destination attributes and compare them based on two assumptions that form either a symmetric or an asymmetric relationship between destination attribute performance and tourist satisfaction. For this purpose, data were collected from tourists coming to Fethiye, Turkey. Multivariate regression analysis was performed on the obtained data based on the linear assumption first. The results revealed that the attitudes of staff and the attitudes of the shopkeepers are the main determinants of tourist satisfaction. Then, penalty-reward-contrast analysis was performed based on the nonlinear assumption. According to analysis results, attitudes of the staff are performance factors; and travel agency services, attitudes of the shopkeepers, security/safety, and beach/sea are classified as excitement factors. The elements that take part in the excitement factor are the attributes that contribute to satisfaction the most.

Section 2
Experiences and Tourism Supply

Chapter 4
Conditions of Network Engagement: The Quest for a Common Good 69
    Veronika Trengereid, Western Norway University of Applied Sciences, Norway & Nord
        University, Norway

There is growing research interest in innovation network dynamics. Based on an explorative case study of a regional innovation network for the tourism industry, this chapter contributes to a better understanding of network engagement as a dynamic and social construct. By following the microfoundational trend, the chapter anchors the concept of engagement at a lower level in order to increase the depth of understanding of the conditions of network engagement. As there are many different notions of engagement, the chapters start by providing an overview of the different notions of engagement in innovation and network literature. Then, inspired by the critical incident technique, a narrative presents the findings, showing the dynamic and social aspect of network engagement, followed by a discussion of the conditions of network engagement and theoretical contributions.

Chapter 5
Hospitality in the Experience Economy 85
    Aditya Ranjan, Jamia Millia Islamia, India
    Shweta Chandra, Jamia Millia Islamia, India
    Rohan Bhalla, Jamia Millia Islamia, India
    Sumedha Agarwal, Sharda University, India

Experience economy plays a predominant role in the hospitality industry. Consumer experience has always been of great importance for the hospitality business. As consumer experience evolved, businesses needed and still need to find new ways to differentiate themselves. To remain competitive and stay in the market, hospitality firms are working towards creating outstanding and memorable experiences that exceed guest expectations. In the context of Pine and Gilmore's experience economy conceptual model, the chapter attempts to theorize and explain how hospitality businesses are curating consumer experiential encounters. Digital nomads are the ignition source of driving an experience economy. The chapter further highlights how technology would additionally ease hospitality enterprises to frame excellent strategies focused on supplying the value to the digital consumers and then expecting their customers to generate additional business.

Chapter 6
Corporate Museum Experiences in Enogastronomic Tourism 107
Mario Ossorio, University of Campania "Luigi Vanvitelli", Italy

Over the last years, an evolution of museum function has occurred. Museums are no longer considered just a treasure house but a place that matches cultural and commercial needs. Recently, the literature sheds light on their relevance to customers' experiences. The chapter aims to explore a specific category of museums, highlighting their many functions. More specifically, the chapter analyses the relevance of corporate museums in the enogastronomic industry. Two Italian corporate museums in the pasta industry are explored, highlighting their relevance for visitor experience needs.

Chapter 7
If You're Happy, I'm Happy: Emotion Contagion at a Tourist Information Center 122
Ondrej Mitas, Breda University of Applied Sciences, The Netherlands
Marcel Bastiaansen, Breda University of Applied Sciences, The Netherlands & Tilburg University, The Netherlands
Wilco Boode, Breda University of Applied Sciences, The Netherlands & Tilburg University, The Netherlands

An increasing body of research has addressed what a tourism experience is and how it should best be measured and managed. One conclusion has been to recommend observational methods such as facial expression analysis. The chapter uses facial expression analysis to determine whether the emotions of employees in the tourism industry affect the emotions of their customers, following a pattern of emotional contagion. The findings show that emotional valence and arousal are both contagious. Furthermore, the findings show that arousal is less contagious at a higher likelihood to recommend, likely due to higher employee arousal during approximately the middle third of their conversation. Furthermore, findings demonstrate that emotion measurement is now possible at reasonable convenience for the tourism industry and gives a unique insight into tourists' actual experiences that is more precise and valid than self-report alone, though with certain costs and stringent methodological limitations.

Chapter 8
New Paradigms of the Tourist Guide Profession 141
Ilídia Carvalho, Lusíada University, Lisbon, Portugal

In this chapter, using the Portuguese tourist guides as an example, the author intends to expose the reality of the profession and how it is nowadays necessary to adapt it to the new tourism paradigms. The pandemic, which has suddenly and deeply affected tourist guides, will also be one of the topics. A brief historical background of the profession will be given to be able to understand what a tourist guide is today, as well as the skills needed for the profession obtained through education and training, which are also one of the topics presented. The way these professionals have been dealing with digitals and how new technological tools are being used for the profession will be explained. Issues like authenticity, responsibility, and the contribution of tourist guides to develop tourism destinations will also be covered in the text.

Section 3
Managing Experiences in Tourism Products

Chapter 9
Innovative Certifications in Adventure Tourism: Attributes and Diffusion 161
    Dorthe Eide, Nord University, Norway
    Anne-Mette Hjalager, University of Southern Denmark, Denmark
    Marcus Hansen, Wrexham Glyndwr University, UK

Certifications, quality systems and standardization carriers systemic innovativeness, since they usually are established after a lengthy period of research, evidence-finding and testing. Ideally, they incorporate the most decisive best practices that will benefit firms, customers, and wider groups of stakeholders in communities. Such systems can be seen as driving forces for innovation, and memberships in them is likely to enhance prospective changes in the any industry. This chapter addresses the prospects of diffusion of innovation through certification and quality systems, using Rogers (1995) diffusion theory explaining adoption based on the five attributes. Findings from a qualitative multi-case study of the national tourism quality certifications of VisitScotland (Quality Assurance), New Zealand (Qualmark) and Iceland (Vakinn) is used to illustrate and explain diffusion. The study shows that relative advantage and compatibility seem most critical for adoption. Complexity and observability are important too, while trialability seems less obtainable in this particular context.

Chapter 10
Community-Based Tourism Experiences in Nepal: A Path to Sustainable Tourism in the Post-
COVID-19 Era 176
    Sandeep Basnyat, Macao Institute for Tourism Studies (IFTM), China
    Trijya Kafle, Nepal College of Management, Nepal

This chapter presents a case study of community-based tourism (CBT) in Nepal. Based on the Nepalese experiences, this chapter demonstrates that the CBT approach not only helps to economically empower the local community, revitalize local culture, and enhance appreciation for the natural and cultural environment, but also ultimately helps to promote socially responsible and environmentally conscious sustainable tourism practices. Identifying policies and appropriate practices for the sustainable development of tourism is critical because of the recent crisis of COVID-19 that has almost paralyzed the entire travel and tourism industry. Furthermore, based on CBT approaches, the knowledge derived from the Nepalese experiences can be used in various developing countries that aim to develop sustainable tourism development models for the post-COVID-19 era.

Chapter 11
Surfing the Creative Wave: Designing Surfing as a Creative Tourism Experience 189
    Rui Carvalho, GOVCOPP, University of Aveiro, Portugal & ISLA Santarém, Portugal
    Patrícia Reis, GOVCOPP, University of Aveiro, Portugal & ISLA Santarém, Portugal &
        Polytechnic Institute of Leiria, Portugal

Creative tourism experiences constitute clear examples of the experience economy principles. They address new tourists' necessities. They can activate tangible and intangible resources, contribute to the development of local skills while offering the chance to engage with the overall social agents of the tourism system addressing key tourism challenges of the 21st century. Over the past few years, surf tourism has aroused the interest of many people, and surf tourists are increasingly more experienced, demanding and seeking a wide range of engaging experiences. To connect surf tourism to creative tourism, the authors developed a model focused on a creative surf experience. The chapter presents several contributions to the development of creative experiences of surf tourism where surf destinations can focus on and develop a greater audience that searches for such experiences.

Chapter 12
Wellness Tourism Experience on the Rise Post COVID: Behavioural Demand Trends and Expectations 215
    Nasim Hekmat, University Portucalense, Portugal
    Makhabbat Ramazanova, University Portucalense, Portugal
    Jorge Marques, University Portucalense, Portugal
    Joana Alegria Quintela, University Portucalense, Portugal

This chapter synthesizes the emergence of the growing wellness tourism segment in an era of post-COVID-19 travel when consumer mentality has been radically changed and shifted towards different needs. This includes any activity that allows tourists to work on themselves mentally or physically and present several considerations and recommendations for the wellness industry to take full advantage of tourism opportunities moving forward. It aims to help understand consumer behaviour and preferences by predicting wellness tourism trends and developments, acknowledging the gaps in the research available for understanding wellness tourism post covid and reflecting the experience economy perspective in the sector. A research method was developed, including a literature review and survey application to potential wellness tourists. Discussion of results is provided, along with main conclusions, allowing the identification of trends and development measures to help improve wellness tourism in a post-COVID era.

Section 4
Smart-Based Experiences

Chapter 13
Developing Smart Experiences 239
    Abbie-Gayle Johnson, The Hong Kong Polytechnic University, Hong Kong

Studies have drawn on single theoretical perspectives to examine smart experiences; however, this chapter proposes a multi-theoretical perspective for understanding the development of smart experiences. This is an alternate perspective to exploring the planning and management processes that precede the formation of smart initiatives. Different theoretical perspectives, focused on stakeholder involvement, are drawn upon to understand the engagement in developing smart experiences. This development has created various smart experiences, which was possible due to core collaboration components and varying factors. The chapter calls for empirical investigations into smart tourism through the lens of tourism collaboration to deepen understanding of this development. Practitioners can also benefit from using this perspective, as it provides insights useful for developing smart experiences at the destination level, which is currently lacking in public discourse.

Chapter 14
Experience Toward Smart Tour Guide Apps in Travelling: An Analysis of Users' Reviews on
Audio Odigos and Trip My Way... 255
Arvind Mahajan, Lovely Professional University, India
Sana Maidullah, Lovely Professional University, India
Mohammad Rokibul Hossain, Premier University, Bangladesh

The integration of navigation systems and smart tour guide apps has gained popularity among travellers with the rapid development of the internet, mobile technology, and the wide acceptance of smartphones. The purpose of the study is twofold: (1) to assess the growth of smart tour guide apps in India and (2) to examine the tourists' experiences in using smart tour guide apps. To achieve the purpose of the study, a content analysis method was employed to analyse the users' reviews on the "Audio Odigos" and the "Trip My Way," which are very popular tour guide apps in India. The results reveal that smart tour guide apps are more preferred than the human tour guide. An app-based tour guide facilitates exceptional experiences for accurate and useful information on historical monument tours, city tours, and destination tours. Thus, the findings can be used to improve the existing apps and develop more sophisticated apps in the future that can ensure sustainable smart tourism.

Chapter 15
Accessible Tourism Experiences in Smart Destinations: The Case of Breda (Netherlands) 274
Fatih Ercan, Zonguldak Bülent Ecevit University, Turkey

Accessible tourism is among the issues that have been emphasized in recent years. Smart technologies which have developed and become widespread nowadays are seen as an important tool in ensuring accessibility in destinations. Today, destinations are trying to improve the tourism experiences of individuals with some form of disability by using smart technologies. This study aims to reveal the current accessible tourism applications in smart destinations with the example of the city of Breda. Data were obtained using the document analysis technique, which is one of the qualitative data collection methods. As a result of the data analysis, it has been determined that technologies such as destination websites, mobile applications, virtual reality are used extensively for accessible transportation and information about the destination in Breda.

Section 5
Authenticity

Chapter 16
Authenticity in Tourism Experiences: Determinants and Dimensions... 302
Sumedha Agarwal, Sharda University, India
Priya Singh, Jamia Millia Islamia, India

Authenticity is a term that emerged from the modern era. Travellers are demanding authentic, experientially oriented opportunities with more meaningful interactions with locals. Travellers of the new generation want to have meaningful travel which is sustainable as well as experiential. The rise of an experience economy that concentrates on entertainment, education, escapism, and esthetics has made authentic travel experiences more critical. The tourists are more aware of their needs and are motivated towards places that offer real experiences. The chapter aims to explain the concept of authenticity and relate it to the tourism and hospitality industry. The discussion around various kinds of authenticity as described in the literature has been done. A case study demonstrating authentic experiences in rural homestays has been included in the chapter. Further authentic experiences derived from various tourism and hospitality sectors like food, accommodation, and entertainment have been explained.

Chapter 17
Promoting the Tourist Experience Economy in LEDCs Through Authentic Fair-Trade
Handicrafts: A Conceptual Framework 318
    Peter Marwa Ezra, Clemson University, USA
    Lauren Duffy, Clemson University, USA

The handicraft sector plays an important role in providing economic benefits of tourism to local communities. However, this sector is threatened by globalized supply chains. This conceptual chapter explores the synergistic value of linking the experience economy, creative tourism, and fair-trade principles to increase the benefits of the handicraft sector to local communities while supporting positive tourist experiences. The handicraft sector contributes to the livelihoods of marginalized members of the supply chain side of a destination by opening opportunities for adding value to their tangible products through co-created experiences. Furthermore, the creative potential allows tourists to create memories, connecting with producers in interesting and meaningful ways, when fair-trade principles are integrated as part of the tourist experience. To ensure a balanced synergy and active connection between experience economy, creative tourism, and fair-trade concepts, well-trained and skilled artists, art managers, and creative entrepreneurs are needed in tourist destinations.

Compilation of References 337

About the Contributors 397

Index 405

Preface

In the last years, tourism has been facing a new paradigm. The introduction of experiences in the market changed how tourism is developing, the destinations' management and promotion (Oh et al., 2007; Stamboulis & Skayannis, 2003). Many authors consider experiences as the nature of tourism (Cohen, 1979a; Quan & Wang, 2004; Song et al., 2015; Sternberg, 1997; Uriely, 2005), leading to several studies on this area (Aho, 2001; Binkhorst, 2005; Binkhorst & Dekker, 2009; Jennings, 2006; Kim et al., 2012; Larsen, 2007; Li, 2000; Oh et al., 2007; Quan & Wang, 2004; Quinlan Cutler & Carmichael, 2010; Ryan, 2002; Selstad, 2007; Stamboulis & Skayannis, 2003; Tung & Ritchie, 2011; Urry, 2002; Volo, 2009).

Researchers try to understand this phenomenon, using frameworks to better explain the experience process, dividing them into phases or stages (Aho, 2001; Clawson & Knetsch, 1966; Cohen, 1979b; Kim et al., 2012; Otto & Ritchie, 1996; Quan & Wang, 2004; Cutler & Carmichael, 2010; Tung & Ritchie, 2011; Volo, 2009). These tourism experience models offer good insight and provide an excellent understanding of this field of study, although they only take into analysis the experience per se. A way to integrate the tourism experience in destinations and their relationship with tourists will provide an important development on the industry and help destinations become even more competitive, offering tourists an experience even more suitable to their needs and demands.

But for this evolution to occur, the knowledge on tourism experience must be supported by the broader comprehension of the experience phenomenon. To apprehend how the experience concept evolved through the years, how to define it and how to create it can help apply these same principles in a more specific context. The experience economy was studied firstly in a non-consumption perspective (Abrahams, 1986; Arnould & Price, 1993; Csikszentmihalyi, 1975a, 1975b, 1990, Maslow, 1959, 1962, 1964, Privette, 1981, 1983; Turner & Bruner, 1986) and later brought these initial ideas to consumption and marketing (Ambler et al., 2002; Boswijk et al., 2007; Brakus et al., 2009; Carbone & Haeckel, 1994; Gentile, Spiller, & Noci, 2007; Holbrook & Hirschman, 1982; Pine II & Gilmore, 1998, 1999; Poulsson & Kale 2004; Prahalad & Ramaswamy, 2004b; Schmitt, 1999a; Schouten et al., 2007), offering different points of view on this concept. The desire for memorable experiences (Berry & Bendapudi, 2003; Berry et al., 2002), the search for social status and less boredom in life, and to find identity and involvement in an increasingly affluent society (Lorentzen, 2009; Sundbo, 2009) led to Pine II and Gilmore's (1998) concept of experience economy.

For Pine II and Gilmore (1998), the experience is as real as a product or service. The authors argue that there is experience when business organisations use the services that they have available as a stage, and their products as props to lead consumers to feel involved, thus ending up providing them with a memorable event. Mitchell (2000, cited in McLuhan, 2000) agrees with that perspective, stating that

Preface

experiences are the basis of the memory, which allows strengthening marketing by taking advantage of the emotions and the senses.

According to Pine II and Gilmore (1998), we live in the era of a consumer who increasingly seeks to buy experiences. Thus, it is natural that there is an increase in demand for destinations that can provide their visitors with unique experiences, which there would not be the possibility to perform elsewhere, or at least not with the same authenticity (Soares, 2009). The authors also argue that the experience is linked to the senses, i.e., using them, either to a greater or lesser extent, will be a decisive factor in building the experience. The concept of experience addressed so far presents the possibility that, when visiting a place, there is a unique, memorable, and special moment that takes place at different times of life (Schmitt, 2002).

MacCannell (1989) was one of the authors who demonstrated interest in the influence of experience in tourism, indicating that tourists increasingly seek authentic experiences, and destinations are seen as means to achieve this end, staging an authenticity that the tourist does not find in their daily lives. Stamboulis and Skayannis (2003) argue that tourism has focused on the tourist's experience of visiting, seeing, learning, enjoying, and living a different lifestyle. Therefore, the authors consider that everything that tourists encounter in a destination can be considered an experience. This line of thought leads to the belief that experiences are no longer just a way to add value to tourism, but something mandatory in the tourism supply (Larsen, 2007).

Buhalis (1999) and Brown and Getz (2005) argue that the experience adds value to the tourism product and may thus be a competitive advantage for the destination. It is verified that there is not only one theory to define experiences; however, the existing concepts are interconnected and complementary, despite being a very complex theme. There is agreement among authors that the experience is something as real as a product or service, and that, in general, a consumer who acquires an experience is a more satisfied consumer than one who acquires a product or service. The already mentioned Pine II and Gilmore's approach divides the experience into four categories based on the participation of consumers and the connection that binds them to the experience. Throughout the analysis, one realises that experiences, creativity, innovation, design, and new technologies are increasingly common words in business organisations, and it is also considered that not using them may lead to great difficulty in maintaining the business.

Smith (2006) also dedicated to studying experience tourism and put forward a set of assumptions that contribute to its understanding and implementation. For the author, experience tourism results from a global movement towards experiential learning, through which people create meanings through direct experience. Experience tourism stimulates visitors to active participation and promotes activities that attract and emerge people in cultures, communities, among others. Experience tourism is the opposite of mass tourism, which traditionally focuses on package tours with low levels of personal involvement. In this sense, it is significantly more interesting for the promotion of sustainable tourism and sustainable development.

Many scholars have tried to gather all the ramifications of experience (Carù & Cova, 2003; Same & Larimo, 2012; Tynan & McKechnie, 2009; Verhoef et al., 2009), but their research always failed to appoint one of two dimensions mentioned by previous studies. The literature does not offer a broader analysis of all dimensions of the experience economy and tourism experiences. This book intends to bring together these highly interrelated concepts, including several chapters that address the broad concept of 'experience economy' and its application to the many dimensions of tourism, bringing together theoretical and applied perspectives.

The book is organised into five sections and 17 chapters. A brief description of each of the chapters follows.

SECTION 1: TOURISM DESTINATIONS

Chapter 1, "Cognitive Science of Tourism Experiences," introduces a cognitivist psychology approach to experience research. Such theoretical discussion may seem of little practical use, but the chapter argues that it is fundamental to understanding how and why experiences are created. The chapter applies theory and concepts from cognitive science (cognitive psychology and neuroscience) in the study of tourism experiences, providing a different psychological paradigm to the behavioural approach currently in use in much research. The chapter describes the scope of cognitive psychology and neuroscience, its main concepts of cognitive psychology (perception, attention, emotion, memory, consciousness, learning) and their neuronal basis (neuroscience). These concepts are then applied in three topic areas related to tourism experiences: decision making, emotion and attention. Several applications to tourism experience research are noted. Finally, the chapter discusses the way cognitive psychology concepts can be used in tourism research.

Chapter 2, "Destination Image and Tourism Experiences," starts by acknowledging that the development of world tourism and the increase in the number of tourism destinations has led to the development of competition. Therefore, to gain a competitive advantage, efforts to create a destination image have gained importance. It is necessary to create an image for the destinations and communicate this image clearly to the visitor. An accurate and effective strategy should be pursued in creating the destination image, and the impression and perception that will create behavioural intention should be given importance. It is crucial to include tourism experiences because of the undeniable need of managing and marketing services and experience in tourism. Destination image consists of the sum of the information individuals have about a region, their experiences, and impressions. Therefore, effective and efficient use of tourism experiences is essential for a positive destination image.

Chapter 3, "Prioritisation of the Destination Attributes: The Case of Fethiye, Turkey," aims to identify the destination attributes and compare them based on two assumptions that form either a symmetric or an asymmetric relationship between destination attributes' performance and tourist satisfaction. For this purpose, data were collected from tourists coming to Fethiye, Turkey. Multivariate regression analysis was performed on the obtained data, based on the linear assumption first. The results revealed that the attitudes of staff and the attitudes of the shopkeepers are the main determinants of tourist satisfaction. Then, penalty-reward-contrast analysis was performed based on the nonlinear assumption. According to analysis results, attitudes of the staff are performance factors; and travel agency services, attitudes of the shopkeepers, security/safety, and beach/sea are classified as an excitement factor. The elements that take part in the excitement factor are the attributes that contribute to satisfaction the most.

SECTION 2: EXPERIENCES AND TOURISM SUPPLY

Chapter 4, "Conditions of Network Engagement: The Quest for a Common Good," contributes to a better understanding of network engagement as a dynamic and social construct, based on an explorative case study of a regional innovation network for the tourism industry. By following the microfoundational

Preface

trend, the chapters anchor the concept of engagement at a lower level to increase the depth of understanding of the conditions of network engagement. As there are many different notions of engagement, the chapter starts by providing an overview of the different notions of engagement in innovation and network literature. Then, inspired by the critical incident technique, a narrative presents the findings, showing the dynamic and social aspect of network engagement, followed by a discussion of the conditions of network engagement and theoretical contributions.

Chapter 5, "Hospitality in the Experience Economy," is based on the role played by the experience economy in the hospitality industry. Consumer Experience has always been of great importance for the hospitality business. As consumer experience evolved, companies needed and still need to find new ways to differentiate themselves. To remain competitive and stay in the market, hospitality firms are working towards creating outstanding and memorable experiences that exceed guest expectations. In the context of Pine and Gilmore's experience economy conceptual model, the chapter attempts to theorise and explain how hospitality businesses are curating consumer experiential encounters. Digital nomads are the ignition source of driving an experience economy. The chapter further highlights how technology would additionally provide ease hospitality enterprises to frame excellent strategies focused on supplying the value to the digital consumers and then expecting their customers to generate additional business.

Chapter 6, "Corporate Museum Experiences in Enogastronomic Tourism," highlights that the functions played by museums have evolved in the last years. Museums are no longer considered just a treasure house but a place that matches cultural and commercial needs. Recently, the literature sheds light on their relevance to customers' experiences. The chapter aims to explore a specific category of museums, highlighting their several functions. More specifically, the chapter analyses the relevance of corporate museums in the enogastronomic industry. Two Italian corporate museums in the pasta industry are explored, highlighting their relevance for visitors' experience needs.

Chapter 7, "If You're Happy, I'm Happy: Emotion Contagion at a Tourist Information Center," is grounded on a wide body of research that has addressed what a tourism experience is and how it should best be measured and managed. One conclusion has been to recommend observational methods such as facial expression analysis. The present chapter uses facial expression analysis to determine whether the emotions of employees in the tourism industry affect the emotions of their customers, following a pattern of emotional contagion. The findings show that emotional valence and arousal are both contagious. Furthermore, the findings show that arousal is less contagious at a higher likelihood to recommend, likely due to higher employee arousal during approximately the middle third of their conversation. Furthermore, findings demonstrate that emotion measurement is now possible at reasonable convenience for the tourism industry and gives a unique insight into tourists' actual experiences that is more precise and valid than self-report alone, though with certain costs and stringent methodological limitations.

Chapter 8, "New Paradigms of the Tourist Guide Profession," using the Portuguese tourist guides as an example, intends to expose the reality of the profession and the current need to adapt it to the new tourism paradigms. The pandemic, which has suddenly and deeply affected tourist guides, will also be one of the topics. A brief historical background of the profession are provided to understand what a tourist guide is nowadays, as well as the skills needed for the profession obtained through education and training, which are also one of the topics presented. The way these professionals have been dealing with digitals and how new technological tools are being used for the profession are explained. Issues like authenticity, responsibility and the contribution of tourist guides to develop tourism destinations are also be covered in the text.

SECTION 3: MANAGING EXPERIENCES IN TOURISM PRODUCTS

Chapter 9, "Innovative Certifications in Adventure Tourism: Attributes and Diffusion," aims to examine the role of the function of certification and quality systems in encouraging innovation in adventure tourism. The main assumption is that certification, quality labelling, and standardisation are significant carriers of systemic innovativeness in whatever forms they take. Accordingly, in this understanding, innovations are embedded in such systems since they usually are established only after a lengthy period of research, evidence-finding and testing. Ideally, they incorporate the most decisive best practices that will benefit firms, customers and wider groups of stakeholders in communities. In this perspective, certifications can be said to accumulate and synthesise innovative endeavours and make them more rapidly available than they would be if every organisation had to invent them in its own capacity. Following this rationale, certifications and quality systems can be seen as driving forces for innovation, and membership is likely to enhance prospective changes in any industry.

Chapter 10, "Community-Based Tourism Experiences in Nepal: A Path to Sustainable Tourism in the Post-COVID-19 Era," presents a case study of community-based tourism (CBT) in Nepal. Based on the Nepalese experiences, this chapter demonstrates that the CBT approach helps to economically empower the local community, revitalise local culture and enhance appreciation for the natural and cultural environment, and helps to promote socially responsible and environmentally conscious sustainable tourism practices. Identifying policies and appropriate practices for the sustainable development of tourism is critical because of the recent crisis of COVID-19 that has almost paralysed the entire travel and tourism industry. Furthermore, based on CBT approaches, the knowledge derived from the Nepalese experiences can be used in various developing countries that aim to develop sustainable tourism development models for the post-COVID-19 era.

Chapter 11, "Surfing the Creative Wave: Designing Surfing as a Creative Tourism Experience," addresses the relationship between creative tourism and the experience economy. Creative tourism experiences constitute clear examples of the experience economy principles. They address new tourists' necessities. They can activate tangible and intangible resources, contribute to the development of local skills while offering the chance to engage with the overall social agents of the tourism system addressing key tourism challenges of the 21st century. Over the past few years, surf tourism has aroused the interest of many people, and surf tourists are increasingly more experienced, demanding and seek a wide range of engaging experiences. To connect surf tourism to creative tourism, the authors developed a model focused on a creative surf experience. The chapter presents several contributions to the development of creative experiences of surf tourism where surf destinations can focus on and develop to a greater audience that searches for such experiences.

Chapter 12, "Wellness Tourism Experience on the Rise Post COVID: Behavioural Demand Trends and Expectations," synthesises the emergence of the growing wellness tourism segment in an era of post-COVID-19 travel when consumer mentality has been radically changed and shifted towards different needs. This includes any activity that allows tourists to work on themselves mentally or physically and present several considerations and recommendations for the wellness industry to take full advantage of tourism opportunities moving forward. It aims to help understand consumer behaviour and preferences by predicting wellness tourism trends and developments, acknowledging the gaps in the research available for understanding wellness tourism post covid, and reflecting the experience economy perspective in the sector. A research method was developed, including a literature review and survey application

Preface

to potential wellness tourists. Discussion of results is provided, along with main conclusions, allowing to identify trends and developments measures to help improve wellness tourism in a post COVID era.

SECTION 4: SMART-BASED EXPERIENCES

Chapter 13, "Developing Smart Experiences," proposes a multi-theoretical perspective to understanding the development of smart experiences. This is an alternate perspective to exploring the planning and management processes that precede smart initiatives' formation. Different theoretical perspectives focused on stakeholder involvement are drawn upon to understand the engagement for developing smart experiences. This development resulted in the creation of various smart experiences. These initiatives were possible due to core collaboration components and influences associated with various theories used to examine tourism collaboration. Finally, the chapter calls for empirical investigations in smart tourism to be conducted through the lens of collaboration to deepen understanding of development. Practitioners can also benefit from insights using this perspective as it provides insights useful for developing smart experiences at the destination level that are currently lacking in public discourse.

Chapter 14, "Experience Toward Smart Tour Guide Apps in Travelling: An Analysis of User Reviews on Audio Odigos and Trip My Way," approaches the integration of navigation systems and smart tour guide apps, which has gained popularity among travellers with the rapid development of the internet, mobile technology, and the wide acceptance of smartphones. The purpose of the study is twofold: (i) to assess the growth of smart tour guide apps in India, and (ii) to examine the tourists' experience in using smart tour guide apps. A content analysis method was employed to analyse the users' reviews on the "Audio Odigos" and the "Trip My Way", which are very popular tour guide apps in India. The results reveal that smart tour guide apps are more preferred than the human tour guide. Besides, an app-based tour guide facilitates exceptional experiences for accurate and useful information on historical monument tours, city tours, and destination tours. Thus, the findings can be used to improve the existing apps and develop more sophisticated apps in the future that can ensure sustainable smart tourism.

Chapter 15, "Accessible Tourism Experiences in Smart Destinations: The Case of Breda (The Netherlands)," focuses on an important issue, which is the use of smart technologies to improve accessible tourism experiences. Accessible tourism is among the issues that have been emphasised in recent years. Smart technologies which have developed and become widespread nowadays are seen as an important tool in ensuring accessibility in destinations. Today, destinations are trying to improve the tourism experiences of individuals with some form of disability by using smart technologies. This study aims to reveal the current accessible tourism applications in smart destinations with the example of the city of Breda. Data were obtained using the document analysis technique, which is one of the qualitative data collection methods. As a result of the data analysis, it has been determined that technologies such as destination websites, mobile applications, virtual reality are used extensively for accessible transportation and information about the destination in Breda.

SECTION 5: AUTHENTICITY

Chapter 16, "Authenticity in Tourism Experiences: Determinants and Dimensions," is based on the assumption that travellers are demanding authentic, experientially oriented opportunities with more meaningful interactions with locals. Travellers of the new generation want to have meaningful travel which is sustainable as well as experiential. The rise of an experience economy that concentrates on entertainment, education, escapism and aesthetics have made authentic travel experiences more critical. The tourists are more aware of their needs and are motivated towards places that offer real experiences. The present chapter aims to explain the concept of authenticity and relate it to the tourism and hospitality industry. The discussion around various kinds of authenticity as described in the literature has been done. A case study demonstrating authentic experiences in rural homestays has been included in the chapter. Further authentic experiences derived from various tourism and hospitality sectors like food, accommodation, and entertainment have been explained.

Chapter 17, "Promoting the Tourist Experience Economy in LEDCs Through Authentic Fair-Trade Handicrafts: A Conceptual Framework," is a conceptual work that explores the synergistic value of linking the experience economy, creative tourism, and fair-trade principles to increase the benefits of the handicraft sector to local communities while supporting positive tourist experiences, considering that the handicraft sector plays an important role in providing economic benefits of tourism to local communities, despite being threatened by globalised supply chains. The handicraft sector contributes to the livelihoods of lesser marginalised in the supply side of a destination by opening opportunities for adding value to their tangible products through co-created experiences. Furthermore, the creative potential allows tourists to create memories, connecting with producers in interesting and meaningful ways, when fair-trade principles are integrated as part of the tourist experience. To ensure a balanced synergy and active connection between experience economy, creative tourism and fair-trade concepts, well-trained and skilled artists, art managers and creative entrepreneurs are needed in tourist destinations.

REFERENCES

Abrahams, R. D. (1986). Ordinary and extraordinary experiences. In V. W. Turner & E. M. Bruner (Eds.), *The anthropology of experience* (pp. 45–72). University of Illinois Press.

Aho, S. K. (2001). Towards a general theory of touristic experiences: Modelling experience process in tourism. *Tourism Review*, *56*(3/4), 33–37. doi:10.1108/eb058368

Ambler, T., Bhattacharya, C. B., Edell, J., Keller, K. L., Lemon, K. N., & Mittal, V. (2002). Relating brand and customer perspectives on marketing management. *Journal of Service Research*, *5*(1), 13–25. doi:10.1177/1094670502005001003

Arnould, E. J., & Price, L. L. (1993). River Magic: Extraordinary experience and the extended service encounter. *The Journal of Consumer Research*, *20*(1), 24. doi:10.1086/209331

Berry, L. L., & Bendapudi, N. (2003). Clueing in customers. *Harvard Business Review*, *81*(2), 100–106. PMID:12577657

Berry, L. L., Carbone, L. P., & Haeckel, S. H. (2002). Managing the total customer experience. *MIT Sloan Management Review*, *43*(3), 85–89. doi:10.1002/arp.339

Binkhorst, E. (2005). *The co-creation tourism experience*. Whitepaper Co-Creations.

Preface

Binkhorst, E., & Den Dekker, T. (2009). Agenda for co-creation tourism experience research. *Journal of Hospitality Marketing & Management*, *18*(2–3), 311–327. doi:10.1080/19368620802594193

Boswijk, A., Thijssen, T., & Peelen, E. (2007). *The experience economy: A new perspective*. Pearson Education.

Brakus, J. J., Schmitt, B. H., & Zarantonello, L. (2009). Brand experience: What is it? How is it measures? Does it affect loyalty? *Journal of Marketing*, *73*(May), 52–68. doi:10.1509/jmkg.73.3.052

Brown, G., & Getz, D. (2005). Linking wine preferences to the choice of wine tourism destinations. *Journal of Travel Research*, *43*(3), 266–276. doi:10.1177/0047287504272027

Buhalis, D. (1999). Tourism on the Greek Islands: Issues of peripherality, competitiveness and development. *International Journal of Tourism Research*, *1*(5), 341–358. doi:10.1002/(SICI)1522-1970(199909/10)1:5<341::AID-JTR201>3.0.CO;2-0

Carbone, L. P., & Haeckel, S. H. (1994). Engineering customer experiences. *Marketing Management*, *3*(3), 8–19.

Carù, A., & Cova, B. (2003). Revisiting consumption experience: A more humble but complete view of the concept. *Marketing Theory*, *3*(2), 267–286. doi:10.1177/14705931030032004

Clawson, M., & Knetsch, J. L. (1966). *Economics of outdoor recreation*. Resources for the Future by Johns Hopkins Press.

Cohen, E. (1979a). A phenomenology of tourist experiences. *Sociology*, *13*(2), 179–201. doi:10.1177/003803857901300203

Cohen, E. (1979b). Rethinking the sociology of tourism. *Annals of Tourism Research*, *6*(1), 18–35. doi:10.1016/0160-7383(79)90092-6

Csikszentmihalyi, M. (1975a). *Beyond boredom and anxiety*. Jossey-Bass Publishers.

Csikszentmihalyi, M. (1975b). Play and intrinsic rewards. *Journal of Humanistic Psychology*, *15*(3), 41–63. doi:10.1177/002216787501500306

Csikszentmihalyi, M. (1990). *Flow: The psychology of optimal experience*. HarperCollins Publishers.

Gentile, C., Spiller, N., & Noci, G. (2007). How to sustain the customer experience: An overview of experience components that co-create value with the customer. *European Management Journal*, *25*(5), 395–410. doi:10.1016/j.emj.2007.08.005

Holbrook, M., & Hirschman, E. (1982). The experiential aspects of consumption: Consumer fantasies, feelings, and fun. *The Journal of Consumer Research*, *9*(September), 132–141. doi:10.1086/208906

Jennings, G. (2006). Perspectives on quality tourism experiences: An introduction. In G. Jennings & N. P. Nickerson (Eds.), *Quality tourism experiences* (pp. 1–22). Elsevier B.V. doi:10.1016/B978-0-7506-7811-7.50005-5

Kim, J.-H., Ritchie, J. R. B., & McCormick, B. (2012). Development of a scale to measure memorable tourism experiences. *Journal of Travel Research*, *51*(1), 12–25. doi:10.1177/0047287510385467

Larsen, S. (2007). Aspects of a psychology of the tourist experience. *Scandinavian Journal of Hospitality and Tourism, 7*(1), 7–18. doi:10.1080/15022250701226014

Li, Y. (2000). Geographical consciousness and tourism experience. *Annals of Tourism Research, 27*(4), 863–883. doi:10.1016/S0160-7383(99)00112-7

Lorentzen, A. (2009). Cities in the experience economy. *European Planning Studies, 17*(6), 829–845. doi:10.1080/09654310902793986

MacCannell, D. (1989). *The tourist*. Academic Press.

Maslow, A. H. (1959). Cognition of being in the peak experiences. *The Journal of Genetic Psychology, 94*(1), 43–66. doi:10.1080/00221325.1959.10532434 PMID:13641628

Maslow, A. H. (1962). Lessons from the peak experience. *Journal of Humanistic Psychology, 2*(9), 9–18. doi:10.1177/002216786200200102

Maslow, A. H. (1964). *Religions, values, and peak experiences*. Penguin Books Limited.

McLuhan, R. (2000, Oct. 26). Go live with a big brand experience. *Marketing*.

Oh, H., Fiore, M., & Jeoung, M. (2007). Measuring experience economy concepts: Tourism applications. *Journal of Travel Research, 46*(2), 119–132. doi:10.1177/0047287507304039

Otto, J. E., & Ritchie, J. R. B. (1996). The service experience in tourism. *Tourism Management, 17*(3), 165–174. doi:10.1016/0261-5177(96)00003-9

Pine, B. J. II, & Gilmore, J. H. (1998). Welcome to the experience economy. *Harvard Business Review, 76*(4), 97–105. PMID:10181589

Pine, B. J. II, & Gilmore, J. H. (1999). The experience economy: Work is theatre & every business a stage. *Business (Atlanta, Ga.), 40*. Advance online publication. doi:10.1080/02642069700000028

Poulsson, S. H. G., & Kale, S. H. (2004). The experience economy and commercial experiences. *The Marketing Review, 4*(3), 267–277. doi:10.1362/1469347042223445

Prahalad, C. K., & Ramaswamy, V. (2004). Co-creation experiences: The next practice in value creation. *Journal of Interactive Marketing, 18*(3), 5–14. doi:10.1002/dir.20015

Privette, G. (1981). Dynamics of peak performance. *Journal of Humanistic Psychology, 21*(1), 57–67. doi:10.1177/002216788102100106

Privette, G. (1983). Peak experience, peak performance, and flow: A comparative analysis of positive human experiences. *Journal of Personality and Social Psychology, 45*(6), 1361–1368. doi:10.1037/0022-3514.45.6.1361

Quan, S., & Wang, N. (2004). Towards a structural model of the tourist experience: An illustration from food experiences in tourism. *Tourism Management, 25*(3), 297–305. doi:10.1016/S0261-5177(03)00130-4

Quinlan Cutler, S., & Carmichael, B. (2010). The dimensions of the tourist experience. In M. Morgan, P. Lugosi, & J. R. B. Ritchie (Eds.), *The tourism and leisure experience: Consumer and managerial perspectives* (pp. 3–26). Channel View Publications. doi:10.21832/9781845411503-004

Preface

Ryan, C. (2002). *The tourism experience* (2nd ed.). Continuum.

Same, S., & Larimo, J. (2012). Marketing theory: Experience marketing and experiential marketing. In *The 7th International Scientific Conference "Business and Management 2012". Selected papers* (pp. 480–487). Vilnius, Lithuania: Vilnius Gediminas Technical University Publishing House Technika. 10.3846/bm.2012.063

Schmitt, B. H. (1999a). *Experiential marketing*. Free Press.

Schmitt, B. H. (2002). *Marketing mxperimental*. Nobel.

Schouten, J. W., McAlexander, J. H., & Koenig, H. F. (2007). Transcendent customer experience and brand community. *Journal of the Academy of Marketing Science, 35*(3), 357–368. doi:10.100711747-007-0034-4

Selstad, L. (2007). The social anthropology of the tourist experience. exploring the "Middle Role.". *Scandinavian Journal of Hospitality and Tourism, 7*(1), 19–33. doi:10.1080/15022250701256771

Smith, W. L. (2006). Experiential tourism around the world and at home: Definitions and standards. *International Journal of Services and Standards, 2*(1), 1–14. doi:10.1504/IJSS.2006.008156

Soares, T. C. (2009). *Características do turismo de experiências: Estudos de caso em Belo Horizonte e Sabará sobre inovação e diversidade de valorização dos clientes*. Universidade Federal de Minas Gerais.

Song, H. J., Lee, C.-K., Park, J. A., Hwang, Y. H., & Reisinger, Y. (2015). The influence of tourist experience on perceived value and satisfaction with temple Stays: The experience economy theory. *Journal of Travel & Tourism Marketing, 32*(4), 401–415. doi:10.1080/10548408.2014.898606

Stamboulis, Y., & Skayannis, P. (2003). Innovation strategies and technology for experience-based tourism. *Tourism Management, 24*(1), 35–43. doi:10.1016/S0261-5177(02)00047-X

Sternberg, E. (1997). The iconography of the tourism experience. *Annals of Tourism Research, 24*(4), 951–969. doi:10.1016/S0160-7383(97)00053-4

Sundbo, J. (2009). Innovation in the experience economy: A taxonomy of innovation organisations. *Service Industries Journal, 29*(4), 431–455. doi:10.1080/02642060802283139

Tung, V. W. S., & Ritchie, J. R. B. (2011). Exploring the essence of memorable tourism experiences. *Annals of Tourism Research, 38*(4), 1367–1386. doi:10.1016/j.annals.2011.03.009

Turner, V. W., & Bruner, E. M. (1986). *The anthropology of experience*. University of Illinois Press., doi:10.1093/oxfordhb/9780199736362.013.0005

Tynan, C., & McKechnie, S. (2009). Experience marketing: A review and reassessment. *Journal of Marketing Management, 25*(5–6), 501–517. doi:10.1362/026725709X461821

Uriely, N. (2005). The tourist experience: Conceptual developments. *Annals of Tourism Research, 32*(1), 199–216. doi:10.1016/j.annals.2004.07.008

Urry, J. (2002). *The Tourist Gaze* (2nd ed.). SAGE Publications Ltd.

Verhoef, P. C., Lemon, K. N., Parasuraman, A., Roggeveen, A., Tsiros, M., & Schlesinger, L. A. (2009). Customer experience creation: Determinants, dynamics and management strategies. *Journal of Retailing, 85*(1), 31–41. doi:10.1016/j.jretai.2008.11.001

Volo, S. (2009). Conceptualising experience: A tourist-based approach. *Journal of Hospitality Marketing & Management, 18*(2–3), 111–126. doi:10.1080/19368620802590134

Acknowledgment

We would like to acknowledge the assistance of all academics and researchers who contributed to the successful completion of the book, in particular, the authors and the colleagues who took part in the review process. Without their support, this publication would not have been possible to bring to light.

Rui Augusto da Costa
GOVCOPP, University of Aveiro, Portugal

Filipa Brandão
GOVCOPP, University of Aveiro, Portugal

Zélia Breda
GOVCOPP, University of Aveiro, Portugal

Carlos Costa
GOVCOPP, University of Aveiro, Portugal

Section 1
Tourism Destinations

Chapter 1
Cognitive Science of Tourism Experiences

Noel Scott
University of the Sunshine Coast, Australia & Edith Cowan University, Australia

Ana Claudia Campos
https://orcid.org/0000-0002-5816-5137
University of Algarve, Portugal

ABSTRACT

While other disciplinary approaches such as sociology and anthropology are important, this chapter introduces a cognitivist psychology approach to experience research. Such theoretical discussion may seem of little practical use, but the chapter argues that it is fundamental to understanding how and why experiences are created. The chapter applies theory and concepts from cognitive science (cognitive psychology and neuroscience) in the study of tourism experiences. This provides a different psychological paradigm to the behavioural approach currently in use in much research. The chapter describes the scope of cognitive psychology and neuroscience, its main concepts of cognitive psychology (perception, attention, emotion, memory, consciousness, learning), and their neuronal basis (neuroscience). These concepts are then applied in three topic areas related to tourism experiences: decision making, emotion, and attention. Several applications to tourism experience research are noted. Finally, the chapter discusses the way cognitive psychology concepts can be used in tourism research.

INTRODUCTION

The experience economy paradigm emphasises the importance of experiences and, consequently, the need to better understand them. Accordingly, studies of tourism experiences are increasingly common, using perspectives from anthropology, sociology, marketing or psychology (Larsen, 2007). This chapter approaches experiences from the sub-field of cognitive psychology. It discusses how cognitive psychology addresses mental processes usually involved in tourist experiences, such as decision-making, emotion and attention. In summary, this chapter's objectives are: (i) to argue the relevance of cognitive psychology to

DOI: 10.4018/978-1-7998-8775-1.ch001

study the tourist experience; (ii) to clarify the cognitive psychology approach to the tourist experience; (iii) to showcase the cognitive paradigm as applied to three cognitive processes involved in the tourist experience, (iv) to highlight problems and potential of application of cognitive psychology approach and assumptions to tourism; and lastly, (5) to illuminate the practical implications of cognitive psychology to the management of tourism experiences.

EMBRACING UNPOPULAR IDEAS

The study of experiences is a popular topic in the tourism literature and has been a central theme in research (E. Cohen, 1979; Larsen, 2007; Mannell & Iso-Ahola, 1987; O'Dell & Billing, 2005; Ooi, 2003; Otto & Brent Ritchie, 1996; Prentice, Witt, & Hamer, 1998; Ryan, 1997; Uriely, 2005). An experience is considered the principal 'product' of travel. Tourism marketing and travel agents provide a "marketplace" and tourists with the "mental places" where experiences occur (Volo, 2009, p. 119). Prior investigations into tourism experiences have adopted two main approaches: those seeking to understand the meaning of an experience and those trying to understand how an experience is "produced" in the human mind (Skavronskaya et al., 2017). This distinction is analogous to the distinction between the content of a television program and how the content is created, transmitted, and displayed on a television, the television process. In this chapter, we focus on the mental processes that support "having an experience" rather than discussing what the experience "means".

A tourism business operator may consider that, from a practical perspective, understanding the mental processes involved in "having an experience" is not particularly important. After all, the operator may say, I understand my customers and can observe that they are satisfied with their experiences. I do not need to know how they are thinking and why they are satisfied. The authors argue that understanding the cognitive psychology of "having an experience" is useful in understanding a visitor's decision-making process, their emotional responses and what they notice and pay attention to. This knowledge can then be used to improve or change the experience to improve the outcomes from customer experiences and increase profitability. Further, this chapter discusses some of the problems with 'folk psychology' or our everyday understanding of how we think that is incorrect. Thus, an understanding of cognitive psychology can inform the management of experiences. Cognitive science (cognitive psychology, neuroscience, and related fields) is the discipline that studies the mental processes that support "having an experience".

Other disciplines such as anthropology (Ellis, Park, Kim, & Yeoman, 2018; Graburn, 1983; Selstad, 2007) and sociology (Cohen & Cohen, 2019) are important in understanding what experiences mean normatively for a culture or group. In cognitive psychological terms, these disciplines focus on understanding how individual mental processes are determined by the often subconscious, mental schema of shared culture or group norms. They also may examine how an object shapes an individual's actions with a normative meaning (a heart shape that means 'love') or a narrative with cultural or group associations. Clearly, these are important in 'having an experience'. However, an experience is also discussed as unique and individual, and thus a person's experience is also influenced by the mental processes occurring in the brain. Indeed, a cognitive psychologist would say our mental processes determine our thoughts and experiences as they provide the mechanism by which our thoughts exist. However, we may consider four levels of analysis concerning human experiences that can be discerned: group, individual, cognitive process and neural (Figure 1).

Cognitive Science of Tourism Experiences

Figure 1. Levels of analysis used to study tourism experiences
Source: own elaboration

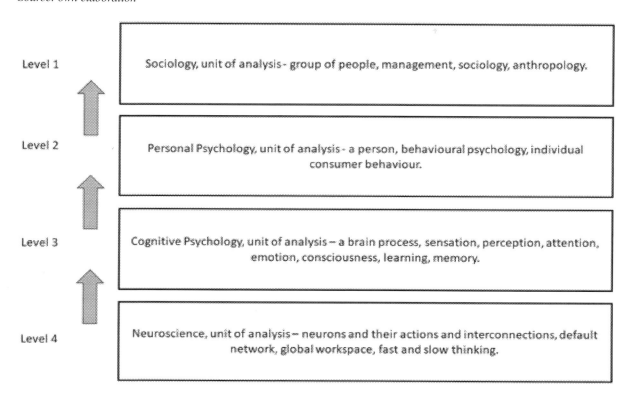

Some researchers use concepts from anthropology (Ellis et al., 2018; Graburn, 1983; Selstad, 2007) or sociology to explore the meaning of an experience (Ford & Brown, 2006; Matteucci, 2014; Moscardo & Pearce, 2007; Russell, 1995), shown as Level in Figure 1. For example, Matteucci (2014) examines the meaning of flamenco dancing and the shaping of identity through stories and myths. Level two is the most common level of analysis to study individual attitudes and behaviour before, during or after an experience. For example, memorable tourism experience (MTE) studies examine the relationship between a servicescape and an individual's post-experience memories, attitudes, or summary evaluations (i.e., satisfaction). These studies usually collect individual data but analyse and report only group results (Kim, 2010, 2018; Kim & Brent Ritchie, 2014). While some more individual-based studies are available, including the seminal "River Magic: Extraordinary Experience and the extended service encounter" by Arnould and Price (1993), most of them do not try to explain the relationship between a person's experience (stimulus -S) and an individual's emotions, feelings, and memories (response-R).

Level 3 experience studies examine an individual's mental processes to provide an explanation for these S-R relationships. This explanation is based on an understanding of, for example, how an individual perceives, pays attention to, appraises, elicits emotions and feelings, and responds to the stimulus. Our knowledge of level three processes has expanded rapidly over the past half-century, and tourism researchers have begun to use cognitive appraisal processes (Scherer, Schorr, & Johnstone, 2001) and the effect of emotion on perception (Zadra & Clore, 2011).

Level 4 experience studies are based on neuroscience, relating stimuli to the actions of neurons in our brain. For example, Stienmetz, Kim, Xiang, and Fesenmaier (2021) discuss work on fast and slow thinking (Kahneman, 2011), judgement and decision-making biases (Kahneman, 2000), and the 'parsing' of a stream of perception into a mental 'event' (Zacks, Speer, Swallow, Braver, & Reynolds, 2007). However, the steady increase in the application of cognitive science concepts in tourism research requires some caution, as discussed below.

The first issue for tourism researchers in using concepts from cognitive psychology is the translation problem (Francken & Slors, 2018). This concerns the difficulties of relating everyday 'common sense' words such as emotion and memory into well-defined concepts such as semantic, episodic, autobiographical, long term and working memory or for emotion, high arousal, and positive valence. The terms and concepts used by tourism researchers may be derived from folk psychology, such as the everyday beliefs about the mind, rather than cognitive science (Sibicky, Klein, & Embrescia, 2020). For example, we must distinguish between two common ways of thinking about the experience, immediate consciousness or the moment-by-moment lived experience, and post hoc satisfaction or the evaluated experience (Mannell & Iso-Ahola, 1987).

The second problem is that academic discussion of cognition is based on 100 years of psychology studies that have used different paradigms, definitions, and concepts. For example, many common decision-making models used in tourism are based on a rational and conscious mental process and ignore heuristic or emotional effects. In addition, tourism is an applied field and so derives its theories from other disciplines. However, there is a tendency for a theory to be stuck to, long after it has been abandoned in the original discipline. These expired theories are called 'zombie theories' (Quiggin, 2012). A third problem is the "mix and match" use of concepts and theories from different disciplines without considering their underlying assumptions. For these reasons, the application of cognitive science to study tourism phenomena requires adopting a particular cognitive paradigm and translating the everyday language used by respondents into its well-defined terms.

THE COGNITIVE PARADIGM

The tourism literature has tended to study experiences using a behavioural paradigm and theory. Take, for example, a stream of research by Jong-Hyeong Kim, who has developed a memorable tourism experience (MTE) scale (Kim, 2010, 2014) and applied it to examine the effects of MTEs on loyalty (Kim, 2018). This research aimed to build "a linkage between destinations' specific attributes and memorable experiences" (Kim, 2014, p. 41). The author provided an interesting discussion of the psychology of memory, noting that memory is enhanced by emotion. Kim (2010) determines that experiences of refreshment, involvement and local culture are likely to be recalled. Later, a scale to measure Memorable Tourism Experiences was developed (Kim, Ritchie, & McCormick, 2012), including several dimensions of experiences that are likely to be memorable (Figure 2).

In this stream of literature, Kim and his co-authors seek to correlate either destination attributes or the characteristics of a tourism experience with positive or negative emotion and memorability (Kim, 2021). They rightly indicate that stronger emotions are antecedents of a stronger recall of an experience. However, the reason why one dimension of a destination may lead to stronger emotion is not discussed. Therefore, the MTE scale is a profiling tool that can be used to compare destinations (destination X is higher than destination Y on dimension Z) but does not help understand why individuals react in this way. Further, an attribute may have been experienced – I was excited - but this does not guarantee that it is memorable – excitement may have been incidental only and not relevant to the experience. Memorability and emotion derive from goal relevance and other situationally determined evaluation dimensions (called appraisal dimensions).

Figure 2. Memorable tourism experience scale
Source: after Kim et al., 2012

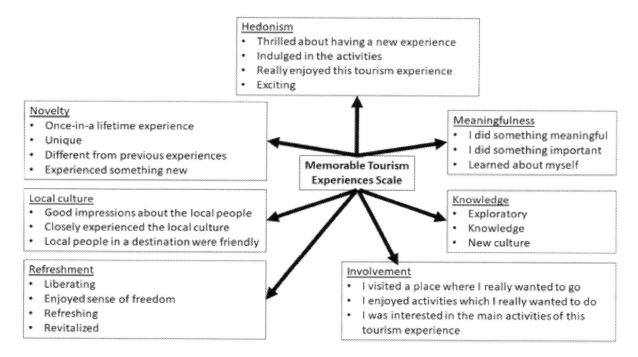

The lesson in studying individuals to explain why a particular experience was associated with an emotion or memory is that it is necessary to consistently understand and use cognitive psychology's assumptions and theories. Jong-Hyeong Kim (2021) describes memory from a cognitive psychology perspective but fails to use the related cognitive psychology of the cognitive appraisal theory of emotion, which explains why a strong memory is found.

The cognitive paradigm assumes:

1. Our thought processes determine the meaning of an object. There is no such thing as an authentic object, separate from our prior knowledge and experience. Objects do not have an a priori meaning. Instead, the meaning of an object is learned. Thus, a person going to a theme park may experience sadness or happiness depending on their mental appraisal. Our association of a theme park with excitement and happiness is due to the relative frequency of excitement amongst all the people who attend a park. We may be able to say that most visitors will be excited, but we cannot say that all will be. This is important as experiences are individual.

2. All humans think, but that does not mean they understand how their brain works. One of the important implications of the study of Levels 3 and 4 is that many of our common beliefs (assumptions) about how we think and make decisions are incorrect. Much of neuroscience and cognitive psychology work seeks to explain why the brain does not work as expected.
3. Cognitive models of our brain are complex. The brain has developed through evolutionary processes and consists of multiple recursively interactive systems. Therefore no one model is generally used. For example, our reactions to environmental stimuli are based on the interplay of a reflective, conscious, deliberative system that is controlled but effortful, and a quicker automatic system that responds in line with habits and emotions (Kahneman, 2011). The nature of our experience is then determined by which system is dominant, and this is determined by the nature of the stimulus (a dangerous lion versus a gentle massage) and the current internal state (goals, memories of prior experiences, etc.). In most previously experienced 'normal' situations, the habit and emotion system are dominant, although most research is based on rational conscious (effortful) cognition.
4. Our brain capacity and mental processes place limitations on our ability to understand the world around us. For example, each of our sense organs has a restricted ability; our eyes cannot see in the infrared, our hearing has restrictions both in low and high frequencies. Despite this, the volume of sensory stimuli available means a need to limit our mental processes to only the most salient at any one point in time. Therefore, we use habits and emotions to deal with many situations.

SOME PROBLEMS OF EXPERIENCES AND THEIR COGNITIVE 'SOLUTION'

Decision Making

Tourism as a field of study has adapted its theories of visitor decision-making and behaviour from economics and psychology (McCabe, Li, & Chen, 2016). Foxall (1990) and Decrop (2014) classify decision-making models into five theoretical types: economic, psychodynamic, behaviourist, cognitive, and humanistic. Furthermore, both Foxall (1990) and Decrop (2014) consider cognitive models characterised by explicitly conscious and rational mental processes. This is the first point of terminological confusion as cognitive science recognises different types of mental processes used during decision making.

Behaviourist and rationalist psychological theories of decision making assume that people assess the desirability and likelihood of possible outcomes of choice alternatives and integrate this information through some type of expectation-based calculus to arrive at a decision (Loewenstein, Weber, Hsee, & Welch, 2001). In cognitive psychology, researchers recognise that there are several different types of decision processes, and that emotional processes are important in decisions. Indeed, most actions taken may be based on emotions and subsequent feelings, intuition, or habit (Duhigg, 2013), although we are not reflexively self-aware of these thought processes. However, the effect of emotions can be measured experimentally. 'Feelings-as-information theory' (Avnet, Pham, & Stephen, 2012; Schwarz, 2011) considers those human sensations termed 'feelings' as the result of emotional activity of which we are not conscious. Indeed, we are unaware of most normal bodily sensations, although we are aware of those sensations called 'feelings" and abnormal sensations we register as pain (Damasio, 1995).

Many decision-making models also implicitly assume that such unconscious mental activity is not rational. However, the concept of rationality is also complex, has a long history, and is associated with logic, reasoning rather than intuition, and an absence of emotion. Thus, Herbert Simon instead defined rationality in a social science sense as actions or thoughts that:

Contribute to certain goals, where these goals may be the pleasure or satisfaction of an individual or the guarantee of food or shelter for the members of a society. [..] When awareness and intention are present, the function is usually called manifest, otherwise it is a latent function." (Simon, 1978, p. 3).

Using this definition, 'rational' goal-directed decision-making models can be characterised as exhibiting manifest rationality. However, the definition also attributes latent rationality to actions undertaken to achieve a goal even if a consumer is not consciously aware of that goal at that time. Most mental activity is unconscious. Thus, researchers should examine experience choice using decision-making processes from the cognitive paradigm.

Emotion and Feelings

There is a range of different experiential outcomes or types of experiences ranging from ordinary to extraordinary (Duerden et al., 2018). Memorable tourism experiences (MTE) tend to be associated with strong emotions and feelings, suggesting that we need to understand the mental processes responsible for emotional elicitation and feelings. There are several competing theories concerning how emotion is elicited (Figure 3 and Table 1). Cognitive Appraisal Theory (CAT) and Constructivist Theory (Barrett & Satpute, 2019; Volo, 2021) are two important types of theories today (Scarantino & de Sousa, 2021). The tourism literature has used Behaviourist (Kim, 2010), Stimulus-Organism-Response (Chen, So, Hu, & Poomchaisuwan, 2021), Basic emotions (Faullant, Matzler, & Mooradian, 2011), Constructivist (Volo, 2021), and Appraisal Theories (Hosany, 2012; Ma, Gao, Scott, & Ding, 2013). These theories vary in terms of their assumptions concerning how emotions are elicited. Behaviourist (Stimulus-Response) theory treats the brain as a black box with emotions not discussed and only behaviour of importance. SOR theory provides the person with a limited role in the elicitation of emotion based on personality factors, such as novelty seeking. Cognitive appraisal is a process that detects and assesses the significance of the environment for well-being (Moors, Ellsworth, Scherer, & Frijda, 2013). "Significance for well-being" means the achievement or obstruction of concerns, such as an individual's needs, attachments, values, current goals, and beliefs (Frijda, 2007). Therefore, moods are different from emotions as they have no target (Scarantino & de Sousa, 2021). Significance is based on a few dimensions, such as goal congruence and importance, and degree of novelty. Most recently, constructivist theories of emotion have been introduced by Volo (2021). Although no mechanism is specified, the constructivist approach shares some similarities with appraisal theories in its focus on the core effect. However, the constructivist approach emphasises a particular emotion being recognised based on cultural learning rather than an independently determined type. This means that their prior learned associations determine a person's emotional response. The individualisation of an emotional response to a stimulus is determined, in appraisal theory, by personal goals and prior experience.

Figure 3. Theories of emotion

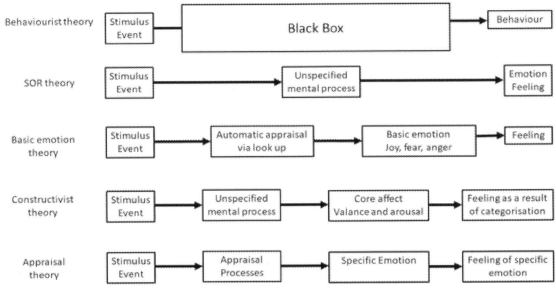

Table 1. Characteristics of theories of emotion.

	Behaviourism	SOR	Basic	Constructivist	Appraisal
Cause of emotion	Event	Environment	Automatic appraisal	Core affect determined by processes including appraisal.	Jointly determined by dimensions including prior experience (novelty) and reappraisal
Process	Learned association	Deterministic	Deterministic	Strongly constructed	Mildly constructed
Main determinant	Learned association	Environment characteristics	Genetic	Cultural learning and determinants of core emotion (unspecified).	Current goals Prior experience Agency, etc.

Both constructivist and CAT approaches consider that "it is not the event itself that generates the emotions, but rather the way individuals evaluate or appraise the event" (McColl-Kennedy et al., 2017, p. 249). Thus, emotion is transactional and involves an interaction between a person and an event (Lazarus, 1991). Further, for all theories, emotions are no longer considered structurally opposed to reason (Scarantino & de Sousa, 2021). Emotions are also agreed to correlate with changes in motivation to do things (Scarantino & de Sousa, 2021).

One interesting consequence of recognising the importance and ubiquity of emotions in everyday experience is that concepts, such as satisfaction and value, may be considered associated with emotional processes and feelings. For example, the risk is associated with worry, anxiety, or fear (Marion, 2016). Worry has been shown to be a better predictor of behaviour than risk perceptions (Wolff, Larsen, & Øgaard, 2019). Similarly, several authors have discussed satisfaction as a feeling (Ma, Scott, Ding, & Gao, 2017) as well as a summative evaluation.

Attention

Our everyday life is dependent on our mental attention processes, whether people are aware of them or not. Human beings are limited in their capacity to deal with the almost infinite external sensory and internal information available to them (Cohen, 2014). Not all information is always relevant to every individual or situation. Attention concerns those processes that allow individuals to deal with perceptual information and remains a key research topic in cognitive psychology. More recently, neuroscience has been contributing to further understanding of attentional phenomena. Attention processes may be thought of as a gate for information to flow into or within the brain (Cohen, 2014). Think of the following examples.

- A guide explains a painting to a group of tourists.
- A young couple visits Temple Bar in Dublin for the first time.
- A visitor to a wildlife park swims with dolphins.
- A tourist participates in a local gastronomy workshop.
- A travel party gathers at Buckingham Palace during changing of the guard.

Each of these examples of tourism experiences emphasises different facets of attention. For example, listening to someone's explanation of a painting at a museum or art gallery involves a degree of concentration, i.e. attempting at understanding what is being said about the painter and the painting techniques used mobilises the individual to attend to the auditory and visual stimuli signalled by the guide while avoiding distractors.

Visiting the iconic Temple Bar area in Dublin is quite challenging from the individual's cognitive point of view, as stimuli are multisensory, may be associated with symbolic meaning for many people, and our attention may be directed to many different parts of the scene. Attention is a selective process through which one stimulus is prioritised over another. For example, does one attend to auditory information or visual, noise from the surroundings (e.g., music), visual icons (e.g., a famous pub) or passers-by conversations? It may be that visitors may shift attention from one stimulus, a band playing music, to another, a street juggler.

Swimming with dolphins in a semi-captive environment is a voluntary behaviour, involving explicit intention to perform specific tasks, like touching the animals or doing acrobatic moves with them. Task performance is influenced by goal importance, and attention is implicitly directed towards stimuli that contribute to the achievement of that goal. For example, the animal trainer will usually be the best source of information about how to behave to achieve the goal (interact with the dolphin) successfully, then the individual will (top-down) direct attention to this target.

A gastronomy workshop requires a combination of fine motor movements and task performance for goal achievement. The workshop experience requires participant attention, and combines both automatic and intentional attention, as well as the ability to sustain attentional performance over the timespan of the workshop. Watching the chef preparing a special dish requires effortful attention in a highly distracting environment. Also, active participation in the preparation of the ingredients and the processing of the sequential tasks to have the dish completed guides goal-oriented responses; in this case, response intentions influence orienting of attention to specific targets (e.g., the participant looks at the chef's hands and movements rather than at their clothes).

The changing of the guard at Buckingham Palace is a temporary ceremony that attracts many people to the area. The crowded environment involves people, colours, sounds and movements. Enthusiastic visitors are exposed to many stimuli in a short time (e.g., the person beside you, the military manoeuvres, the guards matching, etc.). Individuals in such a stimulus context may need to direct attention between equally goal-relevant sources of information and to discern meaningful signals from irrelevant noise (e.g., a group of turbulent and talkative nearby visitors may be noise, as opposed to the goal-relevant sound of a guard issuing ceremonial orders).

Introducing Attention: The Gate to the Brain

The brain is an organ with no direct access to the external world; thus, it depends on sensory organs for perceptual information. The brain's neural cells are connected, through electrochemical signals, with these sensory organs (Eagleman, 2015). Attention allows our brain to deal with our immersion in the world and the need to respond to external and internal demands. Attention has been described as "the interface between the vast amount of stimulation provided by our complex environment and the more limited set of information of which we are aware" (Rosario Rueda, Pozuelos, & Cómbita, 2015, p. 184). It manifests in physiological (e.g., heartbeat or pupil dilation), behavioural and motor responses (e.g., turning the head towards the source of a loud sound). Such attentional physiological and behavioural responses occur by cognitive processes taking place in the brain's neural circuitry. Cognitive processes include reasoning, planning, decision-making and execution, response monitoring, behaviour adjustment, memory (encoding, storage, and retention), perception, and (for some) emotions. For them to take place, attention is critical as all depend on the brain's ability to select those stimuli that deserve priority (Anderson, 2013). Conceptually, attention has been considered a multidimensional construct (Rosario Rueda et al., 2015) as research describes many empirical phenomena that do not correspond to a single system of the brain which unitarily and coherently could be labelled as "attention" (Hommel et al., 2019).

Filter for Information Processing

Attention is best described as a collection of processes that have physiological, cognitive, and neural bases, and produce observable effects (Cohen, 2014). It is part of daily life and accounts for many behavioural responses and actions, leading to adaptive behaviour. This is possible since attention enables the selective processing of information because of the constant bombarding of the senses (Pratte, Ling, Swisher, & Tong, 2013). In broad terms, attention is the process of selecting a subset of the available sensory information for preferential processing (Pitts, Lutsyshyna, & Hillyard, 2018). Attention and information processing are not the same, although they are interrelated. Information processing refers to memory stimulus recognition, response rate, and information load capacity, whereas attention involves initiation or activation, selection, sustaining, shifting, and control (Rueda et al., 2015).

Functions of Attention

The functions of attention involved in everyday life are based on the neural network of the brain (Rueda et al., 2015). Activation is linked to the energetic state of the individual as a biological organism which exchanges energy with the environment; this energetic state is called arousal, and by combining the organism's physiological state, behavioural activity, and environmental factors, produces and impacts attentional performance (Cohen, 2014). Selection allows prioritisation of stimuli due to their abundance and the limited capacity of processing information. Prioritisation involves the orienting network of the brain in charge of sensory input. Control voluntarily guides goal-oriented action, if necessary, by counteracting automatic behaviour, which requires low levels of attention or none at all. (Rueda et al., 2015) identify attention control with the brain's executive network, responsible for decision-making processes, thoughts, or conflict resolution.

Attention Constraints

Individuals differ in their attention skills and efficiency (Rueda et al., 2015). Differences are observable and measured through behaviour; however, by the application of neuroimaging techniques, neuroscience has shown the neurological basis for these differences. Thus, attention to the internal and the external worlds is affected by several factors of different categories, as structural (related to genetics and brain neuroanatomy and physiology), but also energetic (termed arousal), and environmental (dependent on the individual internal and external circumstances, such as maturation level of the individual, family context or educational).

An individual's number of attentional resources are determined by brain organisation (neural circuitry and structure), information processing speed, memory capacity and processes, the contextual environment, and the relationship between attention and consciousness (Cohen, 2014). The contextual environment includes the individual's experience, family context and socio-economic status (Rueda et al., 2015). For instance, processing speed depends on an individual's rate of processing characteristic, but structurally is affected by working memory capacity and contextually by information presentation. Accordingly, it is claimed that attentional capacity is roughly proportional to processing speed (Cohen, 2014). There are many neural cell types. How their anatomy influences functional properties, responds to complex or specific stimuli, or connects in groups to form networks is a way to describe and understand brain organisation and attentional constraints.

Attentional Processes

Selective and Focused Attention: One Thing at a Time

An intuitive way of describing attention is to say that it is the focusing of the mind on something. In fact, focusing has been identified as one salient characteristic of attention. Focusing means concentrating cognitive resources on specific information, while ignoring other types of information, more specifically that information that is irrelevant to the situation. Thus, selection is the process that allows this concentration. Concentration is possible because information is prioritised according to demands imposed by a situation, and the need for adaptive behaviour, e.g., as time and space constraints, as attention, is limited in capacity. Selection and focusing are complementary facets of attention, as focus refers to the informational load accepted by the selection process, which is set in motion due to the need to pursue goals and activities in a new context. The selective nature of attention is indisputable, but the same is not true as to the processing mechanisms of selection, which seem to affect perception and control in the performance of tasks (Swallow & Jiang, 2013). Theoretical explanations to provide a consistent model of selection are not yet fully developed or indeed accepted.

Attentional processes are useful to understand tourism experiences. No matter how exciting the experience environment is, and regardless of the multisensorial stimuli one may find in it, tourists will always focus on some stimuli to the exclusion of others. Therefore, experiences should be aware of human attentional characteristics and emphasise stimuli relevant to the context of the experience and the activities involved. This will influence a participant's adaptive behaviour and enhance opportunities for successful perceptual and cognitive processing and behaviour. Tour guides are attention mediators who may try to concentrate a tourist's attention on aspects of the environment (Ooi, 2005).

Attention Shift and Division: Humans Wander, Externally and Internally

Attention shifting describes the condition of the flexibility of attention as it shifts back and forth between multiple tasks, operations, or mental sets (von Suchodoletz, Fasche, & Skuballa, 2017). Attention shifting is a common phenomenon when a multitude of stimuli that count as potential sources of information compete for people's limited attention. The world is stimuli-cluttered, and some of the stimuli are found in the external environment (e.g., purposely multisensorial). In contrast, others are located internally in the individual as engaged in top-down attention-competing tasks (as in driving and using a phone). This requires individuals to learn how to discern relevant sources from irrelevant ones and what signal and noise are. Research confirms that switching between tasks is effortful and expensive regarding attentional resources and time, leading to "switch costs" (Corbetta & Shulman, 2002).

Switch costs may be mitigated but not eliminated, and mitigation depends on allowing time to prepare for the switching. Neurophysiological studies on human vision have found that attention operates at two levels using complementary mechanisms, noise filtering and amplification. At one stage, attention operates by applying the noise filtering process, through which a reduction of responses occurs to non-relevant stimuli, and only then amplifies noise-reduced ones. This points to the fact that the brain presents a hierarchy in its systems, as in the visual (Pratte et al., 2013). Everyday life provides plenty of evidence of people engaging in multitasking, suggesting the need of switching attention from one task to another. This process involves prioritising tasks and allocating an amount of attention, which is also dependent on several different factors (Farmer, Janssen, Nguyen, & Brumby, 2018). The division of attention may create problems of interference of stimuli, compromising attentional performance, particularly in demanding scenarios (Cohen, 2014), because there is a need to adapt behaviour to an adequate response. In this, a distinction should be made between automatic and effortful tasks, as the more automatic a task is, the less affected is the performance of the other. Recent research has shown that although people perform well at multitasking by adjusting behaviour, they do not reach optimal outcomes (Farmer et al., 2018).

Tourism experiences usually occur in sensorially cluttered environments, and many stimuli compete for the tourist's attention. As there is evidence that stimuli interference occurs in divided attention situations, experience managers should consider a single task orientation, so that tourist performance enhances chances of successful completion. Additionally, as automatic behaviour leaves room for allocating more attentional resources to controlled attention, planned activities should integrate opportunities to automatic performance, which is easier to find among routine, non-surprising activities. A cooking workshop, for example, presents tourists with familiar tasks combined with non-familiar ones.

Sustained and Effortful Attention: Is There Easy or Difficult Attention?

Sustained attention is "a fundamental component of attention characterised by the subject's readiness to detect rarely and unpredictably occurring signals over prolonged periods of time" (Sarter, Givens, & Bruno, 2001, p. 146). Ko, Komarov, Hairston, Jung, and Lin (2017, p. 1) consider sustained attention as the "process that enables the maintenance of response persistence and continuous effort over extended periods of time". When individuals must pay attention to something that may randomly enter the visual field, their response capacity depends on the maintenance of attentional effort. This is called vigilance. Vigilance is said to require little response but a high persistence capacity (Cohen, 2014), and time duration per se may be taxing to good performance. If there is a relationship between attention and time devoted to a task, in a sense, all sustained attention is also effortful and potentially leads to fatigue (Ko et al., 2017). However, effort depends also on the demands of the task itself. Thus, there are differences in the degree of task effort, and consequently in attentional performance. Sustained and effortful attention demand control over behaviour, and thus the executive function of attention.

Some activities in a tourism context may be physically and/or mentally effortful and may compromise attentional performance, e.g., parachuting from a skyscraper or cage diving to shark-watching. Activities involving a combination of concentration and physical activity represent a high risk for individual safety, impacting the body's physiological responses, impairing attention to the broader environment. The effort demanded may require concurrent tasks (watching the shark and using underwater equipment properly), thereby dividing attention between different goals (to dive, to watch the shark, to master the equipment, to keep safe and alive). Other experiences, like dog sledging, which require tourists to enact the role of an experienced racer, are also physically and mentally demanding, especially for those visitors lacking relevant prior knowledge and experience (i.e., dealing with race dogs, snowy trails, or the sledges). Everyday automobile driving is s a complex activity because it involves multitasking, human-specific functioning, and a dangerous situation itself (Groeger & Murphy, 2021). Non-familiar tasks, such as operating a dog sledge, qualify as a novel stimulus prioritised over familiar ones, and attention increases because of novelty (biased attention) (Horstmann & Herwig, 2016). If a stimulus is unfamiliar, attention increases towards the environment, which in turn increases the perception of risk; therefore, the allocation of attention to behaviours relevant to the performance of the specific tasks is greater than in low perceived risk (Mrkva, Cole, & Van Boven, 2021).

Bottom-Up and Top-Down Attention: From External to Internal

Bottom-up (salience-driven; exogenous; automatic) and top-down (goal-driven; endogenous) attention concepts (Pitts et al., 2018) both enhance the neuronal activity for information processing, and thus facilitate discrimination between signal and noise (Sarter et al., 2001). Bottom-up attention occurs as an effect of the salient characteristics of a stimulus and its sensory context (Corbetta & Shulman, 2002); thus, responses to the external environment involve automatised performance at the sensory-physiological and motoric levels, requiring low levels of effort or awareness. There are some intrinsic qualities of objects that, relative to the environment, make them particularly salient for attention. Research findings show that cue presentation facilitates identification of the stimulus, and that sensory cues make this identification more rapidly than cognitive ones (Corbetta & Shulman, 2002). Novel, surprising, distinctive, and salient objects and events capture the brain's attention and "are processed at the expense of ongoing behaviour and neural activity" (Corbetta & Shulman, 2002, p. 201). This quick response of the brain is interpreted as an ability to act upon a stimulus that may bear important implications to survival and well-being, by leading to obtaining a reward or preventing a negative outcome from happening (Anderson, 2013).

In real-life situations, the two attentional processes, bottom-up and top-down, interfere with one another resulting in stimuli becoming salient if a goal is called into consideration (Corbetta & Shulman, 2002). This interference highlights a state of cognitive competition (Romaniuk & Nguyen, 2017). The dichotomy between bottom-up and top-down attention is not consensual (Awh, Belopolsky, & Theeuwes, 2012). Research indicates a mutual influence and the same underlying neural basis (Katsuki & Constantinidis, 2014).

Selective attention and stimuli prioritisation are set in motion by goals and the performance of tasks required to achieve them. Cognitive processes guide perceptual activity to highlight the relevant stimuli in a situation (Corbetta & Shulman, 2002). The process is described as attentional priority or goal-driven attentional control (Anderson, 2013). The interpretation of the external world is a function of the representation of what is important in a specific situation: it can be either the prey we want to catch, the friend we want to spot in a gathering, or the "small animal playing a musical instrument" in the painting (Corbetta & Shulman, 2002, p. 201). Controlled attention (e.g., focused on an area or an object feature) reduces distraction, especially if stimuli are known in advance, as in the case of the prey we are hunting and expecting to see at a particular location. In this case, top-down attention is said to be contingent (Anderson, 2013), and immediate benefits are seen in the individual's quick response to the situation.

The combination of bottom-up and top-down attention has been studied in the context of tourism experiences (Campos, Pinto, & Scott, 2020). According to these findings, bottom-up attention processes were stronger than top-down ones, which may be due to the paramount importance of the unusual, non-familiar environments where tourist experiences take place. This combination of the two directions of the selection process (Rosario Rueda et al., 2015) can be emphasised in tourism experiences, especially in those adopting a co-creation approach (e.g., many types of creative tourism experiences), as these require performance of tasks and goal achievement; these many examples of co-creative experiences demand voluntary non-automatic) and top-down attention.

CONCLUSION

This chapter has discussed concepts from cognitive psychology and their application to tourism research. The chapter contends that a cognitive psychology approach can help tourism researchers better understand tourism experiences and hence provide meaningful results for practitioners. It has highlighted three areas, decision-making, emotion, and attention, central to understanding experiences. Several other topic areas have not been discussed due to a lack of space: consciousness, sensation and perception, prospection and retrospection, memory and so on. The application of cognitive psychology to tourism provides a rich and fruitful area for further research.

The chapter has also highlighted several problems that become evident in applying theory from cognitive psychology. First, the translation problem is changing how other researchers describe a situation using 'zombie theories' or folk concepts into the terms used in the cognitive paradigm. The second problem is that strictly applying cognitive concepts requires a deep understanding of them, which is difficult to achieve in an applied field. As disciplinary theory changes, the transfer of the appropriate concepts to the applied field requires innovative ideas that can face a conservative academic audience. It is vital to use appropriate theory, but, even within the field of cognitive psychology, several theories are vying for acceptance. This is the situation currently between cognitive appraisal theories and the constructivist theories of emotion (Volo, 2021).

Further, it is difficult for a tourism academic to be aware of the relevant theory to use. Tourism academics must be concerned about whether using a new theory will make a difference to the results of a study. For example, the importance of understanding attention processes is that this knowledge can provide useful information for reinterpreting and understanding the confusion of a servicescape (Ooi, 2005), the outcomes of an experience (Campos et al., 2020), and the goals of a consumer through an eye-tracking study (Scott et al., 2019). The importance of using cognitive psychology to study decision making is to emphasise the importance of emotions (Achar, So, Agrawal, & Duhachek, 2016) and habit (Mitev & Irimiás, 2020) in that process.

Similarly, in understanding emotion, cognitive psychology can indicate the reason for individual differences in the emotions elicited by two people having the same apparent experience. Cognitive psychology moves tourism research on from the belief that the environment is determinant. But as Volo (2021) discussed, there is always a new theory that can be applied. Here the relevant issue is not whether there is a new theory but whether that new theory makes a difference to the results of an experiment or provides new insights. The differences between constructivist and appraisal theory in terms of their implications for tourism research are unclear. The advantages of adopting a cognitive psychological approach are significant; that of adopting a cognitivist and constructivist approach is less clear.

There are many areas for applying cognitive psychology concepts in tourism, and emotional experiences are a natural fit. However, many other concepts can be studied in experience research, such as worry (Jiang, Li, Huang, & Scott, 2020), awe (Coghlan, Buckley, & Weaver, 2012), memorability (Campos et al., 2017), mindfulness (Chen, Scott, & Benckendorff, 2017), imagery processing (Dung Le, Scott, & Lohmann, 2019), and so on. It may be that a better understanding of psychology can help in promoting pro-environmental messages. Indeed, there is much that warrants attention from researchers wanting to address new ideas and challenges.

There are many practical applications of cognitive psychology in the study of tourism experiences. After all, tourism is simply another human activity where our brain must understand and respond to the external environment. Several useful methods developed in cognitive psychology research may be useful in studying experiences, such as eye-tracking (Le, Hadinejad, Moyle, Ma, & Scott, 2020) or skin conductance (Li, 2020). These can help understand objectively a visitor's the focus of a visitor's attention or their physiological reactions to an experience. More generally, cognitive psychology highlights the importance of understanding a person's goals and the degree of novelty of the experience in determining their emotional outcomes, memories, and foci of attention. Further, cognitive psychology highlights that visitors are active in interpreting and interacting with their environment and co-creating their experiences in it.

ACKNOWLEDGMENT

This chapter is financed by National Funds provided by FCT–Foundation for Science and Technology through project UIDB/04020/2020.

REFERENCES

Achar, C., So, J., Agrawal, N., & Duhachek, A. (2016). What we feel and why we buy: The influence of emotions on consumer decision-making. *Current Opinion in Psychology*, *10*, 166–170. doi:10.1016/j.copsyc.2016.01.009

Anderson, B. A. (2013). A value-driven mechanism of attentional selection. *Journal of Vision (Charlottesville, Va.)*, *13*(3), 1–16. doi:10.1167/13.3.7 PMID:23589803

Arnould, E., & Price, L. L. (1993). River Magic: Extraordinary experience and the extended service encounter. *The Journal of Consumer Research*, *20*(1), 24–45. doi:10.1086/209331

Avnet, T., Pham, M. T., & Stephen, A. T. (2012). Consumers' trust in feelings as information. *The Journal of Consumer Research*, *39*(4), 720–735. doi:10.1086/664978

Awh, E., Belopolsky, A. V., & Theeuwes, J. (2012). Top-down versus bottom-up attentional control: A failed theoretical dichotomy. *Trends in Cognitive Sciences*, *16*(8), 437–443. doi:10.1016/j.tics.2012.06.010 PMID:22795563

Barrett, L. F., & Satpute, A. B. (2019). Historical pitfalls and new directions in the neuroscience of emotion. *Neuroscience Letters*, *693*, 9–18. doi:10.1016/j.neulet.2017.07.045 PMID:28756189

Campos, A. C., Mendes, J., Oom do Valle, P., & Scott, N. (2017). Co-creating animal-based tourist experiences: Attention, involvement and memorability. *Tourism Management*, *63*, 100–114. doi:10.1016/j.tourman.2017.06.001

Campos, A. C., Pinto, P., & Scott, N. (2020). Bottom-up factors of attention during the tourist experience: An empirical study. *Current Issues in Tourism*, *23*(24), 3111–3133. doi:10.1080/13683500.2019.1681383

Chen, G., So, K. K. F., Hu, X., & Poomchaisuwan, M. (2021). Travel for affection: A stimulus-organism-response model of honeymoon tourism experiences. *Journal of Hospitality & Tourism Research (Washington, D.C.)*. Advance online publication. doi:10.1177/10963480211011720

Chen, I.-L., Scott, N., & Benckendorff, P. (2017). Well-being benefits from mindful experience. In N. Scott, J. Gao, & J. Ma (Eds.), Tourism experience design (pp. 174-188). CABI.

Coghlan, A., Buckley, R., & Weaver, D. (2012). A framework for analysing awe in tourism experiences. *Annals of Tourism Research*, *39*(3), 1710–1714. doi:10.1016/j.annals.2012.03.007

Cohen, E. (1979). A phenomenology of tourist experiences. *Sociology*, *13*(2), 179–210. doi:10.1177/003803857901300203

Cohen, R. A. (2014). Neuropsychology of attention: Synthesis. In R. A. Cohen (Ed.), *The neuropsychology of attention* (pp. 931–963). Springer. doi:10.1007/978-0-387-72639-7_28

Cohen, S. A., & Cohen, E. (2019). New directions in the sociology of tourism. *Current Issues in Tourism*, *22*(2), 153–172. doi:10.1080/13683500.2017.1347151

Corbetta, M., & Shulman, G. L. (2002). Control of goal-directed and stimulus-driven attention in the brain. *Nature Reviews. Neuroscience*, *3*(3), 201–215. doi:10.1038/nrn755 PMID:11994752

Damasio, A. R. (1995). Toward a neurobiology of emotion and feeling: Operational concepts and hypotheses. *The Neuroscientist, 1*(1), 19–25. doi:10.1177/107385849500100104

Decrop, A. (2014). Theorising tourist behavior. In S. McCabe (Ed.), *The Routledge handbook of tourism marketing* (pp. 251–267). Routledge.

Duerden, M. D., Lundberg, N. R., Ward, P., Taniguchi, S. T., Hill, B., Widmer, M. A., & Zabriskie, R. (2018). From ordinary to extraordinary: A framework of experience types. *Journal of Leisure Research, 49*(3-5), 196–216. doi:10.1080/00222216.2018.1528779

Duhigg, C. (2013). *The power of habit: Why we do what we do and how to change*. Random House.

Eagleman, D. (2015). *The brain: The story of you*. Canongate Books.

Ellis, A., Park, E., Kim, S., & Yeoman, I. (2018). What is food tourism? *Tourism Management, 68*, 250–263. doi:10.1016/j.tourman.2018.03.025

Farmer, G. D., Janssen, C. P., Nguyen, A. T., & Brumby, D. P. (2018). Dividing attention between tasks: Testing whether explicit payoff functions elicit optimal dual-task performance. *Cognitive Science, 42*(3), 820–849. doi:10.1111/cogs.12513 PMID:28653447

Faullant, R., Matzler, K., & Mooradian, T. A. (2011). Personality, basic emotions, and satisfaction: Primary emotions in the mountaineering experience. *Tourism Management, 32*(6), 1423–1430. doi:10.1016/j.tourman.2011.01.004

Ford, N., & Brown, D. (2006). *Surfing and social theory: Experience, embodiment and narrative of the dream glide*. Routledge.

Foxall, G. (1990). *Consumer psychology in behavioral perspective*. Beard Books.

Francken, J. C., & Slors, M. (2018). Neuroscience and everyday life: Facing the translation problem. *Brain and Cognition, 120*, 67–74. doi:10.1016/j.bandc.2017.09.004 PMID:28899576

Frijda, N. H. (2007). *The laws of emotion*. Erlbaum.

Graburn, N. H. H. (1983). The anthropology of tourism. *Annals of Tourism Research, 10*(1), 9–33. doi:10.1016/0160-7383(83)90113-5

Groeger, J. A., & Murphy, G. (2021). Driving and cognitive function in people with stroke and healthy age-matched controls. *Neuropsychological Rehabilitation*, 1–24. doi:10.1080/09602011.2020.1869566 PMID:33428553

Hommel, B., Chapman, C. S., Cisek, P., Neyedli, H. F., Song, J. H., & Welsh, T. N. (2019). No one knows what attention is. *Attention, Perception & Psychophysics, 81*(7), 2288–2303. doi:10.375813414-019-01846-w PMID:31489566

Horstmann, G., & Herwig, A. (2016). Novelty biases attention and gaze in a surprise trial. *Attention, Perception & Psychophysics, 78*(1), 69–77. doi:10.375813414-015-0995-1 PMID:26486643

Hosany, S. (2012). Appraisal determinants of tourist emotional responses. *Journal of Travel Research, 51*(3), 303–314. doi:10.1177/0047287511410320

Jiang, Y., Li, S., Huang, J., & Scott, N. (2020). Worry and anger from flight delay: Antecedents and consequences. *International Journal of Tourism Research*, *22*(3), 289–302. doi:10.1002/jtr.2334

Kahneman, D. (2000). Evaluation by moments: Past and future. In D. Kahneman & A. Tversky (Eds.), *Choices, values, and frames* (pp. 693–708). Cambridge University Press. doi:10.1017/CBO9780511803475.039

Kahneman, D. (2011). *Thinking, fast and slow*. Macmillan.

Katsuki, F., & Constantinidis, C. (2014). Bottom-up and top-down attention: Different processes and overlapping neural systems. *The Neuroscientist*, *20*(5), 509–521. doi:10.1177/1073858413514136 PMID:24362813

Kim, J.-H. (2010). Determining the factors affecting the memorable nature of travel experiences. *Journal of Travel & Tourism Marketing*, *27*(8), 780–796. doi:10.1080/10548408.2010.526897

Kim, J.-H. (2014). The antecedents of memorable tourism experiences: The development of a scale to measure the destination attributes associated with memorable experiences. *Tourism Management*, *44*, 34–45. doi:10.1016/j.tourman.2014.02.007

Kim, J.-H. (2018). The impact of memorable tourism experiences on loyalty behaviors: The mediating effects of destination image and satisfaction. *Journal of Travel Research*, *57*(7), 856–870. doi:10.1177/0047287517721369

Kim, J.-H. (2021). Destination attributes affecting negative memory: Scale development and validation. *Journal of Travel Research*.

Kim, J.-H., & Brent Ritchie, J. R. (2014). Cross-cultural validation of a memorable tourism experience scale (MTES). *Journal of Travel Research*, *53*(3), 323–335. doi:10.1177/0047287513496468

Kim, J.-H., Brent Ritchie, J. R., & McCormick, B. (2012). Development of a scale to measure memorable tourism experiences. *Journal of Travel Research*, *51*(1), 12–25. doi:10.1177/0047287510385467

Ko, L. W., Komarov, O., Hairston, W. D., Jung, T. P., & Lin, C. T. (2017). Sustained attention in real classroom Settings: An EEG study. *Frontiers in Human Neuroscience*, *11*, 388. doi:10.3389/fnhum.2017.00388 PMID:28824396

Larsen, S. (2007). Aspects of a psychology of the tourist experience. *Scandinavian Journal of Hospitality and Tourism*, *7*(1), 7–18. doi:10.1080/15022250701226014

Lazarus, R. S. (1991). *Emotion and adaptation*. Oxford University Press.

Le, D., Hadinejad, A., Moyle, B., Ma, J., & Scott, N. (2020). A review of eye-tracking methods in tourism research. In M. Rainoldi & M. Jooss (Eds.), *Eye tracking in tourism*. Springer. doi:10.1007/978-3-030-49709-5_2

Le, D., Scott, N., & Lohmann, G. (2019). Applying experiential marketing in selling tourism dreams. *Journal of Travel & Tourism Marketing*, *36*(2), 220–235. doi:10.1080/10548408.2018.1526158

Li, S. (2020). Using self-report and skin conductance measures to evaluate theme park experiences. *Journal of Vacation Marketing*.

Loewenstein, G. F., Weber, E. U., Hsee, C. K., & Welch, N. (2001). Risk as feelings. *Psychological Bulletin, 127*(2), 267–286. doi:10.1037/0033-2909.127.2.267 PMID:11316014

Ma, J., Gao, J., Scott, N., & Ding, P. (2013). Customer delight derived from theme park experiences: The antecedents of delight based on cognitive appraisal theory. *Annals of Tourism Research, 42*, 359–381. doi:10.1016/j.annals.2013.02.018

Ma, J., Scott, N., Ding, P., & Gao, J. (2017). Delighted or satisfied? Positive emotional responses derived from theme park experiences. *Journal of Travel & Tourism Marketing, 34*(1), 1–19. doi:10.1080/10548408.2015.1125824

Mannell, R. C., & Iso-Ahola, S. E. (1987). Psychological nature of leisure and tourism experience. *Annals of Tourism Research, 14*(3), 314–331. doi:10.1016/0160-7383(87)90105-8

Marion, K. (2016). Risk and uncertainty in travel decision-making: Tourist and destination perspective. *Journal of Travel Research, 57*(1), 129–146.

Matteucci, X. (2014). Forms of body usage in tourists' experiences of flamenco. *Annals of Tourism Research, 46*(0), 29–43. doi:10.1016/j.annals.2014.02.005

McCabe, S., Li, C., & Chen, Z. (2016). Time for a radical reappraisal of tourist decision making? Toward a new conceptual model. *Journal of Travel Research, 55*(1), 3–15. doi:10.1177/0047287515592973

McColl-Kennedy, J. R., Danaher, T. S., Gallan, A. S., Orsingher, C., Lervik-Olsen, L., & Verma, R. (2017). How do you feel today? Managing patient emotions during health care experiences to enhance well-being. *Journal of Business Research, 79*, 247–259. doi:10.1016/j.jbusres.2017.03.022

Mitev, A. Z., & Irimiás, A. (2020). Travel craving. *Annals of Tourism Research*. PMID:34566201

Moors, A., Ellsworth, P. C., Scherer, K. R., & Frijda, N. H. (2013). Appraisal theories of emotion: State of the art and future development. *Emotion Review, 5*(2), 119–124. doi:10.1177/1754073912468165

Moscardo, G., & Pearce, P. L. (2007). The rhetoric and reality of structured tourism work experiences: A social representational analysis. *Tourism Recreation Research, 32*(2), 21–28. doi:10.1080/02508281.2007.11081273

Mrkva, K., Cole, J. C., & Van Boven, L. (2021). Attention increases environmental risk perception. *Journal of Experimental Psychology. General, 150*(1), 83–102. doi:10.1037/xge0000772 PMID:32700924

O'Dell, T., & Billing, P. (Eds.). (2005). Experiencescapes: Tourism, culture and economy. Kopenhavn: Business School Press.

Ooi, C. S. (2003). *Crafting tourism experiences: Managing the attention product*. Paper presented at the 12th Nordic Symposium on Tourism and Hospitality Research, Norwegian School of Hotel Management, Stavanger, University College, Norway.

Ooi, C. S. (2005). A theory of tourism experiences: The management of attention. In T. O'Dell & P. Billing (Eds.), *Experiencescapes: Tourism, culture and economy* (pp. 51–68). Copenhagen Business School Press.

Otto, J. E., & Brent Ritchie, J. R. (1996). The service experience in tourism. *Tourism Management, 17*(3), 165–174. doi:10.1016/0261-5177(96)00003-9

Pitts, M. A., Lutsyshyna, L. A., & Hillyard, S. A. (2018). The relationship between attention and consciousness: an expanded taxonomy and implications for 'no-report' paradigms. *Philosophical Transactions B, 373*(1755).

Pratte, M. S., Ling, S., Swisher, J. D., & Tong, F. (2013). How attention extracts objects from noise. *Journal of Neurophysiology, 110*(6), 1346–1356. doi:10.1152/jn.00127.2013 PMID:23803331

Prentice, R., Witt, S. F., & Hamer, C. (1998). Tourism as experience: The case of heritage parks. *Annals of Tourism Research, 25*(1), 1–24. doi:10.1016/S0160-7383(98)00084-X

Quiggin, J. (2012). *Zombie economics: How dead ideas still walk among us*. Princeton University Press.

Romaniuk, J., & Nguyen, C. (2017). Is consumer psychology research ready for today's attention economy? *Journal of Marketing Management, 33*(11-12), 909–916. doi:10.1080/0267257X.2017.1305706

Rosario Rueda, M., Pozuelos, J. P., & Cómbita, L. M. (2015). Cognitive Neuroscience of Attention - From brain mechanisms to individual differences in efficiency. *AIMS Neuroscience, 2*(4), 183–202. doi:10.3934/Neuroscience.2015.4.183

Russell, C. L. (1995). The social construction of orangutans: An ecotourist experience. *Society & Animals, 3*(2), 151–170. doi:10.1163/156853095X00134

Ryan, C. (1997). *The tourist experience*. Cassell.

Sarter, M., Givens, B., & Bruno, J. P. (2001). The cognitive neuroscience of sustained attention: Where top-down meets bottom-up. *Brain Research. Brain Research Reviews, 35*(2), 146–160. doi:10.1016/S0165-0173(01)00044-3 PMID:11336780

Scarantino, A., & de Sousa, R. (2021). Emotion. In E. N. Zalta (Ed.), *The Stanford Encyclopedia of Philosophy*.

Scherer, K. R., Schorr, A., & Johnstone, T. (2001). *Appraisal processes in emotions: Theory, methods, research*. Oxford University Press.

Schwarz, N. (2011). Feelings-as-information theory. In P. Van Lange, A. Kruglanski, & E. Higgins (Eds.), *Handbook of theories of social psychology* (pp. 289–308). Sage.

Scott, N., Zhang, R., Le, D., & Moyle, B. (2019). A review of eye-tracking research in tourism. *Current Issues in Tourism, 22*(10), 1244–1261. doi:10.1080/13683500.2017.1367367

Selstad, L. (2007). The social anthropology of the tourist experience: Exploring the "middle role". *Scandinavian Journal of Hospitality and Tourism, 7*(1), 19–33. doi:10.1080/15022250701256771

Sibicky, M., Klein, C. L., & Embrescia, E. (2020). Psychological misconceptions and their relation to students' lay beliefs of mind. *Teaching of Psychology, 48*(2), 103–109. doi:10.1177/0098628320959925

Simon, H. A. (1978). Rationality as process and as product of thought. *The American Economic Review, 68*(2), 1–16.

Skavronskaya, L., Scott, N., Moyle, B., Le, D., Hadinejad, A., Zhang, R., & Shakeela, A. (2017). Cognitive psychology and tourism research: State of the art. *Tourism Review*, *72*(2), 221–237. doi:10.1108/TR-03-2017-0041

Stienmetz, J., Kim, J., Xiang, Z., & Fesenmaier, D. R. (2021). Managing the structure of tourism experiences: Foundations for tourism design. *Journal of Destination Marketing & Management*, *19*, 100408. doi:10.1016/j.jdmm.2019.100408

Swallow, K. M., & Jiang, Y. V. (2013). Attentional load and attentional boost: A review of data and theory. *Frontiers in Psychology*, *4*, 274. doi:10.3389/fpsyg.2013.00274 PMID:23730294

Uriely, N. (2005). The tourist experience: Conceptual developments. *Annals of Tourism Research*, *32*(1), 199–216. doi:10.1016/j.annals.2004.07.008

Volo, S. (2009). Conceptualising experience: A tourist based approach. *Journal of Hospitality Marketing & Management*, *18*(2), 111–126. doi:10.1080/19368620802590134

Volo, S. (2021). The experience of emotion: Directions for tourism design. *Annals of Tourism Research*, 86.

von Suchodoletz, A., Fasche, A., & Skuballa, I. T. (2017). The role of attention shifting in orthographic competencies: Cross-sectional findings from 1st, 3rd, and 8th grade students. *Frontiers in Psychology*, *8*, 1665. doi:10.3389/fpsyg.2017.01665 PMID:29018387

Wolff, K., Larsen, S., & Øgaard, T. (2019). How to define and measure risk perceptions. *Annals of Tourism Research*, *79*, 102759. doi:10.1016/j.annals.2019.102759

Zacks, J. M., Speer, N. K., Swallow, K. M., Braver, T. S., & Reynolds, J. R. (2007). Event perception: A mind-brain perspective. *Psychological Bulletin*, *133*(2), 273–293. doi:10.1037/0033-2909.133.2.273 PMID:17338600

Zadra, J. R., & Clore, G. L. (2011). Emotion and perception: The role of affective information. *Wiley Interdisciplinary Reviews: Cognitive Science*, *2*(6), 676–685. doi:10.1002/wcs.147 PMID:22039565

Chapter 2
Destination's Image and Tourism Experiences

Gökhan Akel
https://orcid.org/0000-0003-4353-7855
Antalya Akev University, Turkey

ABSTRACT

The development of world tourism and the increase in the number of tourism destinations has led to the development of competition. Therefore, to gain a competitive advantage, efforts to create a destination image have gained importance. It is necessary to create an image for the destinations and communicate this image clearly to the visitor. An accurate and effective strategy should be pursued in the creation of the destination image, and the impression and perception that will create behavioural intention should be given importance. It is very important to include tourism experiences because of the undeniable necessity of managing and marketing services and experience in tourism. Destination image consists of the sum of the information individuals have about a region, their experiences, and impressions. Therefore, effective and efficient use of tourism experiences is very important for a positive destination image.

INTRODUCTION

Tourism is seen as a phenomenon that is researched and studied for its development by both academicians, practitioners, and managers. The tourism industry contributes economically to countries in terms of consumption, foreign exchange input, and employment on a regional and global basis (Buhalis, 1999; Kandampully, 2000). The economic contribution of tourism to countries is not only in the tourism industry, but also supports the development of many industries. With the development of the transportation sector and technology in recent years, tourism has become easier on a global scale, and the tourism sector has gained value. The development of world tourism and the increase in the number of tourism destinations has led to the development of competition. So, efforts to create a destination image have gained importance for gaining a competitive advantage. Because, to gain an advantage in the competition in the tourism industry, it is necessary to develop a positive image for destinations (Baloglu & McCleary, 1999b). Also, it is necessary to know the destination image in the minds of tourists and the strengths and

DOI: 10.4018/978-1-7998-8775-1.ch002

weaknesses of the destination (Chen & Uysal, 2002) to gain a competitive advantage. Today, competition is valid not only for products, institutions, companies, individuals but also within countries and destinations. Therefore, the destination image is also very important for a competitive advantage. Creating a positive image, especially in the tourism industry, requires comprehensive and strategic planning due to the industry's structure (Akyurt & Atay, 2009). Another issue that is as important as the clarity of the destination image and its clear transfer to the individual is the positive result of the experience gained by the individual from this touristic activity because the individual positive experience will make the stronger of the destination image. In addition to the competitive advantage, tourists' changing expectations and needs and the fact that similar services are offered in many destinations have caused tourists to seek diversity and diversity. These tourist expectations have brought many changes in the tourism industry. In addition to the goods and services in the tourism industry, focusing on tourism experiences is considered very important in contributing to the destination image. Destinations refer to certain geographic areas such as continent, country, region, city. It consists of a combination of touristic features that offer interconnected services to visitors. In creating destinations, many features of the region such as cultural characteristics, geographical conditions, historical importance, ethnic cuisine, and having an endemic species are taken into consideration. Destination image consists of the sum of the information, experiences, and impressions that individuals have about a region. So, tourism experiences are very valuable. If people's experiences reinforce the destination image, the destination image becomes even more important.

Pine and Gilmore (1999) highlight the impact of experience on economic growth, arguing the change of the global economy towards products, services, and experience. The competition between products, services, and experiences in the tourism industry and the constant change in the demands and expectations of tourists reveal the necessity of managing and marketing tourism destinations by evaluating them from a strategic perspective. So, image plays an important role in the success of destinations. Furthermore, destination image has an impact on consumer behaviour because it is related to the resources and attractive aspects of a tourism destination and is considered as a mental indicator of consumers' knowledge, emotion, and perception towards a particular destination (Crompton, 1979; Fakeye & Crompton, 1991; Stabler, 1995).

When the cultural and social activities of destinations in tourism are evaluated in terms of marketing, they are very important in attracting tourists. Marketing activities should be carried out in an integrated manner with tourism experience elements, taking into account the elements of tourism experience. Such activities are offered to serve positioning in a competitive market. From this point of view, a positive idea about the destination will contribute to innovation, diversity, and difference. In addition to innovation, diversity, and differences in tourism, attractive aspects, natural beauties, entertainment activities, and unforgettable experiences also attract tourists (Lew, 1987). For this reason, touristic destinations need to progress with strategic planning and management for the destination image. Also, it is necessary to create an image for the destinations and transfer this image clearly to the visitor.

In tourism management, the perception of destination in the minds of consumers is very important for visitors to choose destinations. It is necessary to understand, correctly evaluate and effectively manage the perception of destination in the minds of consumers. So, it is very important in terms of marketing, sales, and management that countries care about destination image and tourism experiences while determining effective tourism policies and strategies. If positive attitudes and expectations are formed in potential consumers, the image that will appear in the mind will contribute to the positive outcome of the destination evaluation (Hughes, 2008).

Tourism image is generally examined together with consumer behaviour. Research shows that tourism image is a direct antecedent of perceived quality, satisfaction, revisit intention, and willingness to recommend the destination (Bigne et al., 2001). Therefore, while creating a destination image in tourism, a difference can be made by focusing not only on goods and services but also on elements of the tourism experience such as hedonism, novelty, local culture, refreshment, meaningfulness, involvement, and knowledge. Also, destination image and tourism experiences need to be taken into account in tourism planning and management strategies to create behavioural intentions. Therefore, the destination image should not be considered independently of the tourism experience.

Therefore, the key concepts of this book chapter are destination image and tourism experiences. Therefore, this book chapter first provides an overview of destination image and tourism experiences. It then clarifies the importance of elements of tourism experiences in destinations and the relationship between tourism experiences and destination image. For this purpose, this book chapter will consist of the titles introduction, background, main focus of the chapter, solutions, and recommendations, future research directions, and conclusion.

BACKGROUND

Destinations are areas that have created a certain image in the minds of tourists. Regions with unique touristic features, hosting events such as festivals and carnivals, and attraction centres have the characteristic of being a destination (Hosany et al., 2006). Destinations, which offer interconnected services to visitors and are formed by the combination of touristic features, reflect the culture in which they are located. Therefore, destinations are areas that have created a certain image in the minds of tourists with different and original features. Destination tourism as a whole can be defined as touristic activities carried out in a particular area.

The image, which is expressed as a result of the interaction of one's beliefs, ideas, feelings, expectations, and impressions about an object (Reynolds, 1965; Chon, 1990), has been extensively studied in the tourism literature due to its important role in influencing the decision-making process of tourists. The competition between products, services, and experiences in the tourism industry and the constant change in the demands and expectations of tourists reveal the necessity of managing and marketing tourism destinations by evaluating them from a strategic point of view. So, image, which is a very important concept of marketing and consumer behaviour, especially in the tourism sector, plays an important role in the success of destinations.

Although the definition of the concept of an image differs according to many researchers, it is explained as the sum of beliefs and impressions transmitted from various sources over time and interpreted as an accepted mental output of the features and benefits sought about a product or destination (Gartner, 1994; Mackay & Fesenmaier, 2000; Gallarza et al., 2002). According to another definition, image is expressed as a structure that represents information, feelings, and impressions about an object or destination (Reynolds, 1965; Baloğlu, 1998; Baloglu & McClearly, 1999a). In brief, image is a critical factor in the destination selection process, influencing tourists during the subsequent evaluation of travel and their future intentions, regardless of the possibilities offered by any place (Um & Crompton 1990; Chi & Qu, 2008). Image in tourism has been one of the most important issues in destination studies, especially due to its impact on consumer decision-making and preference (Echtner & Ritchie, 1991; Baloglu & McCleary, 1999a; Kim & Richardson, 2003; Pike & Ryan, 2004). Destination image has been defined

Destination's Image and Tourism Experiences

from various perspectives in the literature but is generally expressed as the impression, attitude, belief, and emotional thoughts about a place (Fridgen 1987; White, 2004; Safitri & Maftukhah, 2018). According to another definition, destination image refers to the impressions a person has about a region where he/she does not reside (Hunt, 1975).

Studies on destination image started in the 1970s by John Hunt with the evaluation of image as an element in tourism development. From this period on, the destination image began to play an important role in tourism research (Hosany et al., 2006; Lin & Huang, 2009). Although destination image is mainly discussed as a tourism and marketing issue, it has been the subject of different understandings of consumer behaviour such as anthropology and sociology (Meethan 1996; Selwyn 1996), semiotics (Sternberg 1997), and geography (Draper & Minca 1997). Thus, the scope of destination image research in the literature is quite wide. In Table 1, some studies in the literature on destination images are given.

Table 1. Literature review on destination image

Topic	Author
Attitudes towards destinations	Ryan & Montgomery, 1994; Muller, 1996
Destination selection process	Chen & Tsai, 2007; Hsu et al., 2009; Tavitiyaman & Qu, 2013; Zhang et al., 2014; Park et al., 2017
Destination image and factors affecting destination selection	Walmsley & Jenkins, 1993; Baloglu ve Bringberg, 1997; Hsu et al., 2009
Destination image formation	Gartner, 1994; Mackay & Fesenmaier, 1997; Baloglu & McClearly, 1999a; Kim & Richardson, 2003; Pike & Ryan, 2004
Measuring of destination image	Echtner & Ritchie, 1993; Driscoll et al., 1994; Stylidis et al., 2008
Change of destination image over time	Dann, 1996; Selby & Morgan, 1996
Destination image management policies	Selby & Morgan, 1996; Lohmann & Kaim, 1999
Effect of previous visits on destination image	Phelps, 1986; Ahmed, 1991; Chon, 1990; Hu & Ritchie, 1993
The relationship of the image with the choice of destination	Fakeye & Crompton 1991; Milman & Pizam, 1995; Baloglu & McCleary, 1999a
The effect of destination image on tourist behaviour	Mansfeld, 1992; Bigne et al., 2001
The relationship of (destination) image with satisfaction	Chen & Myagmarsuren, 2010; Song et al., 2013; Wang et al., 2017; Bhat & Dirzi, 2018
The relationship between satisfaction-based image and tourist behaviour	Chon 1990
The effect of quality satisfaction on destination image	Chi & Qu, 2008
Effect of distance on destination image	Ahmed 1991; Ahmed, 1996; Dadgostar & Isotalo, 1996
The effect of tourism image on the choice of holiday destination	Moutinho, 1987; Gartner, 1989; Crompton & Ankomah, 1993
The effect of destination image on behavioural intentions	Bigne et al., 2001; Lee et al., 2005; Chen & Tsai, 2007; Chi & Qu, 2008; Wang & Hsu, 2010;
The relationship of destination image with loyalty	Chi & Qu, 2008; Agapito et al., 2013; Wu, 2016
The effect of destination image on tourists' post-travel evaluations	Baloglu & McCleary, 1999a
Willingness to revisit and recommend destinations	Milman & Pizam, 1995; Court & Lupton, 1997; Baloglu & McCleary, 1999a; Bigne et al., 2001; Joppe et al., 2001; Chen & Tsai, 2007; Tavitiyaman & Qu, 2013; Zhang et al., 2014; Park et al., 2017; Albayrak et al., 2018

Because the services and experiences offered in tourism are intangible, images become more important than reality (Gallarza et al., 2002, p. 57). It is very important for the destination image that the image to be created is clear and the experiences offered at the destinations are positive and memorable. Positive and memorable experiences, as well as products and services, will further strengthen the destination image. Destinations with a strong image are more likely to be evaluated and preferred among alternatives (Echtner & Ritchie, 1991; Alhemoud & Armstrong, 1996).

The perceived post-visit destination image also affects tourist satisfaction and the intention to revisit in the future, depending on the destination's capacity to meet visitor wants and needs and to provide experiences that match the destination image (Chon, 1990; Court & Lupton, 1997; Baloglu & McCleary, 1999a; Bigne et al., 2001; Joppe et al., 2001). Therefore, the destination image is effective in the travel or accommodation selection process. It is very effective in the evaluation of tourists' travel or stays and future intentions. In Table 2, some studies in the literature on destination image and experiences are given.

Table 2. Literature review of destination images and experiences

Topic	Authors
Experience-based tourist satisfaction and willingness to revisit destinations	Chon, 1990; Court & Lupton, 1997; Baloglu & McCleary, 1999a; Bigne et al., 2001; Joppe et al., 2001
Effect of experience on intention to recommend	Anderson, 1998
The impact of tourism experiences on revisit intention	Kim et al., 2010; Chang, Backman, & Huang, 2014; Tsai, 2016; Kim, 2018; Zhang et al., 2018
The effect of nostalgia on the destination image	Akgün et al., 2019
The effect of emotional experiences on destination image	Prayag et al., 2017; Kim 2018
The effect of escape, aesthetics, entertainment, and educational experiences on the destination image	Tan, 2017
The effect of involvement, one of the elements of tourism experience, on the destination image	Beerli & Martin, 2004a
The impact of innovation as an element of tourism experience on the intention to recommend and revisit	Vittersø et al., 2017; Zhang et al., 2018; Dedeoğlu et al., 2018; Roy, 2018
The relationship between innovation, which is an element of tourism experience, and behavioural intentions	Chang et al., 2014; Dedeoglu et al., 2018
The effect of innovation, which is an element of tourism experience, on behavioural intentions.	Bigné et al., 2005; Mitas & Bastiaansen, 2018
The effect of perceived quality of experience on behavioural intentions	Wu et al., 2018
The relationship of tourism experiences with the destination image	Dagustani et al., 2018; Li et al., 2021
The effect of post-travel destination image on tourism experience	Beerli & Martin, 2004a; Smith et al., 2015

Unlike many tangible products, tourists cannot try any destination beforehand and choose accordingly (Gartner, 1989). The tendency of tourists to seek new and different experiences and choose different destinations is an important research subject in marketing and tourism research and applications. While an experience with a destination creates a feedback effect by giving ideas and creating perceptions for the next destination choice, it will also affect the evaluation of alternative destinations. Evaluation of the experiences offered at the destination affects and changes the image (Chon, 1991; Echtner & Ritchie,

1991). Therefore, in addition to variables such as the image causing expectations in the minds of visitors and perceived quality and satisfaction in tourism, the relationship between expectations and experience should be examined (Phelps, 1986; Font, 1997). Bigne et al. (2001) and Lee et al. (2005) argued that individuals with a positive destination image would perceive their experiences as positive, leading to higher satisfaction and behavioural intentions.

In addition to providing goods and services, businesses are trying to achieve sustainable success and sustainable by focusing on memories and experiences. By staging experience, businesses use experience as a strategic tool (Garg et al., 2010). Since the concept of experience economy was introduced into the literature by Pine and Gilmore (1999), it has been applied in many studies in tourism until today. Since the purpose of tourism is to create and offer experiences, tourism is one of the industries at the centre of the experience economy (Quan & Wang, 2004). In the context of the tourism industry, experience has been expressed as a mental state that differs according to visitors (Otto & Ritchie, 1996). Also, visitor experiences in tourism are expressed as events that take place different from daily life and away from routine (Walls et al., 2011).

In industries involving experiential products such as tourism, consumers are constantly in search of information. The data collected for the destination image is usually obtained from sources such as publicity (advertising and brochures), opinions of others (neighbourhood, travel agencies), media reports (newspapers, magazines, news, and documentaries), and popular culture (movies, literature) (Reynolds, 1965; Um & Crompton, 1990; Cohen-Hattab & Kerber, 2004). Apart from the information sources, it is also based on the knowledge and experience obtained (Echtner & Ritchie, 2003).

MAIN FOCUS OF THE CHAPTER

Components of the Destination Image

Previous studies on the components of destination image focused mainly on the cognitive component, and no consensus could be obtained on this issue (Chon, 1991; Fakeye & Crompton, 1991). Moreover, many studies in the literature deal with cognitive and affective characteristics together in the measurement of destination image (Baloglu & McCleary, 1999a; Baloglu, 2001; Hui & Wan, 2003; Kim & Richardson, 2003; Beerli & Martin, 2004b; Michaelidou et al., 2013). Therefore, the coexistence of cognitive and affective components can better explain a tourist's image of a place, which is not completely determined by physical characteristics and includes emotions (Baloglu & Brinberg, 1997; Baloglu & McCleary, 1999a). Therefore, it is useful to examine the image of any destination with a multi-dimensional approach by evaluating it both perceptually/cognitively and affectively (Baloglu & Brinberg, 1997; Baloglu & McCleary, 1999a; Kim & Park, 2015).

The cognitive component, which is related to beliefs or knowledge about the qualities of a destination (Baloglu & McCleary, 1999a), refers to a person's belief or knowledge about the characteristics of a touristic destination (Baloglu, 1999a; Pike & Ryan, 2004). Elements of the cognitive component include "natural environment", "cultural heritage", "tourist infrastructures", or "atmosphere" (San Martín, & Del Bosque, 2008). The affective component is related to the individual's feelings or commitment to the destination (Baloglu & McCleary, 1999a; Kim & Richardson, 2003; Chen & Uysal, 2002; Pike & Ryan, 2004). Therefore, tourists' beliefs and knowledge about a travel destination are called cognitive images, while their emotions and feelings are called affective images (Michaelidou et al., 2013).

Tourism Experience and Tourism Experience Components

The concept of experience has been important in tourism studies since the 1970s (Cohen, 1979). Nowadays, with increasing social interaction, individuals tend to travel to different destinations to gain new experiences. It is stated by Larsen (2007) that the tourism experience includes expectations, events, and memories. Also, Larsen defined the tourism experience as "a past personal travel-related event strong enough to enter into long-term memory". Larsen (2007) approached the concept from a broad perspective and stated that tourist experiences are related to social, cognitive, and personality processes. In the systematic model, Larsen (2007) stated that the tourist experience consists of three processes: expectations, perception, and memories at the destination. The expectation process reflects the purpose. This process also shapes the future tourist behaviour to some extent while inferring the general state and characteristics of the tourist.

The concept of experience economy was first mentioned in the book "The Experience Economy" by Pine and Gilmore (1999). In this book, the age of experience economy, which is stated as the next stage of the industrial economy and service economy, expresses the situation in which societies are involved with the development and differentiation of services (Yuan & Wu, 2008; Pine & Gilmore, 2012). In addition to bed and breakfast, consumption centres in tourism offer their guests an integrated experience of entertainment, aesthetics, escape, and education. Including the elements of the experience economy, consisting of entertainment, aesthetics, escape, and education experience, into experiential marketing strategies, will not be sufficient for market share, competitive advantage, and long-term profitability. Evaluation from this point of view has been adopted in many tourism studies (e.g. Oh et al., 2007; Mehmetoglu & Engen, 2011; Loureiro, 2014). Another example is the experiential marketing approach, where Schmitt (1999) argues that marketers should create sensory, emotional, intellectual, and behavioural experiences. In this respect, there are also some studies in tourism research (e.g. Tsaur et al., 2007; Lee & Chang, 2012; Wang et al., 2012).

In addition to the experience economy elements, Kim et al. (2010), there is a postmodern period in which tourism experience elements such as hedonism, novelty, local culture, refreshment, meaningfulness, involvement, and knowledge must also be taken into account. Tourism experience elements were measured using twenty-five items in seven sub-dimensions developed by Kim (2010). It is necessary to carry out marketing activities considering the elements of experience economy in a way that is integrated with the elements of tourism experience.

Hedonism is expressed as an aspect of the consumption experience that includes multi-dimensional, creative, and emotional elements (Holbrook & Hirschman, 1982). Hedonism, which plays a key role in measuring and evaluating the experience and is an important element among tourism experiences, focuses on the emotion, entertainment, and fantasy encouraged by the experience (Hirschman & Holbrook, 1982). Hedonism, which is defined as pleasurable emotions that excite the person (Kim et al., 2012), is examined as a hedonic service by evaluating experiences emotionally (Pikkemaat & Schuckert, 2007).

Novelty, which is an element of tourism experience, is a difference that separates from daily life while experiencing something new and different (Lee & Crompton, 1992). Tourists seek novelty not because of dissatisfaction, but because they seek different experiences and diversity (Niininen et al., 2004; Bigné et al., 2009; Ma et al., 2013; Mitas & Bastiaansen, 2018: 99). Although the search for innovation in tourism is thought to be the main reason for visiting different destinations, the intention to revisit and pay for different reasons can be carried (Prebensen & Rosengren, 2016). Tourists seek novelty not because of dissatisfaction, but because they seek different experiences and diversity (Niininen et al., 2004; Bigné et al., 2009), and it has been found that some tourists seek novelty more than others (Kim & Kim, 2015). Since tourism is a field based on discovering new places and gaining experiences (Martins et al., 2017), it is not expected that experiences will remain constant in a changing world. Also, innovation in tourism experiences reflects tourists' desire and need to learn new skills and acquire knowledge, in addition to arousing curiosity (Williams & Soutar, 2009).

Since local dishes and cuisines are the most important elements that reflect local values, these elements are among the indispensable elements of the tourism experience as they convey the local culture in the best way (Wijaya et al., 2013; Tsai, 2016). So, tourists can be exposed to cultural change in the destination they reach, thanks to tourism that brings local people and visitors together. Visiting different destinations causes tourists to interact with local people and accumulate new memories (Tussyadiah & Fesenmaier, 2009). In different destinations, the interaction of tourists by meeting with other people will increase the experience of an unforgettable and unique experience (Morgan, 2007).

Refreshment is used in the sense of liberating, renewal, and revitalization in the tourism experience (Kim et al., 2012) and focuses on the state of mind and experiential participation of tourists (Adongo et al., 2015). Also, the experience of refreshment, Kauppinen-Raisanen et al. (2013) suggested that it can be seen as a sensory attraction from trying local cuisines in different destinations.

Meaningfulness is expressed as a sense of great value or importance (Kim et al., 2012). The meaningfulness of experience relates only to the totality of memorable experiences, our interactions with those close to us, and what we learn from them during all experiences (Boswijk et al., 2007).

Involvement, which expresses being physically involved in tourism experiences (Kim et al., 2012), is related to the extent to which the consumer is interested in the message to be given and considers it important (Puccinelli et al., 2009). Therefore, involvement plays an important role in creating an experience, as it means that the customer is in constant interaction with the business. Also, as with consumers, they tend to remember the experiences that their visitors are interested in more (Kim, 2014).

Knowledge is expressed as one of the most important tourism experiences (Tung & Ritchie, 2011) and stems from consumers' desire to learn new things, develop new skills and gain new experiences (Kim et al., 2012). In addition, the element of knowledge from tourism experiences refers to the fact that tourists learn much information during the visit of a historical place when interacting with the local people in any tourism destination (Coudounaris & Sthapit, 2017).

Tourism image is generally examined together with consumer behaviour. Studies show that tourism image is a direct antecedent of perceived quality, satisfaction, revisit intention, and willingness to recommend the destination (Bigne et al., 2001). Therefore, while creating a destination image in tourism, a difference can be created by focusing not only on goods and services but also on elements of the tourism experience. Also, tourism planning and management strategies need to consider destination image and tourism experiences to create behavioural intentions. For this reason, the destination image should not be considered independently of the tourism experience.

SOLUTIONS AND RECOMMENDATIONS

Destination selection is important in influencing the decision-making process, gaining experience after arriving at the destination, then evaluating and forming future behavioural intentions (Mansfeld, 1992; Bigne et al., 2001; Lee et al., 2005). Destination image is as important as perceived quality and satisfaction variables. Therefore, marketers and managers should give the necessary importance to the destination image. Tourists create an image in their minds with their individual experiences, close environment, and social media recommendations. Therefore, tourism destination managers should carefully choose the message they want to convey, and the promised product, service, and experience should be compatible and consistent with the product, service, and experience they offer. Furthermore, tourists' experience and satisfaction with visits will influence their future behaviour intentions. Therefore, destination managers should invest more in destinations to improve the tourist experience. Also, it should not be forgotten that although it is very difficult to change the destination image once it is established, the most important goal is to maintain a positive view.

Destination tourism managers and marketers need to make image creation attractive and better manage their management and marketing strategies to create behavioural intention in the future. Managers and marketers need to approach the image correctly and strategically, as the destination image will affect the tourists' satisfaction with their experience, their intention to recommend, and their intention to revisit. Because the images and experiences tourists perceive about the destination are very important for the success and sustainability of the destination (Byon & Zhang, 2010). Moreover, the success of destination marketing depends on the interaction of destination loyalty with satisfaction and image. No matter how happy tourists are with the product, service, and experience, they may not have the intention to revisit and recommend. To retain customers, their satisfaction is often not enough, as another goal, it is necessary to focus on creating customer loyalty. Therefore, tourism destinations should pay attention to the image they are trying to create and the quality of products, services, and experiences. Moreover, destination managers should offer products, services, and experiences according to tourists from different nationalities to increase tourism competitiveness.

Providing the destination image, which is a critical stimulus in motivating tourists (Cai, 2002), depends on some variables in theory. However, managing all these variables is difficult. Managers and marketers can focus on service quality by right advertising and promotion, and by organizing various cultural and artistic events. By including hotels, restaurants, theme parks, and shopping stores in the general tourism understanding, activities should be carried out to contribute to the destination image in all places.

Destination image, which contributes significantly to behaviours such as destination choice and travel intention (Alcaniz et al., 2009; Liu et al., 2017), is an important determinant in a tourist's destination selection (Chen & Tsai, 2007; Hughes, 2008; Byon & Zhang, 2010; Dixit, 2017). Therefore, effective and efficient use of tourism experiences is very important for a positive destination image. It should be considered that the positive destination image created by the tourism experiences offered will affect the behavioural intentions, and tourism and marketing strategies should be planned accordingly. Managing the tourist experience and destination image is considered a driving force in destination success as it has a significant impact on satisfaction and behavioural intention (Suhartanto et al., 2018).

Destination marketers should determine and implement strategies about the formation of the image and the continuation of the process. Considering that tourists evaluate and use cognitive and affective dimensions together in creating a destination image, destination managers and marketers should emphasize not only the physical characteristics of the destination but also the emotions by focusing on the mind, perception, and impression. While presenting tourism experiences, it should improve and develop the destination image by emphasizing the affective dimensions.

FUTURE RESEARCH DIRECTIONS

Although destination image has been examined in various studies in the literature, there is not enough research. The number of studies on destination image in tourism has increased in recent years, but it is anticipated that future studies will focus more on it. Future studies can examine the variables that affect the purchase intention and purchasing behaviour, such as service quality, satisfaction, loyalty with destination marketing in tourism.

The role of tourism experiences in the formation of the destination image has not been sufficiently clarified. Due to the complex nature of image creation and the complex use of technology, more work is needed to fully understand the destination image's structure. The wide source of information offered by the Internet and social media has made communication between potential visitors more complex. The fact that knowledge creation and modification is fast and easy, and the dissemination of any information to such a large audience has made it more difficult to provide effective destination marketing, image building, and positioning. Some previous studies have focused on destination positioning (Crompton et al., 1992; Echtner and Ritchie 1991; Reilly 1990; Chaudhary, 2000; Rezende-Parker et al., 2003). However, future research may focus on the destination positioning strategy in tourism. Destination positioning can be expressed as reinforcing existing positive images, correcting negative images, or recreating an image (Pike & Ryan, 2004).

In today's competitive environment, providing and managing a positive and appropriate destination image and effective tourism experience elements is very important for competitive advantage. This book chapter highlights the importance of tourism experience elements in image creation in tourists' evaluations of tourism destinations. Therefore, tourism managers and destination marketers should focus on the elements that emphasize the differences and diversity of tourism destinations based on both the cognitive and emotional components of the destination image. Furthermore, it should continuously improve its services and experiences according to the changing technology and today's tourist demands and expectations.

Although this book chapter makes important theoretical contributions to understanding the relationship between destination image and tourism experiences, it contains some limitations. Since it was not based on quantitative research, the results were compiled by supporting the existing literature, and the relationship between the two key concepts was tried to be emphasized. While examining the destination image, future research should also attach importance to emotional images and evaluate destination marketing in tourism from a different perspective by integrating these two concepts. Besides, it is recommended to examine whether socio-cultural values affect the perceived image of destinations. In addition to the destination image and tourism experiences examined within the scope of the study, other factors such as nostalgia experience, memory, the shopping experience can also be included in future research.

CONCLUSION

Destination image has been extensively studied in the literature. Destination image, which is one of the management and planning issues, especially in the field of tourism, has been the area of interest of researchers for the last fifty years. However, the literature on its relationship with tourism experiences is rather sparse. This study is about the planning and management of destination image and tourism experiences in tourism.

Many theoretical and conceptual definitions of destination image have been made. Destination image, which is the subject of research in many ways, is evaluated in an integrated way with the experience offered by experiential marketing and considered as the fourth economic presentation. The point that destinations focus on in creating a destination image and managing it is the experience element. In the field of tourism, which is the subject of the destination image, tourism experiences are indispensable for competitive advantage and sustainable success.

Drawing an experience-based image, starting with the destination image in tourism, is one of the key points that tourism managers should pay attention to in the planning and management process. Because a more positive image will lead to a higher probability of repeat visits to the same destination (Chi & Qu, 2008). In addition to management and marketing strategies aimed at increasing the likelihood of repeat visits, a sustainable success can be laid by establishing the intention to recommend. Since providing a destination image is important not only for existing tourists but also for potential tourists, the intention to recommend greatly influences consumer behaviour in attitude and perception towards a particular destination. With correct and appropriate marketing communication and recommendations, a positive image can be created in attracting tourists to destinations (Govers et al., 2007). Therefore, tourism destinations are likely to achieve success in the future in terms of marketing and management with the positive image they create and the effective use of tourism experiences.

REFERENCES

Adongo, C. A., Anuga, S. W., & Dayour, F. (2015). Will they tell others to taste? International tourists' experience of Ghanaian cuisines. *Tourism Management Perspectives, 15*, 57–64. doi:10.1016/j.tmp.2015.03.009

Agapito, D., Valle, P., & Mendes, J. (2013). The cognitive-affective-cognitive model of destination image: A confirmatory analysis. *Journal of Travel & Tourism Marketing, 30*(5), 471–481. doi:10.1080/10548408.2013.803393

Ahmed, Z. U. (1991). The influence of the components of a state's tourist image on product positioning strategy. *Tourism Management, 12*(4), 331–340. doi:10.1016/0261-5177(91)90045-U

Ahmed, Z. U. (1996). The need for the identification of the constituents of a destination's tourist image: A promotional segmentation perspective. *Tourism Review, 51*(2), 44–57.

Akgün, A. E., Senturk, H. A., Keskin, H., & Onal, I. (2020). The relationships among nostalgic emotion, destination images and tourist behaviors: An empirical study of Istanbul. *Journal of Destination Marketing & Management, 16*.

Akyurt, H., & Atay, L. (2009). Destinasyonda imaj oluşturma süreci. *Aksaray Üniversitesi İktisadi ve İdari Bilimler Fakültesi Dergisi, 1*(1), 1–14.

Albayrak, T., Caber, M., González-Rodríguez, M. R., & Aksu, A. (2018). Analysis of destination competitiveness by IPA and IPCA methods: The case of Costa Brava, Spain against Antalya, Turkey. *Tourism Management Perspectives, 28*, 53–61. doi:10.1016/j.tmp.2018.07.005

Alcaniz, E., Sanchez, I., & Blas, S. (2009). The functional -psychological continuum in the cognitive image of a destination: A confirmatory analysis. *Tourism Management, 30*(5), 715–723. doi:10.1016/j.tourman.2008.10.020

Alhemoud, A. M., & Armstrong, E. G. (1996). Image of tourism attractions in Kuwait. *Journal of Travel Research, 34*(4), 76–80. doi:10.1177/004728759603400413

Anderson, E. W. (1998). Customer satisfaction and word of mouth. *Journal of Service Research, 1*(1), 5–17. doi:10.1177/109467059800100102

Baloglu, S. (1998). An empirical investigation of attitude theory for tourist destinations: A comparison of visitors and nonvisitors. *Journal of Hospitality & Tourism Research (Washington, D.C.), 22*(3), 211–224. doi:10.1177/109634809802200301

Baloglu, S. (2001). Image variations of Turkey by familiarity index: Informational and experiential dimensions. *Tourism Management, 22*(2), 127–133. doi:10.1016/S0261-5177(00)00049-2

Baloglu, S., & Brinberg, D. (1997). Affective images of tourism destinations. *Journal of Travel Research, 35*(4), 11–15. doi:10.1177/004728759703500402

Baloglu, S., & McCleary, K. W. (1999a). A model of destination image formation. *Annals of Tourism Research, 26*(4), 868–897. doi:10.1016/S0160-7383(99)00030-4

Baloglu, S., & McCleary, K. W. (1999b). US international pleasure travelers' images of four Mediterranean destinations: A comparison of visitors and nonvisitors. *Journal of Travel Research, 38*(2), 144–152. doi:10.1177/004728759903800207

Beerli, A., & Martin, J. D. (2004a). Factors influencing destination image. *Annals of Tourism Research, 31*(3), 657–681. doi:10.1016/j.annals.2004.01.010

Beerli, A., & Martín, J. D. (2004b). Tourists' characteristics and the perceived image of tourist destinations: a quantitative analysis: A case study of Lanzarote, Spain. *Tourism Management, 25*(5), 623–636. doi:10.1016/j.tourman.2003.06.004

Bhat, S. A., & Darzi, M. A. (2018). Antecedents of tourist loyalty to tourist destinations: A mediated-moderation study. *International Journal of Tourism Cities, 4*(2), 261–278. doi:10.1108/IJTC-12-2017-0079

Bigné, J. E., Andreu, L., & Gnoth, J. (2005). The theme park experience: An analysis of pleasure, arousal and satisfaction. *Tourism Management, 26*(6), 833–844. doi:10.1016/j.tourman.2004.05.006

Bigné, J. E., Sánchez, I., & Andreu, L. (2009). The role of variety seeking in short and long run revisit intentions in holiday destinations. *International Journal of Culture, Tourism and Hospitality Research, 3*(2), 103–115. doi:10.1108/17506180910962113

Bigne, J. E., Sanchez, M. I., & Sanchez, J. (2001). Tourism image, evaluation variables and after purchase behaviour: Inter-relationship. *Tourism Management, 22*(6), 607–616. doi:10.1016/S0261-5177(01)00035-8

Boswijk, A., Thijssen, T., & Peelen, E. (2007). *The experience economy: A new perspective.* Pearson Education Benelux.

Buhalis, D. (1999). Tourism on the Greek Islands: Issues of peripherality, competitiveness and development. *International Journal of Tourism Research*, *1*(5), 341–358. doi:10.1002/(SICI)1522-1970(199909/10)1:5<341::AID-JTR201>3.0.CO;2-0

Byon, K., & Zhang, J. (2010). Development of a scale measuring destination image. *Marketing Intelligence & Planning*, *28*(4), 508–532. doi:10.1108/02634501011053595

Cai, L. A. (2002). Cooperative branding for rural destinations. *Annals of Tourism Research*, *29*(3), 720–742. doi:10.1016/S0160-7383(01)00080-9

Chang, C. H., Shu, S., & King, B. (2014). Novelty in theme park physical surroundings: An application of the stimulus– organism–response paradigm. *Asia Pacific Journal of Tourism Research*, *19*(6), 680–699. doi:10.1080/10941665.2013.779589

Chang, L. L., Backman, K. F., & Huang, Y. C. (2014). Creative tourism: A preliminary examination of creative tourists' motivation, experience, perceived value and revisit intention. *International Journal of Culture, Tourism and Hospitality Research*, *8*(4), 401–419. doi:10.1108/IJCTHR-04-2014-0032

Chaudhary, M. (2000). India's image as a tourist destination: A perspective of foreign tourists. *Tourism Management*, *21*(3), 293–297. doi:10.1016/S0261-5177(99)00053-9

Chen, C., & Tsai, D. (2007). How destination image and evaluative factors affect behavioural intentions? *Tourism Management*, *28*(4), 1115–1122. doi:10.1016/j.tourman.2006.07.007

Chen, C. F., & Myagmarsuren, O. (2010). Exploring relationships between Mongolian destination brand equity, satisfaction and destination loyalty. *Tourism Cconomics*, *16*(4), 981–994. doi:10.5367/te.2010.0004

Chen, C. F., & Tsai, D. (2007). How destination image and evaluative factors affect behavioral intentions? *Tourism Management*, *28*(4), 1115–1122. doi:10.1016/j.tourman.2006.07.007

Chen, J. S., & Uysal, M. (2002). Market positioning analysis: A hybrid approach. *Annals of Tourism Research*, *29*(4), 987–1003. doi:10.1016/S0160-7383(02)00003-8

Chi, C. G. Q., & Qu, H. (2008). Examining the structural relationships of destination image, tourist satisfaction and destination loyalty: An integrated approach. *Tourism Management*, *29*(4), 624–636. doi:10.1016/j.tourman.2007.06.007

Chon, K. S. (1990). The role of destination image in tourism: A review and discussion. *Tourism Review*, *45*(2), 2–9.

Chon, K. S. (1991). Tourism destination image modification process. Marketing implications. *Tourism Management*, *12*(1), 68–72. doi:10.1016/0261-5177(91)90030-W

Cohen, E. (1979). A phenomenology of tourist experiences. *Sociology*, *13*(2), 179–201. doi:10.1177/003803857901300203

Cohen-Hattab, K., & Kerber, J. (2004). Literature, cultural identity and the limits of authenticity: A composite approach. *International Journal of Tourism Research*, *6*(2), 57–73. doi:10.1002/jtr.470

Coudounaris, D. N., & Sthapit, E. (2017). Antecedents of memorable tourism experience related to behavioral intentions. *Psychology and Marketing*, *34*(12), 1084–1093.

Court, B., & Lupton, R. A. (1997). Customer portfolio development: Modeling destination adopters, inactives and rejecter. *Journal of Travel Research, 36*(1), 35–43. doi:10.1177/004728759703600106

Crompton, J. (1979). An assessment of the image of Mexico as a vacation destination and the influence of geographical location upon the image. *Journal of Travel Research, 17*(4), 18–23. doi:10.1177/004728757901700404

Crompton, J. L., & Ankomah, P. K. (1993). Choice set propositions in destination decisions. *Annals of Tourism Research, 20*(3), 461–476. doi:10.1016/0160-7383(93)90003-L

Crompton, J. L., Fakeye, P. C., & Lue, C. C. (1992). Positioning: The example of the Lower Rio Grande Valley in the winter long stay destination market. *Journal of Travel Research, 31*(2), 20–26. doi:10.1177/004728759203100204

Dadgostar, B., & Isotalo, R. M. (1996). Content of city destination image for near-home tourists. *Journal of Hospitality & Leisure Marketing, 3*(2), 25–34. doi:10.1300/J150v03n02_03

Dagustani, D., Kartini, D., Oesman, Y. M., & Kaltum, U. (2018). Destination image of tourist: Effect of travel motivation and memorable tourism experience. *Etikonomi, 17*(2), 307–331. doi:10.15408/etk.v17i2.7211

Dann, G. M. (1996). Tourists' images of a destination-an alternative analysis. *Journal of Travel & Tourism Marketing, 5*(1-2), 41–55. doi:10.1300/J073v05n01_04

Dedeoglu, B. B., Bilgihan, A., Ye, B. H., Buonincontri, P., & Okumus, F. (2018). The impact of servicescape on hedonic value and behavioral intentions: The importance of previous experience. *International Journal of Hospitality Management, 72*, 10–20. doi:10.1016/j.ijhm.2017.12.007

Dixit, S. K. (2017). Introduction. In S. K. Dixit (Ed.), *The Routledge handbook of consumer behaviour in hospitality and tourism* (pp. 1–3). Routledge. doi:10.4324/9781315659657-1

Draper, D., & Minca, C. (1997). Image and destination: A geographical approach applied to Banff National Park, Canada. *Tourism Review, 2*, 14–24.

Driscoll, A., Lawson, R., & Niven, B. (1994). Measuring tourists' destination perceptions. *Annals of Tourism Research, 21*(3), 499–511. doi:10.1016/0160-7383(94)90117-1

Echtner, C. M., & Ritchie, J. B. (2003). The meaning and measurement of destination image. *Journal of Tourism Studies, 14*(1), 37–48.

Echtner, C. M., & Ritchie, J. R. B. (1991). The meaning and measurement of destination image. *Journal of Tourism Studies, 2*(2), 2–12.

Echtner, C. M., & Ritchie, J. R. B. (1993). The measurement of destination image: An empirical assessment. *Journal of Travel Research, 31*(4), 3–13. doi:10.1177/004728759303100402

Fakeye, P. C., & Crompton, J. L. (1991). Images differences between prospective, first-time and repeat visitors to the Lower Rio Grande valley. *Journal of Travel Research, 30*(2), 10–16. doi:10.1177/004728759103000202

Font, X. (1997). Managing the tourist destination's image. *Journal of Vacation Marketing, 3*(2), 123–131. doi:10.1177/135676679700300203

Fridgen, J. D. (1987). Use of cognitive maps to determine perceived tourism regions. *Leisure Sciences, 9*(2), 101–117. doi:10.1080/01490408709512150

Gallarza, M. G., Saura, I. G., & Garcia, H. C. (2002). Destination image: Towards a conceptual framework. *Annals of Tourism Research, 29*(1), 56–78. doi:10.1016/S0160-7383(01)00031-7

Garg, R., Rahman, Z., & Kumar, I. (2010). Evaluating a model for analyzing methods used for measuring customer experience. *Journal of Database Marketing & Customer Strategy Management, 17*(2), 78–90. doi:10.1057/dbm.2010.7

Gartner, W. C. (1989). Tourism image: Attribute measurement of state tourism products using multi-dimensional scaling techniques. *Journal of Travel Research, 28*(2), 16–20. doi:10.1177/004728758902800205

Gartner, W. C. (1994). Image formation process. *Journal of Travel & Tourism Marketing, 2*(2-3), 191–216. doi:10.1300/J073v02n02_12

Govers, R., Go, F. M., & Kumar, K. (2007). Promoting tourism destination image. *Journal of Travel Research, 46*(1), 15–23. doi:10.1177/0047287507302374

Hirschman, E. C., & Holbrook, M. B. (1982). Hedonic consumption: Emerging concepts, methods and propositions. *Journal of Marketing, 46*(3), 92–101. doi:10.1177/002224298204600314

Holbrook, M. B., & Hirschman, E. C. (1982). The experiential aspects of consumption: Consumer fantasies, feelings and fun. *The Journal of Consumer Research, 9*(2), 132–140. doi:10.1086/208906

Hosany, S., Ekinci, Y., & Uysal, M. (2006). Destination image and destination personality: An application of branding theories to tourism places. *Journal of Business Research, 59*(5), 638–642. doi:10.1016/j.jbusres.2006.01.001

Hsu, T. K., Tsai, Y. F., & Wu, H. H. (2009). The preference analysis for tourist choice of destination: A case study of Taiwan. *Tourism Management, 30*(2), 288–297. doi:10.1016/j.tourman.2008.07.011

Hu, Y., & Ritchie, J. B. (1993). Measuring destination attractiveness: A contextual approach. *Journal of Travel Research, 32*(2), 25–34. doi:10.1177/004728759303200204

Hughes, H. L. (2008). Visitor and non-visitor destination images: The influence of political instability in South-Eastern Europe. *Tourism: An International Interdisciplinary Journal, 56*(1), 59–74.

Hui, T. K., & Wan, T. W. D. (2003). Singapore's image as a tourist destination. *International Journal of Tourism Research, 5*(4), 305–313. doi:10.1002/jtr.437

Hunt, J. D. (1975). Image as a factor in tourism development. *Journal of Travel Research, 13*(3), 1–7. doi:10.1177/004728757501300301

Joppe, M., Martin, D. W., & Waalen, J. (2001). Toronto's image as a destination: A comparative importance-satisfaction. Analysis by origin of visitor. *Journal of Travel Research, 39*(3), 252–260. doi:10.1177/004728750103900302

Kandampully, J. (2000). The impact of demand fluctuation on the quality of service: A tourism industry example. *Managing Service Quality*, *10*(1), 10–18. doi:10.1108/09604520010307012

Kauppinen-Raisanen, H., Gummerus, J., & Lehtola, K. (2013). Remembered eating experiences described by the self, place, food, context and time. *British Food Journal*, *115*(5), 666–685. doi:10.1108/00070701311331571

Kim, H., & Richardson, S. L. (2003). Motion picture impacts on destination images. *Annals of Tourism Research*, *30*(1), 216–237. doi:10.1016/S0160-7383(02)00062-2

Kim, J. H. (2014). The antecedents of memorable tourism experiences: The development of a scale to measure the destination attributes associated with memorable experiences. *Tourism Management*, *44*, 34–45. doi:10.1016/j.tourman.2014.02.007

Kim, J. H. (2018). The impact of memorable tourism experiences on loyalty behaviors: The mediating effects of destination image and satisfaction. *Journal of Travel Research*, *57*(7), 856–870. doi:10.1177/0047287517721369

Kim, J. H., Ritchie, J. B., & McCormick, B. (2012). Development of a scale to measure memorable tourism experiences. *Journal of Travel Research*, *51*(1), 12–25. doi:10.1177/0047287510385467

Kim, J. H., Ritchie, J. R., & Tung, V. W. S. (2010). The effect of memorable experience on behavioral intentions in tourism: A structural equation modeling approach. *Tourism Analysis*, *15*(6), 637–648. doi:10.3727/108354210X12904412049776

Kim, S., & Kim, H. (2015). Moderating effects of tourists' novelty-seeking tendencies on the relationship between satisfaction and behavioral intention. *Tourism Analysis*, *20*(5), 511–522. doi:10.3727/108354215X14411980111415

Kim, S., & Park, E. (2015). First-time and repeat tourist destination image: The case of domestic tourists to Weh island, Indonesia. *An International Journal of Tourism and Hospitality Research*, *26*(3), 421–433. doi:10.1080/13032917.2014.984233

Larsen, S. (2007). Aspects of a Psychology of the Tourist Experience. *Scandinavian Journal of Hospitality and Tourism*, *7*(1), 7–18. doi:10.1080/15022250701226014

Lee, B., Lee, C. K., & Lee, J. (2014). Dynamic nature of destination image and influence of tourist overall satisfaction on image modification. *Journal of Travel Research*, *53*(2), 239–251. doi:10.1177/0047287513496466

Lee, C., Lee, Y., & Lee, B. (2005). Korea's destination image formed by the 2002 world cup. *Annals of Tourism Research*, *32*(4), 839–858. doi:10.1016/j.annals.2004.11.006

Lee, T. H., & Chang, Y. S. (2012). The influence of experiential marketing and activity involvement on the loyalty intentions of wine tourists in Taiwan. *Leisure Studies*, *31*(1), 103–121. doi:10.1080/02614367.2011.568067

Lee, T. H., & Crompton, J. (1992). Measuring novelty seeking in tourism. *Annals of Tourism Research*, *19*(4), 732–751. doi:10.1016/0160-7383(92)90064-V

Lew, A. A. (1987). A framework of tourist attraction research. *Annals of Tourism Research*, *14*(4), 553–575. doi:10.1016/0160-7383(87)90071-5

Li, T. T., Liu, F., & Soutar, G. N. (2021). Experiences, post-trip destination image, satisfaction and loyalty: A study in an ecotourism context. *Journal of Destination Marketing & Management*, 19.

Lin, C. T., & Huang, Y. L. (2009). Mining tourist imagery to construct destination image position model. *Expert Systems with Applications*, *36*(2), 2513–2524. doi:10.1016/j.eswa.2008.01.074 PMID:32288333

Liu, X., Li, J., & Kim, W. G. (2017). The role of travel experience in the structural relationships among tourists' perceived image, satisfaction, and behavioral intentions. *Tourism and Hospitality Research*, *17*(2), 135–146. doi:10.1177/1467358415610371

Lohmann, M., & Kaim, E. (1999). Weather and holiday destination preferences image, attitude and experience. *Tourism Review*, *54*(2), 54–64.

Loureiro, S. M. C. (2014). The role of the rural tourism experience economy in place attachment and behavioral intentions. *International Journal of Hospitality Management*, *40*, 1–9. doi:10.1016/j.ijhm.2014.02.010

Ma, J., Gao, J., Scott, N., & Ding, P. (2013). Customer delight from theme park experiences: The antecedents of delight based on cognitive appraisal theory. *Annals of Tourism Research*, *42*, 359–381. doi:10.1016/j.annals.2013.02.018

MacKay, K. J., & Fesenmaier, D. R. (1997). Pictorial element of destination in image formation. *Annals of Tourism Research*, *24*(3), 537–565. doi:10.1016/S0160-7383(97)00011-X

MacKay, K. J., & Fesenmaier, D. R. (2000). An exploration of cross-cultural destination image assessment. *Journal of Travel Research*, *38*(4), 417–423. doi:10.1177/004728750003800411

Mansfeld, Y. (1992). From motivation to actual travel. *Annals of Tourism Research*, *19*(3), 399–419. doi:10.1016/0160-7383(92)90127-B

Martins, J., Gonçalves, R., Branco, F., Barbosa, L., Melo, M., & Bessa, M. (2017). A multisensory virtual experience model for thematic tourism: A Port wine tourism application proposal. *Journal of Destination Marketing & Management*, *6*(2), 103–109. doi:10.1016/j.jdmm.2017.02.002

Meethan, K. (1996). Place, Image and Power: Brighton as Resort. In T. Selwyn (Ed.), *The tourist image: Myths and myth making in tourism* (pp. 180–196). Wiley.

Mehmetoglu, M., & Engen, M. (2011). Pine and Gilmore's concept of experience economy and its dimensions: An empirical examination in tourism. *Journal of Quality Assurance in Hospitality & Tourism*, *12*(4), 237–255. doi:10.1080/1528008X.2011.541847

Michaelidou, N., Siamagka, N.-T., Moraes, C., & Micevski, M. (2013). Do marketers use visual representations of destinations that tourists value? Comparing visitors' image of a destination with marketer-controlled images online. *Journal of Travel Research*, *52*(6), 789–804. doi:10.1177/0047287513481272

Milman, A., & Pizam, A. (1995). The role of awareness and familiarity with a destination: The central Florida case. *Journal of Travel Research*, *33*(3), 21–27. doi:10.1177/004728759503300304

Mitas, O., & Bastiaansen, M. (2018). Novelty: A mechanism of tourists' enjoyment. *Annals of Tourism Research, 72*, 98–108. doi:10.1016/j.annals.2018.07.002

Morgan, M. (2007). We're not the Barmy Army!: Reflections on the sports tourist experience. *International Journal of Tourism Research, 9*(5), 361–372. doi:10.1002/jtr.637

Moutinho, L. (1987). Consumer behaviour in tourism. *European Journal of Marketing, 21*(10), 5–44. doi:10.1108/EUM0000000004718

Muller, T. E. (1996). How personal values govern the post-visit attitudes of international tourists. *Journal of Hospitality & Leisure Marketing, 3*(2), 3–24. doi:10.1300/J150v03n02_02

Niininen, O., Szivas, E., & Riley, M. (2004). Destination loyalty and repeat behaviour: An application of optimum stimu-lation measurement. *International Journal of Tourism Research, 6*(6), 439–447. doi:10.1002/jtr.511

Oh, H., Fiore, A. M., & Jeoung, M. (2007). Measuring experience economy concepts: Tourism applications. *Journal of Travel Research, 46*(2), 119–132. doi:10.1177/0047287507304039

Otto, J. E., & Ritchie, J. B. (1996). The service experience in tourism. *Tourism Management, 17*(3), 165–174. doi:10.1016/0261-5177(96)00003-9

Park, S. H., Hsieh, C.-M., & Lee, C.-K. (2017). Examining Chinese college students' intention to travel to Japan using the extended Theory of Planned Behavior: Testing destination image and the mediating role of travel constraints. *Journal of Travel & Tourism Marketing, 34*(1), 113–131. doi:10.1080/10548 408.2016.1141154

Phelps, A. (1986). Holiday destination image: the problem of assessment: An example developed in Menorca. *Tourism Management, 7*(3), 168–180. doi:10.1016/0261-5177(86)90003-8

Pike, S., & Ryan, C. (2004). Destination positioning analysis through a comparison of cognitive, affective, and conative perceptions. *Journal of Travel Research, 42*(4), 333–342. doi:10.1177/0047287504263029

Pikkemaat, B., & Schuckert, M. (2007). Success factors of theme parks: An exploration study. *Turizam: Međunarodni Znanstveno-Stručni Časopis, 55*(2), 197–208.

Pine, B. J., & Gilmore, J. H. (1999). *The experience economy: Work is theatre and every business a stage*. Harvard Business School Press.

Pine, B. J., & Gilmore, J. H. (2012). Deneyim ekonomisi. İstanbul: Optimist Yayınları.

Prayag, G., Hosany, S., Muskat, B., & Del Chiappa, G. (2017). Understanding the relationships between tourists' emotional experiences, perceived overall image, satisfaction, and intention to recommend. *Journal of Travel Research, 56*(1), 41–54. doi:10.1177/0047287515620567

Prebensen, N. K., & Rosengren, S. (2016). Experience value as a function of hedonic and utilitarian dominant services. *International Journal of Contemporary Hospitality Management, 28*(1), 113–135. doi:10.1108/IJCHM-02-2014-0073

Puccinelli, N. M., Goodstein, R. C., Grewal, D., Price, R., Raghubir, P., & Stewart, D. (2009). Customer experience management in retailing: Understanding the buying process. *Journal of Retailing*, *85*(1), 15–30. doi:10.1016/j.jretai.2008.11.003

Quan, S., & Wang, N. (2004). Towards a structural model of the tourist experience: An illustration from food experiences in tourism. *Tourism Management*, *25*(3), 297–305. doi:10.1016/S0261-5177(03)00130-4

Reilly, M. D. (1990). Free elicitation of descriptive adjectives for tourism image assessment. *Journal of Travel Research*, *28*(4), 21–26. doi:10.1177/004728759002800405

Reynolds, W. H. (1965). The role of the consumer in image building. *California Management Review*, *7*(3), 69–76. doi:10.2307/41165634

Rezende-Parker, A. M., Morrison, A. M., & Ismail, J. A. (2003). Dazed and confused? An exploratory study of the image of Brazil as a travel destination. *Journal of Vacation Marketing*, *9*(3), 243–259. doi:10.1177/135676670300900304

Roy, S. (2018). Effects of customer experience across service types, customer types and time. *Journal of Services Marketing*, *32*(4), 100–413. doi:10.1108/JSM-11-2016-0406

Ryan, C., & Montgomery, D. (1994). The attitudes of Bakewell residents to tourism and issues in community responsive tourism. *Tourism Management*, *15*(5), 358–369. doi:10.1016/0261-5177(94)90090-6

Safitri, C., & Maftukhah, I. (2018). Pengaruh kualitas layanan, promosi dan citra destinasi terhadap kepuasan melalui keputusan pengunjung. *Management Analysis Journal*, *6*(3), 310–319.

San Martín, H., & Del Bosque, I. A. R. (2008). Exploring the cognitive–affective nature of destination image and the role of psychological factors in its formation. *Tourism Management*, *29*(2), 263–277. doi:10.1016/j.tourman.2007.03.012

Selby, M., & Morgan, N. J. (1996). Reconstruing place image: A case study of its role in destination market research. *Tourism Management*, *17*(4), 287–294. doi:10.1016/0261-5177(96)00020-9

Selwyn, T. (1996). Introduction. In T. Selwyn (Ed.), *The tourist image: Myths and myth making in tourism* (pp. 1–32). Wiley.

Smith, W. W., Li, X. R., Pan, B., Witte, M., & Doherty, S. T. (2015). Tracking destination image across the trip experience with smartphone technology. *Tourism Management*, *48*, 113–122. doi:10.1016/j.tourman.2014.04.010

Song, Z., Su, X., & Li, L. (2013). The indirect effects of destination image on destination loyalty intention through tourist satisfaction and perceived value: The bootstrap approach. *Journal of Travel & Tourism Marketing*, *30*(4), 386–409. doi:10.1080/10548408.2013.784157

Stabler, M. J. (1995). The image of destination regions: Theoretical and empirical aspects. In B. Goodall & G. Ashworth (Eds.), *Marketing in tourism industry: The Promotion of destination regions* (pp. 133–159).

Sternberg, E. (1997). The iconography of the tourism experience. *Annals of Tourism Research*, *24*(4), 951–969. doi:10.1016/S0160-7383(97)00053-4

Stylidis, D., Terzidou, M., & Terzidis, K. (2008). Islands and destination image: The case of Ios. *Tourismos*, *3*(1), 180–189.

Suhartanto, D., Clems, M., & Wibisono, N. (2018). How experiences with cultural attractions affect: Destination image and destination loyalty. *Tourism, Culture & Communication*, *18*(3), 177–189. doi:10.3727/109830418X15319363084463

Tan, W. K. (2017). Repeat visitation: A study from the perspective of leisure constraint, tourist experience, destination images, and experiential familiarity. *Journal of Destination Marketing & Management*, *6*(3), 233–242. doi:10.1016/j.jdmm.2016.04.003

Tavitiyaman, P., & Qu, H. (2013). Destination image and behavior intention of travelers to Thailand: The moderating effect of perceived risk. *Journal of Travel & Tourism Marketing*, *30*(3), 169–185. doi:10.1080/10548408.2013.774911

Tsai, C. T. (2016). Memorable tourist experiences and place attachment when consuming local food. *International Journal of Tourism Research*, *18*(6), 536–548. doi:10.1002/jtr.2070

Tsaur, S. H., Chiu, Y. T., & Wang, C. H. (2007). The visitors behavioral consequences of experiential marketing: An empirical study on Taipei Zoo. *Journal of Travel & Tourism Marketing*, *21*(1), 47–64. doi:10.1300/J073v21n01_04

Tung, V. W. S., & Ritchie, J. B. (2011). Exploring the essence of memorable tourism experiences. *Annals of Tourism Research*, *38*(4), 1367–1386. doi:10.1016/j.annals.2011.03.009

Tussyadiah, I. P., & Fesenmaier, D. R. (2009). Mediating tourist experiences: Access to places via shared videos. *Annals of Tourism Research*, *36*(1), 24–40. doi:10.1016/j.annals.2008.10.001

Um, S., & Crompton, J. L. (1990). Attitude determinants in tourism destination choice. *Annals of Tourism Research*, *17*(3), 432–448. doi:10.1016/0160-7383(90)90008-F

Vitterso, J., Prebensen, N. K., Hetland, A., & Dahl, T. (2017). The emotional traveler: Happiness and engagement as predictors of behavioral intentions among tourists in Northern Norway. In J. S. Chen (Ed.), *Advances in hospitality and leisure* (pp. 3–16). Emerald Publishing Limited. doi:10.1108/S1745-354220170000013001

Walls, A., Okumus, F., Wang, Y., & Kwun, D. (2011). An epistemological view of consumer experiences. *International Journal of Hospitality Management*, *30*(1), 10–12. doi:10.1016/j.ijhm.2010.03.008

Walmsley, D. J., & Jenkins, J. M. (1993). Appraisive images of tourist areas: Application of personal constructs. *The Australian Geographer*, *24*(2), 1–13. doi:10.1080/00049189308703083

Wang, B., Yang, Z., Han, F., & Shi, H. (2017). Car tourism in Xinjiang: The mediation effect of perceived value and tourist satisfaction on the relationship between destination image and loyalty. *Sustainability*, *9*(1), 22. doi:10.3390u9010022

Wang, C., & Hsu, M. K. (2010). The relationships of destination image, satisfaction, and behavioral intentions: An integrated model. *Journal of Travel & Tourism Marketing*, *27*(8), 829–843. doi:10.1080/10548408.2010.527249

Wang, W., Chen, J. S., Fan, L., & Lu, J. (2012). Tourist experience and wetland parks: A case of Zhejiang, China. *Annals of Tourism Research*, *39*(4), 1763–1778. doi:10.1016/j.annals.2012.05.029

White, C. (2004). Destination image: To see or not to see. Part 1. *International Journal of Contemporary Hospitality Management*, *16*(5), 309–314. doi:10.1108/09596110410540285

Wijaya, S., King, B., Nguyen, T. H., & Morrison, A. (2013). International visitor dining experiences: A conceptual framework. *Journal of Hospitality and Tourism Management*, *20*, 34–42. doi:10.1016/j.jhtm.2013.07.001

Williams, P., & Soutar, G. N. (2009). Value, satisfaction and behavioral intentions in an adventure tourism context. *Annals of Tourism Research*, *36*(3), 413–438. doi:10.1016/j.annals.2009.02.002

Wu, C. W. (2016). Destination loyalty modeling of the global tourism. *Journal of Business Research*, *69*(6), 2213–2219. doi:10.1016/j.jbusres.2015.12.032

Wu, H. C., Li, M. Y., & Li, T. (2018). A study of experiential quality, experiential value, experiential satisfaction, theme park image, and revisit intention. *Journal of Hospitality & Tourism Research (Washington, D.C.)*, *42*(1), 26–73. doi:10.1177/1096348014563396

Yuan, Y. H., & Wu, C. (2008). Relationships among experiential marketing, experiential value and customer satisfaction. *Journal of Hospitality & Tourism Research (Washington, D.C.)*, *32*(3), 387–410. doi:10.1177/1096348008317392

Zhang, H., Fu, X., Cai, L. A., & Lu, L. (2014). Destination image and tourist loyalty: A meta-analysis. *Tourism Management*, *40*, 213–223. doi:10.1016/j.tourman.2013.06.006

Zhang, H., Wu, Y., & Buhalis, D. (2018). A model of perceived image, memorable tourism experiences and revisit intention. *Journal of Destination Marketing & Management*, *8*, 326–336. doi:10.1016/j.jdmm.2017.06.004

ADDITIONAL READING

Ashworth, G., & Goodall, B. (1988). Tourist images: Marketing considerations. In B. Goodall & G. Ashworth (Eds.), *Marketing in the tourism industry: The promotion of destination regions* (pp. 213–238). Routledge.

Boulding, W., Kalra, A., Staelin, R., & Zeithaml, V. A. (1993). A dynamic process model of service quality: From expectations to behavioral intentions. *JMR, Journal of Marketing Research*, *30*(1), 7–27. doi:10.1177/002224379303000102

Christopher, M., Payne, A., & Ballantyne, D. (1993). *Relationship marketing: Bringing quality, customer service and marketing together*. Butterworth-Heinemann.

Cooper, C., Fletcher, J., Gilbert, D., & Wanhill, S. (1993). *Tourism: Principles & practice*. Pitman Publishing.

Goodall, B. (1988). How tourists choose their holidays: An analytical framework. In B. Goodall & G. Ashworth (Eds.), *Marketing in the tourism industry: The promotion of destination regions* (pp. 1–17). Routledge.

Kent, P. (1990). People, places and priorities: Opportunity sets and consumers holiday choice. In G. Ashworth & B. Goodall (Eds.), *Marketing tourism places* (pp. 42–62). Routledge.

Kotler, P., Bowen, J., & Makens, J. (1996). *Marketing for hospitality and tourism*. Prentice Hall.

Ross, G. F. (1991). Tourist destination images of the wet tropical rainforests of North Queensland. *Australian Psychologist*, 26(3), 153–157. doi:10.1080/00050069108257241

Ross, G. F. (1993). Ideal and actual images of backpacker visitors to Northern Australia. *Journal of Travel Research*, 32(2), 54–57. doi:10.1177/004728759303200208

Stabler, M. (1990). The concept of opportunity sets as a methodological framework for the analysis of selling tourism places: The Industry view. In G. Ashworth & B. Goodall (Eds.), *Marketing tourism places* (pp. 23–41). Routledge.

Witter, B. S. (1985). Attitudes about a resort area: A comparison of tourists and local retailers. *Journal of Travel Research*, 24(1), 14–19. doi:10.1177/004728758502400103

KEY TERMS AND DEFINITIONS

Destination Image: Can be expressed as the visitor's subjective and cognitive perception of the destination reality.

Revisit Intention: Is expressed as the desire of the tourists to revisit the destination in another time period.

Satisfaction: Can be defined as the general degree of pleasure felt by the visitor, resulting from the travel experience meeting the traveller's wishes, expectations and needs.

Tourism: Is an industry that offers experience by its essence and foundation.

Tourism Experience: Is expressed as the moment of value creation when tourism consumption and tourism production meet.

Chapter 3
Prioritization of the Destination Attributes:
The Case of Fethiye, Turkey

Özgür Davras
Süleyman Demirel University, Turkey

ABSTRACT

This chapter aims to identify the destination attributes and compare them based on two assumptions that form either a symmetric or an asymmetric relationship between destination attribute performance and tourist satisfaction. For this purpose, data were collected from tourists coming to Fethiye, Turkey. Multivariate regression analysis was performed on the obtained data based on the linear assumption first. The results revealed that the attitudes of staff and the attitudes of the shopkeepers are the main determinants of tourist satisfaction. Then, penalty-reward-contrast analysis was performed based on the nonlinear assumption. According to analysis results, attitudes of the staff are performance factors; and travel agency services, attitudes of the shopkeepers, security/safety, and beach/sea are classified as excitement factors. The elements that take part in the excitement factor are the attributes that contribute to satisfaction the most.

INTRODUCTION

The tourism sector, which is increasingly developing every year, plays an important role in the economic development of countries with its income-increasing effect and employment rates. According to the World Tourism Organization (2021) data, the number of international tourists, which was 25 million in 1950, reached approximately 1.5 billion people in 2019, with an increase of 3.8% (approximately 54 million people) compared to the previous year. Today, although the tourism sector is experiencing difficult days due to the pandemic (Covid-19), the number of international tourists in 2030 is predicted to be around 1 billion 800 million, according to the long-term estimates of the same organisation. Although tourism is one of the fastest-growing sectors, parallel to the rapid development in the world economy, the number of tourism destinations is increasing day by day, and the differences between them are becoming

DOI: 10.4018/978-1-7998-8775-1.ch003

Copyright © 2022, IGI Global. Copying or distributing in print or electronic forms without written permission of IGI Global is prohibited.

less obvious. In an increasingly competitive environment, it is difficult for the destination to compete and maintain its position in the international market if it cannot maintain or improve its resources and destination pull factors (Davras, 2021).

In the global tourism market wherein a fierce competition environment, the success of the destinations depends on providing higher visitor satisfaction. Because visitor satisfaction is accepted as the antecedent of loyalty and repurchase behaviour and, it positively affects profitability (Albayrak & Caber, 2013). Visitor satisfaction is created by a combination of various attributes of the destinations. Therefore, determining the most important features of a destination that, in the formation of general visitor satisfaction, is one of the most important tasks of destination authorities and tourism marketers. Identifying the most important destination attributes that affect tourists' experiences before, during and after travel allows destination managers to segment the market and better meet tourist demands and needs. In this way, by determining the destination attributes that increase tourist satisfaction, destination managers will be able to transfer their limited resources to the right attributes. Therefore, destination management organisations need to make an intense effort to develop and market the tourism sector, which provides economic and social contributions to get a competitive advantage. The purpose of destination marketing is to make and develop the destination identity created by attributes of a destination even more attractive with effective communication tools for potential tourists. The competitiveness and success of a destination in tourism depend on providing high-quality service and creating and developing customer satisfaction. This is because customer satisfaction positively affects profitability and is defined as a pioneer of purchasing behaviour. Customer satisfaction, which is defined as pleasure with specific destination attributes, is a combination of various attributes of the destination. In other words, it could be the result of the performance of the destination attributes (Albayrak & Caber, 2013). Considering the effects of each destination attribute on customer satisfaction, it is important to identify which attribute should be taken into consideration for destination management organisations (DMOs) to invest their limited resources in improving the right product.

Since tourist satisfaction plays an important role in the success of destinations, tourism research has focused on tourists' perceptions of quality about destination attributes and the effects of these attributes on overall satisfaction. Therefore, researchers advise destination managers to allocate more resources to underperforming attributes to improve the quality of their destination attributes. However, considering the limited resources of destinations, managers should also base their resource allocation decisions on a priority assessment of attributes. For this purpose, researchers have generally used analysis techniques such as multivariate regression and structural equation modelling for identifying resource priorities. The common purpose of these statistical techniques is to guide managers in their efforts to increase customer satisfaction in terms of making rational decisions. The common point of the related techniques is that they are based on the assumption that there is a linear relationship between the performance of the product attributes and customer satisfaction. However, some studies conducted in recent years (Fuchs & Weiermair, 2003; Allegre & Garau, 2011) revealed that there might be a non-linear relationship between product attributes and customer satisfaction. According to this non-linear approach, the negative performance of a product attribute has more of an impact on customer satisfaction than the positive performance of the same attribute (Albayrak & Caber, 2013). In other words, the impact of a product on customer satisfaction may vary depending on the perceived performance of the attribute. Among the most preferred techniques to reveal the non-linear relationship between the performance of product attributes and customer satisfaction, take part Kano Technique, Critical Incident Technique, Dual Importance Mapping, and Penalty-Reward Contrast Analysis with the help of regression analysis with dummy variables. According to the researchers who adopt the non-linear approach, when traditional methods are predicated on, there is a risk of transferring the limited resources of the enterprises to the wrong attributes. To annihilate this risk, it is necessary to determine the product attributes that need to be increased with the correct methods.

In summary, some researchers prefer the linear approach, while others adopt the non-linear approach to determine the relationships between product attributes and customer satisfaction. Although both approaches have scientific value, it has become increasingly important today to investigate how the results obtained differ according to these two different approaches and to decide which one provides the correct results. Today, although the importance of the relationship between high product quality and customer satisfaction has been understood, discussions related to improving product features are still ongoing. The product attributes that managers need to transfer resources to increase customer satisfaction differ according to the assumption discussed (symmetric relationship / asymmetric relationship). It would be appropriate for managers to consider the results of the analysis performed with different assumptions while making a decision. Otherwise, it may be possible to use the limited resources in the wrong attributes.

This book chapter aims to identify and compare the symmetric and asymmetric influences of destination attributes on visitor satisfaction. To achieve these objectives, the book chapter was constituted as follows: first, the literature on destination attributes was examined and explained, and then the relationship between destination attributes and overall visitor satisfaction was investigated using two different methods. The chapter concludes with a discussion of the research findings together with their managerial implications.

DESTINATION ATTRIBUTES

A tourism destination is a place where visitors experience several natural and/or artificial attributes of that place that are perceived to be its major sources of attraction (Albayrak & Caber, 2013). According to another definition is a physical space in which a tourist spends at least one overnight. It includes tourism products, such as support services, attractions, and tourist resources within one day's return travel time (Vanhove, 2011:21). Destination attributes are the assignment of utility values to various ''parts'' of the destination alternative for the destination choice. The set of attributes is constructed in the tourist's mind as a result of perceived needs and expectations derived from a given destination, constraints to be faced, and the information collected while pursuing a destination choice process (Zhang et al., 2004).

A tourism destination has a complex structure consisting of both tangible and intangible dimensions. While the tangible dimensions consist of the physical stock of tourism businesses, visitor attractions, parking facilities, etc., intangible dimensions consist of historical and cultural values, etc. (Palmer & Bejou, 1995). Each destination has some unique attributes. Researchers (Baloğlu & Uysal, 1996) exhibited that the destination attributes consist of two main categories based on Dann's push-pull motivations framework. Pull factors are those that attract travellers to destinations where tourism products are provided. Beaches, cultural and historical centres, shopping and natural scenery are factors that motivate travellers. Push factors are the internal forces demanded by the psychological motives of the travellers, such as the desire to escape from the environment, rest, relaxation, experience and socialisation.

Destination attributes which are considered synonymously with different concepts in the literature such as destination attractions, destination resources, pull factors, destination product, and destination quality, can be expressed as the combination of various elements that attract visitors to the region. Destination decision-makers aim to make the destination attractive by bringing natural and cultural elements together, as well as many other different elements, into a tourism product (Albayrak & Caber, 2013).

Since the destinations generally have different attributes, they will differ from each other. Therefore, destination characteristics are classified into different types in the literature. For example, Karasakal's (2019) study, in which he examined 32 studies conducted in 16 different countries, determined that 638 destination attributes were discussed. These attributes were classified under 24 groups. These attributes consist of accommodation, shopping, food and beverage, hygiene and cleanliness, security, price, access, activities and events, infrastructure, facilities, attitude/hospitality, cultural and historical elements, religious elements, entertainment, natural environment, atmosphere, service, image, sightseeing, communication, informativeness, supporting elements, other attractions, and negative elements.

Tourists perceive the tourism destination, which consists of different components as a whole. Therefore, destination managers who want to increase local economic and social development have to offer quality tourism products to ensure tourist satisfaction and loyalty. However, it is very unlikely that managers will be successful and provide quality service without understanding the tourists' wishes and needs. Therefore, they need to determine the destination characteristics that determine tourist satisfaction and loyalty. The basic attributes that can be in a destination are explained in detail below.

Price

Price is one of the most influential factors affecting tourist decisions and is seen as one of the elements with destination attractiveness. Price is generally defined as the monetary value of a product or service (Kotler et al. l., 1999: 681). In terms of tourism, it is related to the visitors' evaluation of the products offered at the destination as the price and value. Tourism studies have revealed that travellers are highly-priced sensitive (Lee et al., 1996). The cost of a tourism experience (such as transportation costs, expenditures at the destination) affects the travel decisions of tourists (Dwyer & Kim, 2003).

The perception of value is important. In other words, the relationship between the prices and perceived value of the touristic products offered in the destination affects the behavioural intentions of the tourists towards the destination. One of the challenges that destinations face is providing value for money. Destination and tourism managers can apply different pricing techniques. However, what is the tourist's perception of those prices and the value that counts? For example, Kozak and Rimmington (2000) concluded that the money-perceived value relationship positively affects tourists' destination satisfaction.

On the other hand, the general price level of a destination affects not only the tourist's travel decision, but also the tourist's holiday budget and the expenditures in the destination. Davras (2021), in her study on winter tourism destinations in Turkey, revealed that the price is determined as the most important attribute that can increase satisfaction according to the non-linear assumption. Therefore, the price policies to be implemented by the destination management organisations can be effective on the destination preferences of the tourists, as well as on the accommodation, food and beverage preferences, and shopping preferences in the destination.

Cultural and Historical Values

A destination's culture, history, heritage, traditions and customs, architectural features, cuisine, arts, crafts, music, dance are important attractions for potential tourists (Dwyer & Kim, 2003). These values are seen as attraction elements for mostly cultural tourism tourists. Values such as archaeological and historical artefacts, structures, architectural and artistic works, customs and traditions of the people living in the region, culinary culture and hospitality in the destination are considered within the scope of historical and cultural attractions.

Some destinations in the world have witnessed historical events and hosted many civilisations. Destinations that can preserve and carry these elements to the present create a great potential for cultural tourism. For example, cities such as Istanbul, Prague, London, Paris, Krakow are some of the culturally and historically important destinations. Since cultural and historical values in a destination are unique, they cannot be imitated and play an important role in differentiating from other destinations.

Socio-cultural resources in a destination can be listed as places worth seeing, cultural opportunities, cultural and sports activities. Cultural resources in tourism contain multiple dimensions. Cultural resources can be listed as follows (Fernandez et al., 2007);

- Art, historical areas and sites: monuments, museums, cultural exhibitions and world cultural heritage.
- Human activities in cultural interests: popular religious celebrations, music, cinema, theatre, dance, crafts and popular architecture, traditional gastronomy, cultural routes.
- Economic events in areas of cultural interest: industrial and mining heritage, agriculture and livestock, trade fairs.
- Natural and cultural values: Natural parks and cultural parks.

Entertainment and Events

Entertainment opportunities for a destination are not just a product created for local people, but also an element to be considered for visitors. This attribute encompasses activities such as concerts, dances, shows, games, movies, nightclubs, discos, and gambling (Loi, 2008). Especially gambling can be an important attraction for some destinations. Every year, thousands of tourists go to destinations like Las Vegas and Cyprus to gamble. Besides these, the theme park is also an important entertainment element. Theme parks contribute to the region's attractiveness and have a great economic contribution thanks to the employment they provide to thousands of people. Entertainment activities are tourism products developed to meet the needs of tourists and provide them with unforgettable moments. Entertainment opportunities not only contribute to the attractiveness of the destination but also provide an economic return. For this reason, many destinations have focused on developing a leisure-based tourism product.

The events are internationally recognised as they contribute to the economic development of tourism. If tourism products are diversified in a tourism destination, the attractiveness of that destination will increase. For example, in Las Vegas, the organisation of entertainment and family-oriented events alongside casinos has provided the destination to continue to evolve.

Events are attractive factors for destinations looking for urban development, international market recognition and local economic development (Derrett, 2004). Moreover, events that contribute significantly to the success and attractiveness of tourism destinations create economic effects for destinations. In addition to this economic effect, it creates motivation to travel to the destination and constitutes a revisit intention. In addition, events prolong the tourist season and increase tourists' loyalty (McHone and Rungeling, 2000). Tourism destinations carry out national and international events and activities for reasons such as increasing the variety of touristic products, increasing the number of tourists, generating more income and providing a competitive advantage. For example, Hernandez-Mogollon et al.1 (2018), in a study they conducted in Spain, determined that cultural events contribute to the development of the destination image.

Image

Image is defined as the impression that an individual or business leaves in the minds of other individuals or businesses. According to another definition, image is the result of how consumers perceive a business, and it is an individual's thoughts, beliefs and feelings about a business. Thus, although the image emerges as a function of people's attitudes, knowledge, imagination, prejudices and experiences, it is also expressed as the image formed in perceptions resulting from a series of information (Çetin, 2017, p. 92). On the other hand, destination image can be defined as the visual or mental impression of a tourist about a travel experience or the beliefs, ideas, and impressions they have about a destination. According to another definition, it can be expressed as tourists' thoughts and value judgments about a country, a region or a brand (Turkay, 2014: 210). Destination image is the situation in which the features of a destination (such as landscape, activity) reflect the destination and bring it to the tourist's mind. These features can be a source of motivation for tourists to visit the destination. Destination image is accepted as an important dimension of brand equity as an important component in the process of destination brand value formation in the field of tourism and accommodation (Boo et al., 2009).

Some studies in the literature have revealed that the destination image affects the tourist's holiday destination choice process and their revisit intention. For example, Im et al. (2012) and Yang et al. (2015) determined that the destination image positively affected destination loyalty. Hernandez-Lobato et al. (2006) determined that destination image has an effect on destination satisfaction.

Many researchers argue that the destination image consists of cognitive/perceptual and emotional dimensions. However, some researchers include behavioural dimensions as well as cognitive and emotional dimensions. Cognitive destination image includes the evaluations made by the tourist in line with their knowledge and beliefs about the destination and taking the destination characteristics into account. Emotional destination image, on the other hand, expresses the tourist's feelings towards a destination or loyalty to the destination. As a result of cognitive and emotional evaluations about the destination, the overall image of the destination is formed (Ünal and Caber, 2019).

Shopping

Shopping, which is a destination attraction feature and motive for travel, is an indispensable activity for tourists (Moscardo, 2004). While shopping can be a single reason for people to travel, it can also be a supportive factor. Especially, shopping festivals organised together with organisations to increase the number of tourists in destinations increase the attractiveness of tourist destinations. For example, Dubai, known as the shopping centre of the Middle East, is an important destination that has made significant investments in this area and has positioned itself in people's minds with the shopping festivals organised.

Destinations give importance to shopping opportunities to increase both their economic income and their attractiveness. Tourists buy souvenirs or gifts at the destination they visit. Souvenir shopping is one of the main spending areas of tourists, and it is seen that some tourists travel only for shopping, and tourism has a strong effect on retail trade, touristic shopping is an attraction power besides its economic contribution. The use of cultural elements in the design of touristic products contributes to the originality and quality of the products and enriches the visiting experience of tourists.

Shopping increases tourists' satisfaction with the destination. Yau & Chan (1990), in their study on the determination of Hong Kong holiday destination attributes, revealed that shopping opportunities are one of the most important factors affecting visitor satisfaction. A study conducted in Indonesia determined that shopping facilities are important for tourist satisfaction and destination image (Suhartanto and Triyuni, 2016).

Cuisine/Gastronomy

Along with the fact that eating meets a physiological need, in parallel with the developments in the developing food and beverage industry, this need has been met outside, and it has turned into a leisure activity. For people, meeting the need for food no longer just means meeting a physiological need, but also means enjoying food, atmosphere and other conditions. However, eating is not only a leisure activity but also a part of tourism behaviour. Kivela and Crotts (2005) found that motivation to travel for gastronomy reasons is a valid construct. Also, they have revealed that gastronomy has an impact on tourists' destination experiences and positively affects tourists' revisit intentions. Similarly, Guan and Jones (2015) revealed that tourists' local culinary experiences positively affect their perception of the destination.

Local food culture is one of the most important elements of destinations. Destinations should develop and present quality food and beverages as a touristic product and tourist experience for that destination. Decision-makers, who understand the importance of food for tourism, have started to create a gastronomic image to differentiate destination attractiveness and be competitive (Kivela and Crotts, 2005). Therefore, the kitchen is primarily used as a marketing tool for some destinations. For example, Singapore aims to attract gastronomic tourists using the slogan "Singapore: the Food Capital of Asia". Similarly, food is an important tourist attraction for the cities of Tuscany and Lyons in France. Therefore, if the variety of food and beverage within the destination is managed correctly, it will contribute positively to the competitiveness of the destination.

Natural Resources

The natural resources of a destination define the environmental framework within which the tourist enjoys the destination. Natural resources are important elements of attraction in the region that are formed by themselves in time. They include physiography, climate, flora and fauna, scenery and other physical assets (Dwyer and Kim, 2003). Since tourism is a sector dependent on the natural environment, it is one of the sectors that will be affected most quickly by the destruction that may occur. Environmental awareness of the tourists is increasing, and, in this case, it can affect their destination preferences. Lo et al. (2017) concluded that natural resources positively affect destination competitiveness from tourists' perspectives. On the other hand, since the natural environment is a very effective factor for a region to be a tourism destination, DMOs should determine the number of tourists that will destroy the natural environment and manage tourist mobility well. In other words, planning should be done considering the carrying capacity of the destination.

Prioritization of the Destination Attributes

Environment

With the increase in the number of environmentally conscious tourists in recent years, environmental quality has become even more important for destinations. Destinations that attach importance to environmental quality will be more advantageous than their rivals (Gooroochurn & Sugiyarto, 2005). Campo and Garau (2008) concluded that environmental factors are the most important dimension affecting tourist satisfaction, in their study on tourists coming to the Balearic Islands.

Among the environmental factors, the quality of the beaches and seawater, and the coastline's presence and cleanliness strengthen the destination's position in the market. On the other hand, the average temperature, type and amount of precipitation, and humidity can enable the destination to have an advantageous position against its rivals.

Accommodation

Accommodation businesses play a central role in the tourism industry and are a basic product for the destination. Comfort, variety and quality of accommodation establishments are indispensable elements in tourism destinations. Nowadays, different accommodation options are preferred destinations for tourists. The product of accommodation establishments, such as building and design, decoration, furniture, human resources, food and beverage, equipment and materials, check-in and check-out processes are among the determinants of service quality.

Accommodation service quality plays an important role in tourist satisfaction. For example, Caber (2013) indicated that "Accommodation" is one of the important attributes which affect overall visitor satisfaction. According to this result, the authors recommended the DMOs should allocate their limited resources mostly to 'Accommodation'' facilities. Similarly, Kwanisai and Vengesayi (2016) found in their study in Zimbabweans that accommodation had the greatest contribution towards destination satisfaction.

Activities

One of the attractions of the destination is the activities that tourists can perform at the destination. They are accepted as important tourism attractors. Activities can be expressed as elements including cultural, natural and sportive activities, entertainment, and services that tourists participate in during their holidays. This category is intended to capture those activities where the visitor tends to be highly involved as a participant or those events where simply being there is significant. For example, summer activities such as golf and tennis; winter activities such as skiing; water sport activities such as swimming, fishing and boating; Special interest activities such as adventure tourism, ecotourism, heritage/cultural tourism, night clubs/nightlife are included in this category (Dwyer and Kim, 2003).

Research on destination choice models in the literature has revealed that activities are an important attribute for the destination. For example, Law et al. (2004) revealed that travel activities are essential for Hong Kong travellers. Moscardo et al. (1996) argued that there is a link between travel motivation and activities. Therefore, it can be said that the managers' development of different activity strategies in the destination will play an important role in attracting more tourists.

Climate/Weather Conditions

The climate and weather conditions of a destination are considered important factors in the destination preference of tourists. At the same time, it has a positive effect on the development of sustainable tourism in the destination. This attribute includes subjects such as temperature, humidity, wind, cooling effects, radiation. Other issues such as wind speed or snow depth are important for winter tourism destinations (Becken & Wilson, 2013). Climate is defined as the long-term observed condition in a region. Weather is the manifestation of the climate at a particular time. Tourists will experience real weather conditions that may deviate from the expected climatic conditions in a destination. Therefore, tourists are more likely to be affected by weather rather than climate.

Although economic variables are effective in tourists' decision-making, the climate is a driving and important factor for tourism destinations. For example, the climate is the main source of tourism for coastal destinations. Climate can also be reflected in the destination image (Becken & Wilson, 2013).

Accessibility

Since the distribution system in the tourism sector is the reverse, tourists have to travel and from the destination they choose. Therefore, accessibility is seen as the main component of tourism. The accessibility of a destination refers to the transportation-related technology and infrastructure necessary to visit the destination and benefit from all kinds of activities within the destination, or it is the proximity of destinations with high attractiveness to the target audience in the market and the possibility of reaching them at a low cost. It is comprised of a variety of elements, including seaways, highways, airlines, railways, frequency and quality of transportation, competition between companies, entry permits and visa procedures, etc. Costly or difficult to obtain visas can be a deterrent to visiting tourists. Countries may impose restrictions on domestic tourists who wish to participate in foreign tourism (Dwyer and Kim, 2003). Prideaux (2000) argued that the choice of destination is affected by the comfort levels of vehicles, travel times and transportation systems.

Accessibility is one of the key attributes for destinations. In addition, accessibility contributes to the attractiveness of a destination. If destinations do not have accessibility opportunities, other attractions of the destination will not make sense for tourists because tourists do not prefer to travel to places where accessibility is difficult or problematic. Accessibility opportunities and developments in transportation have a great contribution to the development of tourism and its reaching today's volume. The accessibility of the destinations may be the reason for preference in the selection of the destination. If it is desired to attract visitors to a destination, the means of transportation and facilities of that destination must be developed. The development of tourism in terms of destinations depends on the efficiency, quality and capacity of the transportation network (Prideaux, 2000). For this reason, it is not possible for destinations with unqualified and low-quality transportation networks to develop and attract large numbers of tourists. Access to destinations can be eased by establishing different and wide distribution channels and expanding sales networks. Improving links between transport systems can also increase destination competitiveness. (Dwyer & Kim, 2003).

Researches reveal the importance of transportation for a destination. For example, Yau and Chan (1990), in their study on the determination of Hong Kong holiday destination characteristics, revealed that transportation is one of the most important factors affecting visitor satisfaction. Similarly, in their study in Bangladesh, Biswas et al. (2020) concluded that transportation positively affects tourist satisfaction. Kozak (2001), in their study comparing Turkey and Spain destinations, revealed that transportation services are the most important factor affecting the intention to revisit.

Tourism Infrastructure

Tourism infrastructure comprises the basis of the tourism resources of the destination and is very important for tourism development. Tourism infrastructure includes all the services that tourists need during their stay in a destination (Jovanovic & Ivana, 2016). The general infrastructure of a destination includes airports, highways, transportation systems, water supply, sewerage, health facilities, hygiene and sanitation, wastewater facilities, solid waste facilities, recycling facilities, communication systems, and computer services). On the other hand, Tourism infrastructure includes food and beverage services, fast food outlets, accommodation facilities, themed attractions, transportation facilities, harbours, tour operators, travel agencies, car rental companies, convention offices, nightclubs and tourist information offices. In addition to this, it covers places such as shopping centres, vehicle repair shops, pharmacies, gas stations, markets, hairdressers, laundries, administration offices (Dwyer & Kim, 2003).

Infrastructure is very important and necessary for a tourism destination. No matter how attractive a destination is, if its connection with the means of transportation is not at a good level, there may be problems in the marketing of the relevant destination, and as a result, a decrease in tourist flow may occur. It can be said that transportation infrastructure has an impact on tourist flow. In general, areas with well-developed transport facilities have been the first preferred destinations for visitors (Prideaux, 2000).

A destination with insufficient infrastructure is unlikely to be successful. In a quality destination, infrastructure and superstructure problems should be eliminated. The inability or lack of infrastructure investments significantly impacts tourists' perception of destination quality, alongside other products. Due to this important effect of infrastructure investments to achieve the quality of the destination, it should be considered together with other factors in ensuring customer satisfaction and creating quality products. Murphy et al. (2000) found that inadequate tourism infrastructure negatively affects tourist experiences.

Security and Safety

In recent years, tourism and security incidents have become an integral part of each other. Security incidents such as terrorism, war, theft or fighting that may occur in a tourism destination will undoubtedly affect that destination negatively. While security measures have been in place since the dawn of modern tourism, they became even more important after the al-Qaeda attacks on the United States on September 11, 2001. Such events destabilise the global tourism industry and force the industry to operate under high levels of uncertainty and risk (Mansfeld & Pizam, 2006).

The safety and security element is vital to deliver quality in tourism destinations. This element includes attributes such as terrorist incidents, political instability, corruption, unhygienic products, epidemics, crime rates and inadequate healthcare (Dwyer and Kim, 2003). The ability of tourism destinations to carry out activities that provide other economic returns only depends on the provision of a safe environment. The security element includes the visitors coming to the destination to feel safe against physical and financial dangers, and the services provided are free from danger and risk (Parasuraman et al., 1985).

As tourism is linked to the concept of security, destinations are deeply affected by tourists' perceptions of security and security and risk management (Hall et al., 2012). Therefore, safety and security are important factors both for tourists in destinations to have a comfortable and peaceful holiday and for choosing a destination. Zhang et al. (2004), in their study on tourists coming to Hong Kong destinations, determined that safety is the most important factor in tourists' destination preference.

Local People

One of the factors that determine the service quality of the destination is the "local people". Local people consist of tourism employees, tradespeople, other customers coming to the destination or residents, which tourists may encounter in a tourism area. Positive relations between tourists and local people are very important for the development of sustainable tourism. The relationships of local people with tourists, their behaviour towards them, and their approach to tourists can play an important role in tourists' positive evaluation of the destination and the formation of their satisfaction and loyalty. In other words, destination image or loyalty is affected not only by the employees providing the service, but also by the positive interactions of tourists with local people. Tourists' perception of local people in a destination can play an important role in tourist behaviour (Nam et al., 2016).

The local people's perception of tourism, their perspective and evaluation of tourism are guiding for the development and marketing of the destination. Cultural relations between tourists and local people are among the reasons for social irresponsibility in tourism movements. Language problems, in particular, hinder the establishment of close relations and mutual cultural exchange. However, factors such as the structure of the local community, the types of visitors, the attitude of the local people towards tourists, the behaviour of tourists that do not fit the local community structure, conflicts of interest, communication problems, differences in lifestyle, the level of development of tourism and the effects of mass tourism affect the relations between tourists and local people (Cengiz & Kırkbir, 2007). The development of tourism in a destination is possible by providing the benevolent behaviour of individuals with whom tourists can interact. Suppose the helpful and positive attitudes of the local people cannot be ensured. In that case, the high quality of the products and services offered in the tourism establishments and the benefits provided by the public to the tourists may fail the tourism efforts.

Tourism Employee (Human Resources)

One of the most important attributes of the tourism sector is that the enterprises in the sector are labour-intensive based. In labour-intensive enterprises, production and service are mostly provided by the workers. This situation reveals that the quality of products and services offered to consumers in tourism establishments is determined by the employees. In other words, since the quality and efficiency of the service are the basic elements of the tourism industry, there is a need for an educated and skilled workforce. Tourism businesses operating in the destination are obliged to take this factor into account. Employing experienced/trained people and providing the necessary training or education to the person will increase the level of service quality offered at the destination (Gooroochurn and Sugiyarto, 2005).

In the tourism sector, where competition is intense, tourism enterprises effectively use their existing production resources to increase their profitability and efficiency. Among these resources, human resources should be used effectively and should be invested in. In this context, tourism managers should employ talented people with tourism education. In addition, it should provide job satisfaction by motivating its employees well. This will increase the performance and productivity of the employees as well as increase customer satisfaction. Destinations that provide high customer satisfaction will also provide a competitive advantage in an intensely competitive environment.

There are findings in the literature that tourism employees are important for the tourism sector. Alhelalat et al. (2017), in their study on restaurant employees in Jordan, concluded that the attitudes and behaviours of the staff affect tourist satisfaction. Gu and Siu (2009) found that high job satisfaction increases the performance of the employees in their study on tourism workers in Macao.

Information

Undoubtedly, one of the most important issues among the expectations of tourists who will visit a tourism destination begins with obtaining accurate and reliable information about the destination. Holiday plans, especially for distant destinations, are made after in-depth research, taking the economic and time cost into account. Tourists can access this information from different sources such as the website of the business or destination, e-mail, search engines, webcasting, podcasting, online review platforms. The point to be considered here, of the information related to tourism products that take part in these resources, is the quality, accuracy, accessibility, and ease of use (Kozak, 2019). After the destination selection, reliable information in the destination, a well-functioning tourism information office, guiding and clear direction signs and signboards, and not experiencing language problems in information services are required for quality service delivery in destinations.

Albayrak ve Caber (2013) indicated that "Information" is one of the important attributes which affects overall tourist satisfaction. Moutinho et al. (2012) also revealed that information positively affects the perceived value from the destination.

Service Quality

Service quality, which is the basis of marketing and consumer behaviour, is defined as the result of comparing the expectations of consumers from a product and the performance of that product after the experience. (Parasuraman et al., 1985). In other words, it is the general evaluation of a product/service. Destination service quality can be expressed as the quality of service related to tourism products offered in a destination in the minds of tourists (Kayat & Hai, 2014), or it is the evaluation of the performance of the products offered by the destination service providers by the tourists. Destination quality includes not only physical products but also the services offered. Destination service quality perceptions of tourists include the natural beauties of the destination and the services offered in the destination. In the literature, destination quality can be subdivided further into destination service quality and destination natural quality. Destination service quality covers the accommodation, local transport cleanliness, hospitality, activities, language, and airport, while destination natural quality covers location, culture, and pure beauty (Tosun et al., 2015).

The service dimension of the tourism experience is vital. Go and Govers (1999) stated that the service quality standard should be provided in destinations, and a total quality management approach should be adopted for tourist satisfaction. At the same time, providing quality and high standard services plays an important role in the competitive advantage of destinations. Destination managers need to develop some strategies to provide quality service. For example, service standards can be provided in tourism enterprises, training can be provided for tourism employees, and the complaints of incoming visitors can be resolved.

The literature emphasises that destination service quality has a positive effect on tourist behaviours. For example, Kim et al. (2013), in their studies in the Orlando region, revealed that the quality of destination service strongly affects both the satisfaction and loyalty of tourists. Akroush et al. (2016) investigated the destination service perceptions of tourists coming to Dead Sea destinations. The results of the study revealed that all service quality dimensions positively affect tourists' destination image perceptions.

Health/Hygiene

The element of cleanliness and hygiene refers to the cleanliness and order that tourists want to see in a tourism destination in all product and service businesses. Tourists travelling for various purposes benefit from many businesses that offer services and products in destinations during their travels. All offered products or services must be produced in a way that is clean, attentive, and most importantly, protecting the health of the customer. An unhealthy and unclean environment affects customers negatively, and accordingly, it causes a decrease in service quality and destination image. Elements of cleanliness and hygiene in tourism destinations can be listed in the form of general cleanliness, clean and hygienic tourism establishments, the destination being free from air pollution, the cleaning of public toilets, the cleaning of streets and the cleaning of public transport vehicles (Seakhoa-King, 2007). On the other hand, this attribute also includes health considerations, of tourists concerning the local cuisine. Because tourists are particularly concerned with the hygiene of the local food, which affects their food consumption (Promsivapallop & Kannaovakun, 2019).

Studies in the literature reveal the importance of cleanliness and hygiene. For example, Albayrak and Caber (2013), in their study on the tourists coming to Side-Manavgat destination, determined that cleanliness and hygiene are the most important attributes after the accommodation and information. Kayar and Kozak (2010) found that Health and Hygiene is the most significant attribute along with transport infrastructure and natural and cultural resources in determining destination competitiveness. Promsivapallop and Kannaovakun (2019) determined that health/hygiene attribute is an effective factor in destination preference.

Local Transportation

Local transportation services are one of the basic elements of the touristic product that enables the visitors to move to the destination (Hacıoğlu, 2010). It is possible that destinations with easy and quality transportation facilities can positively affect behavioural intention by supporting memorable experiences (Dwyer and Kim, 2003).

Local transportation systems define as a set of services that include transportation systems and transportation services, modes of transportation, terminals and their operation and connections with each other, which tourists benefit from during their vacations at the destination (Prideaux, 2000). In this context, the importance of transportation infrastructure emerges. Economical, safe and comfortable local transportation vehicles (taxi, public transportation, metro, tram, minibus, bus, etc.) can contribute positively to the competitiveness of the destination in the tourism market. On the other hand, infrastructure facilities such as bridges, tunnels, underpasses, highways, connected roads, intersections, viaducts, highways, level crossings must also be available in the destination (Sakai, 2006). Albayrak and Caber (2013) argued that local transportation is one of the features that affect tourists' satisfaction.

Geographical Location

One of the indispensable elements of destinations is their geographical location. The fact that the visited destination has a worth seeing and admirable nature enriches the tourists' holidays and makes their experiences different by leaving positive memories in their memories. There are many natural wonders among the geographical location components, especially natural landscapes, natural formations, mountains, sea, beaches, fjords, forests, canyons, rivers, valleys, paths, waterfalls, etc. The characteristic geographical attributes of the visited destination are undoubtedly one of the most important factors that attract tourists to the region. Destinations with unique geographical and climatic characteristics gain a significant advantage in competitive market conditions. However, it is important to present this natural heritage to make a difference among other destinations to have a strong place in the total visit experience (Dwyer & Kim, 2003).

Tourist Satisfaction

Customer satisfaction, which is the driving force behind the business performance, competitiveness and profitability of businesses, is defined as the general evaluation of the performance of different attributes that constitute the product/service. Nowadays, it is highly likely that businesses will achieve high customer satisfaction by increasing the performance of their products/services. In the literature, it has been determined that high customer satisfaction enables businesses to acquire new customers, positively affects the financial performance of businesses, decreases price sensitivity among consumers, and increases customer loyalty (Bartikowski & Llosa, 2004).

Tourist satisfaction is a cognitive-emotional situation that the tourist obtains from the destination experience. In other words, it can be defined as the general evaluation of the performances of the different attributes that constitute the destination by the tourists. It is highly probable that high destination satisfaction will be achieved by increasing the performance of the features that make up the destination. As a result of increases in tourism demand for package holidays over the past two decades, destinations also have become more important than individual attractions. Therefore, tourist satisfaction with a destination, rather than with a facility, might create repeat visits (Kozak & Rimmington, 2000). Previous research findings also demonstrate that there is a significant relationship between tourist satisfaction, revisit intention, and positive word-of-mouth communication.

METHOD

A survey technique was used to obtain study data. Based on the literature review in line with the objectives of the study, Albayrak and Caber (2013) scale in their study have been selected. The survey consisted of two sections. The first section included seven questions about participant demographics. The second section consists of 15 items designed to identify destination attributes with an impact on tourist satisfaction. Also, one item measuring the overall level of satisfaction of participants was included in the survey. Items are formulated to have a total assessment scale (1: Strongly disagree,... 5: Strongly agree). The questionnaire was originally developed in Turkish, then translated into English by professional translators.

The target population of the study consists of tourists who have come to Fethiye-Turkey. As it was not possible to reach the entire universe, a convenience sampling method was preferred. The questionnaire was filled by tourists between September 10 and October 10 2020, in two cafeterias (with the permission of the cafe owners), where tourists show great interest. A total of 600 questionnaires were left in both cafeterias, and 398 questionnaires were returned. Data obtained through answers given by participants were analysed with SPSS 25. Firstly, frequency distribution was made to identify the demographic characteristics of the participants. Afterwards, the linear relationships between the destination attributes and OCS were measured by multivariable regression analysis, and the non-linear relationships were measured by penalty-reward-contrast analysis.

FINDINGS

To identify demographic characteristics of the participants, questions relating to gender, age, marital status and level of education have been asked. Table 1 shows the data obtained through descriptive statistics.

Table 1. Demographics of the participants

Gender	n	%	Marital status	n	%
Male	235	59.3	Married	264	66.8
Female	161	40.5	Single	131	33.2
Total	396	100	Total	398	100
Age	n	%	**Education level**	n	%
20 and below	25	6.6	High School	76	19.7
Between 20 and 29	86	22.9	Undergraduate	254	65.8
Between 30 and 39	120	31.9	Postgraduate	56	14.5
40 and above	145	38.6			
Total	376	100	Total	386	100
Duration of the holiday	n	%	**Times of the visit to the destination**	n	%
Less than 1 week	58	14.7	First time	220	55.7
Between 7-13 days	239	60.5	2 and more times	175	44.3
More than 2 weeks	98	24.8			
Total	395	100	Total	395	100
Nationality	n	%			
British	145	36.6			
Turkish	78	19.6			
Russian	42	10.6			
Dutch	40	10.0			
French	38	9.5			
German	24	6.0			
Others	31	7.7			
Total	398	100			

Prioritization of the Destination Attributes

When Table 1 is examined, it is seen that most of the participants are male (59.3%), married (66.8%), and 40 years old and above (38.6%). In addition, 65.8% have an undergraduate degree, 40.5% of the participants stay between 7-13 days, 24.8% stay more than two weeks, and 14.7% stay less than one week. Moreover, 36.6% are British, 19.6% are Turkish, 10.6% are Russian, 10% are Dutch, and 9.5% are French. Further, 55.7% of the participants visited the destination as first-time visitors, and 44.3% of them were frequent visitors.

Descriptive statistics for items that measured participants' perceptions about the performance of destination attributes are shown in Table 2. The reliability of the measurement tool was tested by Cronbach's alpha, which was found to be 0.86. This was considered sufficient, since values above 0.70 are generally considered acceptable. Items that had the highest mean ratings were "beach and sea" (6.71), "natural resources" (6.44), "security and safety" (6.31), and "recreational activities" (6.24). The item which had the lowest arithmetic mean (5.54) was about "shopping centre services". It was followed by "tourism information services" (5.67), "attitudes of the shopkeepers" (5.70), "environmental cleaning" (5.71), "attitudes of the staff" (5.72), and "travel agency services" (5.73).

Table 2. Descriptive statistics for the destination attributes

Attributes	Frequency	Means*	Std. Error	Var.
Environmental cleaning	397	5.71	1.106	1.22
Food quality	396	6.01	.939	.88
Beverage quality	395	6.10	.922	.85
Natural resources	395	6.44	.783	.61
Attitudes of the staff	396	5.72	1.101	1.21
Accommodation services	395	5.92	.918	.84
Shopping center services	396	5.54	1.065	1.13
Tourism information services	396	5.67	1.028	1.05
Travel agency services	397	5.73	1.000	1.00
Price in general	395	5.78	1.111	1.23
Local transportation	395	5.96	1.010	1.02
Recreational activities	395	6.24	.927	.86
Attitudes of the shopkeepers	398	5.70	1.102	1.21
Security and safety	397	6.31	.848	.71
Beach and sea	397	6.71	.549	.30

*1= Very bad; 5= Very good

By examining symmetric relationships first, destination attributes performance and their impacts on tourist satisfaction were identified with the purpose of understanding which attributes needed to be prioritised for improvement of the tourist's satisfaction. Multivariate regression analysis was performed to determine the linear relationships between the performance of destination attributes and tourist's satisfaction (Table 3).

Table 3. Symmetric relationships among the destination attributes and tourist satisfaction

Destination attributes	VIF	β	t	p
Environmental cleaning	1.469	.082	2.075	.039**
Food quality	2.744	.103	1.907	.057***
Beverage quality	2.452	.072	1.418	.157
Natural resources	1.214	.083	2.300	.022**
Attitudes of the staff	1.667	.142	3.363	.001*
Accommodation services	1.881	.041	.925	.355
Shopping center services	1.897	.064	1.427	.155
Tourism information services	2.313	.011	.221	.825
Travel agency services	2.003	.128	2.776	.006*
Price in general	1.312	.126	3.387	.001*
Local transportation	1.917	.058	1.284	.200
Recreational activities	1.664	.089	2.109	.036**
Attitudes of the shopkeepers	2.085	.142	3.011	.003*
Security and safety	1.631	.121	2.912	.004*
Beach and sea	1.171	.103	2.933	.004*

*p<0.01; **p<0.05; ***p<0.1 R^2:0.619; F: 38.831 Dependent variable: Tourist satisfaction

As a result of the analysis, it was found that the model (F: 38.831; p = 0.000) was significant, and, in total, 62% of the variance in tourist satisfaction could be explained by destination attributes. Standardised beta coefficients of ten destination attributes were found to be significant, and the beta coefficient of the remaining five destination attributes were found to be insignificant. The results showed that the attitudes of staff and the attitudes of the shopkeepers are the most important destination attributes in determining tourist satisfaction. The variance inflation factor (VIF) was also determined to examine multicollinearity in multivariate regression analysis. The result showed minimal levels of multicollinearity, as the VIF presented values below the threshold of 3.3 (Vazquez et al., 2017).

Then, penalty-reward-contrast analysis was performed with the help of dummy variable regression analysis to determine the non-linear relationships between the performance of destination attributes and tourist satisfaction. The Penalty-Reward Contrast Analysis was first proposed by Brandt (1987; cited in Tontini et al., 2017) to identify product attributes that create higher customer satisfaction. This analysis also enables to classify of product attributes as the basic, performance and excitement according to their effects on customer satisfaction at their low and high-performance levels. At low or high levels of performance, services reveal to have varying influences on customer satisfaction. Hence, this approach suggests that there are asymmetries in the relationships between the service attributes or dimensions and overall customer satisfaction. For performing penalty-reward-contrast analysis, destination attributes were firstly re-coded as low, middle and high performing with dummy regression analysis. One set of dummy variables was created and used to quantify satisfying attributes, while another set was created to quantify dissatisfying attributes. After this coding of low and high-performance values for ten variables which standardised beta coefficients were found to be significant, a total of twenty dummy variables as the independent and tourist satisfaction as the dependent variable was used in the regression model.

Prioritization of the Destination Attributes

Analysis suggests two separate coefficients that indicate the impact of each dimension on tourist satisfaction at the low and high-performance levels. According to the obtained beta coefficients, the importance of destination service quality varies according to the performance levels of each attribute (Table 4).

Table 4. Classification of destination attributes

Destination attributes	Low Performance	VIF	High Performance	VIF	IR-Value	Classification
Environmental cleaning	-.160*	1.300	.010	1.422	.06	Basic
Food quality	-.136*	1.561	.065	1.308	.48	Basic
Natural resources	-.032	1.194	.016	1.359	.50	-
Attitudes of the staff	-.110*	1.329	.112*	1.379	1.02	Performance
Travel agency services	-.035	1.208	.149*	1.333	4.26	Excitement
Price in general	-.101**	1.389	.087**	1338	.86	Basic
Recreational activities	-.114*	1.317	.060	1.413	.53	Basic
Attitudes of the shopkeepers	-.059	1.480	.084***	1.526	1.42	Excitement
Security and safety	-.074***	1.326	.116*	1.590	1.56	Excitement
Beach and sea	-.038	1.052	.119*	1.413	3.13	Excitement

*p<0.01; **p<0.05; *** p<0.1 R²:0.559; F: 22.962 Dependent variable: Tourist satisfaction

Classification of destination attributes according to non-linear effects on satisfaction is based on the IR proposed by Matzler and Renzl (2007). The IR value is calculated by dividing the beta coefficient of the reward variable by the beta coefficient of the penalty variable. Absolute value, which is expressed as the range of impact on satisfaction for each attribute, was used in IR value calculation. Accordingly, if the obtained value is less than 0.9, that attribute is a basic factor; if the value is greater than 1.1, that attribute is an excitement factor. If the value is between 0.9 and 1.1, it is classified as a performance factor. Basic attributes are the basic functions of a product. If they are not submitted to the customers, it creates dissatisfaction. On the other hand, submitting them does not create satisfaction because they accept these attributes as prerequisites (Matzler & Sauerwein, 2002). For performance attributes, satisfaction is proportional to the performance level – the higher the performance, the higher the customers' satisfaction and vice versa. Excitement attributes are the key factors for customer satisfaction. If they are present or their performance is sufficient, they would create a superior level of satisfaction. On the other hand, if they are not present, customers would not be dissatisfied. These attributes are neither demanded nor expected by the customers (Albayrak and Caber, 2013).

According to the penalty-reward-contrast analysis results, environmental cleaning, food quality, price, and recreational activities are basic factors; attitudes of the staff are performance factors; and travel agency services, attitudes of the shopkeepers, security/safety, and beach/sea are classified as an excitement factor. Since the beta coefficients of the natural resources attribute are meaningless, no classification has been made for this attribute.

DISCUSSION AND CONCLUSION

Destination management organisations try to get the maximum benefit from the attributes of their destinations. In this context, they measure tourist perceptions regarding existing attributes to provide satisfactory services in the future. Marketing strategies cannot be expected to become successful in a highly competitive marketplace, without knowing which product attributes are more influential on tourist satisfaction than others. Therefore, the effects of destination attributes on tourist satisfaction have been extensively discussed in the literature. In these studies, it is generally assumed that there is a linear relationship between the performance of product attributes and customer satisfaction. However, some studies conducted in recent years have revealed that this relationship may not be linear. While many researchers prefer the linear approach to determine the relationships between product attributes and satisfaction, others prefer the non-linear approach. Although both assumptions have scientific value, it has become more important to decide which assumption provides accurate and detailed information. In this study, the effects of Turkey-Fethiye destination attributes on tourist satisfaction were examined according to two different assumptions.

Firstly, the multiple regression analysis results, which was performed according to the linear assumption, revealed the attitudes of staff and the attitudes of the shopkeepers as the determinant of satisfaction. It is possible to provide higher customer satisfaction by increasing the performance of these two destination attributes. Secondly, the test of asymmetric impacts by penalty-reward-contrast analysis indicates that travel agency services, attitudes of the shopkeepers, security/safety, and beach/sea attributes are excitement factors. In other words, these attributes increase satisfaction if delivered, but they don't cause dissatisfaction if not delivered. Travel agency services, security/safety, and beach/sea features have a low effect on satisfaction according to the linear assumption, while their effect on satisfaction is high according to the non-linear assumption. On the other hand, the attitudes of the shopkeeper's attribute are the most important determinant of satisfaction according to both linear and non-linear assumptions. The attributes of environmental cleaning, food quality, price, and recreational activities are classified among the basic factors. If the expectations of the tourists for these attributes are not met, there will be dissatisfaction. On the other hand, the attitudes of the staff are performance factors according to the analysis of the results. While the high performance of this attribute causes customer satisfaction, its low performance causes customer dissatisfaction.

DMOs have to offer high-quality and satisfactory products to their customers to keep their current customer potential. If they cannot keep the performance of the attributes that are included in the basic factors at the appropriate levels, customer (dis)satisfaction can be high. However, since dissatisfaction does not mean a guarantee of customer satisfaction, DMOs must also allocate resources to excitement factors as well as investing in basic factors to achieve higher customer satisfaction. In other words, since customer satisfaction cannot be achieved by increasing the performance of only basic factors, they need to exceed customer expectations in terms of both basic factors and excitement factors. According to the results of this study, it can be said to be sufficient that DMOs should keep current performance levels of environmental cleaning, food quality, price, and recreational activities for customer satisfaction. To provide higher customer satisfaction, they need to transfer their resources to attributes taken part in the excitement factors. Accordingly, it is required that they increase the performance level of travel agency services, attitudes of the shopkeepers, security/safety, and beach/sea attributes. On the other hand, Albayrak & Caber (2013) stated that excitement attributes are not expressed by the customers, as these are the attributes they do not expect. Therefore, detection of excitement factors is more difficult than other factors. Traditional surveys (pre-structured questionnaires) used in marketing research are not able to inform managers about which product or attributes can be converted into excitement factors. So, DMOs should focus on tourists' suggestions by using qualitative research methods and determining the excitement factors.

In summary, the performance of destination attributes is perceived differently by tourists. It is important that DMOs provide services at an acceptable level according to the varying effects of attributes on tourist satisfaction. DMOs will be able to allocate their limited resources to the right attributes in order to provide higher tourist satisfaction, taking the outcomes of two different assumptions into account. If the changing customer behaviours are not identified and followed, the tourism products offered may fail in the marketplace. Rapidly changing tourism trends and service practices put stress on DMOs. To keep their market positions locally and globally, DMOs have to achieve high service quality and maintain 'delighted' customers (Davras, 2021). For this purpose, they should periodically measure customer perceptions about the service.

There are a number of limitations to this study. First, since the non-probability sampling method was preferred, the generalisability of results to the population might be limited. Second, as the study was conducted at Fethiye-Turkey, the results cannot be generalised to other tourism destinations. Therefore, further studies may focus on different tourism destinations such as mountain, cruise and winter tourism destinations, so that destination attributes and their asymmetric influences on satisfaction can be compared, depending on destinations and tourists' demographics.

REFERENCES

Akroush, M. N., Jraisat, L. E., Kurdieh, D. J., AL-Faouri, R. N., & Qatu, L. T. (2016). Tourism service quality and destination loyalty: The mediating role of destination image from international tourists' perspectives. *Tourism Review, 71*(1), 18–44. doi:10.1108/TR-11-2014-0057

Albayrak, T., & Caber, M. (2013). The symmetric and asymmetric influences of destination attributes on overall visitor satisfaction. *Current Issues in Tourism, 16*(2), 149–166. doi:10.1080/13683500.2012.682978

Alhelalat, J. A., Ma'moun, A. H., & Twaissi, N. M. (2017). The impact of personal and functional aspects of restaurant employee service behaviour on customer satisfaction. *International Journal of Hospitality Management, 66*, 46–53. doi:10.1016/j.ijhm.2017.07.001

Allegre, J., & Garau, J. (2011). The factor structure of tourist satisfaction at sun and sand destinations. *Journal of Travel Research, 50*(1), 78–86. doi:10.1177/0047287509349270

Baloglu, S., & Uysal, M. (1996). Market segments of push and pull motivations: A canonical correlation approach. *International Journal of Contemporary Hospitality Management, 8*(3), 32–38. doi:10.1108/09596119610115989

Bartikowski, B., & Llosa, S. (2004). Customer satisfaction measurement: Comparing four methods of attribute categorisations. *Service Industries Journal, 24*(4), 67–82. doi:10.1080/0264206042000275190

Becken, S., & Wilson, J. (2013). The impacts of weather on tourist travel. *Tourism Geographies, 15*(4), 620–639. doi:10.1080/14616688.2012.762541

Biswas, C., Deb, S. K., Hasan, A. A. T., & Khandakar, M. S. A. (2020). Mediating effect of tourists' emotional involvement on the relationship between destination attributes and tourist satisfaction. *Journal of Hospitality and Tourism Insights*. doi:10.1108/JHTI-05-2020-0075

Boo, S., Busser, J., & Baloğlu, S. (2009). A model of customer-based brand equity and its application to multiple destinations. *Tourism Management, 30*(2), 219–231. doi:10.1016/j.tourman.2008.06.003

Campo, S., & Garau, J. B. (2008). The influence of nationality on the generation of tourist satisfaction with a destination. *Tourism Analysis, 13*(1), 81–92. doi:10.3727/108354208784548779

Cengiz, E., & Kırkbir, F. (2007). A structural model suggestion about relationship between total tourism affect perceived by local residents and tourism support. *Anadolu University Journal of Social Sciences, 7*(1), 19–37.

Çetin, İ. (2017). *Brand value and value creation in hotel businesses*. Detay Publication.

Davras, G. M. (2021). Classification of winter tourism destination attributes according to three factor theory of customer satisfaction. *Journal of Quality Assurance in Hospitality & Tourism, 22*(4), 496–516. doi:10.1080/1528008X.2020.1810195

Derrett, R. (2004). Festivals, events and the destination. *Festival and Events Management*, 32-64.

Dwyer, L., & Kim, C. (2003). Destination competitiveness: Determinants and indicators. *Current Issues in Tourism, 6*(5), 369–414. doi:10.1080/13683500308667962

Fernandez, A. G., Blanco, M. C., Barreto, M., & Santos, C. R. (2007). Comperative analysis of international tourists in inland cultural destinations: The case of Castilla y Leon, Spain. In G. Richards (Ed.), *Cultural tourism: Global and local perspectives*. Taylor & Francis Group.

Fuchs, M., & Weiermair, K. (2003). New perspective of satisfaction research in tourism destinations. *Tourism Review, 58*(3), 6–14. doi:10.1108/eb058411

Go, F. M., & Govers, R. (1999). The Asian perspective: Which international conference destinations in Asia are the most competitive? *Journal of Convention & Exhibition Management, 4*(1), 37–50. doi:10.1300/J143v01n04_04

Gooroochurn, N., & Sugiyarto, G. (2005). Competitiveness indicators in the travel and tourism industry. *Tourism Economics, 11*(1), 25–43. doi:10.5367/0000000053297130

Gu, Z., & Siu, R. C. S. (2009). Drivers of job satisfaction as related to work performance in Macao casino hotels. *International Journal of Contemporary Hospitality Management, 21*(5), 561–578. doi:10.1108/09596110910967809

Guan, J., & Jones, D. L. (2015). The contribution of local cuisine to destination attractiveness: An analysis involving Chinese tourists' heterogeneous preferences. *Asia Pacific Journal of Tourism Research, 20*(4), 416–434. doi:10.1080/10941665.2014.889727

Hacıoğlu, N. (2010). *Tourism Marketing*. Nobel Publishing.

Hall, C. M., Timothy, D. J., & Duval, D. T. (2012). *Safety and security in tourism: Relationships, management, and marketing*. Routledge. doi:10.4324/9780203049464

Hernandez-Lobato, L., Solis-Radilla, M., Molinar-Tena, M. A., & Sanchez-Garcia, J. (2006). Tourism destination image, satisfaction and loyalty: Ixtapa-zihuatanejo, Mexico. *Tourism Geographies*, *8*(4), 343–358. doi:10.1080/14616680600922039

Hernandez-Mogollon, J. M., Duarte, P. A., & Folgado-Fernandez, J. A. (2018). The contribution of cultural events to the formation of the cognitive and affective images of a tourist destination. *Journal of Destination Marketing & Management*, *8*, 170–178. doi:10.1016/j.jdmm.2017.03.004

Im, H. H., Kim, S. S., Elliot, S., & Han, H. (2012). Conceptualising destination brand equity dimensions from a consumer-based brand equity perspective. *Journal of Travel & Tourism Marketing*, *29*(4), 385–403. doi:10.1080/10548408.2012.674884

Jovanovic, S., & Ivana, I. L. I. C. (2016). Infrastructure as important determinant of tourism development in the countries of Southeast Europe. *Ecoforum Journal*, *5*(1).

Karasakal, S. (2019). *Effect of destination attributes on flow experience, positive emotion and overall satisfaction: Case of Antalya* (Doctoral Thesis). Akdeniz University Social Sciences Institute.

Kayar, Ç. H., & Kozak, N. (2010). Measuring destination competitiveness: An application of the travel and tourism competitiveness index (2007). *Journal of Hospitality Marketing & Management*, *19*(3), 203–216. doi:10.1080/19368621003591319

Kayat, K., & Hai, A. M. (2014). Perceived service quality and tourists' cognitive image of a destination. *Anatolia: An International Journal of Tourism and Hospitality Research*, *25*(1), 1–12. doi:10.1080/13032917.2013.814580

Kim, S. H., Holland, S., & Han, H. S. (2013). A structural model for examining how destination image, perceived value, and service quality affect destination loyalty: A case study of Orlando. *International Journal of Tourism Research*, *15*(4), 313–328. doi:10.1002/jtr.1877

Kivela, J., & Crotts, J. C. (2006). Tourism and gastronomy: Gastronomy's influence on how tourists experience a destination. *Journal of Hospitality & Tourism Research (Washington, D.C.)*, *30*(3), 354–377. doi:10.1177/1096348006286797

Kotler, P., Armstrong, G., Saunders, J., & Wong, V. (1999). *Principles of marketing*. Prentice Hall Inc.

Kozak, M. (2001). Repeaters' behavior at two distinct destinations. *Annals of Tourism Research*, *28*(3), 784–807. doi:10.1016/S0160-7383(00)00078-5

Kozak, M., & Rimmington, M. (2000). Tourist satisfaction with Mallorca, Spain, as an off-season holiday destination. *Journal of Travel Research*, *38*(3), 260–269. doi:10.1177/004728750003800308

Kozak, N. (2019). *Tourism Marketing*. Detay Publishing.

Kwanisai, G., & Vengesayi, S. (2016). Destination attributes and overall destination satisfaction in Zimbabwe. *Tourism Analysis*, *21*(1), 17–28. doi:10.3727/108354216X14537459508775

Law, R., Cheung, C., & Lo, A. (2004). The relevance of profiling travel activities for improving destination marketing strategies. *International Journal of Contemporary Hospitality Management*, *16*(6), 355–362. doi:10.1108/09596110410550798

Lee, C. K., Var, T., & Blain, T. (1996). Determinants of inbound tourism expenditures. *Annals of Tourism Research*, *23*(3), 527–542. doi:10.1016/0160-7383(95)00073-9

Lo, M. C., Mohamad, A. A., Chin, C. H., & Ramayah, T. (2017). The impact of natural resources, cultural heritage, and special events on tourism destination competitiveness: The moderating role of community support. *International Journal of Business & Society*, *18*.

Loi, K. I. (2008). Gaming and entertainment tourist destinations: A world of similarities and differences. *Tourism Recreation Research*, *33*(2), 165–183. doi:10.1080/02508281.2008.11081303

Mansfeld, Y., & Pizam, A. (2006). *Tourism, security and safety*. Routledge. doi:10.4324/9780080458335

Matzler, K., & Renzl, B. (2007). Assessing asymmetric effects in the formation of employee satisfaction. *Tourism Management*, *28*(4), 1093–1103. doi:10.1016/j.tourman.2006.07.009

Matzler, K., & Sauerwein, E. (2002). The factor structure of customer satisfaction: An empirical test of the importance grid and the penalty-reward-constrant analysis. *International Journal of Service Industry Management*, *13*(4), 314–332. doi:10.1108/09564230210445078

McHone, W. W., & Rungeling, B. (2000). Practical issues in measuring the impact of a cultural tourist event in a major tourist destination. *Journal of Travel Research*, *38*(3), 300–303. doi:10.1177/004728750003800313

Moscardo, G. (2004). Shopping as a destination attraction: An empirical examination of the role of shopping in tourists' destination choice and experience. *Journal of Vacation Marketing*, *10*(4), 294–307. doi:10.1177/135676670401000402

Moscardo, G., Morrison, A. M., Pearce, P. L., Lang, C. T., & O'Leary, J. T. (1996). Understanding vacation destination choice through travel motivation and activities. *Journal of Vacation Marketing*, *2*(2), 109–122. doi:10.1177/135676679600200202

Moutinho, L., Albayrak, T., & Caber, M. (2012). How far does overall service quality of a destination affect customers' post-purchase behaviours? *International Journal of Tourism Research*, *14*(4), 307–322. doi:10.1002/jtr.856

Murphy, P., Pritchard, M. P., & Smith, B. (2000). The destination product and its impact on traveller perceptions. *Tourism Management*, *21*(1), 43–52. doi:10.1016/S0261-5177(99)00080-1

Nam, M., Kim, I., & Hwang, J. (2016). Can local people help enhance tourists' destination loyalty? A relational perspective. *Journal of Travel & Tourism Marketing*, *33*(5), 702–716. doi:10.1080/10548408.2016.1167386

Palmer, A., & Bejou, D. (1995). Tourism destination marketing alliances. *Annals of Tourism Research*, *22*(3), 616–629. doi:10.1016/0160-7383(95)00010-4

Parasuraman, A., Zeithaml, V. A., & Berry, L. L. (1985). A conceptual model of service quality and its implications for future research. *Journal of Marketing*, *49*(4), 41–50. doi:10.1177/002224298504900403

Prideaux, B. (2000). The role of the transport system in destination development. *Tourism Management*, *21*(1), 53–63. doi:10.1016/S0261-5177(99)00079-5

Promsivapallop, P., & Kannaovakun, P. (2019). Destination food image dimensions and their effects on food preference and consumption. *Journal of Destination Marketing & Management*, *11*, 89–100. doi:10.1016/j.jdmm.2018.12.003

Sakai, M. (2006). Public investment in tourism infastructure. In International handbook on the economics of tourism (pp. 266-280). Edward Elgar Publicition.

Seakhoa-King, A. (2007). *Conseptualising 'quality of tourism destination': An investigation of the attributes and dimensions of quality of a tourism destination* (PhD dissertation). University of Bedforshire.

Suhartanto, D., & Triyuni, N. (2016). Tourist loyalty toward shopping destination: The role of shopping satisfaction and destination image. *European Journal of Tourism Research*, *13*, 84–102.

Tontini, G., Bento, G. S., Milbratz, T. C., Volles, B. K., & Ferrari, D. (2017). Exploring the non-linear impact of critical incidents on customer' general evaluation of hospitality services. *International Journal of Hospitality Management*, *66*, 106–116. doi:10.1016/j.ijhm.2017.07.011

Tosun, C., Dedeoğlu, B. B., & Fyall, A. (2015). Destination service quality, affective image and revisit intention: The moderating role of past experience. *Journal of Destination Marketing & Management*, *4*(4), 222–234. doi:10.1016/j.jdmm.2015.08.002

Turkay, O. (2014). *Destination management: functions, approaches and tools from the perspective of management*. Detay Publishing.

Ünal, C., & Caber, M. (2019). The effect of tourist guides' professional competences on destination image and satisfaction. *Anatolia: Journal of Tourism Research*, *30*(1), 82–92.

Vanhove, N. (2011). *The economics of tourism destinations* (2nd ed.). Elsevier Insights. doi:10.4324/9780080969978

Vazquez, M. V., Verdugo, M. C., & Garcia, A. O. (2017). Shopping value, tourist satisfaction and positive word of mouth: The mediating role of souvenir shopping satisfaction. *Current Issues in Tourism*, *20*(13).

Yang, Y., Liu, X., & Li, J. (2015). How customer experience affects the customer-based brand equity for tourism destinations. *Journal of Travel & Tourism Marketing*, *32*(sup1), 97–S113. doi:10.1080/10548408.2014.997959

Yau, O. H., & Chan, C. F. (1990). Hong Kong as a travel destination in South-East Asia: A multidimensional approach. *Tourism Management*, *11*(2), 123–132. doi:10.1016/0261-5177(90)90028-8

Zhang, H. Q., Qu, H., & Tang, V. M. Y. (2004). A case study of Hong Kong residents' outbound leisure travel. *Tourism Management*, *25*(2), 267–273. doi:10.1016/S0261-5177(03)00096-7

Section 2
Experiences and Tourism Supply

Chapter 4
Conditions of Network Engagement:
The Quest for a Common Good

Veronika Trengereid
https://orcid.org/0000-0003-0952-1876
Western Norway University of Applied Sciences, Norway & Nord University, Norway

ABSTRACT

There is growing research interest in innovation network dynamics. Based on an explorative case study of a regional innovation network for the tourism industry, this chapter contributes to a better understanding of network engagement as a dynamic and social construct. By following the microfoundational trend, the chapter anchors the concept of engagement at a lower level in order to increase the depth of understanding of the conditions of network engagement. As there are many different notions of engagement, the chapters start by providing an overview of the different notions of engagement in innovation and network literature. Then, inspired by the critical incident technique, a narrative presents the findings, showing the dynamic and social aspect of network engagement, followed by a discussion of the conditions of network engagement and theoretical contributions.

INTRODUCTION

While the creation of tourism experiences has gained considerable research interest following Pine and Gilmore's (1998) notion of the experience economy, less attention has been devoted to the transition towards the experience economy in the tourism industry and the role of innovation networks in such transformation processes. To develop complete tourism experiences, various stakeholders in non-linear relationships need to work together (Baggio, 2008). However, the limited resources of the numerous small and medium-sized tourism organisations (Kofler & Marcher, 2018; Novelli et al., 2006) and territorial attachment of the sector (Hjalager, 2000; Scott et al., 2008) makes the transition to cooperate in developing such new and complete tourism experiences challenging. Tourism organisations also need to balance the fine line between competition and cooperation to gain competitiveness and survive during

DOI: 10.4018/978-1-7998-8775-1.ch004

the experience economy transition. Innovation, particularly collaborative innovation, becomes vital for success (Marasco et al., 2018; Pikkemaat et al., 2019). To facilitate a successful transition towards the experience economy, keeping or increasing organisation and destination competitiveness is challenging. This chapter sheds light on the role of innovation networks in such transitions that require network participants to innovate, mainly due to an innovation network that developed alongside the experience turn, showing that different participants have different transition paces and emphasising the cognitive and social aspects of achieving such a transformation as the experience turn.

Regardless of the type of innovation concerned, how organisations engage in learning and innovation (Wenger, 2000) is vital. Understanding the dynamic nature of network engagement processes is an important research area (Li et al., 2017). While the literature suggests that engagement is essential for the success of inter-organisational innovation processes (Hammarfjord & Roxenhall, 2017; Weisenfeld, 2003), little is known about the conditions of engagement and how engagement processes can be managed and supported. Following the microfoundational trend (e.g. Felin et al., 2015), the chapter aims to increase the understanding of the more general notions of engagement and "make the theory more relevant for managers" (Storbacka et al., 2016, p. 309). By anchoring concepts like engagement on a lower level, the theoretical explanations aim to increase their depth (Felin et al., 2015; Storbacka et al., 2016). Thévenot's (2001) notion of engagement constitutes the framework in this chapter. It follows the microfoundational trend, as it provides a better explanation of how actors relate to and grasp the societal and economic environment with which they interact as members of a regional innovation network.

The chapter explores the following research question: what are the conditions of multi-actor engagement in regional innovation networks, and how can these be managed? The research question is examined through a qualitative explorative case study of a regional innovation network for the tourism industry. It shows how network participants grasp the environment in different ways and the conditions of network engagement in a regional innovation network taking on the experience turn.

REGIONAL INNOVATION NETWORK

In this chapter, innovation network is defined as "a group of agents who interact with each other in order to produce an innovation" (Gallouj et al., 2013, p. 4). When the agents are dispersed over a region, covering multiple destinations, it is referred to as a regional network. Innovation is understood as a new or significantly improved idea made available to users or brought into practice (OECD, 2005; OECD & Eurostat, 2018). The innovation may be a product (good, service, experience), process, concept or business model, and may be market-related, organisational or institutional (Hjalager, 2010; Schumpeter, 1934). The innovation process is open and interactive (Chesbrough, 2011; Fuglsang, 2008), particularly within tourism, where innovations frequently involve various agents and interaction within and between organisations (Marasco et al., 2018). The agents in the regional innovation network studied in this chapter are organisations, making collaboration and engagement more complex, as the network becomes more fluid and primarily socially constructed (e.g. Orton & Weick, 1990).

In the last few years, scholars have begun to take an interest in collaborative innovation dynamics (Marasco et al., 2018). The network-level research focuses mainly on network structure and relations among organisations, while there is less focus on the social and contextual side of networking. According to Newell et al. (2009), there are two theoretical approaches to social networks. The more common approach, network as channels, focuses attention on connections between individuals and organisations, often relying on social network analysis (Scott et al., 2008). The second approach, networks as communities, focuses on the quality of the relations and how interaction between actors shapes and creates the network's results. This network approach is in line with the microfoundational trend, a trend that is a counter-reaction to research that neglects social interaction and treats individuals as homogenous (Felin et al., 2015). This chapter follows the microfoundational trend and uses the community of practice approach (see Newell et al., 2009; Wenger, 2000) to network research. Another benefit of this approach is that work, learning and innovation are linked (Brown & Duguid, 1991). The practice-based approach to innovation and learning views boundary crossings (interaction across traditional communities), brokering, bandwagon effects and scaffolding as vital for learning and innovation (Fuglsang & Eide, 2013; Wenger, 2000). Exploring how actors engage with their social environment can expand the understanding of the dynamics involved in such processes.

ENGAGEMENT

Different theoretical perspectives have used the notion of engagement to analyse economic development. However, the different approaches have quite different notions of engagement. While most of these focus primarily on actors involvement and the result of that involvement, the practice-based approach views engagement as a mode of belonging and a source of collective identity (Wenger, 1998, 2000). The engagement component is about doing things together and how actors engage with one another shapes their perceptions (Wenger, 2000). However, the practice-based approach focuses mainly on communities of practice within an organisation – and lacks an explanation of people's dynamic confrontation with the world (Thévenot, 2001). Thévenot's (2001) notion of engagement addresses this issue by focusing on human dependence on the environment. In this notion, engagement is understood as a social construct attentive to action dynamics (Thévenot & Jacobs, 2007), emphasising that humans need to constantly change their scope of engagement, moving between "modes of interventions and agency engaged in local or individual circumstances and those modes oriented towards the general and public" (Thévenot, 2001, pp. 3-4), taking into account that humans communise based on "a highly personal, local experience of the world" (Thévenot & Jacobs, 2007, p. 411).

Viewing engagement as a cognitive construct draws attention to interdependencies between actors and between actors and the environment, often neglected by other theories (Thévenot & Jacobs, 2007). However, it can strengthen our understanding of practices and how human agents engage in practice and networks. The regimes of engagements give researchers a framework for describing how the actors relate to and grasp the societal environment they interact with (Fuglesang, 2015; Fuglsang, 2008). This is relevant for studying the development of experiences and innovation in tourism, as both practices usually involve several agents. This notion of engagement also takes into account that actors may have different drives and perspectives on engaging with their social and economic environment. The literature has, however, devoted little attention to the cognitive formats of the interactive process of how actors grasp the environment (Fuglsang, 2018).

Regimes of Engagement

Thévenot (2001) identifies three pragmatic regimes of engagement:

1. familiar engagement – engages actors in personal or local convenience within a familiar environment, turning to the intermediate surroundings and "using familiar, appropriate things and inhabited places when acting" (Thévenot & Jacobs, 2007, p. 416). This form of engagement is highly dependent on local and personal clues and can be difficult for the actor to articulate. The convenience of the good governs this regime of engagement.
2. engagement in a plan – engages actors in successfully realising a plan, requiring actors to project themselves into the future. The convenience of good that governs this regime is the prospect of being an individual endowed with authority (Thévenot & Jacobs, 2007). It requires the agent to coordinate action and use conventions to accomplish the plan, which means that the plan and arguments need to be understandable for more people.
3. engagement in justifiable action – engages actors in an aptly qualified common good, relying on the persons' engagement with their surroundings to legitimise and qualify a common good. This regime of engagement involves the actor in the broader world, where it is no longer sufficient just to be restricted to a joint plan or local and personal convenience. The convenience of good that governs this regime of engagement is a conventional qualification understood as an actors attempt to justify a specific action or conventions in terms of a collective good that they intend to produce (Fuglsang & Nordli, 2018).

These different forms of engagement do not explain the structure of relations, but are different interaction formats (Thévenot, 2001; Thévenot & Jacobs, 2007). Nor is the engagement static; agents usually fluctuate between the personalised and generalised relation to the environment (Thévenot, 2001). The generalised forms of engagement give actors access to more resources and the wider environment and require more coordination with other actors. On the other hand, the personalised formats of engagements increase convenience for the actors, while also narrowing the scope of action.

The engagement regimes have limited use in an innovation network, and there is a lack of research on how innovation may also depend on actor capability and skills to progress societal engagement (Fuglsang & Nordli, 2018). Furthermore, the research seems to neglect the conditions for engagement in regional innovation networks, even though this may be vital to enhancing innovation.

Conditions of Engagement

While the practice-based approach to engagement focuses primarily on the collective processes and enabling factors of the emergence and development of communities, this chapter focuses on the individual network participants and their social skills and ability to drive societal engagement. The framing of engagement as a cognitive construct allows an exploration of the dynamic and social interactions between network members, network management and the broader society. The conceptions of the good become vital when exploring the conditions of engagement in regional innovation networks and the engaged reality. The common good that engages the different formats in Thévenot's (2001) theory on engagement is not stated clearly. In an interview with Blokker and Brighenti (2011), Thévenot elaborates on this issue, focusing on the moral elements in the various conceptions of the common good, as actors can have various understandings of the good. To understand the common good and forces of each regime, one must also explore which reality is engaged, thereby opening up a new perspective on *"the dynamic institutions of both personalities and communities as integrating a moving combination of engagement"* (Blokker & Brighenti, 2011, p. 389). The different participants in a network may have different horizons and ambitions for engaging with their social and economic environment. Consequently, participant engagement formats also rely on how they deal cognitively and emotionally with their social environment (Fuglsang & Nordli, 2018).

METHOD

The method is an explorative case study of NCE Tourism, a regional innovation network of the tourism industry supported for the most extended period by the Norwegian policy innovation program, ARENA and the Norwegian Centers of Expertise. NCE Tourism was one of the early regional innovation networks established in the early stages of the application of the concept of experience design and experience-based tourism. Norwegian tourism organisations have traditionally had little experience with collaboration and innovation, further challenging the facilitation of collaborative innovation for its members. However, networking is challenging in many ways, as shown by periods of struggles and progress over the network operating decade (Jakobsen & Arnesen, 2020). The findings shed light on some of these struggles and the progress made by the network and its participants, focusing on the transition from a service innovation focus to an experience focus in developing the tourism industry on the western coast of Norway.

Case

NCE Tourism and its development are largely studied in retrospect. In 2005, a group of professionals from the industry, research and public supporting organisations began exploring the conditions for establishing a tourism network on the western coast of Norway. During this phase, a steering group was established, and two hired tourism consultants began developing the initiative more systematically and obtaining funding for a tourism network. Admission into the Norwegian innovation program in 2007 secured long-term funding and formally established the networks. The goal was to increase the industry's international competitiveness by increasing collaborative innovation and addressing the industry's challenges of short seasons, little revenue, little market knowledge and an immature and underdeveloped tourism experience offered to tourists. An explorative case study design (Flyvbjerg, 2001) was chosen to explore the development of the network's experience focus, as obtaining the contextual expertise of experts seems essential to understanding the phenomenon of regimes of engagement and conditions of engagement in a regional innovation network. The strength of case designs is to explore unclear phenomena, and the conditions of societal engagement in regional innovation networks are such a phenomenon with unclear boundaries (Yin, 2012). NCE Tourism was chosen as a case due to its development alongside the experience turn in the Norwegian tourism industry and its ambition to bring together a broad range of relevant professionals for developing the tourism industry on the western coast of Norway. The network also had a large number of members, with up to 200 members at most, making the task even more challenging, although most of the time it has just under 100 members. While the research and public supporting professionals have remained largely the same, there have been changes to the industry members. However, there have been members representing the entire value chain of transport, accommodation, visitor centres and experiences at all times. Despite the development of the experience organisations, they are still mostly smaller than the other members of the tourism value chain. These aspects make NCE Tourism an extreme case. An extreme case is a type of case selection used to activate more participants and reveal more information about the mechanism in the studied situation (Flyvbjerg, 2001). The dynamic of the industry participants is further elaborated in the findings. Additional selection criteria were a network that pursues innovation, collaborates with industry, research and development participants and the public sector, is within the experience-based tourism industry and geographically dispersed.

The study is situated in the interpretive constructionist paradigm (see Guba & Lincoln, 1994), assuming that human context, relations and time are essential for meaning construction and how reality is engaged and common goods constructed (Alvesson & Sköldberg, 2000; Lindberg et al., 2014). The explorative case design involves dialogue, triangulation, context and processes (Flyvbjerg, 2001). Through "recursive cycling among the case data, emerging theory, and later, extant literature", case studies can be used for theory building (Eisenhardt & Graebner, 2007, p. 25). The engagement phenomenon was discovered inductively in the data material, but the theoretical construct of engagement has been used together with the data to theorise the conditions of engagement in regional innovation networks.

Data

In-depth retrospective interviews with key representatives of the different groups of network professionals were the primary data source. Secondary data in the form of reports, other studies of the network, news articles in both the media and from the network was used as a supporting data source, as the informants also discussed issues retrospectively and sometimes forget details like names and specific times. The primary data consists of interviews with 15 informants and covers the different types of organisations participating in the network: seven of the informants represented the network's business members, three the network's management, two originated from research and development organisations and three from public and other supporting organisations. Having several informants with different angles and perspectives helps bias the retrospective sense-making (Eisenhardt & Graebner, 2007). On average, the interviews lasted 60 minutes. The interviews were semi-structured and started by asking the informants to describe the development of the network and explain the critical incidents in the development process from their perspective. Inspired by Flanagan's (1954) critical incident technique, the study focuses on network' development and informant involvement. The technique follows the interpretative paradigm and builds on the overall situatedness of the study. It should also be mentioned that a critical incident only needs to be significant for the informant; it does not need to be spectacular (Serrat, 2017). The strength of the technique is that it helps gauge abstract constructs, such as common goods and reality, and that incidents provide in-depth information more readily than observations (Serrat, 2017).

Narrative

Narratives provide a rich framework through which it is possible to investigate how humans experience the world described through their stories (Webster & Mertova, 2007). The narrative in this chapter focuses on the story of the network's experience turn. A critical incident analysis is used to develop the narrative. First, the critical events need to be identified, which is done based on the impact on the storyteller (Mertova & Webster, 2020). Furthermore, critical events relate first and foremost to the profound effect they have on the people involved. Examples of these are entering the network, participating (or not participating) in general network activities and participating in collaborative innovation through the network. Based on the various data sources, a narrative for developing the network focusing on scenes where participant engagement or a lack of engagement became central. The experiential quality of the narrative is created by the scene and plot working together (Connelly & Clandinin, 1990). The scene is

Conditions of Network Engagement

where the story happened, but time can also be a vital part of the plot. The final narrative is a condensed version of the complete sequence of the development of the network. The condensed version is based on the author's interpretations of the data. Even though Flanagan's (1954) critical incident technique inspired the analysis, a broader and more hermeneutical approach to critical events was used to develop the narrative.

FINDINGS

The findings are presented in the form of a brief narrative that has been codified, employing the three critical incidents shaping the transition towards the experience economy, which also shed light on the conditions of network engagement: network formation, development & growth and stagnation. The codification is also grounded in the conditions of network engagement at a lower level and make it more relevant for network managers. The types of engagement forms involved and the condition of engagement in these situations are outlined under each incident.

Network Formation

Western Norway has a 200-year history as an international tourist destination and was one of few Norwegian regions with a regional destination management organisation (Fjord Norway AS) with a marketing focus, aiming to attract both national and international tourists to the region. Due to an established regional focus and contact with both the region's tourism organisations and public supporting organisations, Fjord Norway quickly assumed a central position in the development of the network. In addition, stakeholders like county administrators, researchers, Innovation Norway's regional representative and a number of representatives from the industry also took part in a steering group that laid the groundwork for a network initiative. The group's goal was to apply for admission into the Norwegian policy program for innovation and industry development. However, this also meant that the network needed to meet the program admission requirements regarding stakeholder representation and innovation and development ambitions. Furthermore, transportation and accommodation businesses were considered vital industry stakeholders in terms of development and for providing industry financing. Of the ten members of the steering group, one was a small accommodation.

Coincidentally, following the rejection of the first application for funding a regional tourism innovation network through the Norwegian policy program for innovation and industry development, a steering group member heard two consultants during a lecture criticise the existing overall strategy for tourism development. These two consultants had a background in activity-based tourism. One of these consultants had also been a consultant in the southeastern regional tourism innovation network, the first tourism network admitted into the Norwegian policy program for innovation and industry development. The consultants held a series of lectures for politicians and public supporting organisations, advocating a transition from developing offers around services and visits to attractions to focusing on activity-based attractions and developing complete experiences. Despite being hired to develop a second application based on the lectures, the consultants soon experienced resistance in the steering group:

During the first meeting we attended, the experience organisations were referred to as 'garnish organisations.'...It was like an audition for us, as our take on tourism development was that the tourist does not travel to the fjords to take the bus or sleep at a hotel. (Network manager, a)

The discussions often reflected on the different stakeholders' ambitions and ideas about the future. Many spoke on behalf of the destination they represented, others for their organisation as vital financial stakeholders in the network. The tension between the different participants' ambitions and views on forming the network were described as tangible. During this process, the two hired consultants assumed an active role in advocating the development of active experiences, the network's main aim, using the experience economy literature as an argument alongside the growing market trend towards international tourists wanting more active vacations, and focusing on how to make the region more competitive internationally. Eventually, some of the larger organisations began to agree:

...then some of these so-called infrastructure representatives began understanding the argument in which more professionalism in sub-vendor links was essential for some of them and pulled the others in the same direction. (Network manager, a)

The steering group then agreed that the goal should be to become a leading international tourist destination for experiencing nature and culture. However, to anchor the network idea in the industry, they needed to broaden the network's focal areas. The three focal areas chosen for the network were round trips, theme travel and location & identity development. In addition, developing relations between the members, developing and sharing knowledge and learning, focusing on segmentation and developing new tourist offerings were established as supporting processes. During this initial establishment phase of the network, the hired consultants, who would later became the network managers, assumed an active role in the formation of the network:

The network leaders need to be proactive and take responsibility for some of the work themselves, working operationally to build the new concepts, launch them and anchor them. This is why we succeeded with the team travel area. I do not believe in projects where you only facilitate [projects]. (Network manager, b)

Development and Growth

Carrying out projects within the different focal areas was an essential part of the development and growth phase of the network and involved new stakeholders in designing and carrying out the projects. An example of such a project is the hiking project. The network focused on the segments and development of complete concepts. The project involved identifying attractive hiking destinations and hiking summits and developing the related infrastructure, from grading and marking trails to challenging and supporting guiding companies in developing their offerings and developing market communication around these hiking destinations and selected destination summit hikes like Trolltunga and Preikestolen. Different participants were involved in the different aspects of the project. For instance, applying for public and private financing funds was essential for grading and marking hiking trails. Although local hiking groups often carried out the grading and marking of trails, identifying and grading them also involved destination management organisations (DMO) and industry organisations, while the regional destination management organisation, Fjord Norway, became involved in developing and carrying out the market communications for the hiking destinations. However, the network not only worked on large specific projects, but the network managers also researched upcoming trends and developed stories about the future based on market data. They began challenging industry professionals to create joint strategies and scenarios. They also invited international industry professionals from more developed destinations to present their development and offers. The resulting inspiration brought together industry participants in initiating joint projects.

The network considered participation in the national innovation and industry program to be vital. Consequently, after two years in the introduction program, the network submitted an application for admission into an extended industry development program. The extended program [Norwegian Center of Expertise] could last for up to nine years if the evaluation and new agreement every third year were approved. Also, the network's funding would be higher than the introduction program. In the application, the network narrowed its focus to theme tourism: winter tourism, hiking tourism, outdoor adventure and arts & culture. Being in an extended industry development program also involved an expectation of an increase in research-industry relations. However, such admission also meant higher financial contributions from the network participants, resulting in changes to who participated. Despite this, the network had strong storytelling elements around the importance of the small nature and activity organisations and how these were a prioritised group:

At first [on joining the Norwegian Center of Expertise program], several actors were inspired by a good 'introduction sale', so they did not really know what they were in for, but once they saw that there was a need for something, and this was something that happened on the west coast, it became imperative to join. (Research participant)

Two stagnation periods followed the admission into the Norwegian Centre of Expertise program (NCE). These periods of stagnation are described in a separate section below. In this section, we progress to the subsequent development and growth phase that followed after significant changes were made to the network's management group and a further narrowing of the network scope. When applying for the second period of the NCE program, the network now clearly stated that the goal was to develop active, nature-based experiences within the areas of skiing, hiking, biking, fishing, kayaking and river sports, as well as architecture. Also, some joint activities were carried out, like a booking system project, which particularly benefited the smaller organisations:

…e.g. the booking system projects, which can be highly challenging knowledge-wise for a single organisation, but, by connecting partners with knowledge in that field, you end up with partners with different knowledge that are joined in a cluster, with better results: two plus two equals five. (Tour operator)

During this time, the network managers focused on listening to member needs. However, it also became important to plan projects:

…all of the projects we now carry out involve a project template … so, we have a goal for the project, which in turn attracts participants. (Network manager, c)

The network also developed projects in collaboration with other networks, such as the Vidden projects, in which participants of the NCE Media network used media technology to develop an app to enhance the visitor hiking experience and make it possible to send essential information to visitors. The network divided the members into groups, tailoring the activities to each specific group, and facilitating and following up on active members. However, there was little coupling between these groups.

Stagnation

Less than a year after the admission into the NCE-programme, the two network managers from the previous phases decided to leave the network, and the network hired a new manager. As newly admitted into the NCE-programme, a detailed plan for activities for the subsequent phases still were under discussion in the steering group. Some felt that the network focused a lot on internal issues. When the network manager became sick, this feeling became even more prominent amongst the network actors not involved in the steering group. However, many industry members continued their membership, despite little activities and, at times, also little communication from the network. They believed in networking as an essential tool to stay competitive internationally:

I think I enjoy the 'commune' idea, i.e. that we are better together, …we are stronger together. I'm just one man sitting in my office, going on walks, taking care of my own business, but together with others we can constitute a cluster that is competitive in a larger market… (Activity-based organisation, b)

Some actors also had a self-critical take on the lack of involvement in the network, recognising that they critically consider potential benefits before participating in any network activities. Also, some felt that the networked later focused too much on introductory courses that did not present new knowledge to skilled firms. Others had internal affairs to attend to, leaving little time to participate in network activities. However, some activities took place, and some industry actors carried out projects supported by consultants or the network management team.

The network used the feedback from the first period of stagnation to create a new growth and development phase, as described in the above section. However, approaching the end of the NCE-programme, new discussions about the future of the network began. They discussed the possibility of applying for the next level in the Norwegian industry development program, continuing as a division within the RDMO, and other solutions. There was, however, not enough support for applying to the next-level public industry program, and even though the RDMO aimed at taking over part of the network's activities, the formal network of NCE Tourism was closed down in 2019.

DISCUSSION

The findings have shown how actors relate to and grasp their societal environment when engaging in a regional innovation network, highlighted by the tourism industry paradigm change. Furthermore, it supports Thévenot and Jacobs's (2007) notion of engagement as dynamic, as actors constantly change their scope of engagement and fluctuate between more personalised and generalised engagement formats. Understanding the common good and the forces governing each engagement regime is vital in exploring the condition for network engagement. Therefore, the section starts by discussing each regime of engagement before paying attention to the dynamics between the regimes.

Particularly in the forming phase, it is evident that the different actors disagree on what reality to consider. This process of developing a network idea that gives meaning to and pulls together diverse actors in a network is described as a 'bandwagon effect' (Fuglsang & Eide, 2013) which is similar to the alignment component in the community of practice theory (Wenger, 2000). While the Fuglsang and Eide (2013) paper focuses on creating collaboration by defining a shared meaning and embracing a joint journey, this chapter instead focuses on the difference in reality and how the dynamic confrontation with 'the world' opens the scope of action. The findings show how forming a network exposes participants to a wider environment, where their local convenience is not necessarily seen as justifiable by others. Despite creating many discussions and disagreements, it also means that the network participants need to decide what constitutes a common good when encountering the wider world through an innovation network. The discussion in the forming phase seems to fluctuate between the different actors' views of convenience. To settle on a common goal, some of the actors need to leave their convenience. Familiar engagement is by Thévenot (2001) described as being governed by convenience, keeping within a familiar milieu. When the network managers try to convince the steering group to prioritise active nature experience by referring to the growing trend of experiences using the experience economy and market trend as arguments, it is a form of confrontation with the world. The large accommodation and transportation firms are confronted with a new reality where the small and nature-based activity experiences matter more. This confrontation is probably more evident as the network was formed during the experience turn. Still, the network needed to find a common goal that the wider environment could legitimise due to seeking public funding and admission into the national industry development program. The finding also gives insight into the conditions of the regimes of justifiable engagement. The network managers used a combination of economic theories, market data, and with time, also other actors to make the steering group engage in a common good, but persistence in discussions was also important. This common good turned out to be the aim of becoming a leading international provider of active and nature-based experiences.

While the narrative of the network formation sheds light on the regime of justifiable action, the narrative of the development and growth phase sheds light on the regime of engagement in a plan. Thévenot and Jacobs (2007) argue that actors need to project themselves into the future to realise a plan successfully. However, the findings also show that developing a project template is vital for successfully realising a plan. Small firms' resource restrictions can make the conditions for engagement in plan difficult. However, teaching the participants how to develop a project template, and following up on firms and projects progress, is also shown to improve the conditions for engagement in plan. Showcases of what similar firms have done with success also seem vital for engagement in plan. The community of practice literature describes such tools and processes as boundary objects and brokering (Wenger, 2003). However, while the boundary objects facilitate and utilise the tension between merging different practices, it is used here to explain how managers can enhance the condition of the engagement in plan regime. The motivational effect of boundary objects is also described in Fuglsang and Eide's (2013) paper, even though using a different notion of engagement. The good governing this engagement regime is the participants' goal or prospected output. The findings show that project templates are a condition for engagement as it aids participants in articulating goals and plans so that they are understandable for others. Furthermore, the experience turn also shows the importance of knowledge-building. What constitutes an experience or how to develop an experience is not necessarily understood similarly by different participants.

Networking is not easy. Networks do not continually develop and grow. Sometimes they also stagnate. The findings show how stagnation phases can stimulate new development and growth or result in the termination of the network. The stagnation phases described in the findings seem to be recognised by the lack of contact with the participants and few or no network activities. Thus, making even familiar engagement difficult. Thévenot and Jacobs (2007) argue that convenience is governing this format of engagement. After the first stagnation phase, the network managers seemed mainly occupied with what the participants found useful and wanted. It seems that there was less focus on challenging the members with the broader world. Even though the network collaborated across industries on the Vidden project, the confrontation did not evoke the same need for change. Familiar engagement instead seems to be the primary format of engagement. By talking and listening to members at meetings, gatherings, or sometimes having industry knowledge, the network managers can facilitate convenient network activities within the participants' familiar milieu. However, such personalised formats of engagement also narrow the participants' scope of actions (Thévenot, 2001). The findings suggest that it also reduces the newness in the network activities, suggesting more incremental and less radical innovations. Also, the practice-based literature suggests that the potential for innovation lies in the tension between different practices and knowledge (Wenger, 2003).

All three engagement formats were present at all network phases despite highlighting one format in each phase narrative. Also, the reality engaged differentiates between members and members over time as their ambitions and horizons for engaging with the environment differ. While much network literature interprets this as a lack of network engagement, this chapter interprets it as natural fluctuation and changes between scopes of engagement in line with Thévenot's (2001) notion of engagement. Network participation, network managers, and other network actors may shape and change actors' perception of the reality engaged and the ambitions and horizons for their engagement.

FUTURE RESEARCH DIRECTIONS

The development of complete tourist experiences and the transition to the new paradigm should be understood as a cognitive and social process as actors' engagement is closely linked to how actors relate to their social environment. However, few have taken this approach when exploring the different industry actor's roles in changing a paradigm. More research is needed to fully understand how actors engage in new paradigms, e.g., by taking a discursive perspective on the transition or studying engagement from a firm level. Future studies should also include the interactions between even more stakeholders as future experience paradigms may develop a similar understanding of co-creation as one finds in the service-dominant logic. Public supporting organisations, customers, and funding organisations are examples of such stakeholders. Also, the role of innovation networks in the industry's transition into the experience economy should be studied further. The chapter findings build on the narrative of a single tourism network. Networks established earlier or later might have taken a different role than the network in this chapter. Also, network governance may affect the role networks have in changing the industry paradigm.

CONCLUSION

The chapter contributes to new knowledge on the conditions of multi-actor engagement in regional innovation networks and how these can be managed. Building on Thévenot's (2001) pragmatic regimes of engagement, this chapter describes the three formats of engagement in a regional innovation network context. By exploring the goods governing the different engagement formats, the conditions for the different formats of engagement in networks and how to manage these became evident. The chapter's findings extend the current practice-based literature by including the participants' dynamic encounters with the world, which is lacking (Thévenot, 2001). The findings also shed new light on the cognitive and social aspects of the tourism industry's transition towards the experience paradigm. How actors relate to and grasp the social environment is a vital part of such transitions, as a change in paradigm requires that the aptly good that the actors engage in changes. The social environment must legitimise a new common good. The findings have confirmed this as an interdependent process between actors and between actors and their environment. The experience paradigm meant that the tourism industry had to develop in new ways as one now aimed to create complete tourist experiences. The old actions were no longer as easy to justify, challenging actors as the actors needed to leave the familiar milieu in which one has operated, changing the actors' engagement scope. By exploring the transition to the experience paradigm using Thévenot's (2001) concept of pragmatic regimes of engagement, the chapter has given new knowledge on the actors' dynamic confrontation with the world when industry paradigms change. While the community of practice literature narrows the scope of interest to how actors engage in practice, this chapter has increased the understanding of the moral element in practices that shapes the dynamic processes that govern any pragmatic engagement and explaining actors' dynamic confrontation whit the world.

The chapter is based on a retrospective study of one regional innovation network. Despite using secondary data to fill gaps in memories, this is a weakness. While the network studied can shed light on the conditions of network engagement, it may show less of the dynamic between the different formats of engagement due to periods of stagnation. Other networks may generate more knowledge on how the formats of engagement differentiate due to ambitions and horizons.

REFERENCES

Alvesson, M., & Sköldberg, K. (2000). Reflexive methodology: New vistas for qualitative research. Sage (Atlanta, Ga.).

Baggio, R. (2008). Symptoms of complexity in a tourism system. *Tourism Analysis*, *13*(1), 1–20. doi:10.3727/108354208784548797

Blokker, P., & Brighenti, A. (2011). An interview with Laurent Thévenot: On engagement, critique, commonality, and power. *European Journal of Social Theory*, *14*(3), 383–400. doi:10.1177/1368431011412351

Brown, J. S., & Duguid, P. (1991). Organisational learning and communities-of-practice: Toward a unified view of working, learning, and innovation. *Organization Science*, *2*(1), 40–57. doi:10.1287/orsc.2.1.40

Chesbrough, H. (2011). *Open services innovation: Rethinking your business to grow and compete in a new era*. Jossey-Bass.

Connelly, F. M., & Clandinin, D. J. (1990). Stories of experience and narrative inquiry. *Educational Researcher*, *19*(5), 2–14. doi:10.3102/0013189X019005002

Eisenhardt, K. M., & Graebner, M. A. (2007). Theory building from cases: Opportunities and challenges. *Academy of Management Journal*, *50*(1), 25–37. doi:10.5465/amj.2007.24160888

Felin, T., Foss, N., & Ployhart, R. (2015). The microfoundations movement in strategy and organisation theory. *The Academy of Management Annals*, *9*(1), 575–632. doi:10.5465/19416520.2015.1007651

Flanagan, J. C. (1954). The critical incident technique. *Psychological Bulletin*, *51*(4), 327–358. doi:10.1037/h0061470 PMID:13177800

Flyvbjerg, B. (2001). *Making social science matter: Why social inquiry fails and how it can succeed again*. Cambridge University Press.

Fuglesang, L. (2015). Engagement in place: bricolage networking in tourism and the experience economy. In A. Lorentzen, K. Topsø Larsen, & L. Schrøder (Eds.), *Routledge advances in regional economics, science and policy* (pp. 213–228). Routledge. doi:10.4324/9781315885063

Fuglsang, L. (2008). Innovation with care: What it means. In L. Fuglsang (Ed.), *Innovation and the creative process: Towards innovation with care* (pp. 3–21). Edward Elgar. doi:10.4337/9781848440104

Fuglsang, L. (2018). Towards a theory of a practice-based approach to service innovation within spheres of interaction. In A. Scupola & L. Fuglsang (Eds.), *Services, experiences and innovation: Integrating and extending research* (pp. 174–164). Edward Elgar Publishing. doi:10.4337/9781788114301.00015

Fuglsang, L., & Eide, D. (2013). The experience turn as 'bandwagon': Understanding network formation and innovation as practice. *European Urban and Regional Studies*, *20*(4), 417–434. doi:10.1177/0969776412448090

Fuglsang, L., & Nordli, A. (2018). On service innovation as an interactive process: A case study of the engagement with innovation of a tourism service. *Social Sciences*, *7*(12). doi:10.3390/socsci7120258

Gallouj, F., Rubalcaba, L., & Windrum, P. (2013). *Public-private innovation networks in services*. Edward Elgar Pub. Ltd. doi:10.4337/9781781002667

Guba, E. G., & Lincoln, Y. S. (1994). Competing paradigms in qualitative research. In E. G. Guba & Y. S. Lincoln (Eds.), Handbook of qualitative research (Vol. 2, pp. 105–117). Academic Press.

Hammarfjord, M. O., & Roxenhall, T. (2017). The relationship between network commitment, antecedents, and innovation in strategic innovation networks. *International Journal of Innovation Management*, *21*(6), 1750037–1750036p. doi:10.1142/S1363919617500372

Hjalager, A.-M. (2000). Tourism destinations and the concept of industrial districts. *Tourism and Hospitality Research*, *2*(3), 199–213. doi:10.1177/146735840000200302

Hjalager, A.-M. (2010). A review of innovation research in tourism. *Tourism Management*, *31*(1), 1–12. doi:10.1016/j.tourman.2009.08.012

Jakobsen, O., & Arnesen, T. G. (2020). *Sluttevaluering av klyngen NCE Tourism* (152/2020). Menon Economics. https://www.menon.no/publication/sluttevaluering-klyngen-nce-tourism/

Kofler, I., & Marcher, A. (2018). Inter-organisational networks of small and medium-sized enterprises (SME) in the field of innovation: A case study of South Tyrol. *Journal of Small Business and Entrepreneurship*, *30*(1), 9–25. doi:10.1080/08276331.2017.1401202

Li, L. P., Juric, B., & Brodie, R. J. (2017). Dynamic multi-actor engagement in networks: The case of United Breaks Guitars. *Journal of Service Theory and Practice*, *27*(4), 738–760. doi:10.1108/JSTP-04-2016-0066

Lindberg, F., Hansen, A. H., & Eide, D. (2014). A multirelational approach for understanding consumer experiences within tourism. *Journal of Hospitality Marketing & Management*, *23*(5), 487–512. Advance online publication. doi:10.1080/19368623.2013.827609

Marasco, A., De Martino, M., Magnotti, F., & Morvillo, A. (2018). Collaborative innovation in tourism and hospitality: A systematic review of the literature. *International Journal of Contemporary Hospitality Management*, *30*(6), 2364–2395. doi:10.1108/IJCHM-01-2018-0043

Mertova, P., & Webster, L. (2020). *Using narrative inquiry as a research method: An introduction to critical event narrative analysis in research, teaching and professional practice* (2nd ed.). Routledge. doi:10.4324/9780429424533

Newell, S., Robertson, M., Scarbrough, H., & Swan, J. (2009). *Managing knowledge work and innovation* (2nd ed.). Palgrave Macmillan. doi:10.1007/978-0-230-36641-1

Novelli, M., Schmitz, B., & Spencer, T. (2006). Networks, clusters and innovation in tourism: A UK experience. *Tourism Management*, *27*(6), 1141–1152. doi:10.1016/j.tourman.2005.11.011

OECD. (2005). *Oslo manual: guidelines for collecting and interpreting innovation data* (3rd ed.). Organisation for Economic Co-operation and Development.

OECD & Eurostat. (2018). Oslo Manual 2018: Guidelines for Collecting, Reporting and Using Data on Innovation, 4th Edition. The Measurement of Scientific, Technological and Innovation Activities. OECD Publishing. https://doi.org/ doi:10.1787/9789264304604-en

Orton, J. D., & Weick, K. E. (1990). Loosely coupled systems: A reconceptualisation. *Academy of Management Review*, *15*(2), 203–223. doi:10.2307/258154

Pikkemaat, B., Peters, M., & Bichler, B. F. (2019). Innovation research in tourism: Research streams and actions for the future. *Journal of Hospitality and Tourism Management*, *41*, 184–196. doi:10.1016/j.jhtm.2019.10.007

Pine, B. J. II, & Gilmore, J. H. (1998). Welcome to the experience economy. *Harvard Business Review*, *76*(4), 97. PMID:10181589

Schumpeter, J. A. (1934). *The theory of economic development: An inquiry into profits, capital, credit, interest, and the business cycle* (Vol. 46). Harvard University Press.

Scott, N., Baggio, R., & Cooper, C. (2008). *Network analysis and tourism: From theory to practice*. Channel View Publications. doi:10.21832/9781845410896

Serrat, O. (2017). The Critical Incident Technique. In *Knowledge solutions: Tools, methods, and approaches to drive organisational performance* (pp. 1077–1083). Springer. doi:10.1007/978-981-10-0983-9_123

Storbacka, K., Brodie, R. J., Böhmann, T., Maglio, P. P., & Nenonen, S. (2016). Actor engagement as a microfoundation for value co-creation. *Journal of Business Research*, *69*(8), 3008–3017. doi:10.1016/j.jbusres.2016.02.034

Thévenot, L. (2001). Pragmatic regimes governing the engagement with the world. *The practice turn in contemporary theory*, 56-73.

Thévenot, L., & Jacobs, A. (2007). The plurality of cognitive formats and engagements: Moving between the familiar and the public. Authors' reply: Social theory after the cognitive revolution: types of contemporary cognitive sociology. *European Journal of Social Theory*, *10*(3), 409–423. doi:10.1177/1368431007080703

Webster, L., & Mertova, P. (2007). *Using narrative inquiry as a research method: An introduction to using critical event narrative analysis in research on learning and teaching*. Routledge. doi:10.4324/9780203946268

Weisenfeld, U. (2003). Engagement in innovation management: Perceptions and interests in the GM Debate 1. *Creativity and Innovation Management*, *12*(4), 211–220. doi:10.1111/j.0963-1690.2003.00284.x

Wenger, E. (1998). *Communities of practice: Learning, meaning, and identity*. Cambridge University Press. doi:10.1017/CBO9780511803932

Wenger, E. (2000). Communities of practice and social learning systems. *Organisation*, *7*(2), 225–246. doi:10.1177/135050840072002

Wenger, E. (2003). Communities of practice and social learning systems. In D. Nicolini, D. Yanow, & S. Gherardi (Eds.), *Knowing in organisations: A practice-based approach* (pp. 76–99). M.E. Sharpe.

Yin, R. K. (2012). *Applications of case study research* (3rd ed.). SAGE.

Chapter 5
Hospitality in the Experience Economy

Aditya Ranjan
https://orcid.org/0000-0003-1304-5489
Jamia Millia Islamia, India

Shweta Chandra
Jamia Millia Islamia, India

Rohan Bhalla
Jamia Millia Islamia, India

Sumedha Agarwal
https://orcid.org/0000-0002-9856-5661
Sharda University, India

ABSTRACT

Experience economy plays a predominant role in the hospitality industry. Consumer experience has always been of great importance for the hospitality business. As consumer experience evolved, businesses needed and still need to find new ways to differentiate themselves. To remain competitive and stay in the market, hospitality firms are working towards creating outstanding and memorable experiences that exceed guest expectations. In the context of Pine and Gilmore's experience economy conceptual model, the chapter attempts to theorize and explain how hospitality businesses are curating consumer experiential encounters. Digital nomads are the ignition source of driving an experience economy. The chapter further highlights how technology would additionally ease hospitality enterprises to frame excellent strategies focused on supplying the value to the digital consumers and then expecting their customers to generate additional business.

DOI: 10.4018/978-1-7998-8775-1.ch005

INTRODUCTION

Customer experience is the latest catchphrase of the modern economy. Experience is a multi-faceted notion that includes emotional, perceptual, and behavioural components (Schmitt, 1999). Consumers expect incredible products and services from every hospitality business they encounter during their travels. The ever-increasing importance of providing consumers with an outstanding service experience necessitates all stakeholders' collaborative and coordinated effort (Rehman et al., 2020). Such hospitality businesses that fail to create and deliver compelling guest experiences would fall short of modern consumer expectations. Several hospitality companies, like Marriot, are hiring managers in charge of creating and maintaining their customers' experiences. Not only are customer preferences changing in the current economy, but so are service landscapes. Besides, the tech-savvy generations are more racially and ethnically varied than any preceding generation, and they are also the most educated (Page & Williams, 2011). Such digital natives have been born with little or no recollection of the world before smartphones. Therefore, hospitality businesses need to install new and innovative technology platforms that will allow them to manage and create end-to-end guest experiences (Kandampully & Solnet, 2020). The COVID-19 pandemic outbreak, on the other hand, has only accelerated the digitalisation of services that was already speeding up. This article attempts to analyse experience economy through the hospitality industry and evaluate initiatives taken by tourism and hospitality to leverage various experience realms. Every business has a stake, and the Covid-19 pandemic has sped up the need to rethink the experience economy to ensure it becomes world-class. Such a unique set of conditions might be viewed as a great chance to successfully combine technology to produce a unique offering capable of satisfying consumers' experience thirst. The chapter begins by explaining the experience economy and its dimensions as explained by different researchers and then highlights the experience ecosystem in the tourism and hospitality context with relevant industry examples.

UNDERSTANDING EXPERIENCE ECONOMY

Experience Economy includes services, retail, travel, food & beverage, tourism, entertainment, technological, cultural, sporting, and heritage industries (Lorentzen, 2009). It connects multiple components of the economy by bringing together small businesses and regional economies to generate employment. Economies have a dynamic nature with unique progression. Structural change in the economy comes as an inevitable consequence of economic growth (Pine II & Gilmore, 1998). Initially, the financial system began with economies of commodity. A commodity formed the basis of the barter system in an undifferentiated agricultural economy. Gradually the economy evolved to a goods economy. Increasing demand for goods led to the expansion of the industrial sector, which led to the standardisation of goods. For example, today, different cars in the same price range offer almost the same benefits making the selection process more challenging. While discussing hospitality, the same categorisation of hotels has nearly the same set of services and facilities to offer (Cser & Ohuchi, 2008).

Similarly, there is an established classification of restaurants that have similar products and services. Unfortunately, such uniformity produced cutthroat rivalry, as every hospitality operator seeks to outperform their competitor. During the 1980s, when the product economy was dominant in the markets, customer satisfaction was driven by product quality, durability, features, zero defect, and other quality aspects, which lend the competitive advantage. Moreover, many firms adopted cookie-cutter approach,

Hospitality in the Experience Economy

means the same method or style is always applied to provide good or services without customisation (Radder & Louw, 1999). The cookie-cutter approach, successful strategy, and proven business models such as franchisee structure and McDonaldization brought high efficiency and mass production levels but lacked uniqueness (LeBlanc, 2021). On the other hand, the services economy followed the era of the product economy. Instead of goods production, the service economy focused on producing services like maintenance repairs, training, or consulting. As a result, service quality becomes a critical factor in achieving and influencing consumer satisfaction that further impacts customer loyalty (Saleem & Raja, 2014). However, the standardisation of services in the hospitality industry was prime facia for enhancing the customer experience.

Following the service economy came the fourth economic offering, which was the offering of consumer experience. Consumers un-questionably desire experiences and businesses respond by explicitly designing and promoting them (Pine II & Gilmore, 1998). As with goods, services have been increasingly commoditised, paving the way for consumer experiences to emerge as the next stage in the economic evolution (Pine II & Gilmore, 1998). The four-stage evolution of the birthday cake explains it well. Initially, mothers made cakes by mixing the required ingredients (flour, sugar, butter, and eggs). With time and advancement, the Betty Crocker premixes were readily available in the market. Mothers did not mind paying more for those premixes as they offered much comfort and convenience.

With rapid industrialisation, growth, and the onset of the service economy, many ready-made cakes were available at the bakery and grocery stores at a cost ten times more than the raw ingredients. Today the parents do not make the cake or plan the party independently. Still, they hire an event planner, outsource the entire event and thus organise a memorable birthday event for the kids (Pine II & Gilmore, 1998). The pattern of birthday celebrations illustrates the transition from commodities to the goods economy, then to the service economy, and lastly to the experience economy. When the products and service quality no longer distinguish choices, customers turn to seek unique experiences. It became necessary for businesses to provide value-added offerings to existing high-quality products and services to address the need for distinctive and unforgettable consumer experiences. An experience is a tangible offering like any other service, goods, or commodity (Pine II & Gilmore, 1998). To sell better in the emerging experience economy, many organisations simply wrap experiences around their existing services. For example, in the automobile sector, especially car companies make vehicle delivery an enjoyable and memorable experience. A vehicle purchase is an important milestone of life, and the car dealers make that moment special by decorating the car, handing over the key, and getting a picture clicked to the extent they take permission and download your picture from Facebook and play a small video clip. Airlines and restaurants offer a complimentary cake if you happen to be taking their service on your birthday.

Since the early days of the service economy, service delivery has acted as a competitive difference. With the advent of time, customer experience management has emerged as a significant change in the new experience economy. Here, the consumer experience creates value for the business. Firms set up services with goods or commodities, and everything functions together to construct a consumer experience. Experience is multidimensional, including education, esthetics, and recreation as its different facets (Lee et al., 2015). The product economy offers more detailed schemas than does the experience economy (Chang, 2018). The monetary values of services are more than experience. As a result, the average gain and loss values of service are greater than those of experience. So, consumer perceptions of a firm's service are critical and cannot be ignored. Consumers still tend to perceive benefits as being more mainstream than the experience (Chang, 2018). Therefore, good service is the foundation of experience consumption.

Similarly, consumer decision utility has changed to experience utility, focusing on the enjoyment of hedonic quality (Kahneman & Thaler, 2006). Today's customer is aware of spending his money on experiences rather than material possessions. The hospitality businesses have realised the importance of experience, and they connect experience-seeking customers with locals, giving an authentic local experience (Birinci et al., 2018). For example, the Jungle Villa Resort in Chitwan National Park, Nepal, offers Nepalese folk music and dance entertainment services. Since the guests cannot wander outside in the nighttime as it is a wildlife conservation zone, the dance and music performances from the native people keep them entertained. The desert camps provide the same kind of entertainment in the dunes of Jaisalmer, India. The tourists can enjoy an evening of cultural music and dance along with participation in the festivities. Moreover, the aesthetics of the hospitality services are also changing in the backdrop of the experience economy realm. Such transition has made it essential to understand the background and dimensions of experience so that hospitality firms could use it to create a difference.

DIMENSIONS OF EXPERIENCE IN TOURISM AND HOSPITALITY

The experience economy has changed the hospitality landscape in many ways. The dimensions of experience have to be explored to study the transition. Commodities are fungible materials capable of satisfying needs differentiated by price and features. They have an inventory, and the forces of supply and demand determine their availability. The economy is gradually shifting to services and customised activities. Customised services and customerisation riding on service has evolved as the strategy of differentiation. Goods have utility, are tangible, whereas services are intangible, but experiences are memorable, making them an excellent way to connect with the customer (Pine II & Gilmore, 1998). So, today's business target is not only to have a good product but also an excellent service surrounded by a pleasant and memorable experience. It should follow a - no cookie-cutter approach that is personalised, curated, and unique. Experience has taken over the centre stage, and various research studies have been undertaken on the subject providing a deeper understanding of experience.

Experience consists of a complex construct with complex relationships between value, service quality, and satisfaction, forming the basis for consumption (Knutson & Beck, 2004). Experience follows a hierarchical pyramid strategy, with a foundation of product value and quality that extends through serviceability and, lastly, experience. Different researchers have explained experience in the light of varied components. According to Berry et al. (2002), experience consists of the functional and emotional parts. Both these components consist of clues. The valuable functional clues (mechanic clues) come from the cleanliness of the room, timely services, correct billing.

In contrast, the emotional clues (humanistic clues) are perceived by the environment, such as music, lighting, the smile of the front desk staff, the feel of the bedsheet. The combined effect of clues influences customers' emotional perception of service quality, thus impacting their evaluation. Hence the need arose to be clue conscious and work towards designing hints to set the expectations right. According to Mathwick et al. (2001), experience consists of an extrinsic and intrinsic component. The extrinsic part consists of consumption, utility, and product benefits. In contrast, the intrinsic part consists of the experience involved in purchasing. The environment in which the hospitality product or service is delivered influences values, engagement, emotional bond, participation, and stimulation of an experience (Moreira et al., 2017). The room is the extrinsic component in the hospitality context, while the staff's warmth, welcome, courtesy, and care are intrinsic. Wirtz and Bateson (1999) highlighted pleasure and arousal

Hospitality in the Experience Economy

as two components of the experience. Pleasure refers to the hedonic quality of stimuli, extending from extreme displeasure to extreme pleasure. The consumer attitude towards the servicescape is influenced by pleasure intensity affecting evaluation both directly and indirectly. Arousal is a primary, subjective state that an individual may be in, ranging from sleep to frantic excitement. Specifically, pleasure operates as the prime driver of satisfaction, and that excitement serves as an amplifier of the pleasure-satisfaction connection. (Wirtz et al., 2007).

Holbrook (1994) explained that consumption experience could be active or passive. More active the consumption experience, the higher is the participation; hence the experiential value increases. Experience requires absorption that is "occupying customers' attention by bringing the experience into the mind" and immersion that is "becoming physically or virtually a part of the experience itself" (Pine II & Gilmore, 1998). The hospitality businesses enable customers to be in servicescape through offerings for an extended period, engaging consumers creatively and actively (Ballantyne & Nilsson, 2017). For example, hospitality firms use different gestures to connect with consumers and ensure their active involvement. Dramatic notions and principles sometimes often describe the service experience (Grove et al., 2003). In such a case, the performers (service employees), the audience (consumers), the setting (physical environment), and the service itself comprise four critical theatrical components of the service experience (Walls et al., 2011).

As per Mccoll-kennedy et al. (2015), service experience has three approaches: moments of truth, journey mapping, and service blueprinting; (i) moments of truth" are critical dyadic interactions between the customer and the company; (ii) journey mapping" depicts the way the customer engages with the company's service offerings. It maps the service journey from beginning to end as the customer participates in a service encounter to achieve a specific goal; (iii) service blueprints are visual displays that depict all of the processes involved in producing and delivering services, including customer actions, onstage/backstage contact employee actions, service systems, and support processes.

The experience has been explained and discussed in various forms and construct, making it clear that it is multidimensional and an extension of service. Hospitality is a service industry, and so the experience forms its soul. Today in the hospitality industry, the service orientation and the true spirit of experience create an impact. Therefore, given the complexity and multi-faceted nature of the hospitality service experience, co-creating experience calls for thinking beyond the service provider and customer. An illustrative model depicting the stages through which the customer passes in experiential consumption has been shown in figure 1. The complete experience cycle has been divided into three stages: pre-experience, participation, and post-experience. The first stage is the stage where the expectations are set. Word of mouth, eWOM, brand image, and promotions influences the pre-experience stage. The second stage represents the guest's actual real-time experience and includes all encounters throughout the journey with the organisation (Suleri et al., 2021). Post-experience, the final stage of an experience, is the aftermath of the participation; in other words, "it is not over when it is over" (O'Sullivan & Spangler, 1998). With hospitality companies, experiences include everything from online reservations, personal check-in at the front desk or through a central reservation system, to checking in and final bill settlement. Consumer experience is all about the process of acquiring, using, maintaining, and disposing of products and services (Berry et al., 2002).

Hospitality in the Experience Economy

Figure 1. Illustrative diagram depicting the stages in the consumption experience
Source: Knutson & Beck, 2004

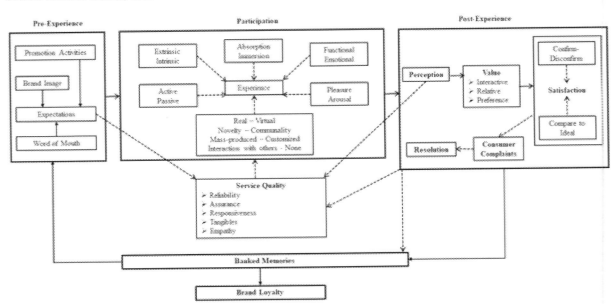

THE HOSPITALITY CUSTOMER EXPERIENCE REALMS

Figure 2. Customer Experience Realms
Source: Pine II & Gilmore, 1998

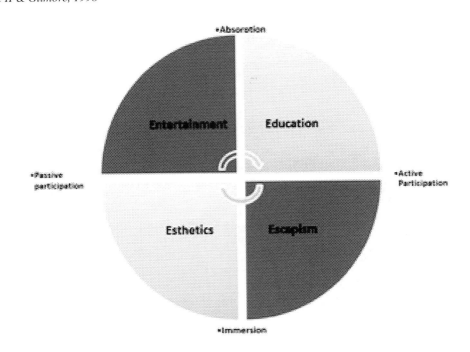

Hospitality in the Experience Economy

The experiences are made up of several components: behaviour, perception, emotion, and cognition. These are often experienced in the tourism industry by visiting, observing, enjoying, and learning in the environment offered by the destination. The four realms, also known as 4Es, were termed by Pine II & Gilmore in 1998. The four realms that consist of "educational, esthetic, escapist, and entertainment" add experiential value to the business in the experience economy (Figure 2). Such experiences are based on the level of customer participation- active or passive-and immersion in such experience.

Educational (Active Participation and Absorption)

Educational experiences are those that are a part of the active participation and absorption quadrant of figure 2. In this category of experiences, the tourists absorb the environment that is offered to them (Pine II & Gilmore, 1998). While absorbing the events that unfold, the tourist also actively participates through physical and mental engagement in such events. Moreover, consumer experiences at the destination help in enhancing the knowledge and skills of the tourists. For example, a tourist can visit art galleries to learn about various art types or visit wineries to strengthen their understanding of wines and the production process.

In the same way, tourists can learn about tea and coffee variety and production by visiting the areas they are grown in. Some tourist attractions are specifically created to educate the tourists. For example, a visit to Happy Valley Tea Estate in Darjeeling city of India can educate tourists about the orthodox method of tea production, which is followed since the time of the British Empire. This place also serves the purpose of museum and tea tasting café to impart education to tourists. This knowledge is further enhanced by promotional brochures, conversations with the experts, and hands-on experiences. For example, the tourists visiting *Choki Dhani* in Jaipur learn about pottery, lac bangles production, embroidery, puppetry, and traditional culinary methods by experts. Thus, a tourist must actively engage the mind and body to enhance their skills and knowledge.

Esthetic (Passive Participation and Immersion)

Passive participation involves an experience that appeals to the senses of tourists (Pine II & Gilmore, 1998). Contrary to the educational experiences, esthetic experience does not affect the mental senses even though the tourists are physically present in the environment (Lorentzen, 2009). Esthetic experiences are more associated with the feeling of *being* that the tourists enjoy at the destination, and it does not alter the nature of the environment they are visiting (Pine II & Gilmore, 1998). The tourists get influenced by the location they are a part of; they appreciate the surroundings and enjoy the appeals of the destination. The level of authenticity of experiences makes little difference to the tourists. Several tourist and hospitality activities fall into this quadrant. Places like beaches, mountains, or valleys allow tourists to enjoy themselves without being physically active (Lorentzen, 2009). The level of involvement is low at these places, and the tourists are not expected to be actively involved. The visitors can appreciate and enjoy the natural surroundings passively and enjoy the feeling of just *being* there. The monuments and historical sites also belong to this category of experiences. For example, an evening on the southernmost tip of the port town of Kanyakumari, India, provides an exceptional experience. This place is known as the union of three major water bodies: Bengal, the Arabian Sea, and the Indian Ocean. The tourists can enjoy a walk along the sea with perfect sunsets and delicious food. The experience, although passive, is highly immersive. Similarly, esthetic servicescapes in resort hotels can also serve as an example. Resorts located in scenic locations offer experiences to guests that all age groups enjoy.

Escapist (Active Participation and Immersion)

Escapist experiences involve the active participation and immersion of the tourists at the destination (Figure 2). The escapist experience requires participation and immersion, greater than education or entertainment (Pine II & Gilmore, 1998). The tourist involved in the escapist experience should affect the performance and outcome of the experience. Playing golf and camping is an example of escapist experiences. Tourism is seen to escape the monotonous daily life (Lee et al., 2015). The researchers have mentioned escapism as one of the most frequent motivations for travelling. The phenomenon of escapism is not clearly defined and has been discussed in various contexts by several researchers. The researchers have concluded that escapism has three significant components- getting away from the monotonous life, immersing in the destination's environment, and involvement in the activities (Lee et al., 2015). The importance of the escapism realm to the hotel and hospitality sector is that all three components must be considered in the marketing of services to address all possible escape motivations of potential guests.

Furthermore, the active consumer and tourist idea encourages hospitality service providers to deliver dynamic experiences for their guests. The leading runners in the experience economy can differentiate themselves by focusing on the experience and escapism domains. The concept of escapism can be discussed through the example of *Ananda in the Himalayas*, Uttarakhand, India. People prefer this place to experience a holistic way of living authentically and understand nature's balance and how the universe affects physical and mental well-being. The guests visiting Ananda can participate in several activities offered by the resort to break the monotony of life. These include meditation, yoga, nature walks and treks, spa treatments, cooking classes, talks with senior *Vedic* scholars. Another example that explains escapism is *Reni Pani* in Madhya Pradesh, India. This place gets its name from a neighbouring tribal village. The resort not only offers guests an authentic wildlife experience in a natural setting, but it also actively contributes to the preservation of the forest, its species, and the residents that rely on them. The guests visit this place to actively participate in activities such as bird watching, anthropological expedition, nature walks, boat, and elephant safari. These activities break the boredom of routine life and provide a medium of escapism to the guests.

Entertainment (Passive Participation and Absorption)

The final realm of the quadrant is entertainment which involves passive participation and absorption of experiences at the destination (Figure 2). The participants do not affect the environment where activities occur and act as spectators while absorbing the performances (Pine II & Gilmore, 1998). Entertainment has been considered essential by researchers for the success of business in the current environment. Entertainment, like the esthetic dimension, necessitates that the offerings capture and occupy the attention and readiness of customers (Pine II & Gilmore, 2011). The tourists passively observe and appreciate the activities and performances of others. The entertainment experience may include listening to music, enjoying a dance performance, reading, or watching other activities. The hospitality service providers nowadays have a variety of entertainment services in the hotels and resorts to enhance the experience of guests' stay. If a guest is entertained, the overall experience of his/her stay would be enriched. It will also enhance the outcome of the trip. For example, the Jungle Villa Resort in Chitwan National Park,

Nepal, offers Nepalese folk music and dance entertainment services. Since the guests cannot wander outside in the nighttime as it is a wildlife conservation zone, the dance and music performances from the native people keep them entertained. The desert camps provide the same kind of entertainment in the dunes of Jaisalmer, India. The tourists can enjoy an evening of cultural music and dance providers and even participate in the festivities. Hence, entertainment is the most effective for enriching stay and memorable experiences (Pine II & Gilmore, 2011).

CREATING EXPERIENCE IN HOSPITALITY

Experience economy plays a dominant role in the hospitality industry (Pine II & Gilmore, 2011). Consumer experiences have always been significant for the hospitality industry, and service providers continuously need to discover innovative methods to stand out. Consumers are likely to spend significantly more money at a hospitality service provider that incorporates a unique theme into its offerings and service (Pizam, 2010). To remain competitive and stay in the market, hospitality firms are working towards creating outstanding and memorable experiences that exceed guest expectations.

Aspiration and Purpose

The first stage in implementing a successful customer-experience transformation is defining the type of experience hospitality businesses intend to provide to their customers (Pine II & Gilmore, 2011). A strong customer-experience aspiration fulfils the hospitality firm's mission and brand promise. For example, Starbucks strives to deliver nurturing experiences in line with its corporate missions. However, while delineating their customer experience aspiration, hospitality firms frequently have problems, as aspirations may be too generic or do not fit snugly with the company's purposes. Hospitality businesses that fall into such traps end up with customer experience transformation plans that are unclear and incoherent. Hospitality firms need to identify the changes in client behaviour that they anticipate to turn customer experience aspirations into expected business value (Pine II & Gilmore, 2011). For example, if a hospitality firm wants to strengthen customer connections, it can assess success by the number of customers who seek their fundamental experiential needs. Hospitality organisations could further anchor their decisions by doing quantitative research and statistical analysis to better prioritise customers' value. Hospitality businesses need to be agile, have cross-functional teams fully invested in their projects with extensive technical expertise, and work with an emphasis on design thinking and continual improvement. Moreover, hospitality managers need to fundamentally identify internal processes and technology capabilities and rethink existing resources while prioritising customer experiences fundamentally. Hospitality firms could combine priority experiences and develop the essential capabilities to produce a roadmap for delivering the consumer experience.

Hospitality Service Experience Ecosystem

The commercial hospitality industry has its roots within two ancient civilisations, Mesopotamia and Greece, as revealed by the archaeological and textual evidence (O'Gorman, 2009). The inscriptions, known as the Code of Hammurabi, consist of laws governing commercial hospitality establishments dating back to 1800 BC. *Hospitiae* were early establishments that offered rooms for rent along with food and drink to overnight guests. Stable was *hospitiae* with facilities to shelter animals; outside the city, the roadside was old motels. Samarqand, located along the Silk Routes, one of the most crucial historical trading routes in the region, had inns for travellers. The industrial revolution pumped in new ideas and brought progress, taking the inn-keeping to the next level.

The initiative of modern-day hospitality was taken in Europe, and it is said to be the birthplace of an organised hotel and lodging industry (Jayapalan, 2001). With time hospitality services and facilities kept on improving. Hotels became grander in architecture and aesthetics. To win and retain the customer, the service standards were increased, the hospitality personnel was trained to deliver superior service and make the guest feel good and welcomed (Berry & Parasuraman, 2004). Their names increasingly addressed the consumers to add a personal touch, thus creating a feeling of being known and recognised. The service-oriented business, especially the hotel industry, focuses on service quality as it increases customer satisfaction, loyalty, and brand image (Saleem & Raja, 2014). Service quality and improvement became the buzzwords. This competition led to the betterment of services. Quote like "customer is always right," "customer is king," and "Customer is God" became the mantras of success. The outcome of good service quality was customer satisfaction, defined as an internal feeling that a customer gets from assessing the service provided, resulting from promised between received service (Parasuraman et al., 1985). On the same ground, Zeithaml et al. (1985) presented the ten practical requirements to measure the quality of services offered to the customers. These are responsiveness, reliability, tangibility, credibility, communication, security, competence, understanding the customers, courtesy, and service accessibility. Parasuraman et al. in 1988 presented the five-dimensional SERVQUAL scale to measure service quality. These dimensions are responsiveness, reliability, assurance, tangibility, and empathy. The service is the critical differentiator in the hospitality sector. With well-researched and tested SOPs and TAT in place, the services have also been standardised to a certain extent. The differentiating factor being the intangibles were added to the service. Experience was considered at the top of the sequential pyramid, and the base been formed by products and services. Hence, the businesses shifted their paradigm from the "delivery-focused" service economy that emphasises high-quality offerings to the "staged" experience economy that creates a memorable consumption experience (Pine II & Gilmore, 2011).

Hospitality landscapes are complex with multiple engagements and complex interplay of service experience contributors/ stakeholders who influence the process of bringing the service experience to life (King et al., 2019). It is a contact-intensive service operation linked with complex internal dynamics to create a meaningful and memorable experience. All involved contributors need to know their roles and responsibilities to provide a sustained, seamless service experience necessary for a competitive advantage in such a system (King et al., 2019). Following the same, even the designations of the hospitality positions are kept as "Customer Experience Officer" or "Customer Delight Officer" and in many places, the 'HAPPY TO HELP BADGES' are worn by the staff to remind them of the customer care constantly.

Hospitality Service Experience Ecosystem (Figure 3) shows people with critical roles and responsibilities in co-producing the service experience (King et al., 2019). Stakeholders are dependent possess different valued resources to be exchanged and help in sustaining the service system and at the same time fulfil their goals. Owners are one of the more powerful stakeholders in the Hospitality Service Experience Eco-System. Their role is to provide the financial capital to establish and sustain the ecosystem where customers can purchase the services. The service provider includes the employees, who are most proximally involved in the service experience, apart from customers themselves. The service provider interacts directly with customers, attends to their needs, and acts as the intermediary between customers and corporate administrators and owners. It establishes the importance of the employees in the entire service experience chain and explains why the hospitality industry highlights employees as their greatest asset. Memorable and pleasurable service encounters are achieved when all stakeholders collaborate and coordinate their efforts towards a shared vision of customer experience (Rehman et al., 2020). One reason customers are called guests in hospitality is that the term guest has the human aspect. In contrast, the words like customer/client/patient objectify the human aspect.

Figure 3. A diagrammatic representation of the hospitality service experience ecosystem
Source: King et al., 2019

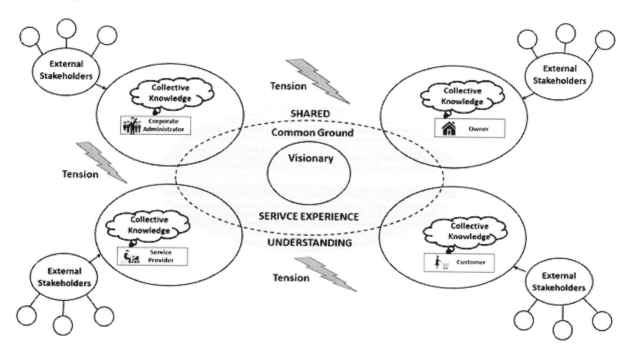

Competing with experiences acts as a double-edged sword. Customers will always experience good, bad, or indifference during any service or product consumption process. The catch is to manage the experience effectively. This need tweaking of service elements and combining functional and emotional benefits in the offerings. Simple gestures have the power to create a WOW effect (Pine II & Gilmore, 2011). For example, the onboard customer Emirates happens to travel on their birthday at 1200 hours the entire crew presents him/her a cake and makes him/her cut the cake. It creates a memorable day for the consumer, and he feels delighted. A guest staying in a hotel who orders milk at bedtime and during his next stay he gets milk at bedtime without asking creates a memorable impact and generates a feeling s/he is being cared for by the hotel. A few years back, the Pizza Hut service staff presented a five-minute medley dance to all the dining guests at the specified time. In case the guest was celebrating his birthday, it was specially done for him. As a result, it became a superhit and motivated people to celebrate their birthdays at Pizza Hut.

On the other hand, it used to re-energise the service staff by breaking from the chores. These acts create emotional bonds between companies and customers, which are difficult for competitors to sever.

Moreover, the holistic nature of these experiential designs makes them very difficult for competitors to copy (Berry et al., 2002). Hence, hospitality companies apply the principles and tools of customer-experience management to strengthen customer loyalty to compete in the market (Kandampully et al., 2018).

DIGITALISATION: CHANGING LANDSCAPE OF EXPERIENCE ECONOMY

Removal of obstacles from trade and tours along with the subsequent expansion in worldwide travel have been key factors in global experiential economy businesses (Dwyer et al., 2009). The product and service economy is globally shifting to the experiential economy, where service delivery as per consumer demand is fundamental to success. Such advancement has been particularly prominent in the hospitality and tourism industries. Globalisation has unleashed the experiential economy potential that has been dormant in the global hospitality industry. It has been observed that in the hospitality sector, consumers' recreational activities have changed due to increased importance to their overall experience. People have become sick and tired of marketing and promotions (Gitlin, 2017). So, they are looking forward to getting an enhanced service experience, as per their requirements. However, the major problem for the hospitality industry is dealing with digital nomads (millennials and Gen Z), new breeds of customers born in the digital age. The digital nomads are born into a fully mechanised world in which they feel that everything is useful. These generations have money and are willing to spend it on memorable experiences (Ramgade & Kumar, 2021).

Moreover, young consumers always keep their social media accounts open and communicate to hospitality service providers when they need something (Bowen & Chen McCain, 2015). Additionally, they do not spend much time on a hospitality service website looking for information that is not readily available. Therefore, they often refuse to participate in a time-consuming process and immediately switch to a competitor's website for hospitality services. The only way hospitality managers could serve them is by being data-driven. When a hospitality business offers an exceptional experience through its service with the aid of technology and is suited to their needs, digital nomads are not hesitant to pay. Digital nomads rapidly utilise search engines and geolocation technology to locate the least expensive, most highly rated, and best-reviewed hospitality goods or services (Ramgade & Kumar, 2021). Such generations demonstrate empathy for the locals who promote them and wish to show them around, especially the hospitality and lodging service providers. Digital nomads instantly express their feelings verbally when they like or dislike the hospitality service provided by the host (Westcott, 2015).

Additionally, such consumers even serve as complimentary brand ambassadors of the hospitality services as they enjoy sharing best practices and contributing to the group. When they enjoy an experience, they influence their peers. Realising the importance of consumers sharing their experiences, some tourism and hospitality firms outperform traditional businesses. Such firms are fueled by the reviews and experiences of the consumers and the host-guest community. Airbnb, for example, utilises the power of the community and sharing economy to empower small apartments and houses that have historically had no place in major online travel agency (OTA) networks (Mody et al., 2019). Without the community's groundbreaking approach by Airbnb, these properties had not surfaced on OTA platforms. The Airbnb platform is the place to find unique local experiences and local guides for travellers looking for it. Visitors want to speak with someone who knows the area well and show them all the hidden gems and provide a wealth of information. Airbnb provides a platform where travellers begin a dialogue with the property owner, serving as a local guide. There is a difference between searching every web post about the area and asking what consumers should see at the service location. Travellers find it easier to connect with other users as soon as they reserve a room with the host, and it aims to create a highly personalised experience for a new guest. The reason is that the user that composes the guest review of an Airbnb user is someone who has used the services of Airbnb.

Changing Customer Preferences

Hospitality businesses have always prioritised the guest experience, and as that experience evolved, firms are required and continue to seek novel ways to differentiate themselves (Deloitte, 2020). Hospitality owners and operators looking to appeal to clients of all ages consider hiring or selecting managers who work with brands to develop distinctive customer experiences. Moreover, hospitality corporations cannot design and serve guests the same way in each hotel they own and, as a result, expect customers to be interested. To be competitive, hospitality firms need to create extraordinary and memorable experiences that go beyond guest expectations. Conventional amenities are not as popular now, as modern travellers want hotels to give their visitors distinctive and individualised experiences rather than providing a wide range of standard amenities. While the digital nomads place a strong emphasis on "enriching their vacation experiences" over other generations, the Gen-X and Baby Boomers also find value in holiday hotel amenities and activities that help to make their holidays particularly unique. So, to succeed in the competitive market, hospitality managers and owners need to cooperate with businesses to provide distinctive customer experiences frequently.

Digitalised Customer Service Experience

Many hospitality businesses are modernising their existing systems to satisfy the growing technological needs of their customers (Naumov, 2019). With these new technologies, small and mid-size hotels that could not previously provide concierge services to their customers now have a cost-effective choice, while high-end luxury hotels are revamping significant aspects of their customer service offerings. Courtyard by Marriott, for example, is updating its hotel technology by placing new digital signage in all of its lobbies. These screens work as high-tech information desks, delivering real-time information like flight status, local weather, activity and restaurant suggestions, and region maps with step-by-step directions to consumers. Other new digital services include broadcasting instructional movies about nearby sites directly to visitors' rooms, chatting with guests via social media such as Twitter, and even providing online ordering apps for room service or groceries for clients staying longer. A great guest experience nowadays requires much more than a clean room and a comfortable bed. Customers nowadays expect hospitality businesses to improve their experiences and interactions by utilising vast amounts of customer data available with the firms. By exploiting consumer data and related insights, hotels may tailor content and experiences to the demands of specific consumers.

ADVANTAGES OF EXPERIENCE ECONOMY

Experience is vital for inclusive global growth, and now it has become a deliberated goal for hospitality organisations. Hospitality businesses have a responsibility to create experiences for future generations so that a wide group of people can use such services. One of the greatest challenges facing hospitality organisations is to assure the accessibility and inclusivity of the consumers while maintaining individuality and distinctiveness in the services.

Personalised Services

Today's consumers want hospitality products or services that are personalised and tailored to their tastes (Naumov, 2019). A free night's stay is one example that would not entice a top-tier guest who has the financial means to book this accommodation but offering an aromatherapy session would serve the purpose. Hospitality service providers can prepare personalised email templates for welcoming the guests and when they leave. Similarly, hospitality businesses could ask guests about their tastes and preferences and record such information for future services. Service providers can use such information to offer up-sells at the right moment, especially when consumers need them. Giving a complimentary gym card to a regular visitor of a hotel, on the other hand, could be a good idea. Service providers may also use recommendation systems and provide the right product or service to the guests at the right moment by utilising big data (Cohen, 2018). Moreover, the hospitality service provider needs to take care of consumer experience and engagement while delivering the service.

Contribute to the Sharing Economy

Hospitality business needs to participate in the community and add value to local businesses by promoting and cooperating with them (Birinci et al., 2018; Sundbo, 2004). Furthermore, hospitality entrepreneurs should try to connect with the visitors and get to know their interests. There is a possibility that consumers of hospitality firms could have some common ground. It would slowly increase the number of people who support and endorse such hospitality services if it happens. For example, suppose a hospitality firm endorses a niche community, such as the LGBTQ+ community. In that case, the entrepreneurs could advertise such events to let visitors know about the event and develop unique experiences. Additionally, hospitality businesses, along with their areas of expertise, could get involved in the community by promoting other local businesses and sharing the local knowledge about their products with customers (Birinci et al., 2018; Sundbo, 2004).

However, to create experiences that captivate customers, hospitality organisations do not need to be affiliated with large hotel chains or brands. Instead, smaller hospitality businesses can take advantage of market trends and employ ingenuity to meet the demands of their customers. For example, Mesa Lane Partners' Autocamp, along with Under Canvas's flagship brand, caters to the growing interest in camping among digital nomads by providing luxury cabin and recreational vehicle (RV) lodgings close to national parks. While these smaller companies may not have as many assets as Marriott, InterContinental, or Hilton Worldwide, they can communicate their companies' stories to a willing audience and immerse that audience in a unique experience to generate revenues.

Developing Hospitality Business as Social Hubs

Today's guests seek out areas to converse and unwind, grab a snack or a cup of coffee, and connect to free Wi-Fi for a few hours. Therefore, hospitality businesses need to construct a social hub at the service delivery points, leading tourists to experience a real taste of the area (Mayfield, 2021). Similarly, establishing an iconic local restaurant or tavern on the local scene would help hospitality firms to help link visitors who are enthusiastic and looking for adventure with residents (Birinci et al., 2018). Hospitality service providers could tap the traveller's motivation to explore the world, while firms could also work on helping such travellers obtain a sense of the local culture (Sundbo, 2004). Similarly, hospitality businesses could work on consumers feel more comfortable interacting with others when they are given the option to do so. Hospitality organisations could also create lobby areas to provide experiences to meet guest and visitor needs (Zach & Krizaj, 2017). Service providers should be equipped with co-working places with outlets and free Wi-Fi these days. For example, consumers need Wi-Fi or internet service to book a cab, post something on social media, or send an email to their office or business partner.

Moreover, hospitality firms would investigate how their goal for providing such facilities should be as simple and trouble-free as possible. Managers need to realise that customers are reluctant to search for plugs or ask for Wi-Fi codes that connect them to the internet. Such cases are more prominent with locals and travellers because they look for living room-style resting areas and want a classy restaurant or bar located right in the action centre.

TRANSFORMED HOSPITALITY EXPERIENCE AMIDST THE PANDEMIC

A short period of time has seen the COVID-19 pandemic wreak devastation on people's lives and livelihoods all over the planet. During COVID-19, there is a significant change in how hospitality businesses engage and provide service to the customers (Diebner et al., 2020). Such hospitality businesses that would refuse to modify will be left behind in the competitiveness. One of such examples is when customer experience has proven valuable throughout history during the last economic downturns. Companies that took customer experience seriously earned more of their shareholders' returns during the recent economic recession (Diebner et al., 2020). During and Post-COVID-19, vulnerable customers and the company's customer service departments have to push their thoughts and reconsider what customer care implies. Hospitality businesses suddenly realised that customer journey and satisfaction indicators are no longer required to inform customers about their needs and demands (Lemon & Verhoef, 2016). For example, before the pandemic, where the customer journey required physical channels, several sectors, including the hospitality business, have considered implementing contactless operations. Now, hospitality businesses are working on establishing some methods to makeover the existing presets of customer experience. Managers and experts believe that a methodology encompassing the fundamental building blocks, one precise vision, an agile approach to change transformation, and enhanced analytics implementation would yield a better customer experience (Bough et al., 2020). Moreover, such a combination would provide a competitive advantage to the hospitality business in the industry.

In a time of COVID-19 crisis, a customer's engagement with a hospitality firm could significantly affect their trust and loyalty (Diebner et al., 2020). As millions are furloughed and withdraw into seclusion, a fundamental indicator of customer experience would be how hospitality businesses can frequently fulfil consumers' new requirements with empathy, care, and concern. Nonetheless, such a situation provides a good time for hospitality firms to step into the lead of instant and long-lasting relationships by analysing the customer behaviour generated from the pandemic crisis. However, it would be critical for the hospitality business to keep themselves well-informed of fast-changing consumer preferences and redesign their offerings to fit into the present consumer experiences. Furthermore, even when the public-health crisis has passed, the global economic consequences will remain for a while. Therefore, leading hospitality businesses would need more focus on the customer experiences emerging as the most important in the "new normal" while also exploring methods of saving and self-funding.

Customer experience post-COVID-19 pandemic includes a lot more than simply customer satisfaction. Therefore, a hospitality business that would care and innovate throughout the pandemic crisis and foresee how customers will modify their post-pandemic behaviour would develop healthier, long-term connections. Maintaining a positive customer experience during a crisis necessitates quick research by hospitality firms to grasp shifting dynamics and new pain areas, as well as exceptional innovation to address them. In a competitive environment, hospitality businesses that adapt to such techniques would value customers in high-priority areas.

FUTURE OF HOSPITALITY EXPERIENCE ECONOMY

By 2030, the experience economy is expected to be worth $8 trillion (Andjelic, 2019). Industries such as hospitality, tourism, travel, retail, wellness, food, beverage, and fashion cannot afford to be one-dimensional any longer. The modern hospitality service providers must keep up their pace with their customers and followers on all social media platforms and provide immediate service (Papasolomou & Melanthiou, 2012). Similarly, hospitality firms are using robotics and AI technology to cater to the demand of the consumers (Naumov, 2019). Robots, for example, can perform simple jobs such as providing Wi-Fi passwords.

Moreover, robots could serve as concierge, steward, bellhops, or customer service assistants within the hospitality service premises to a guest who needs it (Kabadayi et al., 2019). The guest otherwise would have to contact reception or request it in person if there is no chatbot. Thus, such automation could help in saving money on the hospitality service provider's branding initiatives. In addition, these robots use artificial intelligence supported by face and speech recognition technology. Such technological advancements would help the hospitality business impress consumers even more (Samala et al., 2020).

Similarly, chatbots may provide service 24 hours a day, seven days a week (Samala et al., 2020), without the need for the front desk of a hospitality firm to be rude because they have received the same inquiry numerous times. Hospitality service providers could use a chatbot effectively to get the guests into the sales funnel and pre and post-consumption the service like ordering food, room, and housekeeping services (Samala et al., 2020). The hospitality business can benefit from a new sector known as Robotic Process Automation (RPA), in which traditional enterprises automate every tedious process. The data-driven hospitality business could automate these requests, resulting in seamless customer interactions, resulting in increased loyalty and positive guest feedback (Accelirate Inc., 2021). Most hospitality service providers waste a lot of time and resources on repetitive and insignificant chores. Using RPA would help hospitality firms to utilise such funds for more beneficial endeavours.

A chatbot could also leverage the guests' GPS technology to send customised offers right to their phones (Samala et al., 2020). For example, a chatbot can send advance notifications to consumers regarding the information on check-in and check-out timings when they are far-off from the hotel. Similarly, when they reach the hotel, it could also send them details about the happy hours, best prices, and deals that can significantly impact the consumer experience. Modern hospitality service providers can compete with excellent data collection and data analysis. A chatbot can leverage geolocation services to help consumers get the hospitality firm's services when they need them and provide hospitality business information about when to promote their services (Samala et al., 2020).

Digital nomads do not trust advertising messaging these days, especially from unfamiliar persons. Similarly, they do not pay heed to such campaigns which seek their involvement without first providing value. Digital nomads feel free to connect with people who would rather have an emotional connection. People from the digital generation want quick delivery of hospitality services. Furthermore, digital nomads are aware that they have other options whenever they face a roadblock in hospitality services offerings. Therefore, hospitality businesses should try to keep their consumers engaged and give them value regularly. One solution for hospitality service providers could be to create a sales funnel and interact with customers at each stage of their journey (Lemon & Verhoef, 2016). Firms would first focus on supplying value to the consumers and then expect them to generate additional business.

CONCLUSION

The experience economy refers to consumers who choose to spend their money on experiences rather than material possessions. The experience economy is significant in the hospitality, travel, and tourism business. Consumer experience emerges with the interaction with hospitality business while consuming the offered good or services. Such emergence of consumer experience is divided into pre-, during, and post-consumption (Knutson & Beck, 2004; Kandampully et al., 2018; Suleri et al., 2021). Although the steps, procedures, and journeys that two consumers follow to consume goods or services would be the same, each customer would have a unique experience (Lorentzen, 2009).

Moreover, the consumer's experience journey during different consumption phases passes through the various multichannel touchpoints (Lemon & Verhoef, 2016). Therefore, hospitality managers need to arrange each process that offers goods or services at the right place to deliver consumers' experiences (Suleri et al., 2021). Consequently, hospitality businesses need to have clear and comprehensive visibility and awareness of the customer's taste and preferences to effectively confront the complexity of customer experience management. A different approach could identify various factors that illustrate all the customers' points of view before, during, and after their intake of goods or services (Suleri et al., 2021). It is imperative in the hospitality industry to provide exceptional customer service to establish customer loyalty and achieve a competitive advantage (Kandampully et al., 2018). The customer pre-, during, and post-consumption hospitality experience components need to be balanced with a range of other aspects such as price, aesthetic design, atmosphere, product quality, location, and assortment (Ryu & Jang, 2008).

Customer experience in the hospitality industry includes food and beverages, hotel rooms, facilities, and supporting elements and processes that are parts of the customer experience. These include employee knowledge and skills, online and offline interactions, ambience, amenities, and many more (Suleri et al., 2021). In hospitality organisations, customer experience management is viewed as a difficult challenge. Hence, re-evaluating the customer experience is critical for hospitality firms in light of major shifts in technology, social media, and consumer lifestyles (Kandampully et al., 2015). The hospitality managers could work upon digitalising services to provide a personal touch to the customer experience. Customers' increasing demand for exceptional and personalised service emphasises the need for hospitality enterprises to understand the customer journey for seeking such services. Hence, hospitality managers could work on internal communication with such customers. Internal communication is key for hospitality businesses that guarantee mutual understanding among employees while considering the consumer perspective (Sigala, 2005).

The chapter highlights the importance of experience economy and how the COVID-19 pandemic is shaping the hospitality industry. Further, the chapter highlights how the rapid digitalisation and automation process shaping the experience demands of consumers. Therefore, Hospitality enterprises need to prioritise prospects by analysing the different client experiences and then putting these experiences following company values. Hence, by understanding and implementing the hospitality industry's experience economy framework, destination managers and tourism and hospitality suppliers can better craft and communicate their service offering to experience-seeking visitors.

REFERENCES

Accelirate Inc. (2021). *RPA in the Hospitality Industry*. https://www.accelirate.com/industries/hospitality/

Andjelic, A. (2019). *The experience economy is blurring the lines between hospitality and retail: The sociology of business*. https://andjelicaaa.substack.com/p/the-experience-economy-is-blurring-the-lines-between-hospitality-and-retail-34f4d923c0ab

Ballantyne, D., & Nilsson, E. (2017). All that is solid melts into air: The servicescape in digital service space. *Journal of Services Marketing*, *31*(3), 226–235. doi:10.1108/JSM-03-2016-0115

Berry, L. L., Carbone, L. P., & Haeckel, S. H. (2002). Managing the total customer experience. *MIT Sloan Management Review*, *43*(3), 85–89.

Berry, L. L., & Parasuraman, A. (2004). *Marketing services: Competing through quality*. Simon and Schuster.

Birinci, H., Berezina, K., & Cobanoglu, C. (2018). Comparing customer perceptions of hotel and peer-to-peer accommodation advantages and disadvantages. *International Journal of Contemporary Hospitality Management*, *30*(2), 1190–1210. Advance online publication. doi:10.1108/IJCHM-09-2016-0506

Bough, V., Breuer, R., Maechler, N., & Ungerman, K. (2020). *The three building blocks of successful customer-experience transformations*. McKinsey & Company. https://www.mckinsey.com/business-functions/marketing-and-sales/our-insights/the-three-building-blocks-of-successful-customer-experience-transformations

Bowen, J. T., & Chen McCain, S. L. (2015). Transitioning loyalty programs: A commentary on "the relationship between customer loyalty and customer satisfaction". *International Journal of Contemporary Hospitality Management*, *27*(3), 415–430. doi:10.1108/IJCHM-07-2014-0368

Chang, S. (2018). Experience economy in hospitality and tourism: Gain and loss values for service and experience. *Tourism Management*, *64*, 55–63. doi:10.1016/j.tourman.2017.08.004

Cohen, M. C. (2018). Big data and service operations. *Production and Operations Management*, *27*(9), 1709–1723. doi:10.1111/poms.12832

Cser, K., & Ohuchi, A. (2008). World practices of hotel classification systems. *Asia Pacific Journal of Tourism Research*, *13*(4), 379–398. doi:10.1080/10941660802420960

Deloitte. (2020). *The future of hospitality*. Author.

Diebner, R., Silliman, E., Ungerman, K., & Vancauwenberghe, M. (2020). *Adapting customer experience in the time of coronavirus*. McKinsey & Company. https://www.mckinsey.com/business-functions/marketing-and-sales/our-insights/adapting-customer-experience-in-the-time-of-coronavirus

Dwyer, L., Edwards, D., Mistilis, N., Roman, C., & Scott, N. (2009). Destination and enterprise management for a tourism future. *Tourism Management, 30*(1), 63–74. doi:10.1016/j.tourman.2008.04.002

Gitlin, J. (2017). *74% of people are tired of social media ads—but they're effective*. SurveyMonkey.Com. https://www.surveymonkey.com/curiosity/74-of-people-are-tired-of-social-media-ads-but-theyre-effective/

Grove, S. J., Fisk, R. P., & John, J. (2003). The future of services marketing: Forecasts from ten services experts. *Journal of Services Marketing, 17*(2), 107–121. doi:10.1108/08876040310467899

Holbrook, M. B. (1994). The nature of customer value: An axiology of services in the consumption experience. *Service Quality: New Directions in Theory and Practice, 21*(1), 21–71. doi:10.4135/9781452229102.n2

Jayapalan, N. (2001). *Introduction to tourism*. Atlantic Publishers & Dist.

Kabadayi, S., Ali, F., Choi, H., Joosten, H., & Lu, C. (2019). Smart service experience in hospitality and tourism services: A conceptualisation and future research agenda. *Journal of Service Management, 30*(3), 326–348. doi:10.1108/JOSM-11-2018-0377

Kahneman, D., & Thaler, R. H. (2006). Utility maximization and experienced utility. *Journal of Economics*.

Kandampully, J., & Solnet, D. (2020). Competitive advantage through service in hospitality and tourism: A perspective article. *Tourism Review, 75*(1), 247–251. doi:10.1108/TR-05-2019-0175

Kandampully, J., Zhang, T., & Bilgihan, A. (2015). Customer loyalty: A review and future directions with a special focus on the hospitality industry. *International Journal of Contemporary Hospitality Management, 27*(3), 379–414. doi:10.1108/IJCHM-03-2014-0151

Kandampully, J., Zhang, T., & Jaakkola, E. (2018). Customer experience management in hospitality. *International Journal of Contemporary Hospitality Management, 30*(1), 21–56. doi:10.1108/IJCHM-10-2015-0549

King, C., Murillo, E., Wei, W., Madera, J., Tews, M. J., Israeli, A. A., & Kong, L. (2019). Towards a shared understanding of the service experience: A hospitality stakeholder approach. *Journal of Service Management, 30*(3), 410–428. doi:10.1108/JOSM-11-2018-0375

Knutson, B. J., & Beck, J. A. (2004). Identifying the dimensions of the experience construct. *Journal of Quality Assurance in Hospitality & Tourism, 4*(3–4), 23–35. doi:10.1300/J162v04n03_03

LeBlanc, C. (2021). *Cookie cutter or custom: What's the best approach in business?* https://catleblanc.com/cookie-cutter-or-custom-whats-the-best-approach-to-getting-your-business-problems-solved/

Lee, T. H., Jan, F. H., & Huang, G. W. (2015). The influence of recreation experiences on environmentally responsible behavior: The case of Liuqiu Island, Taiwan. *Journal of Sustainable Tourism, 23*(6), 947–967. doi:10.1080/09669582.2015.1024257

Lemon, K. N., & Verhoef, P. C. (2016). Understanding customer experience throughout the customer journey. *Journal of Marketing, 80*(6), 69–96. doi:10.1509/jm.15.0420

Lorentzen, A. (2009). Cities in the experience economy. *European Planning Studies, 17*(6), 829–845. doi:10.1080/09654310902793986

Mathwick, C., Malhotra, N., & Rigdon, E. (2001). Experiential value: Conceptualisation, measurement and application in the catalog and Internet shopping environment. *Journal of Retailing, 77*(1), 39–56. doi:10.1016/S0022-4359(00)00045-2

Mayfield, N. (2021). How your hospitality business can meet the needs of digital nomads. *Forbes.* https://www.forbes.com/sites/forbesbusinesscouncil/2021/03/12/how-your-hospitality-business-can-meet-the-needs-of-digital-nomads/?sh=c6068010d455

Mccoll-kennedy, J., Gustafsson, A., & Friman, M. (2015). *Fresh perspectives on customer experience.* Academic Press.

Mody, M., Suess, C., & Lehto, X. (2019). Going back to its roots: Can hospitableness provide hotels competitive advantage over the sharing economy? *International Journal of Hospitality Management, 76*, 286–298. doi:10.1016/j.ijhm.2018.05.017

Moreira, A. C., Fortes, N., & Santiago, R. (2017). Influence of sensory stimuli on brand experience, brand equity and purchase intention. *Journal of Business Economics and Management, 18*(1), 68–83. doi:10.3846/16111699.2016.1252793

Naumov, N. (2019). *The impact of robots, artificial intelligence, and service automation on service quality and service experience in hospitality.* Emerald Publishing Limited. doi:10.1108/978-1-78756-687-320191007

O'Gorman, K. D. (2009). Origins of the commercial hospitality industry: From the fanciful to factual. *International Journal of Contemporary Hospitality Management, 21*(7), 777–790. doi:10.1108/09596110910985287

O'Sullivan, E. L., & Spangler, K. J. (1998). *Experience marketing: strategies for the new millennium.* Venture Publishing Inc.

Page, R. A., & Williams, K. C. (2011). Marketing to the generations. *Journal of Behavioral Studies in Business, 3*(1), 37–53.

Papasolomou, I., & Melanthiou, Y. (2012). Social media: Marketing public relations' new best friend. *Journal of Promotion Management, 18*(3), 319–328. doi:10.1080/10496491.2012.696458

Parasuraman, A., Zeithaml, V. A., & Berry, L. (1988). *SERVQUAL: A multiple-item scale for measuring consumer perceptions of service quality.* Academic Press.

Parasuraman, A., Zeithaml, V. A., & Berry, L. L. (1985). A conceptual model of service quality and its implications for future research. *Journal of Marketing, 49*(4), 41–50. doi:10.1177/002224298504900403

Pine, J. B. II, & Gilmore, J. H. (1998). Welcome to the experience economy. *Harvard Business Review, 76*(6), 97–105. PMID:10181589

Pine, J. B. II, & Gilmore, J. H. (2011). The experience economy. *Der Markt, 38(3–4)*.

Pizam, A. (2010). Creating memorable experiences. *International Journal of Hospitality Management, 29*(3), 343. doi:10.1016/j.ijhm.2010.04.003

Radder, L., & Louw, L. (1999). Mass customisation and mass production. *The TQM Magazine, 11*(1), 35–40. doi:10.1108/09544789910246615

Ramgade, A., & Kumar, A. (2021). Changing trends of hospitality industry: Emergence of millennials and gen Z as future customers and their influence on the hospitality industry. *Vidyabharati International Interdisciplinary Research Journal, 12*(01), 336–342.

Rehman, J., Hawryszkiewycz, I., Sohaib, O., & Soomro, A. M. (2020). Developing intellectual capital in professional service firms using high performance work practices as toolkit. *Proceedings of the Annual Hawaii International Conference on System Sciences*, 4983–4992. 10.24251/HICSS.2020.613

Ryu, K., & Jang, S. (2008). DINESCAPE: A scale for customers' perception of dining environments. *Journal of Foodservice Business Research, 11*(1), 2–22. doi:10.1080/15378020801926551

Saleem, H., & Raja, N. S. (2014). The impact of service quality on customer satisfaction, customer loyalty and brand image: Evidence from hotel industry of Pakistan. *IOSR Journal of Business and Management, 16*(1), 117–122. doi:10.9790/487X-1616117122

Samala, N., Katkam, B. S., Bellamkonda, R. S., & Rodriguez, R. V. (2020). Impact of AI and robotics in the tourism sector: A critical insight. *Journal of Tourism Futures*. doi:10.1108/JTF-07-2019-0065

Schmitt, B. (1999). Experiential marketing. *Journal of Marketing Management, 15*(1–3), 53–67. doi:10.1362/026725799784870496

Sigala, M. (2005). Integrating customer relationship management in hotel operations: Managerial and operational implications. *International Journal of Hospitality Management, 24*(3), 391–413. doi:10.1016/j.ijhm.2004.08.008

Suleri, J., Meijer, R., & Tarus, E. (2021). Exploring hotel identity by focusing on customer experience analysis. *Research in Hospitality Management, 11*(2), 113–120. doi:10.1080/22243534.2021.1917178

Sundbo, J. (2004). The management of rock festivals as a basis for business dynamics: An example of the growing experience economy. *International Journal of Entrepreneurship and Innovation Management, 4*(6), 587–612. doi:10.1504/IJEIM.2004.005850

Walls, A., Okumus, F., Wang, Y., & Kwun, D. J.-W. (2011). Understanding the consumer experience: An exploratory study of luxury hotels. *Journal of Hospitality Marketing & Management, 20*(2), 166–197. doi:10.1080/19368623.2011.536074

Westcott, M. (2015). Introduction to tourism and hospitality in BC. Academic Press.

Wirtz, J., & Bateson, J. E. G. (1999). Consumer satisfaction with services. *Journal of Business Research, 44*(1), 55–66. doi:10.1016/S0148-2963(97)00178-1

Wirtz, J., Mattila, A. S., & Oo Lwin, M. (2007). How effective are loyalty reward programs in driving share of wallet? *Journal of Service Research, 9*(4), 327–334. doi:10.1177/1094670506295853

Zach, F. J., & Krizaj, D. (2017). Experiences through design and innovation along touch points. In *Design science in tourism* (pp. 215–232). Springer. doi:10.1007/978-3-319-42773-7_14

Zeithaml, V. A., Parasuraman, A., & Berry, L. L. (1985). Problems and strategies in services marketing. *Journal of Marketing*, *49*(2), 33–46. doi:10.1177/002224298504900203

Chapter 6
Corporate Museum Experiences in Enogastronomic Tourism

Mario Ossorio
University of Campania "Luigi Vanvitelli", Italy

ABSTRACT

Over the last years, an evolution of museum function has occurred. Museums are no longer considered just a treasure house but a place that matches cultural and commercial needs. Recently, the literature sheds light on their relevance to customers' experiences. The chapter aims to explore a specific category of museums, highlighting their many functions. More specifically, the chapter analyses the relevance of corporate museums in the enogastronomic industry. Two Italian corporate museums in the pasta industry are explored, highlighting their relevance for visitor experience needs.

INTRODUCTION

In recent years, the traditional cultural museum's mission has gradually lost its centrality, and other functions have become relevant for museum management. In fact, the reduction in public funding, the use of new technologies and customers' propensity to consider museums also as a pleasant experience associated with leisure and not just a treasure house have led museum management to combine cultural and commercial objectives (Caldwell & Coshall, 2002; Kent, 2010; Kesner, 2006). Under these circumstances, museums play a relevant role in the experience economy (Antón et al., 2018; Doering, 1999; Pine & Gilmore, 1999), and collections represent just one part of a wider array of offerings. While museums have been explored from several perspectives (archaeological, museological, managerial, etc.), scant attention has been devoted to the corporate museum (CM), which appears to be underexplored. Nevertheless, this kind of cultural institution has been receiving increasing attention from the business community, public institutions and visitors because of the great relevance connected to it being witness not just of a company but also of an industry and, more generally, of a territory.

The aim of this chapter is to shed light on the role of the CM in enogastronomic industry. The relevance of this topic is linked to the fact that, on the one hand, the recent past has shown how the CM may represent a cultural place to construct a multisensorial experience; on the other hand, the evolution

DOI: 10.4018/978-1-7998-8775-1.ch006

of enogastronomy has pushed customers to appreciate something beyond the strict consumption of food and beverages and also enrich culture, landscape, production methods connected to the food heritage experiences.

In order to investigate the experiences offered to enogastronomic tourists when they visit a CM, the chapter is divided into three sections. A theoretical first section (i) illustrates the changes that have occurred within museum management over the past decades, the factors affecting museum offerings, visitors' needs and the evolution of the museum mission. From this perspective, museums are analysed using the experience economy approach, highlighting that these institutions may offer entertainment, educational, aesthetic and escapist experiences. The second section (ii) describes the relevance of the CM and sheds light on its different scopes: preserving firms' documents and artefacts, strengthening brand identity, supporting firms' marketing mixes and witnessing the transformation of a territory and society. The third section (c) analyses the role of corporate museums in enogastronomic tourism, highlighting the evolution of the concept and the relation with a destination, the main tourists' motivations and the possible enogastronomic experiences. Furthermore, two best practices run by pasta family producers in Gragnano, an old town next to Naples, Italy, and the visitors' experiences connected to them are illustrated. Italy represents an ideal scenario both for the high presence of CMs and for the increasing flow of enogastronomic tourists.

CORPORATE MUSEUMS GENESIS

The Evolution of Museums: New Functions and Visitors' Experiences

Museums represent a relevant heritage destination and a primary tourist attraction for both local and foreign people (Jansen-Verbeke & Rekom, 1996). Over the past few years, museums have enlarged their missions. In the past, people tended to attribute to the museum an educational attainment (Barnard et al., 1980) and learning purposes (Thyne, 2001), and they identified museums as a place with local knowledge (McArthur & Hall, 1996). Over time, visitors have started to perceive museums as a place where they can spend leisure time and compare their visit to a form of consumption (Kesner, 2006). Consequently, while some decades ago Museum Directors and Curators were satisfied to reach a small narrow audience, nowadays they aim on increasing the number of visitors and revenue. Museums are no longer considered just a treasure house that collects and preserves objects but an information centre and a place where leisure, entertainment and identity-formation may be found (Trotter, 1998). Commercial and managerial objectives, combined with the introduction of new technologies and reductions in government budgets, have altered museums' traditional missions (Caldwell & Coshall, 2002; McPherson, 2006; Scott, 2005). Accordingly, museums are now arranging their activities to act as businesses, compete with alternative providers of educational services, and reach a wider audience.

The leisure function connected to museums helps to understand some dimensions often overlooked by museologists and art historians. Once a museum has been legitimately collocated within the leisure-time destinations, they could be logically considered as *constructions to facilitate experience* (Doering, 1999). Accordingly, the museum experience has been converted into a commodity that museums and heritage sites are expected to package and deliver (Kesner, 2006). Because visitors have several and distinct interpretations when they come into contact with exhibits or artefacts, it is important for museum administrators to understand and take them into account in order to adopt adequate managerial choices

(Goulding, 2000). This point is crucial because, on the one hand, museums face competition from other leisure activities, increasing operating costs and decreasing funding; on the other hand, museums have to improve their marketing mix in order to appear more appealing (Geissler et al., 2006). Accordingly, museums should adopt *visitor-oriented strategies* through a deeper analysis of visitors' preferences (Chan, 2009). Nevertheless, museums often delegate the control of exhibitions to curators whose main scope is to serve the art and not the visitor, reducing, consequently, the possibility of gathering more resources (Gofman et al., 2011).

The museum product embodies the sites, shape, lighting and means of stimulating interests (Goulding, 2000) and may be perceived as an experiential product that encompasses a wide set of experiences, such as feelings of fun and enjoyment, a break from routines, spending time with family and friends or learning (Arnould & Price, 1993). Visitors bring back home not so much the exhibits per se but the experiences that link them to their lives (Kent, 2010). Museum experiences involve learning, social, recreational, sensory and aesthetic dimensions (Kotler & Kotler, 2000). The wider the audience that the museum intends to reach, the greater and richer the variety of experiences that visitors require (Hiss, 1990; Kent, 2010; Kotler et al., 2008). Doering (1999) and Pekarik et al. (1999) have identified four clusters of museum experiences: object experiences (e.g. observing rare or valuable objects); cognitive experiences, which include gaining information or knowledge, or enriching understanding; introspective experiences, which focus on private feelings and experiences, such as imagining and reflecting; social experiences, which focus on interactions with friends, family, other visitors or museum staff. Kotler (1999) has pointed out that excitement, playfulness, contemplation and learning are the categories that constitute the range of recreational experiences in a museum (Kesner, 2006; Kotler, 1999).

Visitors' needs are also related to the setting. Bitner (1992) formulated the concept of "servicescape" to shed light on the features of the museum environment, such as temperature, illumination and noise, spatial configuration and functionality, signs and images that affect cognitive and emotional visitors' response to the environment, and, in turn, influence their experiences (Packer, 2008). Consequently, a museum should arrange settings that favour and improve experiences and remove barriers or constraints to them (Doering, 1999). In order to assure the museum's sustainability and survival, the experience it offers should be so gratifying that customers should be stimulated to repeat it (Antón et al., 2018). Accordingly, the museum should "deliver" experiences that emphasise "symbolic meanings, hedonic pleasure and subconscious responses instead of primarily stressing tangible benefits, utilitarian functions and conscious processes" (Holbrook & Hirschman, 1982, p. 132).

The kind of experiences that a visitor may have in a museum may be analysed taking into account the 4E model of Pine II & Gilmore (1999), in which the authors identified the following realms of experiences, depending on the customers' degree of involvement and engagement: entertainment, education, aesthetics and escapism. This model has been used in destination literature, such as bed-and-breakfast accommodation (Oh, Fiore & Jeoung, 2007), cruising tourism (Hosany & Witham, 2010), wine tourism (Quadri-Felitti & Fiore, 2012), musical festivals (Mehmetoglu & Engen, 2011) and in heritage tourism (Antón et al., 2018; Song et al., 2015). It considers two dimensions: customer participation and connection. The first dimension indicates how much the customer is able to influence the performance. At the end of the spectrum lies active participation, referring to customers who play key roles in generating the performance or the event. At the opposite end of the spectrum lies passive participation, where the "guest" joins the event as an observer or listener.

The connection dimension which unites customers on the basis of performance has absorption at one end and immersion on the other end. Being absorbed in an experience entail being mentally involved in the experience. Observing a landscape immersed in the sounds and smell of nature is more immersing than watching a documentary on TV. One of the main motives that stimulate people to attend an event-specific place is to engage in activities that they do not have the possibility of experiencing in daily life and to which they may have access only as a traveller or an eventgoer (Getz, 2008).

Educational experiences in a museum involve more active participation, but the customers' connection is more likely absorption than immersion. Because of their nature, museums offer opportunities for learning, acquiring information or increasing one's knowledge—regardless of the kind of collection—through offerings such as historical amusements, art exhibits, guided tours and audio guides interpreting the museum offerings (Raajpoot et al., 2010; Radder & Han, 2015).

An entertainment experience typically features passive absorption through the senses (Manthiou et al., 2014; Radder & Han, 2015). It entails that the customer is more passively than actively involved in the creation of the performance. Customers tend to be external to the event rather than immersed in the action. Because the observation occurs from outside, there is a low connection with the event. Visiting several rooms and galleries and adopting interactive equipment may represent museum activities that offer fun and pleasure to a visitor (Antón et al., 2018). When social, informative and fun aspects overlap, it is referred to as edutainment (Pine & Gilmore, 1999).

Aesthetic experiences entail that customers are simultaneously immersed in a unique environment and are able to enjoy it passively. In a heritage context, infrastructure, locations and intangible factors are essential to stimulate the imagination as well as visual and haptic perceptions using sensory triggers (Antón et al., 2018; Radder & Han, 2015). Physical space, lighting, colour and means of stimulating interest are essential in a museum (Rentschler & Gilmore, 2002).

Escapist experiences allow the customer to participate actively in an event and, simultaneously, to be immersed in the environment: "The escapist experience is highly immersive wherein consumers are engrossed in a different time or place" (Quadri-Felitti & Fiore, 2012, p. 8). This kind of experience can raise awareness, stimulate the imagination, and help visitors find magic, delight, and ecstasy in artefacts and offer a break from the routine of everyday life (Chauhan, 2006; Timothy & Nyaupane, 2009). Escapism is the main motivation for visiting a museum, followed by learning and sharing time with friends and family (Mannell & Iso-Ahola, 1987; Slater, 2007).

In recent years scholars have focused on a new type of museum, the corporate museum. As described below, it is connected to a company and is used as a marketing device, a source of inspiration for future products, a way to preserve the sense of identity of the organisation. In addition, the peculiar features of a CM make it a place where visitors may have interesting experiences.

Corporate Museums: A Bridge between Culture and Management

Over the last decades, firms have no longer been considered just as organisations producing goods and services aimed at maximising a profit, but, at an increasing pace, they are being viewed as a cultural institution, witnessing the change occurring in society. The contraposition of culture and economy, reflecting both the occidental humanistic culture and the anticapitalistic approach (Calabrò, 2000; Gilodi, 2002; Ruozi & Salvemini, 1999), led for many years to a lack of management of cultural heritage. Historians and archaeological scholars have begun to mitigate the divergence which exists between history and day-to-day life, and, consequently, the history of a civilisation has increasingly become the history of transformation in terms of the production of goods and services aimed at satisfying human needs

Corporate Museum Experiences in Enogastronomic Tourism

(Montella, 2010). Each industrial object represents several histories, and a museum may bear witness to the history of consumption, techniques, designs and tastes (Kaiser, 1988; Quintiliani, 2015).

A corporate museum may be defined as "a corporate facility with tangible objects and /or exhibits, displayed in a museum-like setting that communicates the company history, operations, and /or interests of a company to employees, guests, customers, and /or the public" (Danilov, 1992, p. 4). They are owned by a company, collect and exhibit different objects, and generally are located around the factory or corporate headquarters and are managed by the companies themselves or by the foundation to which companies donated the collection to be shown. They permit retracing not just knowledge about techniques in a certain historical age but also the productive and economic development process generated by the corporation, and therefore by the community in which the firm is situated (Fanfani, 2002). Objects exposed in CMs illustrate firms but also the societies beyond those firms.

In addition, overall organisational culture has gradually shifted from being an object that is interesting from a historical perspective to being one which interesting from a managerial perspective too (Severino & Leombruno, 2008) concerning firms that have existed for a long time and have a history and memory to preserve and exhibit.

Therefore, the great challenge for CM management is to switch from a view where industrial artefacts are considered something to preserve and which visitors can just admire them to a view that offers a learning and experiential process rooted in industrial heirlooms, where visitors are actively engaged, thereby extending the simple and traditional preserving function of the museum (Montemaggi & Severino, 2007; Pozzi, 2016).

Since the end of the 18th century, firms have exhibited the desire to display photographs, technical products and technological know-how (Bonti, 2014; Stigliani & Ravasi, 2007) to collect, document and preserve corporate histories and memories (Nissley & Casey, 2002). CMs collect artefacts, historical documents and corporate legal acts that, on the one hand, testify to the tangible corporate heritage and, on the other hand, represent an asset with great symbolic charge; in that sense, they constitute the intangible corporate heritage (Lehman & Byron, 2007; Quintiliani, 2015; Stigliani & Ravasi, 2007). Restructuring, inventorying and categorising the objects that characterise the different phases of a firm's life cycle are essential to preserve, systematise, and focus the corporate memory (Nissley & Casey, 2002; Severino & Leombruno, 2008).

Clearly collecting elements from a specific firm also entails demonstrating the history and the evolution of the industry in which the firm operates (Danilov, 1991). Furthermore, collecting a firm's artefacts, objects, and machinery allows scholars to better understand the behaviours and the success of that firm. In fact, a resource-based view (Barney, 1991; Wernefelt, 1984) reveals how firms' capabilities, know-how and resources may affect long-term competitive advantage. Consequently, tangible and intangible resources may support scholars to comprehend a firm's performance and, more broadly, the industrial dynamics. The collaborations between management and business history scholars on this topic represent an interesting example of the effort in that regard (Kipping & Üsdiken, 2008; Pozzi, 2016).

If preserving corporate memorabilia may be a spontaneous process, the creation of an archive or a museum implies the investment of financial and human resources, and thus CMs were born at the impulse of great firms. With regard to Italy, only at the end of the 20th century did firms begin to exhibit their memorabilia through archives and museums, also because management considered the firm's documents to be secret and industrial artefacts as something to be jealously protected.

Within managerial studies, CMs have generally been explored from a marketing perspective, which emphasises the relevance of a museum in strengthening organisational identity with respect to internal and external stakeholders (Gilodi, 2002; Martino, 2013; Olins, 1989; van Riel & Balmer, 1997). In a CM, the safeguarding of products, ads and photographs sheds light on what the corporation is and what it symbolises, in other words, organisational identity (Stigliani & Ravasi, 2007). Marketers and designers may consider artefacts archived in a CM to be a source of inspiration based on corporate heritage, for instance, to protect the continuity and uniqueness of style. These tangible manifestations of corporate history may support organisational members in building or protecting a sense of identity for their organisation (Ravasi & Schultz, 2006).

Organisational identity is relevant to differentiate firms from competitors in global competition (Korzeniowski, 2006). In fact, a CM permits a firm's history to be valued, as well as its ancient bonds with a territory, its longevity, the values underlying the brand, and, in turn, the specific traditions of the firm. Not every firm may use this mode of communication. This is particularly true for the sort of firm which has survived for several generations, or which produces cult products. Under these circumstances, CMs represent a marketing channel aimed at strengthening brand awareness. They are used to sustain communication strategies and events that leverage the firm's heritage, e.g. product milestones and leading personalities. This second function has witnessed the evolution of the CM from a passive collection of industrial artefacts to it increasingly becoming a marketing tool (Bonti, 2014; Pastore & Vernuccio, 2006; Gilodi, 2002) and a "good lounge" (Fanfani, 2002).

With regard to the CM's communicational function, it is worth noting that the CM projects messages not just outside but also inside the firm. It protects the firm's culture, which exerts a sense of cohesion (Amari, 1997). In addition, external stakeholders judge a firm mainly by observing the products, their originality, quality, and from these features, they indirectly formulate some ideas on values, beliefs, culture and competencies. When products' features influence positively the prestige and status of the corporation, workers will show a higher level of identification with the firm (Stigliani & Ravasi, 2007).

Corporate heritage may represent a relevant source of inspiration in order to reflect on past iconic products and to revitalise or restyle them or to propose again advertising characters or situations in a modern way: for instance, vintage images of Coca-Cola or the restyling of old Barilla packaging to celebrate the anniversary of the Unification of Italy (Pozzi, 2016).

A further function of the CM is the relationship with the territory and community in which it is situated. Put differently, the CM may express the social responsibility of the company (Bonti, 2014). In fact, on the one hand, the artefacts, photographs and documents exhibited in a CM describe the changes in traditions, habits, competencies and know-how of a certain society. Put differently, a CM is able to show and promote historical, social and cultural values. On the other hand, it may represent an attractive destination in heritage tourism and stimulate other leisure initiatives complementary to the CM, as well as research on business history, the development of creativity and innovation, which, in turn, creates an opportunity for tourism and the territory (Quintiliani, 2015). Under these circumstances, the CM may represent a stronghold for the territory, territorial communities and public institutions.

Lastly, the foundation of a CM may affirm and improve a company's reputation. This is very important both to expand products to new target markets where the firm is not yet well known and to expand into foreign markets. Analysis of the CM experience may be generated through the corporate storytelling narrated via objects, photographs, characters, iconic cult products aimed at enriching customers' learning and leisure needs. Visitors may satisfy their needs during a visit to a CM and, according to the arrangement of physical layout, be actively engaged or, conversely, passive spectators. Piatkowska (2014) analysed several CMs founded by automotive companies and identified several experiences that may have visitors equate the *thrill associated with sports cars to the aesthetic character of euphoria* and experience an interactive exhibition of design process and marketing strategies aimed at strengthening the exclusivity of the brand.

Corporate Museums in Enogastronomic Tourism

Enogastronomic Tourism: Definitions, Tourist Motivations and the Role of Experiences

In this section, two corporate museums producing pasta will be analysed. In order to comprehend more deeply the experiences offered by these corporate museums and required by their visitors and because of the relevance of the industry, an overview of the features of enogastronomic tourism is illustrated in the next paragraphs

Over the last years, several socio-economic features have led to a rise in enogastronomic tourism (Guzel & Apaydin, 2016; Tikkanen, 2017). The actual concept goes beyond the strict consumption of local speciality food, which still continues to represent part of a wider array of products and services. In fact, many enogastronomic products exhibit symbolic traits and offer emotional sensations because they directly evoke a certain territory and its ancient traditions and culture and permit to hand down people's behaviours to the next generations (Asero & Patti, 2009). The land of origin of food or wine specialities represents not only a simple logistic context but becomes a central element of a destination's offering. In this perspective, the consumption of local food and beverages represents a relevant attraction, such as exploring local culture and territories.

Enogastronomic tourism represents a social phenomenon that mixes the environment (climate and geography) and culture (religion, history, ethnic diversity, traditions, values and beliefs) (Seyitoğlu & Ivanov, 2020), incorporating the latter in foods and beverages that are peculiar to a geographical area. It also encompasses the materials, techniques, flavours, recipes and manners that belong to a specific region (Harrington, 2005). In fact, through food and drink, travellers may appreciate an abstract culture using tangible means (Lin & Mao, 2015). Because of its strong connections with the territories of its origin, food can be considered to be a linkage between the authenticity of a territory and tourists who are stimulated by an increasing motivation for genuine and engaging experiences that are closely connected to the peculiarities of the territory visited (de Salvo et al., 2013; Nocifora et al., 2011).

Gastronomic tourism may be represented by a travel experience in an area with distinct gastronomy that implies visits to food producers, gastronomic and culinary events, rural markets and other activities strictly related to food. In this approach, gastronomy represents the main driver for choosing a tourist destination. (Pavlidis & Markantonatou, 2020; Sharples & Hall, 2004). Smith & Xiao (2008) pointed out travels where experience is not the first objective, but it is considered to be very relevant in selecting the travel destination, because tourists eat not just to satisfy their hunger but also to learn, value and experience local culture through local ethnic gastronomic products. Long (2004) revealed that the gastronomic tourist is driven to discover new flavours, and food represents an extraordinary means to discover new cultures and lifestyles.

The abovementioned definitions emphasise the relevance of the experience for travellers. In other words, each tourist is not satisfied with just tasting typical foods and beverages. The individual intends to feel engaged in the typical context that they are visiting. Many studies on gastronomic tourism have focused on the motivations and typologies of tourists towards gastronomy (Seyitoğlu & Ivanov, 2020). Hjalager (2004) identified diversionary and recreational travellers as ones who prefer familiar food and are not much interested in local foodstuffs. Consequently, they do not consider food as a peak experience. On the other side, existential and experiential travellers have a stronger interest in local food, which is perceived as a peak experience. Boyne et al. (2003) considered travellers' effort to seek food-related information during their travel and identified the following groups: (a) travellers who actively seek information on food when they travel to a destination; (b) passive travellers, who may be interested in information on food only when they come cross it; and (c) uninterested travellers who may join in food-related activities anyway. Local food may be actively sought out by authenticity seekers; it is consumed but not actively searched for by passive travellers, and it is not preferred by comfort seekers, who seek familiar food in a familiar environment.

Björk and Kauppinen-Räisänen (2016) identified the following categories of gastronomic tourists: (i) experiencers, who judge food and food-related activities as essential; (ii) enjoyers, who also value gastronomy during their vacation, although their main scope is not gastronomic activities; and (iii) survivors, who view the local food as a means to satisfy their physiological needs.

Through the different typologies offered by previous studies, Quan and Wang (2004) emphasised that local food may represent a peak experience if it is perceived as the main motivation of the traveller, or it is a supporting experience if food just represents a need. Under these circumstances, travellers who value local food will particularly appreciate gastronomic events because they allow a high-value multisensorial experience. On the other hand, gastronomic events are able to boost the attractiveness of a place, generating economic benefits for the community.

Therefore, within enogastronomic literature, scholars have emphasised the relevance of the experience connected to the consumption of food and beverages. Over the last decades, experience has increasingly become a firm's source of a durable competitive advantage: "As services, like goods before them, increasingly become commoditised—think of long-distance telephone services sold solely on price—experiences have emerged as the next step in what we call the progression of economic value" (Pine II & Gilmore, 1998). Firms' efforts to differentiate themselves in the experience economy leverage services as the stage and products as the props in order to package and offer memorable experiences. While previous economic offerings, such as commodities, goods or services, are not personal, experience lives only in the mind of an individual and cannot be the same as the experience of another individual. Each experience is exclusive because it is created by the interaction between the staged event and the state of mind of the individual (Pine II & Gilmore, 1998). Accordingly, a corporate museum in enogastronomic industry represents a relevant setting to explore under the experience economy perspective. In fact, on the one hand, corporate museums allow to have a wide range of experiences such as recreational, celebrating, visual, esthetic, sensory, sociable, educational (Kotler & Kotler, 2000; Radder & Han, 2015). On the other hand, as described above, many enogastronomic tourists consider the experience a relevant factor in choosing the enogastronomic tourism is featured destination.

CORPORATE MUSEUMS PRAXIS

Enogastronomic Experiences in La Fabbrica Della Pasta Di Gragnano and in Il Museo Della Pasta

The surveys presented below were carried out in freshly constructed corporate museums in Italy: La Fabbrica della Pasta di Gragnano and Il Museo della Pasta. The examples were chosen because of their location (in a single country) and business branch that provides similar general circumstances.

La Fabbrica Della Pasta di Gragnano

The town of Gragnano (Na) has been well known for its excellent pasta producers since the fifteenth century. Breezes coming from the sea and from the mountains generate a unique dry microclimate that makes Gragnano an ideal setting to produce pasta. The ancient pasta tradition was evident from the high number of pasta sellers in Gragnano in the seventeenth century, which led to the need to regulate a minimum distance between different shops through a Papal Decree in 1641. The production process became more and more mechanised from the end of the 19th century on[1].

Fabbrica della Pasta di Gragnano, run by the Moccia family, is a CM located in the factory, which hosts a collection of ancient artefacts coming from the first family-controlled factories. The location is featured on tiles on the walls that recall the colour of wheat. The museum exhibits ancient wooden presses of extraordinary workmanship, bamboo canes for drying pasta, ancient dies and tools, and very rare images and photos of Gragnano. More than 500 tools, some of which date back to the eighteenth century, are jealously preserved and displayed.

During the tour of the CM, many ancient anecdotes are told about things such as roads full of carts loaded with sacks of durum wheat semolina during the past centuries, the scent of dried pasta hanging on bamboo canes "caressed" by the winds of the Lattari mountains and the Sorrento gulf, the noise made by the "*scugnizzi*" (street urchins), who picked up the broken pasta, and the trumpets of street vendors. During the tour, the ancient pasta production methods, such as hand pressing (in ancient times) and the mechanical ones, such as the precious mixture pushed through a bronze die, are shown, and il "Pastaio" explains some of the 32 secrets of the "true" pasta of Gragnano, making the guided tour evocative of "time travel". The experience comes to an end with tastes of creative dishes, both traditional and innovative, based on pasta.

Il Museo Della Pasta

Museo Pasta Cuomo is a CM run by one of the oldest family businesses operating in the pasta industry and hosted in ancient spaces occupied by the old "Antica Fabbrica di Paste Alimentari Cuomo". This CM illustrates the family's efforts to invest in corporate culture to strengthen brand identity and differentiate themselves from many other producers in a global and competitive arena.

This museum offers multiple kinds of experiences. First, the location hosting the museum represents a very precious example of archaeology and cultural heritage. In fact, it represents the ancient building where the durum wheat was taken to be transferred to the ancient Cuomo mill in the back of the building to be minced. This is the only building in Gragnano with iron ceilings and vaults made entirely of bricks.

It has been renovated in full compliance with the originally conceived architectural, urban and stylistic characteristics, reflecting respect for the territory's ethic, aesthetic, and cultural value.

Second, the ancient places in which the oldest pasta producers lived over the last 200 years, namely the old mill and pasta factory of 1904 belonging to the Cuomo family, are virtually recreated to permit the visitors to experience the ancient atmosphere under the guidance of the avatar of the ancestor Niccolino Cuomo. Old documents and archaeological finds may be admired, and visitors may appreciate a sensorial gallery where they can smell the flavour of typical dishes described during the tour. A room with virtual reality visors allows visitors to know the history of the Cuomo family and the ancient pasta production method in an immersive experience.

In addition, another experience offered by the company is the *fusilli, cooking and granma homemade pasta classes* in order to improve customers' own competencies in the art of make pasta. Lastly, to be fully immersed in the pasta producers' environment, it is possible to spend time in the bed and breakfast run by the Cuomo family, located in the old pasta makers' building.

CONCLUSION

Museums' needs for additional funding, together with visitors' preference to also experience museums in their leisure time, have been turning museums into places not only where objects are preserved and exhibited but into institution with a wider mission and in competition with concurrent providers of educational services. The museums' need to reach a more significant number of customers is stimulating the achievement of both cultural and commercial objectives. This chapter sheds light on the role of experiences offered by museums that permit visitors to consider museums as places where they can spend their leisure time and not just places for learning purposes. More specifically, the chapter has pointed out the particular category of CM and its linkage to the enogastronomic industry, in which customers desire to have an immersive experience connected to food and beverage.

La Fabbrica della Pasta di Gragnano and il Museo della Pasta represent two interesting examples of CMs that may offer visitors unique experiences connected to enogastronomic tourism. In fact, these museums allow visitors to understand the evolution of the pasta industry over the last three centuries and consequently the evolution of the production methods, tools and processes in addition to the history of the old family-controlled factories that to today operate in the competitive pasta industry. In addition, the guided tour permits the discovery of ancient scenes of day-to-day life in that territory where the pasta industry represented a relevant engine of socio-economic development. The sensorial gallery enhances the experience connected to the visit. To make the visitors more engaged, in the case of the Museo della Pasta, classes are offered on hand-made pasta production.

As described in this chapter, over the last decades, the relevance of CMs has been increasingly grown. Simultaneously, the range of CM's functions has become wider. Nowadays, CMs are not just a place where photographs, documents and artefacts are displayed, but they represent a relevant marketing device, strengthens organisational identity, supports designers in developing new products. When CMs are owned by food and beverage producers, they may enhance the attractiveness of the territory it is collocated. In fact, the gastronomic touristss considers very relevant learning the traditions, the culture, and the methods of production featuring the destination they visit, and the visit of a CM allows them to satisfy their needs.

REFERENCES

Amari, M. (2001). *I musei delle aziende: La cultura della tecnica tra arte e storia*. Franco Angeli.

Antón, C., Camarero, C., & Garrido, M. J. (2018). Exploring the experience value of museum visitors as a co-creation process. *Current Issues in Tourism, 21*(12), 1406–1425. doi:10.1080/13683500.2017.1373753

Arnould, E. J., & Price, L. L. (1993). River magic: Extraordinary experience and the extended service experience. *The Journal of Consumer Research, 20*(1), 24–45. doi:10.1086/209331

Asero, V., & Patti, S. (2009). *Prodotti enogastronomici e territorio: La proposta dell'enoturismo*. XVI Rapporto sul turismo italiano.

Barnard, W. A., Loomis, R. J., & Cross, H. A. (1980). Assessment of visual recall and recognition learning in a museum environment. *Bulletin of the Psychonomic Society, 16*(4), 311–313. doi:10.3758/BF03329552

Björk, P., & Kauppinen-Räisänen, H. (2016). Local food: A source for destination attraction. *International Journal of Contemporary Hospitality, 26*(2), 177–194. doi:10.1108/IJCHM-05-2014-0214

Bonti, M. (2014). The corporate museums and their social function: Some evidence from Italy. *European Scientific Journal, 1*.

Boyne, S., Hall, D., & Williams, F. (2003). Policy, Support and promotion for food-related tourism initiatives. *Journal of Travel & Tourism Marketing, 14*(3-4), 131–154. doi:10.1300/J073v14n03_08

Calabrò, A. (2000). L'arte può farsi reddito senza perdere l'anima. Rapporti, ilSole24Ore.

Caldwell, N., & Coshall, J. (2002). Measuring brand associations for museums and galleries using repertory grid analysis. *Management Decision, 40*(4), 383–392.

Chan, J. K. L. (2009). The consumption of museum service experiences: Benefits and value of museum experiences. *Journal of Hospitality Marketing & Management, 18*(2-3), 173–196. doi:10.1080/19368620802590209

Chauhan, R. (2006). Heritage and cultural tourism. Delhi: Vista.

Danilov, V. (1991). *Corporate museums, galleries, and visitor centers: A directory*. Greenwood Press.

Danilov, V. (1992). *A planning guide for corporate museums, galleries, and visitor centers*. Greenwood Press.

de Salvo, P., Hernández Mogollón, J. M., Clemente, E. D., & Calzati, V. (2013). Territory, tourism and local products. The extra virgin oil's enhancement and promotion: A benchmarking Italy-Spain. *Tourism and Hospitality Management, 19*(1), 23–34. doi:10.20867/thm.19.1.2

Doering, Z. (1999). Strangers, guests, or clients? Visitor experiences in museums. *Curator, 42*(2), 74–87. doi:10.1111/j.2151-6952.1999.tb01132.x

Fanfani, T. (2002). Economical profitability and culture: a possible meeting in the historical archives and in the enterprise's museums. *Quaderni della Fondazione, 1*, 102-131.

Geissler, G. L., Rucks, C. T., & Edison, S. W. (2006). Understanding the role of service convenience in art museum marketing: An exploratory study. *Journal of Hospitality & Leisure Marketing, 14*(4), 69–87. doi:10.1300/J150v14n04_05

Getz, D. (2008). Event tourism: Definition, evolution, and research. *Tourism Management, 29*(3), 403–428. doi:10.1016/j.tourman.2007.07.017

Gilodi, C. (2002). Il museo d'impresa: forma esclusiva per il corporate marketing. *Luic Papers, 101*, 10.

Gofman, A., Moskowitz, H. R., & Mets, T. (2011). Marketing museums and exhibitions: What drives the interest of young people. *Journal of Hospitality Marketing & Management, 20*(6), 601–618. doi:10.1080/19368623.2011.577696

Goulding, C. (2000). The museum environment and the visitor experience. *European Journal of Marketing, 34*(3), 261–278. doi:10.1108/03090560010311849

Guzel, B., & Apaydin, M. (2016). Gastronomy tourism, motivation and destinations. In *Global issues and trends in tourism*. St. Kliment Ohridski University Press.

Hjalager, A. M. (2004). What do tourists eat and why? Towards a sociology of gastronomy and tourism. *Tourism (Zagreb), 52*(2).

Holbrook, M., & Hirschman, E. (1982). The experiential aspects of consumption: Consumer fantasies, feelings and fun. *The Journal of Consumer Research, 9*(2), 132–140. doi:10.1086/208906

Hosany, S., & Witham, M. (2010). Dimensions of cruisers' experiences, satisfaction and intention to recommend. *Journal of Travel Research, 49*(3), 351–364. doi:10.1177/0047287509346859

Jansen-Verbeke, M., & van Rekom, J. (1996). Scanning museum visitors: Urban tourism marketing. *Annals of Tourism Research, 23*(2), 364–375. doi:10.1016/0160-7383(95)00076-3

Kent, T. (2010). The role of the museum shop in extending the visitor experience. *International Journal of Nonprofit and Voluntary Sector Marketing, 15*(1), 67–77. doi:10.1002/nvsm.368

Kesner, L. (2006). The role of cognitive competence in the art museum experience. *Journal of Museum Management and Curatorship, 21*(1), 4–19. doi:10.1080/09647770600302101

Kipping, M., & Üsdiken, B. (2008). Business history and management studies. In G. Jones & J. Zeitlin (Eds.), *The Oxford Handbook of Business History* (pp. 96–119). Oxford University Press.

Kotler, N. (1999). Delivering experience: Marketing the museum's full range of assets. *Museum News*, (May/June), 30–61.

Kotler, N. G., & Kotler, P. (2000). Can museums be all things to all people? In R. Sandell & R. J. Janes (Eds.), *Museum management and marketing* (pp. 313–330). Routledge.

Kotler, N. G., Kotler, P., & Kotler, W. I. (2008). *Museum marketing and strategy – Designing missions: Building audiences, generating revenue and resources*. Jossey-Bass.

Lehman, K. F., & Byrom, J. W. (2007). Corporate museums in Japan: Institutionalising a culture of industry and technology. *9th International Conference on Arts & Cultural Management.*

Lin, L., & Mao, P. (2015). Food for memories and culture: A content analysis study of food specialties and souvenirs. *Journal of Hospitality and Tourism Management, 22*, 22. doi:10.1016/j.jhtm.2014.12.001

Long, L. (2004). *Culinary tourism: Exploring the other through food.* The University Press of Kentucky.

Mannell, R. C., & Iso-Ahola, S. E. (1987). Psychological nature of leisure and tourism experience. *Annals of Tourism Research, 14*(3), 314–331. doi:10.1016/0160-7383(87)90105-8

Manthiou, A., Lee, S., Tang, L., & Chiang, L. (2014). The experience economy approach to festival marketing: Vivid memory and attendee loyalty. *Journal of Services Marketing, 28*(2), 22–35. doi:10.1108/JSM-06-2012-0105

McArthur, S., & Hall, C. M. (1996). *Heritage management in Australia and New Zealand: The human dimensions.* Oxford University Press.

McPherson, G. (2006). Public memories and private tastes: The shifting definition of museums and their visitors in the UK. *Museum Management and Curatorship, 21*(1), 44–57. doi:10.1080/09647770600602101

Mehmetoglu, M., & Engen, M. (2011). Pine and Gilmore's concept of experience economy and its dimensions: An empirical examination in tourism. *Journal of Quality Assurance in Hospitality & Tourism, 12*(4), 237–255. doi:10.1080/1528008X.2011.541847

Montella, M.M. (2010). Museo d'impresa come strumento di comunicazione. Possibili innovazioni di prodotto, processo, organizzazione. *Esperienze d'impresa, 2*, 147-164.

Montemaggi, M., & Severino, F. (2007). *Heritage marketing: La storia dell'impresa italiana come vantaggio competitivo.* Franco Angeli.

Nissley, N., & Casey, A. (2002). The politics of the exhibition: Viewing corporate museums through the paradigmatic lens of organisational memory. *British Journal of Management, 13*(S2), 35–45. doi:10.1111/1467-8551.13.s2.4

Nocifora, E., de Salvo, P., & Calzati, V. (2011). *Territori lenti e turismo di qualità, prospettive innovative per lo sviluppo di un turismo sostenibile.* Franco Angeli.

Oh, H., Fiore, A. M., & Jeoung, M. (2007). Measuring experience economy concepts: Tourism applications. *Journal of Travel Research, 46*(2), 119–132. doi:10.1177/0047287507304039

Olins, W. (1989). *Corporate identity: Making business strategy visible through design.* Harvard Business School Press.

Pavlidis, G., & Markantonatou, S. (2020). Gastronomic tourism in Greece and beyond: A thorough review. *International Journal of Gastronomy and Food Science, 21*, 21. doi:10.1016/j.ijgfs.2020.100229 PMID:32834883

Pekarik, A., Doering, Z., & Karns, D. (1999). Exploring satisfying experiences in museums. *Curator, 42*(2), 152–173. doi:10.1111/j.2151-6952.1999.tb01137.x

Piatkowska, K. K. (2014). The corporate museum: A new type of museum created as a component of marketing company. *The International Journal of the Inclusive Museum*, 6(2), 29–37. doi:10.18848/1835-2014/CGP/v06i02/44436

Pine, I. I. J., & Gilmore, J. (1998). *Welcome to the experience economy. Harvard Business Review.* July-August.

Pine, I. I. J., & Gilmore, J. (1999). *The experience economy.* Harvard Business School Press.

Pozzi, D. (2016). *Heritage & profits: La storia come vantaggio competitive per l'impresa.* Liuc papers, 300.

Quan, S., & Wang, N. (2008). Towards a structural model of the tourist experience: An illustration from food experiences in tourism. *Tourism Management*, 25(3), 297–305. doi:10.1016/S0261-5177(03)00130-4

Quadri-Felitti, D., & Fiore, A. M. (2012). Experience economy constructs as a framework for understanding wine tourism. *Journal of Vacation Marketing*, 18(1), 3–15. doi:10.1177/1356766711432222

Quintiliani, A. (2015). Il Museo d'impresa: Rassegna della letteratura. XXVII Convegno annuale di Sinergie Referred Electronic Conference Proceeding Heritage, management e impresa: quali sinergie?

Raajpoot, N., Koh, K., & Jackson, A. (2010). Developing a scale to measure service quality: An exploratory study. *International Journal of Arts Management*, 12(3), 54–69.

Radder, L., & Han, X. (2015). An examination of the museum experience based on Pine And Gilmore's experience economy realms. *Journal of Applied Business Research*, 31(2), 455–470. doi:10.19030/jabr.v31i2.9129

Rentschler, R., & Gilmore, A. (2002). Museums: Discovering services marketing. *International Journal of Arts Management*, 5(1), 62–72.

Ruozi, R., & Salvemini, S. (1999). Cultura ed economia in valore cultura: Sue anni di premio Guggenheim. Impresa & Cultura.

Scott, C. (2005). Museums and impact: How do we measure the impact of museums? *Proceedings of the Eighth International Conference on Arts and Cultural Management.*

Severino, F., & Leombruno, A. (2008). La cultura imprenditoriale nei musei tematici e distrettuali. *Economia della cultura, 4,* 503-509.

Seyitoğlu, F., & Ivanov, S. (2020). A conceptual study of the strategic role of gastronomy in tourism destinations. *International Journal of Gastronomy and Food Science*, 21.

Sharples, L., & Hall, C. M. (2004). The consumption of experiences or the experience of consumption? An introduction to the tourism of taste. In *Food tourism around the world.* Routledge.

Slater, A. (2007). "Escaping to the gallery": Understanding the motivations of visitors to galleries. *International Journal of Nonprofit and Voluntary Sector Marketing*, 12(2), 149–162. doi:10.1002/nvsm.282

Smith, S. L., & Xiao, H. (2008). Culinary tourism supply chains: A preliminary examination. *Journal of Travel Research*, 46(3), 289–299. doi:10.1177/0047287506303981

Song, H. J., Lee, C. K., Park, J. A., Hwang, Y. H., & Reisinger, Y. (2015). The influence of tourist experience on perceived value and satisfaction with temple stays: The experience economy theory. *Journal of Travel & Tourism Marketing*, *32*(4), 401–415. doi:10.1080/10548408.2014.898606

Stigliani, I., & Ravasi, D. (2007). Organisational artefacts and the expression of identity in corporate museums at Alfa-Romeo, Kartell, and Piaggio. In L. Lerpold, D. Ravasi, J. van Rekom, & G. Soene (Eds.), *Organizational Identity in practice* (pp. 197–214). Routledge. doi:10.4324/NOE0415398398.ch11

Thyne, M. (2001). The importance of values research for nonprofit organisations: The motivation-based values of museum visitors. *International Journal of Nonprofit and Voluntary Sector Marketing*, *6*(2), 116–130. doi:10.1002/nvsm.140

Tikkanen, I. (2007). Maslow's hierarchy and food tourism in Finland: Five cases. *British Food Journal*, *109*(9), 721–734. doi:10.1108/00070700710780698

Timothy, D. J., & Nyaupane, G. P. (2009). *Cultural heritage and tourism in the developing world: A regional perspective*. Routledge. doi:10.4324/9780203877753

Trotter, R. (1998). The Changing face and function of museums. *Media International Australia*, *89*(1), 47–61. doi:10.1177/1329878X9808900108

ENDNOTE

[1] www.fabbricadellapastadigragnano.com

Chapter 7
If You're Happy, I'm Happy:
Emotion Contagion at a Tourist Information Center

Ondrej Mitas
https://orcid.org/0000-0002-7916-0511
Breda University of Applied Sciences, The Netherlands

Marcel Bastiaansen
https://orcid.org/0000-0003-2865-7859
Breda University of Applied Sciences, The Netherlands & Tilburg University, The Netherlands

Wilco Boode
Breda University of Applied Sciences, The Netherlands & Tilburg University, The Netherlands

ABSTRACT

An increasing body of research has addressed what a tourism experience is and how it should best be measured and managed. One conclusion has been to recommend observational methods such as facial expression analysis. The chapter uses facial expression analysis to determine whether the emotions of employees in the tourism industry affect the emotions of their customers, following a pattern of emotional contagion. The findings show that emotional valence and arousal are both contagious. Furthermore, the findings show that arousal is less contagious at a higher likelihood to recommend, likely due to higher employee arousal during approximately the middle third of their conversation. Furthermore, findings demonstrate that emotion measurement is now possible at reasonable convenience for the tourism industry and gives a unique insight into tourists' actual experiences that is more precise and valid than self-report alone, though with certain costs and stringent methodological limitations.

INTRODUCTION

An increasing body of research has addressed tourism experiences. Scholars have asserted definitions of what a tourism experience is, how it can be measured, and how it should best be managed. Two develop-

DOI: 10.4018/978-1-7998-8775-1.ch007

ments have recently occurred in this stream of research. First, several authors have presented the argument that emotions are the core component of experiences and offer the best entry point for measuring and managing experiences (Bastiaansen et al., 2019; Li, Scott, & Walters, 2015; Moyle, Moyle, Bec, & Scott, 2017; Skavronskaya et al., 2017). Second, several studies showed that emotions in tourism experiences could be effectively measured using unobtrusive multi-method approaches that capture the ebb and flow of emotion continuously over time from behaviour, the body, and the brain, creating additional insights over self-report alone (Bastiaansen et al., 2019; Bastiaansen et al., 2018; Kim & Fesenmaier, 2015; Shoval, Schvimer, & Tamir, 2018).

The present chapter extrapolates these developments to a novel technological development: facial expression analysis software, which automatically derives metrics of an individual's emotions based on digital video recordings of their facial expressions. The authors of the present chapter apply this software to address an important practical and theoretical issue in tourism: whether the emotions of employees in the tourism industry affect the emotions of their customers. The effect of emotions in one individual triggering a similar emotion in another individual is known as emotion contagion (Hatfield, Cacioppo, & Rapson, 1993). In this study, the researchers concretely use facial expression analysis at an urban tourist information centre to explain emotion contagion between visitors and employees. This study fulfils two goals: to determine if emotion contagion indeed occurs during interactions at a tourist information centre, and to determine if facial expression analysis is a viable methodology for measuring the continuous ebb and flow of emotion during such tourist experiences. These are crucial issues for the design and management of tourist experiences by destination management organisations, and for these organisations to optimally allocate employee selection and training resources.

Before addressing the empirical data, this chapter synthesises literature about tourism experiences in general, then zooms in on the crucial role of emotions, and how continuous emotion measurement such as facial expression detection has become increasingly accessible. The chapter then covers present knowledge about emotion contagion in employee-customer interactions. The context of the tourist information centre in Gent is explained, followed by the methods and findings of the empirical portion of the chapter. The findings highlight that emotion is contagious between information centre employees and visitors, further reinforcing the importance of emotion detection and management uncovered in the literature review. The chapter concludes with discussions of theoretical and practical implications and recommendations for future research.

LITERATURE REVIEW

Models of Experience

In their seminal book The Experience Economy, Pine and Gilmore (2011) asserted that experiences had become the highest level of economic offering. Furthermore, they distinguished four different types of experiences along with two variables: passivity and engagement. They termed passive experiences in which participants have absorbed entertainment, and those which immerse participants as aesthetic experiences. Active absorbing experiences are called educational in their framework, while active immersive experiences are escapist. Tourism scholars quickly recognised the congruence between Pine and Gilmore's central thesis about the crucial role of experiences in contemporary economic activity, and the fleeting yet memorable nature of tourism products (Pearce & Zare, 2017; Scott & Le, 2017).

Numerous models of tourism experience exist, based both on Pine and Gilmore as well as more fundamental scientific disciplines such as psychology. In a thorough and concise review (Scott & Le, 2017) present a number of orienting conclusions about these models: that their perspective is usually dictated by the discipline from which they originate, that it is not readily possible to combine or synthesise them, and that they generally miss opening the 'black box' of the tourists' mind to predict behaviour. In other words, tourism experience models have lacked the explanatory power needed to design experiences for tourists that would lead to predictable outcomes, by way of known psychological mechanisms. Based on these criticisms, Scott and Le (2017) recommend using a cognitive psychology perspective to study tourist experience, in the hopes that cognitive processes offer such mechanisms. They discuss the cognitive psychology variables of attention, emotion, memory, appraisal, and the closely related concepts of engagement, involvement, immersion, and cognitive absorption.

Along the same lines, Pearce and Zare (2017) presented the orchestra model of experience, wherein sensory, cognitive, affective, and behavioural 'sections' of a tourists' mind 'play' together to create what we call experience. By presenting several psychological components that come together in the mind to form an experience, the orchestra model represents a significant advance in understanding tourist experiences. The orchestra model does not show how these components interact to form an experience, however. To build on their metaphor, while they explicate the musical instruments in the orchestra of tourist experience, the harmony and melody of the music remain elusive. For this explanation, a discipline that looks deeper into the mind was needed, namely neuroscience. To that end, building on the work of Pearce and Zare (2017) as well as (Scott & Le, 2017), Bastiaansen et al. (2019) proposed a model of experience (Figure 1) which uses contemporary neuroscience knowledge to explain how different components interact to form the mental phenomenon we call experience.

Figure 1. Model of experience stressing the role of emotions as determining behavioural outcomes
Source: Bastiaansen et al., 2019

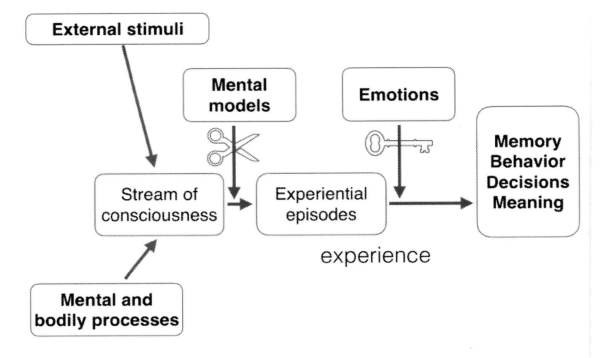

Bastiaansen et al. (2019) propose that external stimuli, such as the sight of a famous building, the sounds of fellow tourists talking on the street, or the taste of local food, combine with internal stimuli, including thoughts and bodily states. This combination produces an individual tourist's continuous, online sense of experiencing, often colloquially called *stream of consciousness*. Mental models such as 'museum visit' or 'dinner' are then used by the mind, much like a pair of scissors, to segment the stream of consciousness into discrete, coherent temporal blocks of experience, sometimes called *experiential episodes*. Most experiential episodes are soon forgotten, but some trigger emotions, such as joy, anger, love, or fear. It is now understood that these emotions are themselves combinations of pre-conscious affective responses, consisting of valence and arousal, and mental models for emotion types, such as joy or fear (Barrett, 2017). These emotions act as a signal to the mind that whatever is happening is important for the future. Thus, emotions act as a sort of key—when turned, emotions prompt an experiential episode to be stored in memory and possibly acted upon with a behavioural response (Fredrickson, 1998). The lack of a process model to explain how experiences are created in the mind, and the consequent neglect of emotions as a key explanatory variable, has been one of the main criticisms levelled at the Pine and Gilmore (2011) experience economy framework (Scott & Le, 2017).

Emotions are short-lived responses to behaviorally relevant stimuli and events. As such, different emotions are likely to occur rapidly and simultaneously during one and the same experiential episode. If the level of emotion during an episode is high enough, the episode is then entered into memory and spurs a tendency toward action (Fredrickson, 1998). Furthermore, it is well known in the psychology literature that stimuli and emotions entered into memory differ from the stimuli and emotions which are actually experienced. In other words, people are systematically inaccurate in recalling their emotions from past experiences (Gilbert, 2006). Emotions are remembered with different levels of intensity and valence than they are actually experienced (Zajchowski, Schwab, & Dustin, 2016). Some of these 'recall biases' have been empirically demonstrated in the context of tourism as well, for example, significant differences between emotions that students expected, reported daily, and recalled from spring break (Wirtz, Kruger, Scollon, & Diener, 2003). In general, this bias is toward predicted and recalled, rather than lived, emotions. In other words, people predict experiences to be more intensely emotional and more strongly balanced (negative or positive) and recall them as being more intensely emotional and more strongly balanced, than how they experience them in the moment (Gilbert, 2006; Wirtz et al., 2003).

Considering that memory is based on emotion, and emotion unfolds continuously over the course of an experience, we propose that measuring emotion continuously over the course of an experience is the key to the 'black box' of the tourist experience. Emotions explain why some experiences are remembered, shared, and acted upon, while others are not (Prayag, Hosany, & Odeh, 2013). Without continuous measurement during experiences over time, however, understanding of tourists' emotions is woefully incomplete.

Continuous Emotion Measurement

Until now, continuous measurements of emotion have been fairly rare in tourism research and carried severe methodological limitations, such as samples of just two participants (Kim & Fesenmaier, 2015). Tourism research has, for several decades, been based on a foundation of self-report data, often within cross-sectional research designs. As we have established, however, the continuous unfolding of emotional experience over time is not accessible to self-report, and requires continuous longitudinal measurement (Bastiaansen et al., 2019). Research participants can be asked to describe or rate how they experienced their emotions over time, sometimes in burdensome detail (Kahneman, Krueger, Schkade, Schwarz, & Stone, 2004), but these recollections are subject to substantial biases (Zajchowski et al., 2016), which are often themselves a topic of research and management interest. The experience can also be interrupted with requests of participants to report their current emotions, as with experience sampling, but then the targeted experience is disrupted and thus changed substantially. Conclusions from experience sampling thus cannot be applied back to the original target experience. This original experience, as designed, would have lacked the disruptions of experience sampling.

These two main limitations—recall biases and experience sampling disruption—have until recently prevented researchers and managers from accessing tourists' emotions as they occur. However, several technological innovations and improvements now enable us to measure emotion continuously and unobtrusively. When combined with self-report to measure behavioural outcomes, these technologies present a unique opportunity to understand emotions at the very moments that participants feel emotions and form memories. Three of these technologies include facial expression detection software, wearable hardware to measure peripheral physiological markers of emotion, such as skin conductance responses, and laboratory equipment to measure brain activity, such as electroencephalography (EEG) devices. All of these are able to measure emotion in a continuous, in-situ, time-based manner. A detailed review of how these technologies afford insights into tourism experiences is available (Bastiaansen et al., 2019). Skin conductance (Kim & Fesenmaier, 2015; Mitas, Mitasova, et al., 2020) and heart rate recordings (Mitas, Cuenen, Bastiaansen, Chick, & van den Dungen, 2020) as well as EEG recordings (Bastiaansen et al., 2018) have been used in tourism contexts. In the present study, we apply the less well-known facial expression analysis during an actual employee-tourist interaction, as this method is ideal for situations where context is held constant and stable facial video recording is possible.

Facial Expression Detection

Psychologists have used coding of facial expressions for emotion research since the development of the Facial Action Coding System (FACS; Ekman & Friesen, 1978). The FACS catalogues all possible muscle contractions or combinations of movements in the face within one of 28 action units. Additional action units describe the movements of the head, eyes, and gross behaviour patterns such as blinking and tilting the head and 'scrunching' the face. This approach has been applied frequently in past decades, and connections between reliable emotion inductions and facial action units are well known (Ekman, 1993; Cohn et al., 2007). Thus, multiple software developers have automated the facial coding process into software packages, which recognise the topography of faces portrayed on still or moving images and calculate the strength of each action unit, and combinations indicating emotion variables such as sadness, love, valence, or arousal. Noldus FaceReader, for example (Lewinski et al., 2014), derives levels of action units, the six basic emotions (joy, surprise, sadness, anger, fear and disgust) often described by Ekman and colleagues (Ekman, 1992), valence, and arousal in still photos and digital video. Digital video is analysed one frame at a time, essentially as a long series of stills. The resulting data need little other processing before analysis, although analysis methods used must be robust against missing data, as the software is very sensitive to shadows, eyeglasses, hairstyles that partly cover the face, head movements, and any other features that obscure a clear view of the face. While typically used with one camera to record the reactions of a single research participant, recording multiple participants within a single interaction using several cameras opens the door to interpersonal emotion expression and induction processes, such as emotion contagion, the main theoretical construct underlying the present study.

Facial expression detection has several substantial limitations. The above-mentioned requirements for the visual quality of the recordings limit its use to contexts that allow clear, stable videography of participants' faces. Also, critiques of facial expression research point out that covariation of facial expressions and emotions is dependent on context and on individual baseline facial behaviours (Barrett, 2017). Thus, research based on facial expression detection must be based on designs where context is held constant, including but not limited to non-target sensory stimuli and participants' cultural backgrounds. Furthermore, research designs for facial expression detection must support within-participant analyses.

Emotion Contagion

In an interaction between two people, an emotional display by one person is known to induce an emotion in the other person (Hatfield et al., 1993). While one sort of emotion in a person (for example, joy which is seen as undeserved) might sometimes prompt a different emotional reaction in another (envy), the emotions induced by emotional expressions of others are often congruent to the emotion expressed. For example, when seeing someone laugh, onlookers often begin to feel amused themselves. During emergencies, fear and panic spread from witnesses to nearby individuals who may be unaware of the original cause of danger. This phenomenon, usually called *emotion contagion*, has been studied in numerous interpersonal and organisational contexts, and at least twice in employee-customer conversations: a real-life experimental simulation of a video rental store (Hennig-Thurau, Groth, Paul, & Gremler, 2006) and a counter café (Barger & Grandey, 2006). Both show evidence that emotion contagion occurs in employee-customer conversations and predicts service outcomes. However, both studies treated emotion as unidimensional, looking at a rather narrow range of facial expressions, and thus of emotions, rather than the full range of emotions a person can experience.

While many conceptualisations of emotions exist in the psychology literature, the most widely accepted are basic emotion theory, which posits that most emotions are a blend of a few basic, foundational types, such as joy, fear, and sadness (Ekman, 1992); and circumplex theory, which posits that emotions are governed by independent systems which regulate their relative strength (arousal) and pleasantness (valence) (Posner, Russell, & Peterson, 2005). According to the circumplex theory, it is necessary to at least measure valence and arousal for a fairly complete picture of emotional experience. Recent work suggests that circumplex theory reflects the neurological underpinnings of emotion, while basic emotions reflect socially sanctioned mental models of the emotional menu in a given context (Barrett, 2017). In that sense, both basic and circumplex models of emotion are valid, while similarly asserting that a single dimension cannot capture emotional experience.

Besides giving an incomplete picture of emotion, both studies of employee-customer conversations miss the moment-to-moment recording of the contagion process, either recording participant emotions only retrospectively with self-report or at three moments during the conversation based only on a single action unit in the face. Thus, we wanted to know if (i) emotion contagion occurs continuously, *from moment to moment* in employee-customer conversations at an urban tourist information center, for valence and arousal, and (ii) if emotion contagion differs in for customers with different levels of intent to recommend the tourist information centre and the city. To address these questions, the employee-customer conversation was our unit of analysis, and while the customer was different in each conversation, the employee was the same across all conversations studied. Thus, there was no need for further nesting of time-ordered data within conversations. Besides extending knowledge on emotion contagion in employee-tourist interactions, our study aimed to test the practical feasibility of facial expression recognition, using widely available commercial hardware and software in an actual tourist experience context. As noted earlier, the context was held constant and primary analyses were within-participants to meet the limitations of facial expression detection. The similarity of context between and within participants and the stable presence of participants' faces during the measured experience made facial expression detection an ideal method for these questions and context.

Context: The Gent Tourist Information Center

Gent is the third-largest city in Belgium and one of Belgium's most popular tourist destinations. The main attractions are the buildings of the largely intact medieval city centre, which includes a UNESCO World Heritage belfry and beguinage, and a large castle and several cathedrals with museum exhibits inside. A handful of notable modern buildings are also frequently visited, along with several art museums. As a mid-sized, contemporary city in Northwestern Europe, Gent offers tourists experiences across the spectra of activity and engagement proposed by Pine and Gilmore (2011).

The Gent destination management organisation *Visit Gent* serves visitors at a Tourist Information Center (TIC) located in the medieval city centre. The TIC office features a wall of brochures and folders and a long table with interactive projections displayed on one end, and 2-3 employees with maps and computer monitors on the other end. Besides providing free maps and information, employees also sell the Gent City Card, which allows visitors access to museums, public transport, bike rental, and a boat tour. At the time of our study, employees of the TIC had recently been trained in soft selling skills, which emphasise the use of empathy and emotion to facilitate sales interactions. Thus, the Gent TIC was an ideal context in which to examine emotion contagion theory. By absorbing visitors and requiring their active participation, a conversation with a Gent TIC employee is best categorised as an *educational* experience in the entertainment-aesthetic-educational-escapist typology of Pine and Gilmore (2011).

METHODS

Sample and Data Collection

We measured emotion contagion between visitors and an employee at the Gent TIC using a convenience sample of 24 undergraduate student visitors. Using such a sample precluded generalising to a larger population but was important for the feasibility of the study in the first place, considering the multiple technical challenges involved. Transport by bus to Gent for the day was arranged for the entire sample. All participants were free to explore the city between 10:00 and 17:00 on the day of the data collection. Each participant was asked to visit the Gent TIC during a specific time slot during the day. During their visit to the TIC, they were instructed to converse with the employee in order to "get the most out of their day in Gent." To preserve the ecological validity of the experience, we did not further direct or specify the content of the conversation. Limiting the target experience to this conversation ensured that context was held constant across time and across participants, a requirement for facial expression detection research. Participants filled out brief questionnaires measuring their self-reported emotions before and after actually visiting the TIC. The post-visit questionnaire also asked participants to report their intent to recommend Gent and the TIC using 11-point Net Promotor Score® (NPS) items (Reichheld, 2003).

If You're Happy, I'm Happy

Facial Expression Recording

Each participant's visit inside the TIC was recorded using the smartphone cameras on two Samsung Galaxy S6s devices. One camera was situated behind the TIC employee and aimed at the face of the participant. The other was, conversely, behind the participant and aimed at the face of the employee. Both camera positions maintained an approximate distance of 3 meters between the camera and the participant. Figure 2 provides a reference to the view of the cameras in relation to the individuals being recorded. This placement allowed fairly unobtrusive, yet well-lit and direct-angle recording of both employee and participant's faces. Several weeks prior to the day of data collection, we conducted a small-scale pilot study with 7 participants to test for the technical feasibility of collecting the desired data. The design and location of the pilot study were identical to the main data collection. In the pilot study, we used additional Canon 550D DLSR cameras, as well as a set of GoPro Hero 4 Action Cameras, including Zoom Lenses (Figure 3). We then conducted planned data processing on both DSLR and smartphone camera data. Results and feedback from participants revealed that closer camera placement was disruptive and that camera angle, not resolution or size of the face, was crucial in producing recordings that the facial expression detection software could analyse. These pilot study outcomes justify our choice of smartphone camera use for the main data collection.

Figure 2. The uncropped camera angles for participants and employee. The camera was placed approximately 3 meters from the face, as to provide an unobstructed view and record the face even if the individual moved from their initial position

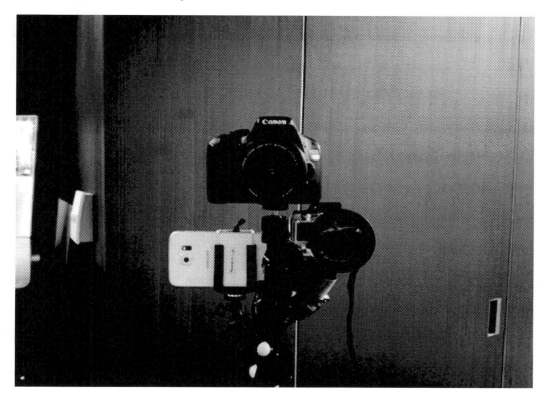

Figure 3. Setup used to test a variety of cameras and lenses on both the Participant and Employee side of the study. A Samsung S6 Smartphone, Canon 550D DLSR Camera, and a GoPro Hero 4 with Zoom Lens were used to determine video quality, usable distance, and view obstruction

Video recordings were edited to optimise lighting so that the target face (participant or employee) was as well-lit and as central as possible. The recordings were occasionally cropped by up to 50% to eliminate other faces from the frame, as the chosen analysis software was specifically developed for single-subject video footage. We ran the editing videos through the analysis function of Noldus FaceReader 7. The analysis produced a frame-by-frame coding of facial action units, as well as general indices of basic emotions, valence, and arousal. The present chapter focuses on valence and arousal. As most digital video records at 30 frames per second, the data were also originally produced at 30 measurements per second (30 Hz). We resampled this to 4 Hz to match other physiological data we recorded for another study. Conversations were resampled to identical durations.

Analysis

We began by graphing the data with points representing each conversation's valence and arousal. Then, we used mixed-effect random intercept linear models in R to model emotion contagion between employee and participant, using the intent to recommend as a moderator. Mixed-effect linear models nest the data within conversations, estimating a different ('random') intercept for baseline levels of the outcome variable in each conversation. The modelling process subsequently estimates the slopes for each coefficient between occasions within the average conversation. Such a within-participants modelling approach, wherein baseline differences between participants are partialed out, is a requirement for facial expression analysis. Separate models were estimated for valence and arousal dimensions of emotion, with participant emotion as the outcome variable and employee emotion, intent to recommend, and the interaction between employee emotion and intent to recommend as predictors. Finally, we averaged facial expression data for participants at each level of intent to recommend for 10% temporal segments of the conversation as a way of graphically probing significant findings from the mixed-effects linear models. While other studies use this 10% segmentation approach as an analytical framework (Nawijn, 2010;

If You're Happy, I'm Happy

Nawijn, Mitas, Lin, & Kerstetter, 2013), the present study preserves the sub-second temporal precision of the data for the initial analysis, using the cruder temporal segment approach only to illustrate and interpret the outcomes.

FINDINGS

Separate plots were produced for participants and employees, with the darkness of each point used to distinguish between conversations that ended with lower (dark) and higher (light) intent to recommend (Figure 4). To display the pattern of the average interaction, we also plotted a smoothed conditional mean over the data points. These graphs show that valence and arousal were generally highest at the beginning and end of the conversation, except for employee arousal, which started high, but remained level over the last quarter of the conversation. Visitor valence was higher at the beginning of the conversation compared to the end, while employee valence was higher at the end compared to the beginning.

Figure 4. Student-visitor participants' (above) and employee's (below) facial expressions showing valence (left panel) and arousal (right panel) in conversations at the Gent TIC

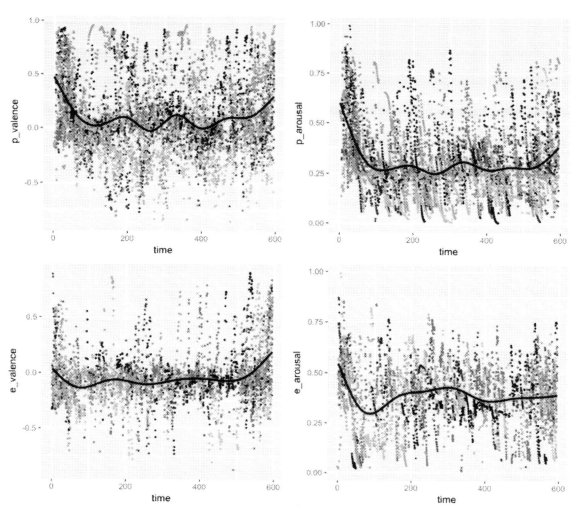

The model for valence showed no significant interaction between employee valence and intent to recommend, and no main effect of intent to recommend. There was a positive, significant effect of employee valence on participant valence (coefficient = 0.602, p < 0.001). In other words, moments of more positive employee facial expressions corresponded to moments of more positive participant facial expressions within the average conversation. Thus, valence between employees and participants was contagious. Furthermore, valence was equally contagious regardless of intent to recommend. The model for arousal showed a significant negative interaction between intent to recommend and employee arousal, indicating that employee arousal predicted participant arousal more strongly at lower levels of intent to recommend (coefficient = - 0.085, p < 0.001). Thus, arousal between employee and participant was also contagious, but more contagious at lower levels of intent to recommend (Table 1).

Table 1. Mixed-effects models of participant facial expression

Outcome	Predictor	Fixed effect coefficient estimate	SE	T	Model AIC
Participant valence					656.9
	(Intercept)	0.1056	0.3407	0.310	
	Intent to recommend	0.00584	0.04034	0.145	
	Employee valence	0.6024	0.01313	4.587***	
	Employee valence * Intent to recommend	-0.01659	0.01585	-1.047	
Participant arousal					-2015.5
	(Intercept)	-0.08607	0.12956	-0.664	
	Intent to recommend	0.04033	0.01532	2.632*	
	Employee arousal	0.93220	0.12859	7.249***	
	Employee arousal * Intent to recommend	-0.08471	0.01525	-5.556***	

Note: *** = p <0.001; ** = p <0.01; * = p <0.05

We graphed the data to determine during which part of the conversation employee and participant arousal differed for participants with high intent to recommend. Levels of participant arousal were averaged for 10 segments of the conversation (first 10% of the conversation, second 10%, and so forth) within each level of intent to recommend. The same was done for employee arousal. We then graphed these data of participant and employee arousal with separate lines representing different levels of intent to recommend (Figure 5). Finally, we took the absolute difference between employee arousal and participant arousal for each segment (first 10% of the conversation, second 10%, and so forth) within each level of intent to recommend. These differences were arranged on a line graph, with difference between employee and participant on the vertical axis, time on the horizontal axis, and each line representing the average of conversations corresponding to a different level of intent to recommend (Figure 6). Thus, the higher the line, the less contagious the emotion at that moment for those individuals. The graph showed that, for intent to recommend of 8, 9, and 10, differences peaked during the middle third of the conversation (segments 3-6). The graphs of employee and participant arousal showed that during these times,

If You're Happy, I'm Happy

in conversations that ended with a high intent to recommend, employee arousal was generally higher. Thus, for more highly recommending participants, the arousal shown in the employees' face—perhaps in the form of curiosity, surprise, or excitement—was not as contagious during the middle part of the conversation.

Figure 5. Average arousal in facial expressions of student-visitor participants (above) and employees (below) for 10% segments in time in conversations at the Gent TIC. Each line represents the average arousal in conversations with a specific level of participants' intent to recommend Gent

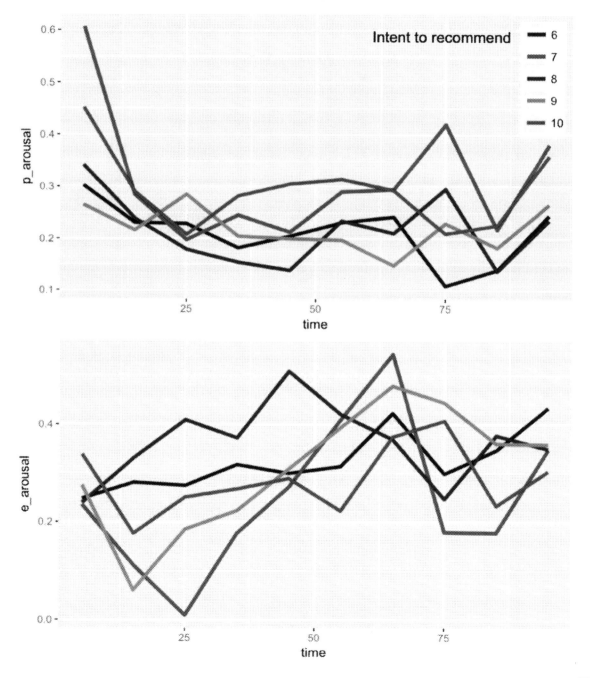

Figure 6. Absolute differences between average arousal in facial expressions of student-visitor participants and employee for 10% segments in time in conversations at the Gent TIC. Each line represents the average participant-employee difference for conversations with a specific level of participants' intent to recommend Gent

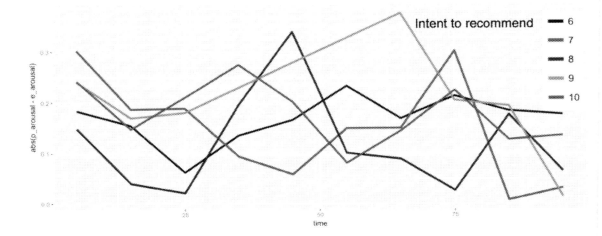

DISCUSSION

The findings show that emotion contagion occurs between tourists and an employee at a TIC, and that both valence and arousal are contagious in this context. This finding supports the use of emotion-based selling trainings in tourism, such as the program implemented at the Gent TIC shortly before the current data collection. Furthermore, the findings show that arousal is less contagious for tourists who are more likely to recommend the destination, likely due to higher employee arousal during approximately the middle third of their conversation. An intriguing possibility to test in future research is that the employee's curiosity or excitement about customers in the middle of the conversation engages them with the information being presented, helping them plan their day without necessarily making them overtly emotional until the end of the conversation. Thus, as part of training, tourism employees might learn that their enthusiasm is valuable even if it does not echo in the faces of tourists during informative interactions.

These findings contribute to existing knowledge on emotion contagion between employees and customers. Previous research used retrospective or self-report measures as evidence for emotion contagion, generally failing to document emotion contagion on the second-to-second temporal scale on which it generally unfolds. With data at this level of detail, we found that emotion contagion occurred both for valence and arousal. Furthermore, intent to recommend Gent moderated emotion contagion of arousal, suggesting that the content of an experience—in this case, an employee providing destination information—can change not only tourists' emotions, but the extent and nature of their emotional connection with an employee. In sum, we conclude that emotion contagion does occur at a TIC, and that TIC employees should receive training to understand and regulate their and their visitors' emotions.

The findings demonstrate that emotion measurement is now possible at reasonable convenience for the tourism industry and gives unique insight into tourists' actual experiences that is more precise and valid than self-report alone. Like all methods, however, facial expression analysis has substantial limitations and demands new analysis procedures. Failure to appreciate the missing data due to indirect camera angles in facial expression data can lead to conclusions that are actually less valid than more conventional self-report methods.

Facial expression detection discriminates between several types of emotion that are expressed in the face, as well as measuring emotional expressions on the valence and arousal dimensions of the circumplex model. However, facial expression detection is practically limited to contexts where clear photos or videos of facial expressions can be obtained without disruptive camera placement. As such, it can be used in the field, but not in situations of poor lighting or where a camera pointed at the face would alter participants' experiences. Although being recorded on video has become increasingly ordinary, due to the dual proliferation of security as well as smartphone cameras, people still react to a camera visibly pointed at their faces. Also, facial expression detection misses emotions that are too mild to be visibly expressed in the face, or where cultural norms suppress expression.

In recent years, facial expression detection has faced serious questions about its cross-cultural and cross-contextual validity (Barrett, 2017). While Ekman (2007) makes relatively strong claims about cross-cultural universality in emotion typology and facial expression, his Facial Action Coding System is designed for detecting variation within, not between contexts. In our study, the tourist information centre employee and customers shared a spatial, relational, and cultural context. In other words, our research design held context constant. It is therefore valid, we argue, to compare and statistically relate facial expressions in this context. Both advocates and critics of facial coding would agree, however, that trying to make such connections across contexts is not valid. Comparing individuals' facial expressions during everyday life to their facial expressions while vacationing in a different culture would not lead to trustworthy interpretations, for example. Furthermore, facial expressions at any given moment may differ between participants for reasons other than emotion. Thus, facial expression analysis is only meaningful when comparing changes in facial expressions within a single participant's experience to that participant's own baseline. Within-participant designs, such as the design used to collect data for the present chapter, are an absolute must.

Finally, we argue that while facial expression analysis is useful and advances insight into tourists' experiences by allowing continuous measurement of emotions, such new approaches to measuring tourists' experiences should always be part of mixed-method research designs that allow benchmarking against more conventional self-report methods. We particularly advise using qualitative research methods, which are uniquely suited to detect confounding variables and contextual influences, alongside behavioural measurement and quantitative self-report measures. Data from interviews, participant observation, or secondary sources such as social media postings can help explain unexpected findings and fill in gaps in video recordings of the face or cognitive biases in participants' recollections. More generally, because self-report data is necessarily retrospective, mixing facial and self-report data affords insight into the substantial yet under-researched differences between ongoing and recalled experiences (Zajchowski et al., 2016). In the case of the present study, for example, self-report was required to measure intent to recommend. Future research could, for example, follow up with participants to uncover if they recommended Gent in the days following the visit.

Furthermore, it is worth pointing out that, like in nearly all in-situ research on tourist experiences, the present study uses a non-probability sample, precluding generalisation to larger populations. Thus, replication of the present study and of empirical tourist experience studies, in general, is of utmost importance to convincingly test and extend existing knowledge on tourist experience.

Implications for Research and Practice

We have argued that emotions are essential ingredients that make experiences memorable, meaningful, and predictive of behaviour (Bastiaansen et al., 2019). Thus, effective tourism experiences can be designed, sold, and managed most effectively if customers' emotions can be measured across touchpoints. For many tour operators and destinations, however, this would entail a massive shift in thinking. They would need to see the experience as something not only designed but measured, and data as something obtained in agreement with customers, rather than passive outcomes of movements and transactions. Furthermore, as emotions come and go rapidly over the course of emotional episodes, unobtrusive and continuous measurement is necessary. Self-report measures of emotions, including smart kiosks and experience sampling on mobile devices, do not offer continuous measurement over time and additionally present a number of validity biases.

Measuring emotions through facial expressions can now complement self-report emotion measurement. We believe that industry practitioners and researchers could both benefit from the cooperation needed to implement such innovative yet challenging methods. For researchers, there is much to learn about the relationships among experienced and recalled emotions, and how these emotions affect downstream behaviour. These processes can best be elucidated using data collected in real-world tourism industry contexts. For tourism industry practitioners, understanding how their customers' minds work and predicting their future behaviour is crucial in the competition for their discretionary income and time. In that respect, continuous emotion measurement benefits the industry greatly, as the cost of emotion measurement technologies such as facial expression analysis continues to decrease.

It is worth pointing out a handful of other up-and-coming technologies here, and the potential they offer. Wearable wristbands such as the Shimmer and Empatica E4 measure heart rate and skin conductivity. These signals correspond with physiological arousal that is associated with emotion, and as such, are much less context-dependent than facial expression detection. Furthermore, wearables do not literally 'stare in the face' of participants. While participants are made aware of wearables at the start of recording, they do not continue to draw attention after that point, according to participants' anecdotal reflections on data collection (Nold, 2009). A shortcoming is that physical movements can introduce overwhelming noise into the signal in the form of artefacts which must be carefully removed from the data. Also, while they detect arousal, it is rather controversial if the signals from these devices also indicate anything about emotion valence (Kreibig, 2010).

Finally, a form of self-report designed to reduce recall biases called experience reconstruction has recently been presented (Strijbosch et al., 2021; Strijbosch et al., 2019). The idea behind experience reconstruction is that breaking an experience down into episodes—which is ideally done by the participant, but can also be done by the researcher—bring the participant cognitively "closer" to the experience being studied, thus making the affective recall more accurate (Kahneman et al., 2004). While overall recalled emotion, experience reconstruction, and arousal measured using wearables have been used simultaneously (Mitas, Cuenen, et al., 2020; Strijbosch et al., 2021), they have not yet been benchmarked against clear emotion inductions or outcomes. Such benchmarking is bound to be a fertile area for future research.

Besides measuring visitors' emotions, tourism managers are urged to pay attention to their employees' abilities to detect, regulate, and express emotions in interpersonal interactions. The Gent TIC undertook a soft selling skills training for employees shortly before the data collection reported here. This training focused on emotion and may have enhanced the positive, recommendable experiences of our participants. The strength of emotion contagion we measured, and the interaction with intent to recommend, suggests that continued attention of tourism managers to their employees' emotion perception and regulation skills is worthwhile.

Future Directions

Much work remains to be done in understanding tourism experiences and in developing experience measurement methods for optimum validity and reliability. As demonstrated, the limitations of facial expression analysis require combining facial video recording with qualitative and quantitative self-report measures. An important direction for future research is to explore how best to integrate data from multiple sources to gain a more valid yet sufficiently rich assessment of the tourism experience. Here, we point to the recent work on experience reconstruction as possible examples (Strijbosch et al., 2021; Strijbosch et al., 2019). Furthermore, the nature of experiences, as well as methodological challenges, are likely to differ across tourism contexts. Walking through a museum is a very different experience from cycling through a city. Facial expressions, in particular, are known to be context-dependent and require different complementary self-report datasets to give a clear picture of experiences therein, unless the context is held constant for the entirety of the study, as in the data presented in this chapter.

Facial expression analysis could be seen as an advance in experience research, but also as an "in-between" stage that produces data used to sharpen and validate ultimately more convenient self-report measures, or new, unforeseen technologies. It seems likely that the technological development which led to the measurement tools we used will continue, so that accuracy and convenience will improve while prices will become more accessible. More importantly, software is developing quickly, especially for open-source platforms such as Python and R.

Ultimately, we hope that better experience measurement will lead the tourism industry to adopt a more evidence-based approach to managing customer experiences, leading to better experiences and competition based on differentiation and quality rather than price. Such a change would have implications beyond the business of tourism, as positive experiences build individuals' quality of life (Lyubomirsky, King, & Diener, 2005). Furthermore, tourism experiences themselves are frequent sources of positive emotions and are important for the quality of life (Mitas, Nawijn, & Jongsma, 2017). Thus, improving the quality of tourism experiences—for example, through enhanced contagion of positive or empathetic emotions, or better employee training aimed at emotion recognition and regulation—could have a broader positive effect on tourists' quality of life, over and above the mere enjoyment of their vacations. Also, designing tourism experiences based on evidence from experience measurement could help tour operators develop equally enjoyable products without the high environmental or social impacts that characterise long-distance vacations (Nawijn & Peeters, 2010).

REFERENCES

Barger, P. B., & Grandey, A. A. (2006). Service with a smile and encounter satisfaction: Emotional contagion and appraisal mechanisms. *Academy of Management Journal*, *49*(6), 1229–1238. doi:10.5465/amj.2006.23478695

Barrett, L. F. (2017). *How emotions are made: The secret life of the brain*. Houghton Mifflin Harcourt.

Bastiaansen, M., Lub, X., Mitas, O., Jung, T. H., Passos Acenção, M., Han, D., & Strijbosch, W. (2019). Emotions as core building blocks of an experience. *International Journal of Contemporary Hospitality Management*, *31*(2), 31. doi:10.1108/IJCHM-11-2017-0761

Bastiaansen, M., Straatman, S., Driessen, E., Mitas, O., Stekelenburg, J., & Wang, L. (2018). My destination in your brain: A novel neuromarketing approach for evaluating the effectiveness of destination marketing. *Journal of Destination Marketing & Management*, *7*, 76–88. doi:10.1016/j.jdmm.2016.09.003

Ekman, P. (1992). An argument for basic emotions. *Cognition and Emotion*, *6*(3-4), 169–200. doi:10.1080/02699939208411068

Ekman, P. (2007). *Emotions revealed: Recognising faces and feelings to improve communication and emotional life*. Macmillan.

Fredrickson, B. L. (1998). What good are positive emotions? *Review of General Psychology*, *2*(3), 300–319. doi:10.1037/1089-2680.2.3.300 PMID:21850154

Gilbert, D. (2006). *Stumbling on happiness*. Alfred A. Knopf.

Hatfield, E., Cacioppo, J. T., & Rapson, R. L. (1993). Emotional contagion. *Current Directions in Psychological Science*, *2*(3), 96–100. doi:10.1111/1467-8721.ep10770953

Hennig-Thurau, T., Groth, M., Paul, M., & Gremler, D. D. (2006). Are all smiles created equal? How emotional contagion and emotional labor affect service relationships. *Journal of Marketing*, *70*(3), 58–73. doi:10.1509/jmkg.70.3.058

Kahneman, D., Krueger, A. B., Schkade, D. A., Schwarz, N., & Stone, A. A. (2004). A survey method for characterising daily life experience: The day reconstruction method. *Science*, *306*(5702), 1776–1780. doi:10.1126cience.1103572 PMID:15576620

Kim, J., & Fesenmaier, D. R. (2015). Measuring emotions in real time: Implications for tourism experience design. *Journal of Travel Research*, *54*(4), 419–429. doi:10.1177/0047287514550100

Kreibig, S. D. J. B. p. (2010). Autonomic nervous system activity in emotion. *RE:view*, *84*(3), 394–421. PMID:20371374

Li, S., Scott, N., & Walters, G. (2015). Current and potential methods for measuring emotion in tourism experiences: A review. *Current Issues in Tourism*, *18*(9), 805–827. doi:10.1080/13683500.2014.975679

Lyubomirsky, S., King, L., & Diener, E. (2005). *The benefits of frequent positive affect: Does happiness lead to success?* American Psychological Association.

Mitas, O., Cuenen, R., Bastiaansen, M., Chick, G., & van den Dungen, E. (2020). The War from both Sides: How Dutch and German Visitors Experience an Exhibit of Second World War Stories. *International Journal of the Sociology of Leisure*, *3*(3), 277–303. doi:10.100741978-020-00062-3

Mitas, O., Mitasova, H., Millar, G., Boode, W., Neveu, V., Hover, M., & Bastiaansen, M. (2020). More is not better: The emotional dynamics of an excellent experience. *Journal of Hospitality & Tourism Research*. doi:10.1177/1096348020957075

Mitas, O., Nawijn, J., & Jongsma, B. (2017). Between tourists: Tourism and happiness. In M. K. Smith & L. Puczko (Eds.), *The Routledge handbook of health tourism* (pp. 47–64). Routledge.

Moyle, B. D., Moyle, C.-l., Bec, A., & Scott, N. (2017). The next frontier in tourism emotion research. *Current Issues in Tourism*, 1–7.

Nawijn, J. (2010). The holiday happiness curve: A preliminary investigation into mood during a holiday abroad. *International Journal of Tourism Research*, *12*(3), 281–290. doi:10.1002/jtr.756

Nawijn, J., Mitas, O., Lin, Y., & Kerstetter, D. (2013). How do we feel on vacation? A closer look at how emotions change over the course of a trip. *Journal of Travel Research*, *52*(2), 265–274. doi:10.1177/0047287512465961

Nawijn, J., & Peeters, P. M. (2010). Travelling 'green': Is tourists' happiness at stake? *Current Issues in Tourism*, *13*(4), 381–392. doi:10.1080/13683500903215016

Nold, C. (2009). Introduction: Emotional geography technologies of the self. In C. Nold (Ed.), Emotional cartography: Technologies of the self. Academic Press.

Pearce, P. L., & Zare, S. (2017). The orchestra model as the basis for teaching tourism experience design. *Journal of Hospitality and Tourism Management*, *30*, 55–64. doi:10.1016/j.jhtm.2017.01.004

Pine, B. J., & Gilmore, J. H. (2011). *The experience economy*. Harvard Business Press.

Posner, J., Russell, J. A., & Peterson, B. S. (2005). The circumplex model of affect: An integrative approach to affective neuroscience, cognitive development, and psychopathology. *Development and Psychopathology*, *17*(3), 715–734. doi:10.1017/S0954579405050340 PMID:16262989

Prayag, G., Hosany, S., & Odeh, K. (2013). The role of tourists' emotional experiences and satisfaction in understanding behavioral intentions. *Journal of Destination Marketing & Management*, *2*(2), 118–127. doi:10.1016/j.jdmm.2013.05.001

Reichheld, F. F. (2003). The one number you need to grow. *Harvard Business Review*, *81*(12), 46–55. PMID:14712543

Scott, N., & Le, D. (2017). Tourism experience: A review. In N. Scott, J. Gao, & J. Ma (Eds.), *Visitor Experience Design* (Vol. 5, p. 30). CABI. doi:10.1079/9781786391896.0030

Shoval, N., Schvimer, Y., & Tamir, M. (2018). Real-time measurement of tourists' objective and subjective emotions in time and space. *Journal of Travel Research*, *57*(1), 3–16. doi:10.1177/0047287517691155

Skavronskaya, L., Scott, N., Moyle, B., Le, D., Hadinejad, A., Zhang, R., & Shakeela, A. (2017). Cognitive psychology and tourism research: State of the art. *Tourism Review*, *72*(2), 221–237. doi:10.1108/TR-03-2017-0041

Strijbosch, W., Mitas, O., van Blaricum, T., Vugts, O., Govers, C., Hover, M., & Bastiaansen, M. (2021). When the parts of the sum are greater than the whole: Assessing the peak-and-end-theory for a heterogeneous, multi-episodic tourism experience. *Journal of Destination Marketing & Management*, *20*, 100607. doi:10.1016/j.jdmm.2021.100607

Strijbosch, W., Mitas, O., van Gisbergen, M., Doicaru, M., Gelissen, J., & Bastiaansen, M. J. (2019). *From experience to memory: on the robustness of the peak-and-end-rule for complex, heterogeneous experiences*. Academic Press.

Wirtz, D., Kruger, J., Scollon, C. N., & Diener, E. (2003). What to do on spring break? The role of predicted, on-line, and remembered experience in future choice. *Psychological Science, 14*(5), 520–524. doi:10.1111/1467-9280.03455 PMID:12930487

Zajchowski, C. A., Schwab, K. A., & Dustin, D. L. (2016). The experiencing self and the remembering self: Implications for leisure science. *Leisure Sciences*, 1–8.

Chapter 8
New Paradigms of the Tourist Guide Profession

Ilídia Carvalho
Lusíada University, Lisbon, Portugal

ABSTRACT

In this chapter, using the Portuguese tourist guides as an example, the author intends to expose the reality of the profession and how it is nowadays necessary to adapt it to the new tourism paradigms. The pandemic, which has suddenly and deeply affected tourist guides, will also be one of the topics. A brief historical background of the profession will be given to be able to understand what a tourist guide is today, as well as the skills needed for the profession obtained through education and training, which are also one of the topics presented. The way these professionals have been dealing with digitals and how new technological tools are being used for the profession will be explained. Issues like authenticity, responsibility, and the contribution of tourist guides to develop tourism destinations will also be covered in the text.

INTRODUCTION

"The work of a tour guide is vastly misunderstood." (Pond, 1993, p. 13)

Tourism is changing and this presents challenges at several levels for those working in this activity. Tourist guides are one of the oldest tourism professions and, for centuries, they have been able to adapt to quite new situations, originating from cyclical or structural factors. Last century they overcame several economic, political, social and even technological changes, and, at this moment, they even need to face a pandemic. Once again, this profession is facing a deep change in tourism, and it needs to adapt simultaneously to new tourism trends and technological evolvement. As proposed by Weiler and Black (2015a, p. 366) "traditional one-way communication appears too limiting in an experience - and consumer centred tourism industry" as we have nowadays. In order to explain better the current situation of these tourist information professionals will be mainly used in this chapter the example of the Portuguese tourist guides.

DOI: 10.4018/978-1-7998-8775-1.ch008

Whenever someone travels in the world, there is always a need for someone to show the way or to interpret the different places and cultures visited. That person is the tourist guide, who even today can take on different roles that are essential for the success of tourism activity. Cohen (1985) mentioned that a tourist guide could be a pathfinder or a mentor, but nowadays not so often anymore there is a need for the tourist guide to find the best route, since today there are so many new technological tools available to reach that aim; but we still need the skills of these professionals mainly as "cultural mediators" (Brito, 2008; Rabotic, 2010; Feldman & Skinner, 2018) or even as "experience brokers" (Weiler & Walker, 2014; Weiler & Black, 2015a). These are important concepts that have to be explored and which are connected with authenticity and the new experience-related tourism, which will be later covered in this chapter.

As Pond (1993) mentions, the purest definition of a tourist guide is someone who conducts a tour. Someone who has the knowledge about several issues or of a particular area whose primary duty is to inform. But tourist guides are much more than that, since they perform a variety of functions, and they work in many different ways and under such diverse conditions. Local guides, city guides, national guides, nature guides are possible names according to their roles. They can also combine these roles with the functions of a tour manager, which gives them even broader responsibilities. They can be employees, but they are mainly independent professionals. They explain subjects in several languages, and for sure they also need to master communication skills, and nowadays even digitals skills. They can have general knowledge or a more specific one, they can travel much or not, but whenever they travel, they are surely not on vacation. Psychology must be one of their main tools, and they must like people, being informative, responsible, patient and polite all the time. As the author has been able to experience for the last three decades of tourist guiding in Portugal, people are often really surprised with the profession when they really hear about it. And those who come to this profession often consider it as their 'passion' or even their 'mission', as stated in several interviews made by the author to some colleagues of the profession, when carrying out an earlier study about the impact of the current pandemic on the tourist guide profession.

But professions also change and, as Pine II and Gilmore (1998) refer, consumers desire experiences, and more and more businesses are responding by explicitly designing and promoting them. All professions, mainly those connected to tourism, will have to adapt. Experiences are taking outstanding importance in tourism, as Pereira, Martins and Baptista (2017) state, when referring to the concept of "tourism of experiences". The above-mentioned authors argue that the tourist experience has evolved together with tourism development. Due to the visitor's psychological character, they may prefer institutionalised, organised and safe experiences or rather look for adventure, risk and unknown experiences. This is highly connected to the theories of the typologies of tourists that started with Cohen (1972), were developed by Plog (1974) with his model of tourist behaviour and were even later completed by Smith (1989). Tourism consists on different experiences, which stimulate our self-confidence and self-esteem, as to remind us of the Maslow's 1940s theory of human motivation.

According to Fortuna (2012), this search for emotional experiences is essential for tourism development, and this author argues that it is not the experiences themselves that generate the emotional reaction of the visitors, but the interpretation they make of those experiences. And the tourist guide, being a professional skilled in interpretation, can play an important role in the tourist experience. Some authors defend that tourist guides are "intermediate interpretation technicians" and "they can add better knowledge and [...] increase the visitors' satisfaction" (Santos Veloso & dos Santos Queirós, 2019, p. 314). The connection between tourist guiding and visitors' satisfaction was also referred by Hsu, Chan and Huang (2009, p. 29) when they defend that "travel managers should bear in mind that tour guide performance directly determines tourist satisfaction with tour guiding service and indirectly [...] with the overall tourism experience". These professionals have then to adapt themselves to the new types of tourism demand, developing new ways of working and creating new kind of experiences for their visitors. We should not forget that the experience economy has been emerging and "leading-edge companies -whether they sell to consumers or businesses- [...] find that the next competitive battleground lies in staging experiences" (Pine II & Gilmore, 1998) and this is also relevant for tourism.

This leads us to several questions about the tourist guide profession, which can be considered to be of great interest, always concerning the theme of adaptation and authenticity. These questions are intended to be answered through the knowledge acquired in a long professional practice of the author, several interviews made to some Portuguese tourist guides and a specific literature review, together with deep reflection.

Question One: How are these professionals adapting to new paradigms in tourism?
Question Two: Are tourist guides facilitators for authentic experiences or rather an obstacle?
Question Three: To what extent are globalisation and digitalisation impacting perceptions on authenticity?

We can say that the main purpose of this chapter will be to provide a better understanding about this profession and how these professionals are dealing with the new paradigms in tourism, bearing in mind that many of these paradigms are also the result of the current crises (technological changings and health concerns) or at least have been much accelerated by them. The author also intends throughout this chapter to present how the tourist guide profession is evolving in Portugal, adapting to all these new situations. To achieve that, it is necessary to know the past for us to be able to understand the present and better prepare for the future.

BRIEF HISTORY OF THE TOURIST GUIDE PROFESSION

The profession has much evolved since ancient times of the Greek festivals and Olympic Games, which attracted many visitors. This travelling is even more encouraged because of the new roads built by the Romans. People needed guides to show them the way and shelter when travelling. As Pond (1993) stated, there were already descriptions of this profession in the travelling stories written by Herodotus in the 5th century BC, even though this historian was somehow suspicious about those guides. It was suggested that Herodotus accepted their function in protecting, but had suspicions about the historical information that some of them gave. "As tourism flourished so apparently did the number of guides" (Pond, 1993, p. 3), and it seems that since there was no guarantee of quality, no education, the experiences were not always the best.

In the Middle Ages, mainly due to the pilgrimages, that have become the main travelling reason, religious places were an attraction and then guides had not only to show the way – like pathfinders –, but also to protect people because travelling was so dangerous. They also needed to understand the different issues related to religion, which fits perfectly in the mentoring aspect of the guide profession. Therefore, priests and monks often took over this function, as Brito (2013; 2010) also mentions.

Later, in the Age of Discoveries, once again, guides were much needed. But, if, at the first moment, translation seems to have been their most important activity, soon interpretation also became fundamental to understand those new societies discovered, trying to avoid war and achieving different kinds of treaties.

However, it should be recognised that the profession has much evolved, mainly with the Grand Tour, when specialised people were needed to systematically accompany the wealthy young nobles around Europe to accomplish their education. "Many of the Grand Tour era tutors and guides were distinguished clergymen, students, schoolmasters, writers and historians" (Pond, 1993, p. 5). They were usually called *cicerones,* some of them being very successful.

In the 17th century, the germ of modern tourism can already be found, since people had started travelling for pleasure and culture. Visitors still needed someone to show them the way and protect them, but then they mostly needed someone to give them information about different cultural subjects. Italy was the most visited country and where many of the 'tourism professionals' were working at that time. Pond (1993) also refers that the competition for the best *cicerone* was keen because not all of them were good professionals. This author even mentions the *vetturini*[1] and some of them could today even be referred to as unscrupulous professionals. Modern tourism was definitively established in the 19th century with the deep social changes, as well as the mobility revolution: the railway.

Tourism activity has then increased, more and more visitors arrived at tourism destinations, and the tourist guide profession must then be regulated for quality to be guaranteed, trying to avoid then some bad practices and experiences from the past. In several countries, it has happened earlier, but, for instance, in Portugal, according to Canário (2013), the first legislation dates back from 1912[2]. Also Carvalho-Oliveira and Cymbron (1994, p. 24) consider this legislation to be "the birth certificate of the Portuguese tourist guides", and it shows that Portuguese official entities already found it necessary on those days to assure correct information to visitors by reliable persons – the tourist guides[3]. Of course, there was a need for education and training, and, still according to Pond (1993), the first courses for tourist guides appeared in England in the Regent Street Polytechnic in 1936, being the main purpose of this course to avoid opportunistic guides with a competitive and aggressive approach towards visitors.

Other countries followed this example after II WW. In Portugal, similar courses were established in 1962[4] only, but even before the *Sociedade Nacional de Informação* already gave a certification[5] to some educated persons, who had proved to have suitable know-how for the profession through an examination. Post-war times were extremely important for the development of tourism, since there was peace and air travelling has become the preferred means of transportation for tourism. Technological development of transportation means has always been very influential on the way tourism develops. People could now travel quickly and easily to different continents. Of course, tourist guides were waiting for them. According to Ap and Wong (2001), they became one of the most important key front-line players in the tourism industry. Also, according to the European Federation of Tourist Guide Associations (FEG)[6], the tourist guide profession has "historically developed for decades as a distinct profession within the tourism industry alongside other complementary professions that also contribute to the visitors' overall experience" and this same institution also states that these professionals "are committed to quality and standards and add value to the visitor experience" (FEG, 2020).

HOW IMPORTANT IS EDUCATION FOR THESE PROFESSIONALS?

According to FEG (2020), the key to high standards and quality service provision are training and qualification. And this can only be achieved through a specific educational plan. In the site of this institution, it can be read that in 2008 European Standards - EN15565 was approved, establishing the minimum standards of training and "never before has there been a pan-European consensus on the minimum hours needed for training, the subjects and competencies to be covered, the relation between knowledge and practical skills and the level of language required" (FEG, 2020: np). It was an important achievement for the profession, allowing uniformity and ensuring the quality of the services provided.

The communication/interpretation process can be easier when related to similar cultures and presenting similar mentalities and concepts, as already mentioned before. But, when this happens in completely different cultural areas, the discourse must be different, and tourist guides have to master the intercultural interpretation. This is a complex phenomenon based on intercultural competence, and not everyone is able to perform it properly since it is an expertise that must be learned and developed. Brito (2017, p. 29) states that "tourism is not only cultural but also intercultural and there is always some degree of cultural exchange when two cultures are in contact. Within the tourism system, guides have a relevant role in cultural contact and eventually cultural change". Thus, it is extremely important to prepare these professionals for a correct and responsible performance by giving them the necessary tools.

Education alone, like experience, is not all that makes a good tourist guide, but it plays a major role in their professional performance. And even though Morales et al. (2009) refer that sometimes the training of tourist guides has been too traditional, and also Santos Veloso and dos Santos Queirós (2019) say that a less generalist oriented training is necessary; others defend that "in the last couple of decades, the training provided by various tourism education institutions [...] ensures high standard of guiding service" (Brito & Farrugia, 2020, p. 8) given them the right skills for a good performance.

Another question is how to evaluate their performance. Some authors argue that "the quality performance evaluation system should include performance assessment on tour guides' knowledge, attitude, and interpersonal skills" (Hsu et al., 2009, p. 29). Santos Veloso and dos Santos Queirós (2019) also state that this evaluation can only rely on the public appreciation. But, indeed, visitors sometimes are not aware of how important it is to have a good professional. Some authors, such as Shani (2017, cited in Brito, 2020, p. 36), even refer that visitors are looking more for entertainment than quality nowadays. This may be the reason why they so easily accept the services from a non-certified tourist guide. Another reason can also lie in the fact that their services are usually less expensive. Visitors can only notice the difference when they have been able to experience a certified tourist guide working; only then they can compare. The problem is that after a bad experience, visitors probably will not wish to try again or at least become suspicious[7]. This is why it is so important to guarantee good performance, and this should always be considered as a serious matter, because it can meddle with the image of a tourism destination. Education and training are therefore necessary, as well as experience to achieve a good performance like in any other profession.

Even though there is a sound tourism education system in Portugal and some other tourism-dependent countries, Brito and Farrugia (2020) refer that the skills of tourist guides are not always recognised and considered essential. As Ap and Wong (2001) state in their study, service professionalism has become an important issue, as destinations compete for tourists in a very competitive environment. Cavalho-Oliveira and Cymbron (1994) stated that the tourist guide performance influences the visitors' opinion about a tourist destination. And also Chan (2004, citedin Hsu et al., 2009, p. 28) stated that "satisfaction with tour guide determined tourist satisfaction with tour experience".

The situation is even more complicated when the tourism stakeholders fail to recognise how important the profession is and use the services of non-certified persons, thus promoting the loss of good professional potential and jeopardising all the efforts made for decades to create a good image of a professional group. For example, the Portuguese (official, professional, licensed, certified or qualified)[8] tourist guides have always contributed to their country's good image and reputation as a tourism destination. Thus, visitors usually consider them as "good ambassadors" of Portugal. And this is only possible when there is a serious commitment, together with specific education and training, which guarantees the required quality standards.

"Nowadays, licensed and unlicensed tourist guides work side by side in most European towns" (Brito & Farrugia, 2020: 7), resulting from "… deregulation decrees (…) published in several European countries as a consequence of the neoliberal market economy" (Brito, 2020: 34/35). This proves to be nonsense in a society where quality and social responsibility are slogans. How can we be sure about the quality of information transmitted by persons that are not certified? Meanwhile, certified professionals are now and then being replaced by the so-called "free guides," who sometimes work just for a tip, which also puts the social responsibility ideals into question. It seems important to ensure that things will not go back to the initial situation, when the profession was sometimes carried out "by people without any qualifications, often incompetent and charlatans" (Brito & Farrugia, 2020: 7). The profession is experiencing difficult, challenging and incoherent times.

New concepts in tourism have appeared, such as slow tourism, smart tourism, creative tourism and intelligent tourism. These new concepts arising from the last tourism trends are certainly also related to digitals evolvement and new kind of experiences wished by visitors, who as Cravidão (2006) so well refers, are more independent, autonomous, and one can even say, more critical and demanding. Nowadays, the trend is also to have strong concerns for sustainability and responsibility, and, of course, safety. These professionals must be prepared through a solid education, since they are being challenged to meet all these new trends and demands. To be able to survive, tourist guides must be able to offer memorable experiences to visitors as soon as tourism recovers from the current pandemic situation. And "to satisfy tourists in search of personalised and meaningful experiences, guides in some cases have to actively engage tourists in the co-creation of their guided tour experiences" (Weiler & Black, 2015a: 364).

THE VARIOUS ROLES OF THE TOURIST GUIDE PROFESSION

Tourist guides are persons with special lifestyle and motivations, who present an extreme devotion towards their profession. In the already above-mentioned interviews made by the author among her colleagues in 2020, these professionals referred to 'live and love their profession'. They seem to like it so much that many of these professionals never thought about trying another profession, and they were even surprised with their success in other areas, when due to Covid-19 and the inherent financial difficulties, they were obliged to look temporarily for other job opportunities, as stated by Carvalho (2020).

The tourist guide is a tourism professional meant to help any visitor to understand the culture being visited. To achieve that, these professionals need to know both cultures very well, since an intercultural interpretation should take place to explain things as accurately as possible, as it has always been expected from good professionals. They have to know very well the issue that is being explained, but they must also be able to know how to explain it properly, i.e., in a way the others will understand it. "Experienced guides make their commentaries meaningful by using common language and by employing analogies, metaphors and other methods of bridging the unfamiliar world of the tour route, content and environment to the things already known and familiar to the group" (Tetik, 2016, p. 47).

This seems to be quite simple, but it can be a real challenge when dealing with different cultures and concepts. This is the secret of the profession: to be able to reach others and transmit the right message in the right way. Additionally, tourist guides must be able to identify the role the visitor wishes him/her to play, because depending on the type of program, nationality, personality of the visitor or even duration of the itinerary, a tourist guide can be seen as a friend, an adviser, a teacher, an organiser, an entertainer, a psychologist or even becoming a 'temporarily family member'. As some authors defend, "their roles and responsibilities are complex and may vary with a number of variables" (Weiler & Black, 2015b, p. 9). The definition of the expected role depends totally on the degree of the relationship established, and it is also often related to the type and length of the travelling together.

Much More Than a Pathfinder or a Mentor

A tourist guide must have a good knowledge of economics, history, geography, gastronomy, among others. For instance, tourist guides presently also need to have concerns and understanding about sustainability, and health and security measures. As some authors point out, tourist guides must also have a role in what "preservation and enhancement of tangible and intangible heritage" (Santos Veloso & dos Santos Queirós, 2019, p. 311) are concerned. They also must show social responsibility and transmit it to their visitors, since "interpretation plays an important role in these environmental innovative tourism forms in general because it influences the consumption and spatial behaviour pattern of visitor and thus represents an effective visitor management instrument" (Tetik, 2016, p. 47).

Similar to educators, these professionals also develop a certain dedication, and they are constantly eager for more information. Brito and Farrugia (2020) presented the acronym SMART (Sophisticated, Memorable, Adaptable, Reliable and Taught) to describe in a single adjective a tourist guide. This gives us a good idea of the complexity of the profession for which education, qualification, responsibility, creativity and experience are fundamental elements. The above-mentioned authors also presented the definition of tour guiding given by FEG, which is the voice of professional tourist guides in Europe and recognised as an advocate of high standards and quality in tourism:

The Art of Guiding is a skill; it is the skill of selecting information and varying it for different audiences; it is the skill of presenting it in a simple and precise way; it is the skill of allowing the visitor to see and to understand; it is a skill which, if well performed, is invisible. (FEG, 2020)

They seem to understand how important their performance can be. As Ap and Wong (2001, p. 559), in their study about tour guiding in Hong-Kong, stated, "through their knowledge and interpretation of a destination's attractions and culture, and their communication and service skills, they have the ability to transform the tourists' visit from a tour into an experience". Also according to FEG, these professionals use "key techniques that combine knowledge and practical skills they help bring alive each location and are often described as 'ambassadors' for their country" (FEG, 2020).

However, some critical voices nowadays stand against the role of the professional tourist guide and defend that other people, namely local people, could/should be the guides in their areas of residence, because they are more authentic and allow visitors to have a 'true' experience. But what is exactly authentic? And what is a true experience? There are so many obstacles for real authenticity. We can never completely embrace the long-sought-after 'truth' because visitors are not locals and their perspectives are different, and so is the way they experience things.

Unquestionably, experience is very important, but a good guide needs more than that. A certified guide will be able to give more and better information, since they have been sensitised and trained for that. As Shani (2017, cited in Brito, 2020, p. 36) refers, the use of a certified tourist guide ensuresthe visitors' ethics, quality and service standards. Tourist guides are professionals with very specific training. It is why some authors defend that it is "necessary to have a basic scientific and technological education" (Santos Veloso & dos Santos Queirós, 2019, p. 315) to be able to acquire the right skills for this job, and for a long time neutrality and objectivity in their speech is a requirement. This means that they have now to adapt to these new trends where personal interpretation became important.

DEALING WITH THE CHALLENGES POSED BY COVID-19

In March 2020, when everyone seemed to be expecting a great year for tourism, which was considered one of the most rentable activities, accounting for a high percentage of GDP in many countries, a pandemic officially started. According to INE (2020)[9], the GVA of tourism in Portugal in 2019 was 8,5%, superior to all other economic sectors in the country, where the tourism percentage of GDP was around 15%,[10] which proves the importance of tourism in this European tourism destination.

The interviewed Portuguese tourist guides stated that their agendas were fully booked at the pandemic's beginning. They were counting upon many visitors to come and to hire their services, and suddenly everything stopped. Tourist guides were obliged to count on their financial reserves, hoping that the disease would be controlled as soon as possible for tourism to (re)start. But, nowadays, we know that the situation has evolved differently, and tourist guides, just like so many other professions connected to tourism, were and still are affected by the pandemic.

As stated by the United Nations World Tourism Organization (UNWTO), "tourism is an activity that is vulnerable to the effects of public health emergencies" (UNWTO, 2020). This organisation also defended that "during times of crisis, tourism has to live up to its responsibility as an integral part of wider society. The sector must put people and their wellbeing first" (UNWTO, 2020) and so it happened. More than one year later, tourism professionals, namely tourist guides, are still waiting for tourism to recover and to become again one of the major engines for the creation of wealth, as it had been happening in many countries for the last decades. But even today, with the vaccination providing to be effective and some baby steps towards international travel, no one can exactly predict the future and the consequences of this crisis. No one knows what will happen in the future, but for sure normality will never be the same. This new normal will certainly present other demands for which other solutions must be found.

Even though "coronavirus continues to disrupt the tourism industry worldwide" (TNI, 2021), there have been some positive reactions and a good example came from Tourism of Northern Ireland (TNI), where a list presenting several trends and opportunities for tourist guides was created (see: https://www.tourismni.com/). One of the first opportunities considered in this document was the domestic market, as well as the specialisation in several thematic aeas, such as: botany, wildlife and Geo-tourism. Another quite important point was to be aware of what visitors' needs and wants are. As Pine II and Gilmore (1998) argue, "experiences, like goods and services, have to meet a customer need; they have to work; and they have to be deliverable. So, "tourist guides might want to develop experience-based products around music, food and drink, genealogy, the great outdoors and others" (TNI, 2021) because the more you personalise the higher the potential of your offer. These are only some examples, but the tourism professionals have to be prepared for all these new trends, and in Portugal some interesting adaptations can already be found.

As already mentioned, during the 1st lockdown in Portugal (March/ April 2020) to understand the situation of the tourist guide profession, a study was carried out by Carvalho (2020), and the results were very interesting because these professionals seemed to be coping very well with the free time they suddenly had. They considered that they just had to use this time properly, doing 'useful' activities for them, such as: staying with their family, organising their libraries, attending training courses and reading, exercising or just enjoying the free time and relaxing. They only complained about their financial situation and the fact that, for some reason, not all were able to obtain the financial support granted by the government, as referred to by Carvalho (2020).

In this same study, Carvalho (2020) also suggests that: tourist guides will probably be one of the last professions to recover, because they mainly work with foreigners, being the direct contact with the client fundamental for the profession and they usually work with groups, which will probably be the last ones to travel again, because of health safety and social distance. These professionals have faced some difficulties because tourism-dependent economies are highly susceptible to being affected by macro-environmental events/factors. Whenever something happens, either at a political or economic level, like the 9/11 attacks or the 2008/2009 financial crisis, tourist guides are usually much affected. The difference now is that never before did they have to face such a long period of crisis, or they had to face a crisis affecting the whole world simultaneously.

They have been experiencing a different situation, and they have been trying to develop several strategies to overcome this challenge. One of the first strategies is to use the time to attend courses and develop new skills, which will be useful in the future, like digitals. Another important strategy is trying to find other jobs temporarily. It does not mean that they are giving up on tourism, but they have to earn some money, and many of them are being successful in Real Estate Agencies, call centres companies or even teaching. It seems they have been successful in other fields, proving that they can also develop new skills and adapt the communication skills they have to other jobs.

Nevertheless, they are all looking forward to working again as tourist guides, but these are examples of resilience and give some hope to other colleagues. Another result of pandemic times is that tourist guides have not been as united as they are now for a long time. The proof of this is the constant way they communicate between them through social networking. Many even became members of the Portuguese Association of Tourist Guides and Tour Managers (AGIC) to be updated and participate in the meetings where important decisions about the profession are taken. The movement *Escolhe bem quem te guia*[11] (Choose well who is guiding you) appeared as a movement of certified tourist guides against free tours and has also played an important role as a platform where tourist guides can exchange their ideas and experiences.

This crisis and the inherent social-economic problems have raised many questions about the recognition of their profession by the official entities. *Turismo de Portugal* and the AGIC are often working together. A good outcome of this cooperation was the creation of the Clean & Safe certificate for tourist guides, which was the first European practical action towards a (re)starting of the activity in safety. This course/certificate gave these professionals information about the correct measures to adopt to prevent infection and protect themselves and their customers. All this learning and training activity became only possible by using the internet. The webinars turned essential and were a complete novelty for the tourist guides. It also presents a new trend that will have consequences in tourism, because these new technologies will probably replace some of the traditional tourism activities in the future.

TOURIST GUIDES AND DIGITALISATION: A DOUBLE SENSE EXPERIENCE

"During the pandemic cyberspace has become the travel agents and tourist information centre. This is where Tourist Guides need to have a presence" (TNI, 2021). As suggested in this website, the online presence of tourist guides is a new trend and must be taken as a serious matter for the future of the profession.

We should not forget how important digitals have been during the lockdown, either at a personal or a professional level. These new technological tools proved to be indispensable for everyone, and for many tourist guides, it was a kind of "deep dive" into technology and that was a challenging experience for them. Authors also argue that "these technological changes and developments have implications for guided tours and tour guides' communication" (Weiler & Black, 2015a, p. 376). Tourist guides want to modernise their profession, because as Black and Weiler (2013) also refer, new technologies should also be used to choreograph memorable experiences for tourists. These professionals also understand that only through these modern communication platforms they will be able to position themselves properly in the tourism market, which as they also know "is evolving due to technological changes and globalisation, phenomena that are shaping the productive chain and services" (Hassan, 2011, p. 46).

But many of the Portuguese tourist guides working today "were not born in the digital age" (Carvalho, 2021, p. 46), and some of them were even sceptical about these new tools, mainly because they did not know or did not master them. As some authors refer, "the growing popularity of internet-based hospitality networks are widening and broadening the field of hospitality actors. They challenge and contribute to a redefinition of professional tour guiding" (Salazar, 2018:114). These professionals had to adapt and had to change their attitude towards digitals, which, according to Carvalho (2021), did happen during the lockdown, since 37.4% of the respondents in her study said to have then changed their attitudes towards digitals.

Tourist guides could have considered all these modern technologies, concurrently to the B2C marketing model, as a strong competitor if not even a threat for their profession, because "in addition to the internet, technology-assisted experiences en route and on-site are more common, ranging from highly interactive visitor centres to mobile phone apps to podcasts in the language of the visitor's choice" (Weiler & Black, 2015b, p.168). Instead of considering these technological tools as a threat, as it would seem logical to happen, because as some authors state: "technology can (indeed) in some cases substitute for what tour guides previously provided" (Weiler and Black, 2015b, p. 168), these professionals seem to consider as their main competitors the persons without certification, who through new technologies can reach the visitors in an easy and uncontrolled way as long as they master digitals. This idea is in line with some authors, who say that "the main competitors to (professional) tour guides are not machines (as some persons may think) but people, partially outside the traditional tourism sectors, who offer guide-like services" (Salazar, 2018, p. 114). Reaching the visitors before arrival is a completely new attitude for Portuguese tour guides to adopt, mainly because "in the past they were not quite allowed to reach directly the client" (Carvalho, 2021, p. 51), being the travel agencies always their preferred partner for work distribution and quality guarantee.

In order to know better the attitude of Portuguese tour guides towards digitals, Carvalho (2021) applied a survey to certified tourist guides only. This study showed that these professionals use digitals more to get information, prepare their itineraries, and communicate with colleagues and less for marketing. Another study about Portuguese tour guides and new technologies was carried out by Chambel (2021) in 2020, with the main purpose of understanding if new technologies were considered an opportunity or a threat by these professionals. Even though the findings of both studies indicate that these professionals conceive digitals more as a facilitator and less as a threat, the truth stated by these studies is also that the potential of the technological tools is not yet properly used for the profession. Also, the age has something to do with a different kind of use given to digitals. These professionals must learn how to explore all the advantages these new tools provide to improve the way they do tour guiding and develop other possibilities for the tour guiding profession.

There are already some good examples of certified tourist guides that decided to conceive different tours based on new technology. This is the case of the blog page turned into a site called "*Teia da Guia*", which even offers online tours today. Also, traditional cooking workshops were created like the one called: "Cooking with Sofia". Other innovative examples, which in a way meet the TNI's guidelines previously mentioned, are some thematic walking tours like "*Viver Amalia*", combining history, sightseeing, and Fado, or "*Lisboa Italiana*", where music and history are also important components, giving a more complete experience to visitors. There are also tourist guides that have specialised in certain areas in Lisbon surroundings that were not considered as tourist areas, so creating a brand, such as Seixal Guided Tours, which is being advertised on Facebook, LinkedIn and Instagram. They have also created professional sites (individual or group) where they offer their services, presenting new tours, many of them already adapted to the current situation and trends. When booking through these sites, the visitor will have a certified tourist guide, being then sure to get a qualified service and ensuring compliance with safety rules.

These professionals understood the importance of digitals and wanted to evolve. Many have enrolled on the 'UpGrade Digital' courses, which were created by *Turismo de Portugal*. No doubt that the pandemic was an important turning point in which technology, tour guiding, and tourism experiences are concerned. These professionals are learning and adapting, and this will have visible and remarkable results in the future, allowing visitors to have a different kind of experience, combining traditional and new guiding technics, and certainly giving better and broader experiences to their guests. But to what extent are these experiences authentic?

SOME REFLECTIONS AND ANSWERS

Authenticity is becoming more and more important, even though this is a complex concept that has already been studied since the last century by several authors, such as Cohen, MacCannell, Wang and others. These authors have presented several approaches to this thematic. Now we would like to present our view about this matter, since it is often questioned if the tourist guide can be authentic.

Tourist guides must interpret, and in Portuguese they are even called '*guias-intérpretes*', which means a professional who interprets several matters and interpretation always carries a certain degree of subjectivity, as pointed out by Santos Veloso and dos Santos Queirós (2019). The information given must be correct, and their communication skills must also be excellent at several levels. Besides giving information, they also accumulate other functions, because, as Salazar (2012) proposes, "apart from providing tourists an unforgettable experience, they can be instrumental in helping communities to have more realistic expectations about tourism development" (Salazar, 2012, p. 20). Their mediation role gives them some big responsibilities[12].

Tourist guides are professionals that have much to do with the image of the destination transmitted to visitors. Salazar (2012) states that tourist guides are often the only 'locals' with whom tourists spend considerable time: they have considerable agency in the image-building process of the peoples and places visited, (re)shaping tourism destination images and indirectly influencing the self-image of those visited, too. This happens either in the most remote areas or in the principal capitals of the world.

When considering that authenticity usually means to be in contact with the 'real situation', with the 'truth', then we can say that many tourism experiences, either in group or individually, are not authentic, because they are often staged situations[13] and do not usually reach the backstage of that society where the authentic reality is to be found. But are not the tourist guides who decide if it happens or not. And is tourism supposed to achieve that? This could only happen when people live for a long time in a certain society, and even in this situation we can ask ourselves if the authenticity of the place will remain, since someone strange to that society is living there and for sure interfering and influencing it. These are only some examples of obstacles to authentic experiences that can be found, but there are even more, and many of them are often not so evident.

Some visitors seem to believe that locals are more authentic and will allow them to know better a certain tourism destination, but for visitors it is also fundamental to see the 'others through the right spectacles'. These spectacles consist of concepts and historical reasons, and this is why usually common locals are not the best ones to explain things. One can even say that they are also too much involved in the reality to be able to explain it. As Morales, Guerra and Serantes (2009) would say, they do a description and not an interpretation. They can describe things as they are and how they feel them, but they do not really know why they do this or that, because they do not usually master the broader perspective. They are not able to explain it properly, and, certainly, they do not always have interpretative skills, not to mention the language skills needed.

On the other hand, people have to be able to understand what they see and listen to. Sometimes visitors are not knowledgeable about certain issues, and they need someone who really can explain the subjects and objects to them. And even more important, to be able to find the right connection between items, which in fact consists of the difficult act of interpreting things, which reveals to be one of the main functions of the tourist guide (see: Brito, 2010, 2013, 2020; Morales et al. 2009, Rabotic, 2010). Being themselves locals with education and trained to transmit accurate information, tourist guides certainly are a good option towards a good tourism experience.

Nowadays, in most countries, we find democracy, and it is possible to explain things in a very accurate way approaching reality through a global perspective without any political control. Whenever visitors come to a tourism destination looking for what they call the "true experience", the tourist guide is the entitled professional to combine different versions and perspectives of the visited reality/context, offering visitors the 'true experience' they are looking for and bringing them to the right spots. Skilled tourist guides will always allow visitors to have their own time to discover things. According to the type of visitor they guide, they should be a mentor, always giving certain liberty for individual discovery. And they will have to consider also that "the more senses an experience engages, the more effective and memorable it can be" (Pine II & Gilmore, 1998).

Curiously, following the current trends of tourism, the authentic is somehow being questioned, because people tend to look more for partial and personal perspectives and especially for the storytelling capabilities of the interpreter, and they care less for the 'reality' or the 'truth', which is to be found in a more global perspective. When Richards (2014) refers to the new trends of cultural tourism, he says that the basic experience consists of an exchange of knowledge and skills between host and guest, which produces a "more locally-driven, equitable and arguably more 'authentic' form of cultural tourism" (Richards, 2014: np). Using the word 'arguably', this author reveals that this perspective is only a possibility. Even the 'authentic' presented today will tend to be later staged, because things in life are unique and do not usually repeat; if they do, they are seldom authentic.

Another interesting aspect is that residents' authenticity seems to be different from what the authentic visitors sometimes look for. As Pereira et al. (2017) refers, many times residents complain that cities are being prepared for visitors and not for them; therefore, they are no longer authentic. This strongly relates to gentrification, which is a terrible process, which really prevents visitors from experiencing the authentic way of life, because residents disappear from the traditional centres, left now for the tourists to use and enjoy. It reminds us of Urry's concept of tourist gaze already presented in the 1990s but still very actual.

Through the reflection presented in the former parts of this chapter, we are able to understand better this profession which reveals to be fundamental for a better comprehension of the visited societies. The questions brought forward in the Introduction above can now be answered.

Question One

How are these professionals adapting to new paradigms in tourism?

The adaptation follows a normal and functional way. Portuguese tourist guides were confronted with the health crises and have reacted positively. The official entities have looked for solutions (ex: Clean & Safe certificate) and new ways to survive the crises (temporary jobs and even online offer). They believe their profession will be able to adapt to a new reality, because they are flexible and skilled, as stated by Carvalho (2020). They have also been able to (re)think the profession and, as shown by some above examples, they have created more experience-centred tours, or inter-active tours; allowing visitors to participate, to deepen their relationship with the destinations, giving them different perspectives, bringing them nearer to authenticity. Considering a new paradigm, they start to understand the need to change the communicative role of a guide, avoiding what Weiler and Black (2015a, p. 366) referred to as "the traditional one-way communication ... [that] ... appears to limit in an experienced – and consumer- centred tourism industry". All this was also often worked out through digitals that have also provided new communication forms, which are also a new trend in tourism. These professionals are now developing digital skills that will prepare them to follow future trends.

Question Two

Are tourist guides facilitators for authentic experiences or rather an obstacle?

We can say that tourist guides are facilitators of authentic experiences and not an obstacle, as it is sometimes meant. As presented throughout the text, they help people to understand what they are seeing and experiencing, "building bridges between the resources and the interests of visitors" (Morales et al., 2009). Some of the aspects discussed above prove that tourist guides are important elements in tourism and should always be residents to be at least able to transmit better the residents' perspective, together with the more global perspective given by education and training, becoming a real and active facilitator agent.

Question Three

To what extent are globalisation and digitalisation impacting perceptions of authenticity?

Both globalisation and digitalisation carry several positive and negative consequences. An example of these negative consequences is certainly the fact that nowadays all cultures quickly and easily apprehend traces from the others. That makes it difficult to find authentic experiences (when considering authentic as something genuine and unique), since globalisation and digitalisation through the spreading of several ideas and concepts of prominent cultures have standardised cultures. Even though authentic experiences are nowadays hard to achieve, all experiences are true ones, even the virtual ones, considering that "the (tourism) product can be created outside the place" (Ferraz, 2017: 87) and nowadays through new technologies can also be consumed elsewhere. All this has strongly impacted our perceptions about society, the world and, of course, authenticity. Nowadays, authenticity is being used by marketers and often used by brands to justify their products as special or better ones. It is an essential element for diversity and identity. When applied to tourism, the usual connotation assigned to authenticity as original, unique and special is a powerful tool that can attract consumers – visitors.

FINAL CONSIDERATIONS

Tourist guides are a professional group that is characterised by big diversity and autonomy. Each professional has a special personality, and, as a freelancer, tourist guides are skilled in leadership, and they are committed and responsible professionals, as referred by Carvalho-Oliveira and Cymbron (1994). The pandemic also gave them time to think about how they work and how the profession could evolve to meet the new types of tourism. Tourist guides, namely the Portuguese ones, have been able to learn about digitals and they started combining their skills to diversify their offer, promoting themselves through digitals, offering new, thematic and creative tours, that are more adapted to the demand and some have even managed to perform them online. Many of these new offers are walking tours, allowing visitors to experience new sounds, tastes and to discover completely different perspectives of a town. According to Pine II and Gilmore (1998), this means they are moving forward to the experience economy, which demands the design of richer thematic experiences, where all senses together with interaction revealed to be fundamental for memorable experiences. This is a turning point for the tourist guide profession, and tourist guiding will certainly evolve to other levels.

Probably this is also the reason why despite all these changings, tourist guides don't seem to be afraid of the virtual reality to replace them, because as Salazar (2018) defends, "human tour guiding is a brokering service that adds to the tourist experience in ways the latest information and communication technologies can impossibly match (yet)" (Salazar, 2018, p. 115). Also Carvalho (2021) was able to state that these professionals are starting to use the new technologies for their profession, and they do also believe that nothing can replace human relationships in tourism and that people will always need the displacement provided by travel. Travelling is undoubtedly a very special time, where several relationships are built and where the feelings of freedom and happiness are also present, because people are far from their everyday life and their usual concerns and they wish to experience other realities. Even though the new paradigms the profession is facing, the Portuguese Tourist guides are sure that they can contribute to visitors' satisfaction towards a tourism destination, adding value and providing them good services and tourism experiences as close as possible to the authentic.

Future Research Directions

Tour guiding is an extremely rich and important issue to be studied, and there are many topics that could and should be deepened. The relationship between tourist guides and digitals and how these new technological tools can be better used to enhance the profession should continue to be studied. We also think that it would be very interesting to conduct another study in a few years to check the results of the changes introduced now into the profession. Also, the way the visitors see the possibility of using the tourist guide services now, when the groups tend to be smaller, would be important to be studied as soon as possible. The perceptions of the youngest generations about the probability and benefits of using a tourist guide, and what would be expected by them from those professionals, would also be an interesting matter to be studied. Finally, it would also be important to enlarge the study of tourist satisfaction now that a new (post-pandemic) reality is coming and maybe even to develop a practical model to check and measure how visitors' satisfaction about a destination is really related to the tourist guide's performances.

CONCLUSION

"Aside from assuring they have sufficient tools in their guiding toolbox, guides need to understand the currency of their services in a global market that is highly unstable and influenced by continuous changes in tourist preferences. This requires them to endlessly vary, reinvent and customise their services" (Salazar, 2018, p. 115). Nowadays, visitors intend to have new emotional experiences, and they are also expecting to have authentic experiences, whatever this may be. New experiences consist of novelty, and this kind of experience should be intended to surprise and impress visitors, enrich their knowledge, and show them different concepts of life, ideas, challenges, and truths. Tourist guides must be able to give them what they are looking for, but with some restrictions, avoiding the fantasy speech or the easy discourse just to please visitors, because that would not be authentic.

Cultures are never static and symbolic representations sometimes change or are even replaced by others. Cultures change, evolve, are influenced and also influence others. Shall we prevent some aspects of our society from changing or disappearing just to present what could be called the staged authentic way of life expected by visitors? Should we freeze some traditions in time just to satisfy the visitor's curiosity? Would it be authentic? We do not think so, if we do not want to create a Disneyland product, which is what happens in some cases when the past is (re)invented. But tourist guides could and should explain how it used to be and why it is like this today. They can and should work with the representations, and for that they need to be skilled in various aspects: historical knowledge, psychology understanding, facts interpretation and mastery of language, and now of digitals as well. All this is needed to be able to enrich their performance, and it is only obtained through education, giving them training and qualification.

Authors defend that "the context in which tour guides are operating has dramatically changed" (Salazar, 2018, p. 114) or that there have been "qualitative changes in the nature of [...] demand" (Richards, 201). These are extremely important statements that must be considered because nothing in life is static and adaptation, following Darwin's theorising, is a necessity to all species. As mentioned before, tourist guides are now facing two different crises, which will profoundly influence how the profession will evolve in the future. One of the crises is cyclical and consists in the fact that this profession was suddenly and deeply affected by the pandemic. The other crisis, being more of structural level, consists of the growing importance that digitals are having and the need to follow this trend, because it will remain and will certainly even increase in the next decades. Thus, tourist guides "must be innovative and marketed as a service that adds value in ways that technology cannot" (Weiler & Black, 2015b, p. 168). They will have to use all their creativity and skills to modernise their profession, providing new and good experiences to the visitors. In order to enhance and reaffirm their profession, tourist guides must adapt now, and they certainly will always have to follow the new paradigms of tourism.

REFERENCES

Ap, J., & Wong, K. (2001). Case study on tour guiding: Professionalism, issues and problems. *Tourism Management, 22*(5), 551–563. doi:10.1016/S0261-5177(01)00013-9

Black, R., & Weiler, B. (2013). Current themes and issues in ecotour guiding. In R. Ballantyne & J. Packer (Eds.), *International handbook on ecotourism* (pp. 336–350). Edward Elgar. doi:10.4337/9780857939975.00033

Brito, M. (2020). The consequences of guiding profession deregulation for the status of training of tourist guides: A Portuguese overview. *International Journal of Tour Guiding Research, 1*(1), 4–12.

Brito, M. (2017). *Intercultural interpretation discourses, techniques and strategies used by tour guides in the Coach Museum, Lisbon: Eight issues.* Nyelv Vilag - Institute of Foreign Languages and Communication of the Budapest Business School, 16-30. httpscomum.rcaap.ptbitstream10400.262296212017.01.006_.pdf

Brito, M. (2013). *Informação tturística – A arte do guia interprete: Entre a cultura do turista e o destino.* Chiado Editora.

Brito, M. (2010). *O guia-intérprete: Facilitador do turismo cultural.* Tese de Doutoramento, Universidade de Évora.

Brito, L. (2008). O guia-intérprete: Mediador intercultural. *Revista Turismo & Desenvolvimento, 10*, 67–84.

Brito, M., & Farrugia, G. (2020). On tourist guiding: Reflecting on a centuries-old profession and proposing future challenges. *International Journal of Tour Guiding Research, 1*(1), 34–44.

Canário, D. (2013). *O papel do guia intérprete no turismo em Lisboa* (Master's dissertation). Instituto das Novas Profissões.

Carvalho, I. (2021). Portuguese tourist guides and the digital age. *International Journal of Tour Guiding Research, 2*(1), 46–62.

Carvalho, I. (2020). A profissão de guia-intérprete e o impacto da COVID-19. *Revista Turismo e Desenvolvimento, 34*, 209–222.

Carvalho-Oliveira, J., & Cymbron, J. (1994). *Ser guia-intérprete em Portugal.* Departamento de Turismo. Instituto Superior de Novas profissões.

Chambel, B. (2021). *As novas tecnologias: Oportunidade ou ameaça para a profissão de guia-intérprete* (Master's dissertation). Escola Superior de Hotelaria e Turismo do Estoril.

Cohen, E. (1972). Towards a sociology of international tourism. *Social Research, 39*(1), 164–182.

Cohen, E. (1985). The tourist guide. The origins, structure and dynamics of a role. *Annals of Tourism Research*, *12*(1), 5–29. doi:10.1016/0160-7383(85)90037-4

Cravidão, F. (2006). Turismo e cultura: dos Itinerários ao lugar dos lugares. In M. L. Fonseca (Coord.), Desenvolvimento e territórios: Espaços rurais pós agrícolas e novos lugares de turismo e lazer (pp. 269-278). Centro de Estudos Geográficos, Universidade de Lisboa.

FEG – European Federation of Tourist Guide Associations. (2020). https://www.feg-touristguides.com/about.php

Feldman, J., & Skinner, J. (2018). Tour guides as cultural mediators: Performance and Positioning. *Ethnologia Europaea*, *48*(2), 5–13. doi:10.16995/ee.1955

Ferraz, J. (2017). Turismo e globalização. In F. Silva, & J. Umbelino (Coord.), Planeamento e desenvolvimento turístico (pp. 79-92). Editora Lidel.

Fortuna, C. (2012). Património, turismo e emoção. *Revista Critica de Ciencias Sociais*, *97*, 23–40.

Hassan, H. (2011). *Tecnologias da informação e turismo: e-tourism* (Master's dissertation). Património e Desenvolvimento da Faculdade de Letras da Universidade de Coimbra.

Hsu, C., Chan, A., & Huang, S. (2009). Tour guide performance and tourist satisfaction: A study of the package tours in Shangai. *Journal of Hospitality & Tourism Research (Washington, D.C.)*, *34*(1), 3–33. doi:10.1177/1096348002026001001

INE – Instituto Nacional de Estatística. (2020). *Conta Satélite de Turismo/Tourism Sattelite Account*. https://www.sgeconomia.gov.pt/noticias/ine-conta-satelite-do-turismo-para-portugal-span-classnovo-novospan.aspx

Morales, J., Guerra, F., & Serantes, A. (2009). *Bases para la definición de competencias en interpretación del património: Fundamentos teóricos y metodológicos para definir las competencias profesionales de especialistas en interpretación del patrimonio en España*. Seminario Permanente de Interpretación del Patrimonio, Centro Nacional de Educación Ambiental - CENEAM.

Pereira, P., Martins, J., & Baptista, L. (2017). A oferta turística e os seus territórios: Autenticidade, patrimonialização e experiência. In F. Silva, & J. Umbelino (Coords.), Planeamento e desenvolvimento turístico (pp. 93-103). Editora Lidel.

Pine, I. I. J., & Gilmore, J. (1998, July). Welcome to the experience economy. Harvard Business Review. July-August. https://hbr.org/1998/07/welcome-to-the-experience-economy

Pond, K. (1993). *The professional guide: Dynamics of tour guiding*. Van Nostrand Reinhold.

Plog, S. (1974). Why destination areas rise and fall in popularity. *The Cornell Hotel and Restaurant Administration Quarterly*, *14*(4), 55–58. doi:10.1177/001088047401400409

Rabotic, B. (2010). Tourist guides in contemporary tourism. In *Proeedings of the International Conference on Tourism and Environment* (pp. 353-364). Sarajevo: Philip Noël-Baker University.

Richards, G. (2014). *Tourism trends: The convergence of culture and tourism*. Academy for Leisure. NHTV University of Applied Sciences. https://www.academia.edu/9491857/Tourism_trends_The_convergence_of_culture_and_tourism

Santos Veloso, A. S., & Santos Queirós, A. (2019). The role of the tourist guide in the context of the conservation and valuation of the tangible and intangible heritage. *Journal of Tourism and Heritage Research, 2*(4), 308–326.

Salazar, N. B. (2012). Community-based cultural tourism: Issues, threats and opportunities. *Journal of Sustainable Tourism, 20*(1), 9–22. doi:10.1080/09669582.2011.596279

Salazar, N. B. (2018). The mechanics and mechanisms of tourism brokering. *Ethnologia Europaea, 48*(2), 111–116. doi:10.16995/ee.1963

Smith, V. (1989). *Hosts and guests: The antropology of tourism*. University of Pensylvannia Press. doi:10.9783/9780812208016

Tetik, N. (2016). The importance of interpretation role of tour guides in geotourism: Can we called them as geotour guides? *International Journal of Education and Social Science, 3*(2), 41–53.

TNI – Tourism Northern Ireland. (2021). *(Post) Pandemic Trends in Tourism – Opportunities for Tourist Guides*. https://www.tourismni.com/build-your-business/sector/tourist-guiding/tourist-guiding-trends-and-opportunities/post-pandemic-trends-in-tourism—opportunities-for-tourist-guides/

UNWTO – United Nations World Travel Organization. (2020). *UNWTO statement on the novel coronavirus outbreak*. https://www.unwto.org/taxonomy/term/356

Urry, J. (1990). *The tourist gaze: Leisure and travel in contemporary societies*. Sage.

Weiler, B., & Walker, K. (2014). Enhancing the visitor experience: Reconceptualising the tour guide's communicative role. *Journal of Hospitality and Tourism Management, 21*, 90–99. doi:10.1016/j.jhtm.2014.08.001

Weiler, B., & Black, R. (2015a). The changing face of the tour guide: One-way communicator to choreographer to co-creator of the tourist experience. *Tourism Recreation Research, 40*(3), 364–378. doi:10.1080/02508281.2015.1083742

Weiler, B., & Black, R. (2015b). *Tour guiding research: Insights, issues and implications. Aspects of Tourism* (Vol. 62). Channel View Publications.

ENDNOTES

[1] *Vetturino* was the driver of an Italian four wheel carriage called *vettura*, who sometimes would exploit the clients or was able to fix arrangements with highway robbers. It seems that this character could have a dubious function and lead to some of the current prejudices about the tourist guide profession.

New Paradigms of the Tourist Guide Profession

[2] The main purpose for the creation of a decree was to offer visitors the best service. Quality had to be assured and on the 16th November 1912 the first legislation appeared, setting out the criteria for becoming a professional guide. This document also ruled the need to obtain a license by passing an examination.

[3] These professionals should wear an uniform and were required to carry a badge.

[4] At the beginning this course took 6 months only, but soon it evolved and its duration reached 3 years, during which several subjects weere studied.

[5] This was an important department created in 1945 to replace the *Secretariado de Propaganda Nacional* at the time of the Estado Novo regime, which thoroughly controlled the entire information sector.

[6] This institution was founded in 1986 in Paris to represent the profession at European level .It played an important role in deliberations about many of the final definition of tourist guiding and tour managing and it is the voice of professional tourist guides in Europe and it is recognised as an advocate of high standards and quality in tourism. It is an active member of several European organisations and groups and a participant or observer in key European forums.

[7] The author herself experienced this situation, when already at the beginning of a tour in Lisbon some clients said that they would not like to go shopping at all, because they had been in Turkey and spent two hours in a shop far from everything. They had felt completely fooled and they did not want this to happen again.

[8] All these adjectives are different expressions that refer to tourist guides who had a specific education and training and have been certified by entities, such as the Portuguese Tourist Guides Association (AGIC) or the Trade Union (SNATTI).

[9] Portugal is one of the countries where the Tourism Satellite Account provides many important statistics about this major activity appearing in the results given by the National Institute of Statistics (INE).

[10] These statistics come from the Tourism Satellite Account and not all countries have it. But when compared worldwide the percentage of tourism for GDP will be of 8%, which brings Portugal to a high ranking, taking into account that in 2018 the OECD average was only of 4, 4% according to the OECD tourism trends and policies in 2020.

[11] This site and blog popular among tourist guides was created in 2020 by a group of certified tourist guides from Oporto, with the aim of disseminating and dignifying the profession. It was so successfully among the tourist guides that they began having meetings every Wednesday and they also give courses and it is similar to an "online Café", as the co-founders stated. This is also a good example of the benefits of the new technological tools for this profession, allowing these professionals to exchange ideas.

[12] This could be a long discussion, although it is beyond the scope of this chapter. The responsibilities of tourist guides are often questioned when comparing to other professions like attorneys or doctors or even economists, but why should cultural aspects be of less importance than others in our society?

[13] There are nowadays agencies hiring local people to meet with tourist groups and talk about their lives. This gives them the impression of having a more authentic experience, but it is not a genuine one, for sure.

Section 3
Managing Experiences in Tourism Products

Chapter 9
Innovative Certifications in Adventure Tourism:
Attributes and Diffusion

Dorthe Eide
Nord University, Norway

Anne-Mette Hjalager
University of Southern Denmark, Denmark

Marcus Hansen
Wrexham Glyndwr University, UK

ABSTRACT

Certifications, quality systems and standardization carriers systemic innovativeness, since they usually are established after a lengthy period of research, evidence-finding and testing. Ideally, they incorporate the most decisive best practices that will benefit firms, customers, and wider groups of stakeholders in communities. Such systems can be seen as driving forces for innovation, and memberships in them is likely to enhance prospective changes in the any industry. This chapter addresses the prospects of diffusion of innovation through certification and quality systems, using Rogers (1995) diffusion theory explaining adoption based on the five attributes. Findings from a qualitative multi-case study of the national tourism quality certifications of VisitScotland (Quality Assurance), New Zealand (Qualmark) and Iceland (Vakinn) is used to illustrate and explain diffusion. The study shows that relative advantage and compatibility seem most critical for adoption. Complexity and observability are important too, while trialability seems less obtainable in this particular context.

INTRODUCTION

Innovation is considered a critical factor and a strategic issue for tourism organisations and destinations to ensure value creation and long-term sustainability (Pikkemaat, Peters, & Bichler, 2019). The commercial adventure tourism has only been possible due to innovation, by making activities traditionally meant for more skilled individuals widely accessible to the masses (Rantala, Rokenes, & Valkonen, 2018; Hansen, Hjalager, & Fyall, 2019). In addition, demand and competition encourage innovation in new industries (Klepper & Malerba, 2010; Roper & Tapinos, 2016). Further, Freel (2000) argued that innovation is essential for competitiveness and satisfies the demand of an ever-changing consumer. This is fuelled by an adventure tourist demanding unique experiences in nature, yet typically approach such activities as casual leisure with a demand for immediate and intrinsic rewards requiring little-to-no training to participate (Stebbins, 1997). Indeed, these tourists often do not possess the required skills to fully participate, thereby creating a need for continual innovation to enable mass participation (Rantala et al., 2018). However, similarly to tourism in general, the challenge for adventure tourism is its fragmented state, whilst it also primarily consists of small-to-medium enterprises with no budgets for research and development (Hjalager, 2018; Hansen et al., 2019).

The purpose of this chapter is to examine the role of the function of certification and quality systems in encouraging innovation in adventure tourism (Blind, 2016). The main assumption is that certification, quality labelling, and standardisation are significant carriers of systemic innovativeness in whatever forms they take. Accordingly, in this understanding, innovations are embedded in such systems, since they usually are established only after a lengthy period of research, evidence-finding and testing. Ideally, they incorporate the most decisive best practices that will benefit firms, customers, and wider groups of stakeholders in communities. In this perspective, certifications can be said to accumulate and synthesise innovative endeavours and make them more rapidly available than they would be if every organisation had to invent them in its own capacity. Following this rationale, certifications and quality systems can be seen as driving forces for innovation, and membership is likely to enhance prospective changes in any industry (Blind, 2016).

There is an increased demand for experience products that are new, extraordinary, personally meaningful and memorable. This has led to an innovation boom, and existing enterprises have diversified their products and services (Margaryan, 2018; Hoaroau-Heemstra & Eide, 2019). Adventure tourism is emerging in peripheral areas, including Arctic areas in Europe, Asia and North America (Saarinen & Varnajot, 2019; Tangeland, 2011). Potentially, these places represent new tourism experiences, but activities are often performed in vulnerable environmental circumstances (Landauer, Goodsite, & Juhola, 2018). In some countries (like New Zealand, Iceland and Norway) there have been periods described as 'the wild west' within some of the adventure sectors as entrepreneurs exploit new areas of tourism on an experimental basis without solid prior knowledge and consolidated methods (Lundberg, Fredman, & Wall-Reinius, 2014). Often there are few entry barriers. The successful introduction of certification and quality systems may serve to promote a greater degree of regulation and professionalising.

Innovation and standardisation are often at cross purposes, and adventure tourism offers a good example. On the one hand, innovativeness is spurred by demand from exploration-seeking tourists; secondly, by the availability of and access to spaces and places; and, thirdly, by supportive technologies such as ICT and mobility tools. On the other hand, there are crucial safety issues in adventure tourism, and a stronger emphasis on the potential environmental implications is emerging (Margaryan & Stensland, 2017). In addition, the distinctive adventure experiences as products call for professionalising using knowledge and tools based on experience design and consumer research (Alsos, Eide, & Madsen, 2014). Thus, innovation and standardisation may seem to be at opposite poles, or even contradictory. Certifications and quality systems promote a higher degree of standardising that, if restrictive, might compromise novelty and diversity (Acemoglu, Gancia, & Zilibotti, 2012; Kondo, 2000). However, there is little knowledge about their impacts on tourism generally nor on how innovativeness is affected in particular. Serious reservations have been expressed about the overall impact and performance of certification systems in sustainable tourism, ecotourism and adventure tourism (Deng-Westphal, Beeton, & Anderson, 2015; Dunk, Gillespie, & MacLeod, 2016). The seemingly non-optimal implementation (Costa, Rodrigues, & Gomes, 2019) and the structural and motivational barriers need to be further investigated (Dodds & Ramsay, 2017).

Certifications are procedures by which an authorised agency establishes, assesses and verifies the attributes and standards (norms, 'best practices') in certified organisational units according to set requirements, achieving an optimal order or uniformity in a given context. This chapter addresses the prospects of diffusion of innovation through certification and quality systems. We use empirical findings from a multi-case study to illustrate and explain diffusion attributes. The study took place in Scotland, Iceland and New Zealand using documents and semi-structured interviews with three types of stakeholders: adventure tourism firms, certification bodies and other stakeholders; only the firms are included here. Illustrations are chosen from findings related to the national tourism quality certifications – VisitScotland Quality Assurance (QA), New Zealand Qualmark (QM) and Iceland's Vakinn. Vakinn was, at the time of the study, in an early adoption phase. QM and Vakinn had specialised criteria for different subsectors within culture and adventure experiences, while QA had specialised criteria for a few larger-sector groups. Unlike the other two, QA did not have an integrated voluntary environmental certification.

INNOVATION AND ADVENTURE TOURISM

Innovation is a critical tool for competitiveness, rejuvenation and sustainability within tourism and, more specifically, adventure tourism (Kuscer, Mihalic, & Pechlaner, 2017; Hansen et al., 2019). At times innovation comes down to a question of survival. Many ski resorts have, for example, been forced to turn to innovative new practices of operation in light of climate change threatening their very existence, leading to less snowfall and thus a poorer quality offering (Kuscer et al., 2017; Perrin-Malterre, 2018). Further, ski resorts have also been facing persistent and increased competition for many years due to limited appeal, as opposed to summer tourists (Zehrer, Smeral, & Hallmann, 2017). This has resulted in several ski resorts in countries such as the US, France and Canada, diversifying their product range and, in turn, extending their typical single season of operation (winter) to effectively become year-round resorts as well (Smith, 2015; Gilani et al., 2018). By doing so, they have not only limited the impact of seasonality, but the resorts have also increased their appeal to a wider audience (Zehrer et al., 2017). As such, by embracing innovation, organisations increase their likelihood of survival (Cefis & Marsili, 2006; Ruhanen & Cooper, 2004). Elsewhere, in the Cambrian Mountain range of Wales, and 7 miles from the nearest coastline, Adventure Parc Snowdonia has turned the site of an old factory into an (unlikely) major surfing destination by creating the world's first inland surf lagoon (Visit Snowdonia, 2020). Whereas tourism operators, in a wider context, have been described as slow innovators, that is clearly not the case in adventure tourism (Williams & Soutar, 2009; Fuglsang, Sundbo, & Sørensen, 2011; Hjalager et al., 2018).

Whilst innovation might come in different shapes, they all share three common elements: creativity, a problem-solving or opportunity approach and a new way of practicing, all of which have been critical to adventure tourism through its commercialisation. This is evidenced in the number of adventure tourism activities, historically only accessible to highly skilled individuals, that are now targeting mass appeal and low-skilled tourists (Mykletun, 2018). This shift in focus has become viable through innovation, particularly in the shape of product innovation (Hansen et al., 2019). As such, innovation is of strategic concern in relation to the short-term and long-term sustainability of adventure tourism organisations and enterprises (Pikkemaat et al., 2019). Research focusing on adventure tourism has been surprisingly sparse despite the importance of innovation in adventure tourism (Hansen et al., 2019).

As the discussion of innovation has evolved within tourism, a more strategic approach to innovation has developed with an increased focus on market orientation, as opposed to Schumpeter's (1934) original work, which emphasises entrepreneurialism (Pikkemaat et al., 2019). Whilst entrepreneurialism is a key part of adventure tourism, this development is critical given the intangibility and interrelatedness of adventure tourism products. As a result, the consumer also plays an essential role in the development of tourism innovation (Grissemann, Plank, & Brunner-Sperdin, 2013). These conditions make it a requisite for the adventure tourism industry to continuously innovate and explore the latest developments in equipment (Williams & Soutar, 2009). This will, in turn, allow them to offer new and challenging experiences and thereby quench the thirst of a consumer otherwise likely to look elsewhere for more unique, challenging and exciting experiences next time.

Innovations can be explored in two different scales: incremental and radical (Hjalager, 2002). Weidenfeld, Williams, and Butler (2010) found that products or processes adopted to improve existing processes and procedures are incremental innovations, whilst radical innovations are new processes or products introduced. Tourism innovation has typically been incremental, yet this is not necessarily the case in the adventure tourism industry (Sigurðardóttir, 2018; Hansen et al., 2019). Incremental innovations include minor and major adaptations of products and services, involving slight differentiation, product line extension as well as changes to the cost/quality ratio of the product (Weidenfeld et al., 2010). On the other hand, commercial adventure tourism seems to thrive on radical innovations (Williams & Soutar, 2009).

Defining innovation is challenging, and the literature has yet to reach a consensus. Yet, innovations share the commonality that they are either new to the organisation in question or the consumer (Hjalager, 2018; Pikkemaat et al., 2019). Past definitions include:

Innovation refers to the process of bringing any new, problem-solving idea into use. Ideas for reorganising, cutting cost, putting in new budgetary systems, improving communication or assembling products in teams are also innovations. Innovation is the generation, acceptance and implementation of new ideas, processes, products or services... Acceptance and implementation is central to this definition; it involves the capacity to change and adapt." (Kanter, cited from Hall & Williams, 2008, p. 5)

Within the wider tourism literature, definitions by Schumpeter (1934) and the OECD (2018) have been employed regularly. For example, the OECD (2018, p. 20) defines innovation as:

A new or improved product or process (or a combination thereof) that differs significantly from the unit's previous products or processes and that has been made available to potential users (product) or brought into use by the unit (process).

Schumpeter (1934) defined innovation by categorising areas in which companies can introduce innovation and which has subsequently been added to by other scholars addressing tourism and experience sectors (Eide & Mossberg, 2013; Alsos, et al. 2014; Eide, Fuglsang, & Sundbo, 2017; Hjalager & Madsen, 2018):

1. **Generation of new or improved products**. The previous example of Adventure Parc Snowdonia is an obvious case of *new or improved products.*
2. **Introduction of new production processes**. This type of innovation includes technology or smarter methods of delivery (Hjalager & Madsen, 2018).
3. **Marketing innovations**. This refers to how products and services are communicated to the consumer before, during and after consumption. Also, it refers to how to select and enter new markets and segments.
4. **Organisational innovations**, which includes new methods for collaborating and managing staff as well as external stakeholders in general (Fuglsang & Eide, 2013; Abelsen, Eide, Kvidal, & Leenheer, 2014; Høegh-Guldberg, Eide, Trengereid, & Hjemdahl, 2018; Hjalager & Madsen, 2018). This categorisation clearly distinguishes innovation from minor changes in the type and delivery of products in the forms of extension of product lines, adding service components or product differentiation (Pieters & Pikkemaat, 2006).

Rogers (1995) enhanced the understanding of innovation and its diffusion. Rogers (1995, p. 5) contended that innovation is "an idea, practice, or object that is perceived as new by an individual or another unit of adoption". He describes adoption as a social process in which some people adopt innovations earlier than others. Different customer or adaptor groups need different strategies to address and influence their innovation adoption behaviour. Rogers (1995) diffusion theory has been applied within the wider tourism context thus far, however only in a limited capacity in adventure tourism (Hansen et al., 2019). Roger's (1995) work is further explored in the following sections as a foundation for scrutinising certifications and their impacts.

DIFFUSION OF INNOVATIONS (DOI): THE CONCEPTUAL FRAMEWORK

Everett Rogers' seminal work on the diffusion of innovations was inaugurated by a publication in 1962. Since then, several versions have emerged, and refinements have been suggested by Rogers as well as a large number of other researchers who have applied the concepts in a variety of fields, sectors and countries, including tourism (Greenhalgh, Robert, Macfarlane, Bate, & Kyriakidou, 2004; Tornatzky & Klein, 1982; Høegh-Guldberg, 2018). This chapter refers to the fourth edition of 'Diffusion of innovations' (Rogers, 1995). Rogers covers different aspects such as the rate and speed of diffusion across industries, over- and underadoption, and how organisations and consumers adopt and with what categories of consequences. Of particular interest in this context is the notion of innovation attributes. According to Rogers, it can be observed that some innovations are implemented very rapidly and pervasively, while others, in spite of their recognised potential, are slow to gain acceptance. Rogers assumes that analysing the attributes of innovations can contribute to an understanding of the patterns governing their adoption. Thus, the diffusion of innovations depends not only on the characteristics of the adopting enterprises and the people involved but also on the characteristics of the innovations themselves.

Rogers' (1995) classification of innovation attributes consists of five categories: relative advantage, compatibility, complexity, trialability and observability. These attributes are explained and illustrated in the sections below in relation to empirical contexts, including how the categories can help understand the adoption of certifications.

Rogers' concepts are usually applied to comprehend the dissemination of a well-defined technology, procedure, or method. However, certification systems in adventure tourism are more complex, and they are bound to be dynamic and ever-changing, reflecting new knowledge and continuous entrepreneurial activity as well as external pressures that will eventually contribute to the gradual maturation of the adventure tourism industry (Deng-Westphal et al., 2015; Dibra, 2019). In order to include the wider dynamics and the relational interaction in the tourism system, Figure 1 distinguishes between micro-, meso- and meta-level dissemination processes. Certification bodies are obliged to undertake the elaboration of workable systems, and these can be considered institutional innovations (Deng-Westphal et al., 2015). As explained above, innovations are embodied in the certifications, and they are straightforwardly accessible to certified enterprises. This process represents 'micro-DOI'. On the other hand, certification systems for adventure tourism are dynamic, and there is continuous feedback from enterprises to the certifications bodies to amend, improve or modify the systems. This is described as 'meso-DOI', in which innovations take place in the certification body itself as a result of consultative processes. 'Meta-DOI' represents an overarching, higher-level innovation dissemination process, which happens trans-nationally, trans-regionally, and across tourism sectors.

Figure 1. Model of innovation dissemination connected to certification systems

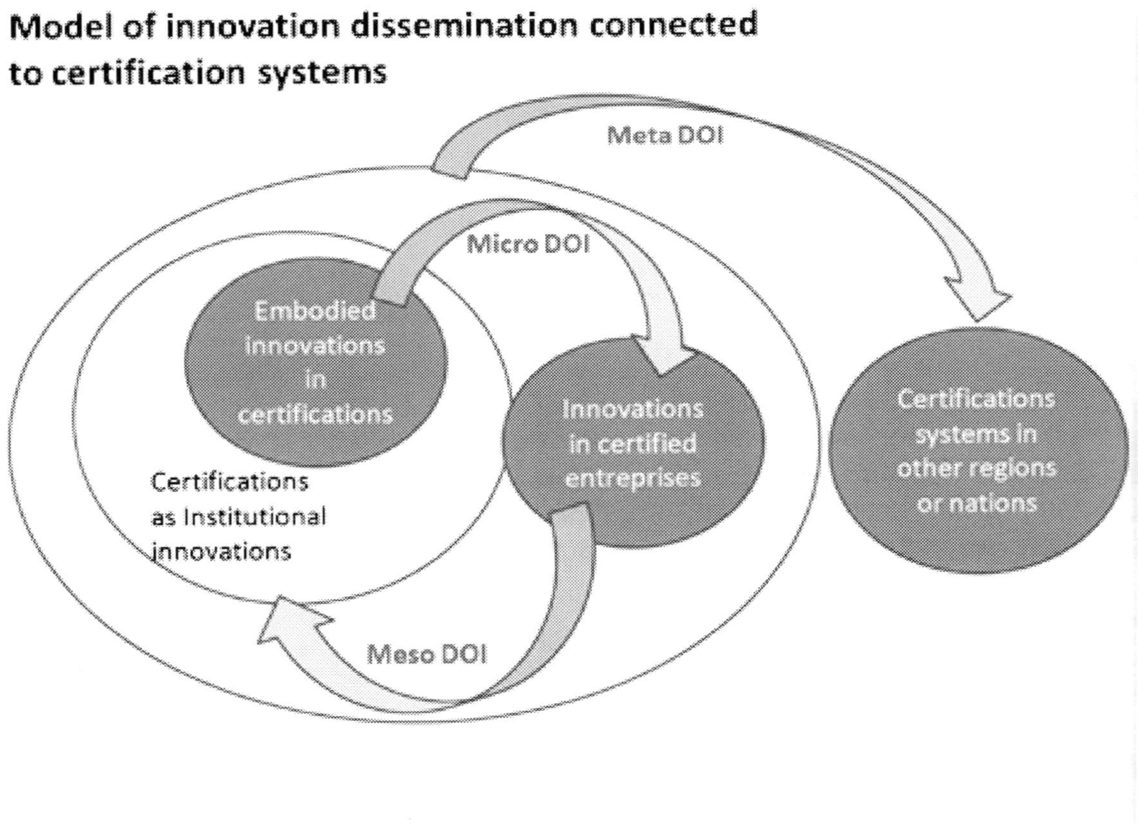

Relative Advantage

Relative advantage is the 'degree to which an innovation is perceived as being better than the idea it supersedes' (Rogers, 1995, p. 212). The sub-dimensions of economic-functional, symbolic and other benefits can follow from innovations. Economic effectiveness in production, marketing or other areas due to cost-effectiveness increases productivity. Increased quality and resulting in higher prices may be another innovation strategy. Traditionally, service sectors have applied one of two main logics: cutting costs or increasing quality (Ritzer, 1998). Symbolic value related to increased social status (identity, brand, image, positive word-of-mouth) can be associated with innovations (e.g. becoming modern, sustainable, high quality). Such associations can be important vis-à-vis customers, partners, employees, suppliers, community actors and other stakeholders. Quality labels and certifications may have symbolic value, increasing sales and justifying higher prices. However, Rogers suggests that relying heavily on status leads to over adoption, which might lessen the benefits once 'many have it'. Generally, a relative advantage is a strong factor, particularly economic profitability. Yet if influential actors subscribe to certain values, other enterprises might implement the innovations even when no profitability improvements are attained. The amount of time that elapses from implementation until the advantage is obtained also matters; long-term advantages can be more questionable. Small firms, in particular, often have limited resources and a short-term focus, and promises of long-term results can be beyond the single firm's capacity for innovative behaviour (Pikkemaat et al., 2019).

In terms of relative advantage, the certification stakeholders refer particularly to market prospects:

A lot of customers book through VisitScotland, and we would not have these customers if we were not part of the QA scheme. (SC-6)

It gives you more opportunities in branding and marketing. It affects the staff, it affects what you are doing, when you have a line that you have to be above. (IC-3)

Also, as referred to particularly in the Icelandic case, the quality system is a catalyst for collaborative effectiveness where the actors in a supply chain or network have a common language. In the systemic setup, there is meso-level diffusion pressure and motivation:

We have taken on Vakinn, and we need other companies that we are selling or working with to have these same standards. If they are also in Vakinn, it makes it easier to work with them.... And it is a pressure to do the same thing. We have to provide some security regulations and go through certain steps in order to be qualified. (IC-3)

If you are buying something from a company, if you have two places of accommodation and one has Vakinn and one doesn't, you would choose, all things equal, the one that has Vakinn. Since you yourself adhere to the 75% rule. (IC-9)

The gradual building up of professionalism and learning of the trade through the certification systems are also emphasised in the study, but to varying degrees, as illustrated in the citations below:

One of the guides that we use said that the Visit Scotland scheme really helped him as it pointed out a couple of things. (SC-6)

Not a great deal of learning involved. It is just nice to have had somebody check what we do and provide...We do not see that the QA system for activities contributes over and above all the certifications and awards that we already have. (SC-7)

So if you don't understand the whole concept of sustainability ... then it could be really useful. (NZ-4)

It teaches those who are not familiar with management what they need to do.... It makes it much easier because there is a checklist of things and they can introduce them into their business. (NZ-1)

It keeps me on my toes. (IC-5)

Compatibility

Compatibility is the degree to which an innovation is "perceived as consistent with existing values, past experience, and needs of potential adopters" (Rogers, 1995, p. 224). Compatibility can be in regard to the entrepreneur's or key staff members' life situations, norms, values or beliefs. Professional cultures, knowledge systems and ways of working may also determine the way people perceive and implement innovations such as certifications. Innovation adoption can be hampered if owners and staff need to 'unlearn' or go through other steep learning curves. Compatibility also depends on how well innovations fit in with previous innovations. Rogers sees previously introduced ideas as 'mental tools' for the actors and suggests that too divergent ideas may be difficult. Compatibility depends on the business model; new ideas and routines may influence not only the firm but customers, financing, business partners, technology and so on. For example, trajectories related to safety may be in opposition to norms, and changes in this area may cause legal liability problems.

Several tourism firms in the study express frustration that the national certification (Scottish QA) is not focused on the particularities of experience products. On the other hand, some New Zealand firms find QM to be focused mainly on backstage processes (routines, management) and too little on in-use practice with customers. This is the main issue in relation to the compatibility attribute; the following excerpts illustrate that the three are perceived differently in certain respects:

...the question is what makes outdoor tourism so different from other parts of tourism, and why we need a different system for that. I think it is because you are dealing with nature, you are dealing with all sorts of elements that you are not dealing with when you are doing culture tours or stuff like, you know, Saga trips or whatever. It is a different risk factor you need to take into account. And then you need different qualifications, you...it is not enough just to be a historian. You need all sorts of skills to be able to survive, so to speak, and return with your group home safely. So I think that is the main difference and why we need a special system for outdoor tourism...I think we have pretty much done – I wouldn't say everything – in Vakinn in terms of safety. (IC-1B)

Because of the knowledge of the snow avalanche. You know, you have to have some knowledge in guiding, in the backcountry and have some ski knowledge and knowledge about the snow conditions and so

Innovative Certifications in Adventure Tourism

on, so I would say that is quite different from another. They require more knowledge about the weather and snow conditions and so on. (IC-1A)

People have to enjoy the tour, but in a safe way.... Because you have this machine [snowmobile] of maybe 250 kilos, you don't want to roll it over. We don't want to be scared all the time. It has to be fun, too, because it is fun. And it is exciting, so this is an experience. They have bought an experience – if you can say it so – from us, so we have to provide that. (IC-2)

It needs to be focused on the product, the delivery of the product. (NZ-4)

You know Qualmark comes from accommodation stars; it has nothing to do with nature tourism. After all, it has been expanded to adventure tourism and transport and all that, but the basic premises are still there. (NZ-3)

They (Visit Scotland) have never gotten it quite right, to be honest, because they historically have not focused on the quality of the outdoor activities and the experiences that we are offering, which is ultimately what matters to the client. Our members were looking at the VS forms a couple of years ago, and, for instance, our car park, which is perfectly satisfactory for our purposes, would have scored two or three stars out of five. Like our toilet facilities, going out of this building to get to the toilets is another factor that will have us marked down in the QA system. When, in reality, what our clients are reporting from their experience with us has to do with other factors. (SC-7)

Complexity

Rogers (1995, p. 242) defines complexity as "the degree to which an innovation is perceived as relatively difficult to understand and use". Difficulties may be technical or related to pre-understanding (competence type and level). High complexity may come about, also, because of fuzzy communication or administrative uncertainty. It can be diminished by organisational measures that simplify operational procedures and ensure transparency of information. What is perceived as complex also depends upon the stakeholders' prior understanding. If the compatibility is low, complexity becomes high.

In particular, firms from Iceland that had no safety procedures already in place argued that certification's complexity and work demands were heavy. In contrast, those having such procedures in place already found it less complex. This result points to the centrality of pre-understanding and pre-practice. However, the learning tools offered by the certification bodies also influence complexity:

It can be overwhelming at first, but once you are in the rhythm, it is fine. (NZ-5)

Compared to ISO, Vakinn is very easy… It gives us gold in the Vakinn environment. (IC-7)

A lot of the things we have been doing already…with risk assessment and security, we had that in place. I just need to put it together in a document. (IC-3)

We have very many criteria that we have to work on, because we have sea kayaking and hiking and biking, riding, and then we have this coffeehouse.... I think it will take some time... But I would say it is work that we would have done anyway, so the cost is not a problem. (IC-1A)

Vakinn organises learning networks and supervision and offers many tools with examples to reduce complexity for firms, particularly as they work on getting certified. New Zealand's QM organises workshops for 'old-timers' to share new knowledge.

Trialability

Trialability refers to the "degree to which an innovation may be experimented with on a limited basis" (Rogers, 1995, p. 243). If different steps or levels are built into the process, an enterprise can undertake gradual assimilation, and it might lapse from the engagement without economic or market risks. Thus, trialability is a distinct part of risk management behaviour. Scalable innovations are most relevant for test implementations. Trialability can include collaboration with customers who are likely to be willing to pioneer new trends, goods and experiences. If they are willing to give the enterprise proper feedback, trialability materialises as a wider co-creation situation, resembling, for example, user-driven innovation.

This empirical study of three national certification systems did not directly reveal information about this category. However, some firms described how they certified only some of their business sector areas, such as accommodation or food, and not their adventure products (found mostly related to Scottish QA). Others started with the easiest or most critical subsectors – for example, safety (found in relation to Vakinn) – and planned to certify more subsectors later. Making the certification dynamic, so that re-certification is based on improvements from the previous round, is a pragmatic way to handle trialability. None of the three systems includes the trialability attribute to any extent.

Observability

Observability relates to "the degree to which the results of an innovation is visible to others" (Rogers, 1995, p. 244). If the benefits of an innovation are visible to potential adopters, it is likely to be adopted more easily. There are tangible aspects, easy to 'gaze', such as specific equipment, written materials and documentation. Soft evidence might be far less visible and open to interpretation by intermediaries.

In the case of certification and quality systems, observability occurs when new adventure tourism operators see such systems in operation, either in their own or other countries. From a distance, they will be able to assess whether and how the systems make a difference. Tourism is a sector that is fairly open to 'friendly espionage'. In quality systems, there is also a significant openness; transparency is part of the logic of a certification system, where not only symbolic evidence, such as labels, signboards, stamps, artefacts, routines and so on, is visible but all award criteria are also widely communicated.

The Norwegian tourism industry examined the quality systems in Scotland, Iceland and New Zealand to develop its own system. Accordingly, Norwegian business and institutional actors used the observability of the systems and the information garnered to draw their conclusions. The New Zealand system, in particular, has a good reputation and has been considered from the outside with admiration. The transnational openness is important for DOI on the meta-level, where tourism systems attempt to learn from one another.

DISCUSSION AND CONCLUSION

This chapter contributes to understanding the role of attributes of innovations in diffusion in the case of certifications. This consideration offers some insight into how certifications can contribute to innovations in adventure tourism. Based on a range of studies, Rogers (1995) concludes that relative advantage tends to be the most important attribute for the diffusion of innovations. However, it often works in combination with others. He demonstrates that DOI is positively related to relative advantage, compatibility, trialability and observability, while being, not surprisingly, negatively related to complexity. Our study shows that relative advantage and compatibility seem most critical for adoption. Complexity and observability are important too, while trialability seems less obtainable in this particular context.

The model attempts to describe how certification systems can diffuse innovations. The firms and quality institutions suggest in their assessments that their systems could ensure faster implementation and consolidation of recognised standards, thus ensuring the embedded, although in many cases quite incremental, categories of innovations. Since certification bodies often perform R&D tasks, they may take on an important role in knowledge development. However, if the certification body is not up to date with the development of tourism, it can instead become an obstacle, hindering the continuous and dynamic meso-innovation stream of knowledge transfer. What is found in this study is that certification bodies facilitate certain innovations and hamper others. Therefore, they can be a good match for some and a mismatch for other tourism firms. The three certifications studied here were perceived with varied degrees of appropriate focus since some had a low focus on experiences (safety, fun and other unique experience quality dimensions); instead, they focused mainly on functional services. The focus seems critical; in addition, the competencies and incentives of which the certification bodies are in possession seem crucial for the recruitment and promotion of the systems and the obtaining of critical mass (Doods & Ramsay, 2017).

The study also reveals the particular difficulties in quality assessment and accurate certification of the specific experience and service dimensions in adventure tourism, here indicated by evidence related to the compatibility attribute. The firms are reluctant to standardise functional services, as these are not a central part of what they do to facilitate value co-creation related to experience products. They fear that a strong focus on functional service may take focus away from the core elements (i.e. the experiences), reducing their differentiation and innovativeness. The latter concern aligns with the discussion in the literature, not only in connection with tourism (Deng-Westphal et al., 2015) but also generally (Blind, 2016).

Research-based evidence about international certification systems is emerging, and the environmental challenges that many types of destinations face tend to stimulate the propensity to develop new systems. Mutual learning from system to system – the meta-DOI – takes place. This suggests that certification systems serve to improve selected aspects of quality and promote the status of relevant policy and the institutional bodies that envision new systems. The Norwegian quality system for experience-based tourism, Varde Experience Quality, which will be implemented in 2021, did to some extent avoid starting from scratch by learning from evidence relating to the three existing systems, particularly the Scottish system. The Norwegian system has done significant innovative work within the experience quality and safety dimensions (Eide & Mossberg, 2019).

A larger innovation agenda frame the points of view expressed in this chapter. Still, the fact remains that governments' stimulation of innovation through regulation has received very little research attention (Hansen et al., 2019; Mahmood & Rufin, 2005). Further research should address the relationships of micro-, meso- and meta-level DOI processes. Moreover, the experience-based tourism contexts are seriously challenging. Neither of the three national certifications was adapted entirely to the experience-economy logic (i.e. value co-creation based on experiences like 'safe and fun'). That mismatch created lower compatibility than expected. This point is critically important to consider not only in future studies, but also in any attempt at innovation policy that may be introduced.

REFERENCES

Abelsen, B., Eide, D., Kvidal, T., & Leenheer, A. (2014). Organisational innovations: Re-organising destination marketing organisations. In G. Alsos, D. Eide, & E. L. Madsen (Eds.), *Handbook of research on innovation in tourism industries* (pp. 277–302). Edward Elgar.

Acemoglu, D., Gancia, G., & Zilibotti, F. (2012). Competing engines of growth: Innovation and standardisation. *Journal of Economic Theory*, *147*(2), 570–601. doi:10.1016/j.jet.2010.09.001

Alsos, G., Eide, D., & Madsen, E. L. (2014). Introduction: Innovation in tourism industries. In G. Alsos, D. Eide, & E. L. Madsen (Eds.), *Handbook of research on innovation in tourism industries* (pp. 1–24). Edward Elgar.

Blind, K. (2016). The impact of standardisation and standards on innovation. In J. Edler, P. Cunningham, & A. Gök (Eds.), *Handbook of innovation policy impact* (pp. 450–483). Edward Elgar. doi:10.4337/9781784711856.00022

Cefis, E., & Marsili, O. (2006). Survivor: The role of innovation in firms' survival. *Research Policy*, *35*(5), 626–641. doi:10.1016/j.respol.2006.02.006

Costa, J., Rodrigues, D., & Gomes, J. (2019). Sustainability of tourism destinations and the importance of certification. *Worldwide Hospitality and Tourism Themes*, *11*(6), 677–684. doi:10.1108/WHATT-08-2019-0050

Deng-Westphal, M., Beeton, S., & Anderson, A. (2015). The paradox of adopting tourism ecolabels. In M. Hughes, D. Weaver, & C. Pforr (Eds.), *The practice of sustainable tourism: Resolving the paradox* (pp. 228–246). Routledge.

Dibra, M. (2015). Rogers theory on diffusion of innovation-the most appropriate theoretical model in the study of factors influencing the integration of sustainability in tourism businesses. *Procedia: Social and Behavioral Sciences*, *195*, 1453–1462. doi:10.1016/j.sbspro.2015.06.443

Dodds, R., & Ramsay, G. (2017). Is economically incentivised participation creating a greater interest into environmental certification? *Journal of Outdoor Recreation and Tourism*, *20*, 31–33. doi:10.1016/j.jort.2017.09.001

Dunk, R. M., Gillespie, S. A., & MacLeod, D. (2016). Participation and retention in a green tourism certification scheme. *Journal of Sustainable Tourism*, *24*(12), 1585–1603. doi:10.1080/09669582.2015.1134558

Eide, D., Fuglsang, L., & Sundbo, J. (2017). Management challenges with the maintenance of experience concept innovations: Toward a new research agenda. *Tourism Management, 63*, 452–463. doi:10.1016/j.tourman.2017.06.029

Eide, D., & Mossberg, L. (2013). Towards more intertwined innovation types: innovation through experience design focusing on customer interactions. In Handbook on the experience economy (pp. 248-268). Edward Elgar. doi:10.4337/9781781004227.00019

Eide, D., & Mossberg, L. (2019). Toward a framework of experience quality assessment: Illustrated by cultural tourism. In D. Jelinčić & Y. Mansfeld (Eds.), *Creating and Managing Experiences in Cultural Tourism* (pp. 101–120). World Scientific. doi:10.1142/10809

Freel, M. S. (2000). Barriers to product innovation in small manufacturing firms. *International Small Business Journal, 18*(2), 60–80. doi:10.1177/0266242600182003

Fuglsang, L., & Eide, D. (2013). The experience turn as bandwagons: Understanding network formation and innovation as practice. *European Urban and Regional Studies, 20*(4), 418–435. doi:10.1177/0969776412448090

Fuglsang, L., Sundbo, J., & Sørensen, F. (2011). Dynamics of experience service innovation: innovation as a guided activity: Results from a Danish survey. *Service Industries Journal, 31*(5), 661–677. doi:10.1080/02642060902822109

Gilani, H. R., Innes, J. L., & De Grave, A. (2018). The effects of seasonal business diversification of British Columbia ski resorts on forest management. *Journal of Outdoor Recreation and Tourism, 23*, 51–58. doi:10.1016/j.jort.2018.07.005

Greenhalgh, T., Robert, G., Macfarlane, F., Bate, P., & Kyriakidou, O. (2004). Diffusion of innovations in service organisations: Systematic review and recommendations. *The Milbank Quarterly, 82*(4), 581–629. doi:10.1111/j.0887-378X.2004.00325.x PMID:15595944

Grissemann, U., Plank, A., & Brunner-Sperdin, A. (2013). Enhancing business performance of hotels: The role of innovation and customer orientation. *International Journal of Hospitality Management, 33*, 347–356. doi:10.1016/j.ijhm.2012.10.005

Hall, C. M., & Williams, A. M. (2008). *Tourism and innovation*. Routledge. doi:10.4324/9780203938430

Hansen, M., Hjalager, A. M., & Fyall, A. (2019). Adventure tourism innovation: Benefitting or hampering operations? *Journal of Outdoor Recreation and Tourism, 28*, 100253. doi:10.1016/j.jort.2019.100253

Hjalager, A. M. (2002). Repairing innovation defectiveness in tourism. *Tourism Management, 23*(5), 465–474. doi:10.1016/S0261-5177(02)00013-4

Hjalager, A. M. (2018). Suppliers as key collaborators for sustainable tourism development. In J. Liburd & D. Edwards (Eds.), *Collaboration for Sustainable Tourism Development* (pp. 187–205). Goodfellow. doi:10.23912/9781911635000-3927

Hjalager, A. M., & Madsen, E. L. (2018). Business model innovation in tourism: Opportunities and challenges. In The Sage handbook of tourism management (pp. 373-390). Sage.

Hoarau-Heemstra, H., & Eide, D. (2019). Values and concern: Drivers of innovation in experience-based tourism. *Tourism and Hospitality Research, 19*(1), 15–26. doi:10.1177/1467358416683768

Høegh-Guldberg, O. (2018). Between company and network practices: Mirroring innovative ideas. *Scandinavian Journal of Hospitality and Tourism, 18*(3), 278–302. doi:10.1080/15022250.2018.1497305

Høegh-Guldberg, O., Eide, D., Trengereid, V., & Hjemdahl, K. M. (2018). Dynamics of innovation network journeys: Phases and crossroads in seven regional innovation networks. *Scandinavian Journal of Hospitality and Tourism, 18*(3), 234–260. doi:10.1080/15022250.2018.1497261

Klepper, S., & Malerba, F. (2010). Demand, innovation and industrial dynamics: An introduction. *Industrial and Corporate Change, 19*(5), 1515–1520. doi:10.1093/icc/dtq043

Kondo, Y. (2000). Innovation versus standardisation. *The TQM Magazine, 12*(1), 6–10. doi:10.1108/09544780010287177

Kuscer, K., Mihalic, T., & Pechlaner, H. (2017). Innovation, sustainable tourism and environments in mountain destination development: A comparative analysis of Austria, Slovenia and Switzerland. *Journal of Sustainable Tourism, 25*(4), 489–504. doi:10.1080/09669582.2016.1223086

Landauer, M., Goodsite, M. E., & Juhola, S. (2018). Nordic national climate adaptation and tourism strategies: (How) are they interlinked? *Scandinavian Journal of Hospitality and Tourism, 18*(sup1), S75-S86.

Lundberg, C., Fredman, P., & Wall-Reinius, S. (2014). Going for the green? The role of money among adventure tourism entrepreneurs. *Current Issues in Tourism, 17*(4), 373–380. doi:10.1080/13683500.2012.746292

Mahmood, I. P., & Rufin, C. (2005). Government's dilemma: The role of government in imitation and innovation. *Academy of Management Review, 30*(2), 338–360. doi:10.5465/amr.2005.16387891

Margaryan, L. (2018). Nature as a commercial setting: The case of adventure tourism providers in Sweden. *Current Issues in Tourism, 21*(16), 1893–1911. doi:10.1080/13683500.2016.1232378

Margaryan, L., & Stensland, S. (2017). Sustainable by nature? The case of (non) adoption of eco-certification among the adventure tourism companies in Scandinavia. *Journal of Cleaner Production, 162*, 559–567. doi:10.1016/j.jclepro.2017.06.060

Mykletun, R. J. (2018). Adventure tourism in the North: Six illustrative cases. *Scandinavian Journal of Hospitality and Tourism, 18*(4), 319–329. doi:10.1080/15022250.2018.1524999

OECD/Eurostat. (2018). Oslo manual 2018: Guidelines for collecting, reporting and using data on innovation (4th ed.). OECD Publishing.

Perrin-Malterre, C. (2018). Tourism diversification process around trail running in the Pays of Allevard (Isère). *Journal of Sport & Tourism, 22*(1), 67–82. doi:10.1080/14775085.2018.1432410

Pikkemaat, B., Peters, M., & Bichler, B. F. (2019). Innovation research in tourism: Research streams and actions for the future. *Journal of Hospitality and Tourism Management, 41*, 184–196. doi:10.1016/j.jhtm.2019.10.007

Rantala, O., Rokenes, A., & Valkonen, J. (2018). Is adventure tourism a coherent concept? A review of research approaches on adventure tourism. *Annals of Leisure Research*, *21*(5), 539–552. doi:10.1080/11745398.2016.1250647

Ritzer, G. (1998). *The McDonaldization thesis*. London: SAGE Publications

Rogers, E. (1995). *Diffusion of innovation*. Free Press.

Roper, S., & Tapinos, E. (2016). Taking risks in the face of uncertainty: An exploratory analysis of green innovation. *Technological Forecasting and Social Change*, *112*, 357–363. doi:10.1016/j.techfore.2016.07.037

Ruhanen, L., & Cooper, C. (2004). Applying a knowledge management framework to tourism research. *Tourism Recreation Research*, *29*(1), 83–88. doi:10.1080/02508281.2004.11081434

Saarinen, J., & Varnajot, A. (2019). The Arctic in tourism: Complementing and contesting perspectives on tourism in the Arctic. *Polar Geography*, *42*(2), 109–124. doi:10.1080/1088937X.2019.1578287

Schumpeter, J. A. (1934). *The theory of economic development*. Harvard University Press.

Sigurðardóttir, I. (2018). Wellness and equestrian tourism: New kind of adventure? *Scandinavian Journal of Hospitality and Tourism*, *18*(4), 377–392. doi:10.1080/15022250.2018.1522718

Smith, M. R. (2015). *Aerial Adventure Park: Trends, statistics and leading practices*. Retrieved from https://www.slideshare.net/MichaelSmith351/2015-aerialadventure-park-trends-statistics-and-leading-practices-52820699

Stebbins, R. A. (1997). Casual leisure: A conceptual statement. *Leisure Studies*, *16*(1), 17–25. doi:10.1080/026143697375485

Tangeland, T. (2011). Why do people purchase adventure tourism activity products? *Scandinavian Journal of Hospitality and Tourism*, *11*(4), 435–456. doi:10.1080/15022250.2011.619843

Tornatzky, L. G., & Klein, K. J. (1982). Innovation characteristics and innovation adoption-implementation: A meta-analysis of findings. *IEEE Transactions on Engineering Management*, *EM-29*(1), 28–45. doi:10.1109/TEM.1982.6447463

Visit Snowdonia. (2020). *Adventure Parc Snowdonia*. Available at: https://www.visitsnowdonia.info/adventure-parc-snowdonia

Weidenfeld, A., Williams, A. M., & Butler, R. W. (2010). Knowledge transfer and innovation among attractions. *Annals of Tourism Research*, *37*(3), 604–626. doi:10.1016/j.annals.2009.12.001

Williams, P., & Soutar, G. N. (2009). Value, satisfaction and behavioral intentions in an adventure tourism context. *Annals of Tourism Research*, *36*(3), 413–438. doi:10.1016/j.annals.2009.02.002

Zehrer, A., Smeral, E., & Hallmann, K. (2017). Destination competitiveness: A comparison of subjective and objective indicators for winter sports areas. *Journal of Travel Research*, *56*(1), 55–66. doi:10.1177/0047287515625129

Chapter 10
Community-Based Tourism Experiences in Nepal:
A Path to Sustainable Tourism in the Post-COVID-19 Era

Sandeep Basnyat
https://orcid.org/0000-0002-2609-8814
Macao Institute for Tourism Studies (IFTM), China

Trijya Kafle
Nepal College of Management, Nepal

ABSTRACT

This chapter presents a case study of community-based tourism (CBT) in Nepal. Based on the Nepalese experiences, this chapter demonstrates that the CBT approach not only helps to economically empower the local community, revitalize local culture, and enhance appreciation for the natural and cultural environment, but also ultimately helps to promote socially responsible and environmentally conscious sustainable tourism practices. Identifying policies and appropriate practices for the sustainable development of tourism is critical because of the recent crisis of COVID-19 that has almost paralyzed the entire travel and tourism industry. Furthermore, based on CBT approaches, the knowledge derived from the Nepalese experiences can be used in various developing countries that aim to develop sustainable tourism development models for the post-COVID-19 era.

INTRODUCTION

The concept of community-based tourism (CBT) evolved around the 1970s as an alternative form of tourism development approach where local communities are involved in the planning, management, decision-making, and execution process (López-Guzmán et al., 2011). Therefore, the CBT approach includes direct local participation in tourism activities and their related processes, and the end benefits are integrated into the local economy (Zielinski, Jeong, & Milanés, 2020). Both micro and macro enter-

DOI: 10.4018/978-1-7998-8775-1.ch010

prises that operate individually or under a common organisational umbrella may support the community and help them embrace control and management, empowerment, conservation of natural and cultural resources, and development through tourism (Zielinski, Jeong, & Milanés, 2020). The advocates of CBT recommend local communities' involvement in planning and management of tourism, especially, because they are not only considered part of the tourism product themselves but also many local communities can adapt to changes quickly (López-Guzmán et al., 2011).

In modern-day tourism, many countries consider CBT an important vehicle for developing rural and remote areas (Zielinski, Jeong, & Milanés, 2020). Numerous studies also exist that point out the relationship between CBT and sustainable tourism and how CBT may help develop tourism sustainably (e.g., Dangi & Jamal, 2016). However, despite enormous potentialities and opportunities, several cases of CBT approaches have failed because of a plethora of factors, including operational, structural, and cultural, among others. This has caused particular difficulty to those interested in either developing a coherent theory or understanding the factors that lead to the successful development of CBT models, especially in developing countries (Dangi & Jamal, 2016; Zielinski, Jeong, & Milanés, 2020).

This chapter presents a case study of the community-based tourism approach being implemented in Nepal and argues that CBT not only helps to economically empower the local community, revitalise local culture and enhance appreciation for the natural and cultural environment but also ultimately helps to promote socially responsible and environmentally conscious sustainable tourism practices (Gyawali, 2020). Based on the Nepalese experiences, this chapter suggests how the countries endowed with cultural and natural attractions can effectively make use of available natural and cultural resources and traditional knowledge system to attract visitors. The chapter further demonstrates how the local community and other stakeholders can actively participate and engage in the tourism experience production process, thereby directing the local community's economic benefits. The CBT model in Nepal has been considered a widely successful one and has been hugely acclaimed. The knowledge derived from the Nepalese experiences can be usefully applied in various developing countries that aim to develop their own sustainable tourism development models for the post-COVID-19 era. After conceptualising CBT and discussing how it is generally managed, this chapter presents a case study of community-based tourism in Nepal, commonly known as homestay tourism or village tourism. The chapter then discusses how socially responsible and environmentally conscious sustainable tourism practices can be promoted to attract visitors in the post-COVID-19 era.

CONCEPTUALISATION OF COMMUNITY-BASED TOURISM

The earlier concept of community-based tourism (CBT) emerged in the 1970s when international donors such as the United Nations and the World Bank introduced the idea of a participatory development process (Zielinski, Jeong, Kim, et al., 2020). In line with this agenda, CBT was conceptualised as an alternative to mass tourism in developing countries and rural tourism in the developed world. It was expected that this initiative would help in grassroots development, resident participation, empowerment, and capacity building of rural communities (Dangi & Jamal, 2016). CBT was considered a viable instrument for poverty reduction for developing countries and would offer opportunities for conservation and rural economic development. Numerous community-development projects based on similar approaches were also started in developing nations, many of which were aided through official development assistance (ODA) (Zielinski, Jeong, Kim, et al., 2020).

CBT initiatives specifically intend to involve the local community in providing services and experiences to the tourists and planning and maintaining the tourism system. In the 1980s, Peter Murphy, based on his research on small communities in British Columbia and the Yukon (Canada), described community-based tourism as an approach where visitors interact with local people (communities) and landscapes and experience tourism products and services. Since then, a variety of concepts and definitions have been proposed by scholars. However, almost all of the definitions agree, in general, that it is a form of tourism that is managed, owned, and controlled by the local communities (Goodwin & Santilli, 2009). Additionally, not only local communities are also actively involved in the planning and development of tourism experiences, but also a major proportion of the benefits remain within the community. As seen, the definition of CBT includes a variety of micro initiatives such as rural tourism, pro-poor tourism, cultural tourism, ecotourism, community benefit tourist initiatives, and community-based enterprises, all of which generally operate in a similar manner (López-Guzmán et al., 2011). Although there might be differences in the way these tourism approaches are defined, at the core, all of them embrace community control and management, empowerment, conservation of natural and cultural resources, and community development through tourism (Zielinski, Kim, et al., 2020).

Since many CBT initiatives are smaller in scale, interactions between visitors and the host community are also particularly suited to rural and regional areas only. Despite this, visitors can see and experience a wide range of tourism products, including local culture, gastronomy, traditional handcraft and folklore, rural communities' lifestyles, and ecology, among others (Eom & Han, 2019). Most recently, some scholars have even suggested the adoption of luxury community-based tourism to localise the ownership of hotels and develop and promote boutique tourism involving the local community (Giampiccoli et al., 2020).

CBT initiatives have been able to foster positive environmental and socioeconomic impacts. Consequently, many development agencies have also used this approach as a community development tool, particularly where other forms of economic development are limited (Mtapuri & Giampiccoli, 2016). The most direct benefits of CBT are the direct economic impact on families, socioeconomic improvements, and sustainable diversification of lifestyles of involved communities (López-Guzmán et al., 2011). Furthermore, it also increases the number of facilities, roads, parks, and recreational and cultural attractions, which benefits communities' quality of life and develops respect for their culture. The use of natural resources, beautiful scenery, and unique flora and fauna also helps increase awareness for the natural environment among local communities and visitors and promote efforts for their conservation (Lee & Jan, 2019). From the tourism industry's perspective, CBT helps create jobs, provides additional income to stakeholders, empowers the community, helps promote conservation efforts, and reduces poverty (Eom & Han, 2019). As a result, many developing countries, including Nepal, India, and Vietnam, among others, emphasise the development of CBT heavily in their tourism policies.

MANAGEMENT OF COMMUNITY-BASED TOURISM

CBT initiatives often experience several challenges both at the start-up as well as during the operation stages. Many such projects have failed either because of the lack of understanding of these challenges or not being able to resolve them. These challenges arise from several factors, including economic, structural, and governance, among others. It has been seen that many CBTs focus on earning profitability without giving due emphasis on local empowerment or participatory approach of decision making as the latter incurs costs (Blackstock, 2005). The operation of several CBT projects relies on external funders, and when the funds dry up, these projects experience financial constraints for maintenance and reinvestments (Goodwin & Santilli, 2009; López-Guzmán et al., 2011). Structural problems, such as the absence of residents' support, and the presence of social inequalities based on class and gender in the community, also lead to the failure of CBT initiatives (Blackstock, 2005).

Governance and operational issues impose significant constraints on the management of CBT. For example, the centralisation of public administration in many countries often leads to slow and complex bureaucratic actions and discourages community ownership and participation in the decision-making process (Dangi & Jamal, 2016). Similarly, the lack of policy direction to support CBT, the lack of access to information and transparency, and potential conflicts between the different public administrations also hinder the success of CBT (Zielinski, Kim, et al., 2020). For these reasons, the concerned stakeholders may need to pay critical attention to the way these projects are managed. It is generally suggested that the local communities should be involved in the planning and management as well as in the decision-making process. Furthermore, measures that indicate economic, socio-cultural, environmental, and community wellbeing should be monitored, and a mechanism should be developed to distribute economic benefits fairly among the residents (Lee & Jan, 2019).

Public administration departments, non-governmental organisations (NGOs), private business enterprises, and the local community should get involved and work together for the successful operation and management of CBT. In general, apart from the local communities, four other important stakeholders are also directly involved in the operation and management of CBT: tourist offices that provide information to visitors; organisations that collaborate with other important institutions such as the tourism industry, government departments, NGOs and universities; companies/people that provide raw materials or materials related to food and accommodation; and intermediaries such as transport or financial business organisations (López-Guzmán et al., 2011). Some companies, such as TourDure in South Korea, foster the local community by supporting the process of tourism business establishment and operation (Eom & Han, 2019). It is important to develop partnerships among the stakeholders to govern and balance benefits and power among them. In practice, two forms of partnerships exist: external, where various entities such as the private sectors, NGOs, and government departments are involved but not the CBT venture itself; and internal, in which CBT venture is also involved.

Various forms of CBT enterprises are in operation. Some operate individually or under a common organisational umbrella. Even those operating under a common organisational umbrella may have collective or individual/family ownership (Zielinski, Kim, et al., 2020). Reviewing different forms of CBT enterprises, conceptually proposed by a number of earlier scholars, Mtapuri and Giampiccoli (2016) highlighted that either the whole family, parts of the community or families, or a joint venture between the community or some of its members and business partner/s may involve in the CBT project. Researchers have also suggested various CBT business models, including a cooperative business, community business, private sector concessions, and non-government organisation (NGO)-private sector partnership, among others.

Partnership with external organisations also helps in the marketing of CBT. Marketing can be done using two approaches, and both approaches are in practice: bottom-up and top-down (Mtapuri & Giampiccoli, 2016). Bottom-up marketing is commonly associated with the domestic/local market, whereas top-down is associated with the international market. Change in the government's policies affects the marketing approaches for CBT. For example, Mtapuri and Giampiccoli (2016) noted that countries like Thailand and Indonesia, where CBT projects were predominantly visited by Western tourists until the mid of 2000, are increasingly visited by urban domestic and regional tourists since then. It has been suggested that a strong connection to the local informal economy helps boost the effects of domestic marketing efforts and benefits the poorer strata of the population, thus encouraging them to participate more actively.

The following section discusses the operation and management of 'homestay', a popular type of CBT practise in Nepal. The discussions are mostly based on the analysis of the primary data collected through interviews with CBT operators/promoters and government employees responsible for planning and implementing policies between April and May 2021.

COMMUNITY-BASED TOURISM PRACTICE IN NEPAL – HOMESTAY

The concept of CBT emerged in the mid of 1980s in Nepal when the government decided to frame a distinct tourism program that would help in the equitable distribution of socioeconomic benefits of tourism and included in its Seventh Plan (1985-90) (Baniya et al., 2018). In its Ninth Plan (1997-2002), the Nepalese government linked the development of tourism with the broad-based poverty eradication strategy. It established the Tourism for Rural Poverty Alleviation Program (TRPAP) under the Ministry of Culture, Tourism and Civil Aviation in 2001. TRPAP was designed to contribute to the poverty alleviation objective of the government by demonstrating sustainable tourism development models in rural areas of Nepal. With technical and financial assistance from the United Nations Development Programme (UNDP), UK's Department for International Development (DFID), and SNV Netherlands Development Organization, Nepal (SNV/Nepal), TRPAP operated in six districts of Nepal[1].

Table 1. Community homestay development trend in Nepal from 2017 to 2019

District	2017 No. of Affiliated House	2017 No. of Room	2017 No. of Bed	2018 No. of Affiliated House	2018 No. of Room	2018 No. of Bed	2019 No. of Affiliated House	2019 No. of Room	2019 No. of Bed
Kathmandu	63	99	214	63	99	176	84	110	188
Bhaktapur				13	14	28	13	14	28
Kavre	49	83	107	61	95	119	61	95	119
Lalitpur	12	24	47	15	28	51	15	28	51
Mugu	5	5	10	5	5	10	5	5	10
Nuwakot	25	33	66	25	33	66	40	48	96
Ramechhap	29	54	96	29	54	96	29	54	96
Chitwon	7	14	28				29	36	72
Makwanpur	7	16	30	7	16	30	7	16	30
Dhading	5	9	18	9	15	18	9	15	18
Udaypur							13	13	18
Saptari							7	7	12
Pyuthan	16	17	34	18	17	34	18	17	34
Total	218	354	650	245	376	628	310	438	742
Total districts with CBT	10			10			13		

(Source: adapted from MoCTCA, 2020)

Community-Based Tourism Experiences in Nepal

The experience of this new initiative demonstrated the importance of including communities for the successful operation and management of tourism projects. Hence, through the new tourism policy of 2008, the government emphasised the development of community-based tourism projects across the country. In 2011, essential directives were issued by the government that formalised the procedures and management of CBTs, especially the homestays. Table 1 provides the trend of community homestay development in Nepal from 2017 to 2019. As Table 1 shows, although the number of districts with community homestay initiatives has remained more or less the same, the registered number of homestay affiliated houses, the number of available rooms and beds for homestay guests have increased over time. It is important to note that the success of community homestay programs has motivated several private business organisations to start similar projects in Nepal. Examination of the homestay projects run by business houses is beyond the scope of this study. However, the profit-oriented private businesses' attraction towards homestays certainly shows the importance and impact of CBT in Nepalese society.

Key Characteristics of Homestay Programs in Nepal

One of the key characteristics of the community-based homestay initiatives in Nepal is that they follow a multi-stakeholder approach to operate the program. Apart from the local community that provides CBT experiences to the visitors, at least three other major stakeholders' supports are involved: Nepal Tourism Board, local government, especially the concerned municipality office, and the association/network. The Ministry of Tourism, through Nepal Tourism Board (NTB), the national tourism organisation, plays important role in promoting homestay programs. NTB works in partnership with local communities, local bodies, and the Homestay Association of Nepal and provides monetary and non-monetary supports. Additionally, NTB, in partnership with other organisations, also conducts capacity-building training programs for the communities in various areas, including front office, guest interactions, and food production, among others. Local municipalities usually do not have their own proactive policies. However, apart from occasional monetary help, local municipalities also support the local CBT initiatives in several ways, such as by protecting the CBT from wildlife and aiding in the development of infrastructures, including electricity, road, and bridges. Privately organised associations and networks play important roles in the management, operation, and promotion of CBT initiatives. These associations and networks explore villages and communities, identify tourism potentials, interact with the communities, and engage them in developing and selling CBTs to potential visitors. Most associations and networks also empower local communities and provide them with the necessary training, including the English language, to develop their skills and sell natural and socio-cultural activities that visitors can enjoy and engage in during their stays. Box 1 demonstrates a general itinerary for the visitors in the homestays in Nepal provided by one of the homestay operators interviewed during the data collection process.

General activities at Ayodhyapuri Bufferzone Community Homestay in Nepal

- Welcome by the community representatives wearing *Magar* (ethnic) dresses
- Demonstration of rooms to the visitors at the community house
- Lunch / Dinner
- Site visit: community lake with fishing and boating activities
- Site visit: community village and cultural/natural attractions such as Baikuntha Jharna (waterfall), and Gadi (places with historic and cultural significance)
- Dinner
- Cultural program at the community center showcasing cultural dances such as Sorathi, Marmi Nach, Lok Geet, Thal Naach, and Kauda Nach.

Special training is provided on greeting and welcoming visitors, and taking care of their needs, including transportation, running water, clean towels, and bedsheets, among others. Additionally, associations and networks promote CBTs through social media, domestic and international travel magazines, and online booking websites such as booking.com or intrepid.com.

The CBT experience in Nepal focuses on people and culture. Homestays provide exotic experiences of distinct Nepalese food and lifestyles to the visitors, including how local communities prepare their food, and sit together and eat their meals with their family members. Most communities identify one signature experience which they provide to the visitors. These communities are considered as 'Namuna' (sample) villages, and the experiences from these village communities are used to replicate and design other CBTs. While designing and developing new CBTs, observation tours are arranged for the representatives of the communities (usually by the CBT associations and networks) to 'Namuna' villages, where they will have an opportunity to obtain first-hand experiences on the operation and management of CBTs. In general, most houses in the community are involved in the CBT programs and act as 'hosts'. To ensure that the benefits of CBTs are properly shared among the community members, bank accounts are opened for each of these hosts.

CBT in Nepal is managed by a 'Homestay Management Committee'. The office secretary in the management committee is responsible for handling bookings, allocating houses that serve the visitors, and communicating with external parties such as Homestay Association. It is important to note that, although the number of international visitors was large in the past, since 2018, the number of domestic visitors has increased incrementally. Instead of paying individual houses where they receive services, visitors make payment through the Homestay Management Committee. The management committee then deducts a certain percentage (usually between 10% and 15%), and deposit the rest of the amount in the host's bank account. The management committee utilises the money to pay for the staff's salary and maintain clean and hygienic conditions in the community. Box 2 provides narratives of one of the CBT operators and the founder of Community Homestay Network, who shared his experiences of managing and operating homestay programs at several districts in Nepal.

Community-based tourism practices in homestays in Nepal as narrated by the founder of Community Homestay Network

> We started community-based tourism from Panauti in Nepal in 2012. Pauauti is rich in cultural attractions. We created a model of homestay project which is managed and run by women in Panauti. We empowered and trained the women in Panauti before formally inviting visitors. In the beginning, only three families participated in the project. Now, around 270 families are involved and have already served more than 7,000 visitors. After the success of Panauti, we replicated the same model in Barauli and other places. Currently, in addition to Panauti, we have been supporting 22 communities across Nepal. We are expanding our reach, and by 2022, we aim to include 50 communities in our network that provide CBT experiences.
>
> Benefits are equally shared and go directly to women. The community where women run the place, women, and the community, both have their own bank account. For every booking, the community homestay network gets 15 percent of the booking, then 85 percent goes to the community. Out of 85 percent, 80 percent goes to the host or the experience provider, and the remaining will go to the community fund and will be invested in community development in the future.
>
> We promote through social media. We also promote through international magazines, booking websites such as booking.com, and through our own travel agency Royal Mountain travel. We continuously send our guides to different villages and ask them to explore the village and identify potentials for CBT. We have a content writer, videographer, and photographer who design CBT experiences for those communities based on their unique practices. We also try to identify one signature experience in each community which we highlight while marketing and promoting CBT. For example, in Panauti, we have a cooking course in family, community hike, local cycle tour in five routes, hand carving, and experience with locals where tourists do everything that the family does. In Bhada, we try to incorporate the daily lives of farmers such as planting rice, wheat, potato, and mustard, and promote them as experiences for visitors.

Most CBT operators and government employees in Nepal argued that the CBT programs have tremendously helped in the conservation and preservation of local culture, thus maintaining the ecosystem in Nepal. The participants perceived that the ecosystem consisted of people and culture, and removing one of these factors may disturb the ecosystem, and tourism experiences become meaningless. Additionally, CBT has also helped to maintain the authenticity of the Nepalese villages' lifestyles and cultures as the community members have realised the economic benefits of doing that. As such, many youths in the local communities are also being increasingly interested in engaging in CBTs. Although comprehensive nationwide data on the socioeconomic benefits of CBT projects in Nepal are not available, Table 2 shows the number of community members, families, and communities who are registered with the Community Homestay Network and have been benefiting from CBT since 2012.

Table 2. Number of community members, families, and communities benefitting from CBT

	2012	2013	2014	2015	2016	2017	2018	2019
Number of community members	52	112	192	192	616	640	828	1350
Number of families	13	28	48	48	154	160	207	270
Number of communities	1	2	3	3	10	11	15	22

(Source: adapted from Community Homestay Network, 2020)

From the community engagement perspective, most local communities have developed their confidence and can interact with the visitors, including in English. As a result, the visitors' experiences at homestays have been enhanced. Additionally, some village communities have started to produce and become self-reliant on agricultural productions such as poultry, fish, and dairy. As reported by Community Homestay Network (2020), a total of 768 jobs were created within their network in 2019, which was an increase of 25% compared to 2018. These jobs included local guides, drivers, cultural performers, trainers, and full-time staff members. Of all the jobs created, 60% were performed by women. The number of cultural performers also increased by 42% compared to 2018 and reached 359 in 2019. Altogether 3,799 international tourists visited the homestays within Community Homestay Network in 2019. On average, the families involved in a CBT project earned up to USD 275 per month during the peak tourist season in Nepal (Community Homestay Network, 2020).

Despite numerous socioeconomic, cultural, and environmental benefits, starting a CBT project has always been a challenging task for most participating operators in this study. As they informed, one of the biggest challenges they had experienced, and continue to experience, is to convince the local community of the benefits of CBT and ensure their participation. Development of CBT is usually a longer-term approach and needs improvements in a variety of areas, including preparation and demonstration of food, hygiene and sanitation, presentation of cultural performances in a professional manner, and welcoming guests with sufficient etiquette. While maintenance of discipline is essential to perform these functions smoothly, community members often need to participate in training programs to upgrade themselves and learn from their own experiences. In order to overcome these challenges, CBT operators usually invite community members and leaders from a potential CBT project area to visit other project villages and provide them with first-hand experience of the operation of CBT, as well as its benefits. Furthermore, the project is started as a part-time initiative for a small number of families and gradually expanded to incorporate others. Additionally, lobbying with the government for developing physical infrastructures and finding an appropriate partner for the promotion of CBT is a continuous and tedious task.

PROMOTION OF SUSTAINABLE CBT PRACTICES FOR THE POST-COVID-19 ERA

It is often argued that tourism activities may lead to negative impacts, such as an unequal distribution of tourism revenue, natural and cultural resource degradation, and a low degree of empowerment, especially in rural communities (Lee & Jan, 2019). These negative impacts may also damage the local economy, culture, and environment, and, subsequently, obstruct sustainable CBT development efforts. Zielinski, Kim, et al. (2020) have argued that most of the barriers for CBT stem from unequal power relations within the community and between the community and other stakeholders and negatively affect the sustainable development of CBT. Therefore, for the successful development of CBT projects, the inclusion of community participation, wellbeing, and local control have been considered integral parts (Blackstock, 2005; Dangi & Jamal, 2016; Okazaki, 2008).

As discussed in the previous section, the CBT approach in Nepal allows visitors to stay at a 'homestay' or a 'family-owned teahouse' and get the authentic local experience while discovering new places, experiencing the real-life of rural areas surrounded by nature, and engaging in various nature- and culture-based tourism activities. While the national tourism organisation and various tourism-related associations/networks actively design, develop and promote CBT for and among the domestic as well as international tourists, management committees, such as the Homestay Management Committee, within the community, provide logistical supports and ensure the fair distributions of economic and social benefits among the community members who are engaged in providing community-based tourism experiences to the visitors. The Nepalese case has shown that such an inclusive approach of CBT practices in Nepal has caused several positive transformative effects among the local communities as they experienced better individual and communal wellbeing with a higher level of satisfaction derived from community empowerment and attachment. Consequently, the CBT model in Nepal has been successful not only in stimulating the local economy but also in enhancing awareness of and appreciation for the preservation of historical and cultural traditions and natural environment among the local communities. Such forms of socially responsible and environmentally conscious sustainable CBT practices in Nepal have increased communities' carrying capacity as a greater number of communities are taking part in CBT initiatives. Furthermore, it has also reduced tourism's negative impacts by ensuring a win-win situation for most rural community members. Considering its effectiveness, the Nepalese government has decided to further expand the CBT practices across the country to recover tourism after the COVID-19. To expedite this process, while a digital database is being developed for planning and policy implementations of community and rural tourism areas with the collaboration of Tribhuvan University (in Nepal), the Nepal Tourism Board (the national tourism organisation) has been working with the international organisations such as the United Nations Development Program (UNDP) and International Finance Corporation (IFC) to digitally market and promote those destinations.

Identifying policies and appropriate practices for the sustainable development of tourism is critical because of the recent crisis of COVID-19 that has almost paralysed the entire travel and tourism industry. UNWTO (2021) has reported that international travel declined by 70% to 75% in the year 2020, which means that international tourism could have returned to levels 30 years ago. It is estimated that the global travel and tourism market saw a loss of 100.8 million jobs worldwide in 2020 because of COVID-19. However, the prospects for 2021 remain uncertain because of a variety of reasons, including the unknown duration of the pandemic across countries, effectiveness, and availability of COVID-19 vaccine, particularly in developing and less resourceful countries, and uncertain policies about travel restrictions, among others (UNWTO, 2021; World Health Organization, 2021).

Furthermore, ongoing studies across the world on the impacts of COVID-19 and the future of travel and tourism, are predicting that the travel and tourism consumption patterns may change in the post-COVID 19 eras. It is expected that, instead of mass tourism, travellers may prefer free and independent travel, luxury trips, and health and wellness tourism. New forms of tourism, including slow tourism and smart tourism, may also drive future tourism activities (Wen et al., 2020). It is being predicted that instead of using crowded public transportation systems, travellers may either use vehicles that would not be crowded (for example, private cars) or travel to destinations that would allow them to experience places without using transportation system at all (Wen et al., 2020). Most popular reasons for travelling may include, among others, relaxation, site seeing, culture, and meeting family and friends. In a recent survey, several potential travellers have expressed their interest in travelling to a remote/isolated destination and staying in a small and remote/isolated hotel (Ivanova et al., 2020). The potential changes in the travel and tourism scenario have propelled many to argue that the travel and tourism industry needs to seriously think of ways to develop practices that may help to recover and sustain tourism in the post-COVID-19 era (Higgins-Desbiolles, 2021). The examination of the successful management and operation of the Nepalese CBT experiences demonstrates that the countries, especially those endowed with cultural and natural attractions in rural communities, can effectively use those resources and traditional knowledge systems to design CBTs that are unique and can attract visitors. However, other countries may need to apply a cautious approach while replicating the Nepalese CBT model in their own contexts. First, although CBT in Nepal started almost four decades ago, as of 2019, it has been applied only in 13 districts (out of 77). These districts are particularly suitable for the initiative because of their abundant natural and cultural endowments and resources. Second, as reported by the Community Homestay Network (2020), the average monthly family income earned by participating in a CBT project during the peak tourist season in Nepal was approximately USD 275 in 2019. The extent to which a monthly income is considered 'good' or not by a society may depend upon a variety of factors including market prices and average living expenditures, and largely affect their choices while engaging in a profession, such as CBT. Third, even though some village communities in Nepal have started to produce and become self-reliant on agricultural products, a number of CBT communities continue to import consumable goods for tourists. Therefore, questions can be raised about the long-term sustainability of such projects. Fourth, except for developing a policy framework, the Nepalese government has largely refrained from providing operational supports to CBT projects in Nepal. As reported by the participants of this study, local governments do not even have their own programs or budget for a CBT. All of such projects are operated and managed by the communities themselves with the support of private agencies. Consequently, despite four decades of involvement, such projects are confined to a limited number of districts in Nepal. Therefore, other countries that strive to replicate the Nepalese CBT model need to carefully examine the types of CBT they choose and fully understand the characteristics of those CBTs and the level of support needed to run them successfully. Regardless, the Nepalese example shows that careful development of CBTs may provide a viable alternative to mainstream tourism in the post-COVID-19 era as it can holistically integrate several components that are considered essential in attracting visitors such as accommodation, food and beverages, complementary services, and other tourism-related subsystems including infrastructure, health, education and environment (López-Guzmán et al., 2011). The presence of these components is vital for the development of sustainable tourism.

CONCLUSION

Based on the Nepalese 'homestay' experiences, this chapter presented a case study of a successful community-based tourism model. As demonstrated, the ways CBT projects are managed and operated play important roles in their success. An inclusive and integrated approach that clearly stipulates roles played by various stakeholders is essential as it helps to balance the power among them and distribute economic benefits equitably. Since CBTs are often presented as an alternative to mainstream tourism, as the Nepalese case shows, they need to focus on providing distinctive experiences to the visitors not only to draw their attention but also to provide them with genuine and authentic experiences that are unique to those tourism areas or villages. While support from the concerned government departments and private sector tourism industry are important in promoting CBTs, the extent to which community members' participation is ensured largely determines their success. Despite challenges, CBT initiatives can be successfully presented not only as an alternative to mainstream tourism but also to revive the tourism industry in the post-COVID-19 era in a more sustainable manner.

REFERENCES

Baniya, R., Shrestha, U., & Karn, M. (2018). Local and community well-being through community based tourism: A study of transformative eff ect. *Journal of Tourism and Hospitality Education*, *8*, 77–96. doi:10.3126/jthe.v8i0.20012

Blackstock, K. (2005). A critical look at community based tourism. *Community Development Journal: An International Forum*, *40*(1), 39–49. doi:10.1093/cdj/bsi005

Community Homestay Network. (2020). *2019 Impact Report*. https://www.communityhomestay.com/impact-report-2019.pdf

Dangi, T. B., & Jamal, T. (2016). An integrated approach to "sustainable community-based tourism". *Sustainability*, *8*(475), 1–32. doi:10.3390u8050475

Eom, T., & Han, H. (2019). Community-based tourism (TourDure) experience program: A theoretical approach. *Journal of Travel & Tourism Marketing*, *36*(8), 956–968. doi:10.1080/10548408.2019.1665611

Giampiccoli, A., Mtapuri, O., & Nauright, J. (2020). Tourism development in the Seychelles: A proposal for a unique community-based tourism alternative. *Journal of Tourism and Cultural Change*, 1–14. doi:10.1080/14766825.2020.1743297

Goodwin, H., & Santilli, R. (2009). Community-based tourism: A success. *ICRT Occasional Paper*, *11*(1), 37.

Goodwin, H., & Santilli, R. (2009). Community-based tourism: A success. *ICRT Occasional Paper, 11*(1), 37.

Gyawali, T. (2020). *Community-based tourism: Support community and immerse in the life of locals.* https://www.nepalsanctuarytreks.com/community-based-tourism-community-support-and-immersing-in-the-life-of-locals/

Higgins-Desbiolles, F. (2020). The "war over tourism": Challenges to sustainable tourism in the tourism academy after COVID-19. *Journal of Sustainable Tourism, 29*(4), 551–569. doi:10.1080/09669582.2020.1803334

Ivanova, M., Ivanov, I. K., & Ivanov, S. (2020). Travel behaviour after the pandemic: The case of Bulgaria. *Anatolia, 32*(1), 1–11. doi:10.1080/13032917.2020.1818267

Lee, T. H., & Jan, F.-H. (2019). Can community-based tourism contribute to sustainable development? Evidence from residents' perceptions of the sustainability. *Tourism Management, 70*, 368–380. doi:10.1016/j.tourman.2018.09.003

López-Guzmán, T., Sánchez-Cañizares, S., & Pavón, V. (2011). Community-based tourism in developing countries: A case study. *Tourismos, 6*(1), 69–84.

MoCTCA. (2020). *Nepal Tourism Statistics 2019*. Ministry of Culture, Tourism and Civil Aviation, Government of Nepal.

Mtapuri, O., & Giampiccoli, A. (2016). Towards a comprehensive model of community-based tourism development. *The South African Geographical Journal, 98*(1), 154–168. doi:10.1080/03736245.2014.977813

Okazaki, E. (2008). A community-based tourism model: Its conception and use. *Journal of Sustainable Tourism, 16*(5), 511–529. doi:10.1080/09669580802159594

UNWTO. (2021). *Impact assessment of the COVID-19 outbreak on international tourism.* https://www.unwto.org/impact-assessment-of-the-covid-19-outbreak-on-international-tourism

Wen, J., Kozak, M., Yang, S., & Liu, F. (2020). COVID-19: Potential effects on Chinese citizens' lifestyle and travel. *Tourism Review, 76*(1), 74–87. doi:10.1108/TR-03-2020-0110

World Health Organization. (2021). *Coronavirus disease (COVID-19) pandemic.* https://www.who.int/emergencies/diseases/novel-coronavirus-2019

Zielinski, S., Jeong, Y., Kim, S.-i., & Milanés, B, C. (. (2020). Why community-based tourism and rural tourism in developing and developed nations are treated differently? A review. *Sustainability, 12*(15), 5938. doi:10.3390u12155938

Zielinski, S., Jeong, Y., & Milanés, C. B. (2020). Factors that influence community-based tourism (CBT) in developing and developed countries. *Tourism Geographies*, 1–33. doi:10.1080/14616688.2020.1786156

Zielinski, S., Kim, S.-i., Botero, C., & Yanes, A. (2020). Factors that facilitate and inhibit community-based tourism initiatives in developing countries. *Current Issues in Tourism, 23*(6), 723–739. doi:10.1080/13683500.2018.1543254

ENDNOTE

[1] There were 75 districts in Nepal when TRPAP was established. After the government of Nepal split two districts in 2017, currently there are 77 districts.

Chapter 11
Surfing the Creative Wave:
Designing Surfing as a Creative Tourism Experience

Rui Carvalho
https://orcid.org/0000-0002-3980-5469
GOVCOPP, University of Aveiro, Portugal & ISLA Santarém, Portugal

Patrícia Reis
https://orcid.org/0000-0002-8184-7515
GOVCOPP, University of Aveiro, Portugal & ISLA Santarém, Portugal & Polytechnic Institute of Leiria, Portugal

ABSTRACT

Creative tourism experiences constitute clear examples of the experience economy principles. They address new tourists' necessities. They can activate tangible and intangible resources, contribute to the development of local skills while offering the chance to engage with the overall social agents of the tourism system addressing key tourism challenges of the 21st century. Over the past few years, surf tourism has aroused the interest of many people, and surf tourists are increasingly more experienced, demanding and seeking a wide range of engaging experiences. To connect surf tourism to creative tourism, the authors developed a model focused on a creative surf experience. The chapter presents several contributions to the development of creative experiences of surf tourism where surf destinations can focus on and develop a greater audience that searches for such experiences.

INTRODUCTION

Experiences are prime manifestations of the experience economy (Geus et al., 2016), presenting themselves as activities that can surpass the conventional providing of services, by telling a story, while providing an ambience and engaging with the customer under new arguments by staging tourism experiences. The 'experiential discourse', in the late 90s, namely through Pine & Gilmore (1998, 1999), offering a new approach to the provision of services while seeking to respond in part to new stimuli, interests, profiles

DOI: 10.4018/978-1-7998-8775-1.ch011

and desires that characterised the demand for services in cultural tourism (van der Ark & Richards, 2006). Here the well-known model of the four realms of Pine annd Gilmore (1998, 1999) provided a new mindset for the holistic approach to experience development.

Contemporary to the experience economy paradigm, the rise of the creative economy is reflective of the larger changes occurring within the global economy marked by the shift from economies based on the production of goods to economies based on the provision of services (Policy Research Group, 2013). Creativity was championed as the main intangible resource (e.g., ideas) for creating value depending on narrative, theming and performance (Richards, 2021).

Creative tourism is based on creativity and its relation to tourism, the specialised consumption as a characteristic of the postmodern tourist and the experience economy paradigm and co-creation (Carvalho et al., 2019). These theoretical underpinnings gain relevance in the present chapter, as creative experiences and co-creation are mandatory for the success of this tourism segment. Creative tourism corresponds to a form of cultural tourism (Ohridska-Olson & Ivanov, 2010; Richards, 2010) where the active involvement of the tourist is sought while developing an authentic and profound touristic experience, arguably, resulting in skill and creative development (Carvalho, 2014) based on the living culture of the destination where such experiences are developed (Cheng & Chen, 2021; Richards, 2011, 2021; Richards & Wilson, 2006, 2007).

Surf tourism can be defined as a type of tourism that includes travel having surfing as the main or secondary motivation, for surf practice or simply to enjoy/or observe the surf activity (e.g., surf events) (Reis, 2020). Thus, it includes practitioners, as well as all types of companions or other people who travel, among other aspects, to passively enjoy the surfing practice (Buckley, 2002; Dolnicar & Fluker, 2003; Martin & Assenov, 2012; Ponting & McDonald, 2013; Reis, 2020). Consequently, surf tourists can be seen as participating more actively or more passively.

Surfing has developed a reputation for having a lifestyle connection based on images from mass media (Ponting & McDonald, 2013) and thereby transcends the practice of sport, as it mixes physical activity, passion, behaviour, leisure, spirituality, energy, and even fantasy (Reis, 2020), and is considered a way of life and expression (Dolnicar & Fluker, 2003), being the surf culture become popular both by surfers and sympathisers (Dolnicar & Fluker, 2003; Reis & Jorge, 2012) and commercialised globally (Moutinho et al., 2007). Surf culture is considered modern, radical, young, daring, and includes values, knowledge, behaviour, symbols (such as objects and language), beliefs, and attitudes related to the surf word (Reis, 2020). It presents a multiplicity of meanings and motivations, and people appropriate it uniquely and singularly (Anderson, 2012). The act of riding the waves has aroused the interest of many people (Reis, 2020) that travel to destinations that, due to the excellent natural conditions for surfing, promote themselves based on surf (Reis, 2015), which gives rise to 'surf destinations' (Reis & Carneiro, in press).

Tourism experience has become a central concept in tourism research (Chen et al., 2020: Hosseini & Garcia, 2021; Wang et al., 2020). On the other hand, touristic destinations are applying creative concepts in response to global competition and innovation (Richards, 2010; Tan et al., 2013) using creativity (i.e., creative cultural elements) to develop environments with a fun and artistic 'creative atmosphere', to create an attractive and distinctive tourism destination (Cheng & Chen, 2021; Richards 2020). Surf tourism is a kind of tourism that sells experiences, suggesting that the use of creativity to develop distinctive surf experiences at surf destinations can become an important development trend.

Although research on creative tourism and surf tourism has increased in the past two decades, no research has been done into the relationship between economic experience, creative tourism experiences and surf tourism, which justifies this research. Moreover, no studies have been identified that analyse the

Surfing the Creative Wave

participation of creative communities in developing surf creative experiences, which makes it important to understand the creative surf experience.

Therefore, this study aims to connect surf tourism to creative tourism and develop and propose a model to design a creative surf experience. The authors try to fill the research gaps by understanding how a creative surf process can be designed, to offer memorable and creative surf experiences at the surf destinations, to enrich and maximise the surf tourists' experience and helping surf creative communities to envisage fruitful ways to improve surf destinations more effectively.

This study takes a more global approach at the level of a surf destination to examine surf creative experiences. It seems that creativity on a surf destination can manifest itself through surf-related products, people, way-of-life, culture, environments, landscape, and activities that serve as stimuli and emotional responses for surf tourists. In addition, the motivations for choosing a surf destination go beyond a simple desire to experience surf practice. This suggests interrelated activities within the overall surf tourism experience: surf environments, surf communities and surf products that can transform them into authentic tourism attractions and memorable surf experiences.

This research approach also has theoretical and practical implications. It contributes to the literature and better understands the conceptual underpinnings that clarify the relations among experience economy, creative tourism, and surf tourism. The model seeks to respond to the need to involve new stakeholders in developing creative surfing experiences, which has not been considered until now. This chapter also intends to reveal that surf creative experiences have a crucial role in surf destinations' image and competitiveness.

To develop the proposed model, in a first step, the authors identified the dimensions of a surf experience, based on the model of the Four Realms of Pine and Gilmore (1998, 1999) to design a 'surf memorable experience'. Next, to characterise the memorability of a surf experience, the seven domains of a *Memorable Tourism Experience Scale* (MTEs) (Kim et al., 2012), were systematised. Then, and inspired by the principles of the creative experiences by Richards (2016) and Tan et al. (2013), the authors add a "co-creative layer" to a surf experience and explain how surfing can be a creative experience. Finally, based on a creative community's environment, the authors design a surf creative experience model, represented in terms of the classic four types of experience consumers, which accommodates the combination of the four dimensions of a memorable surf experience.

The chapter is organised logically, starting with a theoretical background, and continuing with details on the research method, the research results (a surf creative experience design model is presented), solutions and recommendations, and conclusion.

BACKGROUND

Experience Economy

Since the seminal work of Pine and Gilmore (1998, 1999) on the experience economy theory that a new paradigm shift has occurred in tourism consumption emphasising the ever-growing role of tourists as key protagonists of touristic experiences. An economic model based on the staging of "experiences" instead of services, was developed under the assumption that the tourist plays an important role in the final link of the production chain (Andersson, 2007), where its departing point is the individual's personal experience: his or her everyday world and societal context (Boswijk et al., 2005). Thus, the progression of economic value marked by the undifferentiated extraction of commodities and the production of goods and the delivery of services was confronted with the differentiated staging of experiences (Jelinčić & Senkic, 2019; Pine & Gilmore, 1999).

Experiences came to be the "proxy" element where the simple delivery of services was no longer enough to satisfy the client, and costumers converted into "guests" as they not only are confronted with the regular delivery of the service, but they are the "recipient" of a memorable experience (Willett, 2009). According to the author, "Pine and Gilmore´s contribution to knowledge is here, in identifying a common phenomenon and coining a concept to go alongside with it" (Willett, 2009, p. 2). In this context, experiences have emerged as the "next step of the progression of economic value", where the interaction of costumers is where the focus is instead of simple entertainment.

The general characteristics of this new designation are based on experiences that involve the customer in a multidimensional way, creating a memorable and lasting experience. Memorable experiences are remembered and selectively reconstructed by the tourist when describing a particular travel experience (Kim et al., 2012). Authors have developed scales to measure heritage and cultural tourism memorable experiences (Rasoolimanesh et al., 2021; Seyfi et al., 2019) and improved their experiential service design applied, for example, in creative tourism experiences (Chang & Lin, 2019). Enterprises were expected to change the ways they engaged with their clients gaining a competitive advantage, as the concept of staging memorable experiences (Pine & Gilmore, 1998, 1999) expanded to almost every economic sector, including tourism. The influence of the experience economy principles and characteristics of memorable experiences are presented in table 1.

Table 1. Main characteristics of the economy of experience and memorable experiences

Main features of Experience Economy	Main features of Memorable Tourism Experiences (MTEs)
• "An experience is not an amorphous construct; it is a real and offering as any service, good or commodity". (Pine & Gilmore, 1998, p. 98)	• Hedonism – pleasurable feelings that excite oneself, the search for pleasure on an experience • Novelty – a psychological feeling of newness resulting from having a new experience • Local culture – friendly local people and local culture of the destination, that can act as the background where memorable experiences are developed • Refreshment – the state of being refreshed and free • Meaningfulness - doing something meaningful and important • Involvement - personal relevance • Knowledge - obtaining knowledge and learning a new culture during the consumption of memorable tourism experiences (Kim et al., 2012; Kim & Ritchie, 2014; Rasoolimanesh et al., 2021; Sharma & Nayak, 2019; Seyfi et al., 2019)
• "An experience occurs when a company intentionally uses services as the stage, and goods as props, to engage individual customers in a way that creates a memorable event". (Pine & Gilmore, 1998, p. 98)	
• "Experiences are inherently personal, existing only in the mind of an individual who has been engaged on an emotional, physical, intellectual, or even spiritual level". (Pine & Gilmore, 1998, p. 99)	
• "They can be understood as having two dimensions: 1. They depend on the design, marketing, and distribution); 2. They can include active or passive participation causing absorption or immersion)". (Pine & Gilmore, 1998, p. 101)	
• "Between the entertainment or aesthetic experience considered more passive and the more active educational or escapist experience, the guest can absorb the experience or immerse in it" (Pine & Gilmore, 1999, pp. 30-31).	
"Experiences, to be successful, must follow several principles: • Well-defined theme • Harmonisation of impressions and positive 'cues' • Elimination of negative 'cues' • Memorabilia • Involvement of the five senses" (Pine & Gilmore, 1998, pp. 102-105) • Naturalness. (Boswijk et al., 2005, 2007)	

(own elaboration)

Surfing the Creative Wave

The identified characteristics became strategies for designing successful experiences with a lasting effect on the memory of the tourist with different degrees of participation and involvement acting as a fertile base of experience design. Departing from the main principles advanced by Pine and Gilmore, (1998, 1999) recent authors expanded the main principles of experience design, by stressing the importance of the senses in the involvement of the tourist, by adding to a well-defined theme, a solid background (e.g. local culture will be determinant in the development of creative tourism experiences) for the experience, based on a degree of novelty, assuring a meaningful and knowledgeable experience for the tourist and also providing a more active role on the part of the consumer.

Table 1 also highlights the main features of the 'tourism memorable experiences' – MTEs, defined as "a tourism experience positively remembered and recalled after the event occurred" (Kim et al., 2012, p.13). The MTE scale proposed by Kim et al. (2012) includes seven components (hedonism, novelty, local culture, refreshment, meaningfulness, involvement, and knowledge) that are seen as important elements of the tourism experience and affect its memorability for an individual. MTEs also significantly influences behavioural intentions to revisit and recommend a tourist destination (Kim & Ritchie, 2014; Sharma & Nayak, 2019). This seminal scale has been confirmed in other studies and is widely used to measure tourist experiences (e.g., Kim, 2014; Kim & Ritchie, 2014; Rasoolimanesh et al., 2021; Sharma & Nayak, 2019; Seyfi et al., 2019). This study, therefore, adopts this framework.

The theoretical contributions to the experience economy paradigm are twofold: (1) the ontological change of the paradigm on the role of experiences in the tourism value chain; and (2) the experience design and its characteristics. As Björk (2018, p. 22) informs us, "the [experience] concept has been sought by describing its structure, exploring its dimensionality and analysing [its] influencing factors". The fathers of contemporary experience design (Jelinčić & Senkic, 2019) have influenced a wide range of disciplines such as marketing, management, events and especially the staging of tourism experiences in tourism studies. In the last years, several authors have focused on the development experience design (Andersson, 2007; Boswijk et al., 2005; Richards, 2016; Willett, 2009) where the early work of Pine and Gilmore has been highly influential regarding matters of authenticity (Ivanovic & Saayman, 2015), event and festival experiences (Carvalho, 2020, 2021; Geus et al., 2016), transformational experiences (Melo et al., 2021), reflexive tourism experiences (Cohen, 2010; Mkono, 2016) and sport tourism experiences (e.g., Perić et al., 2019; Shipway et al., 2016).

Four Realms of an Experience Pine and Gilmore

Pine and Gilmore (1998, 1999) suggested two dimensions of consumer experience based on customer participation and customer involvement (Figure 1). On the first dimension, customers can participate in the experience in a passive way (passive participation) by not affecting the staged experience and act as listeners and/or observers or can have active participation, playing an important role in co-creating the experience. Regarding the second dimension of experience related to the customer involvement, it should be considered, on one hand, the absorption, which occurs every time someone experiences something without getting deeply involved, and on the other hand, the immersion, which occurs when a consumer becomes involved and immersed with the experience, in physically way. These dimensions outline four types of experiences: (i) educational, (ii) entertainment, (iii) esthetic, and (iv) escapist (Pine & Gilmore, 1998, 1999).

Figure 1. The four realms of an experience
Source: Pine & Gilmore, 1998, 1999

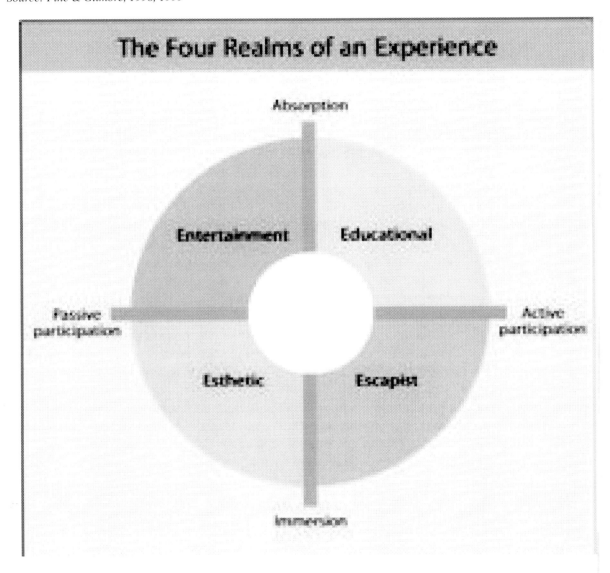

An educational experience (e.g., taking a surf class) is considered a desire to learn something new and actively engages the mind of consumers for the development of their skills and knowledge (Hosany & Witham, 2010; Oh et al., 2007). It is an active and absorptive experience because consumers play a vital role in co-determining their experience. Entertainment experiences (e.g., attending a surf event) involve a passive involvement of the individual in the form of observers or listeners in the experience, without getting involved, and so entertainment reflects absorption (Pine & Gilmore, 1999). An esthetic experience (visiting a surf beach or surf destination) refers to consumers' interpretation of the physical environment around them (Hosany & Witham, 2010). This is when tourists enjoy the environment without affecting or changing its nature (Oh et al., 2007; Pine & Gilmore, 1999). Finally, it is a passive attitude because participants enjoy watching or are influenced by the sensory appeal of the experience and immerse themselves into the experience (immersion) (Hosany & Witham, 2010; Pine & Gilmore, 1999). Escapism experiences (e.g., surfing) allow people to get away from the bustle of surrounding urban life or their dull lives, so they look for exciting and interesting things to relax both physically and emotionally (Oh et al., 2007). These experiences imply greater involvement, are highly immersive and require active participation (Pine & Gilmore, 1999).

In this model, the entertainment and esthetics dimensions entail passive participation, and the consumer does not affect or influence the experiential outcome. In contrast, the education and escapism dimensions involve active participation wherein consumers play a key part in the process. The richest and memorable experiences encompass all four realms and occur in the area where the spectra meet – the "sweet spot". This model will be applied to a memorable surf experience in the following sections.

The context of the experience economy was also prone to developing the so-called creative economy when cultural and creative industries started to have a new role in boosting national economies (Richards, 2011). The creative sectors, creative ideas, and individual creativity were brought to the equation as destinations wanted to differentiate themselves in the tourism market. This relation is highlighted in the next section.

Creative Economy and Creative Tourism Experiences

The creative economy is defined as "the transactions of creative products that have an economic good or service that results from creativity and has economic value" (Howkins, 2002, p. 8) and connected industries which have their origin in individual creativity, skill, and talent and which have a potential for wealth and job creation through the generation and exploitation of intellectual property (DCMS, 1998). Creativity corresponds to the strategical use of both tangible and intangible cultural elements, intellectual products/property of a certain territory/region, or social agents to boost economic development with applications in almost every economic sector where creative clusters, networks, districts, and creative industries are seen as the core of this economical model (Policy Research Group, 2013).

Two highly influential theories have marked the early creative discourse in the first decade of the XXI century. The creative class (Florida, 2002) and the creative city theories (Landry, 2000). Where creative professionals connected to the cultural and creative industries (O'Connor, 2010; Pratt, 2008), including design, education, arts, music, and entertainment (Florida, 2002) and technology-related jobs, these professionals would have an important role in developing of territories. If the experience economy influenced tourism consumption, creativity established a strong connection with tourism, stimulating cultural and creative tourism experiences (Carvalho, 2021; Carvalho et al., 2016, 2019; Richards, 2018, 2021).

In this sense, quickly creative elements started to be included in the design of creative tourism experiences. Based on tangible and intangible cultural elements of the destinations creative atmospheres were idealised, the rise and affirmation of popular culture helped a stronger identity formation in the context of the differentiation in tourism destinations based on the more active involvement of the consumer in the search for deeper and meaningful experiences (Carvalho, 2021; Cheng & Chen, 2021; Richards, 2011, 2020).

This development of creative tourism experiences can be achieved by developing activities based on the specific local culture of the destination, including the process of co-creation (Binkhorst & den Dekker, 2009), that is, the active role of the consumers participating and contributing to their own experience while developing skills related to the theme of the experience and using local culture as a background for such experiences and adding an "authentic" layer to the overall experience. For the development of such experiences, broad use of culture is needed to offer different activities and differentiate the destinations where they are developed. Such experiences can be more active or passive corresponding to the customers' wish and be available as a creative activity (e.g. masterclasses, courses…) or can be present in creative spectacles, events, and festivals or creative networks (Binkhorst, 2007; Carvalho, 2020; Carvalho et al., 2019; Duxbury & Richards, 2019; OECD, 2014; Richards, 2021; Richards & Wilson, 2006). Creative tourists are a group of active stakeholders, and without their participation, creative experiences would not exist (Tan et al., 2013).

'Co-creation' emerged as a new variable to be considered in the experience act forcing, namely, the change of the traditionalist view between supply and demand. According to Prahalad and Ramaswamy, (2004, p, 8), "co-creation is about joint creation of value by the company and the customer […] creating an experiential environment in which consumers can have active dialogue and co-construct personalised experiences". These processes have had a major influence on the involving role of consumers in the overall outcome of tourism experiences which creative tourism experiences constitute a clear example. Here, consumers can have an active dialogue and co-construct personalised experiences. Therefore, the tourist co-creation experience becomes an essential tool for learning, identity formation, and self-development, not only on the part of the consumer but also on the part of the producer (Richards, 2016).

The concept of 'creative local communities' (Carson & Hartmann, 2017) is highly linked to creatives both in urban (Brokalaki & Comunian, 2021; Smith et al., 2021) and rural settings (Bell & Jayne, 2010; Burns & Kirkpatrick, 2008) and marked by their capability to co-create value by organising themselves online and offline (Richards, 2016). One example is the case mentioned by Arriagada (2014, 2015), where new cultural mediators reinforce their role in developing the 'music scene in Chile'. Music fans organise websites to promote indie music, attracting a "set of technologically mediated interactions between different entities – musicians, fans, producers, record labels, corporate brands, and advertisement agencies […] where websites are the key means of making and connecting this diversity of activity to a range of locales" (Arriagada, 2015, p3). Acting like curators they set the conditions in which culture is consumed by "mediating identities, tastes, and lifestyles" (Arriagada 2014, 2015). Related to creative tourism, Carvalho (2021) has studied the involvement of the creative community of Loulé in the Algarve Region in Portugal, engaged in the production, co-creation, and consumption of creative tourism workshops where the local communities collaborate in a creative network (Carvalho, 2021; Carvalho et al., in press).

Creative tourism literature can identify three generations of tourism experiences (Carvalho et al., 2019; Richards, 2011, 2016) and specifically in the experience economy (Alexiou, 2020). According to Richards (2016, p. 2), "this first generation of experiences has been criticised for being too staged, commercial and artificial and therefore not always conducive to current customers". Similarly, due to the existing power shift in company-consumer relations, the strategic staging of experiences has been highly criticised (Binkhorst, 2007; Binkhorst & Den Dekker, 2009). The second generation of experiences is influenced by the concept of co-creation, reserving a more important role to the actors of the experience (e.g. Prahalad & Ramaswamy, 2004). Boswijk et al. (2007) refer that the first-generation producer-oriented experiences described by Pine and Gilmore (1999) were successfully surpassed by the second-generation experiences, based on the co-creation process between consumers and producers. Recently [the emergence] of the third generation of producer and consumer communities is where the differences between the two roles disappear (Richards, 2011). The roles of 'tourist' and 'host' disappear, to be replaced by the creative interaction of equals (Richards, 2016). The latter is marked not only

Surfing the Creative Wave

by "peer-to-peer" tourism experiences co-creation (Dolnicar, 2021) but also virtual communities with offline creative manifestations (Richards, 2016) and digital capital development (Carvalho et al., 2018).

Table 2. Main characteristics of the third generation of experiences and creativity

Characteristics of the third generation of experiences and creativity	Authors
Key elements or qualities for the design of co-creation experiences: • Mutual interest • Interaction • Learning • Creativity	Richards, 2016
Enabling factors for experience design: • Spaces for dialogue • Spaces for creativity • Narrative of place (story, identity, space of flows, etc.) • Integration with landscape and culture • Using a range of senses • Local actors' involvement (within and beyond the destination; working as a network to generate unique experiences (tourism is not isolated from the local community, but part of it). • Putting the local in charge	Richards, 2016
The design process must consider: • Spaces for experience exchange and co-creation • Infrastructure – technical and organisational arrangements (e.g., accommodation, food, and beverage) • Context (shelter, cuisine, environmental, historical, and cultural identity) • Content (core and support experiences)	Richards, 2016
Creativity dimensions in an inner creative experience: • Novelty • Usefulness • Challenge and controlled risk • Experiential • Existential	Tan et al., 2013

Table 2 sums up third-generation experiences' main characteristics and their relation to creativity according to the authors Richards (2011, 2016) and Tan et al. (2013). As we can see (Table 2), Richards (2011, 2016) emphasises the role of creativity in developing experiences as the creative layer is added to co-creation processes. The design of such experiences requires "new physical spaces, linking places and people together (networks), highlighting different aspects of experience, and enabling new power relationships (Richards, 2016, p5). According to Tan et al. (2013), creativity (as inner reflections) constitutes an important theme in a creative tourism design model. The authors highlight that creativity is connected to new things and self-actualisation, connected to the everyday life of the destination, arguably marking the experience and based on several senses. The creative dimension of the model of a creative tourism experience is highlighted by Binkhorst (2007, p128) "experiences can only be creative and unique when people are not only playing an interactive and participative role in them, but also in creating, designing, selecting, and reflecting upon them". Third-generation experience principles will be applied to a creative surf experience in the following sections.

Surf Tourism and Surf Experiences

Over the past few years, the act of riding the waves has aroused the interest of many people (da Rosa et al., 2020; Kruger & Saayman, 2017; Ponting & O'Brien, 2014; Ponting & McDonald, 2013; Reis, 2020; Sotomayor & Barbieri 2016; Towner, 2016), largely due to the proliferation and commercialisation of a set of images of perfect and uncrowded waves, in distant and exotic places (Ponting & McDonald, 2013). Consequently, the number of surfers has grown exponentially, as well as the economic relevance of the surf industry (Barbieri & Sotomayor, 2013; Martin & Assenov, 2012; Ponting & O'Brien, 2014). Surfing is now an activity with global representation (Martin & Assenov, 2011; Ponting & McDonald, 2013), with destinations that, due to the excellent natural conditions for surfing, promote themselves based on surf - surf destinations (Ponting, & O'Brien, 2014; Reis, 2015, Reis, 2020). According to Reis and Carneiro (in press), a surf destination is a "surfing tourist space, consisting of a set of attributes, that interact with each other as a composite product, and involves not only the surf-related attractions, but the whole set of goods and services, infrastructure, equipment, support services, and others whose integrated activities allow surf tourists to realise all kind of surf experiences", which has given rise to the concept of surf tourism.

Surf tourism probably started in the pre-colonial societies of the Hawaiian Islands, which made trips to explore new surf spots (Kampion & Brown, 1998). Surf tourism is thus intrinsically linked to the history of surfing and the relationship between surfing, consumption, and media, having evolved from a cultural practice (Kampion & Brown, 1998). Although it is relatively consensual that surfing is a central component of surf tourism, the various definitions of surf tourism present in literature (Buckley, 2002; Dolnicar & Fluker, 2003; Martin & Assenov, 2012; Ponting & McDonald, 2013) differ in the following aspects: they only consider active participation in the surf, or they integrate both the active practice of surfing and the simple observation of this activity; they impose or not a minimum distance travelled; they consider only foreign residents or also domestic visitors as participants in surf tourism. In this study, it is considered surf tourism definition by Reis (2020), understood as a type of tourism that includes travel having surfing as the main or secondary motivation, for surf practice, to participate in surf events, or simply to enjoy/or observe the surf activity. Thus, it includes practitioners, as well as all types of companions or other people who travel, among other aspects, to passively enjoy the practice of surfing (Buckley, 2002; Dolnicar & Fluker, 2003; Martin & Assenov, 2012; Ponting & McDonald, 2013; Reis, 2020). In the surf tourism context, the practice or appreciation of surfing and the act of travelling is, therefore, associated and complementary. For example, in this context, the search for the perfect wave, an ideal shared by all surfers, results in their predisposition to travel for surf.

Accordingly, to Reis (2020), the following surf tourists can be distinguished: (i) those who travel to get involved in active surf as a central motivation; (ii) those who passively enjoy the surf, and (iii) those who engage in the surf after the visit to the destination, by secondary motives. Each typology of surf tourists represents a different sector of the surf tourism market, and each of these types has different motivations and expectations regarding the surf experience (Barbieri & Sotomayor, 2013; Reis, 2020). These aspects allow Reis (2020) to consider surf tourists into four types (Figure 2): ''professionals', 'regular surfers', 'occasional surfers', and 'sympathisers'. Surf tourism, therefore, includes active surfing participants (professional, regular, and occasional surfers), as well as all types of companions or other people who travel, among other reasons, to passively enjoy the surf, namely, the surf practice or the surf culture (sympathisers). Consequently, each typology of surf tourists has different motivations related to surf.

Figure 2. Surf tourists typologie
Source: Adapted from Reis, 2020

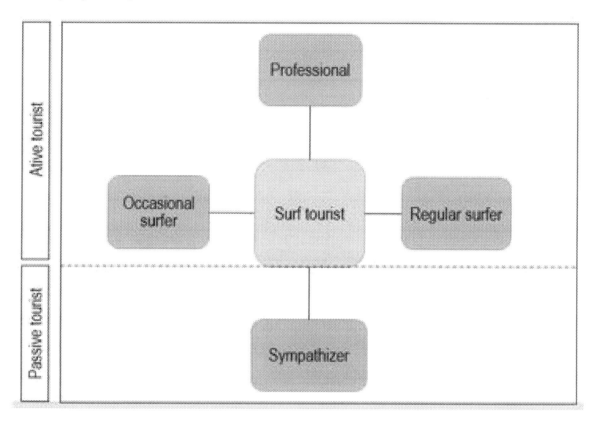

Surfing motivations are many and varied and are dependent on the surf level involvement and surf tourists' characteristics – typologies, interests, needs, goals, surf priorities (Kruger & Saayman, 2017). We can classify them according to physical, interpersonal and status, and prestige motivators.

1. **Physical motivators** are related to health purposes, a quest for health and well-being (de Amaral & Dias, 2008; Anderson, 2012; Buckley, 2012; Fleischmann et al., 2011; Iliuta & Wiltshier, 2018; Kruger & Saayman, 2017); escapism and cathartic purposes, refreshment of body and mind, relaxation, recuperation, stress reduction, and escape from the pressures of everyday life in the sense of "recharging batteries" (Anderson, 2012; Buckley, 2012; Kruger & Saayman, 2017; Reynolds & Nancy, 2012; Towner, 2016; Treadwell et al., 2007); nature purposes, which includes natural/ecological environment contact (de Amaral & Dias, 2008; Anderson, 2012; Treadwell et al., 2007); and pleasure regarding a pleasurable excitement (Booth, 2013; Segabinazzi, 2011).
2. **Interpersonal motivators** are related to the desire to meet other people, integrate, and interact with them, as also, need to belong to the surf community (Koehler, 2006; Segabinazzi, 2011); travel to have fun, to seek new and different experiences, new waves, new environments, and new emotions (Dolnicar & Fluker, 2003; Kampion & Brown, 1998; Ford & Brown, 2005); a quest for sensation seeking, that include variety, novelty, unknown risk, adventure, and complex and excit-

ing and unexpected experiences, related to the emotion that surf produces (Buckley, 2012; Kruger & Saayman, 2017; Stranger, 2017); becoming infected by the spirit of freedom induced by this activity (Koehler, 2006; Reis, 2016); need to escape from routine experiences and socially accepted boundaries (Anderson, 2012; Buckley, 2012), sometimes to have a religious and transcendent experience (Taylor, 2017).

3. **Status and prestige motivators**, related to the surf abilities development, competitiveness, and a desire to win, especially among elite participants; reinforce the sense of belonging and self-confidence within the surf culture (de Amaral & Dias, 2008; Anderson, 2012; Kruger & Saayman, 2017; Reynolds & Nancy, 2012; Treadwell et al., 2007) and development of a self-image related to surf lifestyle and surf culture (Kruger & Saayman, 2017; Reis, 2016, 2020).

Creative tourism is argued to meet the motivations of new tourists who desire to live a multisensorial experience (Richards & Wilson, 2006). Surf tourism is also an experience through all the senses, in which the feeling of the surf materials, tastes, smells, sceneries and sounds combine in rich experience environments (Reis, 2020). In tourism, the more a sensory experience is, the more memorable it will be, and consequently a significant element of the landscape of the creative experience.

Creative tourism experiences constitute a clear example of the experience economy principles. They address new tourists' necessities, and they can activate tangible and intangible resources, contributing to the local development while offering the chance to engage with the tourist stakeholders (Carvalho et al., 2019). On the other hand, surfing provides a diverse range of multisensorial experiences to surf tourists (visual, sensory, esthetic, recreational, sociable, educational, celebrating, enchanting) (Reis, 2020). Surf tourism seems to create new kinds of experiences for surf tourists. When they emerge on the sea, they develop their creative potential and skills through contact with local people and local surf culture, which enhances the atmosphere both locals and tourists appreciate. Surf tourists can choose how they want to participate in the surf experience, depending on surf level involvement and surf participation (professional surfer, regular or occasional surfer, or sympathiser) (Reis, 2020).

Developing and designing a creative tourism experience provides a context in which the experience becomes a framework for learning and self-transformation (Pine & Gilmore, 1999). Therefore, if surf tourists transform themselves through their experiences, as can be seen in the surfing motivations approach, it seems that surf experiences are authentic, memorable, and creative. So, it is important to understand surfing on the spectrum of the creative tourism experience within the surf destination framework.

The Research Method

This study aims to connect surf tourism to creative tourism and develop and propose a model to design a creative surf experience. To achieve these objectives, the research conducted included four stages. First, to design a 'surf memorable experience', the authors identify the dimensions of a surf experience, using the 'Four Realms model' of Pine and Gilmore (1998, 1999) (first experience generation). For this purpose, surf experience dimensions were identified in terms of surf participation (active vs passive), surf involvement (absorption vs immersion), and then four types of surf experiences were delineated: educational, entertainment, esthetic, and escapist, as described below.

Next, to characterise the memorability of a surf experience, the seven domains of a *Memorable Tourism Experience Scale* (MTEs) (Kim et al., 2012), were systematised (hedonism, refreshment, local culture, meaningfulness, knowledge, involvement, and novelty).

Surfing the Creative Wave

On a third stage and inspired by the principles of the creative experiences by Richards (2016) and Tan et al. (2013) (second experience generation), the authors add a "co-creative layer" to a surf experience and explain how surfing can be a creative experience.

Finally, based on a creative community's environment (third experience generation), the authors design a surf creative experience model, represented in terms of the classic four types of consumers experience, which accommodates the combination of the four dimensions of a memorable surf experience.

CREATIVE SURF EXPERIENCES DESIGN MODEL

A Memorable Surf Experience

This section briefly considers the four realms model within a surfing context. Each realm is unique and greatly contributes to the global surf experience, with an ideal combination of aspects of all four realms leading to a 'sweet spot' – a Memorable Surf Experience.

Surf Educational Experience: Education and personal development are important motivations for surf tourists and therefore, learning leads to meaningful experiences. Comprising active participation and absorption, the surf experience impacts significantly by creating memories and generating satisfaction for surf tourists. Surf tourists hope to enhance their knowledge, skills, and ability through an educational experience at the surf destinations. For instance, individuals can learn surf techniques while being close to professional surfers or can improve their surf maneuvres. In addition, they can acquire knowledge about surf rules and surf etiquette. Surfing follows an unwritten code passed down through generations and allows for a healthy coexistence between all those who enjoy the sea (Oliveira et al., 2019). We can also consider surf entrepreneurial intentions as a result of lifestyle factors, as often people travel to surf destinations to learn about potential business ideas (Ratten, 2018), as well as surf workshops as an educational surf activity related to beach preservation, surf breaks, surf techniques, and surf coach or the training of surf judges.

Surf Entertainment Experience: An entertainment experience typically occurs when people passively observe others' activities and/or performances. In surf entertainment experiences, surf tourists want to see, hear, smell, taste, and touch everything related to surfing (Reis, 2020). They are absorbed by performances, having passive participation since they act as observers. In this category, it can be considered surf events or surf competitions, a surf demonstration at the local beach or visiting a surf museum. In this context, surf is considered as an entertainment activity and perceived to be interesting, offering opportunities for entertainment and fun.

Some surf experiences can be both educational and entertaining. To describe this kind of experience- that includes these two types of experiences, we can use the expression *surf edutainment experiences* when surf tourists are eager to learn entertainingly. For instance, surf tourists can engage enthusiastically in a surf tour in which a local and expert guide can transform it into an entertainment experience combined with a learning activity (edutainment) (e.g., visiting a surf museum, a surf spot, surf event; some advice from a local/professional surfer).

Surf Esthetic Experience: The esthetic experience refers to the overall atmosphere and mood of the physical environment of the surfing landscape. On this experience, surf tourists seek to immerse themselves in a surf environment and have predominantly passive participation. Surf tourists want to interact with the surf destination attributes and contemplate the surf-related attractions (e.g., waves, crowd, climate, natural attractions, spots), the other attractions (e.g., surf museum, nightlife, the beauty of the environment), the surf culture and the surf way of life (e.g., surf community, surf traditions, surf spirit), consume products from the surf industry (e.g., surf shops, surf schools), use surf facilities (e.g., lockers, showers), surf-related accommodation, restaurants and cafes, accessibility (e.g., to the surf spots) and others aspects of a surf destination (e.g., popularity, information, hospitality) (Reis, 2020). The esthetic elements in a surf experience stem from the surf attractions, as well as intangible elements, like the surf culture, that engage the imagination of surf tourists using sensory triggers.

Surf Escapist Experience: On this experience, surf tourists search for higher activities and involvement; they truly want to become part of the surf world. They emerge on the landscape with active participation and immersion and connection-level because they attempt to satisfy physical, interpersonal and status and prestige motivations, as discussed above. In this context, surf tourists are looking for more than just surf practice, as surfing is a self-discovery (Anderson, 2012). The more involved they are, the better will be the escapist experience. On a surf escapist experience, people can immerse in the experience and influence their perspectives through physical, mental, and sensory triggers.

'Sweet Spot': A Memorable Surf Experience: To offer a richer and memorable experience, the four different variables of the model defined before should be considered for the experience 'sweet spot'. The general characteristics of this new design are based on a multidimensional approach for creating a memorable and lasting memory. A good example of a memorable surf experience is when the surf experience integrates surf practice (educational dimension) and surf demonstrations (entertainment dimension) with the best surfers, a surf landscape consuming (esthetic dimension) and surfing a perfect and uncrowded wave on a paradise surf destination (escapist dimension).

Considering that at the base of the 'Four Realms' experience is the creation of experiences and emotions that a given product provides to the consumer, allowing individual and unique experiences, it can be verified that surfing is an activity that enables an experience of emotions, involvement, entertainment and sharing of positive memories, essential in the economy of experiences. However, these experiences might differ depending on the surf tourist's needs, interests, motivations, and involvement.

According to the *Memorable Tourism Experience Scale* (MTEs) (Kim et al., 2012), we can also reinforce that a surf experience is a memorable and lasting memory (Table 3). As we can observe, the surf experience presents a multiplicity of meanings and is appropriated uniquely and singularly by its members, depending on surf involvement and surf participation. In this context, a surf experience seems to have its very own identity, related to a way of life in communion with the surrounding environment, where the passion for the sea gives rise to a unique way of living, as well as appropriation and occupation of space. The surf experience reflects how each relates, positions, and places himself in the surfing world, giving it a meaning and a reason for being.

Table 3. Surf memorable experiences

MTES	Surf memorable experiences
• Hedonism	• Incessant search for pleasure (Booth, 2013; Segabinazzi, 2011)
• Novelty	• Surf trips to discover new spots (Gonzalez, 2016) • Search for the perfect wave (Ponting, 2009) • Search from happiness (Stranger, 2011) • Search for adventure and risk (Stranger, 2011)
• Local culture	• Engage in local surf culture and local surf traditions (Reis, 2000) • Surf localism related to a territorial sense of ownership where they traditionally surf (Booth, 2013)
• Refreshment	• 'Surf ideal' related to a healthy life, and environment preservation (Schifino, 2002) • 'Surf nirvana' related to getting away from daily routine and returning to the origins (Ponting & O'Brien, 2014) • Overcoming personal limits (Stranger, 2011)
• Meaningfulness	• 'Flow state' as a state of complete plenitude which leads to a search for happiness through the waves (Stranger, 2011) • 'Get stoked', an embodied feeling of satisfaction, joy, and pride through surf (Kampion & Brown, 1998) • Inner discovery (Taylor, 2017) • The spiritual experience that connects people with the natural environment and God (Taylor, 2017) • Travel to paradise (Taylor, 2017)
• Involvement	• Involvement in the surf scene (Irwin, 1973), surf rituals (Moutinho et al., 2007), surf values and behaviours (Koehler, 2006), surf culture (Reis, 2020), and surf lifestyle (Segabinazzi, 2011) • A feeling of belonging and a friendly atmosphere (Reis, 2020) • Interaction and socialization (Reis, 2016; Segabinazzi, 2011) • Sharing common interests (Koehler, 2006; Reis, 2016) • Confidence and complicity (Koehler, 2006; Reis, 2016)
• Knowledge	• Surfer's code (Oliveira et al., 2019) • Surf techniques (Melo & Fortes, 2009) • Surf culture (Booth, 2001; Reis, 2020) • Surf entrepreneurship (Ratten, 2018) • Through surf media (Melo & Fortes, 2009)

(Own elaboration)

Surfing: A Creative Tourism Experience

Third-generation tourism experiences are based on two principles: co-creation and creativity (Richards, 2016; Tan et al., 2013). Therefore, a memorable surf experience can only be creative and unique when surf tourists are not only playing an interactive and participative role in them, but also in creating, designing, selecting, and reflecting upon them (Binkhorst, 2007), promoting their self-transformation (Pine & Gilmore, 1999). In this regard, to add a "co-creative layer" to a surf experience, one must think of co-creation and creativity as important inputs present in this experience. Consequently, the co-creative role of surf tourists is thus relevant. It should be noted that the model of the four realms has been already applied to creative tourism experiences in other studies (e.g., Chang et al., 2014; Hosany & Witham, 2010), which reinforces its application to surf tourism.

For that intention, it is important to understand what creativity in a surf experience is, and where does creativity in surf tourism comes from. It is worth noting that the active and passive activities that a surf tourist partakes or engages in (through absorption or immersion) during their trip to a surf destination can become meaningful and unique experiences. In this context, surf creative experiences can be designed under Richards (2016) and Tan et al. (2013) creative principles.

According to Richards's (2016) approach, in surf creative experiences, mutual interest, interaction, learning, and creativity between producer (e.g., surf destination stakeholders) and costumer (surf tourist) must be present. Enabling factors for such surf experiences can be present in the use of *spaces for dialogue* on the surf destination (e.g., beach, sea, sand, surf restaurants and bars, streets, surf museums) and *space for creativity* on surf ativities (e.g., surf lessons, surf tours, surfboard treatment techniques, surfboard shaping and design, surf photo sessions); *the narrative of the surf place* (e.g., local surf culture, local surf history, local surf tradition, surf destination image, surf identity) within the surf world (e.g., surf involvement, surf lifestyle, surf entrepreneurship) and *interaction with landscape and culture* (e.g., local surf atmosphere, local surf culture); *surf multisense,* (e.g., ocean's view, texture of surfboards, smell of wax board, surf music sound, surf language); but also the *creative economy apparatus* applied to the tourism system with the *involvement of local actors*, within and beyond the surf destination by the interaction of surf instructors, surf associations, surf schools, surf shops, surf event organisers, surf accommodation, surf related restaurants and bars, surf destination managers, local surf community, among many others. To enhance the surf creative tourism experience, one must envisage the beach as the privileged place for all beach consumers: locals, leisure tourists, surf tourists (professional, regular, and occasional surfers and sympathisers), and the local surf community. We need to face the beach and the sea as the perfect spot for surf events and competitions, several surf activities, surf facilities, sun and sea sport-related activities, and the co-creation of knowledge.

In addition, according to Tan et al. (2013), the presence of creativity in a surf experience should focus on multiple dimensions mentioned above. *'Novelty',* because surf tourists are always looking for new experiences, new surf spots, new waves, new adventures, new and interesting people and destinations, their surf culture, and traditions; an also seeking the *'usefulness'* of the surf experience, namely the reason they engage in surf experiences and what they will do with the knowledge and the sensations acquired. The surf experience also produces useful functions related to the development of social skills and managing feelings. It is a process for self-inspiration and self-transformation, as well as raising environmental awareness and sustainability (*in situ*). Surf tourists are also searching for creative activities with *'controlled risk but a challenging experience'*. Surfing is a voluntary risk-taking activity because it is pursued by the thrills involved, increasing and intensifying the surf level improved as they experience challenging waves. Surfers live for the thrill, and surf is like a drug that simulates the sublime experience of flow (Stranger, 2011). Since surfing involves high levels of risk, it may attract individuals with sensation-seeking tendencies. It is a thrill-seeking creative experience. The *'experiential'* dimension is related to the search for pleasure, satisfaction, good vibes, happiness, freedom, a healthy life, to experience a surf lifestyle, developing friendship and complicity among the surf community. It is a creative experience of well-being. On the other hand, a surf *'existential'* dimension is related to self-awareness and spiritual experience, where surfers search for change, find themselves and improve their self-confidence. A surf experience allows a strong connection and engagement with nature, friends, local community, and family, with positive effects on mental and physical health. Besides, it is a religious experience when men can be connected and stay close to God. It has a transformative effect and is more difficult to achieve since it depends on the surf level involvement and engagement.

In addition to the classic model of Pine and Gilmore (1998, 1999), co-creation processes can be added to the four types of consumers experience, which allow us to design and support a surf creative experience model (Figure 3).

Creative tourism is inseparable from a perspective of quality of life and lifestyle (Ivanovic, 2008), like what happens with the creative surfing experience, which accommodates the combination of four

Surfing the Creative Wave

dimensions of an experience. A creative surf experience is an absorbing and immersive experience, sometimes of self-transcendence and self-transformation, linked to the co-creative role of surf tourists (consumers), which may involve active or passive participation, as well as the producers in the context of surfing experiences during interactions where all parties involved apply skills and resources. Here, consumers engage in active co-creation, resulting in an essential tool to develop skills, identity formation, and self-development for both consumers and producers of the experience (Richards, 2016).

Figure 3. Surf creative experience model
Source: Own elaboration

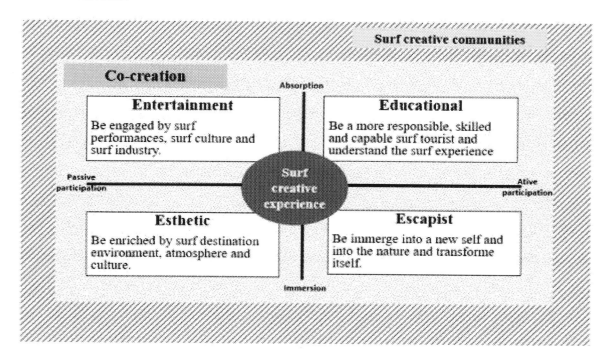

Passively surf tourists engage in surf performances, surf competitions can interact with surf culture, and consume surf industry products (entertainment). Simultaneously, they became delighted by the surf destination landscape, atmosphere, and culture (esthetic). Actively they can change themselves and the others because a responsible surf tourist is not only about keeping the beach clean but also respecting local communities and contributing to sustainable development (escapist), at the same time they learn how to improve their skills and surf level, which contributes to effectively understanding the surfing experience (first and second experience generation). If it is the case, those surf tourists get into the experience process by actively participating in it and co-create it. Therefore, a creative surf experience is an exciting challenge for surf tourists as they are stimulated to participate in the experience by applying some type of personal resources (physical, intellectual, cultural) and stimulating their five senses. For example, they can observe the calm, beauty and inspirational sun, sea, and sand landscape. A sensitive experience comprehends hearing seabirds, the waves, the boats, to smell the sea breeze, touch the sand and taste the saltwater.

However, as suggested by Richards (2011), a creative experience is a shared experience within the creative community, and in this situation involves surf experience consumers (surf tourist) and producers linked directly or indirectly to surf, namely: surf community, local community, the surf industry, surf destination managers, and creative networks (territorial and technological) (third experience generation). Therefore, it is also an exciting challenge for the surf destination – perceived as the creative community. It needs to find adequate facilitating conditions for surf tourists to engage in memorable creative surf experiences, conducting to a definite surf product. Together they can help boost a complete supply of creative surf experiences.

CONCLUSION

Creativity involves adding something new to existing tourism products and experiences and, therefore, is an essential source of competitiveness for surf destinations. From an academic perspective, this chapter significantly contributes to the literature. It allows us to understand better the conceptual underpinnings that clarify the relations among the theoretical concepts analysed: experience economy, creative tourism, and surf tourism. The experience economy paradigm maintains its pertinence to influence the design of memorable experiences in the tourism sector. The creative economy and tourism have helped shape the design of creative experiences, enhancing tourists' role in transforming the meaning of touristic experiences they undertake. Surf tourism is an expanding tourism segment that involves practitioners and sympathisers with surf motivations, and surf tourists are often associated with being creative and adaptive tourists. Building upon these relations, the authors connect the principles of creativity, experience design and co-creation processes to surf tourism. Considering surf tourism experiences, it was possible to map them into the Four Realms of experiences model (Pine & Gilmore, 1998, 1999) and propose a 'memorable surf experience' that can be organised in a surf destination. Analysing the three generations of experiences design alongside the co-creation process and the role of creative communities' networks, the authors present an innovative model of a 'surf creative experience'. This investigation adds to a very limited body of work about surf tourism by providing considerations of the significance of surf tourism experiences.

From a practical perspective, this chapter is considered relevant, as it intended to reveal that surf creative experiences have a crucial role in surf destinations' image and competitiveness. Surf creative experiences can influence behavioural intentions to revisit and recommend a surf destination. Furthermore, adding surf communities to the surf experience can be an interesting innovation tool for surf destinations management. Consequently, planning strategies for a surf destination should involve the various communities existing at the destination: surf community, local community, the surf industry, surf destination managers, and creative networks (territorial and technological). It is recommended that surf destinations inspire surf tourists to have a memorable recollection of their surf travels and share with their friends and families. The proposed model aims to help surf destinations managers and relevant surf stakeholders to develop a suitable surf tourism program that triggers creative principles approach to differentiate themselves in the tourism market, as it seems difficult to find surf creative tourism businesses that provide surf experiences that surf tourists are looking for. Arguably it can be this creative layer that can add meaning to the overall surf experience.

To develop an adequate system of creative surf experiences, surf destination managers need to know and understand the surfing motivations and surf tourist profiles. However, it is important to consider that a creative surf experience is not homogeneous and depends on the characteristic elements of each surf destination and that surf culture is very differentiated and is appropriated uniquely and singularly by each one. In this scope, surfing is not experienced in the same way in all surf destinations. Consequently, one cannot transpose the same surf creative experience model in all surf destinations because they are necessarily different. Therefore, understanding, implementing, and managing the proposed model of surf creative experiences may be crucial for surf destination managers' tasks to attract surf tourists and increase loyalty.

FUTURE RESEARCH DIRECTIONS

Despite the important contributions it provides, this study also has some limitations, and more research is needed. It will be important to continue to study the implications of the design and consumption of creative surf experiences according to the paradigm of the experience economy addressed in this work. More research is needed to frame the surf experience design process better and appraise the outcomes for surf destinations and tourists. Furthermore, it will be interesting to conduct an empirical study with the various typologies of surf tourists to verify whether the model designed here is operational and also, identify creative surf destinations where the model can be applied.

REFERENCES

Alexiou, M. (2020). Experience economy and co-creation in a cultural heritage festival: Consumers' views. *Journal of Heritage Tourism*, *15*(2), 200–216. doi:10.1080/1743873X.2019.1632867

Anderson, J. (2012). Relational places: The surfed wave as assemblage and convergence. *Environment and Planning. D, Society & Space*, *30*(4), 570–587. doi:10.1068/d17910

Andersson, T. D. (2007). The tourist in the experience economy. *Scandinavian Journal of Hospitality and Tourism*, *7*(1), 46–58. doi:10.1080/15022250701224035

Baeker, G. (2008). *Building a creative rural economy*. Retrieved from www.municipalworld.com

Barbieri, C., & Sotomayor, S. (2013). Surf travel behaviour and destination preferences: An application of the serious leisure inventory and measure. *Tourism Management*, *35*, 111–121. doi:10.1016/j.tourman.2012.06.005

Binkhorst, E. (2005). *The co-creation tourism experience*. Retrieved from https://www.researchgate.net/researcher/2002799627_Esther_Binkhorst

Binkhorst, E. (2007). Creativity in tourism experiences: The case of Sitges. In G. Richards & J. Wilson (Eds.), *Tourism, creativity and development* (pp. 125–144)., doi:10.4324/9780203933695

Binkhorst, E., & den Dekker, T. (2009). Agenda for co-creation tourism experience research. *Journal of Hospitality Marketing & Management*, *18*(2-3), 311–327. doi:10.1080/19368620802594193

Björk, P. (2018). Tourist experience value: Tourist experience and life satisfaction. In N. Prebensen, J. Chen, & M. Uysal (Eds.), *Creating experience value in tourism* (pp. 21–30)., doi:10.1079/9781786395030.0021

Boorstin, D. (1992). *The image: A guide to pseudo-events in America* (4th ed.). Vintage Books.

Booth, D. (2001). From Bikinis to Boardshorts: "Wahines" and the paradoxes of surfing culture. *Journal of Sport History, 28*(1), 3–22. PMID:17561560

Booth, D. (2013). History, culture and surfing: Exploring historiographical relationships. *Journal of Sport History, 40*(1), 3–20. PMID:17561560

Boswijk, A., Thijssen, T., & Peelen, E. (2005). *A new perspective on the experience economy*. The European Centre for the Experience Economy.

Boswijk, A., Thijssen, T., & Peelen, E. (2007). The experience economy. A new perspective. Amersterdam: Pearson Education.

Buckley, R. (2002). Surf tourism and sustainable development in Indo-Pacific Islands: The industry and the islands. *Journal of Sustainable Tourism, 10*(5), 405–424. doi:10.1080/09669580208667176

Buckley, R. (2012). Sustainable tourism: Research and reality. *Annals of Tourism Research, 39*(2), 528–546. doi:10.1016/j.annals.2012.02.003

Burns, J., & Kirkpatrick, C. (2008). *Creative industries in the rural East Midlands: Regional study report*. Academic Press.

Campos, A., Mendes, J., Oom, P., & Scott, N. (2015). Current issues in tourism co-creation of tourist experiences: A literature review. *Current Issues in Tourism, 0*(0), 1–32. doi:10.1080/13683500.2015.1081158

Carvalho, R. (2014). A literature review of the role of cultural capital in creative tourism. In J. A. C. Santos, M. Correira, M. Santos, & F. Serra (Eds.), *TMS 2014: Management Studies International Conference* (pp. 17–28). Academic Press.

Carvalho, R. (2020). Understanding the creative tourism experience in cultural and creative events/festivals. *ISLA Multidisciplinary E-Journal, 3*(1), 1–18. Retrieved from http://www.islae-journal.com/index.php/isla/article/view/39

Carvalho, R., Costa, C., & Ferreira, A. M. (2018). New cultural mediators, cocreation, and the cultural consumption of creative tourism experiences. In J. M. Rodrigues, C. M. Ramos, P. J. Cardoso, & C. Henriques (Eds.), *Handbook of research on technological developments for cultural heritage and etourism applications* (pp. 264–283). doi:10.4018/978-1-5225-2927-9.ch013

Carvalho, R., Costa, C., & Ferreira, A. M. (2019). Review of the theoretical underpinnings in the creative tourism research field. *Tourism & Management Studies, 15*(SI), 11–22. doi:10.18089/tms.2019.15SI02

Carvalho, R., Ferreira, A. M., & Figueira, L. M. (2016). Cultural and creative tourism in Portugal. *Pasos: Revista de Turismo y Patrimonio Cultural, 14*(5), 1075–1082. Retrieved from lhttp://ojsull.webs.ull.es/index.php/Revista/article/view/134

Chang, L., Backman, K. F., & Huang, Y. C. (2014). Creative tourism: A preliminary examination of creative tourists' motivation, experience, perceived value and revisit intention. *International Journal of Culture, Tourism and Hospitality Research, 8*(4), 401–419. doi:10.1108/IJCTHR-04-2014-0032

Chang, S., & Lin, R. (2019). A framework of experiential service design in creative tourism. In R. Pl (Ed.), Lecture Notes in Computer Science: Vol. 11577. *Cross-cultural design. culture and society. HCII 2019* (pp. 3–16). doi:10.1007/978-3-030-22580-3_1

Chen, J. S., Prebensen, N. K., & Uysal, M. S. (2018). Dynamic drivers of tourist experiences. In N. Prebensen, J. Chen, & M. Uysal (Eds.), *Creating experience value in tourism* (2nd ed., pp. 11–20). doi:10.1079/9781786395030.0011

Cohen, E. (1979). A phenomenology of tourist experiences. *Sociology, 13*(2), 179–201. doi:10.1177/003803857901300203

Cohen, S. (2010). Reflections on reflexivity in leisure and tourism studies. *Leisure (Waterloo, Ont.), 32*(87), 27–29. doi:10.1360/zd-2013-43-6-1064

da Rosa, S., dos Anjos, F. A., de Lima Pereira, M., & Junior, M. A. (2019). Image perception of surf tourism destination in Brazil. *International Journal of Tourism Cities*.

DCMS. (1998). *Creative industries: Mapping Document*. DCMS.

de Amaral, A. V., & Dias, C. A. G. (2008). Da praia para o mar: Motivos à adesão e à prática do surfe. *LICERE-Revista do Programa de Pós-graduação Interdisciplinar em Estudos do Lazer, 11*(3).

Dolnicar, S. (2019). A review of research into paid online peer-to-peer accommodation: Launching the Annals of Tourism Research curated collection on peer-to-peer accommodation. *Annals of Tourism Research, 75*(January), 248–264. doi:10.1016/j.annals.2019.02.003

Dolnicar, S. (2021). Airbnb before, during and after COVID-19. In Airbnb before, during and after COVID-19. doi:10.14264/ab59afd

Dolnicar, S., & Fluker, M. (2003). Behavioural market segments among surf tourists: Investigating past destination choice. *Journal of Sport & Tourism, 8*(3), 186–196. doi:10.1080/14775080310001690503

Duxbury, N., & Richards, G. (2019). A research agenda for creative tourism. In N. Duxbury & G. Richards (Eds.), *A research agenda for creative tourism*. doi:10.4337/9781788110723

Fleischmann, D., Michalewicz, B., Stedje-Larsen, E., Neff, J., Murphy, J., Browning, K., Nebeker, B., Cronin, A., Sauve, W., Stetler, C., Herriman, L., & McLay, R. (2011). Surf medicine: Surfing as a means of therapy for combat-related polytrauma. *JPO: Journal of Prosthetics and Orthotics, 23*(1), 27–29. doi:10.1097/JPO.0b013e3182065316

Florida, R. (2002). *The rise of the creative class: and how it's transforming work, leisure, community and everyday life*. doi:10.5860/CHOICE.40-2276

Florida, R. (2018). *The rise of the rural creative class*. Retrieved October 3, 2019, from Bloomberg website: https://www.bloomberg.com/news/articles/2018-05-01/what-makes-a-rural-creative-hub-innovation-and-the-arts

Ford, N. J., & Brown, D. (2005). *Surfing and social theory: Experience, embodiment and narrative of the dream glide*. Routledge. doi:10.4324/9780203415023

Geus, S., Richards, G., & Toepoel, V. (2016). Conceptualisation and operationalisation of event and festival experiences: Creation of an event experience scale. *Scandinavian Journal of Hospitality and Tourism*, *16*(3), 274–296. doi:10.1080/15022250.2015.1101933

Goffman, E. (1993). *A representação do eu na vida de todos os dias*. Relógio D'agua.

González, D. S. (2016). *El mundo sobre las olas: Perspectiva de desarrollo turístico a través del surfing* (PhD thesis). Universidad Rey Juan Carlos, Espãna.

Gornostaeva, G., & Campbell, N. (2012). The creative underclass in the production of place: Example of Camden Town in London. *Journal of Urban Affairs*, *34*(2), 169–188. doi:10.1111/j.1467-9906.2012.00609.x

Hosany, S., & Witham, M. (2010). Dimensions of cruisers' experiences, satisfaction, and intention to recommend. *Journal of Travel Research*, *49*(3), 351–364. doi:10.1177/0047287509346859

Howkins, J. (2002). *The creative economy: How people make money from ideas*. Penguin Books.

Iliuta, M. A., & Wiltshier, P. (2018). Spa services and wellness activities within the surf tourism experience: The case study of Jersey, Channel Islands. *International Journal of Spa and Wellness*, *1*(1), 82–94. doi:10.1080/24721735.2018.1432454

Ivanovic, M., & Saayman, M. (2015). Authentic economy shaping transmodern tourism experience. *African Journal for Physical, Health Education, Recreation & Dance*, *2015*(December), 24–36.

Jelinčić, D. A., & Senkic, M. (2019). The value of experience in culture and tourism: The power of emotions. In N. Duxbury & G. Richards (Eds.), *A research agenda for creative tourism* (pp. 41–53). doi:10.4337/9781788110723.00012

Kampion, D., & Brown, B. (1998). *Stoked: A history of surf culture*. Evergreen.

Kim, J. H. (2014). The antecedents of memorable tourism experiences: The development of a scale to measure the destination attributes associated with memorable experiences. *Tourism Management*, *44*, 34–45. doi:10.1016/j.tourman.2014.02.007

Kim, J. H., & Ritchie, J. B. (2014). Cross-cultural validation of a memorable tourism experience scale (MTES). *Journal of Travel Research*, *53*(3), 323–335. doi:10.1177/0047287513496468

Kim, J. H., Ritchie, J. R., & McCormick, B. (2012). Development of a scale to measure memorable tourism experiences. *Journal of Travel Research*, *51*(1), 12–25. doi:10.1177/0047287510385467

Koehler, T. H. (2006). *"Stoked": Os valores da cultura de consumo surf e sua influência no comportamento de compra* (Dissertação de Mestrado). Escola de Administração, Universidade Federal do Rio Grande do Sul, Brazil.

Kruger, M., & Saayman, M. (2017). Sand, sea and surf: Segmenting South African surfers. *S.A. Journal for Research in Sport Physical Education and Recreation*, *39*(2), 115–135.

Landry, C. (2000). *The creative city: A toolkit for urban innovators*. Earthscan.

MacCannell, D. (1999). *The tourist a new theory of the leisure class*. California Press.

Machado, V., Pinto Contreiras, J., & Carrasco, P. (2018). *Local developments of the world summit on sustainable tourism: the municipal sustainable charter of surf in Aljezur*. Sustainable Tourism Law.

Martin, S. A., & Assenov, I. (2012). The genesis of a new body of sport tourism literature: A systematic review of surf tourism research (1997–2011). *Journal of Sport & Tourism, 17*(4), 257–287. doi:10.1080/14775085.2013.766528

Melo, C., Richards, G., & Smith, M. (2021). Transformational tourism experiences : The communication of service providers. In Impact of new media in tourism (pp. 210–233). doi:10.4018/978-1-7998-7095-1.ch013

Melo, V. A. D., & Fortes, R. (2009). O surfe no cinema e a sociedade brasileira na transição dos anos 70/80. *Revista Brasileira de Educação Física e Esporte, 23*(3), 283–296. doi:10.1590/S1807-55092009000300009

Mkono, M. (2016). The reflexive tourist. *Annals of Tourism Research, 57*, 206–219. doi:10.1016/j.annals.2016.01.004

Moutinho, L., Dionísio, P., & Leal, C. (2007). Surf tribal behaviour: A sports marketing application. *Marketing Intelligence & Planning, 25*(7), 668–690. doi:10.1108/02634500710834160

O'Connor, J. (2010). The cultural and creative industries: A literature review. In *Creativity, culture and education*. Retrieved from www.creative-partnerships.com/literaturereviews

OECD. (2014). Tourism and the creative economy. OECD Studies on Tourism. doi:10.1787/9789264207875-en

Oh, H., Fiore, A. M., & Jeoung, M. (2007). Measuring experience economy concepts: Tourism applications. *Journal of Travel Research, 46*(2), 119–132. doi:10.1177/0047287507304039

Ohridska-Olson, R. V., & Ivanov, S. H. (2010). Creative tourism business model and its application in Bulgaria. *Cultural Realms*, 1–17.

Oliveira, F., Eurico, S., & Jorge, J. P. (2019). EBSCode - Eco Based Surf Code: Surfing for a sustainable development of beaches: The Portuguese case. In A. Artal-Tur, M. Kozak, & N. Kozak (Eds.), *Trends in tourist behavior* (pp. 109–123). Springer. doi:10.1007/978-3-030-11160-1_7

Pine, J., & Gilmore, J. (1998). Welcome to the experience economy. *Harvard Business Review*, (July-August), 97–105. PMID:10181589

Pine, J., & Gilmore, J. (1999). *The experience economy: Work is theatre & every business a stage*. doi:10.5860/CHOICE.37-2254

Policy Research Group. (2013). *The creative economy: Key concepts and literature review highlights*. Canadian Heritage.

Ponting, J., & McDonald, M. G. (2013). Performance, agency and change in surfing tourist space. *Annals of Tourism Research, 43*, 415–434. doi:10.1016/j.annals.2013.06.006

Ponting, J., & O'Brien, D. (2014). Liberalising Nirvana: An analysis of the consequences of common pool resource deregulation for the sustainability of Fiji's surf tourism industry. *Journal of Sustainable Tourism, 22*(3), 384–402. doi:10.1080/09669582.2013.819879

Prahalad, C. K., & Ramaswamy, V. (2004). Co-creation experiences: The next practice in value creation. *Journal of Interactive Marketing*, *18*(3), 5–14. doi:10.1002/dir.20015

Pratt, A. C. (2008). Creative cities: The cultural industries and the creative class. *Geografiska Annaler. Series B, Human Geography*, *90*(2), 107–117. doi:10.1111/j.1468-0467.2008.00281.x

Prebensen, N., Chen, J., & Uysal, M. (2018a). Co-creation of tourist experience: Scope, definition and structure. In N. Prebensen, J. Chen, & M. Uysal (Eds.), *Creating experience value in tourism* (2nd ed., p. 273). CABI. doi:10.1079/9781786395030.0001

Prebensen, N., Chen, J., & Uysal, M. (2018b). Creating experience value in tourism. CABI International. doi:10.1079/9781786395030.0000

Prebensen, N., Vitterso, J., & Dahl, T. (2013). Value Co-creation significance of tourist resources. *Annals of Tourism Research*, *42*(xx), 240–261. doi:10.1016/j.annals.2013.01.012

Rasoolimanesh, S. M., Seyfi, S., Hall, C. M., & Hatamifar, P. (2021). Understanding memorable tourism experiences and behavioural intentions of heritage tourists. *Journal of Destination Marketing & Management*, *21*(January), 100621. doi:10.1016/j.jdmm.2021.100621

Ratten, V. (2018). Entrepreneurial intentions of surf tourists. *Tourism Review*, *73*(2), 262–276. doi:10.1108/TR-05-2017-0095

Raunig, G., Ray, G., & Wuggenig, U. (2011). Critique of creativity: Precarity, subjectivity and resistance in the 'creative industries.' *Gene*, 234.

Reis, P. (2015). Peniche: A new use for an old territory. *Proceddings of the Encontro Científico da I2ES – ISLA Santarém*, 113-132.

Reis, P. (2016). O surf como expressão de identidade e de estilo de vida. In N. Abranja, A. A. Alcântara, F. Coelhoso, R. V. Ferreira, A. Marques, & T. Ribeiro (Eds.), Produtos, mercados e destinos turísticos (pp. 131-146). Mangualde: Edições Pedago.

Reis, P. (2020). *The influence of surf culture on the image of surf destinations* (PhD thesis). University of Aveiro, Portugal.

Reis, P., & Jorge, J. P. (2012). Surf tourism: segmentation by motivation and destination choice. In *2nd International Conference on Tourism Recreation Proceedings*. GITUR-Grupo de Investigação em Turismo, Instituto Politécnico de Leiria.

Reynolds, Z., & Hritz, N. M. (2012). Surfing as adventure travel: Motivations and lifestyles. *Journal of Tourism Insights*, *3*(1), 2. doi:10.9707/2328-0824.1024

Richards, G. (2010). Tourism development trajectories: From culture to creativity. *Encontros Científicos: Tourism & Management Studies*, (6), 9–15. doi:10.4324/9780203933695

Richards, G. (2011). Creativity and tourism. The state of the art. *Annals of Tourism Research*, *38*(4), 1225–1253. doi:10.1016/j.annals.2011.07.008

Richards, G. (2016). *Co-designing experiences with consumers: The case of creative tourism*. Retrieved from https://www.academia.edu/26363825/Co-designing_experiences_with_consumers_the_case_of_creative_tourism_Input_for_a_workshop_on_experience_design_Tromsø_27_May_2016

Richards, G. (2018). Cultural tourism: A review of recent research and trends. *Journal of Hospitality and Tourism Management, 36*, 12–21. doi:10.1016/j.jhtm.2018.03.005

Richards, G. (2021). *Rethinking cultural tourism*. Edward Elgar Publishing. doi:10.4337/9781789905441

Richards, G., & Raymond, C. (2000). Creative tourism. *ATLAS News*, (23), 16–20.

Richards, G., & Wilson, J. (2006). Developing creativity in tourist experiences : A solution to the serial reproduction of culture? *Tourism Management, 27*(6), 1209–1223. doi:10.1016/j.tourman.2005.06.002

Richards, G., & Wilson, J. (2007). *Tourism, creativity and development*. doi:10.4324/9780203933695

Schmitt, B. (1999). Experiential marketing. *Journal of Marketing Management, 15*(1-3), 53–67. doi:10.1362/026725799784870496

Segabinazzi, R. C. (2011). *O estilo de vida da Tribo do Surf e a cultura de consumo que a envolve* (Dissertação de Mestrado). Escola de Administração - Universidade Federal do Rio Grande do Sul, Brasil.

Seyfi, S., Hall, C. M., & Rasoolimanesh, S. M. (2019). Exploring memorable cultural tourism experiences. *Journal of Heritage Tourism, 6631*(15), 3. doi:10.1080/1743873X.2019.1639717

Shifino, C. (2002). Previsão de vendas na rede de varejo trópico surf shop. Trabalho de conclusão de curso em administração. Universidade Federal do Rio Grande do Sul –Porto Alegre, Brasil.

Sotomayor, S., & Barbieri, C. (2016). An exploratory examination of serious surfers: Implications for the surf tourism industry. *International Journal of Tourism Research, 18*(1), 62–73. doi:10.1002/jtr.2033

Stranger, M. (2017). *Surfing life: Surface, substructure, and the commodification of the sublime*. Routledge. doi:10.4324/9781315242033

Tan, S. K., Kung, S. F., & Luh, D. B. (2013). A model of "creative experience" in creative tourism. *Annals of Tourism Research, 41*, 153–174. doi:10.1016/j.annals.2012.12.002

Taylor, B. (2017). Surfing into spirituality and a new, aquatic nature religion. *Journal of the American Academy of Religion, 75*(4), 923–951. doi:10.1093/jaarel/lfm067 PMID:20681093

Treadwell, J., Kremer, P., & Payne, W. (2007). The determinants and motives for young people to participate in surfing. *Journal of Science and Medicine in Sport, 10*(6), 68–68.

van der Ark, L., & Richards, G. (2006). Attractiveness of cultural activities in European cities: A latent class approach. *Tourism Management, 27*(6), 1408–1413. doi:10.1016/j.tourman.2005.12.014

Willett, J. (2009). *Cornwall's experience of the experience economy; Longitudinal impacts*. Academic Press.

ADDITIONAL READING

Brochado, A., Stoleriu, O., & Lupu, C. (2018). Surf camp experiences. *Journal of Sport & Tourism*, *22*(1), 21–41. doi:10.1080/14775085.2018.1430609

Campos, A., Mendes, J., Oom do Vale, P., & Scott, N. (2016). Co-creation experiences: Attention and memorability. *Journal of Travel & Tourism Marketing*, *33*(9), 1309–1336. doi:10.1080/10548408.2015.1118424

Fadda, N. (2020). Entrepreneurial behaviours and managerial approach of lifestyle entrepreneurs in surf tourism: An exploratory study. *Journal of Sport & Tourism*, *24*(1), 53–77. doi:10.1080/14775085.2020.1726801

Kladou, S., Rigopoulou, I., Kavaratzis, M., & Salonika, E. (2021). A memorable tourism experience and its effect on country image. *Anatolia*, 1-12.

Valencia, L., Osorio García, M., & Serrano Barquín, R. D. C. (2020). Surf tourism: A review of new lines and topics of research (2012-2018). *Investigaciones Turísticas*, (20), 215–238. doi:10.14198/INTURI2020.20.10

Wallis, L., Walmsley, A., Beaumont, E., & Sutton, C. (2020). 'Just want to surf, make boards and party': How do we identify lifestyle entrepreneurs within the lifestyle sports industry? *The International Entrepreneurship and Management Journal*, *16*(3), 917–934. doi:10.100711365-020-00653-2

KEY TERMS AND DEFINITIONS

Co-Creation: Process through which the customer participates in the production and consumption of products, services or experiences.

Creative Experiences: New ways for tourists to engage in cultural experiences based on activities characteristic of the touristic destination where they are undertaken.

Creative Tourism: Special interest tourism alternative to massive forms of cultural consumption of tourism, where the tourists can develop their creative capital through engaging with locals.

Creativity: Problem-solving strategy or innovation process used to design more engaging and memorable tourism experiences.

Surf Culture: Culture related to surfing, where participants share different values and ideas from the dominant culture.

Surf Destination: Surfing tourist space, consisting of a set of attributes that interact with each other as a composite product.

Surf Tourism: Type of tourism that includes travel by any person who has surfing as their main or secondary motivation, whether for active practice or simply to enjoy/observe the activity and/or participate in surf-related events.

Surf Tourist: A person who travels to a surf destination for a certain time to surf or appreciate the surf practice.

Chapter 12
Wellness Tourism Experience on the Rise Post COVID:
Behavioural Demand Trends and Expectations

Nasim Hekmat
University Portucalense, Portugal

Makhabbat Ramazanova
University Portucalense, Portugal

Jorge Marques
https://orcid.org/0000-0001-5392-5128
University Portucalense, Portugal

Joana Alegria Quintela
https://orcid.org/0000-0002-4475-2744
University Portucalense, Portugal

ABSTRACT

This chapter synthesizes the emergence of the growing wellness tourism segment in an era of post-COVID-19 travel when consumer mentality has been radically changed and shifted towards different needs. This includes any activity that allows tourists to work on themselves mentally or physically and present several considerations and recommendations for the wellness industry to take full advantage of tourism opportunities moving forward. It aims to help understand consumer behaviour and preferences by predicting wellness tourism trends and developments, acknowledging the gaps in the research available for understanding wellness tourism post covid and reflecting the experience economy perspective in the sector. A research method was developed, including a literature review and survey application to potential wellness tourists. Discussion of results is provided, along with main conclusions, allowing the identification of trends and development measures to help improve wellness tourism in a post-COVID era.

DOI: 10.4018/978-1-7998-8775-1.ch012

Copyright © 2022, IGI Global. Copying or distributing in print or electronic forms without written permission of IGI Global is prohibited.

INTRODUCTION

In affluent societies, more and more attention has been paid to healthier and more conscious lifestyles (Koskinen & Wilska, 2019), rejuvenation and self-discovery (Mintel, 2007). There is an undeniable rise in the global popularity of complementary and alternative therapies (House of Lords UK, 2000), such as yoga, meditation, and interest in health and fitness. The tourism industry is swiftly moulding itself to cater to this new consumer demand (Sheldon & Bushell, 2009), which changed significantly, mainly in wellness tourism (Koskinen & Wilska, 2019). Research conducted by Luo et al. (2018) showed that wellness tourism activities can have very positive impacts on an individual's quality of life "and can result in improvements in dealing with problems at work, promoting family harmony, and engaging in social life" (Luo et al., 2018, p. 420). This assumption emphasises the importance of wellness tourism in the current society.

According to the Global Wellness Institute, wellness tourism has recently experienced significant rates of growth, with projections for continued development (GWI, 2018). Estimated at $639.4 billion in 2017, wellness tourism is a fast-growing tourism segment that has been growing by 6.5% annually from 2015-2017 (more than twice the growth rate for general tourism). An expanding global middle class has driven growth, growing consumer desire to adopt a wellness lifestyle, rising interest in experiential travel, and increasing affordability of flights and travel options. Across regions, Europe remains the destination for the largest number of wellness trips, while North America leads in wellness tourism expenditures. However, Asia has made the most gains in the number of wellness trips and wellness tourism expenditures (GWI, 2018).

In this context, the importance of this niche becomes clear, especially in the current era of COVID-19. The pandemic provoked a health crisis that fast turned into a financial decline due to the circulation restraints demanded to control its spreading (IMF, 2020). The lockdown government policies limited individual mobility to the home environment, provoking significant lifestyle changes (Holden, 2020). These limitations and changes affected the tourism business particularly, regarding the fact it results of a lack of the combination among infrastructures, industries, services, and people (Peretta, 2020), with consequences that in certain market areas are not easy to evaluate. The unexpected coronavirus pandemic has had a significant negative impact on many economic sectors worldwide, including tourism. As stated by the United Nations World Tourism Organisation (2021), the tourism sector suffered the most when compared to other economic sectors. Because of the pandemic crisis, the number of international tourist arrivals has decreased by 87% in January 2021, following a drop of 85% at the end of 2020 (UNWTO, 2021).

However, this crisis can simultaneously represent a recovery opportunity for some tourism market segments. Considering this perspective, this text aims to synthesise the emergence of the growing segment of wellness tourism in an era of post-Covid-19 travel, when consumer mentality has been radically changed and shifted towards different needs. This includes any type of activity that allows the tourist to work on themselves mentally or physically, following the experience economy trend. This chapter is also designed to provide a research output and analysis for global wellness tourism industry, namely: by helping to understand consumer behaviour and preferences when choosing a destination for a wellness vacation; by predicting wellness tourism trends and developments; by acknowledging the gaps in the research available for understanding wellness tourism post-Covid-19. The research method was developed to achieve this, including a literature review and survey application to potential wellness tourists. Discussion of results is provided, along with conclusions, identifying trends and development measures to help to improve wellness tourism in a post-Covid-19 era, presenting several considerations and recommendations for the wellness industry.

LITERATURE REVIEW

Experience Economy: A Brief Context

According to research conducted by Luo et al. (2018), Cohen's definition of tourism experience was an important milestone in investigating this topic. According to Cohen (1979), "the tourism experience is derived from the response of a person and his/her spiritual centre", regarding the satisfaction of personal needs that different individuals pursue (Luo et al., 2018, p.411). More recent research takes the definition of the tourist experience to another level, identifying two streams, namely the social science approach and the marketing management approach (Quan & Wang, 2004). From the perspective of social sciences, tourism experience was related to the contrast with the reality, based on the novel changes in the habitual, temporal, and spatial structures, and escape from daily routine (Quan & Wang, 2004). From the perspective of marketing/management, the tourist experience "is all about consumer experience which includes both the peak experience and other supporting experiences that an individual has through any direct or indirect contact with a business." (Luo et al., 2018:412). In this context, Pine and Gilmore (1999), in their groundwork research, suggested that businesses are the stage of the experience economy and customer experience is based on participation extent and relationship with an external stimulus. Thus, the experience should be assessed as a multidimensional concept that includes educational (customer's active involvement in interactions to improve their knowledge and/or skills), esthetic (customer's enjoyment of an enriched and unique physical design), entertainment (draw and engage tourist's attention and readiness to travel through activities and programs), and escapist (customers actively immerse themselves or engage in the activities) dimensions. Therefore, business in the travel industry should consider their economic offerings as an experience rather than mere tourism products (Oh et al., 2007).

Concept of Wellness Tourism

According to Romanova et al. (2015), when speaking of travel based on some form of health-related activities, some terms are mostly used and often interchangeably, such as health tourism, medical tourism, wellness tourism, spa tourism and medical travel. Nevertheless, the term 'wellness' was for the first time presented in 1959 by the American physician Halbert Dunn (Dunn, 1959). The concept of Dunn developed the concept "wellness" in the American language with the combination of the words wellbeing – with a strong 'health + pleasure' component; and "fit-ness" – corresponding to physical fitness, with a very important aesthetic component, whose movement was recognised since the 1950s in the USA through the "sport for all" movement (Nahrstedt, 1999). Dunn considered a special state of health, conceiving the human being, involving an absolute sensation of complete harmony, consisting of body, spirit and mind and being dependent on the surrounding environment, leading to a feeling of great personal contentment, that is, a high level of wellbeing. Thus, it was named "holistic wellness" (Dunn, 1959), redefining the term health to more than just the absence of disease and identifying a new segment of health consisting of mind, body and environment. The term wellness has broadened the focus from physical health to a holistic perspective that integrates an individual's body, mind, and spirit in the social context, enabling to take responsibility for the individual state of health throughout life (Stará, 2017).

On the research level, it should be noted that wellness tourism "has emerged as one of the areas that mostly grows in the interest of academic research" (Hall, 2011, p. 4). However, despite the growing popularity and demand for wellness tourism experiences, there is still a shortage of academic research and the need for better conceptual clarification is noted. Pforr et al. (2014) reveal that a closer look at the literature shows that health and wellness tourism tends to be equated with medical tourism, and frequently is driven by conventional and private health service providers, instead of the specialised tourism industry. According to UNWTO and ETC (2018), wellness tourism and medical tourism are under the umbrella of health. Health tourism has as "primary motivation, the contribution to physical, mental and/or spiritual health through medical and wellness-based activities which increase the capacity of individuals to satisfy their own needs and function better as individuals in their environment and society" (UNWTO & ETC, 2018, p. 2). According to the World Health Organization (WHO), health is a state of complete physical, mental, and social wellbeing and not merely the absence of disease or infirmity (WHO, 1948). The UNWTO defines health tourism as the "supply of some health facilities that use the country's natural resources, especially mineral waters and climate" (Hall, 2011, p. 5). Other researchers (Konu, 2010; Nahrstedt, 2004; Sheldon & Bushell, 2009) also corroborate with this "artificial combination of the words wellbeing and fitness or wellbeing" (Voigt, 2014, p. 19). Wellness tourism improves and balances physical, mental, emotional, occupational, intellectual, and spiritual domains (UNWTO & ETC, 2018). As stated by Dillette et al. (2021, p. 2), "health is considered the goal, while wellness is the pathway to achieve it. Wellness sits within the larger context of overall health." Yet, the concept of wellness is complex and not easy to define (Voigt, 2014). Wellness tourism has been discussed as part of health tourism, or even if it is specifically highlighted as the focus, it is often reduced to spa or thermal tourism (Voigt & Pforr, 2014). Also, health tourism is often marketed as an umbrella term that refers to both wellness tourism and medical tourism, and this has caused confusion between the sectors (Nahrstedt, 2004). Medical and wellness would both fall under the scope of health, but, when it comes to tourism, the Global Wellness Institute (GWI) specifies that wellness tourism and medical tourism are separate areas and should be valued and marketed as such. Wellness tourism is when a person travels to maintain or enhance one's wellbeing. Medical tourism involves the use of evidence-based medical healing resources and services (both invasive and non-invasive) (UNWTO & ETC, 2018), and it occurs when a person travels to receive treatment. This can be either cosmetic or concerning a diagnosis, cure, prevention, and rehabilitation (UNWTO & ETC, 2018). The main factor that separates medical tourism from wellness tourism is their difference in motives, services, employee specialisations, different definitions of heal and their material basis (Voigt, 2013). It is also conceived as a journey seeking health and harmony in body, mind, and spirit (Smith & Puczkó, 2009). Wellness tourism is about self-responsibility and is holistic (Messerli & Oyama, 2004). Individual behavioural patterns, also called "lifestyle", represent the most controllable and determinant areas of influence in human health (Koop et al., 2002). In essence, wellness refers to a lifestyle that incorporates wellbeing (Merriam-Webster Medical Dictionary). Wellness tourism seeks to promote disease prevention and is part of health tourism (Muller & Kaufmann, 2001). As far as the consumer is aware, there is no differentiation between them, as travellers can benefit from a combination of medical procedures and treatments as well as luxury travel packages (Badulescu & Badulescu, 2014). Wellness relates to maintaining a balance and is relative, subjective, and perceptive (Adams, 2003). However, wellness tourism can take a broader range of different niche markets, such as pilgrimage, yoga (Maharani et al., 2020) or babymoon (Gabor & Oltean, 2019). On the other hand, medical tourism can also fall into several areas, such as medical treatments or surgical procedures (Wang et al., 2020). The main differences between medical tourism and wellness tourism can be seen in Figure 1.

Figure 1. Differences between medical tourism and wellness tourism
Source: Maharani et al., 2020

MEDICAL TOURISM
REACTIVE

Travel to recieve treatment for a pre-existing condition.

Motivated by lower cost, high quality care, better access and/or available access to care.

Activities are reactive to the patient's illnesses, medically needed, invasive and/or overseen by a doctor.

WELLNESS TOURISM
PROACTIVE

Travel to manage, maintain or enhance personal wellbeing.

Motivated by healthy living, disease prevention, stress reduction, management of poor lifestyle habits, and/or authentic experiences.

Activities are proactive, voluntary, noninvasive and nonmedical.

Medical tourism is not a new concept, as people have always travelled far and wide for getting the best medical aid they can get. History tells us that people have always travelled to collect the right herbs or seek known physicians (Badulescu & Badulescu, 2014). Medical tourism appeals mainly to two consumer types. One of which is people from developed countries who want easier access to medical procedures or more affordable medical procedures than their home country. At the same time, the second type of consumer is people from countries with underdeveloped healthcare services who can afford to travel to places with better healthcare quality (Chaudhuri, 2008). Wellness tourism, which is usually considered self-care, is often associated with retreats, workshops, cruises, among other contexts (Johnston et al., 2011) (Figure 2). In fact, with the popularisation of yoga and spiritual studies, wellness tourism has flourished. This can also include business workshops that focus on the power of the mind to reach materialistic abundance, as part of the phenomena of wellness tourism and its popularity. Specific types of wellness tourism are location-based experiences (GWI, 2011) and are preferred in their native destination by tourists. Examples of these places are Bali, where their native practices become trends, such as yoga, meditation, Balinese massage, consultation with a healer (Balian) (Darmawijaya et al., 2018), and India (Manhas et al., 2020).

Figure 2. Types of activities of wellness tourism and medical tourism
Source: Johnston et al., 2011

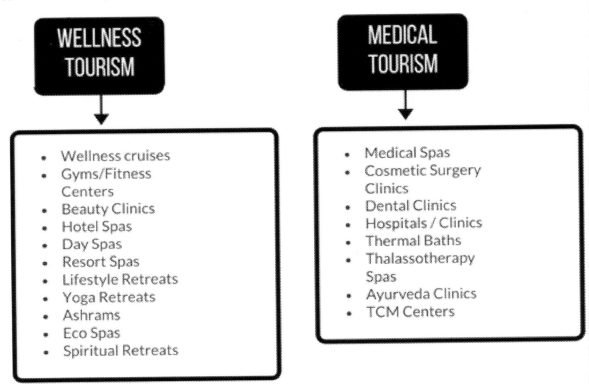

According to the Global Wellness Institute (2020), it is important to differentiate between wellness tourism and medical tourism to avoid confusion. For wellness tourism, generic experiences are identified, such as day spas, beauty clinics, hotel spas, gyms, and wellness cruises (Johnston et al., 2011). For medical tourism, there are location-based experiences, which include any activity or experience that emerges as part of a culture or geographical area. Hence, more and more, the word "experience" is used in the tourism context, like in marketing taglines, destination venues and digital media (Pine & Gilmore, 2013). Although it has been more than 20 years since Pine and Gilmore (1999) announced a new emerging wave of economic history and call it experience economy, there is still an increasing focus on valued experiences, more than on goods and services, considering it as a "mega-trend" (Mehmetoglu & Engen, 2011).

Motivations on Wellness Vacations

Consumers are increasingly turning to holiday travel to improve their health and wellbeing, promoting an offer based on experiences and services that support great outcomes (Lehto & Lehto, 2019). Tourists' motivation has important impacts on their reflective and experiential engagement (Kim et al., 2017). The literature suggests that tourists visit mainly wellness tourism destinations motivated by their intrinsic desires (Koh et al., 2010; Mak et al., 2009), namely related to psychological and emotional attributes (Li & Cai, 2012). Wellness's primary motivation is engagement with preventive, proactive, lifestyle enhancing, fitness and relaxation activities, healthy eating and pampering, and healing treatments (UNWTO & ETC, 2018). Thus, wellness holidays correspond to a new cure (health) and prevention (wellness) product, which gives the spas and thermal baths a context for the inclusion of the two dimensions. The need to escape the pace imposed by modern life and the new aesthetic concerns for the body, combined with the increase in the diversity of treatments and the extension of the period of operation of the resorts, are the main causes of this increase in health and wellness demand. Besides that, wellness tourism can stimulate other types of tourism, encompassing different motivations and at the same time "relating to the specific demographic profile of the clientele" (Sheldon & Bushell, 2009:11). This aspect totally fits on wellness tourist's profile. This kind of tourist look for innovation and knowledge on their vacations. Besides relaxation activities such as fitness, tracking or yoga, also complementary educational programs and prestigious/luxury experiences as cultural and wine and gastronomic activities are included in wellness tourists' motivations to travel (Kim et al., 2017).

The reasons behind the growing interest in wellness tourism, driving the increase in supply and demand for this type of tourism, refer to the expansion of the concept of health from the 1960s onwards, which recognises that consumers are responsible for forging a new, more holistic, positive, and self-responsible understanding of health (Hall & Brown, 2006; Pforr & Voigt, 2014; Sheldon & Bushell, 2009). This trend matches the "wellbeing revolution", an expression presented by Pilzer (2007) in contrast with conventional medicine and pharmaceutical companies. On the other hand, "the wellness industry includes products and services that promote wellness rather than responding to illness" (Pilzer, 2007:28), which includes nutritional supplements, superfoods, and juices, personal trainers, and care alternatives, advocating a healthier lifestyle. Other factors triggering a growing interest in health and wellness are the generalised ageing of the population (particularly in European countries), the acceleration of the pace of life, individualisation, and the search for spirituality (Voigt & Pforr, 2014). According to Baum and Lockstone-Binney (2014), wellness tourism can be developed in different contexts and in its relationship with the surrounding components. Inclusively, it can be included in the corporate context, providing wellness tourism vacations (Hamed, 2015).

METHODOLOGY

The purpose of this section is to present the methodology implemented for this study, namely research strategy and methods applied, population identification and sample selection approach, design and objectives of the survey questionnaire, final sample size and statistical software used to execute the data analysis.

Data Collection and Analysis

A quantitative research strategy was adopted for collecting primary data through the questionnaire survey as a reliable method to collect information from multiple respondents in an efficient and timely manner. It is especially important in this project due to the restrictions of the Covid-19 pandemic, which has made most interactions online. The data collection process was conducted from January till April 2021. The questionnaire was posted on selected Travel Facebook groups in which participants had experience and desire to travel, as well as on WhatsApp and Telegram groups. As a result, 161 valid responses were obtained.

The target population of the empirical study corresponds to all the visitors who had or have a particular interest in wellness tourism. For the study, two specific criteria were applied to select the sample out of the total population; namely, they had to be over the age of 18 and must have had travelled for wellness or have a particular interest in travelling for wellness in an era of post-COVID-19. A convenience sampling approach was applied to select the individuals to participate in the survey questionnaire due to its accessibility and simplicity in reaching the population. The objective of the mentioned approach was to reach out to as diverse a sample as possible, in terms of different nationalities, both people living in their home countries and ex-pats, people from diverse walks of life in terms of financial situations and reasons for wellness travel.

The questionnaire started with explaining the meaning of wellness tourism based on Global Wellness Institute definition. Individuals A positive answer to the previous question allowed them to continue with the next questions. The first section aimed to capture information related to the sociodemographic characteristic of the sample, followed by specific questions such as geographic preferences for a wellness vacation, visitor's specific preferences and expectations of wellness tourism, the experiences looking to enhance the wellness vacation, some aspects related to accommodation, safety, and cleanness among essential factors. The mentioned dimensions were included in the survey questionnaire based on the analysis of previous research and studies in the domain. For data analysis, SPSS statistical software (25.0 version) was applied, and the results are discussed following the set-up objectives at the beginning of the study.

Frequency analysis was executed for the variables describing sample profile and trip characteristics. Concerning the bivariate analyses, the Chi-Square test of independence was used to test the association between willingness to travel in post-COVID-19 period and main goals for wellness vacation, place preferences, as developed in previous studies (Meikassandra et al., 2020).

ANALYSIS AND DISCUSSION OF RESULTS

Sample Profile

Table 1. Countries of residence by region

Regions (classified by UNWTO)	Frequency	Percentage
Asia	98	60,9%
Europe	42	26,1%
Americas	14	8,7%
Africa	7	4,3%
Total	161	100,0%

Source: Authors´ elaboration

The sample encompasses 36 countries (Table 1), allowing the understanding of what wellness tourists expect from their wellness trip irrespective of their country of residence. The objective was to understand what wellness tourists expect from their wellness trip, irrespective of their country.

Table 2. Sample profile

Variables	Frequency	Percentage
Age		
18-24	10	6%
25-34	39	24%
35-44	58	36%
45-54	34	21%
55 and over	20	13%
Gender		
Female	94	58%
Male	67	42%
Occupation		
Employee	77	48%
Self-employee	60	37%
Unemployed	13	8%
Student	6	4%
Retired	5	3%
Monthly Income		
>$500	12	7%
$501-$1,000	17	11%
$1,001-$5,000	71	44%
$5,001-$10,000	25	16%
>$10,000	23	14%
No income	13	8%

Source: Authors´ elaboration

The respondents were mostly aged between 35 and 44 (36%) and 25-34 (24%). Regarding gender, the females are represented by 58% of the respondents and the males by 42% (Table 2). Most of them were employed, shortly followed by self-employed. The monthly income of 44% of respondents were between $1,001-$5,000, significantly higher than the 15% of respondents with the second-highest monthly earnings of $5,000-$10,000.

Regarding the dream destinations of respondents by region described in Table 3, it is possible to observe that travel for wellness is on the incline in developing markets, mainly Asia (61%), followed by Europe (25%). Detailed analysis in this study demonstrates that Indonesia, specifically Bali, as respondents mainly noted, is the most desired location for travel for wellness, closely surpassing Maldives. Some studies also point out that Bali became one of the popular destinations in Asia for a wellness tourism destination in 2017-2018 (Meikassandra et al., 2020). Some respondents selected Americas, Africa, and Australia/Oceania as dream destinations, indicating potential and interest for a wellness vacation in these regions.

Table 3. Dream destinations of respondents by region

Regions (classified by UNWTO)	Frequency	Percentage
Asia	98	60,9%
Europe	40	24,8%
Americas	11	6,8%
Africa	6	3,7%
Australia/Oceania	4	2,5%
Others	2	1,2%
Total	161	100%

Source: Authors´ elaboration

Characteristics of the Wellness Trip

A descriptive statistics analysis was used to characterise the planning of a wellness vacation by potential visitors. First, considering the Covid-19 pandemic, the respondents were asked how likely they were to travel after the pandemic. The results demonstrate that 32% of people are highly likely to travel within the mentioned period and 24% are medium likely, and 24% are likely, leaving very low likelihood at only 12% and 9% for low likelihood (Figure 3).

These results highlight the importance of travel for respondents in the post-pandemic period and their quite optimistic mood. Similar results were presented by Ivanova et al. (2021), stating that most of the Bulgarian respondents were ready to return to travel within two months after the pandemic.

Nevertheless, given that the unexpected pandemic has severely shocked tourists, it is crucial to guarantee appropriate safety and sanitation strategies at destinations. On the other hand, the willingness of most respondents to travel can be explained by their perception of wellness tourism in terms of higher safety and wellness conditions, mental comfort, and relaxation. Regardless of the reason, this is a positive sign for the travel and tourism industry, encouraging and motivating tourism stakeholders to recover the sector more effectively and rapidly.

Figure 3. Willingness to travel in post-Covid-19 period
Source: Authors´ elaboration

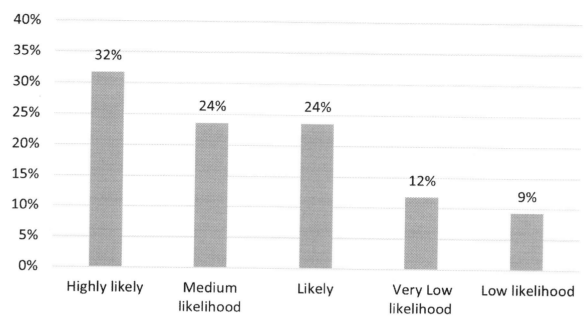

Further, the potential wellness visitors were questions about preference for geographical location when choosing the wellness vacation. A linear scale was used to understand their preferences (1 being the preference to be close to home, and 5 being the willingness to travel far and wide from home). Based on the results, the average value is 4, which indicates that the respondents are willing to travel far from their home country for their wellness trip. 75% of the respondents want to plan their itinerary rather than have a professional travel agent plan their daily activities (Figure 4). This is surprising since often travel is associated with rest and non-decision making, going with the flow and switch-off mindset, but people would like to be part of the planning and know what is, how is and where is of their travel itinerary. Another perspective on these results can be related to the fact that travel agencies are not offering competitive and commoditised packages regarding wellness vacations.

Figure 4. Itinerary planning
Source: Authors´ elaboration

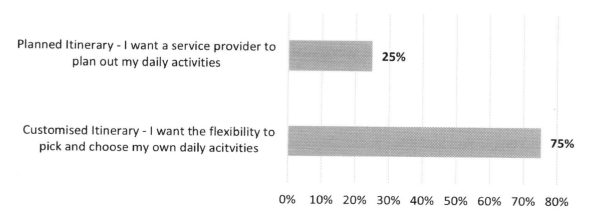

Regarding the place preferences, 76% of the respondents prefer to be in a secluded place to relax with the least amount of people (Figure 5). Not surprisingly, during a pandemic, many respondents prefer to avoid crowded places and less favourable locations to spread the virus. In contrast, only 24% of the respondents chose to be in a group setting or where there is more interaction with other people.

Socialising, meeting new people and active interaction with others was one of the motivations in tourism (Wolf-Watz, 2014). Nevertheless, the consequences of the COVID-19 pandemic crisis have drastically changed this behavioural pattern, resulting in tourists valuing secluded and less crowded places. Earlies studies mention that escapism has been the highest purpose of travel, the notion of getting away and switch-off has often been the primary purpose of tourism (Cohen, 1996; Rojek, 1993),

Figure 5. Atmosphere preference for the wellness vacation
Source: Authors' elaboration

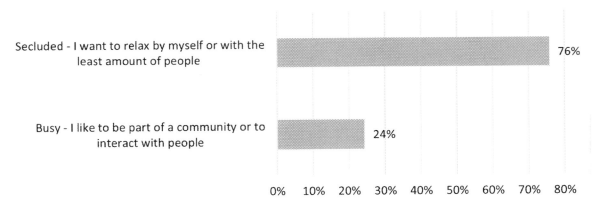

As for the preferred companion, wellness tourism consumers prefer to travel on a wellness vacation with their partner (36%), followed by family (22%), friends (22%) or alone (20%) (Figure 6). Besides the respondents choosing secluded places, they prefer to travel with a companion, the choice of which may depend on various factors. In this context, So & Lehto (2007) explored the travel group segmentation, namely, travelling with family, travelling alone, and travelling with friends among Japanese travellers. The research findings demonstrate that motivations and travel preferences vary among the groups, as well as their participation in different activities. Those who travel alone and with friends tend to be more engaged in activities and socialising with others, while those who travel with family tend to value physical relaxation and active experiential learning.

Also, we aimed to understand the preferred experiences of the travellers. Questions were made about their main objective when going on a wellness vacation, about which activities they believed would help them to achieve their wellness goal, and which wellness activities were most appealing and enjoyable that they would like to include during their trip, and lastly, which activities they would like to include in their trip even if it were not wellness related (Table 4). As it can be noted, the most popular reasons for wellness travel are to rejuvenate and unwind (72%), followed by the goal of mental health (56%), to escape routine (44%) and to work on fitness (27%). When asked how they can enhance their wellness goal, rest and rejuvenation were significantly more popular than the other options. Healthy eating, nutrition and weight loss was the second most popular choice considered by travellers to help them achieve their wellness goal. Yoga and holistic treatments shortly follow, and then below 40% and over 20% of the respondents feel that personal care, beauty, anti-ageing, retreats, shamanic rituals, or fitness boot camps can aid their goal. Only 9% feel that medical treatments can help them reach their goal, and 8% feel transition therapy would help.

Figure 6. Preferred company for the wellness vacation
Source: Authors' elaboration

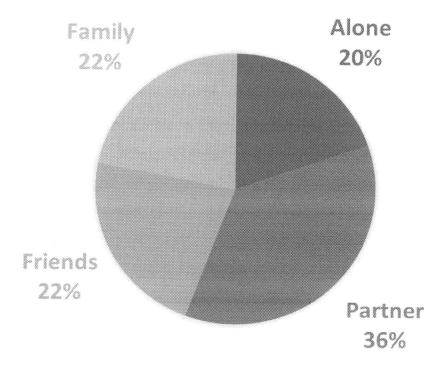

When it comes to wellness activities that visitors would like to add to their itinerary, most respondents preferred walking tours (65%), massages (62%) and spa experiences (61%), thermal/mineral springs (50%), climbing/hiking (48%), facial treatments (27%), new wellness technologies (21%), art therapy (19%), esoteric dancing (19%), vitamin IV drip (14%) and one respondent added their option stating life coaching as an activity.

To deepen into the interests of the travellers during their wellness trip, they were asked which additional activities they would like to be included even if it was not wellness related. Most respondents wanted nature to be included in their trip (81%). Cultural activities were next with 64% and adventure came in at third place with 62%. Rest had 57% and sports had 31%. While 21% of visitors also wanted to visit places, they had seen previously on TV, and 19% of them would include a visit to friends and family during their wellness trip. 17% chose to add "Instagrammable" places into their itinerary, only 1% wanted to visit religious sites, and less than 1% chose temple tours.

Table 4. Desired wellness experience

Variables	Frequency	Percentage
Main objective when going on a wellness vacation		
To rejuvenate and unwind	116	72%
For mental health	91	56%
To escape routine	71	44%
To work on fitness	44	27%
To explore the destination	1	0.6%
Activities to enhance the wellness goal		
Rest & Rejuvenation	131	77%
Healthy eating, nutrition & weight loss	83	48%
Yoga	76	44%
Holistic Treatments	71	42%
Personal care, beauty & anti-aging	63	37%
Retreats	57	33%
Shamanic Rituals	35	21%
Fitness bootcamps	34	20%
Medical Treatments	16	9%
Transition therapy (divorce, job loss)	14	8%
Wellness activity is most appealing for a visitor		
Walking tour	111	65%
Massages	106	62%
Spa experiences	104	61%
Thermal / Mineral springs	85	50%
Climbing / Hiking	82	48%
Facial treatments	46	27%
New wellness technologies – hyperbaric chambers, etc.	36	21%
Art therapy	33	19%
Esoteric dancing	33	19%
Vitamin IV drip	24	14%
Life coaching	1	0.6%
Other experiences that interest the visitors		
Nature	139	81%
Culture	110	64%
Adventure	106	62%
Rest	97	57%
Sport	53	31%
Nightlife	45	26%
Visiting places seen on TV	35	21%
Visiting friends / Relatives	32	19%

Continued on following page

Table 4. Continued

Variables	Frequency	Percentage
Main objective when going on a wellness vacation		
Visiting "Instagrammable" places	29	17%
Religion	26	15%
Temple tours	1	0.6%

(Source: Authors´ elaboration)

Further, the potential travellers were questioned about accommodation preferences when going on a wellness trip and what factors influence their choice of accommodation. The findings illustrate that 53% would opt for luxury hotels while 40% would go for boutique hotels, 28% would choose guest houses, 20% would go camping, and 19% would choose an economy hotel (Figure 7).

Figure 7. Accommodation preferences
Source: Authors´ elaboration

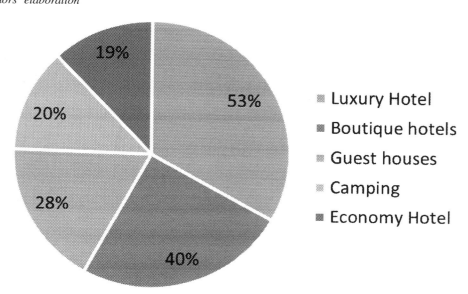

Regarding accommodation, it is possible to analyse in table 5 that cleanliness, safety, and comfort are considered the most important factors for accommodation selection.

Table 5. Importance of the factors for selection accommodation

Factors/ Assessment	Not important at all		Not important		Neutral		Important		Very important		Mean
Safety	2	1%	8	5%	16	10%	37	23%	98	61%	3.37
Cleanliness	4	2%	5	3%	11	7%	24	15%	117	73%	3.52
Comfort	2	1%	7	4%	18	11%	51	32%	83	52%	3.28
Eco friendly	5	3%	21	13%	39	24%	57	35%	39	24%	2.65
Lively environment	8	5%	18	11%	48	30%	47	35%	30	19%	2.52
Close to grocery/ town	12	7%	39	10%	57	35%	52	32%	24	15%	2.37
24 hours service	18	11%	48	14%	53	33%	42	26%	26	16%	2.22
Kitchen access	17	11%	32	20%	65	40%	25	16%	22	14%	2.02

(Source: Authors' elaboration)

What is the Relationship of Willingness for Wellness to Travel with the Goal and Place?

The objective is to examine an association between willingness to travel in the post-Covid-19 period of potential wellness visitors and their goal for a wellness vacation. Considering that both variables are categorical, cross-tabulation was used to examine the relationship between the desire for travelling and the main goals for a wellness vacation, namely the goal to rejuvenate and unwind, escape routine for mental health, and work on fitness and explore the destination. In addition, the Pearson's Chi-squared test of independence was applied for testing the statistical significance of the cross-tabulation table. The results of the cross-tabulation test in this study are presented in table 6.

The results demonstrate a statistically significant association between willingness to travel and the objective to rejuvenate and unwind, with the Chi-Square value 13.566, and p-value 0.009. Further, the positive and statistically significant association is found in the case of the objective to escape routine and desire to make a trip, since the Chi-Square condition is met with the value 8.449 and with a p-value 0.076. It can be concluded that the willingness to travel is associated with the goal to rejuvenate and unwind, as well as with the goal to escape routine. Previous studies in wellness tourism research confirm this trend (Chen & Petrick, 2013; Koskinen & Wilska, 2019; Voigt et al., 2011).

Nevertheless, in the case of the goals to work on fitness and goal for mental health, the results illustrate that there is not enough statistical evidence of an association between the desire to travel and referred objectives of a wellness vacation since the p-value is greater than the significance level ($\alpha = 0.05$).

Table 6. Willingness to travel with the main goals for wellness vacation

Willingness to travel	Main goal for a wellness vacation	Values	Chi-Square Significance
Willingness to travel in post-COVID-19 period	To rejuvenate and unwind	13.566	0.009
	To escape routine	8.449	0.076
	For mental health	1.405	0.843
	To work on fitness	1.121	0.891

(Source: Authors' elaboration)

The following analysis concerns the relationship between willingness to travel and the preferences of potential wellness visitors of a place to be busy and active or secluded with a calm environment. Similarly, Pearson's Chi-squared test was used to investigate if there is a significant association between these two categorical variables. The results are presented in table 7.

Table 7. Willingness to travel in post-Covid-19 period with the place preference

Likelihood for wellness travel / Place preferences	Busy - I like to be part of a community or to interact with people	Secluded - I want to relax by myself or with the least amount of people	Values	Chi-Square Significance
Highly likely	8%	24%		
Likely	8%	15%		
Medium likelihood	5%	19%	4.023	0.403
Low likelihood	1%	8%		
Very low likelihood	2%	10%		
Total	24%	76%		

(Source: Authors´ elaboration)

The findings illustrate that the association between the desire to travel for wellness vacation and preferences of a place is not statistically significant. Potential wellness visitors expressed an appreciation of secluded places with higher frequency values (76%). However, the relationship between the desire to travel and preference of the place was not found. This may be explained by the existence of a diversity of wellness activities, which some visitors may find important to practice during their wellness vacation, regarding the example of spa visitors' attitudes toward healthy living (Koskinen, & Wilska, 2019; Voigt et al., 2011).

CONCLUSION

Over the past few years, there has been growing attention to health and wellbeing issues. It becomes even more relevant today when, on a global scale, a pandemic is being fought. In this context, it is especially important to try to understand which factors influence the behaviour of tourism consumers and, more specifically, wellness tourism consumers. In this way, companies and public and private institutions will have more tools to prepare themselves better to offer the most adequate tourist experience for each consumer profile. While some consumers seek products and services that make them feel younger (Pilzer, 2007), others are more focused on lifestyle (Liu et al., 2018) and believe that "health" not only refers to biomedical matters, but also encompasses leisure, nature, and wellbeing (Young et al., 2018). This belief crucially influences their consumption behaviour reflected in purchasing organic and nutritional food (Lo et al., 2017; Regine, 2011;), participating in wellness programs (Ott-Holland et al., 2019), and choosing wellness tourism (Hritz et al., 2014). This changing consumer behaviour has led to the rise of the wellness economy. As individual needs are altered, so is tourism with (McKercher & Chan, 2005; Trauer, 2006). Global and societal changes have resulted in the need for specific activity focused tourism (McKercher & Chan, 2005; Trauer, 2006), and wellness tourism fulfils the aim of stress management, personal development, reflection, connection and satisfying the urge to find the meaning of life (Kelly, 2010). This type of wellness tourism doesn't just imply changes in the usual tourism concerns like transport and accommodation, but the mental wellbeing of the tourists too (Kelly, 2010). The findings of this study demonstrate that the willingness to travel for wellness vacation is strongly associated with the intention of visitors to rejuvenate and unwind and to escape the usual routine. According to previous studies, escapism has been the highest purpose of travel, the notion of getting away and switch-off has often been the main purpose of tourism (Cohen, 1996; Rojek, 1993), as well as rejuvenation and the urge of self-discovery and self-purpose (Mintel, 2007). Thus, wellbeing can become a type of life of self-discovery in an era of increasing stress. Consequently, wellbeing is generally considered to be a holistic philosophy, supporting temporary feelings of happiness. This book chapter contributes to a better understanding of this niche market, especially relevant in the pandemic context of COVID-19, and to better prepare destinations and stakeholders to answer in a more effective way to the wellness tourist needs and motivations.

FUTURE RESEARCH

Regarding further research, figure as a recommendation the development of longitudinal (cross-temporal) studies that could follow the evolution of the demand behaviour along time. Longitudinal studies may provide greater information about the demand travel behaviour over time, attesting to the changes in wellness tourism demand behavioural trends and expectations.

REFERENCES

Adams, M. (2003). The reflexive self and culture: A critique. *The British Journal of Sociology*, *54*(2), 221–238. doi:10.1080/0007131032000080212 PMID:12945868

Badulescu, D., & Badulescu, A. (2014). Medical tourism: Between entrepreneurship opportunities and bioethics boundaries: Narrative review article. *Iranian Journal of Public Health*, *43*(4), 406–415. PMID:26005650

Baum, T., & Lockstone-Binney, L. (2014). Fit for purpose: Delivering wellness tourism through people. In Wellness tourism. A destination perspective (pp. 130-143). Routledge.

Bushell, R., & Sheldon, P. J. (2009). Introduction to wellness and tourism. In R. Bushell & P. J. Sheldon (Eds.), *Wellness and tourism: Mind, body, spirit, place* (pp. 3–18). Cognizant Communication Corporation.

Chaudhuri, S. K. (2008). Ethics of medical tourism. *Journal of the Indian Medical Association*, *106*, 188. PMID:18714462

Chen, C. C., & Petrick, J. (2013). Health and wellness benefits of travel experiences: A literature review. *Journal of Travel Research*, *52*(6), 709–719. doi:10.1177/0047287513496477

Cohen, E. (1996). A phenomenology of tourist experiences. In Y. Apostopoulos, S. Leivadi, & A. Yiannakis (Eds.), *The sociology of tourism: Theoretical and empirical investigations* (pp. 90–111). Routledge.

Darmawijaya, I. G., Tirtawati, N. M., & Sekarti, N. K. (2018). The typology of wellness tourism in Bali. *3rd International Conference on Tourism, Economics, Accounting, Management, and Social Science (TEAMS 2018)*.

Dillette, A., Douglas, A., & Andrzejewski, C. (2021). Dimensions of holistic wellness as a result of international wellnes tourism experiences. *Current Issues in Tourism*, 24(6), 794–810. doi:10.1080/13683500.2020.1746247

Dunn, H. L. (1959). High-level wellness for man and society. *American Journal of Public Health*, 49(6), 786–792. doi:10.2105/AJPH.49.6.786 PMID:13661471

Gabor, M. R., & Oltean, F. D. (2019). Babymoon tourism between emotional wellbeing service for medical tourism and niche tourism: Development and awareness on Romanian educated women. *Tourism Management*, 70, 170–175. doi:10.1016/j.tourman.2018.08.006

Global Spa Summit. (2011). *Wellness tourism and medical tourism: Where do spas fit?* Available online: https://globalwellnessinstitute.org/industry-research/wellness-tourism-medical-tourism/

Global Wellness Institute. (2011). *Wellness tourism and medical tourism: Where do spas fit?* Available online: https://globalwellnessinstitute.org/industry-research/wellness-tourism-medical-tourism/

Global Wellness Institute. (2018). Available online: https://globalwellnessinstitute.org/industry-research/2018-global-wellness-economy-monitor/

Halden, A. (2020). Responding to the Coronavirus crisis: Parallels for tourism and climate change? In F. Burini (Ed.), *Tourism facing a pandemic: from crisis to recovery* (pp. 57–62). Università degli Studi di Bergamo.

Hall, D., & Brown, F. (Eds.). (2006). *Tourism and welfare: Ethics, responsibility and sustained wellbeing*. CABI., doi:10.1079/9781845930660.0000

Hall, M. C. (2011). Health and medical tourism: A kill or cure for global public health? *Tourism Review*, 66(1/2), 4–15. doi:10.1108/16605371111127198

Hamed, H. M. (2015). Wellness tourism: An Initiative for comprising wellness tourism vacations within the corporate wellness strategy. *American Journal of Tourism Research*, 4(2), 52–67. doi:10.11634/216837861504643

House of Lords. (2000). *Complementary and alternative medicine* (Report of the Select Committee on Science and Technology). HMSO.

Hritz, N. M., Sidman, C. L., & D'abundo, M. (2014). Segmenting the college educated generation Y health and wellness traveler. *Journal of Travel & Tourism Marketing*, 31(1), 132–145. doi:10.1080/10548408.2014.861727

IMF. (2020). *World Economic Outlook, April 2020: The great lockdown*. IMF.

Johnston, K., Puczkó, L., Smith, M., & Ellis, S. (2011). *Wellness tourism and medical tourism: Where do spas fit?* Research Report: Global SPA Summit 2011.

Kelly, C. (2010). Analysing Wellness tourism provision: A retreat operators' study. *Journal of Hospitality and Tourism Management, 17*(1), 108–116. doi:10.1375/jhtm.17.1.108

Kessler, D., Lee, J.-H., & Whittingham, N. (2020). The wellness tourist motivation scale: A new statistical tool for measuring wellness tourist motivation. *International Journal of Spa and Wellness, 3*(1), 24–39. doi:10.1080/24721735.2020.1849930

Kim, E., Chiang, L., & Tang, L. (2017). Investigating wellness tourists' motivation, engagement, and loyalty: In search of the missing link. *Journal of Travel & Tourism Marketing, 34*(7), 867–879. doi:10.1080/10548408.2016.1261756

Koh, S., Jung-Eun Yoo, J., & Boger, C. A. Jr. (2010). Importance-performance analysis with benefit segmentation of spa goers. *International Journal of Contemporary Hospitality Management, 22*(5), 718–735. doi:10.1108/09596111011053828

Konu, H., Tuohino, A., & Komppula, R. (2010). Lake wellness: A practical example of a new service development (NSD) concept in tourism industries. *Journal of Vacation Marketing, 16*(2), 125–139. doi:10.1177/1356766709357489

Koop, C. E., Pearson, C. E., & Schwarz, M. R. (2002). *Critical issues in global health*. Jossey-Bass. doi:10.1097/01445442-200205000-00014

Koskinen, V., & Wilska, T.-A. (2019). Identifying and understanding spa tourists' wellness attitudes. *Scandinavian Journal of Hospitality and Tourism, 19*(3), 259–277. doi:10.1080/15022250.2018.1467276

Lehto, X. Y., & Lehto, M. R. (2019). Vacation as a public health resource: Toward a wellness-centered tourism design approach. *Journal of Hospitality & Tourism Research (Washington, D.C.), 43*(7), 935–960. doi:10.1177/1096348019849684

Li, M., & Cai, L. A. (2012). The effects of personal values on travel motivation and behavioral intention. *Journal of Travel Research, 51*(4), 473–487. doi:10.1177/0047287511418366

Liu, C.-R., Wang, Y.-C., Chiu, T.-H., & Chen, S.-P. (2018). Antecedents and outcomes of lifestyle hotel brand attachment and love: The case of Gen Y. *Journal of Hospitality Marketing & Management, 27*(3), 281–298. doi:10.1080/19368623.2017.1364197

Lo, A., King, B., & Mackenzie, M. (2017). Restaurant customers' attitude toward sustainability and nutritional menu labels. *Journal of Hospitality Marketing & Management, 26*(8), 846–867. doi:10.1080/19368623.2017.1326865

Luo, Y., Lenlung, C., Kim, E., Tang, L., & Song, S. (2018). Towards quality of life: The effects of the wellness tourism experience. *Journal of Travel & Tourism Marketing, 35*(4), 410–424. doi:10.1080/10548408.2017.1358236

Maharani, I. A. K., Wisnu Parta, I. B. M., & Supriadi, I. B. P. (2020). Factors Influencing yoga tourism in bali: Conceptual framework model. *Vidyottama Sanatana: International Journal of Hindu Science and Religious Studies, 4*(1), 20. doi:10.25078/ijhsrs.v4i1.1321

Mak, A. H., Wong, K. K., & Chang, R. C. (2009). Health or selfindulgence? The motivations and characteristics of spagoers. *International Journal of Tourism Research, 11*(2), 185–199. doi:10.1002/jtr.703

Manhas, P. S., Charak, N. S., & Sharma, P. (2020). Wellness and spa tourism: Finding space for Indian Himalayan spa resorts. *International Journal of Spa and Wellness*, 2(14), 1–19. doi:10.1080/24721735.2020.1819705

McKercher, B., & Chan, A. (2005). How special is special interest tourism? *Journal of Travel Research*, 44(1), 21–31. doi:10.1177/0047287505276588

Mehmetoglu, M., & Engen, M. (2011). Pine and Gilmore's concept of experience economy and its dimensions: An empirical examination in tourism. *Journal of Quality Assurance in Hospitality & Tourism*, 12(4), 237–255. doi:10.1080/1528008X.2011.541847

Meikassandra, P., Winarya, S., & Mertha, I. W. (2020). Wellness tourism in Ubud: A qualitative approach to study the aspects of Wellness tourism development. *Journal of Business on Hospitality and Tourism*, 6(1), 79–93. doi:10.22334/jbhost.v6i1.191

Messerli, H. R., & Oyama, Y. (2004). Health and wellness tourism: Global. *Travel & Tourism Analyst*, (August), 1–54.

Mintel. (2007). *Tourism sector report on holistic tourism*. London: Mintel International Group Ltd. Retrieved from http://www.mintel.com

Mueller, H., & Kaufmann, E. L. (2001). Wellness tourism: Market analysis of a special health tourism segment and implications for the hotel industry. *Journal of Vacation Marketing*, 7(1), 5–17. doi:10.1177/135676670100700101

Nahrstedt, W. (1999). Wellness, fitness, beauty, soul: Angebotsanalyse von deuschen Kur und Urlaubsorten. Einleitungsvortrag, 11th ELRA Congress "Leisure and Wellness: Health Tourism in Europe", 7-9/10 Bad Saarow. *Heilbad und Kurort, 51*.

Nahrstedt, W. (2004). Wellness: A new perspective for leisure centers, health tourism, and spas in Europe on the global health market. In K. Wiermair, C. Mathies, & C. Haworth Hospitality (Eds.), *The tourism and leisure industry: Shaping the future*. Bighamton.

Oh, H., Fiore, A., & Jeoung, M. (2007). Measuring experience economy concepts: Tourism applications. *Journal of Travel Research*, 46(2), 119–132. doi:10.1177/0047287507304039

Ott-Holland, C. J., Shepherd, W. J., Ryan, A. M., & Chen, P. Y. (2019). Examining wellness programs generation Y over time: Predicting participation and workplace outcomes. *Journal of Occupational Health Psychology*, 24(1), 163–179. doi:10.1037/ocp0000096 PMID:28872333

Peretta, R. (2020). Commons and the tourism sector facing a pandemic. In F. Burini (Ed.), *Tourism facing a pandemic: From crisis to recovery* (pp. 133–138). Università degli Studi di Bergamo.

Pforr, C., Pechlaner, H., Locher, C., & Jochman, J. (2014). Health regions: Building tourism destinations through networked regional core competences. In C. Voigt & C. Pforr (Eds.), *Wellness tourism. A destination perspective* (pp. 99–111). Routledge.

Pilzer, P. Z. (2007). *The new wellness revolution*. John Wiley & Sons, Inc.

Pine, B. J., & Gilmore, J. H. (1999). *The experience economy: Work is theatre & every business a stage*. Harvard Business Press.

Pine, B. J., & Gilmore, J. H. (2013). The experience economy: Past, present and future. In J. Sundbo, & F. Sørensen (Eds.), Handbook on the experience economy (pp. 21–44). Edward Elgar Publishing. doi:10.4337/9781781004227.00007

Quan, S., & Wang, N. (2004). Towards a structural model of the tourism experience: An illustration from food experiences in Tourism. *Tourism Management, 25*(3), 163–169. doi:10.1016/S0261-5177(03)00130-4

Regine, K. (2011). Generation Y consumer choice for organic foods. *Journal of Global Business Management, 7*(1), 1–13.

Rojek, C. (1993). *Ways of escape: Modern transformations in leisure and travel*. Macmillan Press. doi:10.1057/9780230373402

Romanova, G., Vetitnev, A., & Dimanche, F. (2015). Health and wellness tourism. In F. Dimanche & L. Andrades (Eds.), *Tourism in Russia. A management handbook*. Emerald.

Sheldon, P., & Bushell, R. (Eds.). (2009). *Wellness tourism: Mind, body, spirit, place*. Cognizant.

Smith, M., & Puczkó, L. (2009). *Health and wellness tourism*. Butterworth-Heinemann Elsevier.

Stará, J. (2017). Health and wellness: Conceptual grounding. *Acta Salus Vitae, 5*(2), 3–25.

Sustainable Development Goals. (2015). Available online: https://sdgs.un.org/goals

Trauer, B. (2006). Conceptualising special interest tourism: Framework for analysis. *Tourism Management, 27*(2), 183–200. doi:10.1016/j.tourman.2004.10.004

UNWTO. (2021). *World Tourism Barometer and Statistical Annex*. Available online: https://www.e-unwto.org/doi/abs/10.18111/wtobarometereng.2021.19.1.2?journalCode=wtobarometereng

Voigt, C. (2013). *Wellness tourism: A critical overview*. Retrieved from: http://www.tobewell.eu/media/universityofexeter/businessschool/documents/research/tobewell/Wellness_Tourism_-_Cornelia_Voigt.pdf

Voigt, C. (2014). The Gawler Foundation in Australia: Wellness and lifestyle-based therapeutic retreats for people with serious illnesses. In M. Smith & L. Puczkó (Eds.), *Health, tourism and hospitality: Spas, wellness and medical travel* (pp. 461–465). Routledge.

Voigt, C., Brown, G., & Howat, G. (2011). Wellness tourists: In search of transformation. *Tourism Review, 66*(1/2), 16–30. doi:10.1108/16605371111127206

Voigt, C., & Pforr, C. (2014). *Wellness tourism: A destination perspective*. Routledge.

Wang, K., Xu, H., & Huang, L. (2020). Wellness tourism and spatial stigma: A case study of Bama, China. *Tourism Management, 78*, 104039. doi:10.1016/j.tourman.2019.104039

Wolf-Watz, D. (2014). Traveling for nature? On the paradox of environmental awareness and travel for nature experiences. *Tourism (Zagreb), 62*(1), 5–18.

World Tourism Organization and European Travel Commission. (2018). *Exploring health tourism: Executive summary*. UNWTO. Available online: doi:10.18111/978928442030.8

Young, J., McGrath, R., & Adams, C. (2018). Fresh air, sunshine and happiness: Millennials building health (salutogenesis) in leisure and nature. *Annals of Leisure Research, 21*(3), 324–346. doi:10.1080/11745398.2018.1458634

Section 4
Smart-Based Experiences

Chapter 13
Developing Smart Experiences

Abbie-Gayle Johnson
The Hong Kong Polytechnic University, Hong Kong

ABSTRACT

Studies have drawn on single theoretical perspectives to examine smart experiences; however, this chapter proposes a multi-theoretical perspective for understanding the development of smart experiences. This is an alternate perspective to exploring the planning and management processes that precede the formation of smart initiatives. Different theoretical perspectives, focused on stakeholder involvement, are drawn upon to understand the engagement in developing smart experiences. This development has created various smart experiences, which was possible due to core collaboration components and varying factors. The chapter calls for empirical investigations into smart tourism through the lens of tourism collaboration to deepen understanding of this development. Practitioners can also benefit from using this perspective, as it provides insights useful for developing smart experiences at the destination level, which is currently lacking in public discourse.

INTRODUCTION

Tourism is significantly influenced by technology. As early as the 1940s, industry practitioners were introduced to reservation and global distribution systems (Buhalis, 2019). Since the 2000s, there have been innovations such as social media, sharing economy platforms, virtual reality and smart destinations (Briciu et al., 2020; Jovicic, 2019; Shen et al., 2020; Xu et al., 2017). These innovations provide smart experiences, which are technology-enhanced tourist experiences resulting from the efforts of tourists, tourism businesses and organisations that indirectly contribute to destination development (Gretzel et al., 2015). Destination practitioners continue to share an interest in developing and providing these smart experiences to visitors. Although there is no available statistical data for tracking the number of smart destinations, smart city indices have confirmed that there are over 100 places globally with smart initiatives (IESE, 2019; IMD, 2020).

While this may seem significant, some destinations have yet to develop interconnected systems of diverse stakeholders, despite their interests in smart development. For instance, in 2017, the Jamaican government announced its desire to develop smart cities and destinations. Four years later, the ambas-

DOI: 10.4018/978-1-7998-8775-1.ch013

sador of Japan made a call for the government of Jamaica to proceed with developments while offering Japan's expertise (Jamaica Gleaner, 2021). Nevertheless, there is still a lack of stakeholder collaboration, and plans are yet to be implemented in the country. Furthermore, despite the advancements in smart tourism research and ongoing calls for smart tourism research, there remains a lack of empirical data on the development of these initiatives.

The objective of this chapter is to explore the creation of smart experiences through a multi-theoretical perspective of planning and management processes that precede the formation of smart initiatives. By adopting a holistic view centred on stakeholder involvement, this perspective acknowledges that businesses engage as a result of diverse factors associated with the processes and resources of collaborative tourism development. The chapter first outlines the literature on smart tourism to understand the general context and illustrate the need for further research. This is followed by an examination of the literature on stakeholder involvement. Next, the chapter reveals the method that was applied, namely a case study design with data from Ljubljana, Slovenia, a 2019 and 2020 European Capital of Smart Tourism. The chapter continues with a discussion of the findings and the conclusion.

This study represents one of the first to empirically investigate supplier engagement in the development of smart destination experiences. Findings regarding the success factors that enable this process may be beneficial to industry practitioners involved in smart initiative development and those currently considering implementation. This chapter also applies a tourism collaboration lens to smart tourism, which further develops Ivars-Baidal et al.'s (2019) management approach to smart initiatives.

BACKGROUND

There remains a lack of clear understanding regarding the meaning of smart tourism despite its advancements and ongoing calls for research (Gretzel et al., 2015; Mehraliyev et al., 2020). The word 'smart' plays an integral role in shaping how smart tourism is defined. In order to define smart tourism, there needs to be an examination of the word 'smart', which is the common word found in 'smart tourism' and 'smart experiences'. It denotes a device or phenomenon acting independently (Oxford Dictionaries, 2018). When applied to the tourism context, various definitions have been proposed for 'smart', which include an ever-present information system for tourists driven by technology (Li et al., 2017). According to Gretzel et al. (2015), smart tourism is

'tourism supported by integrated efforts at a destination to collect and aggregate/harness data derived from physical infrastructure, social connections, government/organisational sources and human bodies/ minds in combination with the use of advanced technologies to transform that data into on-site experiences and business value-propositions with a clear focus on efficiency, sustainability and experience enrichment (p. 181)'.

The technological perspective of smart tourism has since shifted to a socio-technical one. Scholars such as Ivars-Baidal et al. (2019) define smart tourism as a destination management approach. According to Gretzel et al. (2015), there are three components of smart tourism: smart destinations, smart experiences and smart business ecosystems. Smart experiences are technology-enhanced, personalised tourism experiences (Buhalis & Amaranggana, 2015; Neuhofer et al., 2015). Based on Gajdosik's (2020) study on smart tourists in Slovakia, global distribution systems (GDSs), online travel agencies (OTAs),

Developing Smart Experiences

destination websites, as well as sharing economy platforms were identified as smart experiences prior to destination visit. During the destination experience, tourists can utilise destination websites, mobile applications, digitised maps, smart cards and social media pages.

The development of smart experiences is dependent on businesses, which are conceptualised as another component of 'smart' – the smart business ecosystem, which involves tourism suppliers and other suppliers who directly exchange resources for the generation of resources and experiences (Gretzel et al., 2015). Del Chiappa and Baggio (2015) utilise the lists offered by destination management organisations (DMOs) to identify stakeholders within smart tourism. These include traditional tourism entities, such as accommodations, restaurants and travel agencies. Koo et al. (2017) identify traditional entities but also include online tourism businesses. While this improves previous studies, this study is limited to online entities and relies solely on the DMOs' perspectives.

The development of smart experiences by businesses in a destination is less researched and understood. Based on Mehyraliyev et al.'s (2020) review of knowledge development in smart tourism, only one study focused on suppliers' views and understandings, while two were based on the adoption of smart tourism. However, these studies shed light based on a single theoretical perspective. For instance, Wang and Cheung (2004), Wang et al. (2016) and Lin (2017) apply technology-related models, such as the technology, organisation and environment (TOE) framework, to examine the factors that influence organisation involvement. Less is known about the influences that affect suppliers' involvement in the formation of these experiences by integrated suppliers. Furthermore, a technological lens limits the ability to examine smart tourism in academic research, as emerging smart tourism initiatives are not all technologically driven in business practice. For instance, in 2018, the European Union (EU) published a list of finalists vying for the title of European Capital of Smart Tourism. Among the winners was Linz, Austria, which showcases art exhibits throughout the city, thus making displays visible beyond art galleries and museums (EU, 2018). The central underpinning of an innovation resulting from a digital ecosystem is collaboration. Thus, in order to build a theoretical understanding of smart tourism within destinations, research should shift its focus to a broader theoretical understanding beyond technology.

Tourism collaboration is a well-established area of research in tourism. However, the traditional context of tourism collaboration differs from that seen in smart tourism, as the latter results from the interconnectivity and interoperability of stakeholders and technologies across physical and virtual environments (Buhalis, 2019). Thus, collaboration moves the smart tourism conversation from technology to the interconnectedness of various stakeholders in a network or system.

TOURISM COLLABORATION

Collaboration is a decision-making process that engages stakeholders of a destination in order to address a problem (Getz & Jamal, 1994; Wood & Gray, 1991). In formulating their collaboration theory, Wood and Gray (1991) outline six elements of collaboration, which are necessary for understanding the collaborative aspect of creating smart experiences. They have provided the foundation for understanding collaboration in tourism settings.

The first element is incorporating stakeholders of a problem domain. This refers to the multiple and diverse organisations and human connections that Gretzel et al. (2015) note in the definition of smart tourism. These can be dynamic, such as hotels, restaurants or sharing economy platforms, or stable, such as Facebook and Expedia (Koo et al., 2017). The second element of collaboration is autonomy. Although stakeholders act together, they all have independent interests that guide their behaviours and decisions in the group (Wood & Gray, 1991). The third element is shared rules, norms and structures. In Barile et al.'s (2017) study, based on the role of mobile applications in the smart tourism ecosystem, it was revealed that there were two types of institutions: static, which is prompted by technology; dynamic, which is initiated by tourism stakeholders, such as signs and dynamic institutions resulting from monitoring the community, including traffic predictions. The fourth aspect of collaboration is the interactive process (Wood & Gray, 1991), in which smart technologies merge the virtual and physical world to allow interaction to occur. The fifth aspect is action or decision. Interactivity facilitates action by stakeholders. The sixth element of collaboration is domain orientation, which signifies that the collaboration is focused on solving a particular issue that is affecting a common group. Collaboration theory signifies that success depends on stakeholders' involvement across domains (Wood & Gray, 1991).

Collaboration can be established based on Selin and Chavez's (1995) tourism partnership model. The model is built on three phases: problem-setting, which includes establishing a facilitator and a shared vision, as well as discussing a problem collectively; direction-setting; and structuring, which involves designating roles and tasks and executing solutions. Augustyn and Knowles (2000) propose a similar model to Selin and Chavez (1995) but identify critical success factors for public-private partnerships. These factors include having a leader, clear objectives, structure and efficient actors (Augustyn & Knowles, 2000). In addition, each member of this established partnership must act together within the ecosystem to generate a solution for an identified problem (Gray, 1989). Also, members should possess the necessary skills, knowledge and resources to execute the assigned tasks (Jamal & Getz, 1995).

Collaboration among public, private and local residents leads to the development of tourist experiences (Jovicic, 2019). These stakeholders, specifically tourism suppliers, can be influenced to participate by a variety of reasons. A review of the tourism collaboration literature results in the following common factors: governance, legitimacy, benefits, resources (Jamal & Getz, 1995; Sigala, 2013; Waddock, 1989; Zemla, 2014) and relational ties (Beritelli, 2011; Jamal & Getz, 1995). While the factors are specific to the context of tourism collaboration, this chapter reveals insights for understanding those that emerge within the context of smart experiences. In order to do this, Fyall et al. (2012) propose the following theories for examining collaborations: transaction cost economics, relational exchange, resource dependency and institutional theory. Transaction cost economics theory acknowledges that organisations vertically integrate to ensure cost minimisation in production (Beritelli, 2011; Williamson, 1985; Zach & Racherla, 2011). Smart initiatives offer businesses the opportunity to reduce transaction costs for operations by sharing goods (Tedjasaputra & Sari, 2016).

Resource dependency theory emphasises that collaborations emerge due to suppliers' need to acquire resources (Fyall et al., 2012; Salancik & Pfeffer, 1977; Wang & Xiang, 2007). This is also applicable to smart tourism, since stakeholders continuously engage in a process of resource exchange (Gretzel et al., 2015). Meanwhile, relational or social exchange theory emphasises relationships (Ahmed et al., 1999; Macneil, 1980; Thibaut & Kelly, 1959). While previous tourism collaboration studies have applied these theories separately, very few studies have drawn on the needed multiple theoretical frameworks to examine the factors of engagement in destination collaboration contexts (Beritelli, 2011; Fyall et al., 2012; Wang & Fesenmaier, 2007; Wondirad et al., 2020). Against this background, the research was guided by the collaboration theories: transaction cost economics, resource dependency and social exchange.

METHOD

Data was compiled based on a case study methodology in order to understand the development of smart experiences within destinations from stakeholders' perspectives. This research design is known for generating insights in under-researched phenomena (Yin, 2014). Case studies are common in examining tourism collaborations; therefore, they are useful for this study (Lin & Simmons, 2017). This section will continue with a discussion of the site of the study, the sample and the data collection methods used.

Site of Study

The research design employs a case study approach to examine smart development in Ljubljana, Slovenia, a 2019 and 2020 European Capital of Smart Tourism. The destination has over 45 smart initiatives. In order to make the analysis more manageable, the following was taken into consideration when choosing the smart initiatives. Gretzel et al. (2015) suggest that smart experiences bridge the gap between digital and physical environments based on advanced technologies. The result is 10 initiatives being reviewed in order to ascertain their lists of suppliers and an understanding of smart development and engagement. Suppliers include the Green Supply Chains web platform, Taste Ljubljana, the Ljubljana by wheelchair mobile application, multisensory museum guided tours, mobile audio guides, mobile parking, a digital city guide, electric car-sharing, the tourist card Urbana and a bike-sharing scheme.

The following provides a brief explanation of each initiative. The Green Supply Chains web platform connects local food growers to potential buyers via an online platform. The Green Supply Chains web platform is complemented by the Taste Ljubljana initiative, which was designed to spread awareness of authentic local food in hotels and restaurants by offering dishes to tourists. It has been further promoted on DMOs' websites. Ljubljana by wheelchair is a mobile application that provides details of wheelchair-accessible locations. Multisensory museum guided tours enable interactive tourist experiences through technologies that connect with the environment to enable personalised engagement for museum visitors. Mobile audio guides are digital guides located in museums. The mobile parking application is designed to show the availability of parking spaces within the city through the integration of sensors. The digital city guide is a mobile application that promotes sightseeing routes. Electric car-sharing enables access to electric cars when not in use. Availability is detected through technologies that sense the environment, such as cameras and sensors. The tourist card, Urbana, is a city card that gives access to attractions, as well as shows the availability of parking spaces and bicycle-sharing. Last, the bike-sharing scheme is an initiative that enables tourists to access bicycle-sharing, which is accessed within destination at bicycle storage containers that can be located via a mobile application. This application also illustrates the available bicycles and charging stations for electric bikes.

Sample

The smart initiatives were reviewed individually to ascertain a list of their stakeholders in the absence of a smart supplier database. Sixty-one businesses were contacted, resulting in a range of responses: no response (16), decline with a reason (14) and accept (31). The study's 31 interview participants were from nine hotels, eight attractions, four restaurants, three destination marketing and tourism consulting organisations, three transportation service providers, two educational institutions, one technology company and the municipal government.

During the period of February to September 2019, fieldwork provided the opportunity to capture online data and documents and conduct semi-structured interviews to provide insights into suppliers' views and behaviours; interviews and documents are mainly used within tourism collaboration studies (Reed, 1997; Xue & Kerstetter, 2018). Interviews were conducted at the various businesses and took twenty minutes to approximately one hour and six minutes. Documents include tourism reports, planning documents, presentations, brochures and promotional material. Online data was based on details garnered from the online platforms of the smart initiatives. These were stored in a protected bag that could only be accessed by the researcher.

The data was collected and uploaded to NVivo, a data analysis software. The interviews were also transcribed and uploaded on NVivo. Data was thematically analysed, which is a common procedure in tourism collaboration studies. According to Braun and Clarke (2006), thematic analysis is a method for locating patterns in data. Steps are as follows: familiarisation with data, generation of initial codes, search for themes, reviewing of themes, definition of themes, naming of themes and formulation of report. Thematic analysis allowed the researcher to unravel the main stakeholders and factors that were associated with supplier engagement. The names of documents, websites and participants were assigned pseudonyms in order to aid the anonymity of organisations and individuals, as well as the researcher's ease of identification during data analysis.

FINDINGS

A case study methodology provided understandings from suppliers in Ljubljana, thereby filling the lack in depth and in practical views of the development of smart initiatives (Zuzul, 2019). The findings that emerged from the thematic analysis show that the development of smart experiences requires a variety of resources and is influenced by different factors associated with the multi-theoretical framework. Influences that emerged in this study were the DMOs and suppliers from social interactions as well as previous formal arrangements, familiarity through business networks and social groups and ongoing daily and monthly interactions. Prior to examining these factors, a brief overview is given regarding the individuals involved in developing Ljubljana's smart experiences.

Getting to Know the Suppliers Creating Smart Experiences

Smart tourism suppliers have been discussed within different typologies that aim to identify organisations within the local tourism industry (Del Chiappa & Baggio 2015; Gajdosik, 2018; Gretzel et al., 2015; Koo et al. 2017). The case of Ljubljana revealed that traditional tourism businesses were involved in smart tourism as expected; however, findings built upon previous studies highlighted that other local entities were involved in the process of development. Participants in smart tourism initiatives emerged from two groups: the city's group for urban development, which focused on sustainable initiatives, and tourism businesses, such as hotels and attractions. While diverse stakeholders can create challenges in collaboration (Czernek, 2013), this was not the case in Ljubljana due to the separation between the two groups.

Ljubljana's smart tourism ecosystem of suppliers is not new, as observed by Gretzel et al. (2015). Rather, the city has embraced existing businesses to construct its smart ecosystem. This is distinct from other destinations, such as Benidorm, Spain, where collaborations are mainly with private, start-up companies and represent new businesses (Femenia-Serra & Ivars-Baidal, 2018). Departing from previous empirical studies on smart tourism suppliers, the findings indicate that there were other participants involved in smart development that were further afield. This is not usually the case with destination collaborations, as they mainly consist of local community stakeholders (Beritelli et al., 2013). The development of smart initiatives was influenced by regional countries and entities. In this instance, the EU can be considered an example of what Gretzel et al. (2015) call 'other suppliers', as it influenced the city's smart ecosystem but was not directly involved in its operation (p. 561). Representatives from the local municipality in Vienna were also stakeholders of and external influences on the development of Ljubljana's smart experiences. Both destinations share a historical relationship and regional proximity. Having identified the main participants in the development of the city's smart initiatives, the next section focuses on the factors that influence local business involvement.

Supplier Engagement for Developing Smart Experiences

A variety of factors are acknowledged as influences of supplier engagement and will be discussed below to illustrate the benefit of drawing on a multi-theoretical approach. The main themes, DMOs and collaboration between suppliers through social interaction, are associated with three dominant theories: resource dependency, relational exchange and transaction cost economics.

Relationship and Resources Through the DMO

Like tourism collaborations (Fyall et al., 2012; Sigala, 2013), the DMO was recognised as a key influencer by suppliers in smart tourism. The organisation develops relationships with tourism businesses through previous industry collaborations and maintains tourism networks to further promote destinations, which is associated with relational exchange theory. The theory assumes that businesses participate with others because of past relationships (Fyall et al., 2012; Macneil, 1980).

Apart from tourism collaboration studies, the DMO's power to influence stakeholders is based on its resources due to a unique occurrence in Ljubljana. Some local tourism operators could not fund or attend regional and global travel tradeshows to promote their organisations and instead chose to continue their engagement with the DMO. Their confidence in the DMO to ensure successful initiatives is unlike that of businesses in other European destinations, such as Greece and Spain, which view the DMO as being inefficient in collaborations (Martins et al., 2020; Sigala, 2013). This shows the importance of the DMO to tourism suppliers in Ljubljana despite its lack of recognition by some smart tourism studies, such as Zhu et al. (2014).

The details of these smart initiatives were promoted by the DMO in the form of marketing collateral at these events, which gave local suppliers added exposure. Suppliers were denied the networking opportunities these events provided, which have been identified as one of the main factors that influence suppliers' participation in destination collaboration events (Menon et al., 2017). However, Ljubljana's suppliers were more interested in driving awareness of their businesses. Based on this, the DMO provided them with exposure and expertise resources; hence, this can be attributed to resource dependency theory (Salancik & Pfeffer, 1977). It emphasises that suppliers collaborate based on their need for resources, whether in a destination collaboration (Wang & Xiang, 2007) or in smart tourism (Gretzel et al., 2015). Nonetheless, it is important to note here that this scenario differs from the type of resources that smart tourism is known for, namely data sharing (Baggio et al., 2020). In Ljubljana, businesses are provided with marketing opportunities through exposure and knowledge of the industry.

The DMO's move to gain exposure for businesses facilitated the inclusion of stakeholders, which is a core principle for achieving justice in smart destinations (Choi et al., 2021). In addition, the DMO was aware of tourism suppliers' needs and had a desire to make it easier for these organisations to attain success:

'We [DMO] want to develop our big partners with projects like this [smart initiatives] and, yeah. We think that everybody [tourism businesses] deserves to see things as easy as possible'.

This illustrates their commitment to tourism practitioners, as seen in previous tourism collaborations (Pansiri, 2013; Waddock, 1989).

Transactions with Suppliers

Ljubljana's physical and social structure provides suppliers with the ease of frequently interacting with other tourism suppliers who continue to engage based on established social exchanges (Ahmed et al., 1999; Macneil, 1980). At the centre of these engagements is the continuous acknowledgement of the DMO. Nonetheless, other stakeholders were deemed necessary for technical support in the development of smart initiatives. Based on transaction cost economics theory, the frequency of interactions for transactions represents a means by which stakeholders can form collaborations over long periods of time (Ahmed et al., 1999; Williamson, 1985). These organisations were chosen based on previous formal agreements, social groups and daily interactions, which are discussed below. These three aspects account for the main ways in which stakeholders perceive the 'frequency' of interactions; hence, the number of exchanges were not fixed.

Previous Formal Arrangements

In Ljubljana, some tourism suppliers confirmed that they engaged in collaborations with the same stakeholders that were involved in formal agreements, whether as a past employee or a supplier, and this has been evident in tourism collaboration:

'I know the director very well, and we work together good because we used to be colleagues and so it's a bit easier' (Participant 7).

As a past employee at one key entity in smart development, Participant 7 had no reservations about engaging in smart initiatives due to having prior positive working experiences with this stakeholder. Stakeholder engagement based on previous business interactions resonated with the findings of other cases of tourism collaboration (Beritelli, 2011; Selin & Myers, 1998). The same principle applied to suppliers in Ljubljana who were not directly associated with the tourism industry. For instance, Participant 17 spoke about the company's arrangements with stakeholders that provided technical expertise for smart initiatives. According to the participant, they anticipated further involvement over a long period of time with the same supplier on other smart initiatives:

'If you ask me, what will be after these 10 years, we [tourism business] will have another contract with the same company [not a traditional tourism business]' (Participant 17).

Long-term engagement was tied to contractual agreements. These arrangements were made after public entities issued requests for proposals via national tender, and interested suppliers responded. For instance, an invitation to tender was sent out by the government to solicit technical expertise for a smart initiative. A contract was signed in the case of the bicycle-sharing scheme between one of the current suppliers and the municipality 'for 15 years' (Participant 20). Arguably, this is beneficial to those within the network. Continuous collaboration with the same stakeholder results in equity of value based on a relational exchange perspective (Fyall et al., 2012; Macneil, 1980). However, these exchanges do not result in equal consideration for those outside the network, since the same supplier may be chosen due to favouritism. This situation indicates the exercise of power, as suppliers are chosen based on the preference of those in authority:

'I mean, of course there were some smaller problems in regard to that [favouritism], but still again, we always like, uhh, make an agreement and mostly all of the major players are part this partnership, which I told you before'.

There was little regard for the issue of favouritism despite its negative effects, such as the exclusion of stakeholders. Arguably, while a legally binding agreement can speak to the requirements for the process, clear regulations for smart development were still missing in Ljubljana. A process of accountability may aid improvement through fair and transparent engagement, leading to decreased nepotism; this is a possible area for future research.

Familiarity Through Business Networks and Social Groups

Stakeholders will choose to do business with those with whom they have personal relationships rather than based on the nature of transactions (Fyall et al., 2012), which was the case in Ljubljana. As a small destination, stakeholders were familiar with each other through tourism networks and chose to engage with the same businesses, which is the underlying assumption of relational exchange theory (Fyall et al., 2012; Macneil, 1980):

'In Ljubljana, we know everybody. I think it's easier for us. You always know somebody from that organisation' (Participant 5).

This case of familiarity can also be examined through the lens of power. For instance, familiarity among stakeholders allowed for acts of nepotism, which requires the use of power to advance interactions with those favoured by the one in the authority position. Participant 17 recalled that the destination was considered for smart initiatives due to one of its nationals being employed in the EU:

'The last initiative which I presented, maybe one month ago, was from the EU Commissioner; she's from Slovenia and she's responsible for the infrastructure. She's responsible, I think, for the traffic and the infrastructure in the European community, and from her cabinet they send me initiatives'.

Participants also preferred engagement in collaborative initiatives with those who were not only from the same region but also from similar social and political groups:

'In Slovenia, first of all, you only collaborate with people you know. Second of all, you only collaborate with people of your social class. Third of all, you only collaborate with people who vote the same political option, so these are all elements that kind of play a role in collaboration and, I mean, in prohibiting proper collaboration' (Participant 13).

Again, there was no regard for the transaction but, instead, the focus continued to be on relationships in determining suppliers' engagement decisions, which is the underlying assumption of relational exchange theory (Fyall et al., 2012). A similar sentiment was shared by Participant 23, who noted that their business decisions were also influenced by and conducted in social settings:

'If there is an important football match going on, you are going to have all the important CEOs at the Lounge or wherever, and if you are there, you see the match, you have a beer, discuss with them, and this is how you easily do business. You combine fun and pleasure with business'.

The arrangements between suppliers took the form of informal agreements rather than signed contracts. This aligns with relational exchange theory, as engagements in collaborations are social (Fyall et al., 2012; Macneil, 1980). The participant declared that frequent interactions with the same individual through informal arrangements were a necessity for future collaborations. Engaging in smart initiatives at the destination level did not require formal arrangements from his organisation and were therefore favourable. Informal relations are not new to tourism collaborations (Beritelli, 2011; Wondirad et al., 2020) but enhance De Wit's (2017) work, illustrating a link between the frequency and mode of interactions.

At times, individuals changed jobs; however, Participant 1 stated that in these situations, it was the frequency of interactions with the organisation that determined the business' decision to engage in collaboration:

'Uhmm, there were some changes also in the last 22, 3 years. A lot of people have changed, so there are new people. So this could be also a bigger challenge for us but, in the end, this hotel and other companies stayed in the partnership'.

Engagement with those from familiar social groups may have led to the exclusion of some stakeholders, but this requires further investigation. Nevertheless, stakeholders sought to engage with other business representatives that were involved in similar social groups. Members of these groups have similar norms, values and personal relationships, which is the basis of relational exchange theory (Macneil, 1980).

Ongoing and Regular Interactions

Ljubljana suppliers regularly interacted with neighbouring businesses, which led to the sharing of resources, from staff to parking facilities and rooms needed to accommodate hotel group blocks and instances of overbooking. These situations were ongoing occurrences but were mainly linked to frequently held conferences in the city. The Ljubljana Exhibition and Convention Centre, renovated between 2001 and 2008 with a new entrance hall in 2012, has 20 rooms that can host from 15 to 6,000 participants. Since 2020, conference facilities have attracted *'about 500,000 visitors per year and is annually hosting over 200 national and international events'* (Website 1). This has resulted in *'events between 500 and 1,500 people'* (Participant 1). The highest room capacity for one hotel is 214 rooms; therefore, a block of rooms provided by multiple hotels is usually needed to successfully host large event groups in the city, which offers a total of 2,975 hotel rooms that are within walking distance from the city centre or five kilometres from it. Hotel partners from these conference collaborations are contacted in situations of overbookings, when businesses rely on each other for resources such as staff and accommodations, signifying resource dependency (Pfeffer & Salancik, 1978).

However, Participant 9 recalled that this is not always possible during peak seasons. This is not the only case in which suppliers were unable to collaborate with those whom they had regular contact with. It was also evident in smart tourism, as some of the suppliers mentioned that they were not aware of who the other participants were. This was often followed with a question by the researcher regarding meeting attendance. Many of the suppliers responded in the negative or dissociated from the process. For instance, Participant 2, who was active in Taste Ljubljana, stated,

'I wouldn't know. Maybe our F&B [Food and Beverage] manager has to go but, uhmm, no. Not. That was the project, and the plan was done at that time'.

CONCLUSION

This chapter provides an understanding of creating smart experiences by adopting a multi-theoretical perspective based on tourism collaboration. These smart initiatives are possible due to the presence of core collaboration components and the influences of supplier involvement. Traditional tourism businesses are involved in the development of smart experiences. However, findings built upon previous studies highlight that other local entities are involved in the process of development, such as those from the city's group for development. There are also entities further afield, such as regional organisations. Factors include the relationship and the resources from DMO as well as transactions with suppliers, namely previous formal arrangements, familiarity through business networks and social groups and ongoing daily and monthly interactions. These factors align with theories associated with tourism collaboration, such as resource dependency, transaction cost and relational exchange theories. Industry practitioners can gain further knowledge of smart tourism as they seek to develop destinations to create smart experiences. This offers knowledge to destination and government officials who are faced with the challenge of furthering involvement in current smart destinations. The chapter also shares relevant findings to practitioners who wish to generate interest and participation in prospective smart destinations.

Findings from this chapter build upon the work of previous tourism scholars, as smart tourism is conceptualised as a management approach (Ivars-Baidal et al., 2019). Findings extend current understandings on the formation of smart experiences beyond the main acknowledgement of technology-related influences. Following these findings, the chapter calls for empirical investigations of smart tourism to be conducted through the lens of collaboration. Future studies can draw on other newly emerging theoretical lenses from collaboration studies that are better fit to examine smart initiatives. Other similar destination contexts can also be considered by scholars for exploring the development of smart experiences. Nonetheless, this chapter provides useful and relevant empirical insights that can contribute to the development and implementation of smart experiences.

REFERENCES

Ahmed, F., Patterson, P., & Styles, C. (1999). The determinants of successful relationships in international business. *Australasian Marketing Journal, 7*(1), 5–21. doi:10.1016/S1441-3582(99)70197-7

Augustyn, M. M., & Knowles, T. (2000). Performance of tourism partnerships: A focus on York. *Tourism Management, 21*(4), 341–351. doi:10.1016/S0261-5177(99)00068-0

Baggio, R., Micera, R., & Del Chiappa, G. (2020). Smart tourism destinations: A critical reflection. *Journal of Hospitality and Tourism Technology, 11*(3). Advance online publication. doi:10.1108/JHTT-01-2019-0011

Barile, S., Ciasullo, M. V., Troisi, O., & Samo, D. (●●●). The role of technology and institutions in tourism service ecosystems: Findings from a case study. *The TQM Journal, 29*(6), 811–833. doi:10.1108/TQM-06-2017-0068

Beritelli, P. (2011). Cooperation among prominent actors in a tourist destination. *Annals of Tourism Research, 38*(2), 607–629. doi:10.1016/j.annals.2010.11.015

Beritelli, P., Strobl, A., & Peters, M. (2013). Interlocking directorships against community closure: A trade-off for development in tourist destinations. *Tourism Review, 68*(1), 21–34. doi:10.1108/16605371311310057

Braun, V., & Clarke, V. (2006). Using thematic analysis in psychology. *Qualitative Research in Psychology, 3*(2), 77–101. doi:10.1191/1478088706qp063oa

Briciu, A., Briciu, V., & Kavoura, A. (2020). Evaluating how 'smart' Brasov, Romania can be virtually via a mobile application for cultural tourism. *Sustainability, 12*(13), 1–17. https://do.org/10.3390/su12135324. doi:10.3390u12135324

Buhalis, D. (2019). Technology in tourism- from information communication technologies to eTourism and smart tourism towards ambient intelligence tourism: A perspective article. *Tourism Review, 75*(1), 1–4. doi:10.1108/TR-02-2020-405

Buhalis, D., & Amaranggana, A. (2015). *Smart tourism destinations enhancing tourism experience through personalisation of services*. Information and Communication Technologies in Tourism. doi:10.1007/978-3-319-14343-9_28

Choi, J., Lee, S., & Jamal, T. (2021). Smart Korea: Governance for smart justice during a global pandemic. *Journal of Sustainable Tourism, 29*(2-3), 541–550. doi:10.1080/09669582.2020.17777143

Czernek, K. (2013, January). Determinants of cooperation in a tourist region. *Annals of Tourism Research, 40*, 83–104. doi:10.1016/j.annals.2012.09.003

De Wit, B. (2017). *Strategy- an international perspective*. Cengage Learning.

Del Chiappa, G., & Baggio, R. (2015). Knowledge transfer in smart tourism destinations: Analysing the effects of a network structure. *Journal of Destination Marketing & Management, 4*(3), 145–150. doi:10.1016/j.jdmm.2015.02.001

EU. (2018). *European Capital of Smart Tourism*. Retrieved from https://smarttourismcapital.eu/

Femenia-Serra, F., & Ivars-Baidal, J. (2018). Do smart tourism destinations really work? The case of Benidorm. *Asia Pacific Journal of Tourism Research, 26*(4). doi:10.1080/10941665.2018.1561478

Fyall, A., Garrod, B., & Wang, Y. (2012). Destination collaboration: A critical review of theoretical approaches to a multi-dimensional phenomenon. *Journal of Destination Marketing & Management, 1*(1-2), 10–26. https://doi.org/10.1016/j.jdmm.2012.10.002

Gajdosik, T. (2018). Smart tourism: Concepts and insights from Central Europe. *Czech Journal of Tourism, 7*(1), 25–44. https://doi.org/10.1515/cjot-2018–0002

Gajdosik, T. (2020). Smart tourists as a profiling market segment: Implications for DMOs. *Tourism Economics, 26*(6), 1042–1062. https://doi.org/10.1177/1354816619844368

Getz, D., & Jamal, T. (1994). The environment-community symbiosis: A case for collaborative tourism planning. *Journal of Sustainable Tourism, 2*(3), 152–173. https://doi.org/10.1080/09669589409510692

Gretzel, U., Sigala, M., Xiang, Z., & Koo, C. (2015). Smart tourism: Foundations and developments. *Electronic Markets, 25*(3), 179–188. https://doi.org/10.1007/s12525-015-0196-8

IESE. (2019). Retrieved December 31, 2020, from https://blog.iese.edu/cities-challenges-and-management/2020/10/27/iese-cities-in-motion-index-2020/

IMD. (2020). Retrieved December 31, 2020, from https://www.imd.org/smart-city-observatory/smart-city-index/

Ivars-Baidal, J., Celdran-Bernabeu, M., Mazon, J., & Perles-Ivars, A. (2017). Smart destinations and the evolution of ICTs: A new scenario for destination management. *Current Issues in Tourism*, 1-20. doi:10.1080/13683500.2017.1388771

Ivars-Baidal, J., Mazon, J., & Perles-Ivars, A. (2019). Smart destinations and the evolution of ICTs: A new scenario for destination management? *Current Issues in Tourism, 22*(13), 1581–1600. https://doi.org/10.1080/13683500.2017.1388771

Jamaica Gleaner. (2021). *Jamaica Gleaner*. Retrieved August 31, 2021, from https://jamaica-gleaner.com

Jamal, T., & Getz, D. (1995). Collaboration theory and community tourism planning. *Annals of Tourism Research, 22*(1), 186–204. https://doi.org/10.1016/0160-7383(94)00067-3

Jovicic, D. (2019). From the traditional understanding of tourism destination to the smart tourism destination. *Current Issues in Tourism, 22*(3), 276–282. https://doi.org/10.1080/13683500.2017.1313203

Koo, C., Park, J., & Lee, J. N. (2017). Smart tourism- traveler, business, and organisational perspectives. *Information & Management*.

Li, Y., Hu, C., Huang, C., & Duan, L. (2017). The concept of smart tourism in the context of tourism information services. *Tourism Management, 58*, 293–300.

Lin, D., & Simmons, D. (2017). Structured inter-network collaboration: Public participation in tourism planning in Southern China. *Tourism Management, 63*, 315–328. https://doi.org/10.1016/j.tourman.2017.06.024

Lin, S. W. (2017). Identifying the critical success factors and an optimal solution for mobile technology adoption in travel agencies. *International Journal of Tourism Research*, *19*(2), 127–144. https://doi.org/10.1002/jtr.2092

Macneil, I. (1980). *The new social contract: An inquiry into modern contractual relation*. Yale University Press.

Martins, C., Carneiro, M., & Pacheco, O. (2020). Key factors for implementation and success of destination management systems. Empirical evidence from European countries. *Industrial Management & Data Systems*.

McCabe, S., Sharples, M., & Foster, C. (2012). Stakeholder engagement in the design of scenarios of technology-enhanced tourism services. *Tourism Management Perspectives*, *4*(October), 36–44. https://doi.org/10.1016/j.tmp.2012.04.007

Mehraliyev, F., Chan, I., Choi, Y., Koseoglu, M., & Law, R. (2020). A state-of-the-art review of smart tourism research. *Journal of Travel & Tourism Marketing*, *37*(1), 78–91. https://doi.org/10.1080/10548408.2020.1712309

Menon, S., Edward, M., & George, B. (2017). Inter-stakeholder collaboration in event management: A case study of Kerala Travel Mart. *International Journal of Leisure and Tourism Marketing*, *5*(4). https://doi.org/10.1504/IJLTM.2017.087493

Neuhofer, B., Buhalis, D., & Ladkin, A. (2015). Smart technologies for personalised experiences: A case study in the hospitality domain. *Electronic Markets*, *25*, 243–254. https://doi.org/10.1007/s12525-015-0182-1

Oxford Dictionaries. (2018). *Oxford Dictionaries*. Retrieved from http://www.oxforddictionaries.com

Pansiri, J. (2013). Collaboration and partnership in tourism: The experience of Botswana. *Tourism Planning & Development*, *10*(1), 64–84. doi:10.1080/21568316.2012.723039

Pfeffer, J., & Salancik, G. R. (1978). *The External Control of Organizations: A Resource Dependence Perspective*. Harper & Row.

Reed, M. (1997). Power relations and community-based tourism planning. *Annals of Tourism Research*, *24*(3), 566–591. doi:10.1016/S0160-7383(97)00023-6

Salancik, G. R., & Pfeffer, J. (1977). An examination of the need: Satisfaction models of job attitudes. *Administrative Science Quarterly*, *22*, 427–456. https://doi.org/10.2307/2392182

Selin, S., & Chavez, D. (1995). Developing an evolutionary tourism partnership model. *Annals of Tourism Research*, *22*(4), 844–856.

Selin, S., & Myers, N. (1998). Tourism marketing alliances: Member satisfaction and effectiveness attributes of a regional initiative. *Journal of Travel & Tourism Marketing*, *7*(3), 79–94. https://doi.org/10.1300/J073v07n03_05

Shen, S., Sotiriadis, M., & Zhou, Q. (2020). Could smart tourists be sustainable and responsible as well? The contribution of social networking sites to improving their sustainable and responsible behaviour. *Sustainability, 12*, 1–21. https://doi.org/10.3390/su12041470

Sigala, M. (2013). Examining the adoption of destination management systems: An inter-organisational information systems approach. *Management Decision, 51*(5), 1011–1036. https://doi.org/10.1108/MD-11-2012-0800

Tedjasaputra, A., & Sari, E. (2016). Sharing economy in smart city transportation services. *Proceedings of the SEACHI 2016 on Smart Cities for Better Living with HCI and UX.*

Thibaut, J. W., & Kelly, H. H. (1959). *The social psychology of groups*. Wiley.

Waddock, S. (1989). Understanding social partnerships: An evolutionary model of partnership organisations. *Administration & Society, 21*(1), 78–100. https://doi.org/10.1177/009539978902100105

Wang, S., & Cheung, W. (2004). E-business adoption by travel agencies: Prime candidates for mobile e-business. *International Journal of Electronic Commerce, 8*(3), 43–63. https://doi.org/10.1080/10864415.2004.11044298

Wang, Y., & Fesenmaier, D. (2007). Collaborative destination marketing: A case study of Elkhart county, Indiana. *Tourism Management, 28*, 863–875. https://doi.org/10.1016/j.tourman.2006.02.007

Wang, Y., & Xiang, Z. (2007, August). Toward a theoretical framework of collaborative destination marketing. *Journal of Travel Research, 46*, 75–85. https://doi.org/10.1177/0047287507302384

Wang, Y. S., Li, H., Li, C., & Zhang, D. (2016). Factors affecting hotels' adoption of mobile reservation systems: A technology-organization environment framework. *Tourism Management, 53*, 163–172. https://doi.org/10.1016/j.tourman.2015.09.021

Williamson, O. (1985). *The economic institutions of capitalism*. The Free Press.

Wondirad, A., Tolkach, D., & King, B. (2020). Stakeholder collaboration as a major factor for sustainable ecotourism development in developing countries. *Tourism Management, 78*, 104024. https://doi.org/10.1016/j.tourman.2019.104024

Wood, D., & Gray, B. (1991). Toward a comprehensive theory of collaboration. *The Journal of Applied Behavioral Science, 27*(139). https://doi.org/10.1177/0021886391272001

Xu, K., Zhang, J., & Tian, F. (2017). Community leadership in rural tourism development: A tale of two ancient Chinese villages. *Sustainability, 9*, 1–22. https://doi.org/10.3390/su9122344

Xue, L., & Kerstetter, D. (2017). Discourse and power relations in community tourism. *Journal of Travel Research, 57*(6), 757–768. doi:10.1177/0047287517714908

Yin, R. (2014). *Case study research design and methods*. Sage.

Zach, F., & Racherla, P. (2011). Assessing the value of collaborations in tourism networks: A case study of Elkhart County, Indiana. *Journal of Travel & Tourism Marketing, 28*(1), 97–110. https://doi.org/10.1080/10548408.2011.535446

Zemla, M. (2014). Inter-destination cooperation: Forms, facilitators and inhibitors –The case of Poland. *Journal of Destination Marketing & Management*, *3*(4), 241–252. https://doi.org/10.1016/j.jdmm.2014.07.001

Zhu, W., Zhang, L., & Li, N. (2014). Challenges, function changing of government and enterprises in Chinese smart tourism. *ENTER 2014 Conference on Information and Communication Technologies*.

Zuzul, T. (2019). Matter battles: Cognitive representations, boundary objects, and the failure of collaboration in two smart cities. *Academy of Management Journal*, *62*(3), 739–784. https://doi.org/10.5465/amj.2016.0625

KEY TERMS AND DEFINITIONS

Collaboration: A decision-making process that engages stakeholders from a destination in order to address a problem.

Smart: Intelligence for autonomous actions.

Smart Business Ecosystem: Tourism suppliers and other suppliers who directly exchange resources for the generation of resources and experiences.

Smart Experiences: Technology-enhanced tourist experiences.

Thematic Analysis: A method for locating patterns in data.

Chapter 14
Experience Toward Smart Tour Guide Apps in Travelling:
An Analysis of Users' Reviews on Audio Odigos and Trip My Way

Arvind Mahajan
Lovely Professional University, India

Sana Maidullah
Lovely Professional University, India

Mohammad Rokibul Hossain
Premier University, Bangladesh

ABSTRACT

The integration of navigation systems and smart tour guide apps has gained popularity among travellers with the rapid development of the internet, mobile technology, and the wide acceptance of smartphones. The purpose of the study is twofold: (1) to assess the growth of smart tour guide apps in India and (2) to examine the tourists' experiences in using smart tour guide apps. To achieve the purpose of the study, a content analysis method was employed to analyse the users' reviews on the "Audio Odigos" and the "Trip My Way," which are very popular tour guide apps in India. The results reveal that smart tour guide apps are more preferred than the human tour guide. An app-based tour guide facilitates exceptional experiences for accurate and useful information on historical monument tours, city tours, and destination tours. Thus, the findings can be used to improve the existing apps and develop more sophisticated apps in the future that can ensure sustainable smart tourism.

INTRODUCTION

Technology is transforming the tourism industry and introducing new facilities for visitors. With the assistance of smart technology and smart tour guide applications (apps), tourists can enjoy their vaca-

DOI: 10.4018/978-1-7998-8775-1.ch014

tion and have a better experience. The revolutionary positive impact of technology has been foresighted significantly in the travel and hospitality industries (Leung, 2020; Osei et al., 2020; Sigala & Gretzel, 2017). In the hospitality and tourism industry, tourists use new technologies and smartphone apps which mediate travel experiences (Dickinson et al., 2014). The invention and adoption of smart tour guides apps have been increasing gradually over the last few years. Tourist guide apps are handy for tourists who want to use a self-guided tour for a cultural heritage site during a walking tour (Kang et al., 2017). Mr. Iyer created the first smart travel guide app after being unable to locate a government-approved human guide during a visit to a cultural heritage site in 2014. He devised a solution to the issue, and the outcome was the "Pinakin App," a Smart Travel Guide app for the Indian states of Karnataka and Tamil Nadu (Sarumathi, 2018). However, this is a paid app; a one-year subscription is available in 49 and 99 Indian Rs only. This is a very affordable rate offered by the app provider in April 2021. The Ministry of Tourism, Government of India, announced the Audio Guide facility App "Audio Odigos" for 12 sites in India, including iconic destinations, in October 2019 (Press Information Bureau, 2019). This app will be available at 100 locations in India soon. The Audio Odigos app helps tourists learn more about India's cultural heritage places. It is accessible in seven different languages, both national and international. The app includes a summary, extensive history, and podcasts, all of which assist visitors to save time while on tour. According to Google Play, the app has excellent quality, with over 5000 users having downloaded it as of April 2021.

The adoption of smart tourism technology enriches the tourist experience at the destination (Gretzel et al., 2015). Informative, interactivity and personalisation are essential factors affecting tourist experience; intention to revisit the smart tourism destination depends on overall tourist experience and satisfaction (Jeong & Shin, 2020). The adoption of m-tourism in India is influenced by technology-specific, country-specific, and perceived effects (Vinodan & Meera, 2020). Concerning a statistical report of Internet users by Sundhya Keelery, India is the second-largest Internet user market after China, with 560 million Indian users (Sundhya, 2020). India is a developing country and the fastest-growing mobile internet market in the world. Tourists use new technology to find out route, tour planning, tickets or hotel booking, find out tour guide, city information, weather report information, online payment method and operate the various electrical devices in hotel by using a mobile phone.

Tourists use travel apps and websites to replace the traditional manual services, enhancing a sense of participation and saving labour costs (Pai et al., 2021). App-based mobile tour guide performance depends on the smartphone and performance of the app to attract travellers. App providers should focus on efforts required to enhance travel app performance, and travellers can use their app-based mobile tour guide more effectively and comprehensively to fulfil their information need by using the app (Lai, 2013). User experience has been performed by assessing the app's quality and usability, its graphic unit interface, and user experience (Tarantino et al., 2019). self-efficacy indirectly influences the use of travel apps (Lu et al., 2015). Trust in smart technology and enjoyment of technology enrich tourist experience. However, some issues need to be studied in the tourist context (Gretzel et al., 2015). Travel app user experience needs to explore (Choi et al., 2018). App users' experience is an important area for future research (Palos et al., 2020).

Decisions regarding acceptance or rejection of technology have remained an open question in the last few decades (Marangunić & Granić, 2015). Not much research was done on technology acceptance with travel app quality and features, but less research on tourist's point of view. To fulfil the research gap, research questions were prepared, what are the user's expectations from the smart guide app, and which natural exclamation words do users use to share their experience? This research examines the progress of new tourism technology in India and identifies the gap between technology providers and smart guide app users' experience. To achieve the objective, the authors of the book chapter downloaded a few free smart guide app from the google play store, which provides North Indian tourist destinations and similarities of sites. The same app is used by the authors of this book chapter for self-experience. Two apps were identified based on destination criteria, one introduced by the Government of India Ministry Tourism "Audio Odigos" and another one from the private sector app "Trip My way". User reviews were available on the Google play store for both apps. The content analysis method used, and coding has been done scientifically. The important contribution of this book chapter is for smart guide app developers to develop such an app that provides a memorable tour experience at a tourist site. Further researchers need to explore more in this topic in the upcoming modification and development of the apps.

The following is the structure of this book chapter. The first part contains a comprehensive analysis of the literature on the use of tourism apps, technology and tourism experience, technology adoption, and a high-level overview of a smart tourist guide app. The methodology, data analysis, findings, and discussion sections follow. The solution and suggestion and the future direction and conclusion are included in the last part. The goal of the study is to give an overview of the tourist experience related to smart tourist guide technology and usability in tourism, as well as their effect on visitors.

REVIEW OF LITERATURE

Use of Apps and Technology in The Tourism Industry

Customers are rapidly embracing mobile apps, and the number of apps used is constantly growing (Mahardika et al., 2019). Most visitors utilise their mobile phones and the latest accessible information technologies at their destination during tourist travels, which is critical in understanding tourists' experiences (Liberato et al., 2018). The term "digitalisation age" refers to a broad knowledge of technology's impact on society and the economy (Xiang, 2018). Smart technologies employed in the tourist sector completely mediate the connection between digital transformation and relationship performance (Nasiri et al., 2020). Furthermore, the use of technology differs from one age group to another. Those born in the digital age and those aged between 18 to 34 years are familiar with the latest technology, like augmented reality, which moderates the tourism technological experience of this age group (Zhuang et al., 2021).

According to Buhalis (2019), the way technology has developed in the last seventy-five years, from the first computer to Internet networking, has transformed the tourism industry. Looking ahead 75 years, from 2020 to 2095, new technologies such as robotics, cashless payments, augmented reality, and virtual reality will be implemented to varying degrees in different sectors and regions across the globe, resulting in a wave of changes in the tourist industry. Web 3.0 is the third generation of Internet service for websites and apps, facilitating computer-to-computer communication by presenting large amounts of data in a format that software agents can comprehend (Buhalis, 2019). However, the mobile phone is a necessary part of people's lives. Continued mobile app use is rising in daily life, such as health and shopping apps. A novel app for a mobile device was developed for tourists visiting Mexico City as part of a project experiment. The first feature of the app tells tourists whether they should travel by automobile or on foot, the second feature of the app allows them to choose which city or regions they want to see, and the third feature of the app calculates the shortest route for tourists (Zacarias et al., 2015). The "Find Natal app" is a smartphone tour guide. Introduced by Brazil during the 2014 FIFA World Cup as part of the smart city project to improve tourist experience during city tours by providing information depending on location, and such apps are valuable in understanding tourist behaviour, experience during the tour and after the trip (Cacho et al., 2016). The Internet of Things (IoT) refers to a system of interrelated, internet-connected objects that can collect and transfer data over a wireless network without human intervention. Travel in a remote area such device helps tourists to find out routes during a trip between two destinations. Apps like Geographical Routing for Mobile Tourist (GRMT) is helpful during a medical emergency, which guides tourists to the nearest medical centre route. Such technology motivates health concern tourists to travel to remote destinations, and they can enhance their trip experience by using the Internet of Things (Almobaideen et al., 2017). Location-based smart travel guides apps are required for tourists during the tour (Jinendra et al., 2012).

Figure 1. Three tour stages and use of technology on each tour stage
Source: adapted from Jeong & Shin, 2020

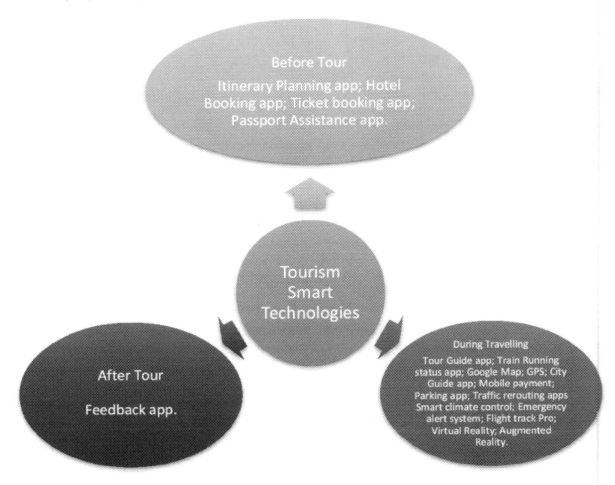

Considering the study done by Navio-Marco needs to revisit progress in information and technology development done by Buhalis & Law in 2008. The Navio-Marco suggested that future research can focus on new technology, that the public and companies will accept the change in technology for implementation in their business (Navío-Marco et al., 2018). Technology advancements like VR and AR, location-based service, virtual assistance robots, and drones offer services in the Hospitality and tourism industry. In the future, a service interruption can be avoided by attention to hyper personalise services, personalised automatic service, and extrasensory experience. There is a positive and negative effect on tourist attitude, satisfaction, participation, and visit intention, and there is a symbiotic relationship between tourists and technology (Buhalis et al., 2019). However, further study needs to be done on the use of AR and VR apps at the museum and cultural heritage sites to understand tourist experience and adoption of technology (Oleksy & Wnuk, 2016). A study by Jeong and Shin reported that five smart tourism destinations are metro cities in the United States of America. Tourist experience about technology, memorable experience of tourists, and smart technology are related to each other. The intention to revisit a destination is dependent on what kind of digital environment is required for tourists (Jeong & Shin, 2020). However, Figure 1 lists the technology used by tourists during various stages of the tour.

Tourist Experience to Use the App

Digital innovation in the tourism industry enhances the tourist experience (Pencarelli, 2020). The role of Tourism 4.0, which is related to big data processing, provides pleasant or unpleasant, well-being, meaningful experience to tourists by tourism technology (Stankov & Gretzel, 2020). Journey Companion' app is an all-in-one app that can fulfil the traveller's requirement to use one app for various destinations, providing information about landmarks, monuments, restaurants, current weather information, currency, holiday information, shopping facilities, picnic spots. Such an app can offer a great travel experience to tourists (V & Sabarish, 2021). Assess tourist experience of smart tourism technology with three values, function, emotion, and social use as the primary foundation of evaluation. Innovative technology is deeply associated with self-efficacy and overall experience in Seoul, South Korea; smart tourism technology is associated with tourist happiness (Lee et al., 2018).

System quality, information quality, and service quality positively impact user engagement with a smartphone travel app. The author suggested that future studies may replicate the theoretical framework model, which was tested in this study, including a multi-dimensional conceptualisation of smartphone app love (Ali et al., 2021). Choi et al. focus on the continued use of travel apps based on the previous experience with a travel app. A situational factor of experience about technology, effect on adoption of travel technology (Choi et al., 2018). Younger tourists utilise mobile travel apps, as compared to older tourists. User experience has social influence, and intention to use the app is not dependent on resource support for the tourism app. Users need to confirm the decision regarding downloading mobile tourism apps and using the app at the destination (Palos et al., 2020). Mobile tourism apps are beneficial to access travel information and share experience. Information quality, perceived ease of use, and perceived usefulness affect using Personalize Location-based Mobile Tourism Application (PLMTA) (Chen & Tsai, 2019). User-generated content platforms allow users to easily use experience and search information, which is available on that platform. User experience and reviews available on online platforms enhance intention to use TripAdvisor, Booking, Expedia, etc. (Assaker et al., 2019). Tourist mobile apps fulfil the tourist requirement, but priority to a given recommendation of a tourist mobile travel app depends on a positive or negative experience. Choosing a mobile app depends on its visual, navigation design, personal aspect, and outcome (Sánchez-Torres & Argila-Irurita, 2021). The performance of mobile electronic guide apps is related to app quality. Users can access apps based on the experience of technology (Tarantino et al.,

2019). Moreover, app technology saves time and money for consumers, which motivates tourists to use mobile apps (Xu et al., 2019). Few tourists are concerned about personal information disclosure, which is an important factor in intention to use the app (Tang et al., 2020).

Adoption of Technology and Apps by Tourists

The adoption of mobile tourism technology is a push factor for invention in the tourism industry in the upcoming future. Based on empirical evidence and scientific reasoning in the context of India, six latent constructs affected on symbolic adoption of m-tourism:

1. Performance expectation (PEX). Under this construct, Vinodan and Meera (2020) identified six more corresponding variables: usefulness, motivation, productivity, performance expectation, comparative advantage. Accomplishments are related to performance issues while adopting m-tourism.
2. Perceived effort time (PEF), ease of use, learning to use, clarity and understanding. Vinodan and Meera (2020) use these indicators for issues related to perceived effort.
3. Technology-specific (TSP) network externalities, trialability, complexity and installation. These four corresponding variables are related to theolog.
4. Country-specific (CSP) language, technical infrastructure, legal barriers, diversity, and exposure. The authors used this variable as a country-specific variable.
5. Facilitation (FCI) financial condition, knowledge level, compatibility, assistance availability, and accessibility. These six facilitating issues are positively related to the adoption of m- tourism.
6. Peer/media influence, trust, aand education level, based on scientific and logical thinking. These three indicators are used for personalising centric factors.

Out of six symbolic adoption factors of m-tourism in India, perceived effort (PEF), technology-specific (TSP), and country-specific (CSP) are affected by the adoption of m-tourism in India (Vinodan & Meera, 2020). Moreover, country-specific variables need to be studied for the acceptance of technology.

According to the theory of planned behaviour, developed by Ajzen in 1985, attitude, subjective norms, and perceived behavioural control are three important components of the theory to shape individual behaviour. Yarimoglu and Gunay (2020) have suggested using different theories to explain attitude and behaviour and adopt such theories for research in the hotel sector. The unified theory of acceptance and the use of technology is useful to study the acceptance and use of technology in the consumer context (Venkatesh et al., 2012).

A literature review, from 1986 to 2013, was done by Marangunic, on the Technology Acceptance Model (TAM), a crucial model for the rejection and acceptance of technology, in order to understand the potential of predictors of human behaviour. Few studies confirmed the model has broad strength applicability of various technologies. Moreover, Marangunic suggested, for further research, the moderating role of individual variables and incorporating additional variables to the technology acceptance model. Investigate actual usage and the relationship between actual use and objective outcome measure, target group of older adults. A growing need for technology, especially in information and communication technology, in the professional and private life of users will undoubtedly enhance the interest in the field of technology acceptance many years to come (Marangunić & Granić, 2015). Moreover, there is research using TAM model on health apps, shopping apps, travel apps and smart tourism technology. Acceptance and rejection of technology is an open question concerning individual users' acceptance.

It is necessary to investigate its contribution to research on individual technology acceptance and use (Tamilmani et al., 2021).

When travellers use a mobile app guide service, their evaluation and feelings towards the services will impact their acceptance level with user context (Chuang, 2020). A study done by Kou et al. on the adoption of mobile apps is useful to motivate travel but investigate the satisfaction of mobile app users (Kuo et al., 2019). The behaviour of adopting app-based hospitality and tourism technology offers a more detailed understanding of the roles of factors in travellers' acceptance model of app-based hospitality and tourism (Lai, 2013). Further research needs to examine mediating processes between personality traits and user behaviour and moderator these relationships (Barnett et al., 2015). Correlation includes tour guide interpretation, tourist satisfaction, and destination loyalty, which are stronger for tourists who perceive a high degree of playfulness and flow in their tourism experience. For future research, perceived trust and perceived value can be examined (Kuo et al., 2016).

An Overview of the Smart Tour Guide Apps

The introduction of the first random-access mobile guide to inform at the Louvre Museum in 1993 marked a significant shift in how museum visitors use mobile guides. The random-access mobile guide at Louvre Museum was the world's first digital wand player (Othman et al., 2013). features in the gaze guidance while adapting the audio content to what has been previously looked at content adoption to obtain a better user experience for a tourist. A study regarding American tourist perceptions unveiled that tourists are satisfied regarding information, but guide quality attitude, behaviour, time management is not up to the mark; therefore, tourists are dissatisfied (Rabotic, 2011). As per Smir, tourists require various information on the region, like police, embassy, regional transportation, tourist safety, tourist places, and tourist guide. Yet, tourists use a mobile device in the region and discover various services and devices. Kwok et al. (2019) did a comparative study of FC-Tour and G-Tour, two types of mobile guides effectiveness, but need to examine experience with a guide. Guided narratives are a novel interaction concept that helps tourists find specific personalised services, which mobile devices can assist (Smirnov et al., 2014.).

Similarly, Lai (2015) has done a literature review on research in technology acceptance between 2003 and 2012. The research was done on a mobile device. Mobile technologies, website, hotel website, online purchase, but only one study was done on mobile electronic tourist guide by Peres Correia and Motilal based on knowledge. The other researchers use the Technology Acceptance Model for studies in the hospitality and tourism industry. In most studies, satisfaction, behaviour, trust, negative and positive effects are investigated (Lai, 2015).

Table 1. Tour guide apps in India

Smart Travel Guide App	Availability of app in No. of Cities	Introduced by	Upcoming Location	Installed by	Reviews
Audio Odigos	New Delhi, Agra, Kutch, Jaipur, Bodhgaya	Ministry of Tourism Govt. of India	100	5,000+	120
Digi Tour	Hampi, Belur, Halebid, Badami, Aihole in Karnataka.,	Digital Technology Pvt. Ltd. And KSTDC	Information not available	1,000 +	35
Trip My Way	New Delhi, Jaipur, Jodhpur, Udaipur, Kota, Mumbai, Pune, Chennai, Itanagar, Srinagar, and More	Ithaka Tales Pvt. Ltd. The Indian National Trust for Art and Cultural Heritage (INTACH) Rajasthan & Delhi Chapters and the Development and Research Organisation for Nature, Arts and Heritage DRONAH foundation.	184	10,000+	230
Hop-On India	New Delhi, Mumbai, Varanasi, Kolkata, Jaipur, Aurangabad, Leh	Desiwalks Tours Private Limited	Information not available	10,000+	128
The Global Vipassana Pagoda	Mumbai with 25 Tour and 122 Paintings	The Global Vipassana Pagoda Research Institute.	Information not available	5,000 +	97
Pinakin App	South India Destination	Aseuro Technologies Private Limited	Information not available	50,000 +	483

(Source: Google Play store app information, April 2021)

Concerning table 1, all apps are tour guide apps and are useful to tourists during the season. When there is a shortage of Government-registered human guides at the cultural heritage site, the above apps are also valuable for group tours to maintain social distance during a pandemic like COVID-19 (Coronavirus Disease 2019). Smart guide apps, like Audio Odigos and others mentioned in table 1, will help tourists in such situations to avoid group gatherings during the guided group tour.

METHODOLOGY

This is exploratory research done to answer the research question of this study. The content analysis method was adopted to analyse the qualitative data of app users' reviews. Review users share their experience on the Google play store in the reviews section, which was easily available to read and copy as part of data collection. The choice for the method has been made based on its particular usability in the context of the emerging field of research, where no solid literature exists. The research method was adopted from Molnar and Moraru's (2017) study. This studies smart tour guide app "Audio Odigos", introduced by the Ministry of Tourism of India, and another app from the private sector, Trip My Way. Both apps were selected based on similar tourist attractions in north India, and tourists can use the app free of cost. For content analysis following steps were followed.

Selection of Apps

Criteria for selecting the two apps are presented in table 1: (i) both apps have maximum smarts cities in North India; (ii) the apps should be available free of cost for users; and (iii) apps' review should be available on online platforms, for example, Google Play Store or Apple App Store. Although the Audio Odigos app was accessible on the Apple App Store, there were no reviews. The Trip My Way app was not accessible for download in the Apple App Store. After that, the Google Play Store discovered both the app and user reviews. Self-experience with app quality and function is critical for a better understanding of users' experiences with both apps. Therefore, the apps were used by the author for two weeks in April 2021.

Data Collection

For the Audio Odigos app, all accessible 120 reviews in the Google Play store were gathered from October 2019 to April 2021. The Trip My Way app's release date is unclear, however between August 2018 and April 2021, all accessible 230 reviews were gathered from the Google Play store. After all app users' reviews were copied from the Google Play Store, a table containing reviews and total ratings for each user was created in Microsoft Word. Data cleaning was done on 120 reviews for Audio Odigos app and 230 for Trip My Way app. To get a better understanding, all reviews have been read five times. A few Hindi language words were translated into English, and spelling was checked. During the data cleaning process, few app users clicked on the like button, so no meaningful changes outcome from such reviews. After removing unwanted data, 100 reviews for Trip My Way app and 74 reviews for Audio Odigos app were considered for data analysis.

Coding Process

Codes were identified with reference to the Technology Acceptance Model (TAM), which is useful to measure the adoption of new technology, and the inductive research approach adopted based on app qualities. The literature review was referred to finalise the coding process. For example, for Trip My Way and Odigos, users used different sentences and words to share their experience about app quality, such as nice, love, great experience quite honestly, excellent, super, greatest, quite good, amazing and very good. Similarly, another code was also designed to analyse the data, which is mentioned in table 2. During the reading of apps users' reviews, based on the coding process, different colours were used for similar words such as yellow, pink, and blue. For example, yellow was used to code "App quality", and green for "App efficiency". Validation and identification of keywords were completed by reading each review five times and preparing nine code keywords for the Audio Odigos app (App Quality, App Efficiency, App Sound Quality, App Content, Image Quantity, Language, App Initiative, Navigation quality, and Negative or Positive Remark about the app). Similarly, eight codes were finalised for the Trip My Way app, for example, App quality App efficiency, App Sound quality, App Content Quantity, Content Quality, Image quantity, Language, and Negative remarks. The frequency of each code group was manually counted, and the count was verified using the search capabilities in Microsoft Office Word.

Table 2. Key elements and frequency of code

Sr. No	App	The key element of reviews and Description of Code	Frequency of code
1	Audio Odigos (Government of India App)	**App Quality** (good, great, superb, nice, really great, best, wow, very good, excellent, awesome, experience too good, fall in love, wonderful, like this app, pleasant)	33
		App Efficiency (useful, helpful, amazing, very much useful, user friendly, much needed)	17
		App Sound Quality (good, excellent, very good, superb, clear sound, helpful)	8
		App Content (add more cities, places, states, location, monuments, sites, content)	40
		Image Quantity (add more pic, images, and photos)	3
		Language (add more language, multilingual, language)	3
		App Initiative (very good, nice, a good app is symbolically launched)	4
		Navigation quality (smooth, nice)	2
		Negative Remark Glitches need to be fixed, Bugs. Can't change language and city as app fails	2
2	Trip My Way (Private Sector App)	**App quality** (nice, love, great experience quite honestly, excellent, super, greatest, quite good, amazing, very good, awesome, must-have app, best, perfect, informative like I was in a movie, beautiful, fantastic, wonderful app, definitely worth it)	58
		App efficiency (useful, helpful, help the most engaging, better than a local guide, fantastic, brilliant and quite interactive, love execution, effective tool, enthusiastic)	20
		App Sound quality (Excellent audio, voice is better than an official guide, must have great audio	9
		App Content Quantity (Explore a new city, add more places, cities, add more heritage sites, add more sites, location. Add more audio tour, add more tour)	11
		Content Quality (great content and awesome, informative narration, fantastic, excellent, often good, very good, engaging, informative, and enjoyable)	9
		Image quantity (great picture, great experience with the picture, the app has photo function)	3
		Language (add more languages)	3
		Negative remark (Not working now, keep crashing, camera option not found, very unstable, unable to reset password, improve the description, unable to download, not good, bad, don't use photo function, installation and listening issues, useless app, can't log in, register, refuse use via email.)	24

Data Analysis and Discussion

To analyse the customer reviews, a reading of reviews has been done, systematic keyword identified based on app function, quality of the app, positive and negative reviews of tourists. The coding process were adopted to identify keywords from the previous study of Lee et al. (2019). Furthermore, the frequency of reviews in code, the proportion of good *vs* negative reviews, repeated app suggestion keyword, the quality of voice, picture, language, music, and information quality, as well as other indications, were all analysed. As demonstrated in table 2, synthesis is a data annualisation method that enables you to combine different terms into one category of chosen indicators.

Audio Odigos App

Audio Odigos app was launched by the Ministry of Tourism Government of India in October 2019. More than 5,000 users have downloaded this app till April 2021 in the Google Play Store. Based on 74 users' reviews, codes and keywords were prepared systematically based on the frequency of each code. As per the above literature, what is the tourist experience about "Audio Odigos App", nine codes were finalised. Out of 74 user reviews, 33 users share and describe their experience on app quality by using different words, such as "like", "good", "great", "superb", "nice", "really great", "best", "wow", "very good", "excellent", "awesome", "experience too good", "fall in love", "wonderful", "like the app", and "pleasant". These 15 words indicate that users found the smart tourist guide app great in quality and developed a positive attitude for it. This was found to be good since users employed adjective words. Eight users shared their experience about the sound quality, saying it was "excellent", "good", "superb", "cleared", and "helpful sound", making the visit to the tourist site excellent. Experience about image quantity was sensed as good by three users, and three users suggested the addition of more regional languages.

Figure 2. Overall rating of apps

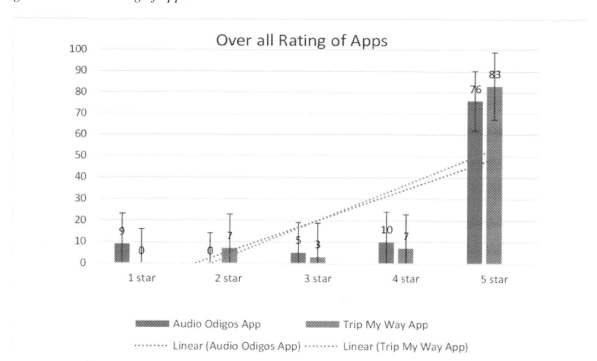

Regarding App efficiency, 17 out of 74 users have indicated that all the app's functions work effectively and shared their views by using words like "useful", "helpful", "amazing", "very much useful", "user friendly", "much needed". These words indicate user experiences about the app's ease of use, where users feel that the app is useful and helpful during a visit to a cultural heritage site. These words indicate an indirect intention to use the app in the future and recommend it to their friends and family.

Two users found the app's navigation system "nice and smoother" during the site visit. Audio Odigos app has Synopsis, Descriptive, and Podcast versions, which tourists can use according to availability of time and need. Regarding app content, 40 users suggested that the app also need improvement to add more cities, places, states, locations, monuments, sites, content.

An important finding is that app developers need to provide more material in terms of more pictures, photos, and images in the Audio Odigos App of India's different cultural sites. The number of reviews indicates that people like the effort made by India's Ministry of Tourism. Such praise shows that the user had a positive experience with the smart tourist guide app. A key result of the app was that just two users expressed dissatisfaction with the app's technology: "Glitches", "Bugs", and "can't change language and city in the app", which need to be fixed.

The overall finding of the present research is that 76% of the users gave a 5-star rating to the app, which means that the app provided a memorable experience to app users. A surprising finding is that no user has given a two-star rating to the app. Figure 2 indicates an overall rating of the app.

Trip My Way App

According to the Google Play Store, Trip My Way is a private sector app with more than 10,000 downloads till April 2021. The following findings are based on a 100-review analysis: 58 users shared their experience about app quality by using words like "great", "nice", "love", "great experience", "excellent", "super", "greatest", "quite good", "amazing", "very good", "awesome", "must-have app", "best", "perfect", "informative, like I was in a movie", "beautiful", "fantastic", "wonderful app", "worth it". These words indicate that the Trip My Way app quality was excellent. App sound quality was described by nine users as "excellent audio", "voice is better than the official guide", "great audio". These words indicate the app sound quality is very good, more than a local tour guide. Content quality is good, according to 9 users.

App efficiency is very important for user experience, and 20 app users say it is "useful", "helpful", "help the most engaging", "better than a local guide", "fantastic", "brilliant, and quite interactive", "lovely execution", "effective tool", "enthusiastic". It indicates that, overall, the app works satisfactorily. In contrast, few users mention that it needs to add more content, city, and sites. In addition, they also mentioned that the app "is not working", "keep crashing", "the camera option was not found", "very unstable", "unable to reset password", "improve the description", "unable to download", "not good", "bad", "don't use photo function", "installation and listening issues", "useless app", "can't log in", "register", "refuse to use via email". It sometimes means that the app works properly, but sometimes users face such difficulty when using it. Figure 2 indicates the overall rating of the app, which is 5-star for 83% of users. It means that the overall experience of the Trip My Way app was very good.

SOLUTIONS AND RECOMMENDATIONS

Based on the study's findings, app developers should conduct regular analyses of tourist reviews and incorporate suggestions by app users to provide a great app experience. Customer reviews provide an opportunity for app developers to interact with both satisfied and dissatisfied customers. In addition, this study suggested some valuable managerial suggestions. To begin with, the research offers empirical insights into consumer responses to useful information on the content of the tourist guide app, which has to be improved in terms of adding new destinations, more history and monuments, and improving the sound and picture quality. Secondly, the research revealed complexity in the technical section that has room for development, such as ease of app installation, the ability to share on social networking sites, the ability to connect with a mail account, and the ability to log in through mobile phone. App quality and app efficiency were suggested as antecedents to future behavioural intents and recommendations based on the study's findings. Thirdly, our research uncovered destination marketing techniques that will assist the Destination Management Organization in implementing creative and appropriate ways to promote the tourist guide app. The main goal is to improve the app's content quality and concentrate on using social networking sites to promote it. DMOs could include and promote quality local cultural heritage goods from destinations, such as historical sites, local cuisines, and hotel accommodations, on social media to enhance their social media marketing operations and increase app viability. Fourthly, DMOs should hire experts familiar with tools and internet statistics to keep track of review and feedback to reveal important key information about tourist guide apps to tourist information to assist in the creation of a database to understand revisiting intentions. Fifthly, a periodic report of social media and destination marketing trends should be sent to the National Tourism Board or The Ministry of Tourism, as this will help researchers and marketing managers strategise on how to make the app very pleasurable and memorable for all app users. Finally, the Ministry of Tourism should ensure that the progress of the tourist guide app is properly managed so that the app records are kept straight in terms of measuring the app development, in terms of technological advancement, so that potential and existing tourist interest is sustained and preserved.

FUTURE RESEARCH DIRECTIONS

In light of the above findings, the author suggests that future research should examine other governmental and private tourist guide app. Future research is recommended to investigate the larger data set related to user experiences with Smart guide apps using different research methods and data collection in different countries and regions. Specifically, surveys and interviews can be used to have a detailed understanding of tourist experience and intention. In this way, the essential factors can be identified for the development of an effective tourist guide app, which may minimise the user's dissatisfaction. Nevertheless, it is evident from the study findings that users appreciate the app quality and efficiency, which is evidently proved that in future intention of use, this app will enhance. So, there is a need to focus on the content part of the experience and on the type of content that is more required for the tourist. In addition, it will be interesting to investigate the tourist experience, tourism satisfaction, loyalty, and intention to recommendation by applying or designing some model related to the use and adoption of technology. Future research can also examine the moderating role of age and gender and mediating role of values and culture. Moreover, in as much as the tourists are satisfied with the tourist guide app, the intention to revisit will be encouraged, and this will translate to the sustainability of the development of the tourist destination.

CONCLUSION

The Ministry of Tourism of the Government of India has launched the Audio Odigos smart guide app, which is free for users. Trip My Way is a private sector app, but it is available free of cost for users. From the positive and negative reviews, few natural exclamation words were found in customer reviews, such as "good", "great", "superb", "nice", "really great", "best", "wow", "very good", "excellent", "awesome", "experience too good", "fall in love", "wonderful", "like this app", "pleasant app". It was confirmed the excellent experience of app users about the App quality.

Audio Odigos app efficiency and sound quality were found up to the mark, yet the content, few cities, and few cultural heritage attractions was found during its use. An important finding was that app developers need to add more cities. Audio Odigos app has features like Synopsis, Descriptive, and Podcast, but lack of awareness was found among app users because only one user described this important feature of the app. Image quality and quantity, navigation quality, and app interactivity experience shared by a few app users and app was found good. At present, the app is available in seven languages, including national and international; however, app users have recommended adding more regional languages. Another important finding was that only two users gave negative reviews, and 24 app users made suggestions for improvement. It indicates that the overall app users' experience was memorable and excellent.

Trip My Way is a very popular private sector app. The app has 24 negative reviews and 11 user suggestions, but it has a 5-star rating. This app has given a fully memorable experience to the tourist. Words like "fantastic", "useful", "helpful", "excellent", "super", "greatest", "quite good", "amazing", "very good", "awesome", "must-have app", "best", "perfect", "informative, like I was in a movie", "beautiful", "fantastic", "wonderful app" address the app quality, indicating an excellent experience using the app. But negative reviews show a need to improve the technology by the app provider to solve issues, such as keep crashing, camera option, save the image, listening, download, registration. Smart guide app saves time for tourists during the tour to find out the availability of Government recognised tour guides. Smart guide apps are available free of cost, which saves money for tourists. Trip My Way and Audio Odigos apps provide authentic information, which is collected from Government sources and recorded by local Government recognised tour guides. Such tour apps enhance tourists at cultural heritage sites, with a great memorable experience. Tour planner travel agents can use an app like Audio Odigos in the upcoming future. It can be used in pandemic situations like coronavirus disease (COVID-19) to maintain social distancing in group tours at the cultural heritage site.

REFERENCES

Ali, F., Terrah, A., Wu, C., Ali, L., & Wu, H. (2021). Antecedents and consequences of user engagement in smartphone travel apps. *Journal of Hospitality and Tourism Technology*. doi:10.1108/JHTT-09-2020-0221

Almobaideen, W., Krayshan, R., Allan, M., & Saadeh, M. (2017). Internet of Things: Geographical routing based on healthcare centers vicinity for mobile smart tourism destination. *Technological Forecasting and Social Change*, *123*, 342–350. doi:10.1016/j.techfore.2017.04.016

Assaker, G., Hallak, R., & El-haddad, R. (2019). *Consumer usage of online travel reviews: Expanding the unified theory of acceptance and use of technology 2 model*. doi:10.1177/1356766719867386

Barnett, T., Pearson, A. W., Pearson, R., & Kellermanns, F. W. (2015). Five-factor model personality traits as predictors of perceived and actual usage of technology. *European Journal of Information Systems*, *24*(4), 374–390. doi:10.1057/ejis.2014.10

Buhalis, D. (2019). Technology in tourism-from information communication technologies to eTourism and smart tourism towards ambient intelligence tourism: A perspective article. *Tourism Review*, *75*(1), 267–272. doi:10.1108/TR-06-2019-0258

Buhalis, D., Harwood, T., Bogicevic, V., Viglia, G., Beldona, S., & Hofacker, C. (2019). Technological disruptions in services: Lessons from tourism and hospitality. *Journal of Service Management*, *30*(4), 484–506. doi:10.1108/JOSM-12-2018-0398

Buhalis, D., & Law, R. (2008). Progress in information technology and tourism management: 20 years on and 10 years after the Internet-The state of eTourism research. *Tourism Management*, *29*(4), 609–623. doi:10.1016/j.tourman.2008.01.005

Cacho, A., Mendes-Filho, L., Estaregue, D., Moura, B., Cacho, N., Lopes, F., & Alves, C. (2016). Mobile tourist guide supporting a smart city initiative: A Brazilian case study. *International Journal of Tourism Cities*, *2*(2), 164–183. doi:10.1108/IJTC-12-2015-0030

Chen, C. C., & Tsai, J. L. (2019). Determinants of behavioral intention to use the Personalised Location-based Mobile Tourism Application: An empirical study by integrating TAM with ISSM. *Future Generation Computer Systems*, *96*, 628–638. Advance online publication. doi:10.1016/j.future.2017.02.028

Choi, K., Wang, Y., & Sparks, B. (2018). Travel app users' continued use intentions: It's a matter of value and trust. *Journal of Travel & Tourism Marketing*, *00*(00), 1–13. doi:10.1080/10548408.2018.1505580

Chuang, C. M. (2020). A current travel model: Smart tour on mobile guide application services. *Current Issues in Tourism*, *23*(18), 2333–2352. doi:10.1080/13683500.2019.1631266

Dickinson, J. E., Ghali, K., Cherrett, T., Speed, C., Davies, N., Norgate, S., Dickinson, J. E., Ghali, K., Cherrett, T., & Speed, C. (2014). *Current Issues in Tourism Tourism and the smartphone app : Capabilities, emerging practice and scope in the travel domain.* doi:10.1080/13683500.2012.718323

Gretzel, U., Werthner, H., Koo, C., & Lamsfus, C. (2015). Conceptual foundations for understanding smart tourism ecosystems. *Computers in Human Behavior*, *50*, 558–563. doi:10.1016/j.chb.2015.03.043

Jeong, M., & Shin, H. H. (2020). Tourists' experiences with smart tourism technology at smart destinations and their behavior intentions. *Journal of Travel Research*, *59*(8), 1464–1477. doi:10.1177/0047287519883034

Jinendra, D., Jadhav, R., Gaidhani Pranav, B. R., Vyavahare, Y., & Achaliyaparag, S. U. (2012). smart travel guide: Application for android mobile. *International Journal of Electronics*.

Kang, K., Jwa, J., & Park, S. E. (2017). Smart audio tour guide system using TTS. *International Journal of Applied Engineering Research*, *12*. http://www.ripublication.com

Keelery, K. (2021). *Topic: Internet usage in India.* Statista. Available at: https://www.statista.com/topics/2157/internet-usage-in-india/

Kuo, T. S., Huang, K. C., Nguyen, T. Q., & Nguyen, P. H. (2019). Adoption of mobile applications for identifying tourism destinations by travellers: An integrative approach. *Journal of Business Economics and Management*, *20*(5), 860–877. doi:10.3846/jbem.2019.10448

Kwok, T. C. K., Kiefer, P., Schinazi, V. R., Adams, B., & Raubal, M. (2019, May 2). Gaze-guided narratives: Adapting audio guide content to gaze in virtual and real environments. *Conference on Human Factors in Computing Systems - Proceedings.* 10.1145/3290605.3300721

Lai, I. K. W. (2015). Traveler acceptance of an app-based mobile tour guide. *Journal of Hospitality & Tourism Research (Washington, D.C.), 39*(3), 401–432. doi:10.1177/1096348013491596

Lee, H., Lee, J., Chung, N., & Koo, C. (2018). Tourists' happiness: Are there smart tourism technology effects? *Asia Pacific Journal of Tourism Research, 23*(5), 486–501. doi:10.1080/10941665.2018.1468344

Lee, L. W., Mccarthy, I. P., & Kietzmann, J. (2019). *Making sense of text: Artificial content analysis.* doi:10.1108/EJM-02-2019-0219

Leung, R. (2020). Hospitality technology progress towards intelligent buildings: A perspective article. *Tourism Review, 76*(1), 69–73. doi:10.1108/TR-05-2019-0173

Liberato, P., Alen, E., & Liberato, D. (2018). Smart tourism destination triggers consumer experience: The case of Porto. *European Journal of Management and Business Economics, 27*(1), 6–25. doi:10.1108/EJMBE-11-2017-0051

Lu, J., Mao, Z., Wang, M., & Hu, L. (2015). Goodbye maps, hello apps? Exploring the influential determinants of travel app adoption. *Current Issues in Tourism, 18*(11), 1059–1079. doi:10.1080/13683500.2015.1043248

Mahardika, H., Thomas, D., Ewing, M. T., & Japutra, A. (2019). Experience and facilitating conditions as impediments to consumers' new technology adoption. *International Review of Retail, Distribution and Consumer Research, 29*(1), 79–98. doi:10.1080/09593969.2018.1556181

Marangunić, N., & Granić, A. (2015). Technology acceptance model: A literature review from 1986 to 2013. *Universal Access in the Information Society, 14*(1), 81–95. doi:10.100710209-014-0348-1

Molnar, E., & Moraru, R. (2017). *Content analysis of customer reviews to identify sources of value creation in the hotel environment.* doi:10.1007/978-3-319-56925-3

Nasiri, M., Ukko, J., Saunila, M., & Rantala, T. (2020). Managing the digital supply chain: The role of smart technologies. *Technovation, 96–97,* 102121. Advance online publication. doi:10.1016/j.technovation.2020.102121

Navío-Marco, J., Ruiz-Gómez, L. M., & Sevilla-Sevilla, C. (2018). Progress in information technology and tourism management: 30 years on and 20 years after the internet: Revisiting Buhalis & Law's landmark study about eTourism. *Tourism Management, 69,* 460–470. doi:10.1016/j.tourman.2018.06.002

Oleksy, T., & Wnuk, A. (2016). Augmented places: An impact of embodied historical experience on attitudes towards places. *Computers in Human Behavior, 57,* 11–16. doi:10.1016/j.chb.2015.12.014

Osei, B. A., Ragavan, N. A., & Mensah, H. K. (2020). Prospects of the fourth industrial revolution for the hospitality industry: A literature review. *Journal of Hospitality and Tourism Technology, 11*(3), 479–494. doi:10.1108/JHTT-08-2019-0107

Othman, M. K., Petrie, H., & Power, C. (2013). Measuring the usability of a smartphone delivered museum guide. *Procedia: Social and Behavioral Sciences*, 97, 629–637. doi:10.1016/j.sbspro.2013.10.282

Pai, C., Kang, S., Liu, Y., & Zheng, Y. (2021). An examination of revisit intention based on perceived smart tourism technology experience. *Sustainability (Switzerland)*, 13(2), 1007. Advance online publication. doi:10.3390u13021007

Palos, P., Jose, S., Saura, R., & Correia, M. B. (2020). Do tourism applications' quality and user experience influence its acceptance by tourists? *Review of Managerial Science*. doi:10.1007/s11846-020-00396-y

Pencarelli, T. (2020). The digital revolution in the travel and tourism industry. *Information Technology & Tourism*, 22(3), 455–476. Advance online publication. doi:10.100740558-019-00160-3

Press Information Bureau. (2019). *PIB Delhi Release ID: 1587157*. https://pib.gov.in/PressReleasePage.aspx?PRID=1587157

Rabotic, B. (n.d.). *American tourists' perceptions of tourist guides in Belgrade*. http://www.vodici-dubrovnik.hr/povijest.php

Sánchez-torres, J. A., & Argila-irurita, A. (2021). *Adoption of tourist mobile applications motivating factors for their use: An exploratory study in Spanish millennials the fourth industrial revolution, which revolves around the latest ICT information and*. March. doi:10.18080/jtde.v9n1.305

Sarumathi, K. (2018). Redefining travel experience through technology. *The Hidu Newspaper, Bengalur*. https://www.thehindu.com/news/cities/bangalore/redefining-travel-experience-through-technology/article22663028.ece

Sigala, M., & Gretzel, U. (2017). *Advances in social media for travel, tourism and hospitality: New perspectives, practice and cases*. Taylor and Francis., doi:10.4324/9781315565736

Smirnov, A., Shilov, N., Kashevnik, A., Teslya, N., & Shchekotov, M. (n.d.). *Intelligent tourist guiding service based on smart-M3 platform*. Academic Press.

Stankov, U., & Gretzel, U. (2020). Tourism 4.0 technologies and tourist experiences: A human-centered design perspective. *Information Technology & Tourism*, 22(3), 477–488. Advance online publication. doi:10.100740558-020-00186-y

Tamilmani, K., Rana, N. P., Fosso, S., & Dwivedi, R. (2021). The extended Unified Theory of Acceptance and Use of Technology (UTAUT2): A systematic literature review and theory evaluation. *International Journal of Information Management*, 57(April), 102269. doi:10.1016/j.ijinfomgt.2020.102269

Tang, J., Akram, U., & Shi, W. (2020). Why people need privacy? The role of privacy fatigue in app users' intention to disclose privacy: Based on personality traits. *Journal of Enterprise Information Management*, 34(4), 1097–1120. https://doi.org/10.1108/JEIM-03-2020-0088

Tarantino, E., De Falco, I., & Scafuri, U. (2019). A mobile personalised tourist guide and its user evaluation. *Information Technology & Tourism*, 21(3).

Te Kuo, N., Chang, K. C., Cheng, Y. S., & Lin, J. C. (2016). Effects of tour guide interpretation and tourist satisfaction on destination loyalty in Taiwan's Kinmen Battlefield tourism: Perceived playfulness and perceived flow as moderators. *Journal of Travel & Tourism Marketing*, *33*(sup1), 103–122. doi:10.1080/10548408.2015.1008670

V, A. K. K., & Sabarish, S. (2021). *Journey companion: An Android travel and tourism application*. Academic Press.

Venkatesh, V., Walton, S. M., & Thong, J. Y. L. (n.d.). *Quarterly consumer acceptance and use of information technology: Extending the unified theory of acceptance and use of technology*. https://about.jstor.org/terms

Vinodan, A., & Meera, S. (2020). M-tourism in India: Symbolic versus intended adoption. *IIMB Management Review*, *32*(2), 177–188. https://doi.org/10.1016/j.iimb.2019.10.004

Xiang, Z. (2018). From digitisation to the age of acceleration: On information technology and tourism. *Tourism Management Perspectives*, *25*(November), 147–150. https://doi.org/10.1016/j.tmp.2017.11.023

Xu, F., Huang, S., & Li, S. (2019). Time, money, or convenience: What determines Chinese consumers' continuance usage intention and behavior of using tourism mobile apps? *International Journal of Culture, Tourism and Hospitality Research*, *13*(3), 288–302. https://doi.org/10.1108/IJCTHR-04-2018-0052

Yarimoglu, E., & Gunay, T. (2020). The extended theory of planned behavior in Turkish customers' intentions to visit green hotels. *Business Strategy and the Environment*, *29*(3), 1097–1108. https://doi.org/10.1002/bse.2419

Zacarias, F., Cuapa, R., De Ita, G., & Torres, D. (2015). Smart tourism in 1-click. *Procedia Computer Science*, *56*(1), 447–452. https://doi.org/10.1016/j.procs.2015.07.234

Zhuang, X., Hou, X., Feng, Z., Lin, Z., & Li, J. (2021). Subjective norms, attitudes, and intentions of AR technology use in tourism experience: The moderating effect of millennials. *Leisure Studies*, *40*(3), 392–406. https://doi.org/10.1080/02614367.2020.1843692

ADDITIONAL READING

Albino, V., Berardi, U., & Dangelico, R. M. (2015). Smart cities: Definitions, dimensions, performance, and initiatives. *Journal of Urban Technology*, *22*(1), 3–21. doi:10.1080/10630732.2014.942092

Ghorbani, A., Danaei, A., Zargar, S. M., & Hematian, H. (2019). Designing of smart tourism organisation (STO) for tourism management: A case study of tourism organisations of South Khorasan province, Iran. *Heliyon*, *5*(6), e01850. Advance online publication. doi:10.1016/j.heliyon.2019.e01850 PMID:31338444

Jiménez-Barreto, J., & Campo-Martínez, S. (2018). Destination website quality, users' attitudes and the willingness to participate in online co-creation experiences. *European Journal of Management and Business Economics*, *27*(1), 26–41. doi:10.1108/EJMBE-11-2017-0048

Koo, C., Shin, S., Gretzel, U., Hunter, W. C., & Chung, N. (2016). Conceptualisation of smart tourism destination competitiveness. *Asia Pacific Journal of Information Systems*, *26*(4), 561–576. doi:10.14329/apjis.2016.26.4.561

Oh, H., Jeong, M., Lee, S., & Warnick, R. (2016). Attitudinal and situational determinants of self-service technology use. *Journal of Hospitality & Tourism Research (Washington, D.C.)*, *40*(2), 236–265. doi:10.1177/1096348013491598

Wang, X., Li, X. R., Zhen, F., & Zhang, J. H. (2016). How smart is your tourist attraction? Measuring tourist preferences of smart tourism attractions via a FCEM-AHP and IPA approach. *Tourism Management*, *54*, 309–320. doi:10.1016/j.tourman.2015.12.003

KEY TERMS AND DEFINITIONS

App Experience: During use of the app, users positive or negative views and how users enjoy app features.

App Information Quality: Authentic information available for app users.

App Navigation: Tourists can use the navigation option at tourist sites to find the way.

Guide: This person gives historical information about various tourist interest places to tourists at cultural heritage sites.

Smart Guide App: Smart Guide is a tourism app that makes it easy to create and enjoy local tour guide experiences during the visit to cultural heritage sites.

Travel Apps: App which is used for travel planning purposes or booking hotels, train tickets, etc.

Travel Technology: Technology which is used in the travel and tourism industry.

Chapter 15
Accessible Tourism Experiences in Smart Destinations:
The Case of Breda (Netherlands)

Fatih Ercan
https://orcid.org/0000-0001-6469-3000
Zonguldak Bülent Ecevit University, Turkey

ABSTRACT

Accessible tourism is among the issues that have been emphasized in recent years. Smart technologies which have developed and become widespread nowadays are seen as an important tool in ensuring accessibility in destinations. Today, destinations are trying to improve the tourism experiences of individuals with some form of disability by using smart technologies. This study aims to reveal the current accessible tourism applications in smart destinations with the example of the city of Breda. Data were obtained using the document analysis technique, which is one of the qualitative data collection methods. As a result of the data analysis, it has been determined that technologies such as destination websites, mobile applications, virtual reality are used extensively for accessible transportation and information about the destination in Breda.

INTRODUCTION

Today, destinations that are trying to increase their income from tourism by attracting more tourists follow various strategies for this. One of these strategies is to make their natural, cultural and historical resources accessible for all. Accessibility is an approach to creating product, service and environmental conditions that allow everyone to use and benefit (Gillovic & McIntosh, 2020). In recent years, the increase in the number of people with disabilities and the prediction that this increase will continue in the future (The World Bank, 2021) increase the importance of accessibility. People with disabilities have the right to travel and participate in tourism activities like other people with no disabilities. However, there is a consensus that their travel and tourism experiences are not sufficiently accessible (Yıldız & Bozyer, 2017; Meskele, Woreta & Weldesenbet, 2018; Devile & Kastenholz, 2018). Allan (2015) reveals in his

DOI: 10.4018/978-1-7998-8775-1.ch015

research that environmental factors are an important travel barrier and intrinsic and interactive factors in the travels of people with disabilities.

The unsuitable physical structure, inadequate physical mobility, inconvenience of transportation activities and their need for assistive travel technologies in the destinations appear as important constraints in the travels of people with disabilities. Tourists with disabilities are more loyal, spend more, stay longer in destinations (Vila, Gonzalez, & Darcy, 2019). However, the increasing value of the accessible tourism market (Bowtell, 2015) makes it necessary to enhance the travel experiences of people with disabilities and to carry out studies on accessible tourism in destinations. Technology is shown as one of the most important factors that change the nature of tourist experiences today (Neuhofer, Buhalis, & Ladkin, 2012; Mayordomo-Martinez et al., 2019). Smart technologies within the digital ecosystem contribute to the accessibility of destinations by allowing information sharing and coordination among tourism components (Cassia et al., 2021). The concept of an inclusive smart city, which refers to the use of smart technologies to make cities more accessible to people with disabilities, enables new experiences to be offered to both tourists with disabilities and no disabilities (Neto, 2018). Here, smart city applications in destinations gain importance.

Smart cities offer new experiences based on smart technologies for the tourists visiting the city as well as the life quality of the local people (OECD, 2020). Smart destinations that are built on a smart city infrastructure are defined as cities or places that use the necessary technological tools, innovations and techniques to create experiences that will satisfy tourists. Here, it is aimed to enrich tourist experiences by using smart destination applications developed in integration with smart city technologies (Jasrotia and Gangotia, 2018). The research results conducted by Huang and Lau (2020) reveal that smart destination experiences strengthen the connection of people with disabilities with the destination, increasing their travel motivation and satisfaction from tourism experiences. Smart technologies are used in destinations for providing accessible information for people with disabilities (Altinay et al., 2016), in vehicles, physical environment (UNWTO, 2020), accommodation enterprises (Suryotrisongko, Kusuma, & Ginardi, 2017), among others.

The aim of this study is to reveal the current accessible tourism applications in smart destinations with the example of the city of Breda. It is seen that technology-supported accessible applications used in destinations are among the research topics that have taken their place in the international literature in recent years. However, it is noteworthy that research on these technologies providing accessible tourism experiences is scarce. Research on what applications provide accessible tourism experiences and how people with disabilities benefit from them gain importance in this respect. Through this research, it is tried to fill this gap in the literature. In the first part of this study, a literature review was made to explain the concepts related to the subject. First, the concepts of smart city, smart tourism, smart tourist and smart destination and their features are discussed. Then, by giving information about the importance of smart technologies in increasing destination accessibility, the relationship between accessibility and technology is revealed. Within the scope of the case study, the Breda city is examined. Documents such as websites of the municipality, destination management organisations, private organisations and news containing information about the city's general structure and destination characteristics are analysed for the purpose of research. Within the scope of this study, detailed information about the accessible smart applications of the Breda will contribute significantly to the development of the relevant literature. It's thought that this study will be a guide for tourism managers as well as academics. Besides that, this study will be an important scientific resource for readers on improving and enhancing the tourism experiences of tourists with disabilities by using accessible smart applications in destinations.

RESEARCH BACKGROUND

In recent years, it is seen that social awareness about accessibility has increased around the world. Accessibility in cities and public spaces is one of the issues that are emphasised as a policy in Europe (Mollá-Sirvent et al., 2018). However, accessibility is among the current issues that attract attention and discussed by researchers in the field of tourism (Darcy, Cameron and Pegg, 2010; Michopoulou, Darcy, Ambrose and Buhalis, 2015; Meskele, Woreta, & Weldesenbet, 2018; Gillovic & McIntosh, 2020). The increase in people's life quality as a result of the developments in technology causes the growth of the accessible tourism market. In this regard, some European countries regulations' are given as examples (Vila, González, & Darcy, 2019). The research conducted by Bowtel (2015) reveals the value of the accessible tourism market in Europe. The author considers accessible tourism an important future market opportunity for European countries and states that there is a potential to generate 88.6 billion Euros from this market by 2025.

It is seen that the use of smart technologies for accessibility is increasing in destinations nowadays. The purpose of these practices is to enhance the accessible tourism experiences of people with disabilities before, during and post-travel (Mayordomo-Martìnez et al., 2019). In addition, accessibility and use of technology are among the most important factors determining the competitiveness of destinations (Mira, Moura, & Breda, 2016). Liberato, Alén-González, and Liberato (2018) state that smart technologies make destinations more attractive and accessible to both locals and tourists. According to the authors, it's possible to enhance tourists' accessible experiences by using smart technologies in destinations. However, these technologies are able to increase the mobility of people with disabilities within the destination (Buhalis and Amaranggana, 2014). While smart tourism technologies are an important tool for providing unique personalised experiences (Wan, 2018), different smart technologies are used to improve destination accessibility. Tourist information tools such as mobile applications and assistive technologies such as travel assistants are smart technologies that can be used by people with disabilities in smart destinations (Darcy, McKercher, & Schweinsberg, 2020).

Thanks to smart technologies, information accessibility increases and transportation and transfer vehicles compatible with the needs of people with disabilities can be used at the destinations. Mobile applications increase the mobility of tourists with disabilities within the destination (Cassia, Castellani, Rossato, & Baccarani, 2021). Smart technologies developed for the special needs of people with disabilities in smart destinations reduce their travel restrictions. In addition, smart destination technologies enhance tourist experiences with information and guidance functions, and thus creating smart tourism experiences (Ribeiro, Silva, Barbosa, Silva, & Metrōlho, 2018).

Organisations such as the European Network for Accessible Tourism (ENAT), established in Europe, are working on accessibility in smart tourism destinations. Accessibility management, smart technologies and smart destination applications constitute the main theme of these activities (ENAT, 2020). Therefore, it is seen that smart destination technologies have been given great importance in enhancing accessibility in European countries in recent years. The European Capital of Smart Tourism award is granted by the European Union in four different categories (accessibility, sustainability, digitalisation, cultural heritage & creativity) each year. Applications such as barrier-free digital accessibility, physical accessibility, accessible information, audio guides are among the best accessibility applications in smart destinations. The 2020 European Capital of Smart Tourism award was given to Breda in the Netherlands for its work in accessible tourism. With its projects and applications, from transportation and communication to accessible information, the Breda city is seen as Europe's most successful smart destination in the accessibility category in 2020 (European Commission, 2021). Therefore, a case study on accessibility practices in Breda will make a significant contribution to the relevant literature.

LITERATURE REVIEW

Use of "Smart" Concept in Tourism

It is seen that the rapid developments in technology in the 21st century have led to the emergence of new concepts. Especially, developments in mobile devices and internet technologies cause the concept of "smart" to be used as a common technological term today. Smart technology is basically a concept that refers to electronic devices with software that adds intelligence to systems. The "Smart" refers to being aware of and interacting with the environment through the sensors (Holnicki-Szulc, Motylewski and Kolakowski, 2008). The term smart is used to point out devices using this type of technology. Silverio-Fernández, Renukappa and Suresh (2018) divide the features that smart devices should have into three main categories:

1. Autonomy: It means that devices perform tasks autonomously without the direct commands of the users. Smart devices perform autonomous tasks due to their features. These tasks can be multiple. For example, mobile devices process information autonomously.
2. Connectivity: It refers to establishing a connection with a network of any size. This connection aims to provide Internet access or share information with other devices on the same network. Transactions performed on mobile devices generally require an internet connection. Devices on the same network can establish wireless connections between each other.
3. Context-Awareness: It refers to the ability of smart devices to collect information around them through sensors such as cameras, microphones and GPS. The information collected with the help of sensors can then be used to make autonomous decisions or to provide direct assistance to the user.

Developments in technology along with the Industry 4.0 revolution allow connected smart devices to be used in different areas. One of these business areas is the tourism industry. Tourism enterprises and destinations create new experiences for tourists by using smart technologies in their service delivery. With the increasing use of smart technologies in tourism, concepts such as smart tourism, smart destination (Corréa & Gosling, 2020), smart city (Gretzel & Koo, 2021) and smart tourist (Femenia-Serra, Neuhofer, & Ivars-Baidal, 2019) are frequently used in the relevant literature.

Smart Tourism

Smart technologies show the current situation as a result of the developments in the field of technology from the past to the present. The tourism industry quickly adopts these technologies and uses them in tourism activities. Being "smart" is seen as an important requirement in order to survive in the highly competitive tourism industry today. Smartness is necessary at every stage, from the acquisition of information to its sharing. The activities carried out by businesses, destinations and tourists in the tourism industry using smart technologies form the basis of smart tourism (Jasrotia & Gangotia, 2018). It's possible to define smart tourism as interactive information communication technologies (ICTs) that support tourists throughout their travels and are used to promote destinations and tourism marketing (Liberato, Alen, & Liberato, 2018). According to another definition, smart tourism is information and communication technology applications such as mobile communication, cloud computing, artificial intelligence and virtual reality used to develop tourism with innovative tools and approaches (Rodrigues, Cardoso, Monteiro, & Ramos, 2020).

Pai, Liu, Kang and Dai (2020) state that traditional tourism has changed with the development of smart technologies and these technologies are widely used in the tourism industry. The authors also emphasise that the ultimate goal of smart tourism is to provide more convenient and enjoyable travel experiences. Stankov and Gretzel (2020) conceptualise smart tourism as Tourism 4.0 and emphasise that smart technologies enrich tourist experiences and increase communication between all stakeholders in the tourism industry. However, due to the diversity of products and services in the tourism industry, it's seen that there are many smart applications used. Smart tourism technologies are designed and developed to increase tourist satisfaction (Sabou & Maiorescu, 2020).

Smart City

It is seen that the concept of "smart" is one of the popular words that have been used frequently in many fields with the emergence of new technologies in recent years. In this context, the smart environment is a structure in which ICTs are widely used, which allows all stakeholders to access information easily, and thus facilitating their activities and providing value to its users (Baggio, Micera, & Chiaappa, 2020). As the use of smart technologies becomes widespread among people, social life and the environment are affected. The rapid population growth and the depletion of resources in cities cause difficulties for people to receive the most basic services. Therefore, most of the cities around the world are turning into smart cities. Smart cities can be explained as a technological initiative that plays an important role in providing direct services to the local population through the optimal use of ICTs. Here, there is an urban transformation that aims to provide basic services to local people and tourists using technology (Habeed & Weli, 2020).

Table 1. Examples of smart city applications

Application Area	Description of Application	Examples of Application
Smart buildings	Smart buildings combine the advantages of communication and control systems	Optimising heating and air conditioning systems
Education, medical and social care	Applications that allow the development in these domains and ensure that all citizens have access to high-quality service	Monitoring systems elderly, telemedicine applications
Smart energy	Smart electrical energy that offers all functions to the service users with smart infrastructure	SmartGrid applications, network optimisation, comply the environment standards, smart lighting
Smart grid (smart metering of natural gas, water, electrical energy)	Real-time consumption metering energy, water and natural gas.	Online consumption information, wireless smart meters
Smart Utilities (smart water distribution and smart waste management)	Intelligent management of water distribution systems and wastewater	Smart wastewater systems, real-time solid waste monitoring
Smart parking	Managing the parking places using sensors, CCTV (Close Circuit TeleVision)	Monitoring systems of the vehicles
Integrated supply systems	Synchronising the supply with the demand, measurement, monitoring and organisation of the transportation	
Smart and integrated transport	Traffic monitoring using and combining all transportation means	CCTV for traffic, smart parking networks, minimising the impact on the environment

(Source: Eremia, Toma, & Sanduleac, 2017)

Accessible Tourism Experiences in Smart Destinations

The ISO 37120/2014 standard, entitled Sustainable Development of Societies, defines 17 main indicators to evaluate the performance of urban services and quality of life. These are economy, energy, education, environment, finance, fire and emergency response, management, health, recreation, safety, shelter, solid waste, telecommunications and investment, transportation, urban planning, wastewater, water and sanitation. For more livable, sustainable, resilient and economically attractive cities, these indicators serve as a reference for politicians, researchers, planners and other professionals (Eremia, Toma and Sanduleac, 2017). Table 3 contains some directions and application examples for the development of smart cities. These applications regarding the systems, services and management that should be found in smart cities show the main features of a smart city.

Smart Destination

Increasing competition between destinations forces destination management organisations to pursue new strategies. In addition, destinations are obligated to offer products and services suitable for the new tourist profile that uses technology extensively. In this context, smart technologies offer significant advantages in producing unique products and services in destinations (Cimbaljevìc, Stankov, & Pavluković, 2019). Furthermore, the increasing amount of information and access to this information makes the use of smart technologies in destinations an important necessity. Applications such as recommender app that are effective in the decision-making process of tourists can be shown as examples of smart destination applications. Internet of things (IoT), social media, augmented and virtual reality, big data are other examples of technologies used in smart destinations (Sabou & Maiorescu, 2020). At destinations, cloud services provide remote access to applications, software and data, while IoT provides services to optimise the interaction between tour operators and users. However, end-user technologies allow users to access tourism-related services with many smart tools and applications (Baggio, Micera, & Chiappa, 2020).

Smart destination refers to an approach in which new technologies are used in destination management. Elements in the digital ecosystem such as social networks and mobile applications facilitate the destination-tourist interaction process. As a result of this interaction, a large amount of data is created, and a "smart environment" is formed. By using these data in destination management, tourists are served in a smart environment (Gomes, Gândara, & Ivars-Baidal, 2017). For this reason, smart destinations serve to provide better service to tourists by using technology, developing technology-based solutions, introducing innovations, and increasing information sharing. All of these create value and new experiences for tourists visiting the destination (Liberato, Alen and Liberato, 2018). In addition, smart destination applications are an important determinant in competition today. However, smart destination is also shown as an important component of smart tourism. Smart destination applications enable smart tourism development and the emergence of the new "smart tourist" type (Liberato, Alén-González, & Liberato, 2018).

Smart Tourist

Developments in ICTs make cities more attractive to both local residents and tourists. Furthermore, increasing communication and information sharing opportunities cause more use of smart technologies by tourists in destinations (Buhalis & Amaranggana, 2014). Thus, it's seen that a new type of tourist, which is described as smart tourist has emerged. In smart tourism, the increasing dependence of destinations, businesses and tourists on ICTs creates smart tourists (Gretzel, Sigala, Xiang, & Koo, 2015).

Therefore, smart tourist can be shown as a new term within the concept of smart tourism. The smart tourist is defined as the type of tourist who uses smart technologies in his/her travel experience, adopts new technologies and shares information. The prominent features of smart tourists are their willingness to share information, tendency to use smart technologies, being ready to interact/co-create through smart tourism technologies, sharing data with stakeholders, using smart technologies to create touristic experiences (Femenia-Serra, Neuhofer, & Ivars-Baidal, 2019).

Smart tourists get smart tourism experiences by using technology during their travels. The occurrence of smart experiences within the scope of tourism is called smart tourism experience. Smart tourists are in social change with the stakeholders in the destination (other tourists, tourism businesses, destination management organisations, etc.). Smart devices that support the creation of smart experiences have an important place in this social change (Corrêa & Gosling, 2020). Smart tourists enhance their tourism experiences by actively using devices such as mobile smartphones, smartwatches and tablets, which are becoming widespread today. Tourists benefit more from smart tourism technologies in a destination. The superior functions of Tourism 4.0 technologies change tourist behaviour and increase information sharing and interaction (Stankov & Gretzel, 2020). As a result, smart tourists are more knowledgeable, interactive, and sophisticated, equipped with new technologies. In other words, it is possible to define the smart tourist as the new tourist type that combines tourism experiences with smart technologies.

Accessible Destination Concept and Features

Tourism is based on the touristic travels people make from one place to another for touristic purposes. A successful destination is a place that meets the needs of different types of tourists. Accessibility of the tourist attraction elements, businesses and services in the destination draws attention among the issues that are given importance in tourism (Ferri, 2014). Safe, convenient, low-cost transportation and other tourism infrastructure are key factors in the success of tourism. Destinations that do not have the necessary tourism infrastructure for people with disabilities pose an important travel restriction for them. The fact that they do not have equal conditions with other people regarding mobility within the destination or access to information negatively affects the participation of people with disabilities in tourism (UNWTO-World Tourism Organization, 2013). Therefore, accessibility can be shown as one of the important issues for people with disabilities and tourism activities today.

Accessibility, disability and inclusive tourism are interrelated concepts. Accessibility for people with disabilities is the basis of inclusive tourism. Accessibility refers to the structure formed by the development of products, services and environments that everyone (disabled or non-disabled) can use and benefit from. Disability, on the other hand, is a situation that restricts people's participation in the social life on an equal basis with other individuals. It is stated that 15% or 1 billion people of the total world population are disabled (Gillovic & McIntosh, 2020). People with disabilities who are physically or mentally different and constitute a significant part of the world population can participate in social life with some arrangements made according to their needs. Today, it is seen that there is an increasing social awareness about accessibility due to the increase in the number of people with disabilities worldwide (Mollá-Sirvent et al., 2018).

The increasing number of people with disabilities and their positions in the general population in most European countries, America and other regions are better understood today. According to universal human rights, it is seen that the rights of people with disabilities are respected, and the regulations on accessibility are emphasised. In this context, countries are now more active in providing accessibility for people with disabilities, and they are making their tourism infrastructures more accessible (Darcy, Cameron and Pegg, 2010). Cities need to be made livable for people with disabilities as well as for other individuals. Providing services that will ensure the mobility of people with disabilities and support their activities are among the issues that can be considered in this context. Considering that the participation of people with disabilities in social life is still at low levels (Devile & Kastenholz, 2018), it is clear that more attention should be given to activities to ensure their accessibility.

Accessibility is an issue that everyone may need. Due to conditions such as temporary or permanent disability, illness, physical injury, pregnancy and old age, people need an accessible environment, products and services. Accessibility can be increased by making environmental conditions accessible for the daily life of people with disabilities. Accessible arrangements made in cities improve the life quality of residents and enrich the tourist experience (UNWTO, 2016). Participation of people with disabilities in tourism activities and their mobility within the destination can be shown among the research topics that have been frequently studied academically in recent years (Allan, 2015; Meskele, Woreta, & Weldesenbet, 2018; Gillovic and McIntosh, 2020). The main issues addressed in these studies are the travel motivation of tourists with disabilities, tourism enterprises, and accessibility barriers in the destination environment. In order to increase the participation of people with disabilities in tourism activities, there is a need for the development of inclusive tourism or tourism for all approach.

Accessibility of destinations gains importance within the scope of inclusive tourism activities. Today, destinations realise the tourism potential of people with disabilities and make their attractive resources accessible to them. In this context, physical infrastructure is developed with different alternatives according to their access needs. But, only physical infrastructure arrangements are not enough. The importance of accessible information is also emphasised. The fact that access to information is easy for people with disabilities is as important as physical accessibility in destinations (VisitEngland, 2021). In this context, it's possible to define the concept of accessible destinations as destinations with a tourism infrastructure where physical facilities are made suitable for people with disabilities in the environment, their mobility is supported, and they can easily access information. Both physical infrastructure and easy access to information can be considered important factors affecting the accessibility degree of destinations.

Destinations try to understand the needs of people with disabilities and determine their attitudes and behaviours towards tourism activities. So, they can offer more accessible services for them. Making the physical infrastructures of destinations accessible according to their needs, providing access to touristic attractions, and easy access to all information about the destination draw attention as the features that make a destination accessible (Devile & Kastenholz, 2018). Most of the European countries carry out important works on accessibility and make various regulations. The aim is to make the services offered in destinations accessible to everyone and to eliminate physical or organisational barriers. The accessibility of touristic products and services to more people without any special assistance or vehicle is possible via universal design. In the universal design approach, standards regarding accessibility are determined, products and services for the use of people with disabilities are developed. Ensuring accessibility in transportation, attractions, and facilities is a long process that requires the participation of all stakeholders, including people with disabilities (Michopoulou et al., 2015).

Tourism service providers operating in public and private sectors in destinations act in a coordinated manner to meet the demands of the growing accessible tourism market. The inclusivity of the services and tourism resources comes to the fore in these activities (Mayordomo-Martìnez et al., 2019). Successful destinations in competition have two important features. The first is the accessibility of the entire transportation network within the destination (Buhalis & Amaranggana, 2014; Mira, Moura, &

Breda, 2016), and the other is the ease of access to information about the destination (Neto, Dimmock, Lohmann, & Scott, 2020). The availability of the vehicles in the transportation network for the people with disabilities means the accessible transportation network, the accessibility of the people with disabilities to obtain information from certain points within destination by using the Internet and mobile applications means accessible information (VisitEngland, 2021). Therefore, accessible information about a destination's tourism resources and the accessibility of the transportation network can be considered important factors for destinations to gain a competitive advantage.

Role of Smart Technologies in Destination Accessibility

Crowded cities and the increasing number of people with disabilities worldwide make it necessary to follow new strategies to ensure accessibility. In this context, it is seen that smart city applications have been rapidly adopted in recent years. The smart city approach is an important tool in increasing the life quality of people with disabilities in society. Both local people and tourists visiting the city can benefit from the disabled-friendly practices and accessible environment in smart cities (Suryotrisongko, Kusuma, & Ginardi, 2017). Tourism, a business area where many services are offered, is rapidly adapting to smart technology, and smart applications are used extensively. In smart destinations built on smart city infrastructure, smart applications are developed to offer services tailored to the needs and behaviours of tourists. In addition, it is aimed to enhance accessibility in the destination with special services and applications provided for people with disabilities (Sabou & Maiorescu, 2020).

Liberato, Alen, and Liberato (2018) emphasise the importance of developing destinations based on innovation, sustainability and accessibility in line with developing technologies. The authors state that smart destination applications provide differentiation from competitors and positively affect the quality of the services offered at the destination. However, smart technologies are very important in ensuring instant information flow to tourists and easy access to information. Going to certain places, finding a location, searching for information, and indoor audio guidance are technology-supported accessible services offered in smart destinations. Mobile tour guides and smart travel guides are today's modern form of old audio guides (Lee, 2017). In addition, mobile applications can function as information sources for people with disabilities and their families. These applications aim to show places and spaces that are easily accessible for people with disabilities. In addition, mobile applications include accessible website links of tourism service providers and their accessibility degree (not accessible, partially accessible, fully accessible, etc.) (Ferri, 2014).

The maps in mobile applications contain the destination information and accessible service points that people with disabilities need. Accessible service points (tourism businesses, service providers, etc.) within the destination are shown with special signs on the map. Information about the accessible features of these points can be found here. In addition to written information, audio information can also be found on these maps (Mollá-Sirvent et al., 2018). This feature makes it easier for people with disabilities to benefit from the application, and they can learn before the trip that the place they will go is suitable for their access needs. In addition to mobile applications, destination websites can be considered an important source of information for people with disabilities. Therefore, destination websites are one of the most important tools for destination accessibility. Accessible websites play an important role in influencing the purchasing decisions of people with disabilities by providing them with visual and audio information (Sambhanthan & Good, 2013). The design of destination websites should be accessible to

Accessible Tourism Experiences in Smart Destinations

everyone according to universal standards. Destination websites are classified as low (A), medium (AA) and high (AAA) accessible according to their degree of accessibility (Vila, González, & Darcy, 2019).

Most of the studies on smart cities focus on the technological infrastructure and competence of cities. The efficiency of smart technologies used in cities is the important factor here. For this reason, all systems, infrastructure and services in cities must be managed in an integrated manner using the internet network. In addition to mobile apps, virtual reality technologies used in smart cities today are also important smart technologies for accessibility (Nam and Pardo, 2011). Mobile technologies can be used for information purposes at bus stops and stations by integrating with transportation systems. With the help of audio guides, visually impaired individuals can obtain information about routes and stops/stations. However, with the help of virtual reality technology, people with disabilities can visit museums in a virtual environment (Sambhanthan & Good, 2013). Virtual reality technology is used in tourism to search for information about tourist places, learn their accessibility levels, and visit inaccessible places for people with disabilities in a virtual environment. This technology increases accessibility for tourists with disabilities and creates new experiences for them. Tourists can easily use virtual reality technology through destination websites or mobile applications (Marrasco & Balbi, 2019).

In addition to public transit systems in smart destinations, there are also applications for making city tours on foot. For example, the AccessMap mobile app was implemented in the city of Seattle within the Open Sidewalks project. This application shows the parks, concert venues and transportation alternatives to participate in the trips. Sidewalks for people with disabilities, curb ramps, construction information and alternative roads required for wheelchair users are marked in the AccessMap app. Therefore, this app functions as a tour planning tool for people with disabilities (Korngold, Lemos, & Rohwer, 2017). Another smart destination application as an example for accessibility is the City24/7 app developed for New York City. Through this app, the elderly, hearing and visually impaired individuals and wheelchair users are informed about the services in the city using Smart Screen technology (Frazier & Touchet, 2012).

Figure 1. Access city map
Source: www.accessmap.io

Accessibility can be enhanced by using smart technologies in destinations, and people with disabilities can travel independently and easily. For example, it's possible to direct, guide and inform people with disabilities by using smart technologies in a museum. Audio guide service can be provided by scanning the QR code next to the works exhibited in the museum with a smartphone. It is possible to get information about the attractions and their accessibility features without any help from another person. Therefore, the information in these apps should be kept up-to-date, and the technological infrastructure that will increase the access of people with disabilities to smart technologies should be developed (Corréa & Gosling, 2020). People with disabilities increase their physical access by using smart apps to experience a more accessible travel experience.

RESEARCH METHODOLOGY

The aim of this study is to reveal the current accessible tourism applications in smart destinations with the example of Breda city. Breda is a city in the North Barabant province of the Netherlands. Its population is 184.069 in 2020 (European Commission, 2021). The Breda city, which can be described as a typical Dutch city, draws attention with its historical structure bearing the traces of the Middle Ages. Since the middle of the 20th century, this city has developed with its initiatives in sustainability and technology. Aiming to become a climate-neutral city, Breda gives importance to the use of technology in transportation and other services. In addition, it is aimed to use transportation systems more effectively in the city to shorten transportation times and increase people's mobility (Ron Bos & Temme, 2014). Today, Breda strives to be modern, high-tech and cultural city. Industrial development based on high-tech and creative technology continues rapidly in the city. For this reason, Breda promotes itself as the "game valley" and encourage the "game designers" of the future. Along with developing industries such as textiles, chocolate, beer and fruit products, logistics services, knowledge and the hospitality industry are some of the industries desired to be developed in Breda (van Heelsum, 2009). Therefore, Breda can be described as a city where the development of service industries such as tourism, as well as the manufacturing industry, is aimed.

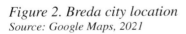

Figure 2. Breda city location
Source: Google Maps, 2021

Accessible Tourism Experiences in Smart Destinations

Services in the Breda city are tried to be provided with the support of high-tech technology. Environmentally friendly trains are used extensively in transportation. In addition to alternatives such as buses and taxis, the railway is also an important transportation vehicle both within the city and nearby cities and rural areas. Local people and tourists can benefit from this transportation network together. Electric cars and taxis draw attention as sustainable, environmentally friendly, and modern technology equipped transportation vehicles. There are technologies such as easy payment systems (public transport chip cards) and information screens in transportation vehicles (Ministry of Transport, Public Works and Water Management, 2010). In Breda city, cutting-edge technology is used in street lighting as well as transportation vehicles. Breda is the first city in Europe to use remote-controlled colour-changing LED technology for street lighting. These streetlights can change into any colour and create a different ambience. This technology enables more efficient energy savings. In addition, smart guide applications are developed to support tourists' participation in various activities such as art and festivals (European Union, 2019).

In recent years, initiatives to enhance accessibility have increased rapidly in Breda. Accessibility of public spaces and transportation is seen as a strategic goal for Breda. In order to achieve this goal, city and transportation planning should be handled together with an interdisciplinary approach. The Breda city uses accessibility as part of its development process within the Strategic Urban Development Plan "Breda 2030". Breda considers accessibility as an important factor that increases the quality and attractiveness of the destination (Bos, Straatemeier, & Temme, 2014). Ensuring more accessible services to both people with disabilities and tourists makes the Breda stand out among other destinations. Breda won the 2019 Access City Award for its consistent and ongoing projects on accessibility. Therefore, Breda is cited as a source of inspiration for other cities (Figg, 2018). The Breda destination also won the 2020 European Capital of Smart Tourism award in the accessibility category. The Breda city, which uses smart technologies in the best way to increase both the life quality and accessibility, is shown among the exemplary smart destinations of the future (European Commission, 2021). In this city, important initiatives have been taken to increase accessibility through digitalisation in recent years, especially the projects on accessible information, the use of smart technologies and the philosophy of accessibility for all bring the Breda city to the fore in this field (Gemeente Breda, 2021). In addition, Breda received the 2019 "Access City Award" and the 2020 "European Capital of Smart Tourism" award in the accessibility category (European Commision, 2021). These factors were effective in choosing Breda city as an exemplary smart destination in this study.

Figure 3. Case study research process
Source: Runeson & Höst, 2009

Case Study is shown as an ideal method for developing theory, examining situations, events in depth, evaluating and revealing the current situation (Baxter & Jack, 2008). In addition, case studies provide theoretical inferences by limiting the subjects to a single sample (George & Bennett, 2005). Within the scope of the case study, document analysis technique was used as a data collection tool in this research. All types of documents, such as books, records, advertisements, handbooks, brochures, newspapers, maps, projects, pictures, electronic resources, websites and news, can be used for data collection in document analysis technique. It is stated that document analysis is frequently used in case studies and a very useful method in this type of research (Bowen, 2009). Documents containing information about the Breda city's structure, destination characteristics and smart applications were collected by examining the websites of the municipality, destination management organisation, private organisations, news and online EU reports. In addition, detailed information about the Breda city was obtained by analysing existing data on accessible smart web and mobile applications and projects. Then, the collected large amount of text/visual data were analysed by the content analysis method.

The collected data were coded, categorised and summarised in a table as Breda city accessible applications. Based on the literature review and collected data, accessible applications in the Breda city are defined as website accessibility, shops accessibility, city accessibility, accommodation accessibility, public transportation accessibility, destination accessibility, event accessibility and trip accessibility. Then, the data were coded according to predetermined categories. Accessible applications in the Breda city, accessible points, users and accessible features/technologies are summarised in a table and then given detailed information about these. In this research, an intercoder agreement test was performed to ensure data coding reliability. The same data was re-coded in NVİVO 12 software by another academician who carried out academic studies about this research subject. The intercoder agreement rate was calculated as 96.1% in this research. 80% and above agreement rate considered as perfect agreement (O'Connor & Joffe, 2020).

RESEARCH FINDINGS

In this part of the study, the findings obtained from the analysis of the collected data are included. In addition, by examining the Breda municipality and destination website, text news, reports, projects and other related online information sources, findings were obtained about the existing accessible smart applications in the Breda destination. It is noteworthy that smart technology-supported solutions have been developed for individuals such as physically people with disabilities, the elderly, pregnant women and families with children. Thus, services offered in the city have become inclusive for everyone.

Table 2 shows the areas where accessible experiences occur in the Breda destination, accessible features and applications, users who benefit from these applications and accessibility types. The collected data is coded under different accessibility types. Findings of different accessibility types and applications are given in sub-headings detailed.

Table 2. Breda city accessible applications

Accessible Points	Users	Accessible Features/Technologies	Type of Accessibility
https://www.breda.nl/, www.welkominbreda.nl, etc.	Visually, Sensory, Hearing Impaired People, Visitors	Understandable, Readable for Everyone, Multiple Language and Communication Options	Website Accessibility
Shops	Individuals with Physical Disability, Limited Mobility (Family with Child, Pregnants, Elderly) Visitors	Mobile Pin Machine for Contactless and Easy Payment	Shops Accessibility
Streets	Inhabitants, Tourists, Visitors with Disabilities	Remote Control, Color Changing LED Technology, More Illuminated and Visible for Visually Impaired	City Accessibility
Hotels	Visitors with Disabilities	Sensor Door	Accommodation Accessibility
Transportation Stations	Visually Impaired People	Audio Guide, Navigation and City Map Apps	Public Transportation Accessibility
Destination	Wheelchair Users, Hearing Impaired Visitors	Virtual Reality City Tour, Pre-Experience of Destination	Destination Accessibility
Events	Limited Mobility Tourists	Mobile Apps, Live-Stream Event Videos	Event Accessibility
Transportation Vehicles	Limited Mobility Tourists, Wheelchairs Users	Trip Organiser Tools (Website, Mobile Apps)	Trip Accessibility

(Source: own elaboration)

Website Accessibility

The Breda municipality and destination websites are fully accessible to local residents (including sensory impairments). These websites have also been made accessible to foreign visitors using the English language option. In addition to visual communication, the accessibility of websites is increased with audio communication options for people with disabilities. To increase the accessibility of the website, special software is used, periodic controls are made, and training is given to the employees, website editors on accessibility. Text, image and video format information are used to be more accessible for everyone. The Breda municipality cooperates with people with disabilities and visitors to quickly resolve website accessibility problems reported through various communication channels. The findings obtained from the content analysis reveal that more than 25 websites in the Breda destination are designed to be fully accessible for people with disabilities. Website accessibility guidelines are implemented on all websites to ensure accessibility and provide service quality.

Shops Accessibility

As a result of the content analysis, one of the tourism units in which accessible smart applications are used in the Breda destination has been identified as stores and shopping centres. The mobile pin machine which can be found in most stores or shopping centres in the Breda city is a technology that enables physically disabled people to make contactless payments via their mobile phones. This technology can be used during payment transactions at the reception in hotels. These technologies increase the access of tourists with disabilities visiting the city to the services offered (Liere, 2019). In the Breda destination, such technologies are used to increase easy payment options and store accessibility for families with children, pregnant, and the elderly with limited mobility.

City Accessibility

In the Breda city, LED lighting and animations are used to illuminate iconic structures (such as the castle of Breda). In addition, smart lighting technologies are also used on the streets. So, remote-controlled, colour-changing LED streetlights to increase the brightness of the city. Especially for visually impaired individuals, this technology makes nighttime accessibility of the city possible. However, various tourist structures in the city are illuminated, creating a different ambience and attractiveness.

Accommodation Accessibility

Some hotel businesses in the Breda city have door cameras with sensors at the entrances for people with disabilities, and the door opens automatically (Yates, 2019). So, it is ensured that hotel businesses are more accessible for physically, visually impaired people or the elderly.

Public Transportation Accessibility

Navigation applications developed for visually impaired individuals function as audio guides at many points from the city centre to transportation stations (Yates, 2019). All bus stops and train stations in the Breda have digital information and mobile navigation apps. By using these technologies, accessible information about transportation and the city environment is offered to the tourists. People with disabilities are informed about the accessible services and tourist attraction points (European Commission, 2019). Within the city and intercity bus network (Flix Bus), the train network (NS website) are the Breda destination's online travel and transportation systems. Direct transportation from Breda to other European cities is provided by train and road. For this, there are international trip planner applications (Figure 4).

Destination Accessibility

One of the technologies used in the Breda destination is virtual reality. Before travelling, it is possible to have a pre-experience about Breda and to visit attractive places in a virtual environment. It is possible to see hard-to-reach places while travelling in the city by using this technology. Virtual reality technology enhances the travel experiences of people with physical disabilities, wheelchair users, the visually impaired and other people with disabilities (Netherlands, 2021). It will be possible to visit museums and rural areas and even visit other capitals of Europe through virtual reality centres planned to be established in different places of the city. Thus, the entire city and region will be accessible to tourists.

Accessible Tourism Experiences in Smart Destinations

Figure 4. nsinternational.com International trip planner
Source: www.nsinternational.com/

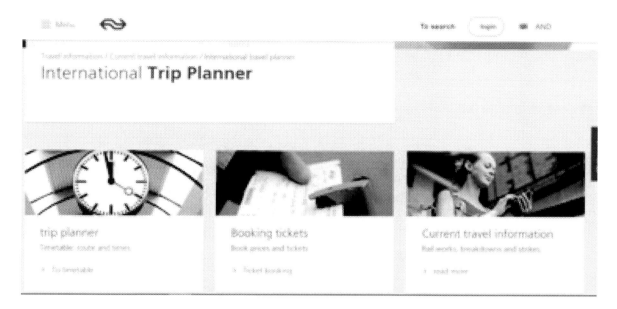

Event Accessibility

This research shows that various technologies are used to increase accessibility to events organised in the Breda destination. Mobile applications and smart screens where all activities and events in the city can be followed live are planned to increase the interaction between the tourist and the destination. This increasing interaction through IoT, sensors and smart applications causes an increase in the amount of big data. By using this big data, the Breda destination management organisation will be able to develop more beneficial projects for tourists (Gemeente Breda, 2021). Furthermore, these accessible applications are used by people with disabilities, enabling them to follow and actively participate in tourism activities in the city.

Trip Accessibility

It's aimed to enhance the smart tourism experiences of people with disabilities with accessible digital route maps in Breda (Cleverciti, 2021). The destination website developed for Breda (https://www.welkominbreda.nl/visit-breda) contains guiding information about transportation alternatives for visitors. Tourists can plan their transportation through websites such as https://9292.nl/, http://www.flixbus.nl/ and https://www.ns.nl/. People with disabilities can plan their travels by getting information about accessible transportation opportunities through these websites. Accessible services for people with disabilities can be provided through these websites. For example, by using the 9292 planner, accessible stops and stations can be searched, and assistive vehicles for transportation can be provided. Thus, by choosing the best transportation vehicle and route, they can provide an accessible transportation experience to the entire city. Besides the website, the 9292 mobile applications can also be used.

Figure 5. 9292 Website
Source: 9292.nl/

E-Scooters (mopeds) are considered assistive vehicles that facilitate the trip of people with disabilities in Breda city. There are mobile applications developed for the rent these vehicles. One of them is the Go Sharing mobile app. By using this app, people can check the availability of mopeds in their region and rent them by making the payment. So, an easy and more accessible destination experience is created. Another mobile app is Breda SmartGuide. In this app, information about the Breda destination is given, and guidance service is provided. This app, which is suitable for people with disabilities, also has an audio guide and navigation features.

SOLUTIONS AND RECOMMENDATIONS

When the globally changing tourist profile is examined, it is noteworthy that there is an increase in the participation of people with disabilities in tourism. One billion people around the world live with some form of disability. They travel as at least two or three people and spend more than tourists without any disabilities. In addition to people with disabilities, the elderly, families with children, pregnant women, etc. recognised among people with special access needs (UNWTO, 2020). Therefore, the accessible tourism market creates great tourism potential for destinations around the world. Destinations that are trying to get more share from this market give more importance to accessibility today. It is observed that the practices aimed at increasing the accessibility of the destination have changed over time and the efficiency of the technology has increased as well.

Developing assistive and facilitating applications for the travel of people with disabilities draws attention among the most important strategies adopted by destinations. Today, it is seen that the developing ICTs are actively used in transportation within the destination and surrounding cities. Eichhorn and Buhalis (2011) state that lack of knowledge is an important travel limiting factor for people with disabilities. Here, technology is shown as the most important information source for people with disabilities. In recent years, rapidly developing smart technologies have been used effectively for accessibility in tourism. Accessibility is emerging as the most important driving force in the development of smart destinations today (Porto, Rucci and Ciaschi, 2018). The findings of this research reveal that Breda effectively uses smart technologies in destination information and transportation. Various mobile applications and destination websites are accessible for people with disabilities in Breda. However, the information obtained from these sources functions as an assistive tool in the travels of tourists with disabilities. It is possible to access information about Breda's accessible places and services from the website and mobile applications. Rebstock (2017) states that increasing accessibility in transportation will positively affect the destination economy and draw attention to the role of transportation systems in the development of accessible tourism. Therefore, increasing the accessibility of transportation by using smart technologies is an important factor for the economic development of the Breda destination.

One of the remarkable findings in this research is that virtual reality, one of the technologies that have become widespread recently, is used to increase accessibility in the Breda destination. Virtual reality technology has the feature of enriching the travel experiences of tourists with limited mobility and providing pre-experience (Lee & Kim, 2021). Virtual reality is used to virtually visit the hard-to-reach points of Breda for people with disabilities. In addition, smart LED lighting systems located at different points in Breda both create a different ambience in the city and help visually impaired individuals. Accessible digital route maps developed for people with disabilities are another example of smart technology that creates an accessible tourism experience in the Breda destination. Technologies such as accessible tour planner websites, applications, audio guides, sensors, contactless and easy payment mobile pin machines have been identified in this research results as applications that make Breda an accessible smart destination. For this reason, Breda is shown as a leading city and source of inspiration in the accessibility category for other cities in Europe (Figg, 2018). Other destinations in Europe and worldwide can use smart technologies in their own cities by examining applications in Breda. Thus, it will be possible to make all destinations more accessible for people with disabilities. As a result of these developments in accessibility, the number of tourists, economic income and value of the destinations will be increased.

DISCUSSION AND CONCLUSION

The use of smart technologies to increase accessibility in destinations is among the very popular innovations in recent years. Successful implementation of this requires the development of strong smart city infrastructure first. This requires cooperation between all tourism stakeholders in the destination. In addition to the physical arrangements in the city (sidewalks, ramps, walking paths, etc.), Breda has developed smart technologies for the use of people with disabilities and enabled tourists with disabilities to benefit from this. The working group that was formed with the participation of the municipality, central government, tourism organisations, businesses and people with disabilities has an important role in Breda's being an inspiring accessible smart destination. From these findings, it is possible to conclude that wide participation of all stakeholders in the city is required to be successful in becoming an accessible smart destination. Destination accessibility can be increased with applications specific to the needs of each type of person with disabilities. Thus, the tourism experiences of people with disabilities in the destination will be enriched.

The Breda city can be shown as an important model for other cities in developing accessible smart destination applications. However, analysing and developing the shortcomings is important for its sustainability. The absence of any foreign language options other than English on the Breda municipality and destination website can be considered one of the major shortcomings limiting accessibility. Rodrìguez Vázquez and O'Brien (2017) emphasise the importance of making websites accessible to everyone, regardless of their (dis)abilities. For this reason, increasing language options on Breda destination websites can be considered as a critical factor in terms of accessibility. In addition, more attention should be paid to visual and auditory applications on these websites for visually and hearing-impaired individuals. Accessibility of website content is shown as an important determinant in the travel planning and destination preferences of people with disabilities (Buhalis & Michopoulou, 2011; Vila, González, & Darcy, 2018). An inclusive website design can be created by using text alternatives, the content presented in different ways, navigating and assistive accessible applications on destination websites.

Smart applications such as mobile pin machines, hotel door cameras with sensors, IoT applications in the event centres emerge as a result of this research as distinguishing features of the Breda from other competing destinations. In order for Breda to continue its success as the best accessible smart destination in Europe, it needs to constantly follow both its competitors and the developments in technology. By examining the smart applications of competing destinations, it may be possible for Breda to overcome its shortcomings. For example, in destinations such as Copenhagen, Lyon, Ljubljana, Tallinn, smart city cards are used in public transportation and to enter tourist attractions. In addition, guidance services can also be provided for people with disabilities with these applications (SmartTourismCapital.eu). By using such smart applications, it will also be possible to increase the public transportation, trip and event accessibility in the Breda destination. Smart technologies are considered an important assistive tool in enhancing the tourism experience of people with disabilities (Huang & Lau, 2020). Therefore, up-to-date smart technologies should be adopted and offered to tourists with disabilities to create better and accessible tourism experiences in destinations.

Enriching the experiences of tourists with disabilities in the destination using smart technologies can be considered a necessity to gain a competitive advantage in the international arena. People with disabilities who have significant tourism potential throughout the world are a key factor for destinations that strive to increase tourism demand and income. In this chapter, successful applications in the Breda city are examined, and accessible smart destination applications that can be an example for other destinations are defined. When considering the future project plans, it is predicted that the Breda city will continue its development towards being a smarter destination. Smart destinations developed using smart city infrastructure can be shown as one of the most important experience providers of the 21st century for accessible tourism.

FUTURE RESEARCH DIRECTIONS

The ongoing developments in smart technologies also increase the effects of this development on tourism. Destinations are trying to increase their accessibility and number of tourists by using smart technologies. For this purpose, it is important to investigate the smart technologies' effectiveness, eliminate the existing deficiencies, and create more accessible destinations. In future research, primary data can be obtained by using the method of interviewing destination management organisations, tourism managers and tourists with disabilities. Next time, a study can be conducted on destination accessibility and the role of smart technologies with a different perspective. Relevant literature and theoretical infrastructure can be developed by obtaining in-depth information.

In addition to destinations, accessible smart applications in main tourism businesses (hotel, restaurant, travel agency, etc.) and other tourism service providers (shops, cafes, recreation centres, etc.) can also be examined. Satisfaction with accessible smart applications can be measured by collecting data from tourists with disabilities in these businesses by survey technique. Determining the effect of accessible smart applications on visiting the business or destination can be considered research that will contribute to the scientific literature.

REFERENCES

2021). Retrieved from https://9292.nl

AccessMap. (2021). *Access map application for Seattle city*. Retrieved from https://www.accessmap.io/?region=wa.seattle&lon=-122.3381214&lat=47.6069591&z=14.5

Allan, M. (2015). Accessible tourism in Jordan: Travel constrains and motivations. *European Journal of Tourism Research, 10*, 109–119.

Altinay, Z., Saner, T., Bahçelerli, N. M., & Altinay, F. (2016). The role of social media tools: Accessible tourism for disabled citizens. *Journal of Educational Technology & Society, 19*(1), 89–99.

Baggio, R., Micera, R., & Chiappa, G. D. (2020). Smart tourism destinations: A critical reflection. *Journal of Hospitality and Tourism Technology, 11*(3), 559–574.

Baxter, P., & Jack, S. (2008). Qualitative case study methodology: Study design and implementation for novice researchers. *Qualitative Report, 13*(4), 544–559.

Bos, R., Straatemeier, T., & Temme, R. (2014). Joint accessibility design: Strategic urban development plan Breda 2030. *Citta 7th Annual Conference on Planning Research: Bridging the Implementation Gap of Accessibility Instruments and Planning Support Systems*.

Bowen, G. A. (2009). Document analysis as a qualitative research method. *Qualitative Research Journal, 9*(2), 27–40.

Bowtell, J. (2015). Assessing the value and market attractiveness of the accessible tourism industry in Europe: A focus on major travel and leisure companies. *Journal of Tourism Futures, 1*(3), 203–222.

Breda. (2021a). *Public transport to and in Breda*. Retrieved from https://www.welkominbreda.nl/visit-breda/public-transport-to-and-in-breda

Breda. (2021b). Retrieved from https://tr.wikipedia.org/wiki/Breda

Buhalis, D., & Amaranggana, A. (2014). Smart tourism destinations. In Z. Xiang & I. Tussyadiah (Eds.), *Information and communication technologies in tourism* (pp. 553–564). Springer. doi:10.1007/978-3-319-03973-2_40

Buhalis, D., & Michopoulou, E. (2011). Information-enabled tourism destination marketing: Addressing the accessibility market. *Current Issues in Tourism, 14*(2), 145-168.

Cassia, F., Castellani, P., Rossato, C., & Baccarani, C. (2021). Finding a way towards high-quality, accessible tourism: The role of digital ecosystems. *The TQM Journal, 33*(1), 205–221.

Cimbaljevìc, M., Stankov, U., & Pavluković, V. (2019). Going beyond the traditional destination competitiveness: Reflections on a smart destination in the current research. *Current Issues in Tourism, 22*(20), 2472–2477.

Cleverciti. (2021). *9 European smart tourism destinations to watch and learn from*. Retrieved from https://www.cleverciti.com/en/resources/blog/9-european-smart-tourism-destinations-to-watch-and-learn-from

Corréa, S. C. H., & Gosling, M. S. (2020). Travelers' perception of smart tourism experiences in smart tourism destinations. *Tourism Planning & Development*. doi:10.1080/21568316.2020.1798689

Darcy, S., Cameron, B., & Pegg, S. (2010). Accessible tourism and sustainability: A discussion and case study. *Journal of Sustainable Tourism, 18*(4), 515–537.

Darcy, S., McKercher, B., & Schweinsberg, S. (2020). From tourism and disability to accessible tourism: A perspective article. *Tourism Review, 75*(1), 140–144.

Devile, E., & Kastenholz, E. (2018). Accessible tourism experiences: The voice of people with visual disabilities. *Journal of Policy Research in Tourism, Leisure & Events, 10*(3), 265–285.

Eichhorn, V., & Buhalis, D. (2011). Accessibility: A key objective for the tourism industry. In D. Buhalis & S. Darc (Eds.), *Accessible tourism: Concepts and issues* (pp. 46–61). Channel View Publications.

ENAT-European Network Accessible Tourism. (2020). *Accessibility at smart tourism destinations: 2nd edition of the TUR4all congress* (Webinar series). Retrieved from https://www.accessibletourism.org/?i=enat.en.events.2188

Eremia, M., Toma, L., & Sanduleac, M. (2017). The smart city concept in the 21st century. *Procedia Engineering, 181*, 12–19.

European Capitals of Smart Tourism. (2021). Retrieved from https://smarttourismcapital.eu/cities-2020-winners/

European Commission. (2019). *Access city award 2019 examples of best practice in making EU cities more accessible*. Retrieved from https://ec.europa.eu/social/main.jsp?catId=1141

European Commission. (2021a). *Compendium of best practices 2020*. Retrieved from https://smart-tourism-capital.ec.europa.eu/best-practices_en

European Commission. (2021b). *Noord-Brabant*. Retrieved from https://ec.europa.eu/growth/tools-databases/regional-innovation-monitor/base-profile/noord-brabant

European Commission. (2021c). *Winners of the European capitals of smart tourism 2020 competition*. Retrieved from https://smart-tourism-capital.ec.europa.eu/competition-winners-2020_en

European Union. (2019). *Compendium of best practices "2019 European capital of smart tourism competition"*. Retrieved from https://smarttourismcapital.eu/wp-content/uploads/2019/07/Compendium_2019_FINAL.pdf

Femenia-Serra, F., Neuhofer, B., & Ivars-Baidal, J. (2019). Towards a conceptualisation of smart tourists and their role within the smart destination scenario. *Service Industries Journal*, *39*(2), 109–133.

Ferri, M. A. (2014). A business model for accessible tourism. In L. Aiello (Ed.), *Handbook of research on management of cultural products: E-Relationship marketing and accessibility perspectives* (pp. 287–302). IGI Global. doi:10.4018/978-1-4666-5007-7.ch014

Figg, H. (2018). *Breda wins 2019 access city award for making the city more accessible to citizens with disabilities*. Retrieved from https://www.eltis.org/discover/news/breda-wins-2019-access-city-award-making-city-more-accessible-citizens-disabilities

Frazier, J., & Touchet, T. (2012). *Transforming the city of New York new platform for public-private cooperation ushers in smart cities of the future*. Retrieved from https://www.cisco.com/c/dam/en_us/about/ac79/docs/ps/motm/City-24x7_PoV.pdf

Gemeente Breda. (2021a). *Bredata masterplan digitalisation Breda*. Retrieved from https://smartcity-breda.com/storage/2020/11/0178_20-BREDATA_masterplan_ENG_V2_internet.pdf

Gemeente Breda. (2021b). Retrieved from https://www.breda.nl/en

George, A. L., & Bennett, A. (2005). *Case studies and theory development in the social sciences*. MIT Press.

Gillovic, B., & McIntosh, A. (2020). Accessibility and inclusive tourism development: Current state and future agenda. *Sustainability*, *12*, 1–15.

Gomes, E. L., Gândara, J. M., & Ivars-Baidal, J. A. (2017). Is it important to be a smart tourism destination: Public managers' understanding of destinations in the state of Paraná. *Brazilian Journal of Tourism Research*, *11*(3), 503–536.

Google Maps. (2021). *Breda*. Retrieved from https://www.google.nl/maps/place/Breda,+Hollanda/

Gretzel, U., & Koo, C. (2021). Smart tourism cities: A duality of place where technology supports the convergence of touristic and residential experiences. *Asia Pacific Journal of Tourism Research*, *26*(4), 352–364.

Gretzel, U., Sigala, M., Xiang, Z., & Koo, C. (2015). Smart tourism: Foundations and developments. *Electronic Markets*, *25*, 179–188.

Habeeb, N. J., & Weli, S. T. (2020). Relationship of smart cities and smart tourism: An overview. *HighTech and Innovation Journal*, *1*(4), 194–202.

Holnicki-Szulc, J., Motylewski, J., & Kolakowski, P. (2008). Introduction to smart technologies. In J. Holnicki-Szulc (Ed.), *Smart technologies for safety engineering* (pp. 1–9). John Wiley & Sons, Ltd.

Huang, L., & Lau, N. (2020). Enhancing the smart tourism experience for people with visual impairments by gamified application approach through needs analysis in Hong Kong. *Sustainability*, *12*, 1–27.

Jasrotia, A., & Gangotia, A. (2018). Smart cities to smart tourism destinations: A review paper. *Journal of Tourism Intelligence and Smartness*, *1*(1), 47–56.

Korngold, D., Lemos, M., & Rohwer, M. (2017). *Smart cities for all: A vision for an inclusive, accessible, urban future*. Retrieved from https://g3ict.org/publication/smart-cities-for-all-a-vision-for-an-inclusive-accessible-urban-future#:~:text

Lee, S. J. (2017). A review of audio guides in the era of smart tourism. *Information Systems Frontiers*, *19*, 705–715.

Lee, W., & Kim, Y. H. (2021). Does VR tourism enhance users' experience? *Sustainability*, *13*, 806.

Liberato, P., Alen, E., & Liberato, D. (2018). Smart tourism destination triggers consumer experience: The case of Porto. *European Journal of Management and Business Economics*, *27*(1), 6–25.

Liberato, P., Alén-González, E., & Liberato, D. (2018). Digital technology in a smart tourism destination: The case of Porto. *Journal of Urban Technology*, *25*(1), 75–97.

Liere, L. (2019). *Access city award 2019: Quick wins from Breda, the Netherlands*. Retrieved from https://nexttourismgeneration.eu/access-city-award-2019-quick-wins-from-breda-the-netherlands/

Marrasco, A., & Balbi, B. (2019). Designing accessible experiences for heritage visitors through virtual reality. *Ereview of Tourism Research*, *17*(3), 426–443.

Mayordomo-Martìnez, D., Sánchez-Aarnoutse, J.-C., Carrillo-de-Gea, J. M., Garcìa-Berná, J. A., Fernández-Alemán, J. L., & Garcìa-Mateos, G. (2019). Design and development of a mobile app for accessible beach tourism information for people with disabilities. *International Journal of Environmental Research and Public Health*, *16*, 1–16.

Meskele, A. T., Woreta, S. L., & Weldesenbet, E. G. (2018). Accessible tourism challenges and development issues in tourist facilities and attraction sites of the Amhara region world heritage sites, Ethiopia. *International Journal of Hospitality and Tourism Systems*, *11*(1), 26–37.

Michopoulou, E., Darcy, S., Ambrose, I., & Buhalis, D. (2015). Accessible tourism futures: The world we dream to live in and the opportunites we hope to have. *Journal of Tourism Futures*, *1*(3), 179–188.

Ministry of Transport, Public Works and Water Management. (2010). *Public transport in Netherlands*. Retrieved from https://www.emta.com/IMG/pdf/brochure.pdf

Mira, M. R., Moura, A., & Breda, Z. (2016). Destination competitiveness and competitiveness indicators: Illustration of the Portuguese reality. *Tékhne – Review of Applied Management Studies*, *14*, 90–103.

Mollá-Sirvent, R. A., Mora, H., Gilart-Iglesias, V., Pèrez-delHolyo, R., & Andùjar-Motonya, M. D. (2018). Accessbility index for smart cities. *Proceedings*, *2*, 1–6.

Nam, T., & Pardo, T. A. (2011). Conceptualising smart city with dimensions of technology, people, and institutions. *The Proceedings of the 12th Annual International Conference on Digital Government Research*.

Netherlands. (2021). *Virtual ways to experience the Netherlands*. Retrieved from https://www.holland.com/global/tourism/travel-inspiration/virtual-ways-to-experience-the-netherlands.htm

Neto, A. Q., Dimmock, K., Lohmann, G., & Scott, N. (2020). Destination competitiveness: How does travel experience influence choice? *Current Issues in Tourism*, *23*(13), 1673–1687.

Neto, J. S. O. (2018). *Inclusive smart cities: Theory and tools to improve the experience of people with disabilities in urban spaces*. Universite Paris Saclay (COmUE). Universidade de Sao Paulo.

Neuhofer, B., Buhalis, D., & Ladkin, D. (2012). Conceptualising technology enhanced destination experiences. *Journal of Destination Marketing & Management*, *1*(1-2), 36–46.

O'Connor, C., & Joffe, H. (2020). Intercoder reliability in qualitative research: Debates and practical guidelines. *International Journal of Qualitative Methods*, *19*(1), 1–13.

OECD-Organisation for Economic Co-operation and Development. (2020). *Smart cities and inclusive growth*. Retrieved from https://www.oecd.org/cfe/cities/OECD_Policy_Paper_Smart_Cities_and_Inclusive_Growth.pdf

Pai, C.-K., Liu, Y., Kang, S., & Dai, A. (2020). The role of perceived smart tourism technology experience for tourist satisfaction, happiness and revisit intention. *Sustainability*, *12*, 1–14.

Porto, N., Rucci, A. C., & Ciaschi, M. (2018). Tourism accessibility competitiveness. A regional approach for Latin American countries. *Journal of Regional Research*, *42*, 75–91.

Rebstock, M. (2017). *Economic benefits of improved accessibility to transport systems and the role of transport in fostering tourism for all*. Retrieved from https://www.itf-oecd.org/sites/default/files/docs/improved-accessibility-fostering-tourism-for-all.pdf

Ribeiro, F. R., Silva, A., Barbosa, F., Silva, A. P., & Metrōlho, J. C. (2018). Mobile applications for accessible tourism: Overview, challenges and a proposed platform. *Information Technology & Tourism*, *19*, 29–59.

Rodrigues, J. M. F., Cardoso, P. J. S., Monteiro, J., & Ramos, C. M. Q. (2020). Augmented intelligence: Leverage smart systems. In J. Rodrigues, P. Cardoso, J. Monteiro, & C. Ramos (Eds.), *Smart systems design, applications, and challenges* (pp. 1–22). IGI Global. doi:10.4018/978-1-7998-2112-0

Rodrìguez Vázquez, S., & O'Brien, S. (2017). Bringing accessibility into the multilingual web production chain. In M. Antona, & C. Stephanidis (Eds.), *International Conference of Universal Access in Human-Computer Interaction: Design and Development Approaches and Methods* (pp. 238-257). Springer.

Ron Bos, M. S., & Temme, R. (2014). A roadmap towards sustainable mobility in Breda. *Transportation Research Procedia*, *4*, 103–115.

Runeson, P., & Höst, M. (2009). Guidelines for conducting and reporting case study research in software engineering. *Empirical Software Engineering*, *14*(2), 131–164.

Sabou, G.-C., & Maiorescu, I. (2020). The challenges of smart tourism: A case of Bucharest. *Sciendo-Studia Universitatis Economics Series*, *30*(2), 70–82.

Sambhanthan, A., & Good, A. (2013). A second life based virtual community model for enhancing tourism destination accessibility in developing countries. *International Journal of Collaborative Enterprise*, *3*(4), 269–286.

Silverio-Fernández, M., Renukappa, S., & Suresh, S. (2018). What is a smart device? A Conceptualisation within the paradigm of the Internet of Things. *Visualisation in Engineering*, *6*(3), 1–10.

SmartTourismCapital. (2021). *Compendium of best practices*. Retrieved from https://smart-tourism-capital.ec.europa.eu/system/files/2021-04/Compendium_2020_FINAL.pdf#page=13

Stankov, U., & Gretzel, U. (2020). Tourism 4.0 technologies and tourist experiences. *Information Technology & Tourism, 22*, 477–488.

Suryotrisongko, H., Kusuma, R. C., & Ginardi, R. H. (2017). Four-hospitality: Friendly smart city design for disability. *Procedia Computer Science, 124*, 615–623.

The World Bank. (2021). *Disability inclusion*. Retrieved from https://www.worldbank.org/en/search?q=disability

UNWTO-World Tourism Organization. (2013). *Recommendations on accessible tourism*. Retrieved from https://www.e-unwto.org/doi/book/10.18111/9789284415984

UNWTO-World Tourism Organization. (2015). *Manual on accessible tourism for all*. Retrieved from https://www.e-unwto.org/doi/book/10.18111/9789284416585

UNWTO-World Tourism Organization. (2016). *Accessible tourism for all: An opportunity wthin our reach*. Retrieved from https://www.e-unwto.org/doi/pdf/10.18111/9789284417919

UNWTO-World Tourism Organization. (2020). *UNWTO inclusive recovery guide – Sociocultural impact of COVID-19 issue 1: Persons with disabilities*. Retrieved from https://www.e-unwto.org/doi/epdf/10.18111/9789284422296

van Heelsum, A. (2009). *Diversity policy in employment and service provision:– Case study: Breda, the Netherlands. European foundation for the improvement of living and working conditions*. Retrieved from http://www.eurofound.europa.eu/publications/htmlfiles/ef091714.htm

Vila, T. D., González, E. A., & Darcy, S. (2018). Website accessibility in the tourism industry: An analysis of official national tourism organisation websites around the world. *Disability and Rehabilitation, 40*(24), 2895–2906.

Vila, T. D., González, E. A., & Darcy, S. (2019). Accessible tourism online resources: A Northern European perspective. *Scandinavian Journal of Hospitality and Tourism, 19*(2), 140–156.

VisitEngland. (2021). *Destinations for all a guide to creating accessible destinations*. Retrieved from https://www.visitbritain.org/sites/default/files/vb-corporate/dmo_guide_final.pdf

Wan, C. K. B. (2018). Flourishing throught smart tourism: Experience patterns for co-designing technology mediated traveller experiences. *The Design Journal, 21*(1), 163–172.

Yates, E. (2019). *People aren't disabled, their city is: Inside Europe's most accessible city*. Retrieved from https://www.theguardian.com/cities/2019/may/28/people-arent-disabled-their-city-is-inside-europes-most-accessible-city

Yıldız, Z., & Bozyer, S. (2017). Erişilebilir turizm ve Türkiye'de erişilebilir turizmin geleceğine yönelik bir projeksiyon. *The First International Congress on Future of Tourism: Innovation, Entrepreneurship and Sustainability*.

ADDITIONAL READING

Gondos, B., & Narái, M. (2019). The opportunities in accessible tourism. *The USV Annals of Economics and Public Administration*, *19*(1), 48–57.

Lestari, N. S., Wiastuti, R. D., & Triana, I. (2019). An overview of accessible tourism information at Taman Mini Indonesia Indah Jakarta. *African Journal of Hospitality, Tourism and Leisure*, *8*(4), 1–11.

Machado, P. (2020). Accessible and inclusive tourism: Why it is so important for destination branding? *Worldwide Hospitality and Tourism Themes*, *12*(6), 719–723. doi:10.1108/WHATT-07-2020-0069

Moura, A. F. A., Kastenholz, E., & Pereira, A. M. S. (2018). Accessible tourism and its benefits for coping with stress. *Journal of Policy Research in Tourism, Leisure & Events*, *10*(3), 241–264. doi:10.1080/19407963.2017.1409750

Ribeiro, F. R., Silva, A., Barbosa, F., Silva, A. P., & Metrolho, J. C. (2018). Mobile applications for accessible tourism: Overview, challenges and a proposed platform. *Information Technology & Tourism*, *19*(1-4), 29–59. doi:10.100740558-018-0110-2

Rubio-Escuderos, L., Garcìa-Andreu, H., & Rosa, J. U. (2021). Accessible tourism: Origins, state of the art and future lines of research. *European Journal of Tourism Research*, *28*, 1–24.

Ryabev Anton, A., & Balandina Iryna, S. (2018). Several problems and prospects of development of accessible tourism and hotel economy in Ukraine. *Bìznes Ìnform*, *10*, 235–240.

Somnuxpong, S., & Wiwatwongwana, R. (2020). The ability to support accessible tourism in Chiang Mai, Thailand. *African Journal of Hospitality, Tourism and Leisure*, *9*(1), 1–16.

Vila, T. D., González, E. A., & Darcy, S. (2019). Accessible tourism online resources: A Northern European perspective. *Scandinavian Journal of Hospitality and Tourism*, *19*(2), 140–156. doi:10.1080/15022250.2018.1478325

Zsarnoczky, M. (2018). The future challenge of accessible tourism in the European Union. *Vadyba Journal of Management*, *33*(2), 39–43.

KEY TERMS AND DEFINITIONS

Accessible Destination: Tourist services offered in a destination are equally accessible for all (disabled and non-disabled).

Accessible Technology: Technologies offered to tourists with disabilities that make their holiday experiences easier and accessible.

Accessible Tourist Experience: Accessible experiences of tourists with disabilities before, during and post travel.

Smart City: It is a city model where smart technologies are used to increase the life quality of local people, improve and manage the services offered to them.

Smart Destination: It is the type of destination where tourist experiences and services are supported and developed with smart technologies such as mobile applications, IoT, artificial intelligence and big data.

Smart Technology: It is a new generation technology that increases the interaction between human-machine and machine-machine through an Internet connection.

Smart Tourism: It is a type of tourism where smart technologies (IoT, mobile apps, big data, etc.) are used by destinations, tourism enterprises, public and private organisations and tourists in tourism activities and services.

Smart Tourism Experience: It is the travel experience of tourists by actively using smart technologies during the entire holiday process.

Section 5
Authenticity

Chapter 16
Authenticity in Tourism Experiences:
Determinants and Dimensions

Sumedha Agarwal
https://orcid.org/0000-0002-9856-5661
Sharda University, India

Priya Singh
Jamia Millia Islamia, India

ABSTRACT

Authenticity is a term that emerged from the modern era. Travellers are demanding authentic, experientially oriented opportunities with more meaningful interactions with locals. Travellers of the new generation want to have meaningful travel which is sustainable as well as experiential. The rise of an experience economy that concentrates on entertainment, education, escapism, and esthetics has made authentic travel experiences more critical. The tourists are more aware of their needs and are motivated towards places that offer real experiences. The chapter aims to explain the concept of authenticity and relate it to the tourism and hospitality industry. The discussion around various kinds of authenticity as described in the literature has been done. A case study demonstrating authentic experiences in rural homestays has been included in the chapter. Further authentic experiences derived from various tourism and hospitality sectors like food, accommodation, and entertainment have been explained.

INTRODUCTION

Authentic experiences have been considered a significant motivational factor in the tourism and hospitality industry. Tourists travel to distant places in search of authentic experiences. With the rise of internet technologies, travellers are more knowledgeable than ever and are not satisfied with artificial and staged experiences. The literature has shown that tourists hunger for an authentic experience (Chhabra et al., 2013; MacCannell, 1973; Yeoman & McMahon-Beattie, 2006). Tourism, in this view, is seen as driven

DOI: 10.4018/978-1-7998-8775-1.ch016

Authenticity in Tourism Experiences

by curiosity to see how others live their lives. They want to move out of the 'tourist bubble' and experience the real side of the destination. Authentic experiences may include various components ranging from food, culture, architecture, customs, rituals, and people (Cohen, 1988; Paulauskaite et al., 2017; Sims, 2009; Vredeveld & Coulter, 2019).

However, there are many other types of authenticity, each with its respective definition or theoretical orientation: constructive authenticity, symbolic authenticity, existential authenticity, cool authenticity, activity-related authenticity, object/objectivist authenticity, emotional authenticity, performative authenticity, and so on (Aziz & Selamat, 2016; Holt, 2012; Jyotsna & Maurya, 2019; Kirillova et al., 2016). Authenticity in tourism has also been discussed by the researchers in the context of staged authenticity. MacCannell (1973) explained that the visitors might be satisfied with the staged authenticity as sometimes they are unable to experience the real side of the destination due to a large number of visitors present there. This is also coined as constructive authenticity. Staged authenticity, however, does not portray the true sense of the destination. The other kind of authenticity is where the tourists can experience or observe the 'local' life without any artificial staging and see the destination's real side and people. While having authentic experiences, the tourists often explore the 'new self' and get transformative feelings. This kind of authenticity is called existential authenticity. In existential, authenticity comprises the feelings, emotions, and perceptions of the tourists.

The issue of authenticity in tourism is widely discussed, with several researchers offering alternative views. (Reisinger & Steiner, 2006). It has been pointed out that the tourist experience's authenticity depends on tourists' choices, interests, and knowledge, and it can differ from one individual to the other. The understanding of authenticity also depends upon who is experiencing or consuming the service or product (Newman, 2019; Terziyska, 2012). But even after all the debate, a study of authentic experiences becomes necessary to understand the motivations of those tourists who choose destinations that are not so popular with the masses and travel extensively to observe culture and people or be alone in a natural setting. In this context, this chapter addresses the concept of authenticity in the tourism and hospitality industry. It presents several practical examples that deliver authentic tourism experiences while considering different dimensions of authenticity in the literature.

UNDERSTANDING AUTHENTICITY

Authenticity has been a debatable topic for more than four decades now, having a diversity of definitions. It is a "substantive-hungry word" with multiple meanings and cannot be interpreted unless its reference is known (Terziyska, 2012). Authenticity can be discussed under two fields: psychology and philosophy. According to Newman (2019), the psychological dimension of authenticity (or inauthenticity) have been shown to affect people's judgments and behaviour across a wide variety of domains like food, arts, music, etc. Authenticity served as a means to assess good and bad experiences of the people. The existential philosophers have presented interesting views on the subject of authenticity. (Heidegger 1962) linked authenticity with creativity. People must seek authenticity and should not get confused with what is given or claimed authentic (Baird and Kaufmann, 2008). Another philosopher stated that "authenticity depends on an individual finding authentic faith and becoming true to oneself and in order to obtain authenticity, one must face reality and derive one's estimation of existence" (Holt, 2012).

Authenticity belongs to one's perception of identifying what is real or genuine, and it raises the concerns of questioning 'what is' and 'what-is-not' authentic (MacCannell, 1973). This concept was first applied to the objects displayed in the museum so that the tourist visiting the museum could differentiate between the real and the false items (Trilling, 1972). Despite the multiplicity of the meanings attached to the term 'Authenticity', what is common and consistent across the literature is that authenticity enfolds to what is real or true.

Authenticity has multi-dimensions and is a subject of open discussion. It broadly relates to the idea of originality and feeling of association to any place, tradition or custom. The researchers give different arguments to derive the meaning of authenticity. Social constructivists associate authenticity with history and culture. The label of 'authenticity is often used for marketing cuisine, handicrafts, handlooms, fairs or festivals. This gives local people a sense of involvement in showcasing their indigenous customs and traditions (Wang, 1999). According to Cohen (2007), authenticity can be described in six unique ways, "authenticity as customary practice or long usage; authenticity as genuineness in the sense of an unaltered product; authenticity as sincerity when applied to relationships; authenticity as creativity with special relevance to cultural performances including dance and music; authenticity as the flow of life in the sense that there is no interference with the setting by the tourism industry or other managers, and authenticity as an unadulterated state, particularly of nature, such as in 'pristine tropical paradise.'

Authenticity plays a pivotal role in creating experiences for tourism and hospitality. It is identified as the critical variable in compounding tourist satisfaction. Today, tourists prefer to travel to places that offer them authentic experiences in food, culture, heritage, rituals and people. Each tourist has a different quest for authentic experiences. The diverse tourists' experience makes it difficult to generalise the concept of authenticity, and it is still the subject of debate for various stakeholders.

AUTHENTICITY IN TOURISM

Authenticity in tourism has captured a lot of interest and controversies indeed. The following three approaches are used to understand the concept of tourism authenticity: objectivism, constructivism and postmodernism.

The objectivist theory stated that authenticity is not linked with a tourist's perception but is associated with the toured object. This further led to the debate about the tourist motivation or what does tourist really seeks- authentic or inauthentic experiences. According to Boorstin (1961), the modern tourist did not look for authenticity and is aware of the pseudo-events that were inauthentic. Moreover, the ancient tourists were curious to experience authenticity, while today's tourist appreciates modernity and superficial experiences. On the contrary, (MacCannell, 1973)stated that "the prime tourist motivator is the quest for authenticity". The alienated tourist desires to visit virgin, primitive, and natural locations, giving the feeling of genuine and authenticity. On the other hand, today tourist appreciates local cuisines, culture, and handicraft to experience the originality of the destination.

Also, tourist experiences in terms of authenticity are yet another essential question that needs to be addressed. Tourists do not always receive authentic experiences. Whatever they witness is 'Staged Authenticity', an artificial space developed where tourists undergo false and inauthentic tourist experiences. A tourist is mainly exposed to the 'frontstage' area, which is devoid of ethnic experiences. Whereas the real authenticity lies in the 'backstage' of any destination, a place where the hosts live, this is not accessible to the tourist (MacCannell, 1973). The tourist exposure in various stages of Staged Authenticity is explained in table 1.

Authenticity in Tourism Experiences

Table 1. Staged authenticity

S.no	Stages	Tourist Exposure
1.	Stage 1	The front region which is accessible to tourists, and they try to go beyond that.
2.	Stage 2	The front region which resembles a back area to create an authentic atmosphere.
3.	Stage 3	The front region which is totally changed to give the impression of a back region.
4.	Stage 4	The back region which is accessible to tourists.
5.	Stage 5	The back region which is slightly changed and is accessible to tourists.
6.	Stage 6	The ultimate backstage, which the tourist never reaches.

(Source: MacCannell, 1973)

The constructivism approach reconsidered the object-tourist relation. As there is no objective or absolute truth, similarly, authenticity also does not permanently rely on the toured object and can be socially constructed. Different people can perceive different authenticity from the same objects based on their beliefs, knowledge, etc. Based on this ideology, the concept of 'Emergent Authenticity' was introduced. After that, it was believed that even a fake event could be gradually accepted as authentic (Cohen, 1988).

In contrast to objectivism and constructivism, postmodernism claimed that authenticity could be detached from any existing real or original object (Bruner, 1994). Authenticity can also be activity-based which refers to tourist experience and not to toured objects. Wang (1999) introduced a different perspective on authenticity – 'Existential Authenticity' –, which refers to "a potential existential state of being that is to be activated by tourist activities. Correspondingly, authentic experiences in tourism are to achieve this activated existential state of being within the liminal process of tourism. Existential authenticity can have nothing to do with the authenticity of toured objects". Tourists are more willing to travel to faraway places and create unique experiences for them. Experiential tourism has been the first choice of the tourists as he also gets a chance to spend some time in isolation and have a much deeper cultural experience. Tourists seek to experience some relief from the mundane and exhausting daily activities which often threaten to overtake their lives. Consequently, they travel to escape and experience existential Authenticity (Pearce and Moscardo, 1986).

Thus, authenticity in tourism is perceived as a tangible tourism destination and an existential tourist experience. Therefore, tourists interpret authenticity in a double dimension, i.e. object-based or existential authenticity, and the concept of authenticity may have different meanings depending on the destination characteristics.

TYPES OF AUTHENTICITY

Objective Authenticity

The term authenticity has been borrowed from the studies of the museum where the experts examined the objects and works of art and explained if they are actually worth the admiration they claim. In tourism, this concept has been extended to explain objective authenticity. The museum-linked definition has been applied to evaluate the perception of tourists for the tourism products. Tourism products or objects are said to possess the quality of authenticity (Fu & Wang, 2020). The various cultural products like arts, crafts, rituals, and customs are considered authentic by tourists because they are locally produced. However, there are certain specific criteria to measure objective authenticity, and it is assumed that tourists are unable to perceive or affect the level of authenticity. Thus, objective authenticity has an undistorted criterion to assess what is or is not genuine. A search for it is seen as a search for "originals" or "truths" that underpin the logic of modernity rather than genuineness (authentic) (Paulauskaite et al., 2017).

Constructive Authenticity

The constructive authenticity belongs to the constructivist view and views authenticity as a product of social construction. This concept is both subjective and negotiable. It represents an attribute projected onto toured objects by tourists or tourism suppliers based on their imagery, expectations, preferences, or powers. This concept explains that authenticity and inauthenticity are a result of individual perceptions and interpretations. All tourism experiences and judgements are personal in nature, so the basis of authenticity is both social and personal. Prentice (2001) explained that learned authenticity, which he defines as "constructed around the professional opinion of tour guides and other authorities," is a closely related idea. Tourists may refer to these 'experts" subjective assessments and revise their perceptions. As a result, authenticity is shaped by a variety of personal and social factors.

Existential Authenticity

Tourist activities trigger a potential existential state of being in the tourists called existential authenticity. Authentic tourism experiences, on the other hand, aim to reach this awakened existential state of being as a part of the core tourism process. As a result, existential authenticity may have little bearing on the authenticity of toured objects (Fu & Wang, 2020).

Wang (1999) divides existential authenticity into two subcategories: interpersonal and intrapersonal authenticity. He also believes that this newly established notion will be able to describe more travel experiences than before, as well as improve the illustrative quality of the "authenticity quest" depiction. Intrapersonal authenticity can be broken down into two parts. First, bodily feelings are the sensations of being on tours, such as recreation, relaxation, and rejuvenation. 'Self-making' is the second component of intrapersonal authenticity, suggesting that a break from societal norms and constraints, through tourism, can provide a structure in which individuals can act spontaneously, in line with their true feelings and authentic self. Interpersonal authenticity is the second dimension of existential authenticity, also composed of two parts – family ties and *communitas*. Wang (1999) explains that tourists are not just seeking an authentic Other or a 'true' self, but they are also in search of authenticity among and between their fellow travellers. Thus, the existentially authentic tourism experience is not only a result of seeing sights of socially constructed importance but also about collectively performing and experiencing the journey (Kirillova et al., 2016; Rickly-Boyd, 2013).

Table 2. Types of authenticity

Pseudo-etic approach	Object-related authenticity	• Objective authenticity refers to the authenticity of originals. • Correspondingly, authentic experiences in tourism are equated to an epistemological experience (cognition) of the authenticity of originals. • 'Constructive authenticity' refers to the authenticity projected onto toured objects by tourists or tourism producers in terms of their imagery, expectations, preferences, beliefs, powers and so on. There are various versions of authenticities regarding the same objects.
Pseudo-emic approach	Activity-related authenticity	• Correspondingly, authentic experiences in tourism and the authenticity of toured objects are constructive of one another. In this sense, the authenticity of toured objects is in fact symbolic authenticity. • Correspondingly, authentic experiences in tourism are to achieve this activate existential state of being within the luminal process of tourism. Existential authenticity may have nothing to do with the authenticity of toured objects.

(Source: adapted from Wang, 1999)

Experiential Authenticity

Experiential authenticity involves helping the individual or group define their sense of self, foster family or team dynamics', often implying a sense of creativity, imagining or creative understanding (Vredeveld & Coulter, 2019). This concept has been used concerning music, dance and even sport tourism experiences involving groups and individuals. Experiential authenticity is also a key issue of contention for tourism events and attractions, particularly cultural and arts heritage. Exploiting an attraction, event, place, site or person for tourism also necessitates a reflection on the rearticulating created (Ferrara, 1998). Although there has been much interest in authenticity in terms of consumption, there has been limited attention paid to the desire for experiential authenticity on the part of the producer of the experience (Pearce & Moscardo, 1986)

Staged Authenticity

Another popular concept used in tourism research is "staged authenticity". MacCannell (1973) proposed this concept in reaction to an increasing number of famous examples of local culture being commodified. He came up with this idea to show how tourists are frequently presented with experiences or performances that are purposefully staged or orchestrated to fit their expectations. As a result, they are often superficial, reflecting merely the "front stage" of a society. As a result, tourists seeking "the real" or "the genuine," i.e., access to the "backstage" of the local community in order to obtain a thorough understanding of culture, have to compromise with artificial and staged experiences. MacCannell (1973) states: "as cultural products lose their meaning for the locals, and as the need to present the tourist with ever more spectacular, exotic and titillating attractions grows, contrived cultural products are increasingly staged for tourists and decorated to look authentic".

When discussing MacCannell's concept of staged authenticity, Żemła and Siwek (2020) raised two points worth noting. First, a brief, few-hour visit to a specific area does not offer tourists a thorough picture of that destination's culture. Instead, tourists are presented with cultural events or performances that are glimpses of significant cultural characteristics that can be used to entertain and educate them. Furthermore, despite having money and being eager to pay for these experiences, tourists are not allowed to visit the "back region" unless local communities are willing to show them around. Thus, it should be up to local communities to decide what they think tourists should see and do. Second, despite criticism from "authenticity" supporters, staged authenticity has been a frequent practice in the tourism sector. Mass tourism and the associated activities have increased demand, and many destination communities are adopting the staged-experience approach to manage tourism activities more efficiently. Furthermore, according to (Cohen, 1988), tourists are aware of their participation in staged cultural events and embrace this condition because it allows them to feel protected while also satisfying their entertainment needs.

EXPERIENCING AUTHENTICITY IN VARIOUS TOURISM PRODUCTS

Authentic Food

Food and drink consumption play a key role in contributing to an overall tourist experience. Tourists enjoy indigenous food, particularly items of local or ethnic nature, which can be linked to their quest for authenticity. Consumers are involved in the process of "authentic-seeking" – a process which describes "consumers searching for authenticity from a range of products, services and experiences, and looking for it within themselves (Yeoman, Brass, & McMahon-Beattie, 2006). The range of products tourists tend to purchase, like food or drink, can be associated with existential authenticity, which provides an authentic sense to tourists post their purchase.

Furthermore, knowledge of the local, regional and national cuisine has become an interest for tourists. Local food can be an asset to integrated tourism development due to its ability to symbolise place and culture, provide a moral "feel good" factor associated with its consumption and enable visitors to experience a sense of connection to their destination both during and after their visit.

Food has always served as a means of cultural identification. While consuming a particular regional food, tourists can closely associate to the culture of that destination. Food provides an authentic representation of the culture, thus enriching the cultural tourism of that particular destination. The literature reveals the potential role of food in sustaining the regional identity and contributing to regional development (Steinmetz, 2010). Local food represents the geography, history, and people of a country and is used for marketing those destinations as it is one of the main sources of tourist attraction.

Food is an essential component of intangible heritage which gives a sense of authenticity to the tourist. Regional food depicts out the tradition, culture and rituals related to food served in that region. Local cuisine offers an authentic cultural experience by serving unique food, thus preserving the destination's intangible heritage. The culinary heritage of a destination gives a fair idea about the mentality, behaviour and character of the society and thus becomes relevant for creating a unique destination identity (Bessiere, 1998). The different rituals and eating traditions determine the tourists well appreciate the society's culture and this diversity in culture. An example of authentic food experiences can be studied through the case of Chowki Dhani in Rajasthan, India (Box 1).

Box 1. Chowki Dhaani Restaurant – Experiencing Food and Beyond!

> Chowki Dhaani Restaurant, Jaipur, has been one of the most innovative tourism projects offering an authentic taste of Rajasthani cuisine to its visitors. It is an ideal place to experience the traditional hospitality and culture of Rajasthan. The essence of authenticity in its food preparation makes it one of the most popular gastronomic destinations in India. Tourists visiting this place develop an understanding of the traditional ways of cooking Rajasthani cuisine and also get a chance to enjoy the ethnic food in the indigenous environment. This place also aims at preserving the local heritage of Rajasthan. The experience of having food while enjoying the live performances given by the folk artists is one of its kind. Chowki Dhaani restaurant is a culturally rich destination, and one must indeed visit the place for an authentic food experience.

Source: Trip Advisor (https://www.tripadvisor.in)

Authentic Accommodation

The search for authenticity has been recognised as an essential tourist motivation. Authenticity in tourism is established as a linkage between a tourist and toured objects/places/cultural elements/ individuals (MacCannell, 1973). However, authenticity cannot solely rely on places and things. Instead, it is also concerned with people's connection to the everyday world and the surrounding environment (Hall, 2007).

In the above context, peer-to-peer accommodation enables the tourists to live an authentic experience. It allows tourists to indulge in real and intimate social relations through intercultural encounters with the residents (Guttentag, 2015). The experience of being exposed to the "real" aesthetic environment adds to tourists' perception of authenticity. Moreover, the tourists accommodating in peer-to-peer accommodation are more likely to experience genuine interactions with guests/ residents belonging to different cross-cultures. Tourist experiences existential authenticity being a part of the community and spending time with the neighbours. This unique and ethnic stay experience guarantees an authentic escape to the tourists.

Homestay accommodation is yet another type, which offers an authentic experience to the tourist. The experience of staying together with a family in their home gives a direct way to access authenticity (Theobald, 1994). Furthermore, tourists staying in homestays are privileged to observe and participate in different cultures and societies. Unlike traditional hotels, homestay guarantees an indigenous environment to the guests with more incredible opportunities to witness other cultures through food, rituals and cultural exchange. Thus, Peer-to-Peer Accommodation and Homestays are the best options suited for guests willing to undergo authentic experiences during their trips.

Case Study: Authentic Experiences and Homestay

The search for authenticity has become a major driving force that motivates tourists to travel to far off places. Travellers, nowadays, are not satisfied by superficial experiences and activities provided at a destination. They search for authentic or real experiences to avoid fake and staged entertainment. They are satisfied with those tourism products that can offer them unexplored tourist experiences. Homestays are one such tourist product that has gained popularity in recent times because they perfectly complement people's quest for authenticity (Aziz & Selamat, 2016; Mura, 2015). The homestays are considered a catalyst for sustaining the rural economy, promoting the development of the rural community, and they also ensure the participation of locals in tourism activities. Homestays are a form of accommodation where a guest can stay with the host or the locals. Apart from dwelling, they also get to share the meals with the family and are considered family members. They also get to learn about the culture and customs of the host family. The tourists enjoy various activities like cooking, eating, participating in local festivals and contributing to the daily chores of the host. The government considers the homestays necessary because they provide an authentic experience to the tourists and preserve and protect the area's authenticity. A glimpse of authentic experiences in a homestay is given through an example of Sunshine Himalayan Cottage in Tirthan Valley of Himachal Pradesh, India (Box 2).

Box 2. Experiencing authentic in Sunshine Himalayan Cottage, India

> Sunshine Himalayan Cottage is a homestay located in the pristine Tirthan Valley, the gateway to the UNESCO World Heritage Site of the Great Himalayan National Park of Himachal Pradesh in India. The six-room cottage is a cocoon of traditional Himachali woodwork, craftsmanship, and cosy, blending in modern amenities and comfort. Each room offers a panoramic view of the river, mountains and forest. The cottage has been built out of respect and love for nature rather than commercial interests. Tirthan Valley is a paradise found for birders, trekkers, adventure sports lovers, wildlife and nature admirers and people who are in search of meaning and miracles. Apart from the beautiful interiors and the stunning environment, this place also serves delicious Himachali dishes. The hosts don't serve food but for pure love and tenderness in all their delicacies. Their food not only serves nourishment to the body but provide all nutrients to the soul. This place is a true amalgamation of local food, architecture, nature and people. The authentic aspects are visible in the reviews given by travellers on TripAdvisor. Some of them are as under:
> "Panki sir's stories are really captivating and will keep you glued to his side late at night. Trust me. This is a place that you absolutely need to visit if you want to truly experience an authentic Tirthan valley."
> "The tree-house room at the top is all the more encaptivating. The food you will eat will surely be delicious and authentic Himachali food you would have ever eaten."
> "Rolling scapes of mountains are dotted with apple, pomegranate, apricot and walnut trees. Besides, the main courtyard bursts with beautiful floral extravaganza."
> "The rooms are so cosy, neat & clean and very nicely done, the interiors give you a feeling of the authentic Himachal architecture."

Source: Trip Advisor, n.d. (https://www.tripadvisor.in); Sunshine Himalayan Cottage, n.d. (https://www.sunshinehimalayancottage.com)

Authentic Attraction

Authenticity has been a motivation for tourists while deciding the destinations. Modern tourists prefer to be involved in the real backstage experience and want to explore deeper locations that are authentic. Therefore, they no longer show interest in exploring popular destinations and are involved in pseudo-events. To escape the mundane daily routine, tourists look for authentic destination experiences which are closer to reality (Kolar, & Zabkar, 2007). As a result, there has been unprecedented growth in the tourists' motivation for visiting unexplored and unspoiled destinations. This has made authenticity a buzzword in context to tourism consumption.

Keeping in view the notion of authenticity, rural destinations have gained much attention from travellers. The visit to rural areas will bring the tourists closer to the real living conditions of the rural people. Unlike pseudo or simulated experiences, the residents in the rural areas will showcase the traditional lifestyle, which will add an authenticity element for the tourist. Rural tourism helps the tourist to have a close picture of the primitive life of the host community, thus unveiling the authentic cultural traditions (Vredeveld & Coulter, 2019). Therefore, touring to any village destination offers a backstage experience to tourists, providing them with an authentic and satisfying experience.

The tangible and intangible cultural heritage resources have been of enormous interest for the tourists seeking authenticity through art, people or culture (Kim & Iwashita, 2016). In the case of intangible heritage, the traditional techniques used by the local community in the form of cooking methods or lifestyle offers authentic experiences to the tourist. Souvenirs are also responsible for providing an authentic experience. While visiting a heritage site, tourists may have a wide range of experiences, including

Authenticity in Tourism Experiences

buildings, local artisans, craftsperson, folk art, traditional rituals and even cultural performances. These experiences may propagate a sense of authenticity in tourists.

Tourists will continue to urge backstage experiences for the quest of authenticity. The preservation of our cultural heritage is of prime importance for keeping the element of authenticity in tourist attractions alive. Jaisalmer, the only living fort in India, is an apt example of authentic attractions (Box 3).

Box 3. Experiencing Jaisalmer's Living Fort

> If there's one place where time can still be felt waiting, it's the Jaisalmer Fort. It is India's only living fort and also a well-known UNESCO world heritage site. When it shimmers in the bright light, the golden stone involuntarily makes the tourist visualise the legends and folklores that blow in the wind of the golden city. Always hosting a mix of tourists and locals, meeting and interacting with those who live in this centuries-old fort is a gateway to walk into a world of authentic traditions of the place. The row of shops selling antique souvenirs gives a royal feeling of everyday fort life. The architectural marvel breathes authenticity and emits mesmerisation.

Source: *History, culture, traditions, communities, monuments, n.d*

Authentic Entertainment

The forms of entertainment offered at any tourist destination are diversified in nature. It may include fairs, festivals, folk dances, etc., which may sometimes also act as a deciding factor for choosing a particular destination. Thus, tourists have varied choices against different forms of entertainment but seek the element of authenticity in common.

Fairs and festivals play a significant role in adding to the cultural restoration of a destination. The traditional fairs and festivals of any particular destination are expressions of the cultural framework of the society. Community-level fairs and festivals serve as the means of social benefits to the community. This further helps nurture community pride and strengthen the relationships among the community people (Grames, 2012). The fairs and festivals provide a reflection of diverse cultures and offer real and authentic experiences to the tourists. It has been observed that these forms of entertainment attract huge crowds spreading to a large geographical area, which helps in bringing people with different cultural values under one roof. Cross-cultural exchange has always been a means to experience authentic traditions and customs.

Music and dance attract huge spectators around the country. The famous folk artists, through their performance, communicate cross-cultural messages to the audience. These performances give a glimpse of living history in the form of aesthetic traditions and history to the audience (Tivers, 2002). Theatres, folk music, and classical dances offer an authentic experience to the tourist through its real and genuine cultural background.

The weakened connection between people and the culture can be strengthened through performing and participating in events. Therefore, tourists should remain motivated to appreciate the forms of tourist entertainment. This will undoubtedly contribute towards the restoration of authenticity within the culture of a destination. The colourful festival of Pushkar is an example of authentic entertainment in tourist experiences (Box 4).

Box 4. Pushkar Fair - Cultural Extravaganza

> Culturally and traditionally rich Puskar Mela is held every year for five days in the city of Pushkar, Rajasthan. It starts from Kartik Ekadashi and continues till Kartik Purnima as per the Hindu calendar. The renowned Pushkar Mela attracts thousands of people from all over the country and abroad. This mega event is usually known for cattle trading, but it is not confined to this activity. The Pushkar fair offers an authentic experience of the traditions followed by the people of Rajasthan. The vibes of this grand fair are truly magical, and it includes musicians, folk dancers and craftspersons all under the same roof. It gives tourists a peek into the cultural heritage of the place. The fair offers a unique experience to the tourists in the form of entertainment. The cross-cultural experience during the event provides an authentic and culturally rich experience to the visitors.

Source: Pushkar Mela, n.d. (https://www.pushkarmela.org)

AUTHENTIC EXPERIENCES AND SHARING ECONOMY

As resources are getting expensive with each passing day, the reduction in consumption is critical. An adequate long term solution to this problem is 'Sharing'. This has led to the emergence of a sharing economy where different consumers share the assets under the common platform. Authenticity is one of the core features of the sharing economy. It collectively offers philosophical, psychological, and spiritual experiences (Kolar & Zabkar, 2007).

Travellers today are looking for authentic, experiential and also meaningful interactions with locals. The sharing economy has been the aptest response to this recent consumer trend. As an answer to this new emerging trend, "Airbnb" is the most recent example.

While exploring the features of Peer-to-Peer accommodation, a range of authentic experiences are being offered to tourists. Tourists have a diversified range of authentic experiences in different accommodation settings. Figure 1 explains the relationship of authenticity, sharing economy and experience economy through an example of Airbnb. Airbnb, which was launched in 2008 in San Francisco, has been praised and criticised at the same time. This new concept of accommodation gives the sense of belongingness and a feeling of being at home. It also offers a unique feel by staying at familiar places (Forno, 2015). The host community gets a chance to earn some revenue from the tourists, whereas the travellers get an opportunity to indulge in real and authentic lifestyles. Thus, sharing economy serves as the common platform to exchange ideas and values among the guest, host and the community. According to this model, the Airbnb travel experience comprises two stages. The first stage is the origin of the guest, and the second is the destination. In the first stage, the guest communicates with the Airbnb and the host through the digital medium at the point of origin. The guest also searches for recommendations and reviews of others through online and offline mediums. This communication continues among various participants during the travel between origin and the destination. When the guest is within the destination, the main interactions are among the guest, host, and local community. The sharing and remembering of the experiences also occur post-trip.

Authenticity in Tourism Experiences

Figure 1. The relationship of authenticity, tourism experiences, and the sharing economy
Source: Paulauskaite et al., 2017

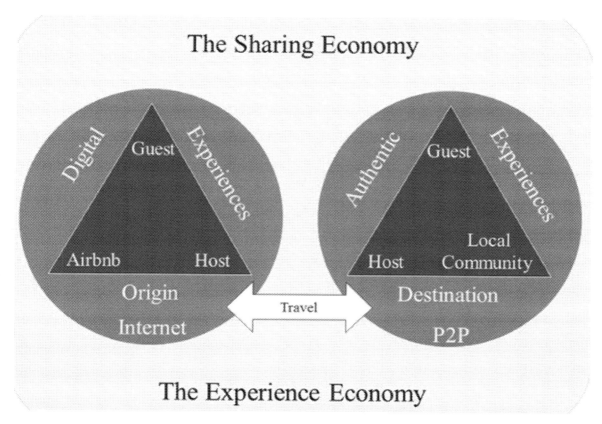

The example of sharing economy in small scale enterprises can be understood by the story of an organisation called NotOnMap, as given in Box 5. This organisation promotes authentic stays and empowers the locals to deliver authentic experiences to tourists.

Box 5. Story of NotOnMap- Live Like Local

> NotOnMap is a social initiative that maintains a sustainable ecosystem of local communities across rural India. They aim to offer the most authentic and unique experience to the tourist by suggesting offbeat locations. This encourages meaningful cultural exchange between tourists and the host community. NotOnMap specialises in providing a deep-rooted backstage experience to travellers by making them live like a local. The unique thing about this initiative is that it does not include any popular destinations on its list. Instead, it looks for very ethnic and authentic places which are primarily virgin and unexplored. Thus, it allows tourists to immerse in local culture, relish local cuisine and engage in learning enriching skills.

Source: Not On Map, n.d

AUTHENTIC TOURIST AND EXPERIENCE ECONOMY

With the introduction of the experience economy, the unique experiential value of tourism products has risen to the forefront of tourism development. It has become the primary value proposition for emerging destinations (Lew, 2011) because the market has evolved into the second-generation experience economy, where unique and personally meaningful experiences are co-created by a firm and a consumer. Staged pleasurable and memorable experiences no longer constitute ultimate economic offerings. Experiences are internal methods of interpreting interactions between people and places, as each individual perceives and understands them uniquely (Pine & Gilmore, 1998). Individuals desire personal significance, a meaningful life, and gratifying relationships with others as co-consumers. Experience has long been seen as a sort of hedonic consumption in the tourist industry, with much research devoted to its pleasurable and satisfying characteristics. Happiness and well-being are commonly thought of as pleasures received from tourism activities, and many researchers have looked into how tourism affects tourists' hedonic well-being. Understanding the eudemonic aspects of tourism experiences conducive to healthy human functioning will become increasingly important as the third-generation experience economy emerges, with its emphasis on personal growth and self-actualisation. A study done by Yeoman and McMahon-Beattie (2006) emphasises the changing trends in an experience economy and their effect on affluent customers. As per the study, luxury has become a mainstream phenomenon in the experience economy and is not reserved for a group of people. Consumers who believe they have all of their material goods and needs are constantly striving for self-esteem and self-actualisation as a result of this accumulation of money. The customer spends money on goods and services that will improve their quality of life and make them feel better about themselves. As a result, as the experience economy expands, customers will dedicate more of their growing wealth to travel and tourism products. As the experience economy evolves, people are more likely to seek and purchase authentic experiences rather than those that are false, fake, or manufactured. The customer is looking for a destination that gives them a sense of place rather than a theme park constructed only for entertainment (Andersson et al., 2007).

CONCLUSION

The chapter analysed the concept of authenticity in the context of the tourism and hospitality industry. The trend of authentic experiences has caught up in recent times, especially after the rise of the experience economy. The level of awareness amongst travellers is high, and they are seeking authentic experiences in place of artificial products. To satisfy the needs of the new-age travellers, the organisation should try to offer experiences that are ethical, natural, simple, rooted and with the human touch. These experiences will not be tainted or manufactured, but will be pure and rooted in the local community's values. The chapter presented several examples encompassing food, architecture, festival and nature that deliver authentic tourism experiences. The chapter outlines various dimensions through which authenticity has been discussed in the literature. The tourists want an experience that is living, local and real. To provide such experiences, the human touch is required because not everything can be mechanised. There is a need to design and develop such tourism products that can deliver the meaning of the place from the perspective of the culture and heritage of the destination too.

The current market trends of sharing economy and experience economy have facilitated the process of providing authentic experiences to tourists. This has also helped the marketers to gain deeper insights into the perceptions of the tourists and the service providers while experiencing any tourism product. With the increasing demand for authentic experiences from the consumers' end, destination marketers have brought significant changes in their marketing strategies and tend to offer experiences in a more local and authentic manner.

REFERENCES

Andersson, T. D., Lemon, K. N., Verhoef, P. C., LeBlanc, C., Knutson, B. J., Beck, J. A. J. A., Kim, S., Cha, J., King, C., Murillo, E., Wei, W., Madera, J., Tews, M. J., Israeli, A. A., Kong, L., Kandampully, J., Zhang, T., Jaakkola, E., Bilgihan, A., ... Andersson, T. D. (2007). The tourist in the experience economy. *Scandinavian Journal of Hospitality and Tourism, 7*(1), 46–58. doi:10.1080/15022250701224035

Aziz, F. S. H., & Selamat, N. H. (2016). Constructing authenticity through hospitality: Examining host-guest relations of a Malay homestay program. *Asian Journal of Tourism Research, 1*(Special). Advance online publication. doi:10.12982/AJTR.2016.0009

Baird, F. E., & Kaufmann, W. (2008). *From Plato to Derrida: Upper Saddle River*. Pearson Prentice Hall.

Bessiere, J. (1998). Local development and heritage: Traditional food and cuisine as tourist attractions in rural areas. European Society for Rural Sociology, 38(1).

Boorstin, D. (1961). *The image: A guide to pseudo-events in America*. Harper and Row.

Bruner, E. M. (1994). Abraham Lincoln as authentic reproduction: A critique of postmodernism. *American Anthropologist, 96*(2), 397–415. doi:10.1525/aa.1994.96.2.02a00070

Chhabra, D., Lee, W., Zhao, S., & Scott, K. (2013). Marketing of ethnic food experiences: Authentication analysis of Indian cuisine abroad. *Journal of Heritage Tourism, 8*(2–3), 145–157. doi:10.1080/1743873X.2013.767816

Cohen, E. (1988). Authenticity and commoditisation in tourism. *Annals of Tourism Research, 15*(3), 371–386. doi:10.1016/0160-7383(88)90028-X

Ferrara, A. (1998). *Reflective authenticity*. Routledge.

Forno, F., & Garibaldi, R. (2015). Sharing economy in travel and tourism: The case of home-swapping in Italy. *Journal of Quality Assurance in Hospitality & Tourism, 16*(2), 202–220. doi:10.1080/1528008X.2015.1013409

Fu, Y. K., & Wang, Y. J. (2020). Experiential value influences authentic happiness and behavioural intention: Lessons from Taiwan's tourism accommodation sector. *Tourism Review*, (April). Advance online publication. doi:10.1108/TR-06-2019-0228

Grames, E. (2012). *Community festivals: Big benefits, but Risks, too*. University of Minnesota Extension.

Guttentag, D. (2015). Airbnb: Disruptive innovation and the rise of an informal tourism accommodation sector. *Current Issues in Tourism, 18*(12), 1192–1217. doi:10.1080/13683500.2013.827159

Hall, C. M. (2007). Response to Yeoman et al: The fakery of "The authentic tourist.". *Tourism Management, 28*(4), 1139–1140. doi:10.1016/j.tourman.2006.09.008

Heidegger, M. (1962). *Being and time*. Blackwell.

History, culture, traditions, communities, monuments. (n.d.). *The Hindu*. Retrieved from https://www.thehindu.com/society/history-and-culture/life-in-jaisalmers-living-fort

Holt, K. (2012). Authentic journalism? A critical discussion about existential authenticity in journalism ethics. *Journal of Mass Media, 27*.

Jyotsna, J. H., & Maurya, U. K. (2019). Experiencing the real village: A netnographic examination of perceived authenticity in rural tourism consumption. *Asia Pacific Journal of Tourism Research, 24*(8), 750–762. doi:10.1080/10941665.2019.1630455

Kim, S., & Iwashita, C. (2016). Cooking identity and food tourism: The case of Japanese udon noodles. *Tourism Recreation Research, 41*(1), 89–100. doi:10.1080/02508281.2016.1111976

Kirillova, K., Lehto, X., & Cai, L. (2016). Mapping existential authenticity and anxiety as outcomes: The tourist in the experience economy. *International Journal of Tourism Research, 19*(1), 13–26. doi:10.1002/jtr.2080

Kolar, T., & Zabkar, V. (2007). The meaning of tourists' authentic experiences for the marketing of cultural heritage sites. *Economic and Business Review for Central and South-Eastern Europe, 9*(3), 235.

Lew, A. A. (2011). Understanding experiential authenticity through the best tourism places. *Tourism Geographies, 13*(4), 570–575. doi:10.1080/14616688.2011.588245

MacCannell, D. (1973). Staged authenticity: Arrangements of social space in tourist settings. *American Journal of Sociology, 79*(3), 589–603. doi:10.1086/225585

Mura, P. (2015). Perceptions of authenticity in a Malaysian homestay: A narrative analysis. *Tourism Management, 51*, 225–233. doi:10.1016/j.tourman.2015.05.023

Newman, G. E. (2019). The Psychology of Authenticity. *Review of General Psychology, 23*(1), 8–18. doi:10.1037/gpr0000158

Not On Map. (n.d.). *About Us*. Retrieved from https://notonmap.com/about-us

Paulauskaite, D., Powell, R., Coca-Stefaniak, J. A., & Morrison, A. M. (2017). Living like a local: Authentic tourism experiences and the sharing economy. *International Journal of Tourism Research, 19*(6), 619–628. doi:10.1002/jtr.2134

Pearce, P. L., & Moscardo, G. M. (1986). The concept of authenticity in tourist experience. *The Australian and New Zealand Journal of Sociology, 22*(1), 121–132. doi:10.1177/144078338602200107

Pine, J., & Gilmore, J. H. (1998). Welcome to the experience economy. *Harvard Business Review, 76*(4), 97–105. PMID:10181589

Prentice, R. (2001). Experiential cultural tourism: Museum and the marketing of the new romanticism of evoked authenticity. *Museum Management and Curatorship, 19*(1), 5–26. doi:10.1080/09647770100201901

Pushkar Mela. (n.d.). Retrieved from https://www.pushkarmela.org

Reisinger, Y., & Steiner, C. J. (2006). Reconceptualising object authenticity. *Annals of Tourism Research, 33*(1), 65–86. doi:10.1016/j.annals.2005.04.003

Rickly-Boyd, J. M. (2013). Existential authenticity: Place matters. *Tourism Geographies, 15*(4), 680–686. doi:10.1080/14616688.2012.762691

Sims, R. (2009). Food, place and authenticity: Local food and the sustainable tourism experience. *Journal of Sustainable Tourism*, *17*(3), 321–336. doi:10.1080/09669580802359293

Steinmetz, R. (2010). *Food, Tourism and Destination Differentiation: The Case of Rotorua*. NewZealand.

Sunshine Himalayan Cottage. (n.d.). Retrieved from https://www.sunshinehimalayancottage.com/

Terziyska, I. (2012). Interpretations of authenticity in tourism. *Science & Research*, *4*(2), 81–87.

Theobald, W. F. (1994). *Global tourism: The next decade*. Butterworth-Heinemann.

Tivers, J. (2002). Performing heritage: The use of live "actors" in heritage presentations. *Leisure Studies*, *21*(3–4), 187–200. doi:10.1080/0261436022000030678

Trilling, L. (1972). *Sincerity and authenticity*. Oxford University Press.

Trip Advisor. (n.d.). Retrieved from https://www.tripadvisor.in/

Vredeveld, A. J., & Coulter, R. A. (2019). Cultural experiential goal pursuit, cultural brand engagement, and culturally authentic experiences: Sojourners in America. *Journal of the Academy of Marketing Science*, *47*(2), 1–17. doi:10.100711747-018-0620-7

Wang, N. (1999). Rethinking authenticity in tourism experience. *Annals of Tourism Research*, *26*(2), 349–370. doi:10.1016/S0160-7383(98)00103-0

Yeoman, I., Brass, D., & McMahon-Beattie, U. (2006). Current issues in tourism: The authentic tourist. *Tourism Management*, *28*(4), 1128–1138. doi:10.1016/j.tourman.2006.09.012

Żemła, M., & Siwek, M. (2020). Between authenticity of walls and authenticity of tourists' experiences: The tale of three Polish castles. *Cogent Arts & Humanities*, *7*(1), 1763893. Advance online publication. doi:10.1080/23311983.2020.1763893

Chapter 17
Promoting the Tourist Experience Economy in LEDCs Through Authentic Fair-Trade Handicrafts:
A Conceptual Framework

Peter Marwa Ezra
https://orcid.org/0000-0002-7305-2608
Clemson University, USA

Lauren Duffy
Clemson University, USA

ABSTRACT

The handicraft sector plays an important role in providing economic benefits of tourism to local communities. However, this sector is threatened by globalized supply chains. This conceptual chapter explores the synergistic value of linking the experience economy, creative tourism, and fair-trade principles to increase the benefits of the handicraft sector to local communities while supporting positive tourist experiences. The handicraft sector contributes to the livelihoods of marginalized members of the supply chain side of a destination by opening opportunities for adding value to their tangible products through co-created experiences. Furthermore, the creative potential allows tourists to create memories, connecting with producers in interesting and meaningful ways, when fair-trade principles are integrated as part of the tourist experience. To ensure a balanced synergy and active connection between experience economy, creative tourism, and fair-trade concepts, well-trained and skilled artists, art managers, and creative entrepreneurs are needed in tourist destinations.

DOI: 10.4018/978-1-7998-8775-1.ch017

Promoting the Tourist Experience Economy in LEDCs Through Authentic Fair-Trade Handicrafts

INTRODUCTION

The handicraft sector is an important segment of the tourism industry, particularly for communities in lesser economically developed countries (LEDCs). Broadly, tourism handicrafts can be described as souvenirs, tokens, or artisan works, representing a destination image or cultural heritage. Carvings, pottery, jewellery, paintings, weavings, metalwork, and other trinkets made of local resources are examples of local handicrafts often found in tourist markets. These pieces are sold to tourists to memorialise or commemorate a visit or experience at a destination (Hume, 2014). While the handicraft sector forms cultural and social elements that contribute to the attractiveness, experience, and memory of a tourist destination (Ritchie & Zins, 1978), it also contributes to the economic engine of a local community (Benson, 2014; Grobar, 2019; Kazungu, 2020; Mahoney, 2012b; Thirumaran, Dam, & Thirumaran, 2014).

This chapter focuses specifically on the handicraft sector within LEDCs where some estimate that the sector employs over 10% of the labour force (Grobar, 2019). Portions, if not all, of a handicraft supply chain could be considered part of the informal economy (Wondirad, Bogale, & Li, 2021). The informal economy represents economic activity that operates without legal recognition, where businesses may or may not have official registrations or licenses, and enumeration for individuals is less formalised or guaranteed (e.g., unpaid family labour, self-employment; Çakmak & Çenesiz, 2020; Portes & Schauffler, 1993; Slocum, Backman, & Robinson, 2011). Work within the informal economy, including the handicraft sector, is accessible to large portions of the population because the sector does not require extensive capital investment, drawing from locally available raw materials (e.g., wood, rock, nuts, grasses) and traditional artisan skills passed down within communities (Timothy & Wall, 1997; Truong, 2018; Truong, Liu, & Pham, 2020). Importantly, the creating and selling of handicrafts that are sold in tourism markets can provide direct access to income-generating opportunities for lesser-educated, lesser-resourced, or marginalised individuals (e.g., Britton, 1982; Carlisle, 2010; Timothy & Wall, 1997). That is, the handicraft sector creates an avenue for direct economic benefits via an income that may sustain their livelihoods (Grobar, 2019; Harris, 2014; Kazungu, 2020; Richard, 2007).

This study adopts the notion of the *experience economy* proposed by Pine and Gilmore (1999) and the related concept of *creative tourism* (Richard & Raymond, 2000; Tan, Kung & Luh, 2013) in the context of the handicraft sector, considering the synergistic opportunities of coupling these ideas with a fair-trade philosophy. The experience economy considers experiences as a form of economic offering that creates a competitive advantage and memorable experiences for tourists. As a subset of this, creative tourism represents a type of tourism where participants actively co-create their experience (Tan et al., 2013). In this vein, this chapter considers the increasing authentic, co-created experiences as a way for the handicraft sector to increase revenue expenditures to local communities. Moreover, this chapter discusses the role of a fair-trade philosophy to guide creative tourism in the handicraft sector so that economic benefits to local communities are maximised through the intentionality of supply chain management.

The practical importance of this conceptual chapter is that it expands on opportunities for local communities to maximise the economic benefits of tourism, adding to the pro-poor tourism agenda. Theoretically, this chapter also demonstrates how *authenticity* weaves across the experience economy, creative tourism, and fair-trade philosophy within the context of the handicraft sector. Bringing these concepts together provides a coherent framework for designing and managing the handicraft sector using the Tanzanian handicraft sector as an example context.

The next section provides an overview of the literature on the handicraft sector, and then expounds on the principles of the fair-trade philosophy. This is followed by a theoretical discussion of the experience economy and creative tourism. The four dimensions (4Es) of the experience economy are presented as a framework to conceptualise the nexus of creative tourism and fair-trade handicraft experiences in the case of Tanzania. The chapter concludes with practical and theoretical implications and future research that outline opportunities for considering ways to increase the economic benefits of tourist handicrafts to local communities.

TOURIST HANDICRAFTS IN LEDCS

Studies have found that the handicraft sector plays an important role in providing direct economic benefits of tourism to the local communities (Benson, 2014; Markwick, 2001a; Richard, 2007; Rylance & Spenceley, 2017; Wondirad et al., 2021). According to Mitchell and Ashley (2009), the handicraft sector is a major avenue for tourists' out-of-pocket spending. Because of this, the handicraft sector is seen as "pro-poor"; rather than spending on mainstream products like hotels and transportation, which have high economic leakage, those involved with handicrafts (from the person who harvests the raw materials to the artisans and to the sellers), receive income directly. For instance, in Ethiopia, the total tourist expenditure on the handicrafts sector was US$12.7 million. Of that spending, US$6.9 million (55%) could be described as pro-poor income or income that moved directly into the hands of the least-resourced in a community. Conversely, tourist expenditures on accommodations were US$98.7 million; only US$10.7 million (11%) could be described as pro-poor (Mitchell & Ashley, 2009).

The ability to retain tourist expenditures in the local community—or reduce economic leakage—is cited by development agencies, governments, and academics as a concern in LEDCs if tourism is to reduce poverty (Anderson, 2013b; Mitchell, 2012; Rylance & Spenceley, 2017; Supradist, 2004; Suryawardani, Bendesa, Antarat, & Wiranathar, 2014). Pro-poor interventions that reduce leakage have been proposed, including the identification of ways to maximise local expenditures through handicraft purchases, increasing the number of locally owned and managed enterprises within the handicraft value chain, and/or improving the quality of handicrafts to capture higher values (Rylance & Spenceley, 2017). It should also be noted that the handicraft sector faces challenges from globalising supply chains, commercialisation, and commodification (Dash, 2015). While this has consequences for creating local revenue, understanding how tourists perceive and consume handicrafts becomes important.

Consumption of Tourist Handicrafts

Besides contributing to the local economy of the host destination, the consumption of souvenirs has been used as "external elicitors of memory, recollections, and emotional value related to an experience" (Elomba & Yun, 2018, p. 104). Tourists purchase souvenirs to keep a memory of their heritage and own authentic products from their destination. Therefore, to foster a long-term tourist-host relationship, souvenirs are used as avenues to improve community relationships, cultural structure, tradition, and heritage (Littrell, Anderson, & Brown, 1993).

Historically, the landscape at tourism destinations has existed with traditional, authentic souvenirs focused on a destination's image and heritage (Hume, 2014). The appeal for traditional and culturally authentic souvenirs dates to the pre-colonial and colonial times, including the conquest and exploration of foreign lands, particularly in LEDCs (Harris, 2014; Mahoney, 2012a; Thirumaran et al., 2014). It was common for European elites to arrange objects gathered from the conquest and exploration of foreign lands into curious or curio cabinets.

Handicrafts form an integral part of cultural products. They carry strong symbolic values from both social and cultural perspectives (Ravasi & Rindova, 2008; Ravasi, Rindova, & Dalpiaz, 2012). The social and cultural meanings associated with a handicraft purchase has individual and social identity formation. According to the theory of consumer behaviour, product consumption entails a steady flow of fantasies, feelings, and fun encompassed by the experiential view (Ravasi & Rindova, 2008).

Literature on tourist consumption of souvenirs has been tackled from various theoretical frameworks, including social psychological approaches on consumer attitudes, economic approaches on willingness to pay for products or services, and sociological approaches on consumer identity (Andorfer & Liebe, 2012; Zukin & Maguire, 2004). In the current globalised era, the contemporary tourists' consumption behaviour is characterised as self-indulgent and hedonistic, connected to identities and sense of belonging, driven by a need to express individualism, and motivated by functional reasons and memorable events (Williams, 2006).

Apart from the social and economic factors, *authenticity* of the handicraft plays a major role in a tourist's decision making. Authenticity has been debated and conceptualised from different schools of thought. MacCannell (1976) proposed authenticity to be what tourists seek when they travel. Individuals seek authenticity as a result of feeling alienated from their modern lives, and when they visit other places and cultures, it is a form of resistance to the alienation they experience in their own lives (Oakes, 2006). Thus, tourists are interested in authentic souvenirs, food, relationships, and experiences.

In this respect, authentic handicrafts can be a source of value because they represent a traditional culture that is genuine, real, and unique (Sharpley, 1994). However, the authenticity of handicrafts can be conceptualised on a spectrum. One end of the spectrum embraces authentic, traditional, handmade, and locally produced handicrafts; the other end is determined by the free market economy, with handicrafts characterised as mass-produced, imported, and commercialised (Scrase, 2003; Varul, 2008). The effects of globalisation and technological advancements have led to mainstreaming and outsourcing within the handicraft sector, threatening the authenticity of tourist handicrafts. A study conducted across South America, Asia, and Africa found a precarious production of handicraft goods and shifting trends in fashion, cultural taste, and aesthetics. This production is linked to globalisation, whereby mass production of cheap factory items are replacing traditional and authentic handicrafts produced by local artisans (Scrase, 2003). Specifically, Yadav and Mahara (2018) found that most handicraft businesses in India face fierce competition from the Chinese markets, creating counterfeit handicrafts at relatively low prices. Instead of globalisation benefiting artisans in LEDCs, it is an obstacle that renders them less access and control in supply chains and production networks (Bissinger & Leufkens, 2020; Herman, 2019; Maertens, 2019; Mookerjee, 2019).

Further studies by Bruner (1991), Elomba and Yun (2018), Mahoney (2012), and Mogindol and Bagul (2014) argued that tourists are not necessarily looking for authentic souvenirs and/or authentic experiences at the time of purchase. For instance, a study conducted in Kenya found that "tourists realised that the native performances on their tour itinerary are constructions of foreign audience and are willing to accept a reproduction, as long as it is a good one" (Bruner, 1991, p. 240).

Still, this chapter argues that the destination's image and geographical context are attributes valued by tourists when it comes to purchasing souvenirs or handicrafts. For example, Koli's (2021) study in India found that 'craft authenticity' was a key criterion for the purchase of handicrafts. Evidence suggests that fair-trade products may compete with mass-produced items in that cost is no longer the only criterion for making purchase decisions. In a study conducted in Malaysia, the findings show that, among other attributes, handicrafts that are made by hand are the most appealing to tourists, especially when background information on the handicraft item is provided (Mogindol & Bagul, 2014). The following section considers how the fair-trade philosophy as a means for protecting authenticity within handicrafts and a way to support local producers.

PHILOSOPHY OF FAIR-TRADE

International and transnational investors dominate the contemporary global tourism industry from more economically developed countries (MEDCs; Bianchi, 2018; Britton, 1991). What ushered in this era of the tourism industry were social and economic policies collectively reflecting *neoliberalism* (Harvey, 2005), which can be characterised as a form of 'late capitalism' (Bansel, 2015). Neoliberal economic policies prevailed in the 1980s and 1990s, favouring free trade through open borders, reducing government restrictions to markets, and increasing privatisation. In addition, structural adjustment policies were promoted to LEDCs as a means to join the global economy through investment from international development organisations (i.e., the World Bank, International Monetary Fund). However, in return for the capital infused into these countries, the countries had to agree to measures that would allow foreign investment and free trade, along with the burden of debt to pay back these loans (Bianchi, 2018; Britton, 1991; Duffy, Stone, Chancellor, & Kline, 2016). Consequently, these policies favoured foreign investors who had more access to capital and greater market reach than businesses in the local community (Duffy et al., 2016). Further, the lack of local ownership – of accommodations, resorts, casinos, airlines – and dominance of foreign investment contributed to high levels of economic leakage (Anderson, 2013a; Mitchell & Ashley, 2007).

Fair-trade philosophy presents an alternative way of thinking about the policies and practices that shape economies. Fair trade broadly seeks greater equity in international trade through dialogue, respect, and transparency. Further, it contributes "to sustainable development by offering better trading conditions to, and securing the rights of, marginalised producers and workers, especially in the South" (World Fair Trade Organization [WFTO], 2021; Elbeshbishi & Al A'ali, 2020). As Elbeshbishi and Al A'ali (2020) note, enhancing the satisfaction of all stakeholders, including producers and consumers, is a premise for fair-trade philosophy. With this, fair trade embraces ethical consumerism and economic fairness. Thus, fair-trade movements are linked to aiding community programs in LEDCs to improve the production of handicrafts and related products that meet the standards and demand for the global tourism market (Doherty, Smith, & Parker, 2015; Molony, 2009; Scrase, 2003).

A defining feature of the fair-trade movement is to maximise the positive elements of globalisation that connect people, communities, and cultures through products and ideas. Additionally, it aims to minimise the negative elements that result in exploitative labour by encouraging the true costs of production to be visible (WFTO, 2021). According to Fairtrade International, fair-trade sales in the consumer markets of Western Europe and North America reached $5.73 billion by 2013, which makes fair-trade one of the most important sectors of ethical consumerism in the world (Doherty et al., 2015). Importantly, fair trade philosophy can be applied to the handicraft sector to ensure that the economic benefits of tourism are retained in local communities. A wave of change in the global tourism market indicates that consumers are beginning to demand more responsible, ethical standards in purchased products and services (Cleverdon & Kalisch, 2000). For instance, Barnett (2001) found that 68% of consumers claimed to pay more for fair-trade products, especially from developing countries. Likewise, Castaldo, Perrini, Misani, and Tencati (2009) showed a positive correlation between a firm's reputation and the behavioural intentions of consumers to purchase fair-trade products. This notion is connected to the interest in the authentic appeal of handicrafts as part of the tourist experience.

Fair-trade philosophy supports the pursuit and appeal of authenticity. To this end, the 10 principles of fair trade from the WFTO (2021) reflect features of authenticity, including the opportunity for disadvantaged producers; transparency and accountability; fair-trade practices, fair payment, and capacity building; fair trade promotion; respect for the environment; no child or forced labour; good working conditions; and no discrimination.

Fair-trade was introduced as an alternative model for business practice and trade policy, responding to the consequences of globalisation. Local communities can also connect handicrafts back to their place-based meaning by focusing on marketing and selling the handicraft *production process*. That is, tourists may not only purchase a handicraft item, but there are opportunities to value-add through the experience of viewing its production as well as the experience of helping create a handicraft item. Fundamentally, this notion of focusing on the process and people involved in the production process embody the ideas of fair-trade philosophy by engaging with the emerging interest in the experience economy.

EXPERIENCE ECONOMY: THEORETICAL FRAMEWORK

Experience can be defined as "a subjective mental state felt by visitors during a service encounter" (Otto & Ritchie, 1996, p. 166). Experience has served as a key construct in travel and tourism research. More recently, intentional experience design and management has gained traction across tourism and leisure fields (see Duerden, 2020; Tussyadiah, 2014). This comes as a result of the seminal work of Pine and Gilmore (1999), on the *experience economy* and its applications to tourism. As Sternberg (1997, p. 954) posited, "tourism's central productive activity is the creation of the touristic experience."

The experience economy is regarded as a paradigm shift of consumer demand from service-based to experience-based products (Pine & Gilmore, 1999). According to Pine and Gilmore (1999, p. 12), "experiences are events that engage individuals in a personal way," leading to personal development and transformation. Considered from consumers' perspective, they look for experiences as "enjoyable, engaging, memorable encounters for those consuming these events" (Oh, Fiore, & Jeoung, 2007, p. 120).

The 4Es

According to Pine and Gilmore (1999), the four realms (or dimensions) of experience, also referred to as the 4Es, are differentiated by the level and form of customer involvement in business offerings, as depicted in Figure 1: (1) education; (2) entertainment; (3) escapism; and (4) esthetics. Along the customer participation axis, passive participation of the customer in business (or destination) offerings characterises the entertainment and esthetic dimensions. Educational and escapist dimensions reflect active participation. The tourist who passively participates in destination activities does not directly affect or influence the performance of the destination (business). An active participant will personally affect the performance or event that becomes part of their experience.

Figure 1. Four realms of experience
Source: Adapted from Pine & Gilmore, 1999

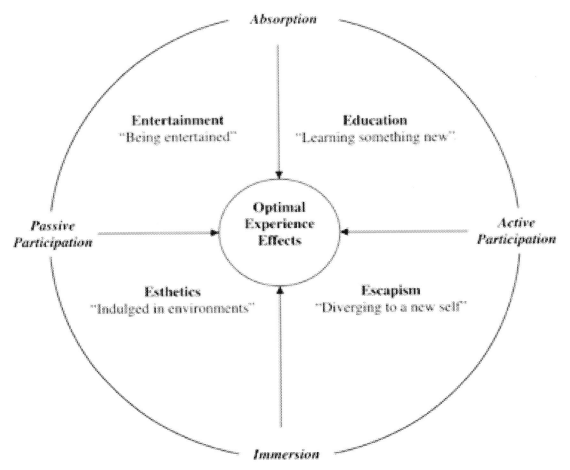

Along the absorption-immersion axis, the tourist typically "absorbs" entertaining and educational offerings of a destination and "immerses" in the destination environment, which results in esthetic or escapist experiences. In this context, absorption is defined as "occupying a person's attention by bringing the experience into the mind" and immersion is "becoming physically (or virtually) a part of the experience itself" (Pine & Gilmore, 1999, p. 31). To genuinely create an educational experience, a tourist must broaden their knowledge and/or abilities by participating in educational activities that actively engage the mind (for intellectual education) and/or body (for physical education; Pine & Gilmore 1999).

Since the inception of the concept of the experience economy, literature has considered experiences within different contexts and sectors of the tourism industry. For instance, Quan and Wang (2004) explored gastronomic experience, demonstrating that food consumption in tourism can be either the peak touristic experience or supporting consumer experience. Williams (2006), after examining the concept of experiential marketing, concluded that tourism practitioners should go beyond service excellence and market experientially to create value in the sector. Additionally, Hayes and MacLeod (2007) examined heritage trails, using the experience economy to find that trails utilise principles of experience design suggested by Pine and Gilmore. They also noted some scope for improvement in terms of positioning and presentational format. Oh et al. (2007) used a quantitative field survey to examine bed and breakfast lodging experiences. Their data supported the four dimensions of the experience economy. Collectively, this work on the dimensions of the experience economy also led to the subsequent development of additional forms of experiential tourism. Of interest in this chapter is creative tourism.

Creative Tourism

Richards and Raymond (2000) defined creative tourism as "tourism which offers tourists the opportunity to develop their creative potential through active participation in courses and learning experiences which are the characteristic of the destination where they are undertaken" (p. 18). Conversely, the United Nations Educational, Scientific and Cultural Organization's (UNESCO, 2006) Creative Cities Network defined creative tourism as "travel directed toward an engaged and authentic, with participative learning in the arts, heritage, or special character of a place, and it provides a connection with those who reside in this place and create this living culture" (p. 3). Richards (2011, p. 1237) further posited that creative tourism incorporates "participative, authentic experiences that allow tourists to develop their creative potential and skills through contact with local people and their culture," which makes it a learning process.

In practice, the concept of creative tourism has evolved and operationalised across various countries, including New Zealand (Creative Tourism New Zealand), Australia (Creative Tourism Australia), France (Creative Paris), and Taiwan (Creative Life; (Tan, Kung, & Luh, 2013). Creative tourism experiences can encompass activities like traditional crafts/handicrafts, gastronomy, perfume making, porcelain painting, and dancing (Richards, 2011).

These creative tourism definitions share common themes, including active participation, creative potential development, learning skills from the locals, and authentic experiences (Richards, 2011; Tan et al., 2013). However, as Ali, Ryu, and Hussain (2016) postulated, most of the current definitions focus on the supply-side of tourism (service providers and industry practitioners); they lack discussion from the tourists' point of view. Moreover, Maitland (2008) argued that the heart of creative tourism is based on demand (from tourists), vis-a-vis exploring what tourists want, their perceptions, and what they enjoy. Even though industry practitioners take the lead in designing and delivering tourist experiences, tourists are viewed as key and active participants in co-creating these experiences while on vacation.

The growing interest in creative tourism experiences can be explained by factors that shape the tourism industry. For instance, the emergence of the concepts of the experience economy, educational tourism, and entertainment economy have made creative tourism more popular and relevant (Ferreira et al., 2019; Pine & Gilmore, 1999; Tan et al., 2013). According to Prahalad and Ramaswamy (2003), "a new point of view is required; one that allows individual customers to actively construct their own consumption experiences through personalised interaction, thereby co-creating unique value for themselves" (p. 12). Active participation has been seen primarily on gastronomical tourism, as tourists participate in wine-making and tasting (Quadri-Felitti & Fiore, 2012), coffee production (Yu & Fang, 2009), and other culinary activities (Quan & Wang, 2004). However, creative tourist participation in authentic souvenir-making and handicraft activities (e.g., carving, weaving, painting) are avenues that need more exploration.

As a final note, understanding the tourist experience has historically been grounded in attempts to understand what tourists seek. Once again, MacCannell (1989), who considered the tourist's quest for authenticity, becomes relevant again to this understanding. However, in the context of experiences, Wang (1999) subsequently introduced the notion of existential authenticity. In this regard, authenticity could be considered in a subjective manner: authenticity could be experienced, sensed, and felt within touristic activities (Kim & Jamal, 2007; Wang, 1999). While some sociologists are concerned with how tourist experiences are staged, packaged, and offered in a commodified setting (see Cohen, 1988; Duffy & Overholt, 2013; Elomba & Yun, 2018; Markwick, 2001b), there is also opportunity to support co-created experiences that help tourists find the authenticity they seek.

THE NEXUS BETWEEN EXPERIENCE ECONOMY, CREATIVE TOURISM, AND FAIR-TRADE CONCEPTS

The following section uses the four dimensions of the experience economy framework to conceptualise the synergy of the experience economy, creative tourism and fair-trade principles in the handicraft sector using Tanzania as a case study (Figure 2).

Figure 2. Typical creative handicraft activities within the 4Es model of the experience economy in Tanzania
Source: Modified from Pine & Gilmore, 1999

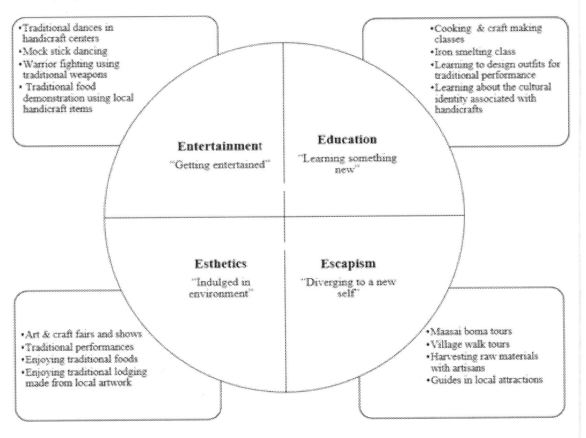

This study argues that the handicraft sector should not limit its scope to the seeing, smelling, listening, and tasting of the tangible handicraft product; handicraft experiences can also engage the tourist in participation in the production process. Further, to strike a balance between being creative and designing an experience that consumers will value and want to engage in, the design of creative experiences in the handicraft sector should take into account consumers' consumption patterns and preferences. As such, using a case study of Tanzania as a LEDCs, what is provided in each of the four dimensions are examples of fair-traded, creative tourism within the handicraft sector.

Education in the Handicraft Sector

There is an increasing demand for educational and learning experiences (Ritchie et al., 2003). Education is considered one motivation for tourists. As shown in Pine and Gilmore's (1999) experience economy framework, the education component is reflected in the active participation and absorption dimensions of the framework. Creative tourism experiences involve activities that provide tourists with the opportunity to learn local skills and traditions (Richards & Wilson, 2006). A traveller engaged in educational experiences absorbs the events before them. This traveller actively participates through interactive mind and/or body engagement. Tourists typically improve their general and specific skills and knowledge through educational experiences at the sites they have visited. The production of handicrafts as a form of creative tourism plays a key role in learning and development. For example, visitors to an art festival can learn about the history of knitting and weaving through many mediums (i.e., brochures, chats with the artist, etc.). In addition, the visitor can improve their abilities by weaving on a basic loom led by the artist's directions (Oh et al., 2007). For instance, artists and artisans in the Dar es Salaam Village Museum, Tanzania, work on a variety of creative handicraft projects with educational potential, including an iron-smelting kiln, Ngalawa, a children's cooking centre, painting lessons, and traditional music and dance (Lwoga & Mapunda, 2017). Others have shown that participating in the creation of handicrafts can increase self-confidence, develop fine motor skills, and strengthen consumers' analytical skills (Farsani, Mortazavi, Bahrami, Kalantary, & Bizhaem, 2017).

In addition to cultural performances, other educational activities allow for tourists' co-creation in designing outfits for a performance, beading jewellery, or preparing food for a ceremony. From a fair-trade perspective, tourists will learn about compliance with fair-trade principles, including conservation and management of tree species commonly used in wood carving, fair pricing of handicraft items, and fair wages to employees. Most importantly, an authentic relationship could be developed between the teacher (i.e., crafter, tradesman) and student (i.e., tourist), ultimately serving as an avenue for increased understanding and empathy.

Entertainment in the Handicraft Sector

Tourism and entertainment are interconnected. From an experience economy perspective, entertainment reflects the passive participation/absorption dimension of the experience economy framework. The entertainment experience occurs when consumers' attention is passively engaged through the observation of activities and/or performances (Manthiou, Lee, Tang, & Chiang, 2014; Oh et al., 2007; Pine & Gilmore, 1999). Taking this further with creative tourism, the tourist is actively engaged in the activity or performance. Besides being one of the oldest forms of experiences, entertainment is one of the most developed and pervasive in today's business environment (Pine & Gilmore 1999).

Entertainment, like the esthetic dimension, necessitates that the offerings capture and occupy customers' attention and readiness. For instance, in most cultural tourism programs in the Northern part of Tanzania, particularly the Arusha and Manyara regions, there are a variety of cultural performances, including traditional dancing, mock stick dancing, and warrior fighting in Maasai cultural *bomas*. These performances are accompanied by the sale of traditional food and handicrafts. Jewellery worn by performers is also sold (Bayno & Jani, 2018; Melubo & Carr, 2019). This could be enhanced if the tourist participates in the traditional dance or helps prepare for a ritual by constructing instruments, weaving hand fans, or preparing food to be served.

Esthetics in the Handicraft Sector

The esthetic experience is a function of the passive participation/immersion dimension of the experience economy framework. It entails the evaluation of the physical environment, overall atmosphere, or mood (Pine & Gilmore, 1999). Tourists enjoy being in the destination environment without affecting or altering the nature of the environment presented to them in esthetic experiences (Oh et al., 2007). Instead, they passively appreciate or are influenced by how the destination appeals to their senses, regardless of the destination's level of authenticity. Such encounters allow the tourist to be present. Many attractions provide esthetic experiences (Oh et al., 2007). For instance, in the Dar es Salaam Village Museum, traditional performances are held at the request of visitors who pay performers on weekends and public holidays. The Village Museum also provides a venue for weddings, cultural shows, meetings, modern music, and handcraft shops (Lwoga & Mapunda, 2017). As an additional example, helping make wood carvings can include the smell of fresh-cut wood and using tools unique to context (e.g., traditional tools, not electric powered saws), alongside local residents performing their normal work. Together, this creates an authentic, co-created experience while also having the consumers connect with the local producers to a greater degree.

Escapism in the Handicraft Sector

As expressed in Pine and Gilmore (1999), escapism is reflected in the active participation and immersion dimensions of the experience economy framework. According to Getz (2007), individuals seek change and novel experiences to escape from daily life's mundane or unpleasant realities. The escapist experience necessitates a greater level of immersion and participation than entertainment or educational experiences. Tourists who partake in escapism embark on a journey by travelling to a location and engaging in activities (Pine & Gilmore 1999).

From a supply-side perspective, destinations offer tourists the opportunity to make handicraft items or actively participate in local festivities, as well as act as guides in local attractions (Dias, González-Rodríguez, & Patuleia, 2020). The escapism experience necessitates that tourists influence performances or occurrences in the real or virtual world (Oh et al., 2007). Further, tourists can spend a day with an artisan/ handicraft producer to harvest material or experience firsthand the labour it took to collect the wood for carvings (escaping from one's own life by being in the shoes of someone else for a day or week). Active participation in harvesting raw materials and traditional tools used in handicraft items (for example, Makonde carvings in Tanzania) could enlighten tourists about the process, creativity, and cultural meaning attached to the handicraft items.

IMPLICATIONS AND FUTURE RESEARCH

Literature has noted the importance of understanding consumer behaviour through the experiential lens (Hayes & MacLeod, 2007; Kim & Fesenmaier, 2015). The experience economy has become a prominent framework for understanding consumer behaviours and preferences in relation to tourism products, services, and experiences (Duerden, 2020; Tussyadiah, 2014). Within this experiential lens, this study used the experience economy to understand the handicraft sector as part of an emerging creative tourism industry, using Tanzania as a case example.

The importance of this is that the handicraft sector provides an opportunity for improved livelihoods for local communities in LEDCs by creating an economic linkage with individuals in local communities (Benson, 2014; Grobar, 2019; Kazungu, 2020; Markwick, 2001a; Mahoney, 2012b; Rylance & Spenceley, 2017; Thirumaran et al., 2014; Wondirad et al., 2021). From the experience economy perspective, local communities could capitalise on the experience of the production of handicrafts. For example, a tourist who participates in procuring raw materials from suppliers will come back to see how they are processed. Further, they can purchase a finished handicraft product or souvenir. Recognising the value of that experience for the tourist, along with the opportunity to engage in the fair-trade model (fair and decent prices), needs exploring. For instance, handicraft businesses could allow tourists to create ceramic products, weave hats, design jewellery, art, and more.

Participation in handicraft processing and souvenir-making is an appropriate example to showcase the relationship between the tourist and the experience economy, creative tourism, and the fair-trade model. This is because handicrafts have become an important element in the contemporary tourism industry, both for tourists who purchase items and for destinations that produce and reproduce their culture and identity within the handicrafts. Specifically, this allows for deeper connections and authentic exchanges between consumer and producer, thereby supporting fair-trade principles. As such, not only would the focus on experiential and creative tourism in the handicraft sector create economic benefits, it could also result in positive socio-cultural affects such as increased cross-cultural understanding and empathy (i.e., tourists will better understand the livelihoods of locals). Finally, these co-created handicraft experiences may also lead to overall tourist satisfaction and increase intention for return visitation to the destination (see Do Valle, Silva, Mendes, & Guerreiro, 2006).

However, to make this possible, there is a need for capacity building and education of those involved in the handicraft sector. Specifically, there needs to be awareness of the possibilities of incorporating creative tourism into their businesses and the skills needed for producers to transition to meaningful co-created experiences. Likewise, both producers and consumers would benefit from a growing awareness of the fair-trade philosophy. Additionally, to further enhance the productivity and efficiency of the handicraft sector, the adoption and utilisation of the latest technology are instrumental. In this respect, craft producers can use 3D technology to improve the design and quality of craft production. Innovation is a transformation of ideas and knowledge into new products or services which involve technology in production, distribution, marketing, and management (Ramadani & Gerguri 2011). Providing capacity development schemes also helps preserve, promote, improve, and transfer the traditional craft production knowledge from generation to generation. Therefore, tourist destinations in LEDCs are required to have well-trained and talented artists, art managers, and creative entrepreneurs to provide a balanced synergy and active link between experience economy, creative tourism, and fair-trade ideals.

Future research should examine how various forms and types of handicraft sectors contribute to the 4Es of the experience economy. As Oh et al. (2007) postulated, the 4Es were not equally important to tourists' evaluation of the bed and breakfast experience in a rural setting. This study argues that the same may be true of the handicraft experience. This information is important for small- to medium-sized tourism business enterprises in developing countries to appropriately allocate limited resources to the correct combination of 4Es in their business settings. Further, as Truong (2018) and Truong et al. (2020) have done with street vendors in Vietnam, future research should explore this issue from the perspective of the handicraft producers, artisans and other stakeholders along the handicraft supply chain.

The existing and growing body of the experience economy literature has broadly addressed a myriad of topics. Yet, it places a major focus on the demand side of tourism (consumers/tourists). Limited knowledge is available on the supply side of tourism in terms of how host communities perceive these consumers/tourists and how such perceptions can determine perceived experiences. This study argues that this Western-dominated and developed country conceptualisation of the experience economy and consumers must be addressed. In response, this study examines the experience economy concept in relation to authentic fair-trade handicrafts and from the perspective of a host community in a developing country.

Finally, this chapter also highlighted how the idea of *authenticity* weaves across the experience economy, creative tourism, and fair-trade philosophy within the context of the handicraft sector. The growth of experience economy and creative tourism can be understood by tourists seeking experiential authenticity (Wang, 1999). Moreover, fair-trade philosophy also supports consumer demand for more authentic products and experiences; that is, the fair-trade philosophy seeks to connect the consumers and producers in reciprocal exchanges that create the basis for authentic exchanges and relationships.

CONCLUSION

This chapter explored the synergistic value of combining the concepts of the experience economy, creative tourism, and fair-trade principles to increase the benefits of the handicraft sector to local communities while promoting positive tourist experiences. Using the 4Es as a framework for application, this chapter considered experiential, creative tourism and fair-trade philosophy in the context of the handicraft sector in Tanzania.

This study focused on the perspective of LEDCs due to the major economic role of traditional handicrafts in local economies. The creative tourism sector, particularly handicrafts, does not require significant investment capital. In addition, it utilises available skills and raw materials. Therefore, this type of creative tourism is appropriate for populations with little education and/or capital. Additionally, incorporating fair-trade principles may improve market linkages between local artisans and tourists.

The growing importance of the experience economy, creative tourism, and fair trade in the tourism and hospitality industry is a wake-up call to academic researchers and business practitioners. These outlets must move with changing consumer behaviours and demands for more tourist experiences. Tourism managers and marketers, as well as local communities, are obliged to be innovative in terms of developing new tourism products as a competitive advantage. There is also a need to change from traditional marketing approaches. For example, we can no longer focus on a destination's physical attributes. Instead, we must consider customer demands and fair-trade principles.

Tourism managers and local artisans need to understand that unique and memorable tourist experiences, consistency in quality products, and good service delivery should be prioritised while considering the creative potential of local and authentic handicrafts. In this sense, memories are likely to act as an important filtering mechanism that links the experience to the tourist's attitudinal outcomes. From a consumer perspective, tourist destination practitioners should consider creative tourists as "active co-creators of their experiences; hence, they should be treated as a heterogeneous group of co-producers who have subjective opinions and feelings toward their creative experiences" (Tan et al., 2014, p. 248).

REFERENCES

Ali, F., Ryu, K., & Hussain, K. (2016). Influence of experiences on memories, satisfaction and behavioral intentions: A study of creative tourism. *Journal of Travel & Tourism Marketing, 33*(1), 85–100. doi:10.1080/10548408.2015.1038418

Anderson, W. (2013). Leakages in the tourism systems: Case of Zanzibar. *Tourism Review, 68*(1), 62–76. doi:10.1108/16605371311310084

Andorfer, V. A., & Liebe, U. (2012). Research on fair trade consumption: A review. *Journal of Business Ethics, 106*(4), 415–435. doi:10.100710551-011-1008-5

Bansel, P. (2015). The subject of policy. *Critical Studies in Education, 56*(1), 5–20. doi:10.1080/17508487.2015.971839

Barnett, P. (2001). Fair trade in tourism. *Industry and Environment, 24*(3), 18–19.

Bayno, P. M., & Jani, D. (2018). Residents' attitudes on the contribution of cultural tourism in Tanzania. *Journal of Tourism and Cultural Change, 16*(1), 41–56. doi:10.1080/14766825.2016.1211663

Benson, W. (2014). *The benefits of tourism handicraft sales at Mwenge Handicrafts Centre in Dar Es Salaam*. Tampere University of Applied Sciences.

Bianchi, R. (2018). The political economy of tourism development: A critical review. *Annals of Tourism Research, 70*(June), 88–102. doi:10.1016/j.annals.2017.08.005

Bissinger, K., & Leufkens, D. (2020). (Fairtrade) certification: Consequences of being a niche market. *Agrekon, 59*(2), 188–201. doi:10.1080/03031853.2019.1699840

Britton, S. (1982). The political economy of tourism in the Third World. *Annals of Tourism Research, 9*(3), 331–358. doi:10.1016/0160-7383(82)90018-4

Britton, S. (1991). Tourism, capital, and place: Towards a critical geography of tourism. *Environment and Planning. D, Society & Space, 9*(June), 451–478. doi:10.1068/d090451

Bruner, E. M. (1991). Transformation of self in tourism. *Annals of Tourism Research, 18*(2), 238–250. doi:10.1016/0160-7383(91)90007-X

Çakmak, E., & Çenesiz, M. A. (2020). Measuring the size of the informal tourism economy in Thailand. *International Journal of Tourism Research, 22*(5), 637–652. doi:10.1002/jtr.2362

Carlisle, S. (2010). *Access and marginalisation in a beach enclave resort – Tourism and Inequality: Problems and prospects*. CABI.

Castaldo, S., Perrini, F., Misani, N., & Tencati, A. (2009). The missing link between corporate social responsibility and consumer trust: The case of fair trade products. *Journal of Business Ethics*, *84*(1), 1–15. doi:10.100710551-008-9669-4

Cleverdon, R., & Kalisch, A. (2000). Fair trade in tourism. *International Journal of Tourism Research*, *2*(3), 171–187. doi:10.1002/(SICI)1522-1970(200005/06)2:3<171::AID-JTR194>3.0.CO;2-K

Cohen, E. (1988). Authenticity and commoditation in tourism. *Annals of Tourism Research*, *15*(2), 371–386. doi:10.1016/0160-7383(88)90028-X

Dash, P. K. (2015). Tourism and community development: A Study on handicraft artisans of Odisha. *International Journal for Innovation Education and Research*, *3*(3), 61–72. doi:10.31686/ijier.vol3.iss3.328

Dias, Á., González-Rodríguez, M. R., & Patuleia, M. (2020). Developing poor communities through creative tourism. *Journal of Tourism and Cultural Change*, *0*(0), 1–21. doi:10.1080/14766825.2020.1775623

Do Valle, P. O., Silva, J. A., Mendes, J., & Guerreiro, M. (2006). Tourist satisfaction and destination loyalty intention: A structural and categorical analysis. *International Journal of Business Science and Applied Management*, *1*(1), 25–44.

Doherty, B., Smith, A., & Parker, S. (2015). Fair Trade market creation and marketing in the Global South. *Geoforum*, *67*, 158–171. doi:10.1016/j.geoforum.2015.04.015

Duerden, M. D. (2020). Experience design and the origins and aims of leisure studies: Shifting the focus from context to experience. *Journal of Leisure Research*, *0*(0), 1–13. doi:10.1080/00222216.2020.1867019

Duffy, L. N., & Overholt, J. R. (2013). Seeking authenticity: Re-conceptualizing adventure tourism. *Illuminare: A Student Journal in Recreation, Parks, and Leisure Studies*, *11*(1), 45–59. Retrieved from https://scholarworks.iu.edu/journals/index.php/illuminare/

Duffy, L. N., Stone, G., Chancellor, C. H., & Kline, C. S. (2016). Tourism development in the Dominican Republic: An examination of the economic impact to coastal households. *Tourism and Hospitality Research*, *16*(1), 35–49. doi:10.1177/1467358415613118

Elbeshbishi, A. N., & Al A'ali, E. A. (2020). Fair trade and ethical consumerism: A complementary perspective. In *Ethical consumerism and comparative studies across different cultures: Emerging research and opportunities* (pp. 101–125). IGI Global. doi:10.4018/978-1-7998-0272-3.ch007

Elomba, M. N., & Yun, H. J. (2018). Souvenir authenticity: The perspectives of local and foreign tourists. *Tourism Planning & Development*, *15*(2), 103–117. doi:10.1080/21568316.2017.1303537

Farsani, N. T., Mortazavi, M., Bahrami, A., Kalantary, R., & Bizhaem, F. K. (2017). Traditional crafts: A tool for geo-education in geotourism. *Geoheritage*, *9*(4), 577–584. doi:10.100712371-016-0211-2

Ferreira, J., Sousa, B. M., & Gonçalves, F. (2019). Encouraging the subsistence artisan entrepreneurship in handicraft and creative contexts. *Journal of Enterprising Communities*, *13*(1–2), 64–83. doi:10.1108/JEC-09-2018-0068

Grobar, L. M. (2019). Policies to promote employment and preserve cultural heritage in the handicraft sector. *International Journal of Cultural Policy*, *25*(4), 515–527. doi:10.1080/10286632.2017.1330887

Harris, J. (2014). Development in practice meeting the challenges of the handicraft industry in Africa : Evidence from Nairobi from Nairobi. *Development in Practice*, *24*(1), 105–117. doi:10.1080/09614524.2014.867478

Harvey, D. (2005). *A brief history of neoliberalism.* Oxford University Press. doi:10.1093/oso/9780199283262.001.0001

Hayes, D., & MacLeod, N. (2007). Packaging places: Designing heritage trails using an experience economy perspective to maximise visitor engagement. *Journal of Vacation Marketing*, *13*(1), 45–58. doi:10.1177/1356766706071205

Herman, A. (2019). Governing fairtrade: Ethics of care and justice in the Argentinean wine industry. *Social & Cultural Geography*, *00*(00), 1–22. doi:10.1080/14649365.2019.1593493

Hume, D. L. (2014). *Tourism art and souvenirs : The material culture of tourism an introduction tourism art and souvenirs – The material culture of tourism.* Academic Press.

Kazungu, I. (2020). Network linkages and performance of exporting micro and small enterprises in Dar es Salaam, Tanzania: Perspectives in the handicraft industry. *Global Business Review*. Advance online publication. doi:10.1177/0972150920934433

Kim, J. J., & Fesenmaier, D. R. (2015). Measuring emotions in real time: Implications for tourism experience design. *Journal of Travel Research*, *54*(4), 419–429. doi:10.1177/0047287514550100

Koli, A. K. (2021). Handmade OK please: Key criteria for purchasing craft items by Indian consumers. *Journal of Cultural Heritage Management and Sustainable Development*. Advance online publication. doi:10.1108/JCHMSD-04-2020-0063

Littrell, M. A., Anderson, L. F., & Brown, P. J. (1993). What makes a craft souvenir authentic? *Annals of Tourism Research*, *20*(6), 197–215. doi:10.1016/0160-7383(93)90118-M

Lwoga, B., & Mapunda, B. B. (2017). Challenges facing accessible tourism in cultural heritage sites: The case of Village Museum in Tanzania. *Revista de Turism: Studii Si Cercetari in Turism*, *0*(24), 45–54.

MacCannell, D. (1976). The tourist: A new theory of the leisure class. University of California Press.

Maertens, M. (2019). Fairtrade does not walk the talk. *Nature Sustainability*, *2*(7), 549–550. doi:10.103841893-019-0332-0

Mahoney, D. (2012). Changing strategies in marketing Kenya's tourist art: From ethnic brands to fair trade labels. *African Studies Review*, *55*(1), 161–190. doi:10.1353/arw.2012.0013

Maitland, R. A. (2008). Conviviality and everyday life: The appeal of new areas of London for visitors. *International Journal of Tourism Research*, *10*(1), 15–25. doi:10.1002/jtr.621

Manthiou, A., Lee, S., Tang, L., & Chiang, L. (2014). The experience economy approach to festival marketing: Vivid memory and attendee loyalty. *Journal of Services Marketing*, *28*(1), 22–35. doi:10.1108/JSM-06-2012-0105

Markwick, M. C. (2001). Tourism and the development of handicraft production in the Maltese islands. *Tourism Economics*, *3*(1), 29–51. doi:10.1080/14616680010008694

Melubo, K., & Carr, A. (2019). Developing indigenous tourism in the bomas: Critiquing issues from within the Maasai community in Tanzania. *Journal of Heritage Tourism*, *14*(3), 219–232. doi:10.1080/1743873X.2018.1533557

Mitchell, J. (2012). Value chain approaches to assessing the impact of tourism on low-income households in developing countries. *Journal of Sustainable Tourism*, *20*(3), 457–475. doi:10.1080/09669582.2012.663378

Mitchell, J., & Ashley, C. (2007). Leakage' claims: Muddled thinking and bad for policy. *ODI Opinion*, *81*(1), 1–2.

Mitchell, J., & Ashley, C. (2009). Value chain analysis and poverty. Overseas Development Institute.

Mogindol, S. H., & Bagul, A. H. B. P. (2014). Tourists' perceptions about an appealing handicraft. *Tourism. Leisure and Global Change*, *1*, 22–24.

Molony, T. (2009). Carving a niche: ICT, social capital, and trust in the shift from personal to impersonal trading in Tanzania. *Information Technology for Development*, *15*(4), 283–301. doi:10.1002/itdj.20127

Mookerjee, M. (2019). Do we still need fair trade? *Journal of Fair Trade*, *1*(2), 1–5. doi:10.13169/jfairtrade.1.2.0001

Oakes, T. (2006). Get real! On being yourself and being a tourist. In Travels in paradox: Remapping tourism (pp. 229–250). Rowman & Littlefield Publishers.

Oh, H., Fiore, A. M., & Jeoung, M. (2007). Measuring experience economy concepts: Tourism applications. *Journal of Travel Research*, *46*(2), 119–132. doi:10.1177/0047287507304039

Otto, J. E., & Ritchie, J. R. (1996). The service experience in tourism. *Tourism Management*, *17*(3), 165–174. doi:10.1016/0261-5177(96)00003-9

Portes, A., & Schauffler, R. (1993). Competing perspectives on the Latin American informal sector. *Population and Development Review*, *19*(1), 33–60. doi:10.2307/2938384

Prahalad, C. K., & Ramaswamy, V. (2003). The new frontier of experience innovation. *MIT Sloan Management Review*, *44*(4).

Quadri-Felitti, D., & Fiore, A. M. (2012). Experience economy constructs as a framework for understanding wine tourism. *Journal of Vacation Marketing*, *18*(1), 3–15. doi:10.1177/1356766711432222

Quan, S., & Wang, N. (2004). Towards a structural model of the tourist experience: An illustration from food experiences in tourism. *Tourism Management*, *25*(3), 297–305. doi:10.1016/S0261-5177(03)00130-4

Ravasi, D., & Rindova, V. (2008). *Symbolic value creation*. doi:10.4135/9781849200394.n49

Ravasi, D., Rindova, V., & Dalpiaz, E. (2012). The cultural side of value creation. *Strategic Organization*, *10*(3), 231–239. doi:10.1177/1476127012452824

Richard, N. (2007). Handicrafts and employment generation for the poorest youth and women. *United Nations Educational, Scientific and Cultural Organization, 17*, 65. Retrieved from https://unesdoc.unesco.org/images/0015/001567/156772e.pdf

Richards, G. (2011). Creativity and tourism:The state of the art. *Annals of Tourism Research, 38*(4), 1225–1253. doi:10.1016/j.annals.2011.07.008

Richards, G., & Raymond, C. (2000). Creative tourism. *ATLAS News*, (23), 16–20. doi:10.1007/978-3-319-01669-6_39-1

Ritchie, J. R. B., & Zins, M. (1978). Culture as determinant of the attractiveness of a tourism region. *Annals of Tourism Research, 5*(2), 252–267. doi:10.1016/0160-7383(78)90223-2

Rylance, A., & Spenceley, A. (2017). Reducing economic leakages from tourism: A value chain assessment of the tourism industry in Kasane, Botswana. *Development Southern Africa, 34*(3), 295–313. doi:10.1080/0376835X.2017.1308855

Scrase, T. J. (2003). Precarious production: Globalisation and artisan labour in the Third World. *Third World Quarterly, 24*(3), 449–461. doi:10.1080/0143659032000084401

Sharpley, R. (1994). Tourism and authenticity. In Tourism, tourists and society (pp. 127–162). Huntingdon: Elm Publications.

Slocum, S. L., Backman, K. F., & Robinson, K. L. (2011). Tourism pathways to prosperity: Perspectives on the informal economy in Tanzania. *Tourism Analysis, 16*(1), 43–55. doi:10.3727/108354211X12988225900045

Sternberg, E. (1997). The iconography of the tourism experience. *Annals of Tourism Research, 24*(4), 951–969. doi:10.1016/S0160-7383(97)00053-4

Supradist, N. (2004). *Economic leakage in tourism sector*. Retrieved from https://lup.lub.lu.se/luur/download?func=downloadFile&recordOId=1329250&fileOId=1329251

Suryawardani, O. I. G., Bendesa, K. G., Antarat, M., & Wiranathar, A. S. (2014). Tourism leakage of the accommodation sector in Bali. *ASEAN Journal on HospitalityandToaism, 13*(1), 3–18. doi:10.5614/ajht.2014.13.1.01

Tan, S., Kung, S.-F., & Luh, D.-B. (2013). A model of 'creative experience' in creative tourism. *Annals of Tourism Research, 41*, 153–174. doi:10.1016/j.annals.2012.12.002

Thirumaran, K., Dam, M. X., & Thirumaran, C. M. (2014). Integrating souvenirs with tourism development: Vietnam's challenges integrating souvenirs with tourism development. *Tourism Planning & Development, 0*(0), 1–11. doi:10.1080/21568316.2013.839471

Timothy, D. J., & Wall, G. (1997). Selling to tourists: Indonesian Street Vendors. *Annals of Tourism Research, 24*(2), 322–340. doi:10.1016/S0160-7383(97)80004-7

Truong, V. D. (2018). Tourism, poverty alleviation, and the informal economy: The street vendors of Hanoi, Vietnam. *Tourism Recreation Research, 43*(1), 52–67. doi:10.1080/02508281.2017.1370568

Truong, V. D., Liu, X., & Pham, Q. (2020). To be or not to be formal? Rickshaw drivers' perspectives on tourism and poverty. *Journal of Sustainable Tourism*, *28*(1), 33–50. doi:10.1080/09669582.2019.1665056

Tussyadiah, I. P. (2014). Toward a theoretical foundation for experience design in tourism. *Journal of Travel Research*, *53*(5), 543–564. doi:10.1177/0047287513513172

Varul, M. Z. (2008). Fair trade marketing between recognition and romantic commodification. *Cultural Studies*, *22*(5), 654–679. doi:10.1080/09502380802245910

WFTO. (2021). *Definition of fair trade*. Retrieved June 19, 2021, from https://wfto.com/who-we-are#definition-of-fair-trade

Williams, A. (2006). Tourism and hospitality marketing: Fantasy, feeling and fun. *International Journal of Contemporary Hospitality Management*, *18*(6), 482–495. doi:10.1108/09596110610681520

Wondirad, A., Bogale, D., & Li, Y. (2021). Practices and challenges of developing handicrafts as a core tourism product in Chencha and Konso, Southern Ethiopia. *International Journal of Cultural Policy*, *00*(00), 1–21. doi:10.1080/10286632.2021.1938560

Yadav, R., & Mahara, T. (2018). An exploratory study to investigate value chain of Saharanpur wooden carving handicraft cluster. *International Journal of System Assurance Engineering and Management*, *9*(1), 147–154. doi:10.100713198-016-0492-5

Yu, H., & Fang, W. (2009). Relative impacts from product quality, service quality, and experience quality on customer perceived value and intention to shop for the coffee shop market. *Total Quality Management & Business Excellence*, *20*(11), 1273–1285. doi:10.1080/14783360802351587

Zukin, S., & Maguire, J. S. (2004). Consumers and consumption. *Annual Review of Sociology*, *30*(1), 173–197. doi:10.1146/annurev.soc.30.012703.110553

KEY TERMS AND DEFINITIONS

Authenticity: The phenomenon of objects, activities, performances, emotions and experiences being genuine, unique, and with the reality of the culture they represent. It reflects the identity of a destination's culture.

Fair Trade: Is a business agreement that is designed to assist producers and artisans in developing countries in establishing long-term and equitable trade relationships with consumers in developed countries. The benefits associated with the fair trade business model include fair export prices, improved wages, and sustainable social and environmental standards.

Souvenirs: Tangible objects purchased or collected by travellers during or at the end of their trips and brought home as a remembrance of their trip. They represent the places, people and memories created during a trip.

Traditional Handicrafts: Objects artistically made using simple traditional tools and by using conventional manual methods (e.g., wooden carvings, weaving, painting, printing textiles, metal works, leather works and the likes).

Compilation of References

European Capitals of Smart Tourism. (2021). Retrieved from https://smarttourismcapital.eu/cities-2020-winners/

2021). Retrieved from https://9292.nl

Abelsen, B., Eide, D., Kvidal, T., & Leenheer, A. (2014). Organisational innovations: Re-organising destination marketing organisations. In G. Alsos, D. Eide, & E. L. Madsen (Eds.), *Handbook of research on innovation in tourism industries* (pp. 277–302). Edward Elgar.

Accelirate Inc. (2021). *RPA in the Hospitality Industry*. https://www.accelirate.com/industries/hospitality/

AccessMap. (2021). *Access map application for Seattle city*. Retrieved from https://www.accessmap.io/?region=wa.seattle&lon=-122.3381214&lat=47.6069591&z=14.5

Acemoglu, D., Gancia, G., & Zilibotti, F. (2012). Competing engines of growth: Innovation and standardisation. *Journal of Economic Theory*, *147*(2), 570–601. doi:10.1016/j.jet.2010.09.001

Achar, C., So, J., Agrawal, N., & Duhachek, A. (2016). What we feel and why we buy: The influence of emotions on consumer decision-making. *Current Opinion in Psychology*, *10*, 166–170. doi:10.1016/j.copsyc.2016.01.009

Adams, M. (2003). The reflexive self and culture: A critique. *The British Journal of Sociology*, *54*(2), 221–238. doi:10.1080/0007131032000080212 PMID:12945868

Adongo, C. A., Anuga, S. W., & Dayour, F. (2015). Will they tell others to taste? International tourists' experience of Ghanaian cuisines. *Tourism Management Perspectives*, *15*, 57–64. doi:10.1016/j.tmp.2015.03.009

Agapito, D., Valle, P., & Mendes, J. (2013). The cognitive-affective-cognitive model of destination image: A confirmatory analysis. *Journal of Travel & Tourism Marketing*, *30*(5), 471–481. doi:10.1080/10548408.2013.803393

Ahmed, F., Patterson, P., & Styles, C. (1999). The determinants of successful relationships in international business. *Australasian Marketing Journal*, *7*(1), 5–21. doi:10.1016/S1441-3582(99)70197-7

Ahmed, Z. U. (1991). The influence of the components of a state's tourist image on product positioning strategy. *Tourism Management*, *12*(4), 331–340. doi:10.1016/0261-5177(91)90045-U

Ahmed, Z. U. (1996). The need for the identification of the constituents of a destination's tourist image: A promotional segmentation perspective. *Tourism Review*, *51*(2), 44–57.

Akgün, A. E., Senturk, H. A., Keskin, H., & Onal, I. (2020). The relationships among nostalgic emotion, destination images and tourist behaviors: An empirical study of Istanbul. *Journal of Destination Marketing & Management*, 16.

Akroush, M. N., Jraisat, L. E., Kurdieh, D. J., AL-Faouri, R. N., & Qatu, L. T. (2016). Tourism service quality and destination loyalty: The mediating role of destination image from international tourists' perspectives. *Tourism Review*, *71*(1), 18–44. doi:10.1108/TR-11-2014-0057

Akyurt, H., & Atay, L. (2009). Destinasyonda imaj oluşturma süreci. *Aksaray Üniversitesi İktisadi ve İdari Bilimler Fakültesi Dergisi*, *1*(1), 1–14.

Albayrak, T., Caber, M., González-Rodríguez, M. R., & Aksu, A. (2018). Analysis of destination competitiveness by IPA and IPCA methods: The case of Costa Brava, Spain against Antalya, Turkey. *Tourism Management Perspectives*, *28*, 53–61. doi:10.1016/j.tmp.2018.07.005

Albayrak, T., & Caber, M. (2013). The symmetric and asymmetric influences of destination attributes on overall visitor satisfaction. *Current Issues in Tourism*, *16*(2), 149–166. doi:10.1080/13683500.2012.682978

Alcaniz, E., Sanchez, I., & Blas, S. (2009). The functional -psychological continuum in the cognitive image of a destination: A confirmatory analysis. *Tourism Management*, *30*(5), 715–723. doi:10.1016/j.tourman.2008.10.020

Alexiou, M. (2020). Experience economy and co-creation in a cultural heritage festival: Consumers' views. *Journal of Heritage Tourism*, *15*(2), 200–216. doi:10.1080/1743873X.2019.1632867

Alhelalat, J. A., Ma'moun, A. H., & Twaissi, N. M. (2017). The impact of personal and functional aspects of restaurant employee service behaviour on customer satisfaction. *International Journal of Hospitality Management*, *66*, 46–53. doi:10.1016/j.ijhm.2017.07.001

Alhemoud, A. M., & Armstrong, E. G. (1996). Image of tourism attractions in Kuwait. *Journal of Travel Research*, *34*(4), 76–80. doi:10.1177/004728759603400413

Ali, F., Terrah, A., Wu, C., Ali, L., & Wu, H. (2021). Antecedents and consequences of user engagement in smartphone travel apps. *Journal of Hospitality and Tourism Technology*. doi:10.1108/JHTT-09-2020-0221

Ali, F., Ryu, K., & Hussain, K. (2016). Influence of experiences on memories, satisfaction and behavioral intentions: A study of creative tourism. *Journal of Travel & Tourism Marketing*, *33*(1), 85–100. doi:10.1080/10548408.2015.1038418

Allan, M. (2015). Accessible tourism in Jordan: Travel constrains and motivations. *European Journal of Tourism Research*, *10*, 109–119.

Allegre, J., & Garau, J. (2011). The factor structure of tourist satisfaction at sun and sand destinations. *Journal of Travel Research*, *50*(1), 78–86. doi:10.1177/0047287509349270

Almobaideen, W., Krayshan, R., Allan, M., & Saadeh, M. (2017). Internet of Things: Geographical routing based on healthcare centers vicinity for mobile smart tourism destination. *Technological Forecasting and Social Change*, *123*, 342–350. doi:10.1016/j.techfore.2017.04.016

Alsos, G., Eide, D., & Madsen, E. L. (2014). Introduction: Innovation in tourism industries. In G. Alsos, D. Eide, & E. L. Madsen (Eds.), *Handbook of research on innovation in tourism industries* (pp. 1–24). Edward Elgar.

Altinay, Z., Saner, T., Bahçelerli, N. M., & Altinay, F. (2016). The role of social media tools: Accessible tourism for disabled citizens. *Journal of Educational Technology & Society*, *19*(1), 89–99.

Alvesson, M., & Sköldberg, K. (2000). Reflexive methodology: New vistas for qualitative research. Sage (Atlanta, Ga.).

Amari, M. (2001). *I musei delle aziende: La cultura della tecnica tra arte e storia*. Franco Angeli.

Anderson, B. A. (2013). A value-driven mechanism of attentional selection. *Journal of Vision (Charlottesville, Va.)*, *13*(3), 1–16. doi:10.1167/13.3.7 PMID:23589803

Compilation of References

Anderson, E. W. (1998). Customer satisfaction and word of mouth. *Journal of Service Research*, *1*(1), 5–17. doi:10.1177/109467059800100102

Anderson, J. (2012). Relational places: The surfed wave as assemblage and convergence. *Environment and Planning. D, Society & Space*, *30*(4), 570–587. doi:10.1068/d17910

Anderson, W. (2013). Leakages in the tourism systems: Case of Zanzibar. *Tourism Review*, *68*(1), 62–76. doi:10.1108/16605371311310084

Andersson, T. D. (2007). The tourist in the experience economy. *Scandinavian Journal of Hospitality and Tourism*, *7*(1), 46–58. doi:10.1080/15022250701224035

Andjelic, A. (2019). *The experience economy is blurring the lines between hospitality and retail: The sociology of business*. https://andjelicaaa.substack.com/p/the-experience-economy-is-blurring-the-lines-between-hospitality-and-retail-34f4d923c0ab

Andorfer, V. A., & Liebe, U. (2012). Research on fair trade consumption: A review. *Journal of Business Ethics*, *106*(4), 415–435. doi:10.100710551-011-1008-5

Antón, C., Camarero, C., & Garrido, M. J. (2018). Exploring the experience value of museum visitors as a co-creation process. *Current Issues in Tourism*, *21*(12), 1406–1425. doi:10.1080/13683500.2017.1373753

Ap, J., & Wong, K. (2001). Case study on tour guiding: Professionalism, issues and problems. *Tourism Management*, *22*(5), 551–563. doi:10.1016/S0261-5177(01)00013-9

Arnould, E., & Price, L. L. (1993). River Magic: Extraordinary experience and the extended service encounter. *The Journal of Consumer Research*, *20*(1), 24–45. doi:10.1086/209331

Asero, V., & Patti, S. (2009). *Prodotti enogastronomici e territorio: La proposta dell'enoturismo*. XVI Rapporto sul turismo italiano.

Assaker, G., Hallak, R., & El-haddad, R. (2019). *Consumer usage of online travel reviews: Expanding the unified theory of acceptance and use of technology 2 model*. doi:10.1177/1356766719867386

Augustyn, M. M., & Knowles, T. (2000). Performance of tourism partnerships: A focus on York. *Tourism Management*, *21*(4), 341–351. doi:10.1016/S0261-5177(99)00068-0

Avnet, T., Pham, M. T., & Stephen, A. T. (2012). Consumers' trust in feelings as information. *The Journal of Consumer Research*, *39*(4), 720–735. doi:10.1086/664978

Awh, E., Belopolsky, A. V., & Theeuwes, J. (2012). Top-down versus bottom-up attentional control: A failed theoretical dichotomy. *Trends in Cognitive Sciences*, *16*(8), 437–443. doi:10.1016/j.tics.2012.06.010 PMID:22795563

Aziz, F. S. H., & Selamat, N. H. (2016). Constructing authenticity through hospitality: Examining host-guest relations of a Malay homestay program. *Asian Journal of Tourism Research*, *1*(Special). Advance online publication. doi:10.12982/AJTR.2016.0009

Badulescu, D., & Badulescu, A. (2014). Medical tourism: Between entrepreneurship opportunities and bioethics boundaries: Narrative review article. *Iranian Journal of Public Health*, *43*(4), 406–415. PMID:26005650

Baeker, G. (2008). *Building a creative rural economy*. Retrieved from www.municipalworld.com

Baggio, R. (2008). Symptoms of complexity in a tourism system. *Tourism Analysis*, *13*(1), 1–20. doi:10.3727/108354208784548797

Baggio, R., Micera, R., & Del Chiappa, G. (2020). Smart tourism destinations: A critical reflection. *Journal of Hospitality and Tourism Technology*, *11*(3). Advance online publication. doi:10.1108/JHTT-01-2019-0011

Baird, F. E., & Kaufmann, W. (2008). *From Plato to Derrida: Upper Saddle River*. Pearson Prentice Hall.

Ballantyne, D., & Nilsson, E. (2017). All that is solid melts into air: The servicescape in digital service space. *Journal of Services Marketing*, *31*(3), 226–235. doi:10.1108/JSM-03-2016-0115

Baloglu, S. (1998). An empirical investigation of attitude theory for tourist destinations: A comparison of visitors and non-visitors. *Journal of Hospitality & Tourism Research (Washington, D.C.)*, *22*(3), 211–224. doi:10.1177/109634809802200301

Baloglu, S. (2001). Image variations of Turkey by familiarity index: Informational and experiential dimensions. *Tourism Management*, *22*(2), 127–133. doi:10.1016/S0261-5177(00)00049-2

Baloglu, S., & Brinberg, D. (1997). Affective images of tourism destinations. *Journal of Travel Research*, *35*(4), 11–15. doi:10.1177/004728759703500402

Baloglu, S., & McCleary, K. W. (1999a). A model of destination image formation. *Annals of Tourism Research*, *26*(4), 868–897. doi:10.1016/S0160-7383(99)00030-4

Baloglu, S., & McCleary, K. W. (1999b). US international pleasure travelers' images of four Mediterranean destinations: A comparison of visitors and nonvisitors. *Journal of Travel Research*, *38*(2), 144–152. doi:10.1177/004728759903800207

Baloglu, S., & Uysal, M. (1996). Market segments of push and pull motivations: A canonical correlation approach. *International Journal of Contemporary Hospitality Management*, *8*(3), 32–38. doi:10.1108/09596119610115989

Baniya, R., Shrestha, U., & Karn, M. (2018). Local and community well-being through community based tourism: A study of transformative eff ect. *Journal of Tourism and Hospitality Education*, *8*, 77–96. doi:10.3126/jthe.v8i0.20012

Bansel, P. (2015). The subject of policy. *Critical Studies in Education*, *56*(1), 5–20. doi:10.1080/17508487.2015.971839

Barbieri, C., & Sotomayor, S. (2013). Surf travel behaviour and destination preferences: An application of the serious leisure inventory and measure. *Tourism Management*, *35*, 111–121. doi:10.1016/j.tourman.2012.06.005

Barger, P. B., & Grandey, A. A. (2006). Service with a smile and encounter satisfaction: Emotional contagion and appraisal mechanisms. *Academy of Management Journal*, *49*(6), 1229–1238. doi:10.5465/amj.2006.23478695

Barile, S., Ciasullo, M. V., Troisi, O., & Samo, D. (•••). The role of technology and institutions in tourism service ecosystems: Findings from a case study. *The TQM Journal*, *29*(6), 811–833. doi:10.1108/TQM-06-2017-0068

Barnard, W. A., Loomis, R. J., & Cross, H. A. (1980). Assessment of visual recall and recognition learning in a museum environment. *Bulletin of the Psychonomic Society*, *16*(4), 311–313. doi:10.3758/BF03329552

Barnett, P. (2001). Fair trade in tourism. *Industry and Environment*, *24*(3), 18–19.

Barnett, T., Pearson, A. W., Pearson, R., & Kellermanns, F. W. (2015). Five-factor model personality traits as predictors of perceived and actual usage of technology. *European Journal of Information Systems*, *24*(4), 374–390. doi:10.1057/ejis.2014.10

Barrett, L. F. (2017). *How emotions are made: The secret life of the brain*. Houghton Mifflin Harcourt.

Barrett, L. F., & Satpute, A. B. (2019). Historical pitfalls and new directions in the neuroscience of emotion. *Neuroscience Letters*, *693*, 9–18. doi:10.1016/j.neulet.2017.07.045 PMID:28756189

Bartikowski, B., & Llosa, S. (2004). Customer satisfaction measurement: Comparing four methods of attribute categorisations. *Service Industries Journal*, *24*(4), 67–82. doi:10.1080/0264206042000275190

Compilation of References

Bastiaansen, M., Lub, X., Mitas, O., Jung, T. H., Passos Acenção, M., Han, D., & Strijbosch, W. (2019). Emotions as core building blocks of an experience. *International Journal of Contemporary Hospitality Management, 31*(2), 31. doi:10.1108/IJCHM-11-2017-0761

Bastiaansen, M., Straatman, S., Driessen, E., Mitas, O., Stekelenburg, J., & Wang, L. (2018). My destination in your brain: A novel neuromarketing approach for evaluating the effectiveness of destination marketing. *Journal of Destination Marketing & Management, 7*, 76–88. doi:10.1016/j.jdmm.2016.09.003

Baum, T., & Lockstone-Binney, L. (2014). Fit for purpose: Delivering wellness tourism through people. In Wellness tourism. A destination perspective (pp. 130-143). Routledge.

Baxter, P., & Jack, S. (2008). Qualitative case study methodology: Study design and implementation for novice researchers. *Qualitative Report, 13*(4), 544–559.

Bayno, P. M., & Jani, D. (2018). Residents' attitudes on the contribution of cultural tourism in Tanzania. *Journal of Tourism and Cultural Change, 16*(1), 41–56. doi:10.1080/14766825.2016.1211663

Becken, S., & Wilson, J. (2013). The impacts of weather on tourist travel. *Tourism Geographies, 15*(4), 620–639. doi:10.1080/14616688.2012.762541

Beerli, A., & Martin, J. D. (2004a). Factors influencing destination image. *Annals of Tourism Research, 31*(3), 657–681. doi:10.1016/j.annals.2004.01.010

Beerli, A., & Martín, J. D. (2004b). Tourists' characteristics and the perceived image of tourist destinations: a quantitative analysis: A case study of Lanzarote, Spain. *Tourism Management, 25*(5), 623–636. doi:10.1016/j.tourman.2003.06.004

Benson, W. (2014). *The benefits of tourism handicraft sales at Mwenge Handicrafts Centre in Dar Es Salaam*. Tampere University of Applied Sciences.

Beritelli, P. (2011). Cooperation among prominent actors in a tourist destination. *Annals of Tourism Research, 38*(2), 607–629. doi:10.1016/j.annals.2010.11.015

Beritelli, P., Strobl, A., & Peters, M. (2013). Interlocking directorships against community closure: A trade-off for development in tourist destinations. *Tourism Review, 68*(1), 21–34. doi:10.1108/16605371311310057

Berry, L. L., Carbone, L. P., & Haeckel, S. H. (2002). Managing the total customer experience. *MIT Sloan Management Review, 43*(3), 85–89.

Berry, L. L., & Parasuraman, A. (2004). *Marketing services: Competing through quality*. Simon and Schuster.

Bessiere, J. (1998). Local development and heritage: Traditional food and cuisine as tourist attractions in rural areas. European Society for Rural Sociology, 38(1).

Bhat, S. A., & Darzi, M. A. (2018). Antecedents of tourist loyalty to tourist destinations: A mediated-moderation study. *International Journal of Tourism Cities, 4*(2), 261–278. doi:10.1108/IJTC-12-2017-0079

Bianchi, R. (2018). The political economy of tourism development: A critical review. *Annals of Tourism Research, 70*(June), 88–102. doi:10.1016/j.annals.2017.08.005

Bigné, J. E., Andreu, L., & Gnoth, J. (2005). The theme park experience: An analysis of pleasure, arousal and satisfaction. *Tourism Management, 26*(6), 833–844. doi:10.1016/j.tourman.2004.05.006

Bigné, J. E., Sánchez, I., & Andreu, L. (2009). The role of variety seeking in short and long run revisit intentions in holiday destinations. *International Journal of Culture, Tourism and Hospitality Research, 3*(2), 103–115. doi:10.1108/17506180910962113

Bigne, J. E., Sanchez, M. I., & Sanchez, J. (2001). Tourism image, evaluation variables and after purchase behaviour: Inter-relationship. *Tourism Management*, *22*(6), 607–616. doi:10.1016/S0261-5177(01)00035-8

Binkhorst, E. (2005). *The co-creation tourism experience*. Retrieved from https://www.researchgate.net/researcher/2002799627_Esther_Binkhorst

Binkhorst, E. (2007). Creativity in tourism experiences: The case of Sitges. In G. Richards & J. Wilson (Eds.), *Tourism, creativity and development* (pp. 125–144)., doi:10.4324/9780203933695

Binkhorst, E., & den Dekker, T. (2009). Agenda for co-creation tourism experience research. *Journal of Hospitality Marketing & Management*, *18*(2-3), 311–327. doi:10.1080/19368620802594193

Birinci, H., Berezina, K., & Cobanoglu, C. (2018). Comparing customer perceptions of hotel and peer-to-peer accommodation advantages and disadvantages. *International Journal of Contemporary Hospitality Management*, *30*(2), 1190–1210. Advance online publication. doi:10.1108/IJCHM-09-2016-0506

Bissinger, K., & Leufkens, D. (2020). (Fairtrade) certification: Consequences of being a niche market. *Agrekon*, *59*(2), 188–201. doi:10.1080/03031853.2019.1699840

Biswas, C., Deb, S. K., Hasan, A. A. T., & Khandakar, M. S. A. (2020). Mediating effect of tourists' emotional involvement on the relationship between destination attributes and tourist satisfaction. *Journal of Hospitality and Tourism Insights*. doi:10.1108/JHTI-05-2020-0075

Björk, P. (2018). Tourist experience value: Tourist experience and life satisfaction. In N. Prebensen, J. Chen, & M. Uysal (Eds.), *Creating experience value in tourism* (pp. 21–30)., doi:10.1079/9781786395030.0021

Björk, P., & Kauppinen-Räisänen, H. (2016). Local food: A source for destination attraction. *International Journal of Contemporary Hospitality*, *26*(2), 177–194. doi:10.1108/IJCHM-05-2014-0214

Black, R., & Weiler, B. (2013). Current themes and issues in ecotour guiding. In R. Ballantyne & J. Packer (Eds.), *International handbook on ecotourism* (pp. 336–350). Edward Elgar. doi:10.4337/9780857939975.00033

Blackstock, K. (2005). A critical look at community based tourism. *Community Development Journal: An International Forum*, *40*(1), 39–49. doi:10.1093/cdj/bsi005

Blind, K. (2016). The impact of standardisation and standards on innovation. In J. Edler, P. Cunningham, & A. Gök (Eds.), *Handbook of innovation policy impact* (pp. 450–483). Edward Elgar. doi:10.4337/9781784711856.00022

Blokker, P., & Brighenti, A. (2011). An interview with Laurent Thévenot: On engagement, critique, commonality, and power. *European Journal of Social Theory*, *14*(3), 383–400. doi:10.1177/1368431011412351

Bonti, M. (2014). The corporate museums and their social function: Some evidence from Italy. *European Scientific Journal*, 1.

Boorstin, D. (1992). *The image: A guide to pseudo-events in America* (4th ed.). Vintage Books.

Boo, S., Busser, J., & Baloğlu, S. (2009). A model of customer-based brand equity and its application to multiple destinations. *Tourism Management*, *30*(2), 219–231. doi:10.1016/j.tourman.2008.06.003

Booth, D. (2001). From Bikinis to Boardshorts: "Wahines" and the paradoxes of surfing culture. *Journal of Sport History*, *28*(1), 3–22. PMID:17561560

Booth, D. (2013). History, culture and surfing: Exploring historiographical relationships. *Journal of Sport History*, *40*(1), 3–20. PMID:17561560

Bos, R., Straatemeier, T., & Temme, R. (2014). Joint accessibility design: Strategic urban development plan Breda 2030. *Citta 7th Annual Conference on Planning Research: Bridging the Implementation Gap of Accessibility Instruments and Planning Support Systems.*

Boswijk, A., Thijssen, T., & Peelen, E. (2007). The experience economy. A new perspective. Amersterdam: Pearson Education.

Boswijk, A., Thijssen, T., & Peelen, E. (2005). *A new perspective on the experience economy.* The European Centre for the Experience Economy.

Boswijk, A., Thijssen, T., & Peelen, E. (2007). *The experience economy: A new perspective.* Pearson Education Benelux.

Bough, V., Breuer, R., Maechler, N., & Ungerman, K. (2020). *The three building blocks of successful customer-experience transformations.* McKinsey & Company. https://www.mckinsey.com/business-functions/marketing-and-sales/our-insights/the-three-building-blocks-of-successful-customer-experience-transformations

Bowen, G. A. (2009). Document analysis as a qualitative research method. *Qualitative Research Journal, 9*(2), 27–40.

Bowen, J. T., & Chen McCain, S. L. (2015). Transitioning loyalty programs: A commentary on "the relationship between customer loyalty and customer satisfaction". *International Journal of Contemporary Hospitality Management, 27*(3), 415–430. doi:10.1108/IJCHM-07-2014-0368

Bowtell, J. (2015). Assessing the value and market attractiveness of the accessible tourism industry in Europe: A focus on major travel and leisure companies. *Journal of Tourism Futures, 1*(3), 203–222.

Boyne, S., Hall, D., & Williams, F. (2003). Policy, Support and promotion for food-related tourism initiatives. *Journal of Travel & Tourism Marketing, 14*(3-4), 131–154. doi:10.1300/J073v14n03_08

Braun, V., & Clarke, V. (2006). Using thematic analysis in psychology. *Qualitative Research in Psychology, 3*(2), 77–101. doi:10.1191/1478088706qp063oa

Breda. (2021a). *Public transport to and in Breda.* Retrieved from https://www.welkominbreda.nl/visit-breda/public-transport-to-and-in-breda

Breda. (2021b). Retrieved from https://tr.wikipedia.org/wiki/Breda

Briciu, A., Briciu, V., & Kavoura, A. (2020). Evaluating how 'smart' Brasov, Romania can be virtually via a mobile application for cultural tourism. *Sustainability, 12*(13), 1–17. https://do.org/10.3390/su12135324. doi:10.3390u12135324

Brito, M. (2017). *Intercultural interpretation discourses, techniques and strategies used by tour guides in the Coach Museum, Lisbon: Eight issues.* Nyelv Vilag - Institute of Foreign Languages and Communication of the Budapest Business School, 16-30. httpscomum.rcaap.ptbitstream10400.262296212017.01.006_.pdf

Brito, L. (2008). O guia-intérprete: Mediador intercultural. *Revista Turismo & Desenvolvimento, 10*, 67–84.

Brito, M. (2010). *O guia-intérprete: Facilitador do turismo cultural.* Tese de Doutoramento, Universidade de Évora.

Brito, M. (2013). *Informação tturística – A arte do guia interprete: Entre a cultura do turista e o destino.* Chiado Editora.

Brito, M. (2020). The consequences of guiding profession deregulation for the status of training of tourist guides: A Portuguese overview. *International Journal of Tour Guiding Research, 1*(1), 4–12.

Brito, M., & Farrugia, G. (2020). On tourist guiding: Reflecting on a centuries-old profession and proposing future challenges. *International Journal of Tour Guiding Research, 1*(1), 34–44.

Britton, S. (1982). The political economy of tourism in the Third World. *Annals of Tourism Research*, *9*(3), 331–358. doi:10.1016/0160-7383(82)90018-4

Britton, S. (1991). Tourism, capital, and place: Towards a critical geography of tourism. *Environment and Planning. D, Society & Space*, *9*(June), 451–478. doi:10.1068/d090451

Brown, J. S., & Duguid, P. (1991). Organisational learning and communities-of-practice: Toward a unified view of working, learning, and innovation. *Organization Science*, *2*(1), 40–57. doi:10.1287/orsc.2.1.40

Bruner, E. M. (1991). Transformation of self in tourism. *Annals of Tourism Research*, *18*(2), 238–250. doi:10.1016/0160-7383(91)90007-X

Bruner, E. M. (1994). Abraham Lincoln as authentic reproduction: A critique of postmodernism. *American Anthropologist*, *96*(2), 397–415. doi:10.1525/aa.1994.96.2.02a00070

Buckley, R. (2002). Surf tourism and sustainable development in Indo-Pacific Islands: The industry and the islands. *Journal of Sustainable Tourism*, *10*(5), 405–424. doi:10.1080/09669580208667176

Buckley, R. (2012). Sustainable tourism: Research and reality. *Annals of Tourism Research*, *39*(2), 528–546. doi:10.1016/j.annals.2012.02.003

Buhalis, D., & Michopoulou, E. (2011). Information-enabled tourism destination marketing: Addressing the accessibility market. *Current Issues in Tourism*, *14*(2), 145-168.

Buhalis, D. (1999). Tourism on the Greek Islands: Issues of peripherality, competitiveness and development. *International Journal of Tourism Research*, *1*(5), 341–358. doi:10.1002/(SICI)1522-1970(199909/10)1:5<341::AID-JTR201>3.0.CO;2-0

Buhalis, D. (2019). Technology in tourism- from information communication technologies to eTourism and smart tourism towards ambient intelligence tourism: A perspective article. *Tourism Review*, *75*(1), 1–4. doi:10.1108/TR-02-2020-405

Buhalis, D. (2019). Technology in tourism-from information communication technologies to eTourism and smart tourism towards ambient intelligence tourism: A perspective article. *Tourism Review*, *75*(1), 267–272. doi:10.1108/TR-06-2019-0258

Buhalis, D., & Amaranggana, A. (2014). Smart tourism destinations. In Z. Xiang & I. Tussyadiah (Eds.), *Information and communication technologies in tourism* (pp. 553–564). Springer. doi:10.1007/978-3-319-03973-2_40

Buhalis, D., & Amaranggana, A. (2015). *Smart tourism destinations enhancing tourism experience through personalisation of services*. Information and Communication Technologies in Tourism. doi:10.1007/978-3-319-14343-9_28

Buhalis, D., Harwood, T., Bogicevic, V., Viglia, G., Beldona, S., & Hofacker, C. (2019). Technological disruptions in services: Lessons from tourism and hospitality. *Journal of Service Management*, *30*(4), 484–506. doi:10.1108/JOSM-12-2018-0398

Buhalis, D., & Law, R. (2008). Progress in information technology and tourism management: 20 years on and 10 years after the Internet-The state of eTourism research. *Tourism Management*, *29*(4), 609–623. doi:10.1016/j.tourman.2008.01.005

Burns, J., & Kirkpatrick, C. (2008). *Creative industries in the rural East Midlands: Regional study report*. Academic Press.

Bushell, R., & Sheldon, P. J. (2009). Introduction to wellness and tourism. In R. Bushell & P. J. Sheldon (Eds.), *Wellness and tourism: Mind, body, spirit, place* (pp. 3–18). Cognizant Communication Corporation.

Byon, K., & Zhang, J. (2010). Development of a scale measuring destination image. *Marketing Intelligence & Planning*, *28*(4), 508–532. doi:10.1108/02634501011053595

Compilation of References

Cacho, A., Mendes-Filho, L., Estaregue, D., Moura, B., Cacho, N., Lopes, F., & Alves, C. (2016). Mobile tourist guide supporting a smart city initiative: A Brazilian case study. *International Journal of Tourism Cities, 2*(2), 164–183. doi:10.1108/IJTC-12-2015-0030

Cai, L. A. (2002). Cooperative branding for rural destinations. *Annals of Tourism Research, 29*(3), 720–742. doi:10.1016/S0160-7383(01)00080-9

Çakmak, E., & Çenesiz, M. A. (2020). Measuring the size of the informal tourism economy in Thailand. *International Journal of Tourism Research, 22*(5), 637–652. doi:10.1002/jtr.2362

Calabrò, A. (2000). L'arte può farsi reddito senza perdere l'anima. Rapporti, ilSole24Ore.

Caldwell, N., & Coshall, J. (2002). Measuring brand associations for museums and galleries using repertory grid analysis. *Management Decision, 40*(4), 383–392.

Campo, S., & Garau, J. B. (2008). The influence of nationality on the generation of tourist satisfaction with a destination. *Tourism Analysis, 13*(1), 81–92. doi:10.3727/108354208784548779

Campos, A. C., Mendes, J., Oom do Valle, P., & Scott, N. (2017). Co-creating animal-based tourist experiences: Attention, involvement and memorability. *Tourism Management, 63*, 100–114. doi:10.1016/j.tourman.2017.06.001

Campos, A. C., Pinto, P., & Scott, N. (2020). Bottom-up factors of attention during the tourist experience: An empirical study. *Current Issues in Tourism, 23*(24), 3111–3133. doi:10.1080/13683500.2019.1681383

Campos, A., Mendes, J., Oom, P., & Scott, N. (2015). Current issues in tourism co-creation of tourist experiences: A literature review. *Current Issues in Tourism, 0*(0), 1–32. doi:10.1080/13683500.2015.1081158

Canário, D. (2013). *O papel do guia intérprete no turismo em Lisboa* (Master's dissertation). Instituto das Novas Profissões.

Carlisle, S. (2010). *Access and marginalisation in a beach enclave resort – Tourism and Inequality: Problems and prospects*. CABI.

Carvalho, R. (2014). A literature review of the role of cultural capital in creative tourism. In J. A. C. Santos, M. Correira, M. Santos, & F. Serra (Eds.), *TMS 2014: Management Studies International Conference* (pp. 17–28). Academic Press.

Carvalho, R. (2020). Understanding the creative tourism experience in cultural and creative events/festivals. *ISLA Multidisciplinary E-Journal, 3*(1), 1–18. Retrieved from http://www.islae-journal.com/index.php/isla/article/view/39

Carvalho, R., Costa, C., & Ferreira, A. M. (2019). Review of the theoretical underpinnings in the creative tourism research field. *Tourism & Management Studies, 15*(SI), 11–22. doi:10.18089/tms.2019.15SI02

Carvalho, R., Ferreira, A. M., & Figueira, L. M. (2016). Cultural and creative tourism in Portugal. *Pasos: Revista de Turismo y Patrimonio Cultural, 14*(5), 1075–1082. Retrieved from lhttp://ojsull.webs.ull.es/index.php/Revista/article/view/134

Carvalho, I. (2020). A profissão de guia-intérprete e o impacto da COVID-19. *Revista Turismo e Desenvolvimento, 34*, 209–222.

Carvalho, I. (2021). Portuguese tourist guides and the digital age. *International Journal of Tour Guiding Research, 2*(1), 46–62.

Carvalho-Oliveira, J., & Cymbron, J. (1994). *Ser guia-intérprete em Portugal*. Departamento de Turismo. Instituto Superior de Novas profissões.

Carvalho, R., Costa, C., & Ferreira, A. M. (2018). New cultural mediators, cocreation, and the cultural consumption of creative tourism experiences. In J. M. Rodrigues, C. M. Ramos, P. J. Cardoso, & C. Henriques (Eds.), *Handbook of research on technological developments for cultural heritage and etourism applications* (pp. 264–283). doi:10.4018/978-1-5225-2927-9.ch013

Cassia, F., Castellani, P., Rossato, C., & Baccarani, C. (2021). Finding a way towards high-quality, accessible tourism: The role of digital ecosystems. *The TQM Journal, 33*(1), 205–221.

Castaldo, S., Perrini, F., Misani, N., & Tencati, A. (2009). The missing link between corporate social responsibility and consumer trust: The case of fair trade products. *Journal of Business Ethics, 84*(1), 1–15. doi:10.100710551-008-9669-4

Cefis, E., & Marsili, O. (2006). Survivor: The role of innovation in firms' survival. *Research Policy, 35*(5), 626–641. doi:10.1016/j.respol.2006.02.006

Cengiz, E., & Kırkbir, F. (2007). A structural model suggestion about relationship between total tourism affect perceived by local residents and tourism support. *Anadolu University Journal of Social Sciences, 7*(1), 19–37.

Çetin, İ. (2017). *Brand value and value creation in hotel businesses*. Detay Publication.

Chambel, B. (2021). *As novas tecnologias: Oportunidade ou ameaça para a profissão de guia-intérprete* (Master's dissertation). Escola Superior de Hotelaria e Turismo do Estoril.

Chang, C. H., Shu, S., & King, B. (2014). Novelty in theme park physical surroundings: An application of the stimulus–organism–response paradigm. *Asia Pacific Journal of Tourism Research, 19*(6), 680–699. doi:10.1080/10941665.2013.779589

Chang, L. L., Backman, K. F., & Huang, Y. C. (2014). Creative tourism: A preliminary examination of creative tourists' motivation, experience, perceived value and revisit intention. *International Journal of Culture, Tourism and Hospitality Research, 8*(4), 401–419. doi:10.1108/IJCTHR-04-2014-0032

Chang, S. (2018). Experience economy in hospitality and tourism: Gain and loss values for service and experience. *Tourism Management, 64*, 55–63. doi:10.1016/j.tourman.2017.08.004

Chang, S., & Lin, R. (2019). A framework of experiential service design in creative tourism. In R. Pl (Ed.), Lecture Notes in Computer Science: Vol. 11577. *Cross-cultural design. culture and society. HCII 2019* (pp. 3–16). doi:10.1007/978-3-030-22580-3_1

Chan, J. K. L. (2009). The consumption of museum service experiences: Benefits and value of museum experiences. *Journal of Hospitality Marketing & Management, 18*(2-3), 173–196. doi:10.1080/19368620802590209

Chaudhary, M. (2000). India's image as a tourist destination: A perspective of foreign tourists. *Tourism Management, 21*(3), 293–297. doi:10.1016/S0261-5177(99)00053-9

Chaudhuri, S. K. (2008). Ethics of medical tourism. *Journal of the Indian Medical Association, 106*, 188. PMID:18714462

Chauhan, R. (2006). *Heritage and cultural tourism*. Delhi: Vista.

Chen, I.-L., Scott, N., & Benckendorff, P. (2017). Well-being benefits from mindful experience. In N. Scott, J. Gao, & J. Ma (Eds.), Tourism experience design (pp. 174-188). CABI.

Chen, C. C., & Petrick, J. (2013). Health and wellness benefits of travel experiences: A literature review. *Journal of Travel Research, 52*(6), 709–719. doi:10.1177/0047287513496477

Chen, C. C., & Tsai, J. L. (2019). Determinants of behavioral intention to use the Personalised Location-based Mobile Tourism Application: An empirical study by integrating TAM with ISSM. *Future Generation Computer Systems*, *96*, 628–638. Advance online publication. doi:10.1016/j.future.2017.02.028

Chen, C. F., & Myagmarsuren, O. (2010). Exploring relationships between Mongolian destination brand equity, satisfaction and destination loyalty. *Tourism Cconomics*, *16*(4), 981–994. doi:10.5367/te.2010.0004

Chen, C., & Tsai, D. (2007). How destination image and evaluative factors affect behavioural intentions? *Tourism Management*, *28*(4), 1115–1122. doi:10.1016/j.tourman.2006.07.007

Chen, G., So, K. K. F., Hu, X., & Poomchaisuwan, M. (2021). Travel for affection: A stimulus-organism-response model of honeymoon tourism experiences. *Journal of Hospitality & Tourism Research (Washington, D.C.)*. Advance online publication. doi:10.1177/10963480211011720

Chen, J. S., Prebensen, N. K., & Uysal, M. S. (2018). Dynamic drivers of tourist experiences. In N. Prebensen, J. Chen, & M. Uysal (Eds.), *Creating experience value in tourism* (2nd ed., pp. 11–20). doi:10.1079/9781786395030.0011

Chen, J. S., & Uysal, M. (2002). Market positioning analysis: A hybrid approach. *Annals of Tourism Research*, *29*(4), 987–1003. doi:10.1016/S0160-7383(02)00003-8

Chesbrough, H. (2011). *Open services innovation: Rethinking your business to grow and compete in a new era*. Jossey-Bass.

Chhabra, D., Lee, W., Zhao, S., & Scott, K. (2013). Marketing of ethnic food experiences: Authentication analysis of Indian cuisine abroad. *Journal of Heritage Tourism*, *8*(2–3), 145–157. doi:10.1080/1743873X.2013.767816

Chi, C. G. Q., & Qu, H. (2008). Examining the structural relationships of destination image, tourist satisfaction and destination loyalty: An integrated approach. *Tourism Management*, *29*(4), 624–636. doi:10.1016/j.tourman.2007.06.007

Choi, J., Lee, S., & Jamal, T. (2021). Smart Korea: Governance for smart justice during a global pandemic. *Journal of Sustainable Tourism*, *29*(2-3), 541–550. doi:10.1080/09669582.2020.17777143

Choi, K., Wang, Y., & Sparks, B. (2018). Travel app users' continued use intentions: It's a matter of value and trust. *Journal of Travel & Tourism Marketing*, *00*(00), 1–13. doi:10.1080/10548408.2018.1505580

Chon, K. S. (1990). The role of destination image in tourism: A review and discussion. *Tourism Review*, *45*(2), 2–9.

Chon, K. S. (1991). Tourism destination image modification process. Marketing implications. *Tourism Management*, *12*(1), 68–72. doi:10.1016/0261-5177(91)90030-W

Chuang, C. M. (2020). A current travel model: Smart tour on mobile guide application services. *Current Issues in Tourism*, *23*(18), 2333–2352. doi:10.1080/13683500.2019.1631266

Cimbaljevìc, M., Stankov, U., & Pavluković, V. (2019). Going beyond the traditional destination competitiveness: Reflections on a smart destination in the current research. *Current Issues in Tourism*, *22*(20), 2472–2477.

Cleverciti. (2021). *9 European smart tourism destinations to watch and learn from*. Retrieved from https://www.cleverciti.com/en/resources/blog/9-european-smart-tourism-destinations-to-watch-and-learn-from

Cleverdon, R., & Kalisch, A. (2000). Fair trade in tourism. *International Journal of Tourism Research*, *2*(3), 171–187. doi:10.1002/(SICI)1522-1970(200005/06)2:3<171::AID-JTR194>3.0.CO;2-K

Coghlan, A., Buckley, R., & Weaver, D. (2012). A framework for analysing awe in tourism experiences. *Annals of Tourism Research*, *39*(3), 1710–1714. doi:10.1016/j.annals.2012.03.007

Cohen, E. (1972). Towards a sociology of international tourism. *Social Research*, *39*(1), 164–182.

Cohen, E. (1979). A phenomenology of tourist experiences. *Sociology*, *13*(2), 179–210. doi:10.1177/003803857901300203

Cohen, E. (1985). The tourist guide. The origins, structure and dynamics of a role. *Annals of Tourism Research*, *12*(1), 5–29. doi:10.1016/0160-7383(85)90037-4

Cohen, E. (1988). Authenticity and commoditisation in tourism. *Annals of Tourism Research*, *15*(3), 371–386. doi:10.1016/0160-7383(88)90028-X

Cohen, E. (1996). A phenomenology of tourist experiences. In Y. Apostopoulos, S. Leivadi, & A. Yiannakis (Eds.), *The sociology of tourism: Theoretical and empirical investigations* (pp. 90–111). Routledge.

Cohen-Hattab, K., & Kerber, J. (2004). Literature, cultural identity and the limits of authenticity: A composite approach. *International Journal of Tourism Research*, *6*(2), 57–73. doi:10.1002/jtr.470

Cohen, M. C. (2018). Big data and service operations. *Production and Operations Management*, *27*(9), 1709–1723. doi:10.1111/poms.12832

Cohen, R. A. (2014). Neuropsychology of attention: Synthesis. In R. A. Cohen (Ed.), *The neuropsychology of attention* (pp. 931–963). Springer. doi:10.1007/978-0-387-72639-7_28

Cohen, S. (2010). Reflections on reflexivity in leisure and tourism studies. *Leisure (Waterloo, Ont.)*, *32*(87), 27–29. doi:10.1360/zd-2013-43-6-1064

Cohen, S. A., & Cohen, E. (2019). New directions in the sociology of tourism. *Current Issues in Tourism*, *22*(2), 153–172. doi:10.1080/13683500.2017.1347151

Community Homestay Network. (2020). *2019 Impact Report*. https://www.communityhomestay.com/impact-report-2019.pdf

Connelly, F. M., & Clandinin, D. J. (1990). Stories of experience and narrative inquiry. *Educational Researcher*, *19*(5), 2–14. doi:10.3102/0013189X019005002

Corbetta, M., & Shulman, G. L. (2002). Control of goal-directed and stimulus-driven attention in the brain. *Nature Reviews. Neuroscience*, *3*(3), 201–215. doi:10.1038/nrn755 PMID:11994752

Corréa, S. C. H., & Gosling, M. S. (2020). Travelers' perception of smart tourism experiences in smart tourism destinations. *Tourism Planning & Development*. doi:10.1080/21568316.2020.1798689

Costa, J., Rodrigues, D., & Gomes, J. (2019). Sustainability of tourism destinations and the importance of certification. *Worldwide Hospitality and Tourism Themes*, *11*(6), 677–684. doi:10.1108/WHATT-08-2019-0050

Coudounaris, D. N., & Sthapit, E. (2017). Antecedents of memorable tourism experience related to behavioral intentions. *Psychology and Marketing*, *34*(12), 1084–1093.

Court, B., & Lupton, R. A. (1997). Customer portfolio development: Modeling destination adopters, inactives and rejecter. *Journal of Travel Research*, *36*(1), 35–43. doi:10.1177/004728759703600106

Cravidão, F. (2006). Turismo e cultura: dos Itinerários ao lugar dos lugares. In M. L. Fonseca (Coord.), Desenvolvimento e territórios: Espaços rurais pós agrícolas e novos lugares de turismo e lazer (pp. 269-278). Centro de Estudos Geográficos, Universidade de Lisboa.

Crompton, J. (1979). An assessment of the image of Mexico as a vacation destination and the influence of geographical location upon the image. *Journal of Travel Research*, *17*(4), 18–23. doi:10.1177/004728757901700404

Compilation of References

Crompton, J. L., & Ankomah, P. K. (1993). Choice set propositions in destination decisions. *Annals of Tourism Research*, *20*(3), 461–476. doi:10.1016/0160-7383(93)90003-L

Crompton, J. L., Fakeye, P. C., & Lue, C. C. (1992). Positioning: The example of the Lower Rio Grande Valley in the winter long stay destination market. *Journal of Travel Research*, *31*(2), 20–26. doi:10.1177/004728759203100204

Cser, K., & Ohuchi, A. (2008). World practices of hotel classification systems. *Asia Pacific Journal of Tourism Research*, *13*(4), 379–398. doi:10.1080/10941660802420960

Czernek, K. (2013, January). Determinants of cooperation in a tourist region. *Annals of Tourism Research*, *40*, 83–104. doi:10.1016/j.annals.2012.09.003

da Rosa, S., dos Anjos, F. A., de Lima Pereira, M., & Junior, M. A. (2019). Image perception of surf tourism destination in Brazil. *International Journal of Tourism Cities*.

Dadgostar, B., & Isotalo, R. M. (1996). Content of city destination image for near-home tourists. *Journal of Hospitality & Leisure Marketing*, *3*(2), 25–34. doi:10.1300/J150v03n02_03

Dagustani, D., Kartini, D., Oesman, Y. M., & Kaltum, U. (2018). Destination image of tourist: Effect of travel motivation and memorable tourism experience. *Etikonomi*, *17*(2), 307–331. doi:10.15408/etk.v17i2.7211

Damasio, A. R. (1995). Toward a neurobiology of emotion and feeling: Operational concepts and hypotheses. *The Neuroscientist*, *1*(1), 19–25. doi:10.1177/107385849500100104

Dangi, T. B., & Jamal, T. (2016). An integrated approach to "sustainable community-based tourism". *Sustainability*, *8*(475), 1–32. doi:10.3390u8050475

Danilov, V. (1991). *Corporate museums, galleries, and visitor centers: A directory*. Greenwood Press.

Danilov, V. (1992). *A planning guide for corporate museums, galleries, and visitor centers*. Greenwood Press.

Dann, G. M. (1996). Tourists' images of a destination-an alternative analysis. *Journal of Travel & Tourism Marketing*, *5*(1-2), 41–55. doi:10.1300/J073v05n01_04

Darcy, S., Cameron, B., & Pegg, S. (2010). Accessible tourism and sustainability: A discussion and case study. *Journal of Sustainable Tourism*, *18*(4), 515–537.

Darcy, S., McKercher, B., & Schweinsberg, S. (2020). From tourism and disability to accessible tourism: A perspective article. *Tourism Review*, *75*(1), 140–144.

Darmawijaya, I. G., Tirtawati, N. M., & Sekarti, N. K. (2018). The typology of wellness tourism in Bali. *3rd International Conference on Tourism, Economics, Accounting, Management, and Social Science (TEAMS 2018)*.

Dash, P. K. (2015). Tourism and community development: A Study on handicraft artisans of Odisha. *International Journal for Innovation Education and Research*, *3*(3), 61–72. doi:10.31686/ijier.vol3.iss3.328

Davras, G. M. (2021). Classification of winter tourism destination attributes according to three factor theory of customer satisfaction. *Journal of Quality Assurance in Hospitality & Tourism*, *22*(4), 496–516. doi:10.1080/1528008X.2020.1810195

DCMS. (1998). *Creative industries: Mapping Document*. DCMS.

de Amaral, A. V., & Dias, C. A. G. (2008). Da praia para o mar: Motivos à adesão e à prática do surfe. *LICERE-Revista do Programa de Pós-graduação Interdisciplinar em Estudos do Lazer*, *11*(3).

de Salvo, P., Hernández Mogollón, J. M., Clemente, E. D., & Calzati, V. (2013). Territory, tourism and local products. The extra virgin oil's enhancement and promotion: A benchmarking Italy-Spain. *Tourism and Hospitality Management*, *19*(1), 23–34. doi:10.20867/thm.19.1.2

De Wit, B. (2017). *Strategy- an international perspective*. Cengage Learning.

Decrop, A. (2014). Theorising tourist behavior. In S. McCabe (Ed.), *The Routledge handbook of tourism marketing* (pp. 251–267). Routledge.

Dedeoglu, B. B., Bilgihan, A., Ye, B. H., Buonincontri, P., & Okumus, F. (2018). The impact of servicescape on hedonic value and behavioral intentions: The importance of previous experience. *International Journal of Hospitality Management*, *72*, 10–20. doi:10.1016/j.ijhm.2017.12.007

Del Chiappa, G., & Baggio, R. (2015). Knowledge transfer in smart tourism destinations: Analysing the effects of a network structure. *Journal of Destination Marketing & Management*, *4*(3), 145–150. doi:10.1016/j.jdmm.2015.02.001

Deloitte. (2020). *The future of hospitality*. Author.

Deng-Westphal, M., Beeton, S., & Anderson, A. (2015). The paradox of adopting tourism ecolabels. In M. Hughes, D. Weaver, & C. Pforr (Eds.), *The practice of sustainable tourism: Resolving the paradox* (pp. 228–246). Routledge.

Derrett, R. (2004). Festivals, events and the destination. *Festival and Events Management*, 32-64.

Devile, E., & Kastenholz, E. (2018). Accessible tourism experiences: The voice of people with visual disabilities. *Journal of Policy Research in Tourism, Leisure & Events*, *10*(3), 265–285.

Dias, Á., González-Rodríguez, M. R., & Patuleia, M. (2020). Developing poor communities through creative tourism. *Journal of Tourism and Cultural Change*, *0*(0), 1–21. doi:10.1080/14766825.2020.1775623

Dibra, M. (2015). Rogers theory on diffusion of innovation-the most appropriate theoretical model in the study of factors influencing the integration of sustainability in tourism businesses. *Procedia: Social and Behavioral Sciences*, *195*, 1453–1462. doi:10.1016/j.sbspro.2015.06.443

Dickinson, J. E., Ghali, K., Cherrett, T., Speed, C., Davies, N., Norgate, S., Dickinson, J. E., Ghali, K., Cherrett, T., & Speed, C. (2014). *Current Issues in Tourism Tourism and the smartphone app : Capabilities, emerging practice and scope in the travel domain*. doi:10.1080/13683500.2012.718323

Diebner, R., Silliman, E., Ungerman, K., & Vancauwenberghe, M. (2020). *Adapting customer experience in the time of coronavirus*. McKinsey & Company. https://www.mckinsey.com/business-functions/marketing-and-sales/our-insights/adapting-customer-experience-in-the-time-of-coronavirus

Dillette, A., Douglas, A., & Andrzejewski, C. (2021). Dimensions of holistic wellness as a result of international wellness tourism experiences. *Current Issues in Tourism*, *24*(6), 794–810. doi:10.1080/13683500.2020.1746247

Dixit, S. K. (2017). Introduction. In S. K. Dixit (Ed.), *The Routledge handbook of consumer behaviour in hospitality and tourism* (pp. 1–3). Routledge. doi:10.4324/9781315659657-1

Do Valle, P. O., Silva, J. A., Mendes, J., & Guerreiro, M. (2006). Tourist satisfaction and destination loyalty intention: A structural and categorical analysis. *International Journal of Business Science and Applied Management*, *1*(1), 25–44.

Dodds, R., & Ramsay, G. (2017). Is economically incentivised participation creating a greater interest into environmental certification? *Journal of Outdoor Recreation and Tourism*, *20*, 31–33. doi:10.1016/j.jort.2017.09.001

Doering, Z. (1999). Strangers, guests, or clients? Visitor experiences in museums. *Curator*, *42*(2), 74–87. doi:10.1111/j.2151-6952.1999.tb01132.x

Compilation of References

Doherty, B., Smith, A., & Parker, S. (2015). Fair Trade market creation and marketing in the Global South. *Geoforum*, *67*, 158–171. doi:10.1016/j.geoforum.2015.04.015

Dolnicar, S. (2021). Airbnb before, during and after COVID-19. In Airbnb before, during and after COVID-19. doi:10.14264/ab59afd

Dolnicar, S. (2019). A review of research into paid online peer-to-peer accommodation: Launching the Annals of Tourism Research curated collection on peer-to-peer accommodation. *Annals of Tourism Research*, *75*(January), 248–264. doi:10.1016/j.annals.2019.02.003

Dolnicar, S., & Fluker, M. (2003). Behavioural market segments among surf tourists: Investigating past destination choice. *Journal of Sport & Tourism*, *8*(3), 186–196. doi:10.1080/14775080310001690503

Draper, D., & Minca, C. (1997). Image and destination: A geographical approach applied to Banff National Park, Canada. *Tourism Review*, *2*, 14–24.

Driscoll, A., Lawson, R., & Niven, B. (1994). Measuring tourists' destination perceptions. *Annals of Tourism Research*, *21*(3), 499–511. doi:10.1016/0160-7383(94)90117-1

Duerden, M. D. (2020). Experience design and the origins and aims of leisure studies: Shifting the focus from context to experience. *Journal of Leisure Research*, *0*(0), 1–13. doi:10.1080/00222216.2020.1867019

Duerden, M. D., Lundberg, N. R., Ward, P., Taniguchi, S. T., Hill, B., Widmer, M. A., & Zabriskie, R. (2018). From ordinary to extraordinary: A framework of experience types. *Journal of Leisure Research*, *49*(3-5), 196–216. doi:10.1080/00222216.2018.1528779

Duffy, L. N., & Overholt, J. R. (2013). Seeking authenticity: Re-conceptualizing adventure tourism. *Illuminare: A Student Journal in Recreation, Parks, and Leisure Studies*, *11*(1), 45–59. Retrieved from https://scholarworks.iu.edu/journals/index.php/illuminare/

Duffy, L. N., Stone, G., Chancellor, C. H., & Kline, C. S. (2016). Tourism development in the Dominican Republic: An examination of the economic impact to coastal households. *Tourism and Hospitality Research*, *16*(1), 35–49. doi:10.1177/1467358415613118

Duhigg, C. (2013). *The power of habit: Why we do what we do and how to change*. Random House.

Dunk, R. M., Gillespie, S. A., & MacLeod, D. (2016). Participation and retention in a green tourism certification scheme. *Journal of Sustainable Tourism*, *24*(12), 1585–1603. doi:10.1080/09669582.2015.1134558

Dunn, H. L. (1959). High-level wellness for man and society. *American Journal of Public Health*, *49*(6), 786–792. doi:10.2105/AJPH.49.6.786 PMID:13661471

Duxbury, N., & Richards, G. (2019). A research agenda for creative tourism. In N. Duxbury & G. Richards (Eds.), *A research agenda for creative tourism*. doi:10.4337/9781788110723

Dwyer, L., Edwards, D., Mistilis, N., Roman, C., & Scott, N. (2009). Destination and enterprise management for a tourism future. *Tourism Management*, *30*(1), 63–74. doi:10.1016/j.tourman.2008.04.002

Dwyer, L., & Kim, C. (2003). Destination competitiveness: Determinants and indicators. *Current Issues in Tourism*, *6*(5), 369–414. doi:10.1080/13683500308667962

Eagleman, D. (2015). *The brain: The story of you*. Canongate Books.

Echtner, C. M., & Ritchie, J. B. (2003). The meaning and measurement of destination image. *Journal of Tourism Studies*, *14*(1), 37–48.

Echtner, C. M., & Ritchie, J. R. B. (1993). The measurement of destination image: An empirical assessment. *Journal of Travel Research*, *31*(4), 3–13. doi:10.1177/004728759303100402

Eichhorn, V., & Buhalis, D. (2011). Accessibility: A key objective for the tourism industry. In D. Buhalis & S. Darc (Eds.), *Accessible tourism: Concepts and issues* (pp. 46–61). Channel View Publications.

Eide, D., & Mossberg, L. (2013). Towards more intertwined innovation types: innovation through experience design focusing on customer interactions. In Handbook on the experience economy (pp. 248-268). Edward Elgar. doi:10.4337/9781781004227.00019

Eide, D., Fuglsang, L., & Sundbo, J. (2017). Management challenges with the maintenance of experience concept innovations: Toward a new research agenda. *Tourism Management*, *63*, 452–463. doi:10.1016/j.tourman.2017.06.029

Eide, D., & Mossberg, L. (2019). Toward a framework of experience quality assessment: Illustrated by cultural tourism. In D. Jelinčić & Y. Mansfeld (Eds.), *Creating and Managing Experiences in Cultural Tourism* (pp. 101–120). World Scientific. doi:10.1142/10809

Eisenhardt, K. M., & Graebner, M. A. (2007). Theory building from cases: Opportunities and challenges. *Academy of Management Journal*, *50*(1), 25–37. doi:10.5465/amj.2007.24160888

Ekman, P. (1992). An argument for basic emotions. *Cognition and Emotion*, *6*(3-4), 169–200. doi:10.1080/02699939208411068

Ekman, P. (2007). *Emotions revealed: Recognising faces and feelings to improve communication and emotional life*. Macmillan.

Elbeshbishi, A. N., & Al A'ali, E. A. (2020). Fair trade and ethical consumerism: A complementary perspective. In *Ethical consumerism and comparative studies across different cultures: Emerging research and opportunities* (pp. 101–125). IGI Global. doi:10.4018/978-1-7998-0272-3.ch007

Ellis, A., Park, E., Kim, S., & Yeoman, I. (2018). What is food tourism? *Tourism Management*, *68*, 250–263. doi:10.1016/j.tourman.2018.03.025

Elomba, M. N., & Yun, H. J. (2018). Souvenir authenticity: The perspectives of local and foreign tourists. *Tourism Planning & Development*, *15*(2), 103–117. doi:10.1080/21568316.2017.1303537

ENAT-European Network Accessible Tourism. (2020). *Accessibility at smart tourism destinations: 2nd edition of the TUR4all congress* (Webinar series). Retrieved from https://www.accessibletourism.org/?i=enat.en.events.2188

Eom, T., & Han, H. (2019). Community-based tourism (TourDure) experience program: A theoretical approach. *Journal of Travel & Tourism Marketing*, *36*(8), 956–968. doi:10.1080/10548408.2019.1665611

Eremia, M., Toma, L., & Sanduleac, M. (2017). The smart city concept in the 21st century. *Procedia Engineering*, *181*, 12–19.

EU. (2018). *European Capital of Smart Tourism*. Retrieved from https://smarttourismcapital.eu/

European Commission. (2019). *Access city award 2019 examples of best practice in making EU cities more accessible*. Retrieved from https://ec.europa.eu/social/main.jsp?catId=1141

European Commission. (2021a). *Compendium of best practices 2020*. Retrieved from https://smart-tourism-capital.ec.europa.eu/best-practices_en

European Commission. (2021b). *Noord-Brabant*. Retrieved from https://ec.europa.eu/growth/tools-databases/regional-innovation-monitor/base-profile/noord-brabant

Compilation of References

European Commission. (2021c). *Winners of the European capitals of smart tourism 2020 competition*. Retrieved from https://smart-tourism-capital.ec.europa.eu/competition-winners-2020_en

European Union. (2019). *Compendium of best practices "2019 European capital of smart tourism competition"*. Retrieved from https://smarttourismcapital.eu/wp-content/uploads/2019/07/Compendium_2019_FINAL.pdf

Fakeye, P. C., & Crompton, J. L. (1991). Images differences between prospective, first-time and repeat visitors to the Lower Rio Grande valley. *Journal of Travel Research*, *30*(2), 10–16. doi:10.1177/004728759103000202

Fanfani, T. (2002). Economical profitability and culture: a possible meeting in the historical archives and in the enterprise's museums. *Quaderni della Fondazione*, *1*, 102-131.

Farmer, G. D., Janssen, C. P., Nguyen, A. T., & Brumby, D. P. (2018). Dividing attention between tasks: Testing whether explicit payoff functions elicit optimal dual-task performance. *Cognitive Science*, *42*(3), 820–849. doi:10.1111/cogs.12513 PMID:28653447

Farsani, N. T., Mortazavi, M., Bahrami, A., Kalantary, R., & Bizhaem, F. K. (2017). Traditional crafts: A tool for geo-education in geotourism. *Geoheritage*, *9*(4), 577–584. doi:10.100712371-016-0211-2

Faullant, R., Matzler, K., & Mooradian, T. A. (2011). Personality, basic emotions, and satisfaction: Primary emotions in the mountaineering experience. *Tourism Management*, *32*(6), 1423–1430. doi:10.1016/j.tourman.2011.01.004

FEG – European Federation of Tourist Guide Associations. (2020). https://www.feg-touristguides.com/about.php

Feldman, J., & Skinner, J. (2018). Tour guides as cultural mediators: Performance and Positioning. *Ethnologia Europaea*, *48*(2), 5–13. doi:10.16995/ee.1955

Felin, T., Foss, N., & Ployhart, R. (2015). The microfoundations movement in strategy and organisation theory. *The Academy of Management Annals*, *9*(1), 575–632. doi:10.5465/19416520.2015.1007651

Femenia-Serra, F., & Ivars-Baidal, J. (2018). Do smart tourism destinations really work? The case of Benidorm. *Asia Pacific Journal of Tourism Research, 26*(4). doi:10.1080/10941665.2018.1561478

Femenia-Serra, F., Neuhofer, B., & Ivars-Baidal, J. (2019). Towards a conceptualisation of smart tourists and their role within the smart destination scenario. *Service Industries Journal*, *39*(2), 109–133.

Fernandez, A. G., Blanco, M. C., Barreto, M., & Santos, C. R. (2007). Comperative analysis of international tourists in inland cultural destinations: The case of Castilla y Leon, Spain. In G. Richards (Ed.), *Cultural tourism: Global and local perspectives*. Taylor & Francis Group.

Ferrara, A. (1998). *Reflective authenticity*. Routledge.

Ferraz, J. (2017). Turismo e globalização. In F. Silva, & J. Umbelino (Coord.), Planeamento e desenvolvimento turístico (pp. 79-92). Editora Lidel.

Ferreira, J., Sousa, B. M., & Gonçalves, F. (2019). Encouraging the subsistence artisan entrepreneurship in handicraft and creative contexts. *Journal of Enterprising Communities*, *13*(1–2), 64–83. doi:10.1108/JEC-09-2018-0068

Ferri, M. A. (2014). A business model for accessible tourism. In L. Aiello (Ed.), *Handbook of research on management of cultural products: E-Relationship marketing and accessibility perspectives* (pp. 287–302). IGI Global. doi:10.4018/978-1-4666-5007-7.ch014

Figg, H. (2018). *Breda wins 2019 access city award for making the city more accessible to citizens with disabilities*. Retrieved from https://www.eltis.org/discover/news/breda-wins-2019-access-city-award-making-city-more-accessible-citizens-disabilities

Flanagan, J. C. (1954). The critical incident technique. *Psychological Bulletin*, *51*(4), 327–358. doi:10.1037/h0061470 PMID:13177800

Fleischmann, D., Michalewicz, B., Stedje-Larsen, E., Neff, J., Murphy, J., Browning, K., Nebeker, B., Cronin, A., Sauve, W., Stetler, C., Herriman, L., & McLay, R. (2011). Surf medicine: Surfing as a means of therapy for combat-related polytrauma. *JPO: Journal of Prosthetics and Orthotics*, *23*(1), 27–29. doi:10.1097/JPO.0b013e3182065316

Florida, R. (2002). *The rise of the creative class: and how it's transforming work, leisure, community and everyday life*. doi:10.5860/CHOICE.40-2276

Florida, R. (2018). *The rise of the rural creative class*. Retrieved October 3, 2019, from Bloomberg website: https://www.bloomberg.com/news/articles/2018-05-01/what-makes-a-rural-creative-hub-innovation-and-the-arts

Flyvbjerg, B. (2001). Making social science matter: Why social inquiry fails and how it can succeed again. Cambridge University Press.

Font, X. (1997). Managing the tourist destination's image. *Journal of Vacation Marketing*, *3*(2), 123–131. doi:10.1177/135676679700300203

Ford, N., & Brown, D. (2006). *Surfing and social theory: Experience, embodiment and narrative of the dream glide*. Routledge.

Forno, F., & Garibaldi, R. (2015). Sharing economy in travel and tourism: The case of home-swapping in Italy. *Journal of Quality Assurance in Hospitality & Tourism*, *16*(2), 202–220. doi:10.1080/1528008X.2015.1013409

Fortuna, C. (2012). Património, turismo e emoção. *Revista Critica de Ciencias Sociais*, *97*, 23–40.

Foxall, G. (1990). *Consumer psychology in behavioral perspective*. Beard Books.

Francken, J. C., & Slors, M. (2018). Neuroscience and everyday life: Facing the translation problem. *Brain and Cognition*, *120*, 67–74. doi:10.1016/j.bandc.2017.09.004 PMID:28899576

Frazier, J., & Touchet, T. (2012). *Transforming the city of New York new platform for public-private cooperation ushers in smart cities of the future*. Retrieved from https://www.cisco.com/c/dam/en_us/about/ac79/docs/ps/motm/City-24x7_PoV.pdf

Fredrickson, B. L. (1998). What good are positive emotions? *Review of General Psychology*, *2*(3), 300–319. doi:10.1037/1089-2680.2.3.300 PMID:21850154

Freel, M. S. (2000). Barriers to product innovation in small manufacturing firms. *International Small Business Journal*, *18*(2), 60–80. doi:10.1177/0266242600182003

Fridgen, J. D. (1987). Use of cognitive maps to determine perceived tourism regions. *Leisure Sciences*, *9*(2), 101–117. doi:10.1080/01490408709512150

Frijda, N. H. (2007). *The laws of emotion*. Erlbaum.

Fuchs, M., & Weiermair, K. (2003). New perspective of satisfaction research in tourism destinations. *Tourism Review*, *58*(3), 6–14. doi:10.1108/eb058411

Fuglesang, L. (2015). Engagement in place: bricolage networking in tourism and the experience economy. In A. Lorentzen, K. Topsø Larsen, & L. Schrøder (Eds.), *Routledge advances in regional economics, science and policy* (pp. 213–228). Routledge. doi:10.4324/9781315885063

Fuglsang, L., & Nordli, A. (2018). On service innovation as an interactive process: A case study of the engagement with innovation of a tourism service. *Social Sciences*, *7*(12). doi:10.3390/socsci7120258

Compilation of References

Fuglsang, L. (2008). Innovation with care: What it means. In L. Fuglsang (Ed.), *Innovation and the creative process: Towards innovation with care* (pp. 3–21). Edward Elgar. doi:10.4337/9781848440104

Fuglsang, L. (2018). Towards a theory of a practice-based approach to service innovation within spheres of interaction. In A. Scupola & L. Fuglsang (Eds.), *Services, experiences and innovation: Integrating and extending research* (pp. 174–164). Edward Elgar Publishing. doi:10.4337/9781788114301.00015

Fuglsang, L., & Eide, D. (2013). The experience turn as 'bandwagon': Understanding network formation and innovation as practice. *European Urban and Regional Studies*, *20*(4), 417–434. doi:10.1177/0969776412448090

Fuglsang, L., Sundbo, J., & Sørensen, F. (2011). Dynamics of experience service innovation: innovation as a guided activity: Results from a Danish survey. *Service Industries Journal*, *31*(5), 661–677. doi:10.1080/02642060902822109

Fu, Y. K., & Wang, Y. J. (2020). Experiential value influences authentic happiness and behavioural intention: Lessons from Taiwan's tourism accommodation sector. *Tourism Review*, (April). Advance online publication. doi:10.1108/TR-06-2019-0228

Fyall, A., Garrod, B., & Wang, Y. (2012). Destination collaboration: A critical review of theoretical approaches to a multi-dimensional phenomenon. *Journal of Destination Marketing & Management*, *1*(1-2), 10–26. https://doi.org/10.1016/j.jdmm.2012.10.002

Gabor, M. R., & Oltean, F. D. (2019). Babymoon tourism between emotional wellbeing service for medical tourism and niche tourism: Development and awareness on Romanian educated women. *Tourism Management*, *70*, 170–175. doi:10.1016/j.tourman.2018.08.006

Gajdosik, T. (2018). Smart tourism: Concepts and insights from Central Europe. *Czech Journal of Tourism*, *7*(1), 25–44. https://doi.org/10.1515/cjot-2018-0002

Gajdosik, T. (2020). Smart tourists as a profiling market segment: Implications for DMOs. *Tourism Economics*, *26*(6), 1042–1062. https://doi.org/10.1177/1354816619844368

Gallarza, M. G., Saura, I. G., & Garcia, H. C. (2002). Destination image: Towards a conceptual framework. *Annals of Tourism Research*, *29*(1), 56–78. doi:10.1016/S0160-7383(01)00031-7

Gallouj, F., Rubalcaba, L., & Windrum, P. (2013). *Public-private innovation networks in services*. Edward Elgar Pub. Ltd. doi:10.4337/9781781002667

Garg, R., Rahman, Z., & Kumar, I. (2010). Evaluating a model for analyzing methods used for measuring customer experience. *Journal of Database Marketing & Customer Strategy Management*, *17*(2), 78–90. doi:10.1057/dbm.2010.7

Gartner, W. C. (1989). Tourism image: Attribute measurement of state tourism products using multi-dimensional scaling techniques. *Journal of Travel Research*, *28*(2), 16–20. doi:10.1177/004728758902800205

Gartner, W. C. (1994). Image formation process. *Journal of Travel & Tourism Marketing*, *2*(2-3), 191–216. doi:10.1300/J073v02n02_12

Geissler, G. L., Rucks, C. T., & Edison, S. W. (2006). Understanding the role of service convenience in art museum marketing: An exploratory study. *Journal of Hospitality & Leisure Marketing*, *14*(4), 69–87. doi:10.1300/J150v14n04_05

Gemeente Breda. (2021a). *Bredata masterplan digitalisation Breda*. Retrieved from https://smartcitybreda.com/storage/2020/11/0178_20-BREDATA_masterplan_ENG_V2_internet.pdf

Gemeente Breda. (2021b). Retrieved from https://www.breda.nl/en

George, A. L., & Bennett, A. (2005). *Case studies and theory development in the social sciences*. MIT Press.

Getz, D. (2008). Event tourism: Definition, evolution, and research. *Tourism Management, 29*(3), 403–428. doi:10.1016/j.tourman.2007.07.017

Getz, D., & Jamal, T. (1994). The environment-community symbiosis: A case for collaborative tourism planning. *Journal of Sustainable Tourism, 2*(3), 152–173. https://doi.org/10.1080/09669589409510692

Geus, S., Richards, G., & Toepoel, V. (2016). Conceptualisation and operationalisation of event and festival experiences: Creation of an event experience scale. *Scandinavian Journal of Hospitality and Tourism, 16*(3), 274–296. doi:10.1080/15022250.2015.1101933

Giampiccoli, A., Mtapuri, O., & Nauright, J. (2020). Tourism development in the Seychelles: A proposal for a unique community-based tourism alternative. *Journal of Tourism and Cultural Change*, 1–14. doi:10.1080/14766825.2020.1743297

Gilani, H. R., Innes, J. L., & De Grave, A. (2018). The effects of seasonal business diversification of British Columbia ski resorts on forest management. *Journal of Outdoor Recreation and Tourism, 23*, 51–58. doi:10.1016/j.jort.2018.07.005

Gilbert, D. (2006). *Stumbling on happiness*. Alfred A. Knopf.

Gillovic, B., & McIntosh, A. (2020). Accessibility and inclusive tourism development: Current state and future agenda. *Sustainability, 12*, 1–15.

Gilodi, C. (2002). Il museo d'impresa: forma esclusiva per il corporate marketing. *Luic Papers, 101*, 10.

Gitlin, J. (2017). *74% of people are tired of social media ads—but they're effective.* SurveyMonkey.Com. https://www.surveymonkey.com/curiosity/74-of-people-are-tired-of-social-media-ads-but-theyre-effective/

Global Spa Summit. (2011). *Wellness tourism and medical tourism: Where do spas fit?* Available online: https://globalwellnessinstitute.org/industry-research/wellness-tourism-medical-tourism/

Global Wellness Institute. (2011). *Wellness tourism and medical tourism: W here do spas fit?* Available online: https://globalwellnessinstitute.org/industry-research/wellness-tourism-medical-tourism/

Global Wellness Institute. (2018). Available online: https://globalwellnessinstitute.org/industry-research/2018-global-wellness-economy-monitor/

Go, F. M., & Govers, R. (1999). The Asian perspective: Which international conference destinations in Asia are the most competitive? *Journal of Convention & Exhibition Management, 4*(1), 37–50. doi:10.1300/J143v01n04_04

Goffman, E. (1993). *A representação do eu na vida de todos os dias*. Relógio D'agua.

Gofman, A., Moskowitz, H. R., & Mets, T. (2011). Marketing museums and exhibitions: What drives the interest of young people. *Journal of Hospitality Marketing & Management, 20*(6), 601–618. doi:10.1080/19368623.2011.577696

Gomes, E. L., Gândara, J. M., & Ivars-Baidal, J. A. (2017). Is it important to be a smart tourism destination: Public managers' understanding of destinations in the state of Paraná. *Brazilian Journal of Tourism Research, 11*(3), 503–536.

González, D. S. (2016). *El mundo sobre las olas: Perspectiva de desarrollo turístico através del surfing* (PhD thesis). Universidad Rey Juan Carlos, España.

Goodwin, H., & Santilli, R. (2009). Community-based tourism: A success. *ICRT Occasional Paper, 11*(1), 37.

Google Maps. (2021). *Breda*. Retrieved from https://www.google.nl/maps/place/Breda,+Hollanda/

Gooroochurn, N., & Sugiyarto, G. (2005). Competitiveness indicators in the travel and tourism industry. *Tourism Economics, 11*(1), 25–43. doi:10.5367/0000000053297130

Gornostaeva, G., & Campbell, N. (2012). The creative underclass in the production of place: Example of Camden Town in London. *Journal of Urban Affairs*, *34*(2), 169–188. doi:10.1111/j.1467-9906.2012.00609.x

Goulding, C. (2000). The museum environment and the visitor experience. *European Journal of Marketing*, *34*(3), 261–278. doi:10.1108/03090560010311849

Govers, R., Go, F. M., & Kumar, K. (2007). Promoting tourism destination image. *Journal of Travel Research*, *46*(1), 15–23. doi:10.1177/0047287507302374

Graburn, N. H. H. (1983). The anthropology of tourism. *Annals of Tourism Research*, *10*(1), 9–33. doi:10.1016/0160-7383(83)90113-5

Grames, E. (2012). *Community festivals: Big benefits, but Risks, too*. University of Minnesota Extension.

Greenhalgh, T., Robert, G., Macfarlane, F., Bate, P., & Kyriakidou, O. (2004). Diffusion of innovations in service organisations: Systematic review and recommendations. *The Milbank Quarterly*, *82*(4), 581–629. doi:10.1111/j.0887-378X.2004.00325.x PMID:15595944

Gretzel, U., & Koo, C. (2021). Smart tourism cities: A duality of place where technology supports the convergence of touristic and residential experiences. *Asia Pacific Journal of Tourism Research*, *26*(4), 352–364.

Gretzel, U., Sigala, M., Xiang, Z., & Koo, C. (2015). Smart tourism: Foundations and developments. *Electronic Markets*, *25*(3), 179–188. https://doi.org/10.1007/s12525-015-0196-8

Gretzel, U., Werthner, H., Koo, C., & Lamsfus, C. (2015). Conceptual foundations for understanding smart tourism ecosystems. *Computers in Human Behavior*, *50*, 558–563. doi:10.1016/j.chb.2015.03.043

Grissemann, U., Plank, A., & Brunner-Sperdin, A. (2013). Enhancing business performance of hotels: The role of innovation and customer orientation. *International Journal of Hospitality Management*, *33*, 347–356. doi:10.1016/j.ijhm.2012.10.005

Grobar, L. M. (2019). Policies to promote employment and preserve cultural heritage in the handicraft sector. *International Journal of Cultural Policy*, *25*(4), 515–527. doi:10.1080/10286632.2017.1330887

Groeger, J. A., & Murphy, G. (2021). Driving and cognitive function in people with stroke and healthy age-matched controls. *Neuropsychological Rehabilitation*, 1–24. doi:10.1080/09602011.2020.1869566 PMID:33428553

Grove, S. J., Fisk, R. P., & John, J. (2003). The future of services marketing: Forecasts from ten services experts. *Journal of Services Marketing*, *17*(2), 107–121. doi:10.1108/08876040310467899

Guan, J., & Jones, D. L. (2015). The contribution of local cuisine to destination attractiveness: An analysis involving Chinese tourists' heterogeneous preferences. *Asia Pacific Journal of Tourism Research*, *20*(4), 416–434. doi:10.1080/10941665.2014.889727

Guba, E. G., & Lincoln, Y. S. (1994). Competing paradigms in qualitative research. In E. G. Guba & Y. S. Lincoln (Eds.), Handbook of qualitative research (Vol. 2, pp. 105–117). Academic Press.

Guttentag, D. (2015). Airbnb: Disruptive innovation and the rise of an informal tourism accommodation sector. *Current Issues in Tourism*, *18*(12), 1192–1217. doi:10.1080/13683500.2013.827159

Gu, Z., & Siu, R. C. S. (2009). Drivers of job satisfaction as related to work performance in Macao casino hotels. *International Journal of Contemporary Hospitality Management*, *21*(5), 561–578. doi:10.1108/09596110910967809

Guzel, B., & Apaydin, M. (2016). Gastronomy tourism, motivation and destinations. In *Global issues and trends in tourism*. St. Kliment Ohridski University Press.

Gyawali, T. (2020). *Community-based tourism: Support community and immerse in the life of locals.* https://www.nepalsanctuarytreks.com/community-based-tourism-community-support-and-immersing-in-the-life-of-locals/

Habeeb, N. J., & Weli, S. T. (2020). Relationship of smart cities and smart tourism: An overview. *HighTech and Innovation Journal, 1*(4), 194–202.

Hacıoğlu, N. (2010). *Tourism Marketing.* Nobel Publishing.

Halden, A. (2020). Responding to the Coronavirus crisis: Parallels for tourism and climate change? In F. Burini (Ed.), *Tourism facing a pandemic: from crisis to recovery* (pp. 57–62). Università degli Studi di Bergamo.

Hall, C. M. (2007). Response to Yeoman et al: The fakery of "The authentic tourist.". *Tourism Management, 28*(4), 1139–1140. doi:10.1016/j.tourman.2006.09.008

Hall, C. M., Timothy, D. J., & Duval, D. T. (2012). *Safety and security in tourism: Relationships, management, and marketing.* Routledge. doi:10.4324/9780203049464

Hall, C. M., & Williams, A. M. (2008). *Tourism and innovation.* Routledge. doi:10.4324/9780203938430

Hall, D., & Brown, F. (Eds.). (2006). *Tourism and welfare: Ethics, responsibility and sustained wellbeing.* CABI., doi:10.1079/9781845930660.0000

Hall, M. C. (2011). Health and medical tourism: A kill or cure for global public health? *Tourism Review, 66*(1/2), 4–15. doi:10.1108/16605371111127198

Hamed, H. M. (2015). Wellness tourism: An Initiative for comprising wellness tourism vacations within the corporate wellness strategy. *American Journal of Tourism Research, 4*(2), 52–67. doi:10.11634/216837861504643

Hammarfjord, M. O., & Roxenhall, T. (2017). The relationship between network commitment, antecedents, and innovation in strategic innovation networks. *International Journal of Innovation Management, 21*(6), 1750037–1750036p. doi:10.1142/S1363919617500372

Hansen, M., Hjalager, A. M., & Fyall, A. (2019). Adventure tourism innovation: Benefitting or hampering operations? *Journal of Outdoor Recreation and Tourism, 28,* 100253. doi:10.1016/j.jort.2019.100253

Harris, J. (2014). Development in practice meeting the challenges of the handicraft industry in Africa : Evidence from Nairobi from Nairobi. *Development in Practice, 24*(1), 105–117. doi:10.1080/09614524.2014.867478

Harvey, D. (2005). *A brief history of neoliberalism.* Oxford University Press. doi:10.1093/oso/9780199283262.001.0001

Hassan, H. (2011). *Tecnologias da informação e turismo: e-tourism* (Master's dissertation). Património e Desenvolvimento da Faculdade de Letras da Universidade de Coimbra.

Hatfield, E., Cacioppo, J. T., & Rapson, R. L. (1993). Emotional contagion. *Current Directions in Psychological Science, 2*(3), 96–100. doi:10.1111/1467-8721.ep10770953

Hayes, D., & MacLeod, N. (2007). Packaging places: Designing heritage trails using an experience economy perspective to maximise visitor engagement. *Journal of Vacation Marketing, 13*(1), 45–58. doi:10.1177/1356766706071205

Heidegger, M. (1962). *Being and time.* Blackwell.

Hennig-Thurau, T., Groth, M., Paul, M., & Gremler, D. D. (2006). Are all smiles created equal? How emotional contagion and emotional labor affect service relationships. *Journal of Marketing, 70*(3), 58–73. doi:10.1509/jmkg.70.3.058

Herman, A. (2019). Governing fairtrade: Ethics of care and justice in the Argentinean wine industry. *Social & Cultural Geography, 00*(00), 1–22. doi:10.1080/14649365.2019.1593493

Compilation of References

Hernandez-Lobato, L., Solis-Radilla, M., Molinar-Tena, M. A., & Sanchez-Garcia, J. (2006). Tourism destination image, satisfaction and loyalty: Ixtapa-zihuatanejo, Mexico. *Tourism Geographies*, *8*(4), 343–358. doi:10.1080/14616680600922039

Hernandez-Mogollon, J. M., Duarte, P. A., & Folgado-Fernandez, J. A. (2018). The contribution of cultural events to the formation of the cognitive and affective images of a tourist destination. *Journal of Destination Marketing & Management*, *8*, 170–178. doi:10.1016/j.jdmm.2017.03.004

Higgins-Desbiolles, F. (2020). The "war over tourism": Challenges to sustainable tourism in the tourism academy after COVID-19. *Journal of Sustainable Tourism*, *29*(4), 551–569. doi:10.1080/09669582.2020.1803334

Hirschman, E. C., & Holbrook, M. B. (1982). Hedonic consumption: Emerging concepts, methods and propositions. *Journal of Marketing*, *46*(3), 92–101. doi:10.1177/002224298204600314

History, culture, traditions, communities, monuments. (n.d.). *The Hindu*. Retrieved from https://www.thehindu.com/society/history-and-culture/life-in-jaisalmers-living-fort

Hjalager, A. M., & Madsen, E. L. (2018). Business model innovation in tourism: Opportunities and challenges. In The Sage handbook of tourism management (pp. 373-390). Sage.

Hjalager, A. M. (2002). Repairing innovation defectiveness in tourism. *Tourism Management*, *23*(5), 465–474. doi:10.1016/S0261-5177(02)00013-4

Hjalager, A. M. (2004). What do tourists eat and why? Towards a sociology of gastronomy and tourism. *Tourism (Zagreb)*, *52*(2).

Hjalager, A. M. (2018). Suppliers as key collaborators for sustainable tourism development. In J. Liburd & D. Edwards (Eds.), *Collaboration for Sustainable Tourism Development* (pp. 187–205). Goodfellow. doi:10.23912/9781911635000-3927

Hjalager, A.-M. (2000). Tourism destinations and the concept of industrial districts. *Tourism and Hospitality Research*, *2*(3), 199–213. doi:10.1177/146735840000200302

Hjalager, A.-M. (2010). A review of innovation research in tourism. *Tourism Management*, *31*(1), 1–12. doi:10.1016/j.tourman.2009.08.012

Hoarau-Heemstra, H., & Eide, D. (2019). Values and concern: Drivers of innovation in experience-based tourism. *Tourism and Hospitality Research*, *19*(1), 15–26. doi:10.1177/1467358416683768

Høegh-Guldberg, O. (2018). Between company and network practices: Mirroring innovative ideas. *Scandinavian Journal of Hospitality and Tourism*, *18*(3), 278–302. doi:10.1080/15022250.2018.1497305

Høegh-Guldberg, O., Eide, D., Trengereid, V., & Hjemdahl, K. M. (2018). Dynamics of innovation network journeys: Phases and crossroads in seven regional innovation networks. *Scandinavian Journal of Hospitality and Tourism*, *18*(3), 234–260. doi:10.1080/15022250.2018.1497261

Holbrook, M. B. (1994). The nature of customer value: An axiology of services in the consumption experience. *Service Quality: New Directions in Theory and Practice*, *21*(1), 21–71. doi:10.4135/9781452229102.n2

Holbrook, M. B., & Hirschman, E. C. (1982). The experiential aspects of consumption: Consumer fantasies, feelings and fun. *The Journal of Consumer Research*, *9*(2), 132–140. doi:10.1086/208906

Holnicki-Szulc, J., Motylewski, J., & Kolakowski, P. (2008). Introduction to smart technologies. In J. Holnicki-Szulc (Ed.), *Smart technologies for safety engineering* (pp. 1–9). John Wiley & Sons, Ltd.

Holt, K. (2012). Authentic journalism? A critical discussion about existential authenticity in journalism ethics. *Journal of Mass Media*, *27*.

Hommel, B., Chapman, C. S., Cisek, P., Neyedli, H. F., Song, J. H., & Welsh, T. N. (2019). No one knows what attention is. *Attention, Perception & Psychophysics*, *81*(7), 2288–2303. doi:10.375813414-019-01846-w PMID:31489566

Horstmann, G., & Herwig, A. (2016). Novelty biases attention and gaze in a surprise trial. *Attention, Perception & Psychophysics*, *78*(1), 69–77. doi:10.375813414-015-0995-1 PMID:26486643

Hosany, S. (2012). Appraisal determinants of tourist emotional responses. *Journal of Travel Research*, *51*(3), 303–314. doi:10.1177/0047287511410320

Hosany, S., Ekinci, Y., & Uysal, M. (2006). Destination image and destination personality: An application of branding theories to tourism places. *Journal of Business Research*, *59*(5), 638–642. doi:10.1016/j.jbusres.2006.01.001

Hosany, S., & Witham, M. (2010). Dimensions of cruisers' experiences, satisfaction and intention to recommend. *Journal of Travel Research*, *49*(3), 351–364. doi:10.1177/0047287509346859

House of Lords. (2000). *Complementary and alternative medicine* (Report of the Select Committee on Science and Technology). HMSO.

Howkins, J. (2002). *The creative economy: How people make money from ideas*. Penguin Books.

Hritz, N. M., Sidman, C. L., & D'abundo, M. (2014). Segmenting the college educated generation Y health and wellness traveler. *Journal of Travel & Tourism Marketing*, *31*(1), 132–145. doi:10.1080/10548408.2014.861727

Hsu, C., Chan, A., & Huang, S. (2009). Tour guide performance and tourist satisfaction: A study of the package tours in Shangai. *Journal of Hospitality & Tourism Research (Washington, D.C.)*, *34*(1), 3–33. doi:10.1177/1096348002026001001

Hsu, T. K., Tsai, Y. F., & Wu, H. H. (2009). The preference analysis for tourist choice of destination: A case study of Taiwan. *Tourism Management*, *30*(2), 288–297. doi:10.1016/j.tourman.2008.07.011

Huang, L., & Lau, N. (2020). Enhancing the smart tourism experience for people with visual impairments by gamified application approach through needs analysis in Hong Kong. *Sustainability*, *12*, 1–27.

Hughes, H. L. (2008). Visitor and non-visitor destination images: The influence of political instability in South-Eastern Europe. *Tourism: An International Interdisciplinary Journal*, *56*(1), 59–74.

Hui, T. K., & Wan, T. W. D. (2003). Singapore's image as a tourist destination. *International Journal of Tourism Research*, *5*(4), 305–313. doi:10.1002/jtr.437

Hume, D. L. (2014). *Tourism art and souvenirs : The material culture of tourism an introduction tourism art and souvenirs – The material culture of tourism*. Academic Press.

Hunt, J. D. (1975). Image as a factor in tourism development. *Journal of Travel Research*, *13*(3), 1–7. doi:10.1177/004728757501300301

Hu, Y., & Ritchie, J. B. (1993). Measuring destination attractiveness: A contextual approach. *Journal of Travel Research*, *32*(2), 25–34. doi:10.1177/004728759303200204

IESE. (2019). Retrieved December 31, 2020, from https://blog.iese.edu/cities-challenges-and-management/2020/10/27/iese-cities-in-motion-index-2020/

Iliuta, M. A., & Wiltshier, P. (2018). Spa services and wellness activities within the surf tourism experience: The case study of Jersey, Channel Islands. *International Journal of Spa and Wellness*, *1*(1), 82–94. doi:10.1080/24721735.2018.1432454

IMD. (2020). Retrieved December 31, 2020, from https://www.imd.org/smart-city-observatory/smart-city-index/

Compilation of References

IMF. (2020). *World Economic Outlook, April 2020: The great lockdown*. IMF.

Im, H. H., Kim, S. S., Elliot, S., & Han, H. (2012). Conceptualising destination brand equity dimensions from a consumer-based brand equity perspective. *Journal of Travel & Tourism Marketing, 29*(4), 385–403. doi:10.1080/10548408.2012.674884

INE – Instituto Nacional de Estatística. (2020). *Conta Satélite de Turismo/Tourism Sattelite Account*. https://www.sgeconomia.gov.pt/noticias/ine-conta-satelite-do-turismo-para-portugal-span-classnovo-novospan.aspx

Ivanova, M., Ivanov, I. K., & Ivanov, S. (2020). Travel behaviour after the pandemic: The case of Bulgaria. *Anatolia, 32*(1), 1–11. doi:10.1080/13032917.2020.1818267

Ivanovic, M., & Saayman, M. (2015). Authentic economy shaping transmodern tourism experience. *African Journal for Physical, Health Education, Recreation & Dance, 2015*(December), 24–36.

Ivars-Baidal, J., Celdran-Bernabeu, M., Mazon, J., & Perles-Ivars, A. (2017). Smart destinations and the evolution of ICTs: A new scenario for destination management. *Current Issues in Tourism*, 1-20. doi:10.1080/13683500.2017.1388771

Ivars-Baidal, J., Mazon, J., & Perles-Ivars, A. (2019). Smart destinations and the evolution of ICTs: A new scenario for destination management? *Current Issues in Tourism, 22*(13), 1581–1600. https://doi.org/10.1080/13683500.2017.1388771

Jakobsen, O., & Arnesen, T. G. (2020). *Sluttevaluering av klyngen NCE Tourism* (152/2020). Menon Economics. https://www.menon.no/publication/sluttevaluering-klyngen-nce-tourism/

Jamaica Gleaner. (2021). *Jamaica Gleaner*. Retrieved August 31, 2021, from https://jamaica-gleaner.com

Jamal, T., & Getz, D. (1995). Collaboration theory and community tourism planning. *Annals of Tourism Research, 22*(1), 186–204. https://doi.org/10.1016/0160-7383(94)00067-3

Jansen-Verbeke, M., & van Rekom, J. (1996). Scanning museum visitors: Urban tourism marketing. *Annals of Tourism Research, 23*(2), 364–375. doi:10.1016/0160-7383(95)00076-3

Jasrotia, A., & Gangotia, A. (2018). Smart cities to smart tourism destinations: A review paper. *Journal of Tourism Intelligence and Smartness, 1*(1), 47–56.

Jayapalan, N. (2001). *Introduction to tourism*. Atlantic Publishers & Dist.

Jelinčić, D. A., & Senkic, M. (2019). The value of experience in culture and tourism: The power of emotions. In N. Duxbury & G. Richards (Eds.), *A research agenda for creative tourism* (pp. 41–53). doi:10.4337/9781788110723.00012

Jeong, M., & Shin, H. H. (2020). Tourists' experiences with smart tourism technology at smart destinations and their behavior intentions. *Journal of Travel Research, 59*(8), 1464–1477. doi:10.1177/0047287519883034

Jiang, Y., Li, S., Huang, J., & Scott, N. (2020). Worry and anger from flight delay: Antecedents and consequences. *International Journal of Tourism Research, 22*(3), 289–302. doi:10.1002/jtr.2334

Jinendra, D., Jadhav, R., Gaidhani Pranav, B. R., Vyavahare, Y., & Achaliyaparag, S. U. (2012). smart travel guide: Application for android mobile. *International Journal of Electronics*.

Johnston, K., Puczkó, L., Smith, M., & Ellis, S. (2011). *Wellness tourism and medical tourism: Where do spas fit?* Research Report: Global SPA Summit 2011.

Joppe, M., Martin, D. W., & Waalen, J. (2001). Toronto's image as a destination: A comparative importance-satisfaction. Analysis by origin of visitor. *Journal of Travel Research, 39*(3), 252–260. doi:10.1177/004728750103900302

Jovanovic, S., & Ivana, I. L. I. C. (2016). Infrastructure as important determinant of tourism development in the countries of Southeast Europe. *Ecoforum Journal*, 5(1).

Jovicic, D. (2019). From the traditional understanding of tourism destination to the smart tourism destination. *Current Issues in Tourism*, 22(3), 276–282. https://doi.org/10.1080/13683500.2017.1313203

Jyotsna, J. H., & Maurya, U. K. (2019). Experiencing the real village: A netnographic examination of perceived authenticity in rural tourism consumption. *Asia Pacific Journal of Tourism Research*, 24(8), 750–762. doi:10.1080/1094166 5.2019.1630455

Kabadayi, S., Ali, F., Choi, H., Joosten, H., & Lu, C. (2019). Smart service experience in hospitality and tourism services: A conceptualisation and future research agenda. *Journal of Service Management*, 30(3), 326–348. doi:10.1108/JOSM-11-2018-0377

Kahneman, D. (2000). Evaluation by moments: Past and future. In D. Kahneman & A. Tversky (Eds.), *Choices, values, and frames* (pp. 693–708). Cambridge University Press. doi:10.1017/CBO9780511803475.039

Kahneman, D. (2011). *Thinking, fast and slow*. Macmillan.

Kahneman, D., Krueger, A. B., Schkade, D. A., Schwarz, N., & Stone, A. A. (2004). A survey method for characterising daily life experience: The day reconstruction method. *Science*, 306(5702), 1776–1780. doi:10.1126cience.1103572 PMID:15576620

Kahneman, D., & Thaler, R. H. (2006). Utility maximization and experienced utility. *Journal of Economics*.

Kampion, D., & Brown, B. (1998). *Stoked: A history of surf culture*. Evergreen.

Kandampully, J. (2000). The impact of demand fluctuation on the quality of service: A tourism industry example. *Managing Service Quality*, 10(1), 10–18. doi:10.1108/09604520010307012

Kandampully, J., & Solnet, D. (2020). Competitive advantage through service in hospitality and tourism: A perspective article. *Tourism Review*, 75(1), 247–251. doi:10.1108/TR-05-2019-0175

Kandampully, J., Zhang, T., & Bilgihan, A. (2015). Customer loyalty: A review and future directions with a special focus on the hospitality industry. *International Journal of Contemporary Hospitality Management*, 27(3), 379–414. doi:10.1108/IJCHM-03-2014-0151

Kandampully, J., Zhang, T., & Jaakkola, E. (2018). Customer experience management in hospitality. *International Journal of Contemporary Hospitality Management*, 30(1), 21–56. doi:10.1108/IJCHM-10-2015-0549

Kang, K., Jwa, J., & Park, S. E. (2017). Smart audio tour guide system using TTS. *International Journal of Applied Engineering Research*, 12. http://www.ripublication.com

Karasakal, S. (2019). *Effect of destination attributes on flow experience, positive emotion and overall satisfaction: Case of Antalya* (Doctoral Thesis). Akdeniz University Social Sciences Institute.

Katsuki, F., & Constantinidis, C. (2014). Bottom-up and top-down attention: Different processes and overlapping neural systems. *The Neuroscientist*, 20(5), 509–521. doi:10.1177/1073858413514136 PMID:24362813

Kauppinen-Raisanen, H., Gummerus, J., & Lehtola, K. (2013). Remembered eating experiences described by the self, place, food, context and time. *British Food Journal*, 115(5), 666–685. doi:10.1108/00070701311331571

Kayar, Ç. H., & Kozak, N. (2010). Measuring destination competitiveness: An application of the travel and tourism competitiveness index (2007). *Journal of Hospitality Marketing & Management*, 19(3), 203–216. doi:10.1080/19368621003591319

Compilation of References

Kayat, K., & Hai, A. M. (2014). Perceived service quality and tourists' cognitive image of a destination. *Anatolia: An International Journal of Tourism and Hospitality Research*, 25(1), 1–12. doi:10.1080/13032917.2013.814580

Kazungu, I. (2020). Network linkages and performance of exporting micro and small enterprises in Dar es Salaam, Tanzania: Perspectives in the handicraft industry. *Global Business Review*. Advance online publication. doi:10.1177/0972150920934433

Keelery, K. (2021). *Topic: Internet usage in India.* Statista. Available at: https://www.statista.com/topics/2157/internet-usage-in-india/

Kelly, C. (2010). Analysing Wellness tourism provision: A retreat operators' study. *Journal of Hospitality and Tourism Management*, 17(1), 108–116. doi:10.1375/jhtm.17.1.108

Kent, T. (2010). The role of the museum shop in extending the visitor experience. *International Journal of Nonprofit and Voluntary Sector Marketing*, 15(1), 67–77. doi:10.1002/nvsm.368

Kesner, L. (2006). The role of cognitive competence in the art museum experience. *Journal of Museum Management and Curatorship*, 21(1), 4–19. doi:10.1080/09647770600302101

Kessler, D., Lee, J.-H., & Whittingham, N. (2020). The wellness tourist motivation scale: A new statistical tool for measuring wellness tourist motivation. *International Journal of Spa and Wellness*, 3(1), 24–39. doi:10.1080/24721735.2020.1849930

Kim, E., Chiang, L., & Tang, L. (2017). Investigating wellness tourists' motivation, engagement, and loyalty: In search of the missing link. *Journal of Travel & Tourism Marketing*, 34(7), 867–879. doi:10.1080/10548408.2016.1261756

Kim, H., & Richardson, S. L. (2003). Motion picture impacts on destination images. *Annals of Tourism Research*, 30(1), 216–237. doi:10.1016/S0160-7383(02)00062-2

Kim, J. H., Ritchie, J. R., & Tung, V. W. S. (2010). The effect of memorable experience on behavioral intentions in tourism: A structural equation modeling approach. *Tourism Analysis*, 15(6), 637–648. doi:10.3727/108354210X12904412049776

Kim, J., & Fesenmaier, D. R. (2015). Measuring emotions in real time: Implications for tourism experience design. *Journal of Travel Research*, 54(4), 419–429. doi:10.1177/0047287514550100

Kim, J.-H. (2010). Determining the factors affecting the memorable nature of travel experiences. *Journal of Travel & Tourism Marketing*, 27(8), 780–796. doi:10.1080/10548408.2010.526897

Kim, J.-H. (2014). The antecedents of memorable tourism experiences: The development of a scale to measure the destination attributes associated with memorable experiences. *Tourism Management*, 44, 34–45. doi:10.1016/j.tourman.2014.02.007

Kim, J.-H. (2018). The impact of memorable tourism experiences on loyalty behaviors: The mediating effects of destination image and satisfaction. *Journal of Travel Research*, 57(7), 856–870. doi:10.1177/0047287517721369

Kim, J.-H. (2021). Destination attributes affecting negative memory: Scale development and validation. *Journal of Travel Research*.

Kim, J.-H., & Brent Ritchie, J. R. (2014). Cross-cultural validation of a memorable tourism experience scale (MTES). *Journal of Travel Research*, 53(3), 323–335. doi:10.1177/0047287513496468

Kim, J.-H., Brent Ritchie, J. R., & McCormick, B. (2012). Development of a scale to measure memorable tourism experiences. *Journal of Travel Research*, 51(1), 12–25. doi:10.1177/0047287510385467

Kim, S. H., Holland, S., & Han, H. S. (2013). A structural model for examining how destination image, perceived value, and service quality affect destination loyalty: A case study of Orlando. *International Journal of Tourism Research*, *15*(4), 313–328. doi:10.1002/jtr.1877

Kim, S., & Iwashita, C. (2016). Cooking identity and food tourism: The case of Japanese udon noodles. *Tourism Recreation Research*, *41*(1), 89–100. doi:10.1080/02508281.2016.1111976

Kim, S., & Kim, H. (2015). Moderating effects of tourists' novelty-seeking tendencies on the relationship between satisfaction and behavioral intention. *Tourism Analysis*, *20*(5), 511–522. doi:10.3727/108354215X14411980111415

Kim, S., & Park, E. (2015). First-time and repeat tourist destination image: The case of domestic tourists to Weh island, Indonesia. *An International Journal of Tourism and Hospitality Research*, *26*(3), 421–433. doi:10.1080/13032917.2014.984233

King, C., Murillo, E., Wei, W., Madera, J., Tews, M. J., Israeli, A. A., & Kong, L. (2019). Towards a shared understanding of the service experience: A hospitality stakeholder approach. *Journal of Service Management*, *30*(3), 410–428. doi:10.1108/JOSM-11-2018-0375

Kipping, M., & Üsdiken, B. (2008). Business history and management studies. In G. Jones & J. Zeitlin (Eds.), *The Oxford Handbook of Business History* (pp. 96–119). Oxford University Press.

Kirillova, K., Lehto, X., & Cai, L. (2016). Mapping existential authenticity and anxiety as outcomes: The tourist in the experience economy. *International Journal of Tourism Research*, *19*(1), 13–26. doi:10.1002/jtr.2080

Kivela, J., & Crotts, J. C. (2006). Tourism and gastronomy: Gastronomy's influence on how tourists experience a destination. *Journal of Hospitality & Tourism Research (Washington, D.C.)*, *30*(3), 354–377. doi:10.1177/1096348006286797

Klepper, S., & Malerba, F. (2010). Demand, innovation and industrial dynamics: An introduction. *Industrial and Corporate Change*, *19*(5), 1515–1520. doi:10.1093/icc/dtq043

Knutson, B. J., & Beck, J. A. (2004). Identifying the dimensions of the experience construct. *Journal of Quality Assurance in Hospitality & Tourism*, *4*(3–4), 23–35. doi:10.1300/J162v04n03_03

Koehler, T. H. (2006). *"Stoked": Os valores da cultura de consumo surf e sua influência no comportamento de compra* (Dissertação de Mestrado). Escola de Administração, Universidade Federal do Rio Grande do Sul, Brazil.

Kofler, I., & Marcher, A. (2018). Inter-organisational networks of small and medium-sized enterprises (SME) in the field of innovation: A case study of South Tyrol. *Journal of Small Business and Entrepreneurship*, *30*(1), 9–25. doi:10.1080/08276331.2017.1401202

Koh, S., Jung-Eun Yoo, J., & Boger, C. A. Jr. (2010). Importance-performance analysis with benefit segmentation of spa goers. *International Journal of Contemporary Hospitality Management*, *22*(5), 718–735. doi:10.1108/09596111011053828

Ko, L. W., Komarov, O., Hairston, W. D., Jung, T. P., & Lin, C. T. (2017). Sustained attention in real classroom Settings: An EEG study. *Frontiers in Human Neuroscience*, *11*, 388. doi:10.3389/fnhum.2017.00388 PMID:28824396

Kolar, T., & Zabkar, V. (2007). The meaning of tourists' authentic experiences for the marketing of cultural heritage sites. *Economic and Business Review for Central and South-Eastern Europe*, *9*(3), 235.

Koli, A. K. (2021). Handmade OK please: Key criteria for purchasing craft items by Indian consumers. *Journal of Cultural Heritage Management and Sustainable Development*. Advance online publication. doi:10.1108/JCHMSD-04-2020-0063

Kondo, Y. (2000). Innovation versus standardisation. *The TQM Magazine*, *12*(1), 6–10. doi:10.1108/09544780010287177

Konu, H., Tuohino, A., & Komppula, R. (2010). Lake wellness: A practical example of a new service development (NSD) concept in tourism industries. *Journal of Vacation Marketing*, *16*(2), 125–139. doi:10.1177/1356766709357489

Koo, C., Park, J., & Lee, J. N. (2017). Smart tourism- traveler, business, and organisational perspectives. *Information & Management*.

Koop, C. E., Pearson, C. E., & Schwarz, M. R. (2002). *Critical issues in global health*. Jossey-Bass. doi:10.1097/01445442-200205000-00014

Korngold, D., Lemos, M., & Rohwer, M. (2017). *Smart cities for all: A vision for an inclusive, accessible, urban future*. Retrieved from https://g3ict.org/publication/smart-cities-for-all-a-vision-for-an-inclusive-accessible-urban-future#:~:text

Koskinen, V., & Wilska, T.-A. (2019). Identifying and understanding spa tourists' wellness attitudes. *Scandinavian Journal of Hospitality and Tourism*, *19*(3), 259–277. doi:10.1080/15022250.2018.1467276

Kotler, N. (1999). Delivering experience: Marketing the museum's full range of assets. *Museum News*, (May/June), 30–61.

Kotler, N. G., & Kotler, P. (2000). Can museums be all things to all people? In R. Sandell & R. J. Janes (Eds.), *Museum management and marketing* (pp. 313–330). Routledge.

Kotler, N. G., Kotler, P., & Kotler, W. I. (2008). *Museum marketing and strategy – Designing missions: Building audiences, generating revenue and resources*. Jossey-Bass.

Kotler, P., Armstrong, G., Saunders, J., & Wong, V. (1999). *Principles of marketing*. Prentice Hall Inc.

Kozak, M. (2001). Repeaters' behavior at two distinct destinations. *Annals of Tourism Research*, *28*(3), 784–807. doi:10.1016/S0160-7383(00)00078-5

Kozak, M., & Rimmington, M. (2000). Tourist satisfaction with Mallorca, Spain, as an off-season holiday destination. *Journal of Travel Research*, *38*(3), 260–269. doi:10.1177/004728750003800308

Kreibig, S. D. J. B. p. (2010). Autonomic nervous system activity in emotion. *RE:view*, *84*(3), 394–421. PMID:20371374

Kruger, M., & Saayman, M. (2017). Sand, sea and surf: Segmenting South African surfers. *S.A. Journal for Research in Sport Physical Education and Recreation*, *39*(2), 115–135.

Kuo, T. S., Huang, K. C., Nguyen, T. Q., & Nguyen, P. H. (2019). Adoption of mobile applications for identifying tourism destinations by travellers: An integrative approach. *Journal of Business Economics and Management*, *20*(5), 860–877. doi:10.3846/jbem.2019.10448

Kuscer, K., Mihalic, T., & Pechlaner, H. (2017). Innovation, sustainable tourism and environments in mountain destination development: A comparative analysis of Austria, Slovenia and Switzerland. *Journal of Sustainable Tourism*, *25*(4), 489–504. doi:10.1080/09669582.2016.1223086

Kwanisai, G., & Vengesayi, S. (2016). Destination attributes and overall destination satisfaction in Zimbabwe. *Tourism Analysis*, *21*(1), 17–28. doi:10.3727/108354216X14537459508775

Kwok, T. C. K., Kiefer, P., Schinazi, V. R., Adams, B., & Raubal, M. (2019, May 2). Gaze-guided narratives: Adapting audio guide content to gaze in virtual and real environments. *Conference on Human Factors in Computing Systems - Proceedings*. 10.1145/3290605.3300721

Lai, I. K. W. (2015). Traveler acceptance of an app-based mobile tour guide. *Journal of Hospitality & Tourism Research (Washington, D.C.)*, *39*(3), 401–432. doi:10.1177/1096348013491596

Landauer, M., Goodsite, M. E., & Juhola, S. (2018). Nordic national climate adaptation and tourism strategies: (How) are they interlinked? *Scandinavian Journal of Hospitality and Tourism, 18*(sup1), S75-S86.

Landry, C. (2000). *The creative city: A toolkit for urban innovators*. Earthscan.

Larsen, S. (2007). Aspects of a psychology of the tourist experience. *Scandinavian Journal of Hospitality and Tourism, 7*(1), 7–18. doi:10.1080/15022250701226014

Law, R., Cheung, C., & Lo, A. (2004). The relevance of profiling travel activities for improving destination marketing strategies. *International Journal of Contemporary Hospitality Management, 16*(6), 355–362. doi:10.1108/09596110410550798

Lazarus, R. S. (1991). *Emotion and adaptation*. Oxford University Press.

LeBlanc, C. (2021). *Cookie cutter or custom: What's the best approach in business?* https://catleblanc.com/cookie-cutter-or-custom-whats-the-best-approach-to-getting-your-business-problems-solved/

Le, D., Hadinejad, A., Moyle, B., Ma, J., & Scott, N. (2020). A review of eye-tracking methods in tourism research. In M. Rainoldi & M. Jooss (Eds.), *Eye tracking in tourism*. Springer. doi:10.1007/978-3-030-49709-5_2

Le, D., Scott, N., & Lohmann, G. (2019). Applying experiential marketing in selling tourism dreams. *Journal of Travel & Tourism Marketing, 36*(2), 220–235. doi:10.1080/10548408.2018.1526158

Lee, L. W., Mccarthy, I. P., & Kietzmann, J. (2019). *Making sense of text: Artificial content analysis*. doi:10.1108/EJM-02-2019-0219

Lee, B., Lee, C. K., & Lee, J. (2014). Dynamic nature of destination image and influence of tourist overall satisfaction on image modification. *Journal of Travel Research, 53*(2), 239–251. doi:10.1177/0047287513496466

Lee, C. K., Var, T., & Blain, T. (1996). Determinants of inbound tourism expenditures. *Annals of Tourism Research, 23*(3), 527–542. doi:10.1016/0160-7383(95)00073-9

Lee, C., Lee, Y., & Lee, B. (2005). Korea's destination image formed by the 2002 world cup. *Annals of Tourism Research, 32*(4), 839–858. doi:10.1016/j.annals.2004.11.006

Lee, H., Lee, J., Chung, N., & Koo, C. (2018). Tourists' happiness: Are there smart tourism technology effects? *Asia Pacific Journal of Tourism Research, 23*(5), 486–501. doi:10.1080/10941665.2018.1468344

Lee, S. J. (2017). A review of audio guides in the era of smart tourism. *Information Systems Frontiers, 19*, 705–715.

Lee, T. H., & Chang, Y. S. (2012). The influence of experiential marketing and activity involvement on the loyalty intentions of wine tourists in Taiwan. *Leisure Studies, 31*(1), 103–121. doi:10.1080/02614367.2011.568067

Lee, T. H., & Crompton, J. (1992). Measuring novelty seeking in tourism. *Annals of Tourism Research, 19*(4), 732–751. doi:10.1016/0160-7383(92)90064-V

Lee, T. H., Jan, F. H., & Huang, G. W. (2015). The influence of recreation experiences on environmentally responsible behavior: The case of Liuqiu Island, Taiwan. *Journal of Sustainable Tourism, 23*(6), 947–967. doi:10.1080/09669582.2015.1024257

Lee, T. H., & Jan, F.-H. (2019). Can community-based tourism contribute to sustainable development? Evidence from residents' perceptions of the sustainability. *Tourism Management, 70*, 368–380. doi:10.1016/j.tourman.2018.09.003

Lee, W., & Kim, Y. H. (2021). Does VR tourism enhance users' experience? *Sustainability, 13*, 806.

Lehman, K. F., & Byrom, J. W. (2007). Corporate museums in Japan: Institutionalising a culture of industry and technology. *9th International Conference on Arts & Cultural Management*.

Lehto, X. Y., & Lehto, M. R. (2019). Vacation as a public health resource: Toward a wellness-centered tourism design approach. *Journal of Hospitality & Tourism Research (Washington, D.C.)*, *43*(7), 935–960. doi:10.1177/1096348019849684

Lemon, K. N., & Verhoef, P. C. (2016). Understanding customer experience throughout the customer journey. *Journal of Marketing*, *80*(6), 69–96. doi:10.1509/jm.15.0420

Leung, R. (2020). Hospitality technology progress towards intelligent buildings: A perspective article. *Tourism Review*, *76*(1), 69–73. doi:10.1108/TR-05-2019-0173

Lew, A. A. (1987). A framework of tourist attraction research. *Annals of Tourism Research*, *14*(4), 553–575. doi:10.1016/0160-7383(87)90071-5

Lew, A. A. (2011). Understanding experiential authenticity through the best tourism places. *Tourism Geographies*, *13*(4), 570–575. doi:10.1080/14616688.2011.588245

Liberato, P., Alen, E., & Liberato, D. (2018). Smart tourism destination triggers consumer experience: The case of Porto. *European Journal of Management and Business Economics*, *27*(1), 6–25. doi:10.1108/EJMBE-11-2017-0051

Liberato, P., Alén-González, E., & Liberato, D. (2018). Digital technology in a smart tourism destination: The case of Porto. *Journal of Urban Technology*, *25*(1), 75–97.

Liere, L. (2019). *Access city award 2019: Quick wins from Breda, the Netherlands*. Retrieved from https://nexttourismgeneration.eu/access-city-award-2019-quick-wins-from-breda-the-netherlands/

Li, L. P., Juric, B., & Brodie, R. J. (2017). Dynamic multi-actor engagement in networks: The case of United Breaks Guitars. *Journal of Service Theory and Practice*, *27*(4), 738–760. doi:10.1108/JSTP-04-2016-0066

Li, M., & Cai, L. A. (2012). The effects of personal values on travel motivation and behavioral intention. *Journal of Travel Research*, *51*(4), 473–487. doi:10.1177/0047287511418366

Lin, C. T., & Huang, Y. L. (2009). Mining tourist imagery to construct destination image position model. *Expert Systems with Applications*, *36*(2), 2513–2524. doi:10.1016/j.eswa.2008.01.074 PMID:32288333

Lin, D., & Simmons, D. (2017). Structured inter-network collaboration: Public participation in tourism planning in Southern China. *Tourism Management*, *63*, 315–328. https://doi.org/10.1016/j.tourman.2017.06.024

Lindberg, F., Hansen, A. H., & Eide, D. (2014). A multirelational approach for understanding consumer experiences within tourism. *Journal of Hospitality Marketing & Management*, *23*(5), 487–512. Advance online publication. doi:10.1080/19368623.2013.827609

Lin, L., & Mao, P. (2015). Food for memories and culture: A content analysis study of food specialties and souvenirs. *Journal of Hospitality and Tourism Management*, *22*, 22. doi:10.1016/j.jhtm.2014.12.001

Lin, S. W. (2017). Identifying the critical success factors and an optimal solution for mobile technology adoption in travel agencies. *International Journal of Tourism Research*, *19*(2), 127–144. https://doi.org/10.1002/jtr.2092

Li, S. (2020). Using self-report and skin conductance measures to evaluate theme park experiences. *Journal of Vacation Marketing*.

Li, S., Scott, N., & Walters, G. (2015). Current and potential methods for measuring emotion in tourism experiences: A review. *Current Issues in Tourism*, *18*(9), 805–827. doi:10.1080/13683500.2014.975679

Li, T. T., Liu, F., & Soutar, G. N. (2021). Experiences, post-trip destination image, satisfaction and loyalty: A study in an ecotourism context. *Journal of Destination Marketing & Management*, *19*.

Littrell, M. A., Anderson, L. F., & Brown, P. J. (1993). What makes a craft souvenir authentic? *Annals of Tourism Research*, *20*(6), 197–215. doi:10.1016/0160-7383(93)90118-M

Liu, C.-R., Wang, Y.-C., Chiu, T.-H., & Chen, S.-P. (2018). Antecedents and outcomes of lifestyle hotel brand attachment and love: The case of Gen Y. *Journal of Hospitality Marketing & Management*, *27*(3), 281–298. doi:10.1080/19368623.2017.1364197

Liu, X., Li, J., & Kim, W. G. (2017). The role of travel experience in the structural relationships among tourists' perceived image, satisfaction, and behavioral intentions. *Tourism and Hospitality Research*, *17*(2), 135–146. doi:10.1177/1467358415610371

Li, Y., Hu, C., Huang, C., & Duan, L. (2017). The concept of smart tourism in the context of tourism information services. *Tourism Management*, *58*, 293–300.

Lo, M. C., Mohamad, A. A., Chin, C. H., & Ramayah, T. (2017). The impact of natural resources, cultural heritage, and special events on tourism destination competitiveness: The moderating role of community support. *International Journal of Business & Society*, *18*.

Lo, A., King, B., & Mackenzie, M. (2017). Restaurant customers' attitude toward sustainability and nutritional menu labels. *Journal of Hospitality Marketing & Management*, *26*(8), 846–867. doi:10.1080/19368623.2017.1326865

Loewenstein, G. F., Weber, E. U., Hsee, C. K., & Welch, N. (2001). Risk as feelings. *Psychological Bulletin*, *127*(2), 267–286. doi:10.1037/0033-2909.127.2.267 PMID:11316014

Lohmann, M., & Kaim, E. (1999). Weather and holiday destination preferences image, attitude and experience. *Tourism Review*, *54*(2), 54–64.

Loi, K. I. (2008). Gaming and entertainment tourist destinations: A world of similarities and differences. *Tourism Recreation Research*, *33*(2), 165–183. doi:10.1080/02508281.2008.11081303

Long, L. (2004). *Culinary tourism: Exploring the other through food*. The University Press of Kentucky.

López-Guzmán, T., Sánchez-Cañizares, S., & Pavón, V. (2011). Community-based tourism in developing countries: A case study. *Tourismos*, *6*(1), 69–84.

Lorentzen, A. (2009). Cities in the experience economy. *European Planning Studies*, *17*(6), 829–845. doi:10.1080/09654310902793986

Loureiro, S. M. C. (2014). The role of the rural tourism experience economy in place attachment and behavioral intentions. *International Journal of Hospitality Management*, *40*, 1–9. doi:10.1016/j.ijhm.2014.02.010

Lu, J., Mao, Z., Wang, M., & Hu, L. (2015). Goodbye maps, hello apps? Exploring the influential determinants of travel app adoption. *Current Issues in Tourism*, *18*(11), 1059–1079. doi:10.1080/13683500.2015.1043248

Lundberg, C., Fredman, P., & Wall-Reinius, S. (2014). Going for the green? The role of money among adventure tourism entrepreneurs. *Current Issues in Tourism*, *17*(4), 373–380. doi:10.1080/13683500.2012.746292

Luo, Y., Lenlung, C., Kim, E., Tang, L., & Song, S. (2018). Towards quality of life: The effects of the wellness tourism experience. *Journal of Travel & Tourism Marketing*, *35*(4), 410–424. doi:10.1080/10548408.2017.1358236

Lwoga, B., & Mapunda, B. B. (2017). Challenges facing accessible tourism in cultural heritage sites: The case of Village Museum in Tanzania. *Revista de Turism: Studii Si Cercetari in Turism*, *0*(24), 45–54.

Lyubomirsky, S., King, L., & Diener, E. (2005). *The benefits of frequent positive affect: Does happiness lead to success?* American Psychological Association.

MacCannell, D. (1976). *The tourist: A new theory of the leisure class*. University of California Press.

MacCannell, D. (1973). Staged authenticity: Arrangements of social space in tourist settings. *American Journal of Sociology*, *79*(3), 589–603. doi:10.1086/225585

MacCannell, D. (1999). *The tourist a new theory of the leisure class*. California Press.

Machado, V., Pinto Contreiras, J., & Carrasco, P. (2018). *Local developments of the world summit on sustainable tourism: the municipal sustainable charter of surf in Aljezur*. Sustainable Tourism Law.

MacKay, K. J., & Fesenmaier, D. R. (1997). Pictorial element of destination in image formation. *Annals of Tourism Research*, *24*(3), 537–565. doi:10.1016/S0160-7383(97)00011-X

MacKay, K. J., & Fesenmaier, D. R. (2000). An exploration of cross-cultural destination image assessment. *Journal of Travel Research*, *38*(4), 417–423. doi:10.1177/004728750003800411

Macneil, I. (1980). *The new social contract: An inquiry into modern contractual relation*. Yale University Press.

Maertens, M. (2019). Fairtrade does not walk the talk. *Nature Sustainability*, *2*(7), 549–550. doi:10.103841893-019-0332-0

Maharani, I. A. K., Wisnu Parta, I. B. M., & Supriadi, I. B. P. (2020). Factors Influencing yoga tourism in bali: Conceptual framework model. *Vidyottama Sanatana: International Journal of Hindu Science and Religious Studies*, *4*(1), 20. doi:10.25078/ijhsrs.v4i1.1321

Mahardika, H., Thomas, D., Ewing, M. T., & Japutra, A. (2019). Experience and facilitating conditions as impediments to consumers' new technology adoption. *International Review of Retail, Distribution and Consumer Research*, *29*(1), 79–98. doi:10.1080/09593969.2018.1556181

Mahmood, I. P., & Rufin, C. (2005). Government's dilemma: The role of government in imitation and innovation. *Academy of Management Review*, *30*(2), 338–360. doi:10.5465/amr.2005.16387891

Mahoney, D. (2012). Changing strategies in marketing Kenya's tourist art: From ethnic brands to fair trade labels. *African Studies Review*, *55*(1), 161–190. doi:10.1353/arw.2012.0013

Maitland, R. A. (2008). Conviviality and everyday life: The appeal of new areas of London for visitors. *International Journal of Tourism Research*, *10*(1), 15–25. doi:10.1002/jtr.621

Ma, J., Gao, J., Scott, N., & Ding, P. (2013). Customer delight derived from theme park experiences: The antecedents of delight based on cognitive appraisal theory. *Annals of Tourism Research*, *42*, 359–381. doi:10.1016/j.annals.2013.02.018

Ma, J., Scott, N., Ding, P., & Gao, J. (2017). Delighted or satisfied? Positive emotional responses derived from theme park experiences. *Journal of Travel & Tourism Marketing*, *34*(1), 1–19. doi:10.1080/10548408.2015.1125824

Mak, A. H., Wong, K. K., & Chang, R. C. (2009). Health or selfindulgence? The motivations and characteristics of spagoers. *International Journal of Tourism Research*, *11*(2), 185–199. doi:10.1002/jtr.703

Manhas, P. S., Charak, N. S., & Sharma, P. (2020). Wellness and spa tourism: Finding space for Indian Himalayan spa resorts. *International Journal of Spa and Wellness*, *2*(14), 1–19. doi:10.1080/24721735.2020.1819705

Mannell, R. C., & Iso-Ahola, S. E. (1987). Psychological nature of leisure and tourism experience. *Annals of Tourism Research*, *14*(3), 314–331. doi:10.1016/0160-7383(87)90105-8

Mansfeld, Y. (1992). From motivation to actual travel. *Annals of Tourism Research*, *19*(3), 399–419. doi:10.1016/0160-7383(92)90127-B

Mansfeld, Y., & Pizam, A. (2006). *Tourism, security and safety*. Routledge. doi:10.4324/9780080458335

Manthiou, A., Lee, S., Tang, L., & Chiang, L. (2014). The experience economy approach to festival marketing: Vivid memory and attendee loyalty. *Journal of Services Marketing*, 28(2), 22–35. doi:10.1108/JSM-06-2012-0105

Marangunić, N., & Granić, A. (2015). Technology acceptance model: A literature review from 1986 to 2013. *Universal Access in the Information Society*, 14(1), 81–95. doi:10.100710209-014-0348-1

Marasco, A., De Martino, M., Magnotti, F., & Morvillo, A. (2018). Collaborative innovation in tourism and hospitality: A systematic review of the literature. *International Journal of Contemporary Hospitality Management*, 30(6), 2364–2395. doi:10.1108/IJCHM-01-2018-0043

Margaryan, L. (2018). Nature as a commercial setting: The case of adventure tourism providers in Sweden. *Current Issues in Tourism*, 21(16), 1893–1911. doi:10.1080/13683500.2016.1232378

Margaryan, L., & Stensland, S. (2017). Sustainable by nature? The case of (non) adoption of eco-certification among the adventure tourism companies in Scandinavia. *Journal of Cleaner Production*, 162, 559–567. doi:10.1016/j.jclepro.2017.06.060

Marion, K. (2016). Risk and uncertainty in travel decision-making: Tourist and destination perspective. *Journal of Travel Research*, 57(1), 129–146.

Markwick, M. C. (2001). Tourism and the development of handicraft production in the Maltese islands. *Tourism Economics*, 3(1), 29–51. doi:10.1080/14616680010008694

Marrasco, A., & Balbi, B. (2019). Designing accessible experiences for heritage visitors through virtual reality. *Ereview of Tourism Research*, 17(3), 426–443.

Martin, S. A., & Assenov, I. (2012). The genesis of a new body of sport tourism literature: A systematic review of surf tourism research (1997–2011). *Journal of Sport & Tourism*, 17(4), 257–287. doi:10.1080/14775085.2013.766528

Martins, C., Carneiro, M., & Pacheco, O. (2020). Key factors for implementation and success of destination management systems. Empirical evidence from European countries. *Industrial Management & Data Systems*.

Martins, J., Gonçalves, R., Branco, F., Barbosa, L., Melo, M., & Bessa, M. (2017). A multisensory virtual experience model for thematic tourism: A Port wine tourism application proposal. *Journal of Destination Marketing & Management*, 6(2), 103–109. doi:10.1016/j.jdmm.2017.02.002

Mathwick, C., Malhotra, N., & Rigdon, E. (2001). Experiential value: Conceptualisation, measurement and application in the catalog and Internet shopping environment. *Journal of Retailing*, 77(1), 39–56. doi:10.1016/S0022-4359(00)00045-2

Matteucci, X. (2014). Forms of body usage in tourists' experiences of flamenco. *Annals of Tourism Research*, 46(0), 29–43. doi:10.1016/j.annals.2014.02.005

Matzler, K., & Renzl, B. (2007). Assessing asymmetric effects in the formation of employee satisfaction. *Tourism Management*, 28(4), 1093–1103. doi:10.1016/j.tourman.2006.07.009

Matzler, K., & Sauerwein, E. (2002). The factor structure of customer satisfaction: An empirical test of the importance grid and the penalty-reward-constraint analysis. *International Journal of Service Industry Management*, 13(4), 314–332. doi:10.1108/09564230210445078

Mayfield, N. (2021). How your hospitality business can meet the needs of digital nomads. *Forbes*. https://www.forbes.com/sites/forbesbusinesscouncil/2021/03/12/how-your-hospitality-business-can-meet-the-needs-of-digital-nomads/?sh=c6068010d455

Mayordomo-Martìnez, D., Sánchez-Aarnoutse, J.-C., Carrillo-de-Gea, J. M., Garcìa-Berná, J. A., Fernández-Alemán, J. L., & Garcìa-Mateos, G. (2019). Design and development of a mobile app for accessible beach tourism information for people with disabilities. *International Journal of Environmental Research and Public Health, 16*, 1–16.

McArthur, S., & Hall, C. M. (1996). *Heritage management in Australia and New Zealand: The human dimensions.* Oxford University Press.

McCabe, S., Li, C., & Chen, Z. (2016). Time for a radical reappraisal of tourist decision making? Toward a new conceptual model. *Journal of Travel Research, 55*(1), 3–15. doi:10.1177/0047287515592973

McCabe, S., Sharples, M., & Foster, C. (2012). Stakeholder engagement in the design of scenarios of technology-enhanced tourism services. *Tourism Management Perspectives, 4*(October), 36–44. https://doi.org/10.1016/j.tmp.2012.04.007

Mccoll-kennedy, J., Gustafsson, A., & Friman, M. (2015). *Fresh perspectives on customer experience.* Academic Press.

McColl-Kennedy, J. R., Danaher, T. S., Gallan, A. S., Orsingher, C., Lervik-Olsen, L., & Verma, R. (2017). How do you feel today? Managing patient emotions during health care experiences to enhance well-being. *Journal of Business Research, 79*, 247–259. doi:10.1016/j.jbusres.2017.03.022

McHone, W. W., & Rungeling, B. (2000). Practical issues in measuring the impact of a cultural tourist event in a major tourist destination. *Journal of Travel Research, 38*(3), 300–303. doi:10.1177/004728750003800313

McKercher, B., & Chan, A. (2005). How special is special interest tourism? *Journal of Travel Research, 44*(1), 21–31. doi:10.1177/0047287505276588

McPherson, G. (2006). Public memories and private tastes: The shifting definition of museums and their visitors in the UK. *Museum Management and Curatorship, 21*(1), 44–57. doi:10.1080/09647770600602101

Meethan, K. (1996). Place, Image and Power: Brighton as Resort. In T. Selwyn (Ed.), *The tourist image: Myths and myth making in tourism* (pp. 180–196). Wiley.

Mehmetoglu, M., & Engen, M. (2011). Pine and Gilmore's concept of experience economy and its dimensions: An empirical examination in tourism. *Journal of Quality Assurance in Hospitality & Tourism, 12*(4), 237–255. doi:10.1080/1528008X.2011.541847

Mehraliyev, F., Chan, I., Choi, Y., Koseoglu, M., & Law, R. (2020). A state-of-the-art review of smart tourism research. *Journal of Travel & Tourism Marketing, 37*(1), 78–91. https://doi.org/10.1080/10548408.2020.1712309

Meikassandra, P., Winarya, S., & Mertha, I. W. (2020). Wellness tourism in Ubud: A qualitative approach to study the aspects of Wellness tourism development. *Journal of Business on Hospitality and Tourism, 6*(1), 79–93. doi:10.22334/jbhost.v6i1.191

Melo, C., Richards, G., & Smith, M. (2021). Transformational tourism experiences : The communication of service providers. In Impact of new media in tourism (pp. 210–233). doi:10.4018/978-1-7998-7095-1.ch013

Melo, V. A. D., & Fortes, R. (2009). O surfe no cinema e a sociedade brasileira na transição dos anos 70/80. *Revista Brasileira de Educação Física e Esporte, 23*(3), 283–296. doi:10.1590/S1807-55092009000300009

Melubo, K., & Carr, A. (2019). Developing indigenous tourism in the bomas: Critiquing issues from within the Maasai community in Tanzania. *Journal of Heritage Tourism, 14*(3), 219–232. doi:10.1080/1743873X.2018.1533557

Menon, S., Edward, M., & George, B. (2017). Inter-stakeholder collaboration in event management: A case study of Kerala Travel Mart. *International Journal of Leisure and Tourism Marketing, 5*(4). https://doi.org/10.1504/IJLTM.2017.087493

Mertova, P., & Webster, L. (2020). *Using narrative inquiry as a research method: An introduction to critical event narrative analysis in research, teaching and professional practice* (2nd ed.). Routledge. doi:10.4324/9780429424533

Meskele, A. T., Woreta, S. L., & Weldesenbet, E. G. (2018). Accessible tourism challenges and development issues in tourist facilities and attraction sites of the Amhara region world heritage sites, Ethiopia. *International Journal of Hospitality and Tourism Systems, 11*(1), 26–37.

Messerli, H. R., & Oyama, Y. (2004). Health and wellness tourism: Global. *Travel & Tourism Analyst,* (August), 1–54.

Michaelidou, N., Siamagka, N.-T., Moraes, C., & Micevski, M. (2013). Do marketers use visual representations of destinations that tourists value? Comparing visitors' image of a destination with marketer-controlled images online. *Journal of Travel Research, 52*(6), 789–804. doi:10.1177/0047287513481272

Michopoulou, E., Darcy, S., Ambrose, I., & Buhalis, D. (2015). Accessible tourism futures: The world we dream to live in and the opportunites we hope to have. *Journal of Tourism Futures, 1*(3), 179–188.

Milman, A., & Pizam, A. (1995). The role of awareness and familiarity with a destination: The central Florida case. *Journal of Travel Research, 33*(3), 21–27. doi:10.1177/004728759503300304

Ministry of Transport, Public Works and Water Management. (2010). *Public transport in Netherlands.* Retrieved from https://www.emta.com/IMG/pdf/brochure.pdf

Mintel. (2007). *Tourism sector report on holistic tourism.* London: Mintel International Group Ltd. Retrieved from http://www.mintel.com

Mira, M. R., Moura, A., & Breda, Z. (2016). Destination competitiveness and competitiveness indicators: Illustration of the Portuguese reality. *Tékhne – Review of Applied Management Studies, 14*, 90-103.

Mitas, O., & Bastiaansen, M. (2018). Novelty: A mechanism of tourists' enjoyment. *Annals of Tourism Research, 72*, 98–108. doi:10.1016/j.annals.2018.07.002

Mitas, O., Cuenen, R., Bastiaansen, M., Chick, G., & van den Dungen, E. (2020). The War from both Sides: How Dutch and German Visitors Experience an Exhibit of Second World War Stories. *International Journal of the Sociology of Leisure, 3*(3), 277–303. doi:10.100741978-020-00062-3

Mitas, O., Mitasova, H., Millar, G., Boode, W., Neveu, V., Hover, M., & Bastiaansen, M. (2020). More is not better: The emotional dynamics of an excellent experience. *Journal of Hospitality & Tourism Research.* doi:10.1177/1096348020957075

Mitas, O., Nawijn, J., & Jongsma, B. (2017). Between tourists: Tourism and happiness. In M. K. Smith & L. Puczko (Eds.), *The Routledge handbook of health tourism* (pp. 47–64). Routledge.

Mitchell, J., & Ashley, C. (2009). Value chain analysis and poverty. Overseas Development Institute.

Mitchell, J. (2012). Value chain approaches to assessing the impact of tourism on low-income households in developing countries. *Journal of Sustainable Tourism, 20*(3), 457–475. doi:10.1080/09669582.2012.663378

Mitchell, J., & Ashley, C. (2007). Leakage'claims: Muddled thinking and bad for policy. *ODI Opinion, 81*(1), 1–2.

Mitev, A. Z., & Irimiás, A. (2020). Travel craving. *Annals of Tourism Research.* PMID:34566201

Mkono, M. (2016). The reflexive tourist. *Annals of Tourism Research, 57*, 206–219. doi:10.1016/j.annals.2016.01.004

MoCTCA. (2020). *Nepal Tourism Statistics 2019.* Ministry of Culture, Tourism and Civil Aviation, Government of Nepal.

Mody, M., Suess, C., & Lehto, X. (2019). Going back to its roots: Can hospitableness provide hotels competitive advantage over the sharing economy? *International Journal of Hospitality Management, 76*, 286–298. doi:10.1016/j.ijhm.2018.05.017

Compilation of References

Mogindol, S. H., & Bagul, A. H. B. P. (2014). Tourists' perceptions about an appealing handicraft. *Tourism. Leisure and Global Change, 1*, 22–24.

Mollá-Sirvent, R. A., Mora, H., Gilart-Iglesias, V., Pèrez-delHolyo, R., & Andùjar-Motonya, M. D. (2018). Accessbility index for smart cities. *Proceedings, 2*, 1–6.

Molnar, E., & Moraru, R. (2017). *Content analysis of customer reviews to identify sources of value creation in the hotel environment.* doi:10.1007/978-3-319-56925-3

Molony, T. (2009). Carving a niche: ICT, social capital, and trust in the shift from personal to impersonal trading in Tanzania. *Information Technology for Development, 15*(4), 283–301. doi:10.1002/itdj.20127

Montella, M.M. (2010). Museo d'impresa come strumento di comunicazione. Possibili innovazioni di prodotto, processo, organizzazione. *Esperienze d'impresa, 2*, 147-164.

Montemaggi, M., & Severino, F. (2007). *Heritage marketing: La storia dell'impresa italiana come vantaggio competitivo.* Franco Angeli.

Mookerjee, M. (2019). Do we still need fair trade? *Journal of Fair Trade, 1*(2), 1–5. doi:10.13169/jfairtrade.1.2.0001

Moors, A., Ellsworth, P. C., Scherer, K. R., & Frijda, N. H. (2013). Appraisal theories of emotion: State of the art and future development. *Emotion Review, 5*(2), 119–124. doi:10.1177/1754073912468165

Morales, J., Guerra, F., & Serantes, A. (2009). *Bases para la definición de competencias en interpretación del património: Fundamentos teóricos y metodológicos para definir las competencias profesionales de especialistas en interpretación del patrimonio en España.* Seminario Permanente de Interpretación del Patrimonio, Centro Nacional de Educación Ambiental - CENEAM.

Moreira, A. C., Fortes, N., & Santiago, R. (2017). Influence of sensory stimuli on brand experience, brand equity and purchase intention. *Journal of Business Economics and Management, 18*(1), 68–83. doi:10.3846/16111699.2016.1252793

Morgan, M. (2007). We're not the Barmy Army!: Reflections on the sports tourist experience. *International Journal of Tourism Research, 9*(5), 361–372. doi:10.1002/jtr.637

Moscardo, G. (2004). Shopping as a destination attraction: An empirical examination of the role of shopping in tourists' destination choice and experience. *Journal of Vacation Marketing, 10*(4), 294–307. doi:10.1177/135676670401000402

Moscardo, G., Morrison, A. M., Pearce, P. L., Lang, C. T., & O'Leary, J. T. (1996). Understanding vacation destination choice through travel motivation and activities. *Journal of Vacation Marketing, 2*(2), 109–122. doi:10.1177/135676679600200202

Moscardo, G., & Pearce, P. L. (2007). The rhetoric and reality of structured tourism work experiences: A social representational analysis. *Tourism Recreation Research, 32*(2), 21–28. doi:10.1080/02508281.2007.11081273

Moutinho, L. (1987). Consumer behaviour in tourism. *European Journal of Marketing, 21*(10), 5–44. doi:10.1108/EUM0000000004718

Moutinho, L., Albayrak, T., & Caber, M. (2012). How far does overall service quality of a destination affect customers' post-purchase behaviours? *International Journal of Tourism Research, 14*(4), 307–322. doi:10.1002/jtr.856

Moutinho, L., Dionísio, P., & Leal, C. (2007). Surf tribal behaviour: A sports marketing application. *Marketing Intelligence & Planning, 25*(7), 668–690. doi:10.1108/02634500710834160

Moyle, B. D., Moyle, C.-l., Bec, A., & Scott, N. (2017). The next frontier in tourism emotion research. *Current Issues in Tourism*, 1–7.

Mrkva, K., Cole, J. C., & Van Boven, L. (2021). Attention increases environmental risk perception. *Journal of Experimental Psychology. General*, *150*(1), 83–102. doi:10.1037/xge0000772 PMID:32700924

Mtapuri, O., & Giampiccoli, A. (2016). Towards a comprehensive model of community-based tourism development. *The South African Geographical Journal*, *98*(1), 154–168. doi:10.1080/03736245.2014.977813

Mueller, H., & Kaufmann, E. L. (2001). Wellness tourism: Market analysis of a special health tourism segment and implications for the hotel industry. *Journal of Vacation Marketing*, *7*(1), 5–17. doi:10.1177/135676670100700101

Muller, T. E. (1996). How personal values govern the post-visit attitudes of international tourists. *Journal of Hospitality & Leisure Marketing*, *3*(2), 3–24. doi:10.1300/J150v03n02_02

Mura, P. (2015). Perceptions of authenticity in a Malaysian homestay: A narrative analysis. *Tourism Management*, *51*, 225–233. doi:10.1016/j.tourman.2015.05.023

Murphy, P., Pritchard, M. P., & Smith, B. (2000). The destination product and its impact on traveller perceptions. *Tourism Management*, *21*(1), 43–52. doi:10.1016/S0261-5177(99)00080-1

Mykletun, R. J. (2018). Adventure tourism in the North: Six illustrative cases. *Scandinavian Journal of Hospitality and Tourism*, *18*(4), 319–329. doi:10.1080/15022250.2018.1524999

Nahrstedt, W. (1999). Wellness, fitness, beauty, soul: Angebotsanalyse von deuschen Kur und Urlaubsorten. Einleitungsvortrag, 11th ELRA Congress "Leisure and Wellness: Health Tourism in Europe", 7-9/10 Bad Saarow. *Heilbad und Kurort, 51*.

Nahrstedt, W. (2004). Wellness: A new perspective for leisure centers, health tourism, and spas in Europe on the global health market. In K. Wiermair, C. Mathies, & C. Haworth Hospitality (Eds.), *The tourism and leisure industry: Shaping the future*. Bighamton.

Nam, T., & Pardo, T. A. (2011). Conceptualising smart city with dimensions of technology, people, and institutions. *The Proceedings of the 12th Annual International Conference on Digital Government Research*.

Nam, M., Kim, I., & Hwang, J. (2016). Can local people help enhance tourists' destination loyalty? A relational perspective. *Journal of Travel & Tourism Marketing*, *33*(5), 702–716. doi:10.1080/10548408.2016.1167386

Nasiri, M., Ukko, J., Saunila, M., & Rantala, T. (2020). Managing the digital supply chain: The role of smart technologies. *Technovation*, *96–97*, 102121. Advance online publication. doi:10.1016/j.technovation.2020.102121

Naumov, N. (2019). *The impact of robots, artificial intelligence, and service automation on service quality and service experience in hospitality*. Emerald Publishing Limited. doi:10.1108/978-1-78756-687-320191007

Navío-Marco, J., Ruiz-Gómez, L. M., & Sevilla-Sevilla, C. (2018). Progress in information technology and tourism management: 30 years on and 20 years after the internet: Revisiting Buhalis & Law's landmark study about eTourism. *Tourism Management*, *69*, 460–470. doi:10.1016/j.tourman.2018.06.002

Nawijn, J. (2010). The holiday happiness curve: A preliminary investigation into mood during a holiday abroad. *International Journal of Tourism Research*, *12*(3), 281–290. doi:10.1002/jtr.756

Nawijn, J., Mitas, O., Lin, Y., & Kerstetter, D. (2013). How do we feel on vacation? A closer look at how emotions change over the course of a trip. *Journal of Travel Research*, *52*(2), 265–274. doi:10.1177/0047287512465961

Nawijn, J., & Peeters, P. M. (2010). Travelling 'green': Is tourists' happiness at stake? *Current Issues in Tourism*, *13*(4), 381–392. doi:10.1080/13683500903215016

Compilation of References

Netherlands. (2021). *Virtual ways to experience the Netherlands*. Retrieved from https://www.holland.com/global/tourism/travel-inspiration/virtual-ways-to-experience-the-netherlands.htm

Neto, A. Q., Dimmock, K., Lohmann, G., & Scott, N. (2020). Destination competitiveness: How does travel experience influence choice? *Current Issues in Tourism, 23*(13), 1673–1687.

Neto, J. S. O. (2018). *Inclusive smart cities: Theory and tools to improve the experience of people with disabilities in urban spaces. Universite Paris Saclay (COmUE)*. Universidade de Sao Paulo.

Neuhofer, B., Buhalis, D., & Ladkin, A. (2015). Smart technologies for personalised experiences: A case study in the hospitality domain. *Electronic Markets, 25*, 243–254. https://doi.org/10.1007/s12525-015-0182-1

Neuhofer, B., Buhalis, D., & Ladkin, D. (2012). Conceptualising technology enhanced destination experiences. *Journal of Destination Marketing & Management, 1*(1-2), 36–46.

Newell, S., Robertson, M., Scarbrough, H., & Swan, J. (2009). *Managing knowledge work and innovation* (2nd ed.). Palgrave Macmillan. doi:10.1007/978-0-230-36641-1

Newman, G. E. (2019). The Psychology of Authenticity. *Review of General Psychology, 23*(1), 8–18. doi:10.1037/gpr0000158

Niininen, O., Szivas, E., & Riley, M. (2004). Destination loyalty and repeat behaviour: An application of optimum stimulation measurement. *International Journal of Tourism Research, 6*(6), 439–447. doi:10.1002/jtr.511

Nissley, N., & Casey, A. (2002). The politics of the exhibition: Viewing corporate museums through the paradigmatic lens of organisational memory. *British Journal of Management, 13*(S2), 35–45. doi:10.1111/1467-8551.13.s2.4

Nocifora, E., de Salvo, P., & Calzati, V. (2011). *Territori lenti e turismo di qualità, prospettive innovative per lo sviluppo di un turismo sostenibile*. Franco Angeli.

Nold, C. (2009). Introduction: Emotional geography technologies of the self. In C. Nold (Ed.), Emotional cartography: Technologies of the self. Academic Press.

Not On Map. (n.d.). *About Us*. Retrieved from https://notonmap.com/about-us

Novelli, M., Schmitz, B., & Spencer, T. (2006). Networks, clusters and innovation in tourism: A UK experience. *Tourism Management, 27*(6), 1141–1152. doi:10.1016/j.tourman.2005.11.011

O'Connor, J. (2010). The cultural and creative industries: A literature review. In *Creativity, culture and education*. Retrieved from www.creative-partnerships.com/literaturereviews

O'Connor, C., & Joffe, H. (2020). Intercoder reliability in qualitative research: Debates and practical guidelines. *International Journal of Qualitative Methods, 19*(1), 1–13.

O'Dell, T., & Billing, P. (Eds.). (2005). Experiencescapes: Tourism, culture and economy. Kopenhavn: Business School Press.

O'Gorman, K. D. (2009). Origins of the commercial hospitality industry: From the fanciful to factual. *International Journal of Contemporary Hospitality Management, 21*(7), 777–790. doi:10.1108/09596110910985287

O'Sullivan, E. L., & Spangler, K. J. (1998). *Experience marketing: strategies for the new millennium*. Venture Publishing Inc.

Oakes, T. (2006). Get real! On being yourself and being a tourist. In Travels in paradox: Remapping tourism (pp. 229–250). Rowman & Littlefield Publishers.

OECD & Eurostat. (2018). Oslo Manual 2018: Guidelines for Collecting, Reporting and Using Data on Innovation, 4th Edition. The Measurement of Scientific, Technological and Innovation Activities. OECD Publishing. https://doi.org/doi:10.1787/9789264304604-en

OECD. (2005). *Oslo manual: guidelines for collecting and interpreting innovation data* (3rd ed.). Organisation for Economic Co-operation and Development.

OECD. (2014). Tourism and the creative economy. OECD Studies on Tourism. doi:10.1787/9789264207875-en

OECD/Eurostat. (2018). Oslo manual 2018: Guidelines for collecting, reporting and using data on innovation (4th ed.). OECD Publishing.

OECD-Organisation for Economic Co-operation and Development. (2020). *Smart cities and inclusive growth*. Retrieved from https://www.oecd.org/cfe/cities/OECD_Policy_Paper_Smart_Cities_and_Inclusive_Growth.pdf

Oh, H., Fiore, A. M., & Jeoung, M. (2007). Measuring experience economy concepts: Tourism applications. *Journal of Travel Research*, *46*(2), 119–132. doi:10.1177/0047287507304039

Ohridska-Olson, R. V., & Ivanov, S. H. (2010). Creative tourism business model and its application in Bulgaria. *Cultural Realms*, 1–17.

Okazaki, E. (2008). A community-based tourism model: Its conception and use. *Journal of Sustainable Tourism*, *16*(5), 511–529. doi:10.1080/09669580802159594

Oleksy, T., & Wnuk, A. (2016). Augmented places: An impact of embodied historical experience on attitudes towards places. *Computers in Human Behavior*, *57*, 11–16. doi:10.1016/j.chb.2015.12.014

Olins, W. (1989). *Corporate identity: Making business strategy visible through design*. Harvard Business School Press.

Oliveira, F., Eurico, S., & Jorge, J. P. (2019). EBSCode - Eco Based Surf Code: Surfing for a sustainable development of beaches: The Portuguese case. In A. Artal-Tur, M. Kozak, & N. Kozak (Eds.), *Trends in tourist behavior* (pp. 109–123). Springer. doi:10.1007/978-3-030-11160-1_7

Ooi, C. S. (2003). *Crafting tourism experiences: Managing the attention product*. Paper presented at the 12th Nordic Symposium on Tourism and Hospitality Research, Norwegian School of Hotel Management, Stavanger, University College, Norway.

Ooi, C. S. (2005). A theory of tourism experiences: The management of attention. In T. O'Dell & P. Billing (Eds.), *Experiencescapes: Tourism, culture and economy* (pp. 51–68). Copenhagen Business School Press.

Orton, J. D., & Weick, K. E. (1990). Loosely coupled systems: A reconceptualisation. *Academy of Management Review*, *15*(2), 203–223. doi:10.2307/258154

Osei, B. A., Ragavan, N. A., & Mensah, H. K. (2020). Prospects of the fourth industrial revolution for the hospitality industry: A literature review. *Journal of Hospitality and Tourism Technology*, *11*(3), 479–494. doi:10.1108/JHTT-08-2019-0107

Othman, M. K., Petrie, H., & Power, C. (2013). Measuring the usability of a smartphone delivered museum guide. *Procedia: Social and Behavioral Sciences*, *97*, 629–637. doi:10.1016/j.sbspro.2013.10.282

Ott-Holland, C. J., Shepherd, W. J., Ryan, A. M., & Chen, P. Y. (2019). Examining wellness programs generation Y over time: Predicting participation and workplace outcomes. *Journal of Occupational Health Psychology*, *24*(1), 163–179. doi:10.1037/ocp0000096 PMID:28872333

Otto, J. E., & Brent Ritchie, J. R. (1996). The service experience in tourism. *Tourism Management*, *17*(3), 165–174. doi:10.1016/0261-5177(96)00003-9

Oxford Dictionaries. (2018). *Oxford Dictionaries*. Retrieved from http://www.oxforddictionaries.com

Page, R. A., & Williams, K. C. (2011). Marketing to the generations. *Journal of Behavioral Studies in Business*, *3*(1), 37–53.

Pai, C.-K., Liu, Y., Kang, S., & Dai, A. (2020). The role of perceived smart tourism technology experience for tourist satisfaction, happiness and revisit intention. *Sustainability*, *12*, 1–14.

Pai, C., Kang, S., Liu, Y., & Zheng, Y. (2021). An examination of revisit intention based on perceived smart tourism technology experience. *Sustainability (Switzerland)*, *13*(2), 1007. Advance online publication. doi:10.3390u13021007

Palmer, A., & Bejou, D. (1995). Tourism destination marketing alliances. *Annals of Tourism Research*, *22*(3), 616–629. doi:10.1016/0160-7383(95)00010-4

Palos, P., Jose, S., Saura, R., & Correia, M. B. (2020). Do tourism applications' quality and user experience influence its acceptance by tourists? *Review of Managerial Science*. doi:10.1007/s11846-020-00396-y

Pansiri, J. (2013). Collaboration and partnership in tourism: The experience of Botswana. *Tourism Planning & Development*, *10*(1), 64–84. doi:10.1080/21568316.2012.723039

Papasolomou, I., & Melanthiou, Y. (2012). Social media: Marketing public relations' new best friend. *Journal of Promotion Management*, *18*(3), 319–328. doi:10.1080/10496491.2012.696458

Parasuraman, A., Zeithaml, V. A., & Berry, L. (1988). *SERVQUAL: A multiple-item scale for measuring consumer perceptions of service quality*. Academic Press.

Parasuraman, A., Zeithaml, V. A., & Berry, L. L. (1985). A conceptual model of service quality and its implications for future research. *Journal of Marketing*, *49*(4), 41–50. doi:10.1177/002224298504900403

Park, S. H., Hsieh, C.-M., & Lee, C.-K. (2017). Examining Chinese college students' intention to travel to Japan using the extended Theory of Planned Behavior: Testing destination image and the mediating role of travel constraints. *Journal of Travel & Tourism Marketing*, *34*(1), 113–131. doi:10.1080/10548408.2016.1141154

Paulauskaite, D., Powell, R., Coca-Stefaniak, J. A., & Morrison, A. M. (2017). Living like a local: Authentic tourism experiences and the sharing economy. *International Journal of Tourism Research*, *19*(6), 619–628. doi:10.1002/jtr.2134

Pavlidis, G., & Markantonatou, S. (2020). Gastronomic tourism in Greece and beyond: A thorough review. *International Journal of Gastronomy and Food Science*, *21*, 21. doi:10.1016/j.ijgfs.2020.100229 PMID:32834883

Pearce, P. L., & Moscardo, G. M. (1986). The concept of authenticity in tourist experience. *The Australian and New Zealand Journal of Sociology*, *22*(1), 121–132. doi:10.1177/144078338602200107

Pearce, P. L., & Zare, S. (2017). The orchestra model as the basis for teaching tourism experience design. *Journal of Hospitality and Tourism Management*, *30*, 55–64. doi:10.1016/j.jhtm.2017.01.004

Pekarik, A., Doering, Z., & Karns, D. (1999). Exploring satisfying experiences in museums. *Curator*, *42*(2), 152–173. doi:10.1111/j.2151-6952.1999.tb01137.x

Pencarelli, T. (2020). The digital revolution in the travel and tourism industry. *Information Technology & Tourism*, *22*(3), 455–476. Advance online publication. doi:10.100740558-019-00160-3

Pereira, P., Martins, J., & Baptista, L. (2017). A oferta turística e os seus territórios: Autenticidade, patrimonialização e experiência. In F. Silva, & J. Umbelino (Coords.), Planeamento e desenvolvimento turístico (pp. 93-103). Editora Lidel.

Peretta, R. (2020). Commons and the tourism sector facing a pandemic. In F. Burini (Ed.), *Tourism facing a pandemic: From crisis to recovery* (pp. 133–138). Università degli Studi di Bergamo.

Perrin-Malterre, C. (2018). Tourism diversification process around trail running in the Pays of Allevard (Isère). *Journal of Sport & Tourism*, 22(1), 67–82. doi:10.1080/14775085.2018.1432410

Pfeffer, J., & Salancik, G. R. (1978). *The External Control of Organizations: A Resource Dependence Perspective*. Harper & Row.

Pforr, C., Pechlaner, H., Locher, C., & Jochman, J. (2014). Health regions: Building tourism destinations through networked regional core competences. In C. Voigt & C. Pforr (Eds.), *Wellness tourism. A destination perspective* (pp. 99–111). Routledge.

Phelps, A. (1986). Holiday destination image: the problem of assessment: An example developed in Menorca. *Tourism Management*, 7(3), 168–180. doi:10.1016/0261-5177(86)90003-8

Piatkowska, K. K. (2014). The corporate museum: A new type of museum created as a component of marketing company. *The International Journal of the Inclusive Museum*, 6(2), 29–37. doi:10.18848/1835-2014/CGP/v06i02/44436

Pike, S., & Ryan, C. (2004). Destination positioning analysis through a comparison of cognitive, affective, and conative perceptions. *Journal of Travel Research*, 42(4), 333–342. doi:10.1177/0047287504263029

Pikkemaat, B., Peters, M., & Bichler, B. F. (2019). Innovation research in tourism: Research streams and actions for the future. *Journal of Hospitality and Tourism Management*, 41, 184–196. doi:10.1016/j.jhtm.2019.10.007

Pikkemaat, B., & Schuckert, M. (2007). Success factors of theme parks: An exploration study. *Turizam: Medunarodni Znanstveno-Stručni Časopis*, 55(2), 197–208.

Pilzer, P. Z. (2007). *The new wellness revolution*. John Wiley & Sons, Inc.

Pine, B. J., & Gilmore, J. H. (2012). Deneyim ekonomisi. İstanbul: Optimist Yayınları.

Pine, B. J., & Gilmore, J. H. (2013). The experience economy: Past, present and future. In J. Sundbo, & F. Sørensen (Eds.), Handbook on the experience economy (pp. 21–44). Edward Elgar Publishing. doi:10.4337/9781781004227.00007

Pine, I. I. J., & Gilmore, J. (1998, July). Welcome to the experience economy. Harvard Business Review. July-August. https://hbr.org/1998/07/welcome-to-the-experience-economy

Pine, J., & Gilmore, J. (1999). *The experience economy: Work is theatre & every business a stage*. doi:10.5360/CHOICE.37-2254

Pine, B. J., & Gilmore, J. H. (1999). *The experience economy: Work is theatre & every business a stage*. Harvard Business Press.

Pine, B. J., & Gilmore, J. H. (1999). *The experience economy: Work is theatre and every business a stage*. Harvard Business School Press.

Pine, B. J. II, & Gilmore, J. H. (1998). Welcome to the experience economy. *Harvard Business Review*, 76(4), 97. PMID:10181589

Pine, I. I. J., & Gilmore, J. (1998). *Welcome to the experience economy. Harvard Business Review*. July-August.

Pine, I. I. J., & Gilmore, J. (1999). *The experience economy*. Harvard Business School Press.

Pine, J. B. II, & Gilmore, J. H. (2011). The experience economy. *Der Markt, 38(3–4)*.

Compilation of References

Pitts, M. A., Lutsyshyna, L. A., & Hillyard, S. A. (2018). The relationship between attention and consciousness: an expanded taxonomy and implications for 'no-report' paradigms. *Philosophical Transactions B, 373*(1755).

Pizam, A. (2010). Creating memorable experiences. *International Journal of Hospitality Management, 29*(3), 343. doi:10.1016/j.ijhm.2010.04.003

Plog, S. (1974). Why destination areas rise and fall in popularity. *The Cornell Hotel and Restaurant Administration Quarterly, 14*(4), 55–58. doi:10.1177/001088047401400409

Policy Research Group. (2013). *The creative economy: Key concepts and literature review highlights*. Canadian Heritage.

Pond, K. (1993). *The professional guide: Dynamics of tour guiding*. Van Nostrand Reinhold.

Ponting, J., & McDonald, M. G. (2013). Performance, agency and change in surfing tourist space. *Annals of Tourism Research, 43*, 415–434. doi:10.1016/j.annals.2013.06.006

Ponting, J., & O'Brien, D. (2014). Liberalising Nirvana: An analysis of the consequences of common pool resource deregulation for the sustainability of Fiji's surf tourism industry. *Journal of Sustainable Tourism, 22*(3), 384–402. doi:10.1080/09669582.2013.819879

Portes, A., & Schauffler, R. (1993). Competing perspectives on the Latin American informal sector. *Population and Development Review, 19*(1), 33–60. doi:10.2307/2938384

Porto, N., Rucci, A. C., & Ciaschi, M. (2018). Tourism accessibility competitiveness. A regional approach for Latin American countries. *Journal of Regional Research, 42*, 75–91.

Posner, J., Russell, J. A., & Peterson, B. S. (2005). The circumplex model of affect: An integrative approach to affective neuroscience, cognitive development, and psychopathology. *Development and Psychopathology, 17*(3), 715–734. doi:10.1017/S0954579405050340 PMID:16262989

Pozzi, D. (2016). *Heritage & profits: La storia come vantaggio competitivo per l'impresa*. Liuc papers, 300.

Prahalad, C. K., & Ramaswamy, V. (2003). The new frontier of experience innovation. *MIT Sloan Management Review, 44*(4).

Prahalad, C. K., & Ramaswamy, V. (2004). Co-creation experiences: The next practice in value creation. *Journal of Interactive Marketing, 18*(3), 5–14. doi:10.1002/dir.20015

Pratt, A. C. (2008). Creative cities: The cultural industries and the creative class. *Geografiska Annaler. Series B, Human Geography, 90*(2), 107–117. doi:10.1111/j.1468-0467.2008.00281.x

Pratte, M. S., Ling, S., Swisher, J. D., & Tong, F. (2013). How attention extracts objects from noise. *Journal of Neurophysiology, 110*(6), 1346–1356. doi:10.1152/jn.00127.2013 PMID:23803331

Prayag, G., Hosany, S., Muskat, B., & Del Chiappa, G. (2017). Understanding the relationships between tourists' emotional experiences, perceived overall image, satisfaction, and intention to recommend. *Journal of Travel Research, 56*(1), 41–54. doi:10.1177/0047287515620567

Prayag, G., Hosany, S., & Odeh, K. (2013). The role of tourists' emotional experiences and satisfaction in understanding behavioral intentions. *Journal of Destination Marketing & Management, 2*(2), 118–127. doi:10.1016/j.jdmm.2013.05.001

Prebensen, N. K., & Rosengren, S. (2016). Experience value as a function of hedonic and utilitarian dominant services. *International Journal of Contemporary Hospitality Management, 28*(1), 113–135. doi:10.1108/IJCHM-02-2014-0073

Prebensen, N., Chen, J., & Uysal, M. (2018a). Co-creation of tourist experience: Scope, definition and structure. In N. Prebensen, J. Chen, & M. Uysal (Eds.), *Creating experience value in tourism* (2nd ed., p. 273). CABI. doi:10.1079/9781786395030.0001

Prebensen, N., Chen, J., & Uysal, M. (2018b). Creating experience value in tourism. CABI International. doi:10.1079/9781786395030.0000

Prebensen, N., Vitterso, J., & Dahl, T. (2013). Value Co-creation significance of tourist resources. *Annals of Tourism Research*, *42*(xx), 240–261. doi:10.1016/j.annals.2013.01.012

Prentice, R. (2001). Experiential cultural tourism: Museum and the marketing of the new romanticism of evoked authenticity. *Museum Management and Curatorship*, *19*(1), 5–26. doi:10.1080/09647770100201901

Prentice, R., Witt, S. F., & Hamer, C. (1998). Tourism as experience: The case of heritage parks. *Annals of Tourism Research*, *25*(1), 1–24. doi:10.1016/S0160-7383(98)00084-X

Press Information Bureau. (2019). *PIB Delhi Release ID: 1587157*. https://pib.gov.in/PressReleasePage.aspx?PRID=1587157

Prideaux, B. (2000). The role of the transport system in destination development. *Tourism Management*, *21*(1), 53–63. doi:10.1016/S0261-5177(99)00079-5

Promsivapallop, P., & Kannaovakun, P. (2019). Destination food image dimensions and their effects on food preference and consumption. *Journal of Destination Marketing & Management*, *11*, 89–100. doi:10.1016/j.jdmm.2018.12.003

Puccinelli, N. M., Goodstein, R. C., Grewal, D., Price, R., Raghubir, P., & Stewart, D. (2009). Customer experience management in retailing: Understanding the buying process. *Journal of Retailing*, *85*(1), 15–30. doi:10.1016/j.jretai.2008.11.003

Pushkar Mela. (n.d.). Retrieved from https://www.pushkarmela.org

Quadri-Felitti, D., & Fiore, A. M. (2012). Experience economy constructs as a framework for understanding wine tourism. *Journal of Vacation Marketing*, *18*(1), 3–15. doi:10.1177/1356766711432222

Quan, S., & Wang, N. (2004). Towards a structural model of the tourist experience: An illustration from food experiences in tourism. *Tourism Management*, *25*(3), 297–305. doi:10.1016/S0261-5177(03)00130-4

Quiggin, J. (2012). *Zombie economics: How dead ideas still walk among us*. Princeton University Press.

Quintiliani, A. (2015). Il Museo d'impresa: Rassegna della letteratura. XXVII Convegno annuale di Sinergie Referred Electronic Conference Proceeding Heritage, management e impresa: quali sinergie?

Raajpoot, N., Koh, K., & Jackson, A. (2010). Developing a scale to measure service quality: An exploratory study. *International Journal of Arts Management*, *12*(3), 54–69.

Rabotic, B. (2010). Tourist guides in contemporary tourism. In *Proeedings of the International Conference on Tourism and Environment* (pp. 353-364). Sarajevo: Philip Noël-Baker University.

Rabotic, B. (n.d.). *American tourists' perceptions of tourist guides in Belgrade*. http://www.vodici-dubrovnik.hr/povijest.php

Radder, L., & Han, X. (2015). An examination of the museum experience based on Pine And Gilmore's experience economy realms. *Journal of Applied Business Research*, *31*(2), 455–470. doi:10.19030/jabr.v31i2.9129

Radder, L., & Louw, L. (1999). Mass customisation and mass production. *The TQM Magazine*, *11*(1), 35–40. doi:10.1108/09544789910246615

Compilation of References

Ramgade, A., & Kumar, A. (2021). Changing trends of hospitality industry: Emergence of millennials and gen Z as future customers and their influence on the hospitality industry. *Vidyabharati International Interdisciplinary Research Journal*, *12*(01), 336–342.

Rantala, O., Rokenes, A., & Valkonen, J. (2018). Is adventure tourism a coherent concept? A review of research approaches on adventure tourism. *Annals of Leisure Research*, *21*(5), 539–552. doi:10.1080/11745398.2016.1250647

Rasoolimanesh, S. M., Seyfi, S., Hall, C. M., & Hatamifar, P. (2021). Understanding memorable tourism experiences and behavioural intentions of heritage tourists. *Journal of Destination Marketing & Management*, *21*(January), 100621. doi:10.1016/j.jdmm.2021.100621

Ratten, V. (2018). Entrepreneurial intentions of surf tourists. *Tourism Review*, *73*(2), 262–276. doi:10.1108/TR-05-2017-0095

Raunig, G., Ray, G., & Wuggenig, U. (2011). Critique of creativity: Precarity, subjectivity and resistance in the 'creative industries.' *Gene*, 234.

Ravasi, D., & Rindova, V. (2008). *Symbolic value creation*. doi:10.4135/9781849200394.n49

Ravasi, D., Rindova, V., & Dalpiaz, E. (2012). The cultural side of value creation. *Strategic Organization*, *10*(3), 231–239. doi:10.1177/1476127012452824

Rebstock, M. (2017). *Economic benefits of improved accessibility to transport systems and the role of transport in fostering tourism for all*. Retrieved from https://www.itf-oecd.org/sites/default/files/docs/improved-accessibility-fostering-tourism-for-all.pdf

Reed, M. (1997). Power relations and community-based tourism planning. *Annals of Tourism Research*, *24*(3), 566–591. doi:10.1016/S0160-7383(97)00023-6

Regine, K. (2011). Generation Y consumer choice for organic foods. *Journal of Global Business Management*, *7*(1), 1–13.

Rehman, J., Hawryszkiewycz, I., Sohaib, O., & Soomro, A. M. (2020). Developing intellectual capital in professional service firms using high performance work practices as toolkit. *Proceedings of the Annual Hawaii International Conference on System Sciences*, 4983–4992. 10.24251/HICSS.2020.613

Reichheld, F. F. (2003). The one number you need to grow. *Harvard Business Review*, *81*(12), 46–55. PMID:14712543

Reilly, M. D. (1990). Free elicitation of descriptive adjectives for tourism image assessment. *Journal of Travel Research*, *28*(4), 21–26. doi:10.1177/004728759002800405

Reis, P. (2015). Peniche: A new use for an old territory. *Proceddings of the Encontro Científico da I2ES – ISLA Santarém*, 113-132.

Reis, P. (2016). O surf como expressão de identidade e de estilo de vida. In N. Abranja, A. A. Alcântara, F. Coelhoso, R. V. Ferreira, A. Marques, & T. Ribeiro (Eds.), Produtos, mercados e destinos turísticos (pp. 131-146). Mangualde: Edições Pedago.

Reis, P. (2020). *The influence of surf culture on the image of surf destinations* (PhD thesis). University of Aveiro, Portugal.

Reis, P., & Jorge, J. P. (2012). Surf tourism: segmentation by motivation and destination choice. In *2nd International Conference on Tourism Recreation Proceedings*. GITUR-Grupo de Investigação em Turismo, Instituto Politécnico de Leiria.

Reisinger, Y., & Steiner, C. J. (2006). Reconceptualising object authenticity. *Annals of Tourism Research*, *33*(1), 65–86. doi:10.1016/j.annals.2005.04.003

Rentschler, R., & Gilmore, A. (2002). Museums: Discovering services marketing. *International Journal of Arts Management*, *5*(1), 62–72.

Reynolds, W. H. (1965). The role of the consumer in image building. *California Management Review*, *7*(3), 69–76. doi:10.2307/41165634

Reynolds, Z., & Hritz, N. M. (2012). Surfing as adventure travel: Motivations and lifestyles. *Journal of Tourism Insights*, *3*(1), 2. doi:10.9707/2328-0824.1024

Rezende-Parker, A. M., Morrison, A. M., & Ismail, J. A. (2003). Dazed and confused? An exploratory study of the image of Brazil as a travel destination. *Journal of Vacation Marketing*, *9*(3), 243–259. doi:10.1177/135676670300900304

Ribeiro, F. R., Silva, A., Barbosa, F., Silva, A. P., & Metrōlho, J. C. (2018). Mobile applications for accessible tourism: Overview, challenges and a proposed platform. *Information Technology & Tourism*, *19*, 29–59.

Richard, N. (2007). Handicrafts and employment generation for the poorest youth and women. *United Nations Educational, Scientific and Cultural Organization*, *17*, 65. Retrieved from https://unesdoc.unesco.org/images/0015/001567/156772e.pdf

Richards, G. (2014). *Tourism trends: The convergence of culture and tourism*. Academy for Leisure. NHTV University of Applied Sciences. https://www.academia.edu/9491857/Tourism_trends_The_convergence_of_culture_and_tourism

Richards, G. (2016). *Co-designing experiences with consumers: The case of creative tourism*. Retrieved from https://www.academia.edu/26363825/Co-designing_experiences_with_consumers_the_case_of_creative_tourism_Input_for_a_workshop_on_experience_design_Tromsø_27_May_2016

Richards, G. (2011). Creativity and tourism. The state of the art. *Annals of Tourism Research*, *38*(4), 1225–1253. doi:10.1016/j.annals.2011.07.008

Richards, G. (2018). Cultural tourism: A review of recent research and trends. *Journal of Hospitality and Tourism Management*, *36*, 12–21. doi:10.1016/j.jhtm.2018.03.005

Richards, G. (2021). *Rethinking cultural tourism*. Edward Elgar Publishing. doi:10.4337/9781789905441

Richards, G., & Raymond, C. (2000). Creative tourism. *ATLAS News*, (23), 16–20.

Richards, G., & Wilson, J. (2006). Developing creativity in tourist experiences : A solution to the serial reproduction of culture? *Tourism Management*, *27*(6), 1209–1223. doi:10.1016/j.tourman.2005.06.002

Rickly-Boyd, J. M. (2013). Existential authenticity: Place matters. *Tourism Geographies*, *15*(4), 680–686. doi:10.1080/14616688.2012.762691

Ritchie, J. R. B., & Zins, M. (1978). Culture as determinant of the attractiveness of a tourism region. *Annals of Tourism Research*, *5*(2), 252–267. doi:10.1016/0160-7383(78)90223-2

Ritzer, G. (1998). *The McDonaldization thesis*. London: SAGE Publications

Rodrigues, J. M. F., Cardoso, P. J. S., Monteiro, J., & Ramos, C. M. Q. (2020). Augmented intelligence: Leverage smart systems. In J. Rodrigues, P. Cardoso, J. Monteiro, & C. Ramos (Eds.), *Smart systems design, applications, and challenges* (pp. 1–22). IGI Global. doi:10.4018/978-1-7998-2112-0

Rodrìguez Vázquez, S., & O'Brien, S. (2017). Bringing accessibility into the multilingual web production chain. In M. Antona, & C. Stephanidis (Eds.), *International Conference of Universal Access in Human-Computer Interaction: Design and Development Approaches and Methods* (pp. 238-257). Springer.

Rogers, E. (1995). *Diffusion of innovation*. Free Press.

Rojek, C. (1993). *Ways of escape: Modern transformations in leisure and travel.* Macmillan Press. doi:10.1057/9780230373402

Romaniuk, J., & Nguyen, C. (2017). Is consumer psychology research ready for today's attention economy? *Journal of Marketing Management, 33*(11-12), 909–916. doi:10.1080/0267257X.2017.1305706

Romanova, G., Vetitnev, A., & Dimanche, F. (2015). Health and wellness tourism. In F. Dimanche & L. Andrades (Eds.), *Tourism in Russia. A management handbook.* Emerald.

Ron Bos, M. S., & Temme, R. (2014). A roadmap towards sustainable mobility in Breda. *Transportation Research Procedia, 4*, 103–115.

Roper, S., & Tapinos, E. (2016). Taking risks in the face of uncertainty: An exploratory analysis of green innovation. *Technological Forecasting and Social Change, 112*, 357–363. doi:10.1016/j.techfore.2016.07.037

Rosario Rueda, M., Pozuelos, J. P., & Cómbita, L. M. (2015). Cognitive Neuroscience of Attention - From brain mechanisms to individual differences in efficiency. *AIMS Neuroscience, 2*(4), 183–202. doi:10.3934/Neuroscience.2015.4.183

Roy, S. (2018). Effects of customer experience across service types, customer types and time. *Journal of Services Marketing, 32*(4), 100–413. doi:10.1108/JSM-11-2016-0406

Ruhanen, L., & Cooper, C. (2004). Applying a knowledge management framework to tourism research. *Tourism Recreation Research, 29*(1), 83–88. doi:10.1080/02508281.2004.11081434

Runeson, P., & Höst, M. (2009). Guidelines for conducting and reporting case study research in software engineering. *Empirical Software Engineering, 14*(2), 131–164.

Ruozi, R., & Salvemini, S. (1999). Cultura ed economia in valore cultura: Sue anni di premio Guggenheim. Impresa & Cultura.

Russell, C. L. (1995). The social construction of orangutans: An ecotourist experience. *Society & Animals, 3*(2), 151–170. doi:10.1163/156853095X00134

Ryan, C. (1997). *The tourist experience.* Cassell.

Ryan, C., & Montgomery, D. (1994). The attitudes of Bakewell residents to tourism and issues in community responsive tourism. *Tourism Management, 15*(5), 358–369. doi:10.1016/0261-5177(94)90090-6

Rylance, A., & Spenceley, A. (2017). Reducing economic leakages from tourism: A value chain assessment of the tourism industry in Kasane, Botswana. *Development Southern Africa, 34*(3), 295–313. doi:10.1080/0376835X.2017.1308855

Ryu, K., & Jang, S. (2008). DINESCAPE: A scale for customers' perception of dining environments. *Journal of Foodservice Business Research, 11*(1), 2–22. doi:10.1080/15378020801926551

Saarinen, J., & Varnajot, A. (2019). The Arctic in tourism: Complementing and contesting perspectives on tourism in the Arctic. *Polar Geography, 42*(2), 109–124. doi:10.1080/1088937X.2019.1578287

Sabou, G.-C., & Maiorescu, I. (2020). The challenges of smart tourism: A case of Bucharest. *Sciendo-Studia Universitatis Economics Series, 30*(2), 70–82.

Safitri, C., & Maftukhah, I. (2018). Pengaruh kualitas layanan, promosi dan citra destinasi terhadap kepuasan melalui keputusan pengunjung. *Management Analysis Journal, 6*(3), 310–319.

Sakai, M. (2006). Public investment in tourism infastructure. In *International handbook on the economics of tourism* (pp. 266-280). Edward Elgar Publicition.

Salancik, G. R., & Pfeffer, J. (1977). An examination of the need: Satisfaction models of job attitudes. *Administrative Science Quarterly*, *22*, 427–456. https://doi.org/10.2307/2392182

Salazar, N. B. (2012). Community-based cultural tourism: Issues, threats and opportunities. *Journal of Sustainable Tourism*, *20*(1), 9–22. doi:10.1080/09669582.2011.596279

Salazar, N. B. (2018). The mechanics and mechanisms of tourism brokering. *Ethnologia Europaea*, *48*(2), 111–116. doi:10.16995/ee.1963

Saleem, H., & Raja, N. S. (2014). The impact of service quality on customer satisfaction, customer loyalty and brand image: Evidence from hotel industry of Pakistan. *IOSR Journal of Business and Management*, *16*(1), 117–122. doi:10.9790/487X-1616117122

Samala, N., Katkam, B. S., Bellamkonda, R. S., & Rodriguez, R. V. (2020). Impact of AI and robotics in the tourism sector: A critical insight. *Journal of Tourism Futures*. doi:10.1108/JTF-07-2019-0065

Sambhanthan, A., & Good, A. (2013). A second life based virtual community model for enhancing tourism destination accessibility in developing countries. *International Journal of Collaborative Enterprise*, *3*(4), 269–286.

San Martín, H., & Del Bosque, I. A. R. (2008). Exploring the cognitive–affective nature of destination image and the role of psychological factors in its formation. *Tourism Management*, *29*(2), 263–277. doi:10.1016/j.tourman.2007.03.012

Sánchez-torres, J. A., & Argila-irurita, A. (2021). *Adoption of tourist mobile applications motivating factors for their use: An exploratory study in Spanish millennials the fourth industrial revolution, which revolves around the latest ICT information and*. March. doi:10.18080/jtde.v9n1.305

Santos Veloso, A. S., & Santos Queirós, A. (2019). The role of the tourist guide in the context of the conservation and valuation of the tangible and intangible heritage. *Journal of Tourism and Heritage Research*, *2*(4), 308–326.

Sarter, M., Givens, B., & Bruno, J. P. (2001). The cognitive neuroscience of sustained attention: Where top-down meets bottom-up. *Brain Research. Brain Research Reviews*, *35*(2), 146–160. doi:10.1016/S0165-0173(01)00044-3 PMID:11336780

Sarumathi, K. (2018). Redefining travel experience through technology. *The Hidu Newspaper, Bengalur*. https://www.thehindu.com/news/cities/bangalore/redefining-travel-experience-through-technology/article22663028.ece

Scarantino, A., & de Sousa, R. (2021). Emotion. In E. N. Zalta (Ed.), *The Stanford Encyclopedia of Philosophy*.

Scherer, K. R., Schorr, A., & Johnstone, T. (2001). *Appraisal processes in emotions: Theory, methods, research*. Oxford University Press.

Schmitt, B. (1999). Experiential marketing. *Journal of Marketing Management*, *15*(1–3), 53–67. doi:10.1362/026725799784870496

Schumpeter, J. A. (1934). *The theory of economic development*. Harvard University Press.

Schumpeter, J. A. (1934). *The theory of economic development: An inquiry into profits, capital, credit, interest, and the business cycle* (Vol. 46). Harvard University Press.

Schwarz, N. (2011). Feelings-as-information theory. In P. Van Lange, A. Kruglanski, & E. Higgins (Eds.), *Handbook of theories of social psychology* (pp. 289–308). Sage.

Scott, C. (2005). Museums and impact: How do we measure the impact of museums? *Proceedings of the Eighth International Conference on Arts and Cultural Management*.

Compilation of References

Scott, N., Baggio, R., & Cooper, C. (2008). *Network analysis and tourism: From theory to practice*. Channel View Publications. doi:10.21832/9781845410896

Scott, N., & Le, D. (2017). Tourism experience: A review. In N. Scott, J. Gao, & J. Ma (Eds.), *Visitor Experience Design* (Vol. 5, p. 30). CABI. doi:10.1079/9781786391896.0030

Scott, N., Zhang, R., Le, D., & Moyle, B. (2019). A review of eye-tracking research in tourism. *Current Issues in Tourism*, *22*(10), 1244–1261. doi:10.1080/13683500.2017.1367367

Scrase, T. J. (2003). Precarious production: Globalisation and artisan labour in the Third World. *Third World Quarterly*, *24*(3), 449–461. doi:10.1080/0143659032000084401

Seakhoa-King, A. (2007). *Conseptualising 'quality of tourism destination': An investigation of the attributes and dimensions of quality of a tourism destination* (PhD dissertation). University of Bedforshire.

Segabinazzi, R. C. (2011). *O estilo de vida da Tribo do Surf e a cultura de consumo que a envolve* (Dissertação de Mestrado). Escola de Administração - Universidade Federal do Rio Grande do Sul, Brasil.

Selby, M., & Morgan, N. J. (1996). Reconstruing place image: A case study of its role in destination market research. *Tourism Management*, *17*(4), 287–294. doi:10.1016/0261-5177(96)00020-9

Selin, S., & Chavez, D. (1995). Developing an evolutionary tourism partnership model. *Annals of Tourism Research*, *22*(4), 844–856.

Selin, S., & Myers, N. (1998). Tourism marketing alliances: Member satisfaction and effectiveness attributes of a regional initiative. *Journal of Travel & Tourism Marketing*, *7*(3), 79–94. https://doi.org/ 10.1300/J073v07n03_05

Selstad, L. (2007). The social anthropology of the tourist experience: Exploring the "middle role". *Scandinavian Journal of Hospitality and Tourism*, *7*(1), 19–33. doi:10.1080/15022250701256771

Selwyn, T. (1996). Introduction. In T. Selwyn (Ed.), *The tourist image: Myths and myth making in tourism* (pp. 1–32). Wiley.

Serrat, O. (2017). The Critical Incident Technique. In *Knowledge solutions: Tools, methods, and approaches to drive organisational performance* (pp. 1077–1083). Springer. doi:10.1007/978-981-10-0983-9_123

Severino, F., & Leombruno, A. (2008). La cultura imprenditoriale nei musei tematici e distrettuali. *Economia della cultura*, *4*, 503-509.

Seyfi, S., Hall, C. M., & Rasoolimanesh, S. M. (2019). Exploring memorable cultural tourism experiences. *Journal of Heritage Tourism*, *6631*(15), 3. doi:10.1080/1743873X.2019.1639717

Seyitoğlu, F., & Ivanov, S. (2020). A conceptual study of the strategic role of gastronomy in tourism destinations. *International Journal of Gastronomy and Food Science*, 21.

Sharples, L., & Hall, C. M. (2004). The consumption of experiences or the experience of consumption? An introduction to the tourism of taste. In *Food tourism around the world*. Routledge.

Sharpley, R. (1994). Tourism and authenticity. In Tourism, tourists and society (pp. 127–162). Huntingdon: Elm Publications.

Sheldon, P., & Bushell, R. (Eds.). (2009). *Wellness tourism: Mind, body, spirit, place*. Cognizant.

Shen, S., Sotiriadis, M., & Zhou, Q. (2020). Could smart tourists be sustainable and responsible as well? The contribution of social networking sites to improving their sustainable and responsible behaviour. *Sustainability*, *12*, 1–21. https://doi.org/10.3390/su12041470

Shifino, C. (2002). Previsão de vendas na rede de varejo trópico surf shop. Trabalho de conclusão de curso em administração. Universidade Federal do Rio Grande do Sul –Porto Alegre, Brasil.

Shoval, N., Schvimer, Y., & Tamir, M. (2018). Real-time measurement of tourists' objective and subjective emotions in time and space. *Journal of Travel Research*, *57*(1), 3–16. doi:10.1177/0047287517691155

Sibicky, M., Klein, C. L., & Embrescia, E. (2020). Psychological misconceptions and their relation to students' lay beliefs of mind. *Teaching of Psychology*, *48*(2), 103–109. doi:10.1177/0098628320959925

Sigala, M. (2005). Integrating customer relationship management in hotel operations: Managerial and operational implications. *International Journal of Hospitality Management*, *24*(3), 391–413. doi:10.1016/j.ijhm.2004.08.008

Sigala, M. (2013). Examining the adoption of destination management systems: An inter-organisational information systems approach. *Management Decision*, *51*(5), 1011–1036. https://doi.org/10.1108/MD-11-2012-0800

Sigala, M., & Gretzel, U. (2017). *Advances in social media for travel, tourism and hospitality: New perspectives, practice and cases*. Taylor and Francis., doi:10.4324/9781315565736

Sigurðardóttir, I. (2018). Wellness and equestrian tourism: New kind of adventure? *Scandinavian Journal of Hospitality and Tourism*, *18*(4), 377–392. doi:10.1080/15022250.2018.1522718

Silverio-Fernández, M., Renukappa, S., & Suresh, S. (2018). What is a smart device? A Conceptualisation within the paradigm of the Internet of Things. *Visualisation in Engineering*, *6*(3), 1–10.

Simon, H. A. (1978). Rationality as process and as product of thought. *The American Economic Review*, *68*(2), 1–16.

Sims, R. (2009). Food, place and authenticity: Local food and the sustainable tourism experience. *Journal of Sustainable Tourism*, *17*(3), 321–336. doi:10.1080/09669580802359293

Skavronskaya, L., Scott, N., Moyle, B., Le, D., Hadinejad, A., Zhang, R., & Shakeela, A. (2017). Cognitive psychology and tourism research: State of the art. *Tourism Review*, *72*(2), 221–237. doi:10.1108/TR-03-2017-0041

Slater, A. (2007). "Escaping to the gallery": Understanding the motivations of visitors to galleries. *International Journal of Nonprofit and Voluntary Sector Marketing*, *12*(2), 149–162. doi:10.1002/nvsm.282

Slocum, S. L., Backman, K. F., & Robinson, K. L. (2011). Tourism pathways to prosperity: Perspectives on the informal economy in Tanzania. *Tourism Analysis*, *16*(1), 43–55. doi:10.3727/108354211X12988225900045

SmartTourismCapital. (2021). *Compendium of best practices*. Retrieved from https://smart-tourism-capital.ec.europa.eu/system/files/2021-04/Compendium_2020_FINAL.pdf#page=13

Smirnov, A., Shilov, N., Kashevnik, A., Teslya, N., & Shchekotov, M. (n.d.). *Intelligent tourist guiding service based on smart-M3 platform*. Academic Press.

Smith, M. R. (2015). *Aerial Adventure Park: Trends, statistics and leading practices*. Retrieved from https://www.slideshare.net/MichaelSmith351/2015-aerialadventure-park-trends-statistics-and-leading-practices-52820699

Smith, M., & Puczkó, L. (2009). *Health and wellness tourism*. Butterworth-Heinemann Elsevier.

Smith, S. L., & Xiao, H. (2008). Culinary tourism supply chains: A preliminary examination. *Journal of Travel Research*, *46*(3), 289–299. doi:10.1177/0047287506303981

Smith, V. (1989). *Hosts and guests: The antropology of tourism*. University of Pensylvannia Press. doi:10.9783/9780812208016

Compilation of References

Smith, W. W., Li, X. R., Pan, B., Witte, M., & Doherty, S. T. (2015). Tracking destination image across the trip experience with smartphone technology. *Tourism Management*, *48*, 113–122. doi:10.1016/j.tourman.2014.04.010

Song, H. J., Lee, C. K., Park, J. A., Hwang, Y. H., & Reisinger, Y. (2015). The influence of tourist experience on perceived value and satisfaction with temple stays: The experience economy theory. *Journal of Travel & Tourism Marketing*, *32*(4), 401–415. doi:10.1080/10548408.2014.898606

Song, Z., Su, X., & Li, L. (2013). The indirect effects of destination image on destination loyalty intention through tourist satisfaction and perceived value: The bootstrap approach. *Journal of Travel & Tourism Marketing*, *30*(4), 386–409. doi:10.1080/10548408.2013.784157

Sotomayor, S., & Barbieri, C. (2016). An exploratory examination of serious surfers: Implications for the surf tourism industry. *International Journal of Tourism Research*, *18*(1), 62–73. doi:10.1002/jtr.2033

Stabler, M. J. (1995). The image of destination regions: Theoretical and empirical aspects. In B. Goodall & G. Ashworth (Eds.), *Marketing in tourism industry: The Promotion of destination regions* (pp. 133–159).

Stankov, U., & Gretzel, U. (2020). Tourism 4.0 technologies and tourist experiences. *Information Technology & Tourism*, *22*, 477–488.

Stankov, U., & Gretzel, U. (2020). Tourism 4.0 technologies and tourist experiences: A human-centered design perspective. *Information Technology & Tourism*, *22*(3), 477–488. Advance online publication. doi:10.100740558-020-00186-y

Stará, J. (2017). Health and wellness: Conceptual grounding. *Acta Salus Vitae*, *5*(2), 3–25.

Stebbins, R. A. (1997). Casual leisure: A conceptual statement. *Leisure Studies*, *16*(1), 17–25. doi:10.1080/026143697375485

Steinmetz, R. (2010). *Food, Tourism and Destination Differentiation: The Case of Rotorua*. NewZealand.

Sternberg, E. (1997). The iconography of the tourism experience. *Annals of Tourism Research*, *24*(4), 951–969. doi:10.1016/S0160-7383(97)00053-4

Stienmetz, J., Kim, J., Xiang, Z., & Fesenmaier, D. R. (2021). Managing the structure of tourism experiences: Foundations for tourism design. *Journal of Destination Marketing & Management*, *19*, 100408. doi:10.1016/j.jdmm.2019.100408

Stigliani, I., & Ravasi, D. (2007). Organisational artefacts and the expression of identity in corporate museums at Alfa-Romeo, Kartell, and Piaggio. In L. Lerpold, D. Ravasi, J. van Rekom, & G. Soene (Eds.), *Organizational Identity in practice* (pp. 197–214). Routledge. doi:10.4324/NOE0415398398.ch11

Storbacka, K., Brodie, R. J., Böhmann, T., Maglio, P. P., & Nenonen, S. (2016). Actor engagement as a microfoundation for value co-creation. *Journal of Business Research*, *69*(8), 3008–3017. doi:10.1016/j.jbusres.2016.02.034

Stranger, M. (2017). *Surfing life: Surface, substructure, and the commodification of the sublime*. Routledge. doi:10.4324/9781315242033

Strijbosch, W., Mitas, O., van Gisbergen, M., Doicaru, M., Gelissen, J., & Bastiaansen, M. J. (2019). *From experience to memory: on the robustness of the peak-and-end-rule for complex, heterogeneous experiences*. Academic Press.

Strijbosch, W., Mitas, O., van Blaricum, T., Vugts, O., Govers, C., Hover, M., & Bastiaansen, M. (2021). When the parts of the sum are greater than the whole: Assessing the peak-and-end-theory for a heterogeneous, multi-episodic tourism experience. *Journal of Destination Marketing & Management*, *20*, 100607. doi:10.1016/j.jdmm.2021.100607

Stylidis, D., Terzidou, M., & Terzidis, K. (2008). Islands and destination image: The case of Ios. *Tourismos*, *3*(1), 180–189.

Suhartanto, D., Clems, M., & Wibisono, N. (2018). How experiences with cultural attractions affect: Destination image and destination loyalty. *Tourism, Culture & Communication*, *18*(3), 177–189. doi:10.3727/109830418X15319363084463

Suhartanto, D., & Triyuni, N. (2016). Tourist loyalty toward shopping destination: The role of shopping satisfaction and destination image. *European Journal of Tourism Research*, *13*, 84–102.

Suleri, J., Meijer, R., & Tarus, E. (2021). Exploring hotel identity by focusing on customer experience analysis. *Research in Hospitality Management*, *11*(2), 113–120. doi:10.1080/22243534.2021.1917178

Sundbo, J. (2004). The management of rock festivals as a basis for business dynamics: An example of the growing experience economy. *International Journal of Entrepreneurship and Innovation Management*, *4*(6), 587–612. doi:10.1504/IJEIM.2004.005850

Sunshine Himalayan Cottage. (n.d.). Retrieved from https://www.sunshinehimalayancottage.com/

Supradist, N. (2004). *Economic leakage in tourism sector*. Retrieved from https://lup.lub.lu.se/luur/download?func=downloadFile&recordOId=1329250&fileOId=1329251

Suryawardani, O. I. G., Bendesa, K. G., Antarat, M., & Wiranathar, A. S. (2014). Tourism leakage of the accommodation sector in Bali. *ASEAN Journal on HospitalityandToaism*, *13*(1), 3–18. doi:10.5614/ajht.2014.13.1.01

Suryotrisongko, H., Kusuma, R. C., & Ginardi, R. H. (2017). Four-hospitality: Friendly smart city design for disability. *Procedia Computer Science*, *124*, 615–623.

Sustainable Development Goals. (2015). Available online: https://sdgs.un.org/goals

Swallow, K. M., & Jiang, Y. V. (2013). Attentional load and attentional boost: A review of data and theory. *Frontiers in Psychology*, *4*, 274. doi:10.3389/fpsyg.2013.00274 PMID:23730294

Tamilmani, K., Rana, N. P., Fosso, S., & Dwivedi, R. (2021). The extended Unified Theory of Acceptance and Use of Technology (UTAUT2): A systematic literature review and theory evaluation. *International Journal of Information Management*, *57*(April), 102269. doi:10.1016/j.ijinfomgt.2020.102269

Tangeland, T. (2011). Why do people purchase adventure tourism activity products? *Scandinavian Journal of Hospitality and Tourism*, *11*(4), 435–456. doi:10.1080/15022250.2011.619843

Tang, J., Akram, U., & Shi, W. (2020). Why people need privacy? The role of privacy fatigue in app users' intention to disclose privacy: Based on personality traits. *Journal of Enterprise Information Management*, *34*(4), 1097–1120. https://doi.org/10.1108/JEIM-03-2020-0088

Tan, S. K., Kung, S. F., & Luh, D. B. (2013). A model of "creative experience" in creative tourism. *Annals of Tourism Research*, *41*, 153–174. doi:10.1016/j.annals.2012.12.002

Tan, W. K. (2017). Repeat visitation: A study from the perspective of leisure constraint, tourist experience, destination images, and experiential familiarity. *Journal of Destination Marketing & Management*, *6*(3), 233–242. doi:10.1016/j.jdmm.2016.04.003

Tarantino, E., De Falco, I., & Scafuri, U. (2019). A mobile personalised tourist guide and its user evaluation. *Information Technology & Tourism*, *21*(3).

Tavitiyaman, P., & Qu, H. (2013). Destination image and behavior intention of travelers to Thailand: The moderating effect of perceived risk. *Journal of Travel & Tourism Marketing*, *30*(3), 169–185. doi:10.1080/10548408.2013.774911

Taylor, B. (2017). Surfing into spirituality and a new, aquatic nature religion. *Journal of the American Academy of Religion*, *75*(4), 923–951. doi:10.1093/jaarel/lfm067 PMID:20681093

Compilation of References

Te Kuo, N., Chang, K. C., Cheng, Y. S., & Lin, J. C. (2016). Effects of tour guide interpretation and tourist satisfaction on destination loyalty in Taiwan's Kinmen Battlefield tourism: Perceived playfulness and perceived flow as moderators. *Journal of Travel & Tourism Marketing*, *33*(sup1), 103–122. doi:10.1080/10548408.2015.1008670

Tedjasaputra, A., & Sari, E. (2016). Sharing economy in smart city transportation services. *Proceedings of the SEACHI 2016 on Smart Cities for Better Living with HCI and UX.*

Terziyska, I. (2012). Interpretations of authenticity in tourism. *Science & Research*, *4*(2), 81–87.

Tetik, N. (2016). The importance of interpretation role of tour guides in geotourism: Can we called them as geotour guides? *International Journal of Education and Social Science*, *3*(2), 41–53.

The World Bank. (2021). *Disability inclusion*. Retrieved from https://www.worldbank.org/en/search?q=disability

Theobald, W. F. (1994). *Global tourism: The next decade*. Butterworth-Heinemann.

Thévenot, L. (2001). Pragmatic regimes governing the engagement with the world. *The practice turn in contemporary theory*, 56-73.

Thévenot, L., & Jacobs, A. (2007). The plurality of cognitive formats and engagements: Moving between the familiar and the public. Authors' reply: Social theory after the cognitive revolution: types of contemporary cognitive sociology. *European Journal of Social Theory*, *10*(3), 409–423. doi:10.1177/1368431007080703

Thibaut, J. W., & Kelly, H. H. (1959). *The social psychology of groups*. Wiley.

Thirumaran, K., Dam, M. X., & Thirumaran, C. M. (2014). Integrating souvenirs with tourism development: Vietnam's challenges integrating souvenirs with tourism development. *Tourism Planning & Development*, *0*(0), 1–11. doi:10.1080/21568316.2013.839471

Thyne, M. (2001). The importance of values research for nonprofit organisations: The motivation-based values of museum visitors. *International Journal of Nonprofit and Voluntary Sector Marketing*, *6*(2), 116–130. doi:10.1002/nvsm.140

Tikkanen, I. (2007). Maslow's hierarchy and food tourism in Finland: Five cases. *British Food Journal*, *109*(9), 721–734. doi:10.1108/00070700710780698

Timothy, D. J., & Nyaupane, G. P. (2009). *Cultural heritage and tourism in the developing world: A regional perspective*. Routledge. doi:10.4324/9780203877753

Timothy, D. J., & Wall, G. (1997). Selling to tourists: Indonesian Street Vendors. *Annals of Tourism Research*, *24*(2), 322–340. doi:10.1016/S0160-7383(97)80004-7

Tivers, J. (2002). Performing heritage: The use of live "actors" in heritage presentations. *Leisure Studies*, *21*(3–4), 187–200. doi:10.1080/0261436022000030678

TNI – Tourism Northern Ireland. (2021). *(Post) Pandemic Trends in Tourism – Opportunities for Tourist Guides*. https://www.tourismni.com/build-your-business/sector/tourist-guiding/tourist-guiding-trends-and-opportunities/post-pandemic-trends-in-tourism—opportunities-for-tourist-guides/

Tontini, G., Bento, G. S., Milbratz, T. C., Volles, B. K., & Ferrari, D. (2017). Exploring the non-linear impact of critical incidents on customer' general evaluation of hospitality services. *International Journal of Hospitality Management*, *66*, 106–116. doi:10.1016/j.ijhm.2017.07.011

Tornatzky, L. G., & Klein, K. J. (1982). Innovation characteristics and innovation adoption-implementation: A meta-analysis of findings. *IEEE Transactions on Engineering Management*, *EM-29*(1), 28–45. doi:10.1109/TEM.1982.6447463

Tosun, C., Dedeoğlu, B. B., & Fyall, A. (2015). Destination service quality, affective image and revisit intention: The moderating role of past experience. *Journal of Destination Marketing & Management*, *4*(4), 222–234. doi:10.1016/j.jdmm.2015.08.002

Trauer, B. (2006). Conceptualising special interest tourism: Framework for analysis. *Tourism Management*, *27*(2), 183–200. doi:10.1016/j.tourman.2004.10.004

Treadwell, J., Kremer, P., & Payne, W. (2007). The determinants and motives for young people to participate in surfing. *Journal of Science and Medicine in Sport*, *10*(6), 68–68.

Trilling, L. (1972). *Sincerity and authenticity*. Oxford University Press.

Trip Advisor. (n.d.). Retrieved from https://www.tripadvisor.in/

Trotter, R. (1998). The Changing face and function of museums. *Media International Australia*, *89*(1), 47–61. doi:10.1177/1329878X9808900108

Truong, V. D. (2018). Tourism, poverty alleviation, and the informal economy: The street vendors of Hanoi, Vietnam. *Tourism Recreation Research*, *43*(1), 52–67. doi:10.1080/02508281.2017.1370568

Truong, V. D., Liu, X., & Pham, Q. (2020). To be or not to be formal? Rickshaw drivers' perspectives on tourism and poverty. *Journal of Sustainable Tourism*, *28*(1), 33–50. doi:10.1080/09669582.2019.1665056

Tsai, C. T. (2016). Memorable tourist experiences and place attachment when consuming local food. *International Journal of Tourism Research*, *18*(6), 536–548. doi:10.1002/jtr.2070

Tsaur, S. H., Chiu, Y. T., & Wang, C. H. (2007). The visitors behavioral consequences of experiential marketing: An empirical study on Taipei Zoo. *Journal of Travel & Tourism Marketing*, *21*(1), 47–64. doi:10.1300/J073v21n01_04

Tung, V. W. S., & Ritchie, J. B. (2011). Exploring the essence of memorable tourism experiences. *Annals of Tourism Research*, *38*(4), 1367–1386. doi:10.1016/j.annals.2011.03.009

Turkay, O. (2014). *Destination management: functions, approaches and tools from the perspective of management*. Detay Publishing.

Tussyadiah, I. P. (2014). Toward a theoretical foundation for experience design in tourism. *Journal of Travel Research*, *53*(5), 543–564. doi:10.1177/0047287513513172

Tussyadiah, I. P., & Fesenmaier, D. R. (2009). Mediating tourist experiences: Access to places via shared videos. *Annals of Tourism Research*, *36*(1), 24–40. doi:10.1016/j.annals.2008.10.001

Um, S., & Crompton, J. L. (1990). Attitude determinants in tourism destination choice. *Annals of Tourism Research*, *17*(3), 432–448. doi:10.1016/0160-7383(90)90008-F

Ünal, C., & Caber, M. (2019). The effect of tourist guides' professional competences on destination image and satisfaction. *Anatolia: Journal of Tourism Research*, *30*(1), 82–92.

UNWTO – United Nations World Travel Organization. (2020). *UNWTO statement on the novel coronavirus outbreak*. https://www.unwto.org/taxonomy/term/356

UNWTO. (2021). *Impact assessment of the COVID-19 outbreak on international tourism*. https://www.unwto.org/impact-assessment-of-the-covid-19-outbreak-on-international-tourism

UNWTO. (2021). *World Tourism Barometer and Statistical Annex*. Available online: https://www.e-unwto.org/doi/abs/10.18111/wtobarometereng.2021.19.1.2?journalCode=wtobarometereng

Compilation of References

UNWTO-World Tourism Organization. (2013). *Recommendations on accessible tourism*. Retrieved from https://www.e-unwto.org/doi/book/10.18111/9789284415984

UNWTO-World Tourism Organization. (2015). *Manual on accessible tourism for all*. Retrieved from https://www.e-unwto.org/doi/book/10.18111/9789284416585

UNWTO-World Tourism Organization. (2016). *Accessible tourism for all: An opportunity wthin our reach*. Retrieved from https://www.e-unwto.org/doi/pdf/10.18111/9789284417919

UNWTO-World Tourism Organization. (2020). *UNWTO inclusive recovery guide – Sociocultural impact of COVID-19 issue 1: Persons with disabilities*. Retrieved from https://www.e-unwto.org/doi/epdf/10.18111/9789284422296

Uriely, N. (2005). The tourist experience: Conceptual developments. *Annals of Tourism Research*, *32*(1), 199–216. doi:10.1016/j.annals.2004.07.008

Urry, J. (1990). *The tourist gaze: Leisure and travel in contemporary societies*. Sage.

V, A. K. K., & Sabarish, S. (2021). *Journey companion: An Android travel and tourism application*. Academic Press.

van der Ark, L., & Richards, G. (2006). Attractiveness of cultural activities in European cities: A latent class approach. *Tourism Management*, *27*(6), 1408–1413. doi:10.1016/j.tourman.2005.12.014

van Heelsum, A. (2009). *Diversity policy in employment and service provision:– Case study: Breda, the Netherlands. European foundation for the improvement of living and working conditions*. Retrieved from http://www.eurofound.europa.eu/publications/htmlfiles/ef091714.htm

Vanhove, N. (2011). *The economics of tourism destinations* (2nd ed.). Elsevier Insights. doi:10.4324/9780080969978

Varul, M. Z. (2008). Fair trade marketing between recognition and romantic commodification. *Cultural Studies*, *22*(5), 654–679. doi:10.1080/09502380802245910

Vazquez, M. V., Verdugo, M. C., & Garcia, A. O. (2017). Shopping value, tourist satisfaction and positive word of mouth: The mediating role of souvenir shopping satisfaction. *Current Issues in Tourism*, *20*(13).

Venkatesh, V., Walton, S. M., & Thong, J. Y. L. (n.d.). *Quarterly consumer acceptance and use of information technology: Extending the unified theory of acceptance and use of technology*. https://about.jstor.org/terms

Vila, T. D., González, E. A., & Darcy, S. (2018). Website accessibility in the tourism industry: An analysis of official national tourism organisation websites around the world. *Disability and Rehabilitation*, *40*(24), 2895–2906.

Vila, T. D., González, E. A., & Darcy, S. (2019). Accessible tourism online resources: A Northern European perspective. *Scandinavian Journal of Hospitality and Tourism*, *19*(2), 140–156.

Vinodan, A., & Meera, S. (2020). M-tourism in India: Symbolic versus intended adoption. *IIMB Management Review*, *32*(2), 177–188. https://doi.org/10.1016/j.iimb.2019.10.004

Visit Snowdonia. (2020). *Adventure Parc Snowdonia*. Available at: https://www.visitsnowdonia.info/adventure-parc-snowdonia

VisitEngland. (2021). *Destinations for all a guide to creating accessible destinations*. Retrieved from https://www.visitbritain.org/sites/default/files/vb-corporate/dmo_guide_final.pdf

Vitterso, J., Prebensen, N. K., Hetland, A., & Dahl, T. (2017). The emotional traveler: Happiness and engagement as predictors of behavioral intentions among tourists in Northern Norway. In J. S. Chen (Ed.), *Advances in hospitality and leisure* (pp. 3–16). Emerald Publishing Limited. doi:10.1108/S1745-354220170000013001

Voigt, C. (2013). *Wellness tourism: A critical overview*. Retrieved from: http://www.tobewell.eu/media/universityofexeter/businessschool/documents/research/ tobewell/Wellness_Tourism_-_Cornelia_Voigt.pdf

Voigt, C. (2014). The Gawler Foundation in Australia: Wellness and lifestyle-based therapeutic retreats for people with serious illnesses. In M. Smith & L. Puczkó (Eds.), *Health, tourism and hospitality: Spas, wellness and medical travel* (pp. 461–465). Routledge.

Voigt, C., Brown, G., & Howat, G. (2011). Wellness tourists: In search of transformation. *Tourism Review*, 66(1/2), 16–30. doi:10.1108/16605371111127206

Voigt, C., & Pforr, C. (2014). *Wellness tourism: A destination perspective*. Routledge.

Volo, S. (2009). Conceptualising experience: A tourist based approach. *Journal of Hospitality Marketing & Management*, 18(2), 111–126. doi:10.1080/19368620802590134

Volo, S. (2021). The experience of emotion: Directions for tourism design. *Annals of Tourism Research*, 86.

von Suchodoletz, A., Fasche, A., & Skuballa, I. T. (2017). The role of attention shifting in orthographic competencies: Cross-sectional findings from 1st, 3rd, and 8th grade students. *Frontiers in Psychology*, 8, 1665. doi:10.3389/fpsyg.2017.01665 PMID:29018387

Vredeveld, A. J., & Coulter, R. A. (2019). Cultural experiential goal pursuit, cultural brand engagement, and culturally authentic experiences: Sojourners in America. *Journal of the Academy of Marketing Science*, 47(2), 1–17. doi:10.100711747-018-0620-7

Waddock, S. (1989). Understanding social partnerships: An evolutionary model of partnership organisations. *Administration & Society*, 21(1), 78–100. https://doi.org/10.1177/009539978902100105

Walls, A., Okumus, F., Wang, Y., & Kwun, D. (2011). An epistemological view of consumer experiences. *International Journal of Hospitality Management*, 30(1), 10–12. doi:10.1016/j.ijhm.2010.03.008

Walls, A., Okumus, F., Wang, Y., & Kwun, D. J.-W. (2011). Understanding the consumer experience: An exploratory study of luxury hotels. *Journal of Hospitality Marketing & Management*, 20(2), 166–197. doi:10.1080/19368623.2011.536074

Walmsley, D. J., & Jenkins, J. M. (1993). Appraisive images of tourist areas: Application of personal constructs. *The Australian Geographer*, 24(2), 1–13. doi:10.1080/00049189308703083

Wan, C. K. B. (2018). Flourishing throught smart tourism: Experience patterns for co-designing technology mediated traveller experiences. *The Design Journal*, 21(1), 163–172.

Wang, B., Yang, Z., Han, F., & Shi, H. (2017). Car tourism in Xinjiang: The mediation effect of perceived value and tourist satisfaction on the relationship between destination image and loyalty. *Sustainability*, 9(1), 22. doi:10.3390u9010022

Wang, C., & Hsu, M. K. (2010). The relationships of destination image, satisfaction, and behavioral intentions: An integrated model. *Journal of Travel & Tourism Marketing*, 27(8), 829–843. doi:10.1080/10548408.2010.527249

Wang, K., Xu, H., & Huang, L. (2020). Wellness tourism and spatial stigma: A case study of Bama, China. *Tourism Management*, 78, 104039. doi:10.1016/j.tourman.2019.104039

Wang, N. (1999). Rethinking authenticity in tourism experience. *Annals of Tourism Research*, 26(2), 349–370. doi:10.1016/S0160-7383(98)00103-0

Wang, S., & Cheung, W. (2004). E-business adoption by travel agencies: Prime candidates for mobile e-business. *International Journal of Electronic Commerce*, 8(3), 43–63. https://doi.org/10.1080/10864415.2004.11044298

Compilation of References

Wang, W., Chen, J. S., Fan, L., & Lu, J. (2012). Tourist experience and wetland parks: A case of Zhejiang, China. *Annals of Tourism Research*, *39*(4), 1763–1778. doi:10.1016/j.annals.2012.05.029

Wang, Y. S., Li, H., Li, C., & Zhang, D. (2016). Factors affecting hotels' adoption of mobile reservation systems: A technology-organization environment framework. *Tourism Management*, *53*, 163–172. https://doi.org/10.1016/j.tourman.2015.09.021

Wang, Y., & Fesenmaier, D. (2007). Collaborative destination marketing: A case study of Elkhart county, Indiana. *Tourism Management*, *28*, 863–875. https://doi.org/10.1016/j.tourman.2006.02.007

Wang, Y., & Xiang, Z. (2007, August). Toward a theoretical framework of collaborative destination marketing. *Journal of Travel Research*, *46*, 75–85. https://doi.org/10.1177/0047287507302384

Webster, L., & Mertova, P. (2007). *Using narrative inquiry as a research method: An introduction to using critical event narrative analysis in research on learning and teaching*. Routledge. doi:10.4324/9780203946268

Weidenfeld, A., Williams, A. M., & Butler, R. W. (2010). Knowledge transfer and innovation among attractions. *Annals of Tourism Research*, *37*(3), 604–626. doi:10.1016/j.annals.2009.12.001

Weiler, B., & Black, R. (2015a). The changing face of the tour guide: One-way communicator to choreographer to co-creator of the tourist experience. *Tourism Recreation Research*, *40*(3), 364–378. doi:10.1080/02508281.2015.1083742

Weiler, B., & Black, R. (2015b). *Tour guiding research: Insights, issues and implications. Aspects of Tourism* (Vol. 62). Channel View Publications.

Weiler, B., & Walker, K. (2014). Enhancing the visitor experience: Reconceptualising the tour guide's communicative role. *Journal of Hospitality and Tourism Management*, *21*, 90–99. doi:10.1016/j.jhtm.2014.08.001

Weisenfeld, U. (2003). Engagement in innovation management: Perceptions and interests in the GM Debate 1. *Creativity and Innovation Management*, *12*(4), 211–220. doi:10.1111/j.0963-1690.2003.00284.x

Wenger, E. (1998). *Communities of practice: Learning, meaning, and identity*. Cambridge University Press. doi:10.1017/CBO9780511803932

Wenger, E. (2000). Communities of practice and social learning systems. *Organisation*, *7*(2), 225–246. doi:10.1177/135050840072002

Wenger, E. (2003). Communities of practice and social learning systems. In D. Nicolini, D. Yanow, & S. Gherardi (Eds.), *Knowing in organisations: A practice-based approach* (pp. 76–99). M.E. Sharpe.

Wen, J., Kozak, M., Yang, S., & Liu, F. (2020). COVID-19: Potential effects on Chinese citizens' lifestyle and travel. *Tourism Review*, *76*(1), 74–87. doi:10.1108/TR-03-2020-0110

Westcott, M. (2015). *Introduction to tourism and hospitality in BC*. Academic Press.

WFTO. (2021). *Definition of fair trade*. Retrieved June 19, 2021, from https://wfto.com/who-we-are#definition-of-fair-trade

White, C. (2004). Destination image: To see or not to see. Part 1. *International Journal of Contemporary Hospitality Management*, *16*(5), 309–314. doi:10.1108/09596110410540285

Wijaya, S., King, B., Nguyen, T. H., & Morrison, A. (2013). International visitor dining experiences: A conceptual framework. *Journal of Hospitality and Tourism Management*, *20*, 34–42. doi:10.1016/j.jhtm.2013.07.001

Willett, J. (2009). *Cornwall's experience of the experience economy; Longitudinal impacts*. Academic Press.

Williams, A. (2006). Tourism and hospitality marketing: Fantasy, feeling and fun. *International Journal of Contemporary Hospitality Management*, *18*(6), 482–495. doi:10.1108/09596110610681520

Williamson, O. (1985). *The economic institutions of capitalism*. The Free Press.

Williams, P., & Soutar, G. N. (2009). Value, satisfaction and behavioral intentions in an adventure tourism context. *Annals of Tourism Research*, *36*(3), 413–438. doi:10.1016/j.annals.2009.02.002

Wirtz, D., Kruger, J., Scollon, C. N., & Diener, E. (2003). What to do on spring break? The role of predicted, on-line, and remembered experience in future choice. *Psychological Science*, *14*(5), 520–524. doi:10.1111/1467-9280.03455 PMID:12930487

Wirtz, J., & Bateson, J. E. G. (1999). Consumer satisfaction with services. *Journal of Business Research*, *44*(1), 55–66. doi:10.1016/S0148-2963(97)00178-1

Wirtz, J., Mattila, A. S., & Oo Lwin, M. (2007). How effective are loyalty reward programs in driving share of wallet? *Journal of Service Research*, *9*(4), 327–334. doi:10.1177/1094670506295853

Wolff, K., Larsen, S., & Øgaard, T. (2019). How to define and measure risk perceptions. *Annals of Tourism Research*, *79*, 102759. doi:10.1016/j.annals.2019.102759

Wolf-Watz, D. (2014). Traveling for nature? On the paradox of environmental awareness and travel for nature experiences. *Tourism (Zagreb)*, *62*(1), 5–18.

Wondirad, A., Bogale, D., & Li, Y. (2021). Practices and challenges of developing handicrafts as a core tourism product in Chencha and Konso, Southern Ethiopia. *International Journal of Cultural Policy*, *00*(00), 1–21. doi:10.1080/10286632.2021.1938560

Wondirad, A., Tolkach, D., & King, B. (2020). Stakeholder collaboration as a major factor for sustainable ecotourism development in developing countries. *Tourism Management*, *78*, 104024. https://doi.org/10.1016/j.tourman.2019.104024

Wood, D., & Gray, B. (1991). Toward a comprehensive theory of collaboration. *The Journal of Applied Behavioral Science*, *27*(139). https://doi.org/10.1177/0021886391272001

World Health Organization. (2021). *Coronavirus disease (COVID-19) pandemic*. https://www.who.int/emergencies/diseases/novel-coronavirus-2019

World Tourism Organization and European Travel Commission. (2018). *Exploring health tourism: Executive summary*. UNWTO. Available online: doi:10.18111/978928442030.8

Wu, C. W. (2016). Destination loyalty modeling of the global tourism. *Journal of Business Research*, *69*(6), 2213–2219. doi:10.1016/j.jbusres.2015.12.032

Wu, H. C., Li, M. Y., & Li, T. (2018). A study of experiential quality, experiential value, experiential satisfaction, theme park image, and revisit intention. *Journal of Hospitality & Tourism Research (Washington, D.C.)*, *42*(1), 26–73. doi:10.1177/1096348014563396

Xiang, Z. (2018). From digitisation to the age of acceleration: On information technology and tourism. *Tourism Management Perspectives*, *25*(November), 147–150. https://doi.org/10.1016/j.tmp.2017.11.023

Xue, L., & Kerstetter, D. (2017). Discourse and power relations in community tourism. *Journal of Travel Research*, *57*(6), 757–768. doi:10.1177/0047287517714908

Xu, F., Huang, S., & Li, S. (2019). Time, money, or convenience: What determines Chinese consumers' continuance usage intention and behavior of using tourism mobile apps? *International Journal of Culture, Tourism and Hospitality Research*, *13*(3), 288–302. https://doi.org/10.1108/IJCTHR-04-2018-0052

Xu, K., Zhang, J., & Tian, F. (2017). Community leadership in rural tourism development: A tale of two ancient Chinese villages. *Sustainability*, *9*, 1–22. https://doi.org/10.3390/su9122344

Yadav, R., & Mahara, T. (2018). An exploratory study to investigate value chain of Saharanpur wooden carving handicraft cluster. *International Journal of System Assurance Engineering and Management*, *9*(1), 147–154. doi:10.100713198-016-0492-5

Yang, Y., Liu, X., & Li, J. (2015). How customer experience affects the customer-based brand equity for tourism destinations. *Journal of Travel & Tourism Marketing*, *32*(sup1), 97–S113. doi:10.1080/10548408.2014.997959

Yarimoglu, E., & Gunay, T. (2020). The extended theory of planned behavior in Turkish customers' intentions to visit green hotels. *Business Strategy and the Environment*, *29*(3), 1097–1108. https://doi.org/10.1002/bse.2419

Yates, E. (2019). *People aren't disabled, their city is: Inside Europe's most accessible city*. Retrieved from https://www.theguardian.com/cities/2019/may/28/people-arent-disabled-their-city-is-inside-europes-most-accessible-city

Yau, O. H., & Chan, C. F. (1990). Hong Kong as a travel destination in South-East Asia: A multidimensional approach. *Tourism Management*, *11*(2), 123–132. doi:10.1016/0261-5177(90)90028-8

Yeoman, I., Brass, D., & McMahon-Beattie, U. (2006). Current issues in tourism: The authentic tourist. *Tourism Management*, *28*(4), 1128–1138. doi:10.1016/j.tourman.2006.09.012

Yıldız, Z., & Bozyer, S. (2017). Erişilebilir turizm ve Türkiye'de erişilebilir turizmin geleceğine yönelik bir projeksiyon. *The First International Congress on Future of Tourism: Innovation, Entrepreneurship and Sustainability*.

Yin, R. (2014). *Case study research design and methods*. Sage.

Yin, R. K. (2012). *Applications of case study research* (3rd ed.). SAGE.

Young, J., McGrath, R., & Adams, C. (2018). Fresh air, sunshine and happiness: Millennials building health (salutogenesis) in leisure and nature. *Annals of Leisure Research*, *21*(3), 324–346. doi:10.1080/11745398.2018.1458634

Yuan, Y. H., & Wu, C. (2008). Relationships among experiential marketing, experiential value and customer satisfaction. *Journal of Hospitality & Tourism Research (Washington, D.C.)*, *32*(3), 387–410. doi:10.1177/1096348008317392

Yu, H., & Fang, W. (2009). Relative impacts from product quality, service quality, and experience quality on customer perceived value and intention to shop for the coffee shop market. *Total Quality Management & Business Excellence*, *20*(11), 1273–1285. doi:10.1080/14783360802351587

Zacarias, F., Cuapa, R., De Ita, G., & Torres, D. (2015). Smart tourism in 1-click. *Procedia Computer Science*, *56*(1), 447–452. https://doi.org/10.1016/j.procs.2015.07.234

Zach, F. J., & Krizaj, D. (2017). Experiences through design and innovation along touch points. In *Design science in tourism* (pp. 215–232). Springer. doi:10.1007/978-3-319-42773-7_14

Zach, F., & Racherla, P. (2011). Assessing the value of collaborations in tourism networks: A case study of Elkhart County, Indiana. *Journal of Travel & Tourism Marketing*, *28*(1), 97–110. https://doi.org/10.1080/10548408.2011.535446

Zacks, J. M., Speer, N. K., Swallow, K. M., Braver, T. S., & Reynolds, J. R. (2007). Event perception: A mind-brain perspective. *Psychological Bulletin*, *133*(2), 273–293. doi:10.1037/0033-2909.133.2.273 PMID:17338600

Zadra, J. R., & Clore, G. L. (2011). Emotion and perception: The role of affective information. *Wiley Interdisciplinary Reviews: Cognitive Science*, 2(6), 676–685. doi:10.1002/wcs.147 PMID:22039565

Zajchowski, C. A., Schwab, K. A., & Dustin, D. L. (2016). The experiencing self and the remembering self: Implications for leisure science. *Leisure Sciences*, 1–8.

Zehrer, A., Smeral, E., & Hallmann, K. (2017). Destination competitiveness: A comparison of subjective and objective indicators for winter sports areas. *Journal of Travel Research*, 56(1), 55–66. doi:10.1177/0047287515625129

Zeithaml, V. A., Parasuraman, A., & Berry, L. L. (1985). Problems and strategies in services marketing. *Journal of Marketing*, 49(2), 33–46. doi:10.1177/002224298504900203

Zemla, M. (2014). Inter-destination cooperation: Forms, facilitators and inhibitors –The case of Poland. *Journal of Destination Marketing & Management*, 3(4), 241–252. https://doi.org/10.1016/j.jdmm.2014.07.001

Żemła, M., & Siwek, M. (2020). Between authenticity of walls and authenticity of tourists' experiences: The tale of three Polish castles. *Cogent Arts & Humanities*, 7(1), 1763893. Advance online publication. doi:10.1080/23311983.2020.1763893

Zhang, H. Q., Qu, H., & Tang, V. M. Y. (2004). A case study of Hong Kong residents' outbound leisure travel. *Tourism Management*, 25(2), 267–273. doi:10.1016/S0261-5177(03)00096-7

Zhang, H., Fu, X., Cai, L. A., & Lu, L. (2014). Destination image and tourist loyalty: A meta-analysis. *Tourism Management*, 40, 213–223. doi:10.1016/j.tourman.2013.06.006

Zhang, H., Wu, Y., & Buhalis, D. (2018). A model of perceived image, memorable tourism experiences and revisit intention. *Journal of Destination Marketing & Management*, 8, 326–336. doi:10.1016/j.jdmm.2017.06.004

Zhuang, X., Hou, X., Feng, Z., Lin, Z., & Li, J. (2021). Subjective norms, attitudes, and intentions of AR technology use in tourism experience: The moderating effect of millennials. *Leisure Studies*, 40(3), 392–406. https://doi.org/10.1080/02614367.2020.1843692

Zhu, W., Zhang, L., & Li, N. (2014). Challenges, function changing of government and enterprises in Chinese smart tourism. *ENTER 2014 Conference on Information and Communication Technologies*.

Zielinski, S., Jeong, Y., Kim, S.-i., & Milanés, B, C. (. (2020). Why community-based tourism and rural tourism in developing and developed nations are treated differently? A review. *Sustainability*, 12(15), 5938. doi:10.3390u12155938

Zielinski, S., Jeong, Y., & Milanés, C. B. (2020). Factors that influence community-based tourism (CBT) in developing and developed countries. *Tourism Geographies*, 1–33. doi:10.1080/14616688.2020.1786156

Zielinski, S., Kim, S.-i., Botero, C., & Yanes, A. (2020). Factors that facilitate and inhibit community-based tourism initiatives in developing countries. *Current Issues in Tourism*, 23(6), 723–739. doi:10.1080/13683500.2018.1543254

Zukin, S., & Maguire, J. S. (2004). Consumers and consumption. *Annual Review of Sociology*, 30(1), 173–197. doi:10.1146/annurev.soc.30.012703.110553

Zuzul, T. (2019). Matter battles: Cognitive representations, boundary objects, and the failure of collaboration in two smart cities. *Academy of Management Journal*, 62(3), 739–784. https://doi.org/10.5465/amj.2016.0625

About the Contributors

Rui Augusto Costa graduated in Management and Tourism Planning at the University of Aveiro in 1988, completed his Master's degree in Innovation and Policy Development at the University of Aveiro and a PhD in Tourism at the same University in 2012. He is Assistant Professor in the Tourism Area in the Department of Economics, Management, Industrial Engineering and Tourism at University of Aveiro. He's member of the executive board of DEGEIT and he's also an Integrated Member of the Research Unit on Governance, Competitiveness and Public Policy in the Research Group on Tourism and Development. Develops his research in the planning and project in Tourism, networks, governance and public policy, territorial dynamics of investment and financing of small and micro enterprises in the tourism sector. Participates in several projects of applied research nationally and internationally, and he's author and co-author of several articles in national and international journals. He is also Associate editor of the Journal of Tourism & Development, member of the Organizing Committee of the International Conference INVTUR and Internship coordinator (bachelor and master).

Filipa Brandão holds a Ph.D. in Tourism and a MSc in Tourism Management and Development from the University of Aveiro. She is Assistant Professor at the at the Department of Economics, Management, Industrial Engineering and Tourism (DEGEIT) of the University of Aveiro. She is a full member of the Research Unit in 'Governance, Competitiveness and Public Policies' of the University of Aveiro (GOVCOPP-UA), Vice- Director of the Master in Tourism Management and Planning, Associate Editor of Tourism & Development Journal. She authored or co-authored books, book chapters and papers published in international journals. She is also involved in applied research and consultancy projects in the field of Tourism and Leisure and is a member of the organizing and scientific committees of international tourism conferences. Her research and scientific production focus on tourism innovation, regional development, social network analysis, and tourism destinations' planning and management.

Zélia Breda holds a PhD in Tourism, a Master's degree in Chinese Studies (Business and International Relations) and a degree in Tourism Management and Planning from the University of Aveiro, where she is Assistant Professor, at the Department of Economics, Management, Industrial Engineering, and Tourism, holding the position of Director of the Master in Tourism Management and Planning. She is a full member of the Research Unit Governance, Competitiveness and Public Policies of the University of Aveiro; a founding member and vice-president of the Observatory of China (www.observatoriodachina.org), and a senior researcher of the spin-off company Idtour (www.idtour.pt). She is also a member of the editorial and scientific boards of a few academic national and international journals, as well as a member of the organizing and scientific committees of international tourism conferences. She has authored and co-authored several national and international papers and communications on tourism, and has been taking part in several research projects in the tourism field, both as a member of the team and as a consultant.

* * *

Sumedha Agarwal is a Junior Research Fellow pursuing her PhD from the School of Business Studies, Sharda University- Noida, India. She has done Masters in Tourism Management from IMS Ghaziabad and holds a Master Degree in Conservation, Preservation and Heritage Management from Indraprastha University, Delhi. She has teaching experience of five years at all levels. She has worked with prestigious institutions like the Department of Tourism and Hospitality Management, Jamia Millia Islamia, New Delhi and Amity University Noida, India. She has one edited book to her credit and ten publications in national and international journals, books and edited books. She has presented her research at several international conferences, including one attended at the University of Kragujevac, Serbia. Presently, she is working in sustainable tourism, women entrepreneurship, community-based tourism, and homestays.

Gökhan Akel is a Research Assistant of Management Information Systems at the University of Antalya AKEV University, Turkey. He has a PhD in Business Administration. Currently, he serves as a Foreign Language Editor for the Business Economics and Management Research Journal. He has an interest in Consumer Behavior and Tourism Marketing Research.

Sandeep Basnyat is an Assistant Professor at the Macao Institute for Tourism Studies (IFTM), Macao, China. He has a PhD Degree in Tourism from the University of Otago, a Master of Arts Degree in International Trade and Economic Cooperation from Kyung Hee University, South Korea. His research areas of interest include employee relationships; human resource management; work, workers and working conditions; and emotion, emotional labour and labour sustainability; destination marketing and branding; place attachment; community tourism and authenticity in the tourism and hospitality industry.

Marcel Bastiaansen obtained a master in Experimental Psychology from Tilburg University (1996) and a PhD in Cognitive Neuroscience (cum laude) in 2000. From 2000 to 2012, he worked as a full-time researcher and Principal Investigator both at the Donders Institute for Cognitive Neuroimaging and the Max Planck Institute for Psycholinguistics in Nijmegen. His research focused on the relationship between brain dynamics and language comprehension, memory and attention during that period. He has developed extensive experience with all major neuroimaging techniques: EEG, MEG and fMRI. In 2013 he joined BUas, where he teaches quantitative research methods courses in the scientific bachelor and master programs of Leisure and Tourism. At BUas he has initiated both fundamental and applied research on the role of emotions in decision-making, on neuromarketing, and on the EEG and physiological correlates of emotions and (consumer) experiences in leisure and tourism. He is currently developing a research program for implementing objective, biologically-based measurements of visitor experiences and emotions. Since 2016, Marcel is also a member of the Cognitive Neuropsychology department at Tilburg University.

Rohan Bhalla is a Senior Research Fellow and a PhD candidate at the Department of Tourism and Hospitality Management, Jamia Millia Islamia, New Delhi, India. A Gold Medallist in Tourism and Management Studies, he has published in journals and books around areas of his expertise, including

About the Contributors

qualitative research and multi-disciplinary approaches to real-time social sciences projects. His primary interests lie in philosophy, spirituality, transformational tourism, regenerative tourism, rural tourism, and gender studies. He also takes an interest in behavioural sciences, emotional and spiritual intelligence, psychology, communication, and personality development programs. Rohan believes in the "transformational power of education and the role of the teacher as a moral propagator of society to make the world a better place to live".

Wilco Boode is a Technical Lab Facilitator and Applied Game Designer in the Academy of Games and Media of the Breda University of Applied Sciences. He is focused on experience measurements using behavioural and biometric methods, on design for immersive media, both virtual and augmented reality, and on the use of augmented reality content to enhance the experience on the university campus.

Ilídia Carvalho, born in Lisbon, has worked as a certified tourist guide for the last 35 years in Portugal. This long and successful professional experience, together with the academic training (PhD in Tourism in 2015), was fundamental for the realization of this chapter and several other published articles. She has also been lecturing for the last four years at Lusíada University. This recent activity has presented itself as a challenge in her life, enabling a perfect articulation between practice and theory, thus being an added value that translates into continuous complementation and updating of knowledge and skills. Although tourism has always been the main subject of interest, human ecology and anthropology were important subjects in her training, contributing to a broader and more varied perspective of life, simultaneously allowing for a richer perception of the tourism activity.

Rui Carvalho holds a PhD in Tourism from the University of Aveiro, an MSc in Development of Cultural Tourism Products and a BA in Cultural Tourism Management from the Polytechnic Institute of Tomar. He is an Adjunct Professor at ISLA Santarém - Higher Institute of Management and Administration, and a Researcher at the Research Unit on Governance, Competitiveness and Public Policies (GOVCOPP) from the University of Aveiro, and researcher collaborator of the Research and Development Unit, in the group of Management, Marketing and Tourism at ISLA Santarém. He is also a reviewer for several scientific journals, author of scientific papers and book chapters. His research interests are creative/cultural tourism, events, co-creation, tourism destination planning, sociology of tourism and epistemology of tourism.

Shweta Chandra is an experienced and passionate Hospitality and Tourism educator with twenty-two years of blended exposure comprising corporate culture and teaching experience, she has worked with various multinational companies and State/Central Hotel Management Colleges. Currently, she is associated with the Department of Tourism and Hospitality Management at Jamia Millia Islamia. An IHM Jaipur Alumina, with an MBA (Hotel and Tourism Management) and a doctorate from IGNOU, her core domain is accommodation management. She has contributed by writing papers, recording educational videos on the SWAYAM portal, conducting several training programs, and organizing workshops and seminars. The compassion fuels her motivation to develop and empower youth, preparing them for a better future. She foresees education as a dynamic force capable of dissolving diversity, equity, inclusion, and harnessing the full potential of humans bringing about global solidarity.

About the Contributors

Ana Cláudia Campos holds a PhD in Tourism, a MA in Tourism Management, and a BA in Philosophy. Currently, she is an Assistant Researcher at the Research Centre for Tourism, Sustainability and Well-being (CinTurs) of the University of Algarve, Portugal. Her research interests are tourism marketing, tourist experience, tourist psychology, experience design, co-creation, storytelling, and living labs and innovation in tourism.

Özgür Davras is an Associate Professor at the Department of Tourism Management of Süleyman Demirel University. He holds a PhD and a Master degree in Tourism and Hotel Management from Akdeniz University. His areas of interest are tourism, tourism marketing, consumer behaviour, and destination management.

Lauren Duffy is an Associate Professor at Clemson University, USA. She has two major research areas that intersect under the umbrella of critical leisure and critical sustainable tourism studies. First, she has an interest in tourism planning and development with a particular focus on how power dynamics influence stakeholder participation throughout a planning process, and how power influences the distribution of tourism impacts (i.e., better understanding who benefits from tourism development projects). Second, she focuses on critical thinking, reflection, and pedagogy. Her research also explores the impact of cross-cultural exchanges, highlighting the importance of learning from, and with, people across the world.

Dorthe Eide is a Professor in organisation and management at the Nord University Business School in Norway. She holds a Dr Polit degree from the University of Tromsø. Her main context focuses on experience sectors/activities (nature, culture and meals), regarding experience-based innovation and value co-creation, particularly different innovation process approaches (network, triple helix, rural, lab, testing, cross-sector) and experience design, -quality and -consumption. Increasingly also sustainability, visitor management and innovation for sustainability. She manages the research group Marketing, Management and Innovation of Experiences (MMIE), teaches at all levels, and manages several research and innovation projects.

Fatih Ercan is an Assistant Professor of Tourism Management at the Zonguldak Bulent Ecevit University. He holds a Bachelor Degree in Tourism and Hotel Management from Bolu Abant Izzet Baysal University (2004), a Master Degree in Tourism and Hotel Management from Bolu Abant Izzet University (2006), and has earned his PhD in Tourism Management from Aydın Adnan Menderes University (2016). In addition, he has industry and teaching experience. His areas of interest include Tourism and Hotel Management, Tourism Marketing, Tourism Technologies and Digital, Smart Tourism. He has presented papers in numerous seminars, conferences. He has also published research papers in journals of repute.

Peter Ezra is a PhD candidate in the Department of Parks, Recreation, and Tourism Management, of the Clemson University. Prior to joining Clemson University, he was a Lecturer in the Department of Tourism and Recreation, Sokoine University of Agriculture, Tanzania. His research interests revolve around community-based tourism, wildlife-based tourism, ecotourism, tourism education, sustainable tourism development, global tourism value chain, and global tourism production networks.

About the Contributors

Marcus Hansen is the programme leader for Hospitality, Tourism and Events at the North Wales Business School of the Wrexham Glyndwr University. He holds a PhD in tourism management from Manchester Metropolitan University (MMU), which explored stakeholder collaboration in adventure tourism. He teaches across various modules within the North Wales Business School at undergraduate and postgraduate levels. These modules include Managing Sustainable Planning & Development, Visitor Attractions Management, Contemporary Issues in Hospitality Management as well as dissertation-related modules. He has a growing list of publications with a particular interest in adventure tourism and accessible tourism. His current research includes exploring the barriers to travelling with assistance dogs, in collaboration with colleagues from the University of Nottingham. Marcus also works with colleagues at five different universities to create dementia-friendly tourism destinations in the EU, the UK, the US, and New Zealand. His work has thus far seen him speak at international conferences in Europe and the US, collaborating with a number of national and international organisations. Before going into academia, he owned and operated aerial adventure parks in the United States for several years. He has also owned a restaurant, serving waffles with savoury and sweet toppings.

Nasim Hekmat is an alumna of Middlesex University with a degree in Psychology and a Masters degree student at University Portucalense with focus on the medical and wellness sector.

Anne-Mette Hjalager is a Professor at the University of Southern Denmark. She works with innovation, economic issues and gastronomy in tourism, and she has an interest in spatial, particularly rural and coastal, aspects. In addition, she has participated in Nordic tourism collaboration projects about wellbeing tourism. She has published widely in all of these fields, and she served in counselling capacities for national and EU policy and educational bodies. Currently, she is the Editor-in-Chief of the Journal of Gastronomy and Tourism.

Mohammad Rokibul Hossain is currently working as an Assistant Professor of Marketing, at the Faculty of Business Studies of Premier University, Bangladesh. His area of concentration is Marketing and his key research interests lie in Tourism Marketing, Customer Engagement, Consumer Behaviour, Sustainable Marketing and Neuromarketing. He published articles on Tourism Marketing, Customer Relationship Management and Agricultural Marketing in different national and international peer-reviewed journals.

Abbie-Gayle Johnson is an Assistant Professor at The Hong Kong Polytechnic University. Her research interests are smart tourism, destination management, sharing economy, value co-creation and social theory. She also has diverse and substantial experience in the hospitality and tourism industry.

Trijya Kafle is a teaching and research faculty at the Nepal College of Management, Kathmandu, Nepal. She has a Master of Business Administration degree from the School of Management, Kathmandu University, Nepal. Her research areas of interest include strategic management of enterprises, financial management, as well as tourism enterprise development and management.

Arvind Mahajan is a Research Scholar at the School of Hospitality and Tourism Management of the Lovely Professional University, Punjab, India. He is currently working as a lecturer at the Department of Travel and Tourism Government Polytechnic Thane. Before joining this institute, he worked with

Sparrow Tours and Travels Pvt. Ltd. Mumbai, India. Since joining this institute, he has taught Diploma students, Tour Operation, Travel agency Management, Tourism Marketing, Travel Documentation, Business Tourism, Medical Tourism, and Tourism Planning. He has worked as a project coordinator for a curriculum revision project for the Maharashtra State Board of Technical Education. He participated and presented a research paper at three international conferences in India on the impact of online travel portals on offline travel agencies, sustainable tourism challenges, and issues in India with travel agent/ tour operator perspective.

Sana Maidullah received a PhD degree in Humanities and Social Sciences in 2019 from the Indian Institute of Technology, Jodhpur, India. She subsequently joined Lovely Professional University, India, where she is currently working as an assistant professor in the Department of Tourism and Airline. Her main research interest is decision-making, consumer behaviour, and motivation. She is also a multidisciplinary design practitioner with experience in tourism products, communication, and environmental design.

Jorge Marques is an Assistant Professor at the University Portucalense (UPT), a researcher at REMIT - Research in Economics, Management and Information Technologies and CEGOT - Centre of Studies on Geography and Spatial Planning. He holds a degree in Hotel Management from the ISESP - Instituto Superior de Espinho, and a PhD in Tourism, Leisure and Culture from the University of Coimbra (Portugal). Over the last few years, he has developed research in the area of events, more specifically in the area of business events (Business Tourism).

Ondrej Mitas is a Lecturer at the NHTV Breda University of Applied Sciences. He is interested in the psychology of tourist and leisure experiences, focusing on emotions and well-being and quality of life outcomes. Specifically, he examines positive emotions in leisure and tourism experiences over time, the mechanisms of enjoyment, positivity, and flow in tourism and leisure experiences, and innovative research methods using longitudinal, visual, and mixed-method approaches.

Mario Ossorio is Assistant professor in Management at Università degli Studi della Campania Luigi Vanvitelli. He earned his Masters in Economics and Finance from the University of Naples "Federico II" and his PhD in Entrepreneurship and Innovation from the University of Naples II. His current research interests include family businesses, corporate museums, enogastronomic tourism, and corporate governance. Recently, he published in Management Decision, Journal of Management and Governance, EuroMed Journal of Business, International Journal of Managerial and Financial Accounting.

Joana Alegria Quintela has a European PhD in Tourism and a MSc in Tourism Management and Development from the University of Aveiro. She occupied several positions in Hotel Industry in Portugal and abroad and she worked as Program Coordinator, Consultant and Professional Trainer in Tourism and Hotel Management. Presently, she is Assistant Professor at University Portucalense, at Porto (Portugal). She is an integrated member of the research unit REMIT - Research on Economics, Management and Information Technologies and an external member of GOVCOPP - Competitiveness, Governance and Public Policies. She participates in national and international conferences since 2009 and she has been publishing several scientific papers, books chapters and opinion articles on specialized tourism publications. She is also member of the editorial and scientific boards of academic national journals, as

About the Contributors

well guest editor of the Sustainability Journal of MDPI. She participates as Coordinator and member of some ERASMUS + projects. Her research interests focus on health and wellness tourism, with specific emphasis on marketing, sustainability, happiness and quality of life.

Makhabbat Ramazanova is an Assistant Professor at the Department of Tourism, Heritage and Culture and a researcher at the REMIT-Research on Economics, Management, and Information Technologies of the University Portucalense, Portugal. She got a PhD degree in Tourism from the University of the Balearic Islands, Spain, a Master's degree in Sustainable Development from the Dublin Institute of Technology, Ireland, and a Bachelor's degree in Finance from Ualikhanov University, Kazakhstan. She is a member of several EU TEMPUS and ERASMUS + projects. Her main research interests are sustainable tourism, tourism and water, consumer behaviour in tourism, and tourism planning and development.

Aditya Ranjan is a Senior Research Fellow, a scholarship awarded by the University Grants Commission and pursuing a PhD in the Department of Tourism and Hospitality Management, Jamia Millia Islamia. He has a research interest in Rurality, Rural Tourism, Destination marketing. He has published research papers and has presented ideas at various national and international conferences. He has edited a book titled "Rurality, Ruralism and Rural tourism: Challenges and Coping Strategies" and has written chapters for different edited books. He has also contributed manuscripts on various terms in the upcoming Encyclopedia of Tourism Management and Marketing. His advisory work involves helping students, researchers, and stakeholders answer difficult tourism questions, specifically rural tourism. Previously, he taught various tourism-related courses as Assistant Professor at the University Institute of Tourism and Hospitality Management, Chandigarh University.

Patrícia Reis holds a PhD in Tourism, an MSc in Sustainable Tourism Management, a BA in Tourism and a BA in International Relations. She is an Adjunct Professor of Tourism at ISLA Santarém and the Polytechnic Institute of Leiria, Portugal. She is the coordinator of the short-cycle Degree in Tourism Management. She is also a researcher at the Research Unit on Governance, Competitiveness and Public Policies (GOVCOPP), of the University of Aveiro; the Research Unit in Management, Marketing, and Tourism (UI&D) of ISLA Santarém; and the Research Cluster on Surfing and Sustainability of Coastal Areas of the Polytechnic Institute of Leiria. She has authored scientific papers and book chapters. Her research interests include surf tourism, surf culture, tourist destinations, destination image and destination competitiveness.

Noel Scott is an Adjunct Professor of Tourism Management at the University of Sunshine Coast, Queensland, and Edith Cowan University, Western Australia, Australia. His research interests include the study of tourism experiences, and destination management and marketing. He is a frequent speaker at international academic and industry conferences, having over 300 scholarly articles published, including 16 books. He has supervised 23 doctoral students to successful completion of their theses. He is on the Editorial Board of 10 journals, a member of the International Association of China Tourism Scholars and a Fellow of the Council for Australasian Tourism and Hospitality Education. Before starting his academic career in 2001, he worked as a senior manager in various businesses, including Manager Research and Strategic Services at Tourism and Events Queensland.

Priya Singh is presently working as an assistant professor, hotel management in Jamia Millia Islamia, New Delhi. She has a doctorate in hotel management and possesses more than ten years of academic teaching and industry experience at various reputed organizations like IHM Kurukshetra, IHM Dehradun, and The Oberoi Amarvilas Agra. She has also qualified UGC-NET/JRF in Tourism Management. She is a budding and passionate researcher, and her core areas of research are Hospitality Education, Culinary Tourism, and Social Media Food Trends. She has presented research papers at various national and International Conferences. She has numerous publications in reputed journals and books. She has also contributed manuscripts on various terms in the upcoming Encyclopaedia of Tourism Management and Marketing. She is also a Certified Hospitality Trainer (CHT), approved by the ministry of tourism. She has expertise in curriculum development and has also designed various skill development programs for different sectors.

Veronika Trengereid is a PhD candidate at Nord University Business School and a lecturer at Western Norway University of Applied Sciences. Her PhD work focuses on network-driven innovation in experience-based tourism. She is part of the Marketing, Management, and Innovation of Experiences research group at Nord University Business School.

Index

A

accessibility 52, 55, 94, 98, 202, 222, 260, 274-277, 280-295, 297-298
Accessible Destination 280, 290, 299
Accessible Experience 274
Accessible Technology 299
accessible tourism 274-276, 281, 284, 290-299, 333
Accessible Tourist Experience 299
App Experience 266, 273
App Information Quality 273
App Navigation 273
asymmetric impacts 44, 62
attention 1-3, 9-21, 30, 32, 69-71, 78, 89, 92, 107, 124, 136-137, 171, 179, 186, 214, 216-217, 231, 259, 276, 280-281, 284-285, 290-292, 307, 310, 324, 327
authentic experiences 143, 152-155, 186, 302-305, 309-314, 316-317, 321, 325
authentic tourism 191, 302-303, 306, 314, 316
authenticity 34, 91, 113-114, 141-143, 147, 151-154, 183, 193, 302-317, 319, 321-323, 325-326, 328, 330, 332, 335-336

B

Breda city 275-276, 284-288, 290-292

C

certifications 161-163, 165-168, 171-172
co-creation 14, 80, 84, 117, 146, 170-172, 190, 195-197, 203-208, 212, 214, 272, 327
cognitive appraisal theory 1, 5, 7, 19, 38
cognitive psychology 1-2, 4-6, 9, 14-15, 21, 124, 139
community-based tourism 176-178, 180-182, 184, 186-187, 252
constructive authenticity 302-303, 306
consumer behaviour 23-25, 29, 32, 35, 39, 55, 85, 215-216, 231, 321, 329
consumer experience 85, 87, 89, 93, 98, 100-101, 105, 193, 217, 270, 296, 324
coping 1, 149, 299
corporate museum 107, 110-111, 114, 120
COVID-19 44, 86, 99, 102, 146, 148, 156, 176, 184-185, 187, 209, 215-216, 222, 224, 226, 232, 262, 268, 298
creative economy 189-190, 195, 204, 206, 210-211
creative experiences 189-191, 196, 201, 203-204, 206-207, 214, 327, 331
creative tourism 14, 34, 146, 189-193, 195-197, 200, 203-204, 206, 208-211, 213-214, 318-320, 325-327, 329-332, 335
creativity 84, 112, 147, 156, 163, 189-191, 195, 197, 203-204, 206-207, 211-214, 276, 303-304, 307, 328, 335
critical incident technique 45, 69, 74-75, 82-83
customer reviews 255, 264, 266, 268, 270

D

decision-making 1-2, 4, 6-7, 10-11, 14, 16, 19, 24, 29, 52, 176, 179, 241, 254, 279
destination attributes 4, 18, 37, 44-47, 50, 57-65, 201, 210
destination image 18, 22-27, 29-43, 49-50, 52, 54, 56, 63, 65, 67, 204, 319
Destination tourism 22, 24, 30
destination website 272, 286, 289, 292
development measures 215-216
diffusion 161, 163, 165, 167, 171-173, 175
disability 274, 280-281, 290, 294, 298
Disabled Tourist 274

E

emotion contagion 122-123, 126-128, 130, 134, 136
engagement 41, 69-75, 78-84, 88, 91, 98-99, 109,

123-124, 128, 170, 183, 204, 221, 234, 239-240, 242-248, 252, 259, 268, 317, 327, 333
enogastronomic tourism 107-108, 113-114, 116
existential authenticity 302-303, 305-306, 308-309, 316, 325
experience economy 1, 27-28, 33, 38-39, 69-70, 75-76, 79-80, 82-83, 85-88, 91-94, 96-97, 100-102, 104-105, 107-108, 114, 119-121, 123, 125, 139, 143, 154, 157, 173, 189-193, 195-196, 200, 206-208, 211, 213, 215-217, 221, 235-236, 302, 312-316, 318-320, 323-330, 333-334
experience tourism 141, 178
experiences 1-7, 9, 12-16, 18-19, 21-24, 26-32, 34, 37-42, 45, 49-50, 53, 56-57, 69, 71, 73, 75-77, 79-83, 85-89, 91-93, 95-103, 105-110, 112-120, 122-126, 128, 134-144, 146, 148-156, 162-164, 169-173, 176-178, 181-186, 189-214, 217-218, 220-222, 226-227, 232-233, 236, 239-246, 249, 252, 254-257, 263, 265, 267, 269, 271-280, 283, 286, 288-289, 291-292, 294-299, 302-321, 323-331, 334, 336
explorative case design 74

F

facial expression 122-123, 126-130, 132, 134-137
fair trade 322-323, 330-334, 336
fair-trade philosophy 318-319, 322-323, 329-330

G

guide 9, 14, 45, 96, 117, 141-148, 151-155, 157-159, 201, 208, 242-243, 255-257, 259, 261-262, 265-273, 275, 284-285, 290, 298, 315, 319

H

handicrafts 304, 318-323, 325, 327-331, 335-336
Health and wellness tourism 185, 215, 218, 235-236
homestay 176-177, 180-186, 309-310, 315-316
Homestay Management Committee 182, 184
Homestay Network 176, 182-183, 185-186
hospitality industry 85-87, 89, 93, 95-96, 101-105, 270, 284, 302-303, 314, 330

I

innovation network 69-70, 72-73, 75, 78-81, 174
Inter-Organizational Network 69

L

Laurent Thévenot 69, 81

M

mobile application 243, 250
multi-case study 161, 163

N

new technologies 97, 107-108, 141, 149-150, 154, 256-257, 278-280

P

pandemic 44, 86, 99-100, 102, 141-142, 146, 148-151, 154-155, 158, 185, 187, 216, 222, 224, 226, 231-233, 235, 250, 262, 268
pasta industry 107, 115-116
penalty-reward-contrast analysis 44, 58, 60-62
Post-COVID-19 Tourism 176
practice-based 71-72, 80-82, 84
practitioners 14, 22, 136, 190, 198, 206, 239-240, 246, 249, 324-325, 330-331

R

regimes of engagement 69, 71, 73, 80-81
regional innovation network 69-70, 73, 78, 80-81
revisit intention 24, 29, 34, 42-43, 48-49, 57, 67, 208, 271, 297

S

servicescape 3, 15, 35, 85, 89, 102, 109
sharing economy 96, 98, 104, 239, 241, 253, 302, 312-316
Smart Business Ecosystem 241, 254
smart city 239, 253, 258, 269, 274-275, 277-279, 282, 291-292, 294, 296, 298-299
smart destination 240, 275-277, 279, 282-283, 285, 291-292, 294-295, 299
smart experiences 239-245, 249, 254, 280
smart guide app 255-257, 267-268, 273
smart technology 255-256, 259, 274, 277, 282, 291, 300
smart tourism 146, 185, 239-245, 249-252, 254-256, 259-260, 268-273, 275-280, 285, 289, 293-298, 300
smart tourism experience 280, 295, 300
surf culture 190, 198, 200, 202, 204-205, 207, 210,

Index

212, 214
surf destination 191, 194, 198, 200-207, 214
surf tourism 189-191, 198, 200, 203, 206, 208-214
surf tourist 202-206, 214
Sustainable Tourism 52, 54, 103, 158, 163, 172-174, 176-177, 180, 186-187, 208, 211, 250-251, 294, 317, 334, 336
Symmetric Impacts 44

T

thematic analysis 244, 250, 254
tourism experience 1, 3-5, 16, 18-19, 23-24, 28-29, 31, 34-35, 38, 40, 43, 47, 55, 73, 119, 122, 124, 137-139, 143, 152, 177, 189-191, 193, 197, 200, 202-204, 207-208, 210, 214-215, 217, 234, 236, 250, 257, 261, 272, 280, 291-292, 295, 300, 306, 317, 333, 335
tourism quality 161, 163
tourist 1-2, 9, 12, 14, 16-21, 23, 26-28, 30-55, 57, 59-67, 75-76, 80-81, 91-92, 108, 113, 120-125, 127-128, 135, 141-159, 162, 178-179, 183, 185, 190-193, 196, 198, 200, 202-214, 216-217, 221, 231-232, 234, 239, 242-243, 250, 254-259, 261-262, 265-269, 271-281, 283, 288-290, 292, 296-299, 303-311, 313-321, 323-334

tourist experience 2, 16, 18, 20-21, 28, 30, 37, 39-42, 50, 120-122, 124-125, 128, 135, 142, 154, 158, 207, 212, 217, 231, 256-259, 265, 267, 281, 299, 303, 305, 308, 316, 318, 323, 325, 334
tourist guiding 141-142, 154, 156, 159, 271
tourist information 53, 122-123, 127-128, 135, 141, 150, 267, 276
tourist satisfaction 26, 34, 40-41, 44-45, 47, 50-52, 55, 57, 59-65, 67, 143, 145, 155, 157, 261, 272, 278, 297, 304, 329, 332
Traditional Handicrafts 330, 336
travel apps 256, 259-260, 268, 273
Travel Technology 259, 273
True Experiences 141

U

Urban tourism 118

V

virtual reality 116, 154, 239, 257, 274, 278-279, 283, 288, 291, 296
visitor experience 107, 118, 139, 144, 158

Recommended Reference Books

IGI Global's reference books are available in three unique pricing formats:
Print Only, E-Book Only, or Print + E-Book.

Shipping fees may apply.

www.igi-global.com

ISBN: 978-1-7998-1048-3
EISBN: 978-1-7998-1049-0
© 2020; 605 pp.
List Price: US$ **285**

ISBN: 978-1-5225-8933-4
EISBN: 978-1-5225-8934-1
© 2020; 667 pp.
List Price: US$ **295**

ISBN: 978-1-7998-0357-7
EISBN: 978-1-7998-0359-1
© 2020; 451 pp.
List Price: US$ **235**

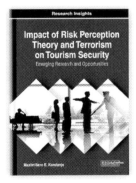

ISBN: 978-1-7998-0070-5
EISBN: 978-1-7998-0071-2
© 2020; 144 pp.
List Price: US$ **175**

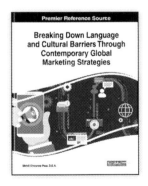

ISBN: 978-1-5225-6980-0
EISBN: 978-1-5225-6981-7
© 2019; 339 pp.
List Price: US$ **235**

ISBN: 978-1-5225-5390-8
EISBN: 978-1-5225-5391-5
© 2018; 125 pp.
List Price: US$ **165**

Do you want to stay current on the latest research trends, product announcements, news, and special offers?
Join IGI Global's mailing list to receive customized recommendations, exclusive discounts, and more.
Sign up at: **www.igi-global.com/newsletters**.

Publisher of Peer-Reviewed, Timely, and Innovative Academic Research

www.igi-global.com | Sign up at www.igi-global.com/newsletters | facebook.com/igiglobal | twitter.com/igiglobal | linkedin.com/igiglobal